RENEWALS 458-4574
DATE DUE

**WITHDRAWN
UTSA Libraries**

Series Contents

1. URBANIZATION
AND THE GROWTH OF CITIES

2. THE PHYSICAL CITY:
PUBLIC SPACE AND THE INFRASTRUCTURE

3. POLITICS AND GOVERNMENT

4. THE ECONOMY

5. THE WORKING CLASS
AND ITS CULTURE

6. TRANSPORTATION
AND COMMUNICATION

7. SOCIAL STRUCTURE
AND SOCIAL MOBILITY

8. INSTITUTIONAL LIFE:
FAMILY, SCHOOLS, RACE, AND RELIGION

VOLUME
2

THE PHYSICAL CITY

PUBLIC SPACE AND THE INFRASTRUCTURE

Edited with introductions by

NEIL LARRY SHUMSKY
*Virginia Polytechnic Institute
and State University*

GARLAND PUBLISHING, INC.
New York & London
1996

Introductions copyright © 1996 Neil Larry Shumsky
All rights reserved

Library of Congress Cataloging-in-Publication Data

The physical city : public space and the infrastructure / edited with
   introductions by Neil Larry Shumsky.
      p.   cm. — (American cities ; v. 2)
   Includes bibliographical references.
   ISBN 0-8153-2187-2 (alk. paper)
      1. City planning—United States—History. 2. Public spaces—
United States—History. I. Shumsky, Neil L., 1944– .
II. Series.
HT123.A6615 1996 vol. 2
[HT167]
307.76'0973 s—dc20
[307.1'216'0973]   95-38499
                                                                CIP

Printed on acid-free, 250-year-life paper
Manufactured in the United States of America

Contents

Series Introduction   vii
Volume Introduction   xi

The Landscape Tradition

The "Rural" Cemetery Movement:
Urban Travail and the Appeal of Nature
Thomas Bender   2

Politics and the Park: The Fight for Central Park
Ian R. Stewart   18

Private Plans for Public Spaces: The Origins of Chicago's Park
System, 1850–1875
Glen E. Holt   51

Frederick Law Olmsted: Landscape Architecture
as Conservative Reform
Geoffrey Blodgett   63

The Landscaper's Utopia Versus the City: A Mismatch
Ross L. Miller   85

The Frederick Law Olmsted Plan for Tacoma
Norman J. Johnston   101

The City Beautiful and the City Efficient

The City Beautiful Movement: Forgotten Origins
and Lost Meanings
Jon A. Peterson   109

The City Beautiful in New York
Harvey A. Kantor   130

A Reconsideration of the 1909 "Plan of Chicago"
Ira J. Bach   154

The Commercial-Civic Elite and City Planning in Atlanta,
Memphis, and New Orleans in the 1920s
Blaine A. Brownell   165

PLANNING COMMUNITIES

Radburn: Planning the American Community
  Mark B. Lapping — 195

Rexford Guy Tugwell: Initiator of America's Greenbelt New Towns, 1935 to 1936
  David Myhra — 212

Frank Lloyd Wright and the American City: The Broadacres Debate
  Stephen Grabow — 225

CONTEMPORARY PLANNING

City Planners and Urban Transportation: The American Response, 1900–1940
  Mark Foster — 235

Historic Planning and Redevelopment in Minneapolis
  David R. Goldfield — 268

Urban Planning as Policy Analysis: Management of Urban Change
  Dennis A. Rondinelli — 279

THE ENGINEERING TRADITION

To Engineer the Metropolis: Sewers, Sanitation, and City Planning in Late-Nineteenth-Century America
  Stanley K. Schultz and Clay McShane — 289

Drainage, Disease, Comfort, and Class: A History of Newark's Sewers
  Stuart Galishoff — 313

"Out of Sight, Out of Mind": The Environment and Disposal of Municipal Refuse, 1860–1920
  Martin V. Melosi — 331

Atlanta's Water Supply, 1865–1918
  John Ellis and Stuart Galishoff — 351

Los Angeles Aqueduct: A Search for Water
  William K. Jones — 369

A Neglected Aspect of the Owens River Aqueduct Story: The Inception of the Los Angeles Municipal Electric System
  Nelson Van Valen — 387

Acknowledgments — 413

SERIES INTRODUCTION

This collection brings together more than 200 scholarly articles pertaining to the history and development of urban life in the United States during the past two centuries. Less than 100 years ago, the Census Bureau revealed that more than half of all Americans live in urban places; barely fifty years ago, historians began to view cities as distinct places worth studying in their own right, and within the past ten years, these earlier developments were supported by the establishment of the Urban History Association.

Urbanization's rapid occurence during the nineteenth century and its brief period of historical study have led to diverse literature about American cities and their history appearing in a wide variety of publications. Because cities are frequently treated as part of states, articles have appeared in state historical journals. Sometimes, an article has covered a discrete institution and appeared in a journal pertaining only to that institution, for example, the family or the church. At still other times, authors have not consciously stressed the urban aspect of a particular subject, so their work has been published in journals that do not receive widespread attention from urbanists.

This series alleviates some of the problem of locating the varied literature by bringing together articles from journals of all types, organizing them, and making them available together for the first time. The articles in this collection emphasize cities—their growth, politics, economy, and so on—and, until now, many of them were accessible only to those members of a particular field who read the specialized journals of that field, whether it be the South, the Progressive Era, labor, or others. All of this seemingly unrelated literature, however, shares a common focus: cities and urban life. The purpose of this series is to bring out that common theme so that literature is more available, the relationship between the articles more easily seen, and the understandings derived from the articles' juxtaposition more thoroughly developed.

The entire collection is structured to highlight questions and problems that concern historians of cities, as well as to acknowledge distinctions among political, economic, social, cultural, and other varieties of history. Urbanization and many of its attendant processes are analyzed in the first volume, which considers not only the growth of cities but also such topics as the relationship between urbanization and the Westward movement, boosterism and urban rivalry, and company towns, concluding with a consideration of suburbs and their place in American urban culture since the middle of the nineteenth century. The physical development of cities and their infrastructure is considered in Volume 2, which focuses on city planning and its origins in the Rural Cemetery Movement, the City Beautiful Movement, and the role of business in advocating more rational and efficient urban places. Volume 2 also contains articles about essential aspects of the urban infrastructure and the provision of basic services essential for urban survival—water, sewer, and transportation systems. The articles about municipal government contained in the third volume include discussions of how rapid urbanization in the early nineteenth century produced a chain reaction, creating first the need for new political institutions, then the rise of machine politics, and, finally, reform movements that designed, advocated, and implemented new institutional structures such as the commission and city manager forms of government. Volume 3 also includes articles that consider the nature of intergovernmental relations at the end of the twentieth century and the connections between the governments of cities and the governments of the regions surrounding them—localities, states, and the nation.

The selections in Volume 4 of the series concern the development of the urban economy since the early nineteenth century. Three groups of articles, each arranged chronologically, deal with three basic sectors of the economy—trade and commerce (especially retailing), manufacturing and industrialization, and finance. Individual articles address subjects as diverse as merchants and shopping malls, flour milling and scientific management, and the Chicago Board of Trade and redlining. Volume 5 contains articles that are closely related but which concentrate specifically on the changing nature of work in American cities during the past two centuries. While they obviously concern the development of the industrial and post-industrial economies, they also recognize that economic transformations are intimately related to cultural change and that economic and cultural change are inseparable and must be considered together. At the same time, taken as a group, the articles reveal differences in experience between black and white Americans, men and women, and native and foreign-born Americans, necessitating that each of these groups be considered separately. The selections also investigate and illuminate questions about the relationships among these different groups and the kinds of actions they have taken to achieve their goals—political protests, boycotts, strikes, and so on.

The relationship between technology and urban life is the focus of the sixth volume. Developments in communication and transportation—bridges, steamships, railroads, street railways, electric trolleys, automobiles, and highways—played a crucial role in the growth of cities and the nature of urban life as did newspapers, telephones, and telecommunications. The articles in this volume examine the significance of the changing technology.

The final two volumes in the series concentrate on social structure and social/political institutions. Volume 7 looks at social class structure and social mobility. Its articles address questions that have intrigued historians for decades. What has been the class structure of American cities during the past two centuries? How much mobility has been possible? For whom has it been possible? What has been the relationship between social and geographic mobility? Finally, how have all kinds of Americans tried to improve their social status? In Volume 8, the focus is on the institutional life of cities. These articles examine institutions that existed in all societies—rural and urban—at all times, including family, religion, and education. They provide a look at how these institutions have changed and developed in concert with the development of cities in the United States. The final sections in Volume 8 discuss several institutions that are uniquely urban: voluntary associations, vigilance committees, and organized police forces. These articles attempt to consider race and ethnicity, class, gender, and the various experiences of different groups of Americans.

INTRODUCTION

For many Americans cities have represented, more than anything else, physical environments that can be manipulated, shaped, or controlled. More important, however, has been the belief that such control in designing and molding the physical structure of cities will subsequently affect urban social, cultural, economic, and political life. With that belief in mind, Americans began trying to "manage" or plan their cities as early as the 1830s and 1840s. Although these first steps were slow and halting, they charted a path whose direction has rarely varied.

Although many towns and cities were deliberately established, planned, and laid out during the colonial era (Philadelphia and Savannah are two notable examples), the origins of modern city planning can be traced back to the rural cemetery movement in the second quarter of the nineteenth century. Beginning at Mount Auburn Cemetery outside of Boston, reformers in New England attempted to do more than merely provide a decent burial place for the dead; they wanted also to preserve part of the natural environment, making it readily accessible to tourists and visitors from the city. The creation of these cemeteries thus established a point-counterpoint ideology between urban and rural that has been inherent in city planning ever since.

The rural cemetery movement marked not only the beginning of an attempt to provide city dwellers with easy access to nature, but also sparked an urban park movement that sought to bring nature into the very heart of the city. For twelve years, a small group of reformers tried to acquire the land that ultimately became New York's Central Park; they promoted it on the basis of public health, urban consciousness, and civic pride. After the city had taken possession of the land and the park opened to the public, it was an immediate success. This success set off a national enthusiasm for constructing urban parks. Piedmont Park in Atlanta and Golden Gate Park in San Francisco are only two of countless examples; some cities, however, like Chicago, were not content with individual parks. There, civic leaders, businessmen, professionals, and real-estate developers laid out a park system that crossed and served the entire city.

As the designers and planners of these parks proceeded with their work, they aspired to more than just bringing open space and nature into the city. They also promoted a distinct set of social and philosophical ideals. Urban life, they believed, was threatening democracy and the parks would therefore permit the lower classes to commune with nature and would reestablish an appropriate setting for democratic society. Frederick Law Olmsted, the greatest American landscape architect of the day and perhaps of all time, designed and built structured, ordered, cultivated parks where he hoped the working class would find solitude away from the chaos of daily life. Olmsted and other Romantics hoped that such parks would guide "lesser folk" to higher and better plateaus of life.

Ultimately, the activities of landscape architects like Olmsted transcended park design, and those artists became fully involved in planning whole cities. Olmsted, for example, prepared a plan for the entire city of Tacoma after the Northern Pacific Railroad Company designated that city as its western terminus. Olmsted's plan stressed aesthetic rather than practical considerations, and the railroad ultimately scrapped it, but the plan testifies to the goals and aspirations of the founders of modern city planning in the United States. It was also a precursor to Olmsted's participation in planning the Chicago World's Fair of 1893, considered by some as the single most important event in the history of American city planning.

By the last decade of the nineteenth century, these earlier developments had begun to coalesce into a reform effort, which came to be known as the City Beautiful Movement. The chief milestone of that reform effort was the World's Columbian Exposition, or Chicago World's Fair of 1893, with its classic-Renaissance architecture, monumental city planning, and municipal art. In reality, however, the City Beautiful Movement did not peak until it produced the New York Improvement Plan of 1907 and Daniel Burnham's 1909 Plan of Chicago. These blueprints continued the tradition of regarding the city in physical terms and trying to effect social change by manipulating the physical environment. The New York plan included neoclassical buildings, civic centers, and massive buildings; the Chicago plan opened up the city with new boulevards, provided recreational facilities, and saved the waterfront. But neither of these plans, nor any of the others at the time, dealt seriously or meaningfully with the economic and social conditions of modern cities. The result was continued haphazard growth, both of the city and its problems.

At about the same time, another reform effort, the City Efficient Movement, was developing. Rather than stressing the physical appearance of cities, the backers of this campaign wanted cities to function more smoothly and provide services in a more businesslike way. Not surprisingly, many of the leading proponents of the City Efficient Movement were businessmen who wanted to create a suitable location for profitable economic activity. They, too, believed that manipulating the physical environment would modify the institutional life of the city.

While many city planners emerged from a tradition of architecture or landscape architecture and gave primary attention to the physical structure and appearance of cities, another tradition was also at work—that of urban engineering. As cities became physically larger with greater populations, the residents were forced to confront critical problems—such as sewerage, refuse disposal, and water supply—that affected the entire city and could best be tackled in a systematic, coherent, citywide fashion. Solving these problems required some kind of central response but also depended on the expertise of engineers with highly specialized knowledge and skills. For many years around the end of the nineteenth century, a large proportion of city managers were trained as engineers, and, although they were able to handle most pressing urban needs, they soon faced some insurmountable problems. A capitalist economy, the sanctity of private property, and the desire to control the cost of public services inhibited the provision of sewers in some cities; and the desire to dispose of wastes cheaply, without understanding the environmental effects, impelled others to pollute the environment and despoil the landscape—even though this did mean providing some public services.

Of all public utilities, perhaps none is more basic to cities than water supply. Because water is essential to the survival of a city and its people, the availability of fresh water was a critical problem for rapidly expanding cities in the late nineteenth and early twentieth centuries. By 1918, Atlanta had committed itself to maintaining a public water supply and paying for it with public funds. While supplying water was an urban priority nationally, it was nowhere a more serious issue than in those cities developing in the arid lands of the Southwest, especially Los Angeles. That city's efforts to provide an ample water supply after 1904 provoked controversy within the city, its surrounding areas, the state, and the national government.

After the first few decades of the twentieth century, disillusionment with attempts to plan, restructure, and provide services for cities began to grow. Cities seemed to have insoluble problems, becoming increasingly out of control and unmanageable. One response was to try planning on a smaller, more limited scale. In 1927, Radburn, New Jersey was heralded as a town that would appeal to the middle class of the motor age. Its designers planned not only the physical form of the town but also its government, economy, and quality of life. A few years later, during the New Deal, Rexford Tugwell used his position as head of the Resettlement Administration to create three new Greenbelt Towns. Recognizing that urban growth was inevitable, Tugwell wanted to relocate the rural poor to the edge of cities, and he believed that housing could be placed in a more attractive setting, allowing a more pleasant environment to emerge. Beginning about the same time but continuing years into the future, Frank Lloyd Wright, possibly the greatest of all American architects, decided to try his hand at city planning, and he designed Broadacre City. Although it was never constructed and became the source of great social and political controversy, Wright's plan reveals many of the same assumptions that had directed most city planners up to that time—especially that modifying the physical form of a city would also change its social characteristics and institutions.

While many planners were attempting to manage urban life by manipulating the physical shape of cities, some of them took a narrower, and probably more realistic, view of what they could accomplish. Rather than seeing the city as a single entity that could be manipulated as a whole, they drew on the tradition of urban engineering and began to analyze and modify discrete parts of the urban setting. During the first half of the twentieth century, many city planners focused their attention on urban transportation, ultimately concluding (perhaps unfortunately) that widespread use of automobiles was preferable to urban mass transportation.

Other groups of planners, especially after World War II, recognized some of the biases traditionally inherent in city planning. One of the most significant biases was the widespread hostility toward cities exemplified by the Rural Cemetery Movement and its idealization of nature and the natural world. When planners began to question this bias, they also began to plan differently. Some of them tried to discover and re-create the positive aspects of life that existed in nineteenth-century cities and to restore those characteristics of urban life that produced a more satisfactory environment. At the same time, some planners recognized the central truth that urban planning is much more than manipulating space and buildings; it is also more than attempting to re-create urban social and economic institutions. Instead, it is a complex political process that involves analyzing, intervening in, and managing the political conflict that accompanies any kind of significant change.

The Physical City

THE "RURAL" CEMETERY MOVEMENT: URBAN TRAVAIL AND THE APPEAL OF NATURE

THOMAS BENDER

THE rural cemetery movement was a widespread cultural phenomenon in mid-nineteenth-century America.[1] Literally a misnomer, "rural cemetery" denoted a burial ground located on the outskirts of a city that was designed according to the romantic conventions of English landscape gardening. Although historians have noted the development of these cemeteries, they have ignored their ideological background and their place in the emerging urban culture.[2]

In *The Making of Urban America*, John W. Reps expresses surprise that the cemeteries were used more as pleasure grounds than as places for burial, and concludes that this "must have astounded and perhaps horrified their sponsors."[3] On the contrary, this phenomenon neither surprised nor outraged anyone. A visit to the local cemetery was considered *de rigueur* for the tourist, and the popular press carried numerous articles on these romantic burial grounds. Many accounts and engravings depict middle-class Americans resorting for pleasure to these park-like cemeteries, empty or nearly empty of graves for many years. America's rural cemeteries were explicitly designed both for the living and for the dead, and the assumptions underlying their widespread popularity were central to mid-nineteenth-century American ideas about the

---

[1] Rural cemeteries were built in every major and in most minor nineteenth-century American cities. For a partial list of the more important cemeteries, with brief descriptions, see *Spring Grove Cemetery: Its History and Improvements...* (Cincinnati, 1869), 129-133.

[2] Neil Harris's *The Artist in American Society: The Formative Years, 1790-1860* (New York, 1966), 200-208, 377-380, is a notable exception. When this article was in proofs, another useful discussion of the cultural significance of rural cemeteries appeared: Stanley French, "The Cemetery as Cultural Institution: The Establishment of Mount Auburn and the 'Rural Cemetery' Movement," *American Quarterly*, XXVI, 37-59 (March, 1974).

[3] John W. Reps, *The Making of Urban America: A History of City Planning in the United States* (Princeton, 1965), 326.

THE "RURAL" CEMETERY MOVEMENT 197

relation of cityscape and landscape in an urbanizing society.

America's first rural cemetery was Mount Auburn, outside Boston. Dr. Jacob Bigelow was the driving force behind its establishment, and many of Boston's elite supported his five-year campaign which culminated with the opening of Mount Auburn in 1831. Bigelow's motives are not entirely clear. His familiarity with European medical literature probably alerted him to the potential menace to public health of cemeteries in the center of densely populated cities. He was also moved by a traditional desire to express respect for the dead through an appropriately serene burial site.[4]

Whatever Bigelow's motives, consecration addresses and other commentary on the cemeteries reveal that rural cemeteries were intended to offer far more than resting places for the dead. Mount Auburn and its imitators were expected, from the beginning, to serve the needs of the living. A month after the consecration of Mount Auburn, Henry Bellows, in his oration at the Harvard Exhibition on October 18, 1831, declared that rural cemeteries "are not for the dead. They are for the living."[5] Writing in 1849, Andrew Jackson Downing asserted that thirty thousand persons visited Mount Auburn in a single season.[6]

Clearly, rural cemeteries had some larger significance for

---

[4] On Bigelow, Mount Auburn, and its influence, see Hans Huth, *Nature and the American* (Berkeley, 1957), 66-69; and Cornelia W. Walter, *Mount Auburn* (New York, 1847). At pages 33-35, Walter reprints a lecture that Bigelow used to promote Mount Auburn.

If the rural cemetery was a key element in the mid-nineteenth-century American effort to develop an ideology that would give meaning, coherence, and some comfort in a rapidly urbanizing and industrializing society, the role of Bigelow is suggestive. According to Perry Miller, Bigelow coined the word "technology" and, along with Joseph Story, who was also involved in the establishment of Mount Auburn, was a leader in accommodating the American mind to the values of a civilization of machines. (Perry Miller, *The Life of the Mind in America* [New York, 1965], 289-293, 298.)

[5] Quoted by Neil Harris, *The Artist in American Society*, 201. At the time of the consecration, the Boston *Courier* predicted that Mount Auburn "will soon be a place of more general resort." (Reprinted in Joseph Story, *An Address Delivered on the Dedication of the Cemetery at Mount Auburn, September 24, 1831* [Boston, 1831], 27.)

[6] [Andrew Jackson Downing,] "Public Cemeteries and Public Gardens," *The Horticulturist*, IV, 10 (July, 1849).

mid-century Americans. But what is the relationship between the cemetery movement and more general changes in American society? How was the American attitude toward the rural cemetery related to thought and feeling about America's increasingly urban environment?

The consecration address delivered by Joseph Story at Mount Auburn suggests the nature of these relationships. After explaining that the "magnificence of nature" in the rural cemetery would be more comforting to the mourner than the "noisy press of business" surrounding a city churchyard, Story made broader claims for the significance of Mount Auburn.[7] "All around us," he observed, "there breathes a solemn calm, as if we were in the bosom of a wilderness." Yet "ascend but a few steps, and what a change of scenery to surprise and delight us.... In the distance, the City—at once the object of our admiration and our love—rears its proud eminences, its glittering spires, its lofty towers, its graceful mansions, its curling smoke, its crowded haunts of business and pleasure." Story then proceeded to refine these images of cityscape and landscape into counterpoints:

There is, therefore, within our reach, every variety of natural and artificial scenery.... We stand, as it were, upon the borders of two worlds; and as the mood of our minds may be, we may gather lessons of profound wisdom by contrasting the one with the other.[8]

A view of the city, Story continued, encourages us to "indulge in the dreams and hope of ambition." The influence of the cemetery's natural landscape, however, will serve as a counterbalance. "The rivalries of the world will here drop from the heart; the spirit of forgiveness will gather new impulses; the selfishness of avarice will be checked; the restlessness of ambition will be rebuked...."[9] Story was suggesting that the influence of the rural cemetery could purify the city without compromising its urbanity.

[7] Story, *Address*, 8, 12. Cf. [Edward Ruggles,] *A Picture of New York* (New York, 1848), 163.
[8] Story, *Address*, 17-18.
[9] Story, *Address*, 20.

THE "RURAL" CEMETERY MOVEMENT 199

Mount Auburn's attraction for the living encouraged imitators. Following the Boston example, Philadelphia established Laurel Hill Cemetery in 1836, and New York City opened Greenwood in 1838.[10] By 1842 New England had several rural cemeteries, including the one opened in Lowell, Massachusetts, in 1841.[11]

The popular image of Lowell, America's first industrial city, illustrates the pertinence of rural cemeteries to the mid-century-American concern about the relationship of the natural and artificial elements of the urbanizing environment. Although it was merely the site of a dozen small farms in 1820, only twenty years later Lowell was acknowledged as "the American Manchester." Because the landscape was altered so rapidly by urbanization, and because the city was a self-conscious and highly visible pioneer of American industrialism, Lowell provides an excellent example for this study.

When Lowell was founded in 1821, the dominant concept of the American landscape was that of "an immense wilderness [turned] into a fruitful field."[12] Art and Nature were blended to define the landscape. Americans assumed that something artificial could be "introduced into the natural order [showing] that man has interposed in some way to improve the processes of nature." However, an extreme departure from nature could not be accommodated within this ideology without upsetting the balance by shifting from the "cultivated" and the good, to the "dissipated and corrupt."[13]

Lowell and other early factory towns were merged within this framework through the use of a factory-in-the-forest image. In 1825, the editor of the *Essex Gazette* emphasized the harmony between the factories and the natural landscape at

[10] Reps, *The Making of Urban America*, 326; Walter, *Mount Auburn*, 11.

[11] In 1842 there were also rural cemeteries in Salem, Worcester, Springfield, and Plymouth, Massachusetts, New Haven, Connecticut, and Nashua and Portsmouth, New Hampshire. See [J. Brazer,] "Rural Cemeteries," *North American Review*, LIII, 390 (Oct., 1841).

[12] Timothy Dwight, *Travels in New-England and New-York* (New Haven, 1821-1822), IV, 516.

[13] John William Ward, *Andrew Jackson: Symbol for an Age* (New York, 1955), 33, 36.

Lowell. "It seemed," he wrote, "to be a song of triumph and exultation at the successful union of nature with the art of man, in order to make her contribute to the wants and happiness of the human family."[14] After two decades of urban growth, however, it appeared that instead of blending with nature, the city was about to overwhelm it. In 1841, a mill-girl poet wrote: "Who hath not sought some sylvan spot/ Where art, the spoiler, ventures not."[15]

When mid-century Lowellians, and Americans in general, abandoned the inadequate imagery of a factory in the forest, they began to visualize the cityscape and natural landscape in terms of the imagery adumbrated by Story. Instead of trying to blend city and country, Americans granted cities their essential urbanity, but insisted upon easy periodic access to nature. In place of a continuous middle landscape, the American landscape would be defined as a counterpoint between Art and Nature, city and country. The rural cemetery movement provides the earliest and most revealing insight into this new ideology in Lowell and in America.

Oliver M. Whipple, the self-made gunpowder manufacturer and civic leader, was the leading spirit in founding Lowell's rural cemetery. The Proprietors were incorporated on January 23, 1841, and through Whipple's generosity, a scenic forty-five-acre site on the outskirts of the city was acquired.[16]

[14] *Essex Gazette*, Aug. 12, 1825, quoted in John O. Green, "Historical Reminiscences," *Proceedings in the City of Lowell at the Semi-Centennial Celebration of the Incorporation of the Town of Lowell, March 1, 1876* (Lowell, 1876), 67-68.

[15] Adelaide, "Alone With Nature," *The Operatives Magazine* (June, 1941), 37. (According to Harriet Robinson, the pseudonym "Adelaide" was used in the *Lowell Offering* by Lydia S. Hall. (Robinson, *Names and Noms De Plume of Writers in the Lowell Offering* [(Lowell, Mass.:?), 1902], ii.) Since it is known that Lydia S. Hall was associated with *The Operatives Magazine*, she was probably "Adelaide" in this case.) See also Anon., "Lowell," [a poem] Lowell *Mercury*, Sept. 5. 1834; F., "Lowell as it was, and as it is," Lowell *Courier*, April 14, 1840; A. R. A., "Pawtucket Falls," *Literary Repository*, I, 128 (1840); and Ella, "The Window Darkened," *Lowell Offering*, v, 265-267 (Dec., 1845).

[16] C. C. Chase, "Brief Biographical Notices of Prominent Citizens of the Town of Lowell—1826-1836," *Contributions of the Old Residents' Historical Association*, IV, 299 (1891); Frank P. Hill, *Lowell Illustrated* (Lowell, 1884), 9; and Amos Blanchard, *An Address Delivered at the Consecration of the Lowell Cemetery, June 20, 1841* (Lowell, 1841), 8.

The cemetery was laid out in the romantic style by George P. Worcester.[17] He had been influenced by the famous French cemetery, Pére-Lachaise, and some commentators believed that Lowell Cemetery, as well as Mount Auburn, were imitations of it. The American cemeteries had indeed imitated the French one to a certain extent, but there was an important difference in their relationship to nature. Pére-Lachaise was an old garden dedicated to a new purpose when it was opened as a cemetery. Mount Auburn and Lowell cemeteries, however, were established on sites of natural beauty with the intention of conserving their original aspect.[18] Mount Auburn and Lowell Cemetery were to be enclaves of natural beauty adjoining the artificial urban environment.

The Reverend Amos Blanchard's consecration address on June 20, 1841, at Lowell reveals the significance of a rural cemetery in an urban society. Although he touched upon such themes as the need for a new burial place in rapidly growing Lowell, and the respect that should be shown for the dead by making burial places beautiful, Blanchard also addressed himself to larger questions. Midway, he began to explain the role of rural cemeteries in enhancing the urban environment. The thrust of his remarks was that America's rapidly growing cities, marked by visual monotony and social chaos, generated distress that could be assuaged through the influence of romantically designed cemeteries.

Blanchard characterized Lowell and, by implication, other American cities as "cities of strangers."[19] Life in the city was impersonal, ever in flux, and more concerned with the next commercial opportunity than with a proper attention to the permanent roots of community life. Urban living seemed more like hotel life than the traditional community of fond memory. Blanchard and his generation were jarred by the discovery that even the bones of the dead, man's sacred link with his com-

[17] Charles Cowley, *Illustrated History of Lowell* (Boston, 1868), 123.
[18] Hans Huth, in *Nature and the American*, 67, makes this point about Mount Auburn.
[19] Blanchard, *Address*, 7.

munal past, were not safe from the next wave of residential and industrial expansion or financial promotion. He informed his audience that "a tomb-stone, in one of our large cities, was lately seen covered with gairish [sic] handbills, announcing schemes of business, and of the idlest of fashionable amusements and follies."[20]

The physical removal of burial places from downtown locations to rural cemeteries would reduce the risk of such desecration. Blanchard further hoped that "the aspirations of vanity, and the pride of distinction in place, wealth, and power [would] here receive an effectual rebuke."[21] Possibly a rural cemetery would remind a society uprooting itself, conquering a continent, and covering it with cities that the past could not be entirely ignored. Blanchard also revealed his "secret wish that when death shall have torn his beloved ones from his embrace, and when himself shall have died, they might repose together, where they should never be disturbed by the encroachments of a crowded and swelling population of the living. . . ." In a dynamic society, the rural cemetery could plausibly serve as a focus for the "cultivation of home attachments towards the city of our abode." Six months after Blanchard's address, the Lowell *Courier* echoed this sentiment, assuring its readers that the cemetery will provide "a new and more sacred and binding tie to this city as our home."[22] In this sense, the rural cemetery movement reflected an anxious search for a sanctuary from the "go a-head" spirit of the age.

But the attraction of the rural cemetery went beyond the

---

[20] Blanchard, *Address*, 15. This issue is prominent in nearly all the rural cemetery commentary of the time. See Story, *Address*, 12; F. W. S. Rev. Frederick William Shelton, "Rural Cemeteries," *Knickerbocker*, XII, 538 (Dec., 1838); and Anon., *The Cincinnati Cemetery of Spring Grove* (Enlarged edition; Cincinnati, 1862), 45.

[21] Blanchard, *Address*, 19.

[22] Blanchard, *Address*, 8; Lowell *Courier*, Dec. 9, 1841. See also Blanchard, *Address*, 6. For more general comments on this point, see Story, *Address*, 5; N. P. Willis, *Rural Letters and Other Records of Thought at Leisure* (New York, 1849), 154; Theodore Dwight, *Travels in America* (Glasgow, 1848), 144-146; [Andrew Jackson Downing,] Rev. of *Designs for Monuments and Rural Tablets . . .*, by J. J. Smith, in *The Horticulturist*, I, 329-330 (Jan., 1847); and Harris, *The Artist in American Society*, 205-206.

conflict between memory and desire in an age of progress. Blanchard explicitly linked the rural cemetery to a complex of beliefs emerging in the middle of the nineteenth century in response to increasing urbanization. The key elements of this ideology were expressed three months before Blanchard's consecration address in a poem entitled "Alone With Nature," written by a Lowell mill girl who signed herself "Adelaide."

> Alone with nature—will not ye
> Who all her beauty daily see,
> Beneath your native, 'house-hold tree,'
>   Enjoy them for the roving stranger!
> I can not relish half her sweets
> Till taught by bustling, crowded streets,
> To sigh for nature's calm retreats,
>   Then task them for the city-ranger.[23]

In the poem, and in the mid-century American mind, the city is sharply distinguished from the natural landscape, and natural beauty is held to be more necessary for urbanites than for rural dwellers.

As the nation became increasingly urban, Americans who had moved from the country to the city tended to romanticize nature. Only an urban society can afford such romanticizing: in a frontier society trees are not scenic; they are potential houses. Roderick Nash argues that the urban "literary gentleman wielding a pen, not the pioneer with his axe," idealized nature.[24] The example of "Adelaide," the pen-wielding mill girl, suggests that the urge to romanticize nature came from more than heavy draughts of Byron and Wordsworth in a library. An intensely felt need was causing gentleman and mill girl alike to turn to the conventions of romanticism to cope with the emergent city. As the urban environment became paved over, more hurried, and commercial, a change of scenery

---

[23] *The Operatives Magazine* (June, 1841), 37. For identification of the author, see note 15 above.

[24] Roderick Nash, *Wilderness and the American Mind* (New Haven, 1967), 44. For a perceptive treatment of one of these intellectuals and the problem of city and country in America, see Michael H. Cowan, *City of the West: Emerson, America, and Urban Metaphor* (New Haven, 1967).

reminiscent of the rural past, a readily accessible natural sanctuary within close proximity to the city, became necessary. A romantic landscape was sought as a counterbalance to the disturbing aspects of the cityscape. This was the attraction of the rural cemeteries on the outskirts of most American cities.[25] Blanchard understood this when he said that the Lowell Cemetery is "accessible at all times, yet so remote from the marts of business as not to be liable to be encroached upon by the spreading abodes of the living: sequestered from the din and bustle of active life...."[26]

Throughout his address Blanchard endeavored to set off the solitude and romantic beauty of the rural cemetery against the bustle and aesthetic barrenness of the city. He contrasted the praiseworthy Roman custom of burials along country highways with the modern notions that until very recent times preferred the location of cemeteries "by the city church-yard, crowded, noisy, and grassless, . . . and never visited by the dew, and the sunshine, and the showers of heaven."[27] This imagery was noted by the editor of Lowell's liveliest nineteenth-century newspaper, the *Vox Populi*. He found the passage in the printed version of Blanchard's address so striking that he checked his copy of Wordsworth's "Essay on Epitaphs," where he found remarkable parallelism, if not outright plagiarism. The editor noted that numerous other expressions in Blanchard's address were nearly identical with passages in the standard romantic authors. Blanchard explained the instances of parallelism by asserting that the boy who had set the type for the printed text must have omitted the quotation marks.[28]

[25] Andrew Jackson Downing makes this point in his "Public Cemeteries and Public Gardens," 9-10.

[26] Blanchard, *Address*, 8. For similar expressions with reference to Mount Auburn, see Theodore Dwight, *Travels in America*, 198; and Story, *Address*, 12-16, 20. All of the consecration addresses that I have been able to read stress this point. Readily available samples may be found in the excerpts reprinted in Brazer's review of several of them in his "Rural Cemeteries," 385-412.

[27] Blanchard, *Address*, 13-14.

[28] *Vox Populi* [Lowell], July 17, 24, 1841. The expressions Blanchard borrowed from Wordsworth can be found in Alexander B. Grosart, ed., *The Prose Works of William Wordsworth* (London, 1876), II, 25-40. The lines here at issue appear on 32-33.

The incident illustrates the manner in which urban Americans like Blanchard turned to a corpus of romantic writings, largely British, borrowed the vocabulary of romantic nature, and used it to cope with American problems.[29]

Americans had been using European romantic conventions to celebrate nature for nearly a half-century, but by 1850 they were using them with a significant difference.[30] Formerly, they had used these conventions to identify America as a rural republic, but now they located the American identity within a counterpoint of romantic nature and the city. The American landscape was no longer visualized as of a piece. For mid-century city dwellers, there was an urban "inside" and a rural "outside." They had developed an adaptive mechanism that would allow them to retain a commitment to nature in an urban and industrial nation. Americans thus avoided an unpalatable choice between city and country. As Frederick Law Olmsted put it, "no broad question of country life in comparison with city life is involved; it is confessedly a question of delicate adjustment" between the natural and the artificial.[31]

A visitor to Lowell in 1843 used the cemetery to describe the city within this new vocabulary. From the city's "busy streets," he passed "through romantic woods" into the cemetery grounds where he was filled with "deep peace." "You stand as it were, beyond the world, beyond its cares, its strifes, its false, *ignis fatuus* hopes, and its griefs. You have entered a realm of quietude, melody and beauty. . . ."[32]

[29] For comments on this "borrowing" tendency in American intellectual history, see Ward, *Andrew Jackson*, 30, 225n; and Nash, *Wilderness and the American Mind*, 44, 50.

[30] On the problem of nature, nationalism, and urbanization, see Perry Miller's essay, "Nature and the National Ego," in *Errand into the Wilderness* (New York, 1964), 204-216, but especially 215-216. Also important are Perry Miller, *The Raven and the Whale: The War of Words and Wits in the Era of Poe and Melville* (New York, 1956); and Harris, *The Artist in American Society*.

[31] Frederick Law Olmsted and Calvert Vaux, *Report of the Landscape Architects and Superintendents to the President of the Board of Commissioners of Prospect Park, Brooklyn* (1868), reprinted in *Landscape into Cityscape: Frederick Law Olmsted's Plans for a Greater New York City*, Albert Fein, Editor (Ithaca, N. Y., 1967), 160.

[32] L. J. B. C., "Lowell Cemetery," *Eastern Argus*, reprinted in the Lowell *Patriot*, January 25, 1844.

Two years later, John Greenleaf Whittier expressed his feelings about the American Manchester's rural cemetery. Whittier, who lived in Lowell for nearly a year as editor of the antislavery *Middlesex Standard,* recorded his impressions of the city in *The Stranger in Lowell* (1845). Lowell stretched "far and wide its chaos of brick masonry and painted shingles." It is the home of the "Wizard of Mechanism," and "WORK is here the Patron Saint." Everywhere the slogan "WORK OR DIE!" glared at the population.[33] After thus describing his first impressions, he wrote of his visit to Lowell's rural cemetery. It is "a quiet, peaceful spot; the city, with its crowded mills, its busy streets and teeming life, is hidden from view. . . . All is still and solemn. . . ." The cemetery, he further observed, is not the resort of only the "aged and the sad of heart," but also of "the young, the buoyant," who relax under its "soothing influence."[34]

Twenty years later, J. W. Meader similarly portrayed the romantic cemetery as a sanctuary within an urban-industrial society. The cemetery, he wrote, is "a symbol of the solitude, though now adorned and beautiful, which covered all this realm around the fine falls of Concord, when it was invaded by the all-subduing and all-conquering Divinity of Mechanism. . . ."[35] Meader's use of "invaded" and "all-conquering" suggests the defensive nature of the counterpoint concept as manifested in the rural cemetery and later park movement. In the early stages of the introduction of the machine into the forest, Americans regarded it as a sort of technological sublime. Both nature and the machine benefited from the blending of the two. By mid-century, however, the dynamic of the machine and the city's power to obliterate the landscape prompted Americans increasingly to use metaphors suggesting conquest instead of conciliation to describe the machine in the garden. Nevertheless, the counterpoint strategy was not developed to

[33] John Greenleaf Whittier, *The Stranger in Lowell* (Boston, 1845), 9-10. Most of the essays collected in this volume first appeared in the *Middlesex Standard.*

[34] Whittier, *Stranger in Lowell,* 42-43.

[35] J. W. Meader, *The Merrimack* (Boston, 1869), 274-275.

roll back technology, or even to prevent further progress; it was designed only to prevent total victory by the "wizard of mechanism." Mid-century Americans attempted to preserve as much of nature as was possible in a nation of cities and machines.

The counterpoint ideology was quickly expanded beyond its connection with the rural cemetery and became the foundation of the American park movement. Dr. Elisha Huntington, several times Mayor of Lowell, realized what increasing numbers of Americans were recognizing: the attractions of cemeteries for the living could be provided in the form of a public park.[36] In his annual address for 1845, Huntington declared: "We have grown up to a city of twenty-six or seven thousand inhabitants, and with a fair prospect of increasing numbers—we are being hemmed in by walls of brick and mortar, shutting out the pure air of heaven. . . ." It is possible, he observed, to walk out of the city "and seek the green, shady fields on our outskirts," but too often one is met with a sign reading "No Trespassers Allowed." The situation demands the establishment of a "public mall or promenade" near the central part of the city. "The value of such, I will not say luxury, but such a necessary of life, as free, open public grounds, is incalculable; we cannot estimate it."[37]

A month later the City Council responded by authorizing the purchase of land at each end of the city where North and South Commons, parks of nine and twenty acres respectively, were subsequently established.[38] The idea of a common, going back to the seventeenth century, took on an added dimension in the mid-nineteenth century. No longer simply the physical

[36] For example, see Downing, "Public Cemeteries and Public Gardens," 11.

[37] Elisha Huntington, *Address of the Mayor of the City of Lowell, on the Organization of the Government, April 7, 1845* (Lowell, 1845), 14-16. Quotations from 14-15. This portion of the address is reprinted and accompanied by a favorable editorial in the *Vox Populi*, Lowell, April 11, 1845.

[38] Hill, *Lowell Illustrated*, 10; and *A Handbook for the Visitor*, 33. North and South Commons were located at what were then considered the Northern and Southern ends of the city. They are shown on H. S. Bradley's map of Lowell (1848) which is printed in F. Hedge, *Pictorial Lowell Almanac*, 1850 (Lowell, 1849).

and symbolic center of the community, the common now served as a counterpoise to the visual monotony and social routine of emerging forms of urban life.

Faced with the reality of urbanization, Lowellians turned away from the strategy of blurring city and country; they now defined them as distinct entities counterbalancing each other. In the 1820's and 1830's the machine, or factory, in the forest seemed like a benign development. What Leo Marx has called the "middle landscape" was preserved, even enhanced.[39] But as machines increasingly dominated life and the cityscape threatened to annihilate nature, rather than reciprocate with it, Americans began to wonder where progress might end. The counterpoint ideology enabled them to draw a line which would not necessarily arrest further development, but would simultaneously ensure an easily accessible natural sanctuary within the larger urban environment. This ideology seems to have taken hold at mid-century and enjoyed success not only in Lowell, but throughout America—most notably in Frederick Law Olmsted's Central Park in New York City.[40]

The mid-century pattern of visualizing the urban environment as a counterpoint of the urban "inside" and the nonurban "outside" began to break down with the approach of the twentieth century. It is clear that by 1893, when James Bayles wrote about contemporary Lowell, the role of the cemetery as a contrast to urban life had been abandoned. He made no mention of "picturesqueness" or the lack of it in his description of Lowell's burial places. In fact, his praise for the cemetery that Blanchard had consecrated as a counterbalance to urban materialism focused upon "the evidence of the expenditure of vast amounts of wealth" to be found there.[41]

[39] *The Machine in the Garden* (New York, 1964), by Leo Marx is an essay in definition of this term; brief explanations of it can be found on 23, 138-140, 226.

[40] For a broader discussion of this ideology and Olmsted's relation to it, see Thomas Bender, Discovery of the City in America: The Development of Urbanism in 19th-Century Social Thought (Ph.D. dissertation, University of California, Davis, 1971), Chap. 7.

[41] James Bayles, *Lowell, Chelmsford, Graniteville, Forge Village, Dracut, Collinsville of To-Day...* (Lowell, 1893), 104-110, quotation from 108. In his apparent abandonment of the older role for the rural cemetery, Bayles went farther than most professional cemetery planners of his generation. The profes-

As Americans became more engrossed in the idea of a civilization of machines and as suburban expansion obscured the divisions between city and country, the vitality of the counterpoint perspective was sapped. It had arisen partly in response to a fear that the city and the machine would overwhelm man and nature, but for a generation that often used machine metaphors to describe the good society, this motive was lacking.[42] Further, for this interpretation of the American landscape, city and country had to be distinct. But in 1906, Frederick W. Coburn, an art critic and the historian of Lowell, noted that city and country were being blurred in suburbia. He observed that since the advent of the streetcar and the automobile, the region stretching from Washington, D. C. to Portland, Maine was becoming one "five-hundred-mile city," essentially urban in character with ubiquitous reminders to suburbanites that they had "not left the city universal behind."[43] America was

---

sional literature at the turn of the century reveals a tendency to at least give lip-service to the older ideal (it was within this tradition that the profession had developed) while emphasizing ideas of keeping cemeteries away from areas of potential industrial expansion, economical land use, and efficient disposal of the dead. These men, while using a lingering rhetoric, saw their task as planners of cemeteries for the dead, not the living. For example, see Alfred Farmar, "The Modern Cemetery," *Overland Monthly*, n.s., XXIX, 443 (April, 1897); Howard E. Weed, *Modern Park Cemeteries* (Chicago, 1912), 15, 25, 94-95, 119-122; Louis Windmuller, "Disposal of the Dead in Cities," *Municipal Affairs*, VI, 473-477 (Fall, 1902); O. C. Simonds, "Landscape Cemeteries," in *The Standard Cyclopedia of Horticulture*, Liberty Hyde Bailey, Editor (3 vols.; continuously paged; New Edition; New York, 1925), III, 1807-1811; and W. D. Cromarty, "Cemeteries of Yesterday and Today: Their Location and Layout in Relation to the City Plan," *Park and Cemetery*, XXX, 320-321 (Feb., 1921).

[42] For example, see Edward Bellamy's image of the ideal urban society functioning like the machinery in a New England textile factory in his *Looking Backward, 2000-1887* (New York, 1960), 164-165. John William Ward has linked Frederick W. Taylor's scientific management principles to this theme in his essay "The Politics of Design," in *Who Designs America?*, Laurence B. Holland, Editor (New York, 1966), 51-85. For more general statements, see Samuel Haber, *Efficiency and Uplift: Scientific Management in the Progressive Era, 1890-1920* (Chicago, 1964); James Weinstein, *The Corporate Ideal in the Liberal State, 1900-1918* (Boston, 1969), Chap. 4; Samuel P. Hays, "The Politics of Reform in Municipal Government in the Progressive Era," *Pacific Northwest Quarterly*, LV, 157-169 (Oct., 1964); Robert H. Wiebe, *The Search For Order, 1877-1920* (New York, 1967), Chap. 6; and Joel H. Spring, *Education and the Rise of the Corporate State* (Boston, 1972), Chaps. 1-3.

[43] Frederick W. Coburn, "The Five-Hundred-Mile City," *World To-Day*, XI, 1251-1260 (Dec., 1906). See also Frederick W. Coburn, *History of Lowell and Its People* (New York, 1920), I, 371.

again becoming a middle landscape, but this one was primarily urban, whereas the earlier one had been essentially arcadian.[44]

In his study of urban planning in America, John W. Reps wondered "why it did not occur to some daring mind that the picturesque curving lines of the local cemetery might serve as a pattern for a successful residential subdivision."[45] The rural cemetery example undoubtedly influenced the romantic suburb movement that began with A. J. Davis's Lewellyn Park (1852) and ended with Riverside (1869), designed by Frederick Law Olmsted and Calvert Vaux.[46] Later suburban development, however, is another matter. Given the nature of late-nineteenth and twentieth-century suburban expansion, the rural cemetery could not serve as a model. The assumptions underlying most of this suburban development were quite different from those at the base of the rural cemetery movement. Suburban expansion in the 1880's and 1890's was spurred by population densities that could not be humanely provided for within the compact city through existing building technology.[47] The result was an extension of the city, whereas the rural cemetery, the park, and the romantic suburb had been designed as counterbalances to the city. The parks and suburban developments in the late-nineteenth and twentieth centuries, despite an occasional curved lane, have been as artificial as the cities of which they are a part.

When the counterpoint scheme lost its force, a new idea emerged. A rural-urban continuum was now thought to provide optimum living and conditions, a concept resulting in a homogenization of the landscape. With the muting of dif-

[44] For a discussion of the suburbanization of the American landscape and the consequent problem of environmental symbolism, see Anselm Strauss, "The Changing Imagery of City and Suburb," *Sociological Quarterly*, I, 15-24 (Jan., 1960).

[45] Reps, *The Making of Urban America*, 326-330.

[46] On this movement, see Christopher Tunnard, "The Romantic Suburb in America," *Magazine of Art*, XL, 184-187 (1947). In his *The City of Man* (New York, 1953), 195, Christopher Tunnard designates Riverside as the last of the "romantic" suburbs.

[47] See Sam Bass Warner, Jr., *Street Car Suburbs: The Process of Growth in Boston, 1870-1900* (Cambridge, 1962).

ferences, the city lost some of its urbanity and the landscape some of its natural beauty. There is no longer any natural sanctuary abutting the city where one might ease the social, psychological, and visual tensions engendered by urban life. To cope with this twentieth-century problem, the nineteenth-century ideology has been reworked, and it now provides the rationale for the wilderness movement.[48] Since there are no longer enclaves within or near the urban area to obtain an alternative to the urban landscape, men periodically leave megalopolis entirely and seek out primitive areas. Suburban sprawl, the bane of social critics, is lost between the antipodal attractions of the city and the wilderness.

[48] Roderick Nash does not explicitly make this argument, but the evidence he presents in *Wilderness and the American Mind* would support it. See also George Butler, "Change in the City Park," *Landscape*, VIII, 10-13 (Winter, 1958-1959); and Sigurd Olson, "The Meaning of Wilderness for Modern Man," *The Carleton Miscellany*, III, 99-113 (Spring, 1962).

Politics and the Park

THE FIGHT FOR CENTRAL PARK

By IAN R. STEWART[*]

CENTRAL PARK is an 840-acre natural preserve set in the midst of what otherwise is one of the world's most densely urbanized environments. For nearly a century and a quarter it has been New York City's largest and most accessible recreational resource. There is no doubt that the park adds immeasurably to the city's attractiveness and the enjoyment of its residents. Although there continue to be numerous arguments about its state of repair and how best to preserve the integrity of its picturesque design, no one seriously questions the fundamental value of the park's presence.

Yet, as with so many civic institutions that later generations have come to prize so highly, the park was neither enthusiastically received nor easily defended when it was first proposed. Why, in fact, should it have been? In the year it was acquired, 1856, the population of the entire city was less than 700,000 people, and open space still abounded both on and near Manhattan island. The built-up portion of the island had just reached Thirty-eighth Street. In addition, the purchase of the park would require the compulsory acquisition of private property and in the process permanently remove more than 7,500 standard building lots from potential development and the tax rolls. And lastly, the projected cost of this "bit of green" would be more than the city's entire budget for the same year. As these and similar arguments would suggest, a civic improvement of this impact and magnitude was unprecedented.

In spite of the obstacles, Central Park was acquired, but it was not an easy matter. More than twelve years were consumed between the

[*] The author is assistant professor in the Department of City and Regional Planning at Cornell University.

Soon after its completion, Central Park's Grand Drive became an immensely popular place for promenading. Harper's Weekly, *December 16, 1865.*

time when it was first publicly proposed and when the city convinced itself and its officials to take title to the land. The last six years, from 1850 to 1856, involved a particularly intense and protracted political struggle. It is important to examine this period in the park's development, for existing historical analysis has focused exclusively on issues emerging after its acquisition in 1856. An examination of this twelve-year controversy will make more evident the exact nature of political behavior and public decision-making in mid-nineteenth-century New York. Furthermore, it is possible to derive a clearer understanding of the motives and issues surrounding the entire urban parks movement since very similar conflicts would shortly arise in other major American cities as each sought to emulate the successful precedent of Central Park.

The first person to urge that New York acquire a large urban open space was William Cullen Bryant. Although a poet of national reputation, Bryant was best known in New York City as the influential and reform-minded editor of the *New York Evening Post*. As early as 1836 Bryant had privately expressed to family and friends his opinion that before it was too late the city should reserve an area of the island's remaining woodland for future use as a public park.[1] The need was clear; for as one commentator noted:

> There was no place within the city limits in which it was pleasant to walk, or ride, or drive, or stroll; no place for skating, no water in which it was safe to row; no field for base-ball or cricket; no pleasant garden where one could sit and chat with a friend, or watch his children play, or, over a cup of tea or coffee, listen to the music of a good band. Theatres, concerts, and lectures were the only amusements within reach of the mass of the people; the sidewalks, the balconies, the back-yards, the only substitutes for the Hyde Park or Tuileries of the Old World, or the ancient freedom and rural beauty of Young New York.[2]

This was not a condition shared by European cities. For many decades, most cities in England and on the Continent had a number of very large open spaces that were rural in aspect and available for multifunctional uses. There are several reasons for this. European cities had been undergoing urbanization for a longer period, and thus the need for and importance of civic open spaces had long been recognized. Secondly, over the course of time more attention had been given to urban planning in European cities, and the reservation of public open spaces within the plan was a more accepted custom. And lastly, vast tracts of open land had long been a tradition within these countries. From medieval and Renaissance times, the large private gardens and hunting preserves of the royal, ecclesiastical, and aristocratic families were a common part of the landscape. By the nineteenth century, when urbanization had engulfed much of this land and when popular revolutions freed others from private control, these preserves were often reclaimed or given over intact to public usage within urban areas.

In America, such large urban open spaces did not exist.[3] For gen-

[1] Frederick Law Olmsted, Jr., and Theodore Kimball, eds., *Frederick Law Olmsted, Landscape Architect, 1822–1903* (New York, 1922), II, 22.
[2] Clarence C. Cook, *A Description of the New York Central Park* (New York, 1869), 13.
[3] Three possible exceptions to this general statement might be suggested: the Boston Common, Philadelphia's Fairmount Park, and Forsythe Park in Savannah. Yet the Common was never really intended for public recreational use until the public gardens were

erations, America had perceived itself as a primarily rural and unsettled territory, but now its young cities were growing as rapidly as any in the Old World. Along with their growth came an increasing recognition that urban land was not an inexhaustible resource for only private use. The need to provide urban amenities, such as large landscaped parks sufficient for the needs of concentrated populations, was becoming clear.

There were, of course, public outdoor amusement centers in New York such as Contoit's, Niblo's, and Vauxhall Gardens where one could sit and have a drink and be entertained. What Bryant had in mind, however, was a large preserve of landscape open to the public at large for out-of-door relaxation and recreation. Aware no doubt of Dickens' remark in 1842 that New York's summer climate was such that it could throw a man into a fever merely to think what the streets would be like if it were not for the daily breezes from the bay, Bryant had also been both frequent witness to and participant in the summer exodus from the city that by this time was becoming ritual. To escape the stifling summer atmosphere in the growing metropolis, hundreds of people flocked whenever possible to the open and cooling reaches of Staten Island or Hoboken. In addition, great numbers of the wealthy fled to Europe, "to walk in the Tuileries, to drive in Hyde Park, to drink coffee under the lindens in Berlin." Others founded the tradition of a summer exodus to Saratoga or Newport. In July and August nobody who was "anybody" was to be found in the city.[4]

On a hot July day in 1844, Bryant went on a walking tour of upper Manhattan to examine several large tracts of land that might be suitable for what he had in mind. He looked at a number of sites and also witnessed the flight of a large number of residents from the city for the forthcoming holidays. Writing for his July 3 issue, he made his thoughts public for the first time:

If the public authorities, who expend so much of our money in laying out the city, would do what is in their power, they might give our vast popula-

---

later added; Fairmount Park was functioning at this time only as a forest preserve for the purpose of protecting the city's watershed; and Savannah's large park was not improved for use until after 1850. The role of rural cemeteries is described later in this article and is treated in general in Thomas Bender, *Toward an Urban Vision* (Lexington, Ky., 1975), 80–83.

[4] Central Park Association, *The Central Park* (New York, 1926), 21–22.

tion an extensive pleasure ground for shade and recreation in these sultry afternoons, which we might reach without going out of town. ... On the road to Harlem, between Sixty-eighth Street on the South, and Seventy-seventh Street on the North, and extending from Third Avenue to the East River, is a tract of beautiful woodland ... thickly covered with old trees, intermingled with a variety of shrubs. ... There never was a finer situation for the public garden of a great city.[5]

The specific site he recommended was commonly known as Jones's Wood. It was a handsome, heavily forested 160-acre site on the upper east side of the island with access to the East River. In spite of the strong case and the specific recommendation made by Bryant, his suggestion aroused very little public interest. Not one to give up a good cause easily, however, Bryant continued to return in his editorials to the city's need for a large public recreation spot.

Less than a year after this first appeal, the editor-in-chief found himself in England. From there he wrote a letter back to his paper in which he glowingly described the verdant expanses he had seen all over the Continent, but especially in London—Hyde Park, St. James's Park, Regent's Park, and Kensington Gardens.[6]

In this letter of June 24, 1845, Bryant introduced two common themes that would often be taken up by the proponents who later joined him in his endeavor to secure a public park for New York City. First, in describing the utility and beauty of the public parks that had so impressed him in Europe, he introduced the idea that these parks were the rightful models for whatever similar improvements New York would undertake. There was also an implied reproach that with all its commercial success, New York had failed to achieve in its urban center the same level of attractiveness and amenity that was so common in most of Europe's industrial and commercial cities. Enthusiastic over what he had seen in Europe, he could not understand why the growing, wealthy cities of America should not also want these attractive examples of urban necessity and sophistication.

This argument had great influence on many New Yorkers, drawing as it did upon strong feelings of national destiny and pride. Not yet a world power but rather in a developing post-colonial position, the

[5] In Allan Nevins, *The Evening Post; a Century of Journalism* (New York, 1922), 194.
[6] William Cullen Bryant, *Letters of a Traveller; Or, Notes of Things Seen in Europe and America* (New York, 1850), 168–73.

young country was sensitive about its status among world nations. Its cities, though burgeoning, were primitive and rough compared to those of the Old World. This mixture of realistic appraisal and youthful insecurity was recognized even by the city fathers:

> The great metropolis of this continent, priding herself on her wealth and commerce, and on the bright auguries that beckon her in the future, ought not to remain, in this particular, so lamentably behind the great cities of the Old World, which, in so many respects, she so vigorously rivals, and confidently hopes to surpass.[7]

Confident of their destiny, but insecure about their present position, Americans, and New Yorkers especially, consciously emulated the fashions, styles, and civic adornments they saw in European capitals. For if they were to be urban, why not also urbane? They knew that tradition, grand public institutions, and civic attractiveness could not be acquired quickly, but their arguments show that they saw the adoption of improvements like the park as an attempt by the New World civilization to rival its European ancestors.[8] As a symbol of the nation's developing pride in its growth, wealth, and culture, the creation of the park was part of the city's emerging urban consciousness and a new, more cosmopolitan, view of itself.

The second argument mentioned in Bryant's letter also became a common theme used to generate support in favor of a park. That is, that parks were the cities' pulmonary organs, inextricably related to its good health, which would by their very nature open up, ventilate, and clear out the city.[9] As the son and grandson of doctors, this no doubt seemed a reasonable conclusion to Bryant.

With his article and the letter, Bryant thrust the issue of a new park for New York firmly into public view and began to outline the arguments he felt should compel the city fathers to act on the matter. The *Evening Post* tirelessly and effectively pursued the idea over the next few years despite little apparent or immediate public response to the proposal. "Its editors had the more faith in it, they said, because while

---

[7] New York City Board of Aldermen, *Document No. 63*, December 27, 1852, 1673.
[8] For further material on this point, see Andrew Jackson Downing, *Rural Essays* (New York, 1869), 139; Amory Mayo, *Symbols of the Capital* (New York, 1859), 40–44; *New York Illustrated* (New York, 1869), 45; Russell Lynes, *The Art-Makers of Nineteenth-Century America* (New York, 1970), 162.
[9] "The Lungs of London," *Blackwood's Magazine*, XLVI (August, 1839), 213–37.

New Yorkers were somewhat slow in adopting plain and homely reforms, they were likely to engage eagerly in any scheme that wore an air of magnificence. They wouldn't take the trouble to keep the streets clean, but they would spend millions to bring a river into the city through the Croton aqueduct, forty miles long. They wouldn't sweep Broadway, but they would cover Blackwell's Island with stately buildings, some of them not needed."[10]

It remained to be seen if it was New York's propensity to indulge more willingly in the larger, more difficult, more visible and impressive public improvements. By the end of the decade, however, one thing was clear. Bryant, by carefully courting public support for what he felt was an eminently worthy public endeavor, had successfully planted the idea and prepared the ground for other proponents who were now prepared to join in the battle.

Bryant could have hoped for no more valuable ally than Andrew Jackson Downing, an immensely popular and well-respected young landscape architect working out of the Hudson Valley community of Newburgh, New York. In 1841, at the age of twenty-six, Downing had published his first book, *A Treatise on the Theory and Practice of Landscape Gardening Adapted to North America*, in which he argued articulately for the adoption in America of the English ideals of landscape architecture that were part of the picturesque gardening principles then popular throughout Europe. The book quickly went through more than six editions, and it brought the young author instant fame. Later books on domestic architecture and horticultural subjects further enhanced his reputation. So widely read were all his books, which contained a mixture of the artistic and practical aspects of house, garden, and decorative design, that he came to hold a preeminent position as an arbiter of public taste.[11]

Downing also edited a journal on rural manners and life called the *Horticulturist and Journal of Rural Art and Rural Taste*, which he

---

[10] Nevins, *The Evening Post*, 196.

[11] Fredrika Bremer, the celebrated Swedish novelist who visited the United States in 1849–51, observed, "nobody, whether he be rich or poor, builds a house or lays out a garden without consulting Downing's works; every young couple who sets up housekeeping buys them." See Fredrika Bremer, *The Homes of the New World* (New York, 1853), 46. For background on Downing, see Russell Lynes, *The Tastemakers* (New York, 1954), 21–28.

Henry Inman's portrait of William Cullen Bryant, a watercolor and pencil sketch, was done shortly after Bryant began his editorial duties with the New York Evening Post. THE NEW-YORK HISTORICAL SOCIETY.

used as a forum in October 1848 to publicly join Bryant in advocating the New York park. Writing an article in the form of a dialogue between the editor and an American traveler returning from Europe after five years, Downing asked the traveler what appeared to be the greatest contrast now between the Old and New Worlds. The traveler responded patriotically, saying that in most things America was more advanced, except for the availability of "public enjoyments" such as museums, libraries, and especially public parks and gardens. He went on to say that having seen the great revolutions, tumult, and bloodshed throughout Europe that year, he was convinced that whatever barrier of class, wealth, and fashion existed in democratic America could be greatly ameliorated by establishing places of resort such as public parks. "By these means you would soften and humanize the rude, educate and enlighten the ignorant, and give continual enjoyment to the educated. Nothing tends to beat down those artificial barriers . . . so much as a community of rational enjoyments."[12]

This sort of argument offered in favor of the park derived from the nineteenth-century romantic notions of the efficacy of nature in countering the presumed evils and chaos of urban life.[13] The United States was still dominantly an agrarian nation, and its values remained rooted in its rural tradition. Many of its citizens believed that by introducing a piece of rural landscape into the city you might also transfer some of the ambiance and moral temper of the countryside with it. The idea of a rural park in the midst of the nation's largest city may be seen as part of this romantic reaction to urbanization. A portion of the broad-based support for Central Park was derived from this romantic impulse and the anticity feelings it encompassed.

A certain immediacy was given to some of the romantics' arguments by those foresighted enough to realize that private development of Manhattan was proceeding at such a rapid rate that the opportunity to reserve land to improve the urban environment would either be

[12] Downing, *Rural Essays*, 139–42.
[13] For a full discussion of the American perception of the role of nature, see Leo Marx, *The Machine in the Garden: Technology and the Pastoral Ideal in America* (New York, 1967); Peter J. Schmitt, *Back to Nature: the Arcadian Myth in Urban America* (New York, 1969); Paul Shepard, *Man in the Landscape* (New York, 1967); Michael H. Cowan, *City of the West: Emerson, America and the Urban Metaphor* (New Haven, 1967).

gone or be too costly to implement if they failed to act quickly.

Less than a year after his initial article appeared, Downing cited further evidence of the latent need for such a park in another article entitled "Public Cemeteries and Public Gardens." Rural cemeteries had been developed near many American cities during the second quarter of the nineteenth century. Greenwood Cemetery in nearby Brooklyn was opened in 1838. While ostensibly nothing more than a burial ground remotely located to permit easy expansion and to protect urban ground wells from pollution, it quickly came to be much more. The site of Greenwood Cemetery had been laid out according to the picturesque principles of the English landscape school. An elaborate network of paths and roadways curved along the natural lines of the terrain. The site was further embellished by artificially constructed ponds and horticultural gardens. As time passed, the landscape was further decorated in classic and Victorian splendor by the opulent tombs, monuments, temples, and sculptural adornments that were often the handiwork of the era's most respected artists and architects. The overall effect, at once a mixture of natural beauty and melancholy sentiment, was one of tremendous appeal to the romantic sensibilities of the city's residents.[14] In one nine-month period, more than 60,000 New Yorkers made the long trek to Greenwood. The reasons for this strong popular response were obvious to Downing:

> The great attraction of these cemeteries, to the mass of the community, is not in the fact that they are burial places, or solemn places of meditation for the friends of the deceased, or striking exhibitions of monumental sculpture, though all of these have their influence. All these might be realized in a burial ground, planted with straight lines of willows and somber avenues of evergreens. The true secret of the attraction lies in the natural beauty of the sites and in the tasteful and harmonious embellishment of these sites by art.... Hence, to an inhabitant of the town, a visit to one of these spots has the united charm of nature and art... the double wealth of rural and moral associations... in the absence of public gardens, rural cemeteries, in a certain degree, supplied their place. But does not this general interest, manifested in these cemeteries, prove that public gardens, established in a liberal and suitable manner near our large cities, would be equally success-

[14] Edmund V. Gillon, Jr., *Victorian Cemetery Art* (New York, 1972), passim; Wilson Flagg, "Rural Cemeteries," *Hovey's Horticulture*, XIX (1853), 486. Also, Joel H. Ross, *What I Saw in New York; or a Bird's Eye View of City Life* (Auburn, N.Y., 1852), 322–26.

ful? [A park] would be the general holiday-ground of all who love to escape from the brick walls, paved streets, and stifling atmosphere of towns.[15]

With Downing now solidly behind the park issue, and with Bryant able to keep it before the public eye through the columns of the *Evening Post*, part of the city's leadership began to coalesce around the issue.

The publicity engendered by these two men had caught the attention of the city's mayor. In his second annual message to the Board of Aldermen on January 7, 1850, Mayor Caleb S. Woodhull reminded the legislators that all the existing public squares below Forty-second Street, in the aggregate, comprised only sixty-three acres, less than one-fourth of that available to London. "The advantages of open squares in a populous city are so apparent, and so important, that no well governed city was ever content to be without them." Not only do open spaces beautify the city and aid public health, Woodhull asserted, but also "They are the great breathing places of the toiling masses who have no other resort in the heat of summer or in time of pestilence, for pure air and healthful recreation, either for themselves or children."[16]

This argument in support of the park reflected the city's deep concern for public-health reform. New York and most other American cities had repeatedly been visited by yellow fever, cholera, and other deadly epidemics. The specter of contagion was real. In the absence of an established germ theory, and as yet unaware of the value of improved sanitation and other public-health measures, an environmental theory of disease held sway. As a result there was a strong feeling that not being able to abandon the unhealthy city, one might, nevertheless, have a positive effect on city-wide health by bringing a bit of the countryside to the urban center. A favorite analogy was that the large urban park could be "the lungs of the city." By helping to ventilate or dissipate the fetid and disease-bearing air of the congested city, a park would act as an effective antidote to this unfortunate by-product of

---

[15] Downing, "Editorial," *The Horticulturist and Journal of Rural Art and Rural Taste*, IV (July, 1849), 9–11.

[16] Quoted in Isaac Newton Phelps Stokes, *Iconography of Manhattan Island, 1498–1909* (6 vols., New York, 1918), V, 1826.

urbanization.[17] Thus, the park gained strong public backing by its promise to help open up the city and relieve its unhealthy state.

Although Woodhull chose not to run for reelection in the mayoral contest of 1850, sufficient public interest had been generated behind the idea of the park so that the two mayoral candidates strongly campaigned for its construction. Fernando Wood, one of the candidates, who had been abroad and who was impressed with the beauty of foreign parks, particularly those of Brussels, was vociferous in pressing this issue. The nominee of the Locofoco party, Wood was a controversial figure, viewed by many as untrustworthy and representative of a new breed of city politicians who were first and foremost concerned with their own self-interest. Although advocates of the park appreciated his support, many agreed with Philip Hone's comment: "Fernando Wood! Let the books of the Mechanics' Bank tell his story . . . Wood, instead of occupying the mayor's seat, ought to be on the rolls of the State Prison. But our blessed universal suffrage will raise a flame with this *Wood* to drive away Whigism, Conservatism, and good honest Democracy as we formerly knew it."[18]

Although Wood lost the election, his opponent, Ambrose C. Kingsland, had also pledged to do something about the public clamor for a park. On April 5, 1851, shortly after taking office, he sent a message to the common council recommending "the purchase and laying out of a park on a scale which will be worthy of the city . . . which would be at once the pride and ornament of the city." The message began by reiterating the arguments which Bryant and Downing had first outlined, but went on to say:

> Such a park, well laid out, would become the favorite resort of all classes. There are thousands who pass the day of rest among the idle and dissolute, in porter houses, or in places more objectionable, who would rejoice in being enabled to breathe the pure air in such a place, while the ride and drive through its avenues, free from the noise, dust and confusion inseparable from all thoroughfares, would hold out strong inducement for the affluent to make it a place of resort.

[17] Charles N. Glaab and A. Theodore Brown, *A History of Urban America* (New York, 1967), 70–71.

[18] Allan Nevins, ed., *The Diary of Philip Hone, 1828–1851* (2 vols., New York, 1927), II, 905.

The ballroom at Niblo's, one of New York's most popular amusement centers. In addition to the ballroom, Niblo's boasted a theater, gardens, and a refreshment center.

There is no park on the island deserving the name ... [and] I think that the expenditure of a sum necessary to produce and lay out a park of sufficient magnitude to answer the purposes above noted would be well and wisely appropriated, and would be returned to us fourfold, in the health, happiness and comfort of those whose interests are specially entrusted to our keeping—the poorer classes.[19]

Although Kingsland recommended no specific site, his action was most important because it forced the council to take formal action on the issue. Clothed as a public panacea—a device to placate the poor, serve the rich, improve public health and happiness—the idea seemed irresistible. The *Evening Post* naturally gave the mayor's message its

[19] In Edward Hagaman Hall, "Central Park in the City of New York," *Sixteenth Annual Report, 1911, of the American Scenic and Historic Preservation Society* (Albany, 1911), 450.

full support, and it seemed sure that a proposal of such broad promise would move ahead without opposition. In spite of this fact, and the mayor's optimistic statement that he could not believe that "anyone can be found to advance an objection against the expediency of having such a one in our midst," forceful and bitter opposition arose almost immediately and did not relent until many years later.[20]

The fight was led by the *Journal of Commerce*, a powerful local business newspaper that generally represented the interests of the commercial community. The cost to the taxpayer for such a scheme would be tremendous, argued the *Journal* editor. Park lands already owned by the city, valued in excess of eight million dollars, and the cool waters and green country surrounding the city, made the proposal unnecessary. The *Evening Post* responded contemptuously that the investment would prove to be an economy, like the money spent for other city improvements. "Every investment of capital that renders the city more healthy, convenient, and beautiful, attracts both strangers and residents, and leads to a liberal patronage of every department of trade." The argument that the city already had eight million dollars worth of parks was labeled as irrelevant, for in spite of the amount of park lands, there were clearly still not enough parks. Lastly, the fact that New York was near water and open green space was no argument at all; so were most European cities, and they had broad urban parks that were greatly used and appreciated by their population.[21]

In spite of this developing controversy, the council moved resolutely ahead. The mayor's message was referred to the Committee on Lands and Places, which shortly recommended that the 160-acre tract on the east side, Jones's Wood—Bryant's originally proposed site—be acquired for the park. The entire common council adopted the recommendations of the committee for the Jones's Wood plan and moved to apply to the state legislature for the enabling legislation that would permit the city to acquire this site and appoint commissioners to assess the value of the land to be condemned. On June 6, 1851, the council authorized the mayor and the comptroller to begin negotiations with the owners of the land prior to the formal appoint-

[20] Ibid.
[21] Nevins, *The Evening Post*, 197.

ment of the commissioners. On July 11, less than one hundred days after the mayor's message, the state legislature, in extra session, approved the city's request by authorizing it to take possession of the territory between Third Avenue and the East River and Sixty-sixth and Seventy-fifth streets.[22]

The site seemed ideal for the purpose outlined. Long a city landmark because of its beautiful, wild condition, it was covered with a good, full growth of mature oak, chestnut, and elm trees. Uncultivated in appearance, and abounding with wildlife, it was a particularly fine example of picturesque scenery. As a park site it was further enhanced by its attractively irregular surface and by its proximity to the river for potential recreational use.

Hardly had the authorization act been published than there arose a chorus of opposition to the proposed site. Surprisingly, Downing led it off by writing a fiery piece called "The New York Park," which was published in the August 1851 issue of the *Horticulturist*. Thanking Mayor Kingsland for his support, he declared that his only objection was that the site was too small. A mere 160 acres would be "only a child's playground" for the world's fourth largest city. "London has over 6,000 acres within its own limits or in the accessible suburbs," he reminded his readers. He went on to castigate those "timid tax-payers, and men nervous in their private pockets of the municipal expenditures," and then urged:

Five hundred acres is the smallest area that should be reserved for the future wants of such a city, *now*, while it might be obtained. Five hundred acres may be selected between Thirty-ninth street, and the Harlem River, including a varied surface of land, a good deal of which is waste area, so that the whole may be purchased at something like a million dollars.[23]

Downing went on to draw a picture of the park he envisioned, with its statues, commemorative monuments, gardens, and artistic adornments. With surprising and prophetic accuracy, he closely outlined the details and picturesque quality of the very park New York would finally build. In addition, Downing took the opportunity with this article to state his arguments more clearly as to the "social influence"

---

[22] New York City, *Proceedings, Approved by the Mayor*, XIX (1851), 241-42, as cited in Stokes, *Iconography*, V, 1834.

[23] Downing, *Rural Essays*, 147-53.

of such a park in New York, which he termed "the most interesting phase of the whole matter." He pointed out that one group of critics of a New York park felt it would be made only "for the 'upper ten', who ride in fine carriages," while another felt that a country park would be "usurped by rowdies and low people." He rejected both criticisms as foolish and instead developed the argument that a public park would be a place where class and social differences need not exist, for "they enjoy together the same music, breathe the same atmosphere of art, enjoy the same scenery, and grow into social freedom by the very influences of easy intercourse, space, and beauty that surround them."[24]

As interesting as the notion was that the environment could have a substantial effect on social conditions, it was not this argument that caught the attention of the public and the council. It was rather the attractive portrait of the large landscaped park that he had described, his concern about the east-side site's insufficient size, its noncentral location, and its inability to absorb the new municipal reservoir that had been projected. These comments seemed to summarize the growing feelings of discontent over Jones's Wood. The council was impressed by Downing's arguments, and thinking that it had perhaps acted too hastily in initially designating the East River site, it accordingly retreated on August 5, 1851. The mayor appointed aldermen Daniel Dodge, Joseph Britton, and William A. Dooley as a committee to examine whether another site was preferable. Two days after this appointment, the council again met. At this session, aldermen who were advocates of the Jones's Wood site tried to force action by offering a resolution that would have directed the corporation counsel to take whatever legal measures were necessary to appoint commissioners of estimate and assessment who could then secure the land immediately. This step was deferred by the full council when it voted to refer the resolution to the special committee appointed a few days before.[25]

Thus the move was on to find a more suitable site, or at least to give further study to the one already designated. By the autumn of 1851, the main groups in the political controversy were divided according to three major interests.[26] First, there was a large and influential group

[24] Ibid., 151.
[25] Hall, "Central Park in the City of New York," 455-56.
[26] Nevins, *The Evening Post*, 198.

of businessmen, represented effectively by the *Journal of Commerce*, who wanted no park at all. Their main contention was that it simply was not needed within the city and that its cost would be disproportionately borne by them. Second, there was a considerable group of citizens who were entirely satisfied with the Jones's Wood proposal, feeling the council had acted appropriately and wisely in initially designating it. And, last, there was a growing group of people who endorsed Downing's criticisms, believing that a larger park carefully laid out in the central portion of the island was more suited to the city's long-term needs. Throughout the fall and winter these contending viewpoints clashed, gaining varying degrees of editorial support in all the local newspapers, while awaiting the report and further recommendations of the special committee.

On January 2, 1852, at the first council meeting of the year, the long-awaited special committee report was presented. Following the direction of the resolution that had created it, the committee comprehensively compared the Jones's Wood tract with what, in its mind, was the only other site on the island that seemed suitable for prospective park use. This was an approximately 760-acre site situated in the geographic center of the island, bounded by Fifth and Eighth avenues on the east and west and by Sixtieth and 106 streets at the southern and northern limits. The relative advantages of each location were analyzed according to four criteria—size, convenience of locality, availability, and probable cost. In each of the first three categories, the committee easily concluded that the central site was superior. It was obviously larger, more readily accessible, and probably easier to acquire.[27]

In terms of cost, it was more difficult to argue in favor of the central location. Nevertheless, after preparing cost estimates for each parcel of land at both sites, the committee produced elaborate calculations and arguments to conclude that the central park would cost $1,407,325 and Jones's Wood $706,705. Although the cost was almose double for the central site, it was nearly five times larger in area than the 160-acre east side tract. Also, it included a site for a new reservoir, which the

[27] New York City Board of Aldermen, *Document No. 83*, January 2, 1852, reprinted in Board of Commissioners of Central Park, *First Annual Report on the Improvement of Central Park, New York* (New York, 1857), 137–58.

city would have to purchase in any event. Thus, it could be viewed as a more economical purchase. To further rationalize the cost differential, it was argued that a greater benefit assessment could be levied. In addition, the long six-mile border of the central site would create many more attractive building sites that in time might be sold off to help pay for the improvement of the park.[28]

The committee was unanimous in its conclusion that the central site was preferable on all counts. It therefore recommended that the Jones's Wood bill be repealed and that the legislature pass a similar act authorizing the acquisition of the central park lands. This committee's long and thorough report is of critical importance to any history of the New York park, for it is here that the present central site was first identified and ably defended. It is also the basic statement of the arguments that ultimately prevailed on the question of location. Furthermore, the report had in no sense been equivocal. As accepted by the council, it was first a very strong reaffirmation of the need for a park, and secondly a conclusive endorsement that there was only one proper location for it.

Despite these facts, the council stalled, for strong and obstinate opposition was still very evident. During the entire year of 1852, the council refused to take positive action to finally settle the issue.[29] As the issue was carried into the spring of 1853, the various interested parties intensified their campaigns as it became certain that by the summer the state legislature would be asked to give approval to one of the sites. The basic positions remained fixed, even if the individual arguments seemed to be constantly shifting. One group wanted no park at all, another felt Jones's Wood should be taken, and the last saw the central park as the obvious and only reasonable choice.

Those who opposed any park were often from the business community, which objected to surrendering any of the island's shoreline to a public pleasure use and, in general, did not approve of the costs it would involve. One writer explained the position in these terms: "Many men of wealth and influence—who through ignorance and lack of mature reflection on the subject, were unable to anticipate any personal advantage from the construction of a park—feared that it would

[28] Ibid.
[29] *New York Times,* May 2, 1852, 2.

only add to their taxes, and thus were led to form the habit of crying down any hopeful anticipations."[30]

Those who were concerned about a rise in taxes were joined in opposing a park by those few who feared that such spots would become centers of crime or at least coarse behavior. Although there was no proof that the other city parks had been reduced to this state, a lead article in one of the local papers painted this menacing picture of the democratic city:

> It is folly to expect in this country to have parks like those in old aristocratic countries. When we open a public park Sam will air himself in it. He will take his friends whether from Church Street, or elsewhere. He will knock down any better dressed man who remonstrates with him. He will talk and sing, and fill his share of the bench, and flirt with the nursery maids in his own coarse way. Now, we ask what chance have William B. Astor and Edward Everett against this fellow citizen of theirs? Can they and he enjoy the same place? Is it not obvious that he will turn them out, and that the great Central Park will be nothing but a great beer garden for the lowest denizens of the city, of which we shall yet pray litanies to be delivered?[31]

In the same article it was argued that a park so described would actually depress the value of property in the neighborhood since much of the bordering property would quickly be taken up "by Irish and German liquor dealers as sites for dram-shops and lager beer gardens."

Perhaps a more serious but unexpected source of opposition to a park came from the respected New York Association for Improving the Condition of the Poor. Its first public report, issued at the beginning of 1853, concluded that appropriating a large space for a public park would be counterproductive to its efforts to improve the condition of the poor:

> It is self-evident that the using of so much of the island as is now designed for this purpose, will so diminish the space otherwise available for dwelling, as directly and indirectly to increase the intolerable grievances of high rents and crowded tenements which multitudes now suffer without affording any compensatory advantages that will benefit the great mass of the population. Its general effects ... will be decidedly unfavorable.[32]

---

[30] Frederick Law Olmsted, "Public Parks and the Enlargement of Towns," reprinted in S. B. Sutton, ed., *Civilizing American Cities* (Cambridge, 1971), 87.
[31] Ibid., 88.
[32] New York Association for Improving the Condition of the Poor, *First Report of a*

Politics and the Park [143]

By May of 1853, it became clear, however, that the idea of having some park had gained too much momentum and public support to enable the small group that took a stance against any park to prevail. Thus, the issue was now reduced to fighting out the choice between the two proposed sites. One indication of this was that even the *Journal of Commerce*, which hitherto had consistently opposed the building of any park, tacitly switched its position to one of modest support. In a May 24 article, it condemned the idea that the existing legislation proposed to charge the entire city with the expense of acquiring and improving the Jones's Wood park site when in fact the increased value of the surrounding property would accrue only to a few landowners. This was an outrage to the general taxpayer, it argued, particularly when it appeared that the central site was preferable. If a park had to be, then the central one was best as it would embrace the site for the reservoir, which the city would in any event have to purchase. "However," it worried aloud and with an obvious lack of enthusiasm, "we do not see the necessity for making it so immensely large."[33]

With the legislature in session, the backers of the two sites now marshaled their forces. The assembly had passed a bill authorizing the taking of Jones's Wood on April 2, 1853, and senate hearings were about to be opened in Albany to argue out once again the merits of the respective sites. On June 9, the city gave its official endorsement to the central site when the Board of Aldermen voted to request the legislature to authorize the opening of a park, the boundaries of which would be southerly by Sixty-third Street, northerly by One-hundredth Street, between Fifth and Eighth avenues.[34] On June 31, the positions that were argued at the state hearings were made generally known when the select committee of the senate released its report.

The report noted first that the only real issue before the committee was whether it should designate Jones's Wood, since this was the only site the assembly had authorized. The report went on to state, however, that because of the common council's recommendation, the

---

Committee on the Sanitary Conditions of the Laboring Classes in the City of New York, with Remedial Suggestions (New York, 1853), 7.
[33] *Journal of Commerce*, May 24, 1853, 3, and June 18, 1853, 3.
[34] Board of Commissioners of Central Park, *First Annual Report*, 167.

committee would also look at the merits of the central site. How fair a hearing the central park site would receive is not clear, for at the very outset the report undermined its objectivity by noting:

> It will be sufficient to call the attention of the Senate to the fact that the Common Council of New York, already infamous for its corruption and venality, in railroads, Russ pavements, and contracts, has been repudiated by its constituency at a recent election, by a vote of ten to one; thirty three thousand to three thousand. Any recommendation from such a source may fairly be suspected, and your committee do not attach to it the slightest importance.[35]

The committee had called at least six professional witnesses who were gardeners, nurserymen, botanists, or landscape designers, and while there was no firm consensus, there was a numerical preference in favor of the Jones's Wood site. In addition, the senate had received numerous petitions from groups in New York City. More than ten thousand citizens had signed an endorsement for the east side site. Nine thousand more remonstrants prayed that Jones's Wood not be taken because it was not sufficiently central. This petition was called into doubt, however, when it was noted that eleven hundred of the signatures were in the same handwriting. A much smaller group petitioned for no park whatsoever. Having considered all the positions argued before it, it was clear that the senate committee was at least in agreement that New York City should have a park. At this point the committee even went so far as to suggest that the acquisition of both sites might indeed be desirable. But, with classic political dexterity, seeing that it might not be wise to intervene in such a controversial local issue—one that had moved so many voters to align themselves in conflicting positions—the committee's final recommendation was to urge that the issue be passed back to the common council by permitting it to make the final choice after the upcoming election.[36]

This decision hardly satisfied anyone, and one of the committee members, Senator James Cooley, immediately issued a sharp minority report. In it he reviewed all the positive arguments in favor of the central site and also called into question the motives of those many thousands who had endorsed the Jones's Wood site. As he saw it, this move

[35] Ibid., 185.
[36] Ibid., 184–85, 189.

A view of the lake in London's Regent's Park, one of the several parks that Bryant referred to as the "lungs of London." THE NEW YORK PUBLIC LIBRARY, PICTURE COLLECTION.

had been spearheaded by a very few who held land near the east side location, those who stood to gain greatly by the increase in land values that such a park designation would bring. Even those whose lands would be taken had lobbied strongly in favor of Jones's Wood; they could not imagine at this time a more generous customer for their land than the city. Accordingly, Cooley recommended the passage of a law for taking the central location. Both reports were distributed to the senate as a whole, and for the next month they were taken under advisement as local newspapers kept the controversy boiling by the frequent publication of letters on all sides of the issue.[37]

Meanwhile, on the very same day that the senate made its report public, the *New York Daily Times* introduced a new complication into the controversy. After reviewing the many virtues that both sides had so strongly put forth in favor of the two sites, the *Times* editor re-

[37] Ibid., 166; *New York Daily Times*, June 21, 1853.

marked, "The friends of each are implacable with anything less than the instant adoption of their favorite competitor. But are not the two perfectly reconcilable? May not both be bought, and the Central Park made to include not only the major part of that embraced within the draft of the Committee, but the whole of Jones's Wood, down to the water's edge?" Why not squeeze the northern and southern boundaries of the central park down to Ninety-sixth and Sixty-sixth streets and extend the western boundary to Ninth Avenue, thus embracing Manhattan Square?

The eastern shall traverse Fourth Avenue from Ninety-Fourth to Seventy-Fifth Street, where, turning towards the River, it shall follow the lines of Jones's Wood. Here all interests are reconciled. No objection is left. Proportion is recovered. Manhattan, Observatory, and Hamilton Squares are brought within the limits of the park. . . . All the recommendations of the Central Park are united with those of Jones's Wood, and nothing omitted but the disadvantages of both.[38]

Two days later, the *Times* offered a further explanation of its proposal, saying that it was only prudent to buy as much land for the park as possible in advance of its need while it was cheap, and, after all, if it were in excess of what was needed, it could always be sold off, probably at treble the price. Bryant and the *Evening Post* thought that taking both sites was a capital idea. "There is now ample room and need enough upon the island for two parks, whereas, if the matter is delayed for a few years, there will hardly be a space left for one."[39] Those opposed to any park at all were filled with rage by this proposal.

The prospect of having two parks or one aggregating nearly one thousand acres was now upon the city. For the *Journal of Commerce* this was the last straw:

What is it, in effect, but a law or laws to drive our population more and more over to Brooklyn, Williamsburgh, Staten Island, Jersey City, etc., by creating a barrier half a mile to two miles wide, north and south, and occupying half the island east and west, over which population cannot conveniently pass? If ever these projects should be carried into effect, they will cost our citizens millions of dollars. . . . Small parks would be a public blessing; and might be as numerous as the health and comfort of our citizens would require, but a perpetual edict of desolation against two and one

[38] *New York Daily Times,* June 21, 1853.
[39] Ibid., June 23, 1853, p. 4; quoted in Nevins, *The Evening Post,* 198.

Politics and the Park [147]

half square miles of this small island might better come from the bitterest enemies of our city than from its friends.[40]

The issue was now out of the hands of the state, and for a brief period during the summer of 1853, the political pressure subsided. The city was no closer to having the issue resolved. Very few believed that the city needed both parks, and certainly the common council's only firm position had been to favor the central site. Thus, not really interested in pursuing the acquisition of two parks as the state had authorized, it still remained for the council to make the difficult choice between them. Realizing this, the various advocates of the two positions simply shifted the direction of their pressure from Albany back to the council.

In spite of the pressure, the council remained resolute in its support of the central site. Accordingly, in the fall of 1853, it made application to the Supreme Court of the First Judicial District for the appointment of commissioners of estimate and assessment, as authorized by the state act, so that it could get on with the acquisition of property. On November 17 the court appointed five men recommended by the city. For the next two and a half years they went about the difficult task of assigning a fair appraised value to the more than 7,500 building lots in question.

With all barriers now cleared for the acquisition of the central site, the common council still had to settle the pending question of what to do with Jones's Wood. This was not an easy matter since a lawsuit was pending. Shortly after passage of the state act permitting the acquisition of the east side site and seeing that the council did not wish to move ahead with it, a group of interested taxpayers initiated a suit to compel the corporation counsel to apply to the court for the appointment of commissioners of estimate. The original enabling law had stated, "it shall be the *duty* of the corporation counsel of the city of New York to cause application to be made . . ." The point at law was hardly a usual one, as Judge James Roosevelt immediately took note:

> Such an application, on its face, is novel and extraordinary, and until now, I believe unprecedented. It proceeds upon the assumption not only of compelling one party to sell but the other to buy against his will—an exercise of

[40] In Nevins, *The Evening Post*, 199.

the power of eminent domain, indicating, it must be admitted, very peculiar if not very hasty legislation.

The corporation accordingly have employed other counsel to resist the action "of the corporation counsel"; and the court is placed in the not very comfortable attitude of recognizing both and of being compelled, should it decide in the favor of the "corporation counsel," to decide against the corporation itself.[41]

Roosevelt failed to resolve the complicated question at hand, noting rather that a new state legislature and common council were about to be in session, and it was his hope that the obvious ambiguities and unconstitutional features within the law would then be taken care of by the action of one of these bodies.

On January 2, 1854, the new common council met for the first time, and as was traditional, the new mayor, Jacob A. Westervelt, delivered the annual message. Much to everyone's surprise, the cause of a park in New York received another minor setback rather than a resolution of its problems. Westervelt came out firmly against any park in the city by detailing the drawbacks in his mind which both sites evidenced.[42] In spite of his fears and lack of interest, however, the whole question had moved too far along to be sidetracked at this point.

A request to repeal the Jones's Wood bill was now pending in Albany, and the assembly committee reported on it first. Its opinion was split. The first group, which decided the city probably did not need both parks, that the site was remote, and that the city certainly could not afford both parks, recommended that the bill be repealed. The other half of the committee disagreed, saying that in its estimation, especially when the public site and reservoirs were subtracted, the central park was not sufficient, and for the good of the city, Jones's Wood ought also to be acquired. Therefore, with no clear consensus from the assembly, the bill to repeal went before the appropriate senate committee, which favored its repeal.[43] There was one other factor, not mentioned by either committee, which had a negative effect on the question of maintaining the law intact. Unlike the bill authorizing the

---

[41] New York State Senate, *Document No. 47*, February 7, 1854.
[42] New York City Board of Aldermen, *Document No. 1*, January 2, 1854.
[43] New York State Assembly, *Document No. 21*, January 18, 1854; *Document No. 18*, January 25, 1854; New York State Senate, *Document No. 47*, February 7, 1854.

taking of the central park, the original Jones's Wood bill had no provision for recouping any part of its cost through a benefit assessment. Rather, the cost of its acquisition and improvement was to be borne by the city taxpayers as a whole, even though it was clear that the small number of adjoining property owners would profit greatly from its construction.[44] This was offensive to a number of residents, and as a result, many of them lobbied earnestly for the bill's defeat. Accordingly, on April 11, 1854, the full legislature voted to repeal the act that had authorized the taking of Jones's Wood, thus finally ending the long struggle regarding the park's location first initiated by Bryant nearly ten years earlier.

With the possibility that it would ever become a public park now gone, Jones's Wood soon became prey to real estate speculators. For a brief period a resort hotel operated out of an old mansion on the site. Then, but three years after the state's action, the *New York Evening Times* reported: "Jones' Woods . . . fairly comes into market to-day for City lots . . . at least 350 lots, scattered over and through the famous 'Woods', are to be offered by Mr. Bleecker to-day, at the Exchange, to the highest bidder."[45] One would think that with the elimination of the east side site from consideration, the city could now proceed in an unencumbered fashion to acquire and construct the central park. Even before the Jones's Wood site was eliminated, however, forces were being marshaled for another skirmish.

Encouraged by the reservation that Mayor Westervelt had expressed, those who in the past had opposed a park found their hopes reinvigorated. In addition, some of those who in the past had enthusiastically endorsed the idea of a park were beginning to develop cold feet as it became apparent from the early work of the commissioners of estimate that the originally estimated cost of $1.4 million would more than likely be trebled.[46] Finally, these two groups were joined by a number of concerned residents who owned property within or near the southern boundary of the park. Together, in the early part of 1854, they initiated a movement to cut back the boundaries and substantially reduce the size of the park.

[44] Board of Commissioners of Central Park, *First Annual Report*, 88–97.
[45] *New York Evening Times*, April 21, 1857, as cited in Stokes, *Iconography*, V, 1868.
[46] Edward Dana Durand, *The Finances of New York City* (New York, 1898), 99–100.

They came before the common council bearing a petition with several thousand signatures and demanding that the park's dimensions be reduced. Public hearings were held, and on March 13, 1854, the Committee on Lands and Places reported a set of recommendations. It proposed to eliminate that portion of the park below Seventy-second Street, as well as a 400-foot strip from each side. A minority of the committee issued a separate report urging instead that only the 400-foot strips be removed while the northern and southern boundaries remain fixed. Opponents to any reduction in the park's area suggested that if a reduction must occur then perhaps the park could extend from Sixth to Eighth or Fifth to Seventh instead of from Fifth to Eighth avenues.[47]

The ubiquitous Bryant showed his usual staunch opposition to any reduction of the park. Protesting vigorously, he reminded his readers that London had more than 1,500 acres of park land, which could no doubt command high prices as building lots, so why should New York be upset about sparing a mere 700. The people of New York, he said, owe it "to the thousands coming after them, who will before many years make this city the first in the world in point of size, to bequeath them pleasure grounds commensurate with its greatness."[48]

On April 3, 1854, the council passed a resolution to petition the state to allow it to reduce the size of the park by nearly one-half, as the committee's majority had recommended. Eighteen fifty-four was an election year, however. Increasingly preoccupied with electioneering activities and hoping to avoid the sort of public controversy this volatile issue had brought forth in the past, the council allowed the rest of the year to slip by without ever formally presenting its petition to the state legislature for action. Late in the year, a state senator, acting independently in response to constituent pressure, had introduced his own bill to reduce the park's area and for "interspersing into the park suitable squares connecting with each other but on which family edifices may be erected." The legislature refused to consider it, and the only response it received was another strong blast from Bryant.[49]

[47] *First Annual Report*, 128, 116–22; Nevins, *The Evening Post*, 200.
[48] In Nevins, *The Evening Post*, 200–201.
[49] Ibid., 200.

Politics and the Park [151]

On January 1, 1855, to the chagrin of many New Yorkers, Fernando Wood, the Democratic candidate, succeeded Westervelt as mayor. He entered office with a history of criminal activity that had just recently come under the scrutiny of a grand jury investigation. His notoriety had been earned. In 1840, at age twenty-eight, he had been elected to Congress, where he quickly gained a reputation as a sharp political operator. It was common knowledge that in 1850, when he unsuccessfully ran for the office of mayor, he had won the nomination by bribing a number of delegates. In the same year, he was also convicted of cheating his business partner and was forced to pay $15,000 in damages.[50] Thus, he hardly appeared in the 1854 election campaign as an exemplary candidate for the office of mayor. One recent historian has spoken of his role in New York City politics in these terms:

> ... Fernando Wood and his organization were the precursors of the Tweed Ring, [and] Wood was, in a very real sense, Tweed's mentor ... Indeed, it has been said that "it was in Wood's school that most of the Tammany leaders of the next generation learned their politics." Wood demonstrated how power could be centralized. As the model of craftiness in government, he was a masterful exponent of applying corrupt practices. His methods were observed by Tweed and he used them later with even more success. Sometimes Tweed learned his lessons the hard way. "I never yet went to get a corner lot," he said, "that I didn't find Wood had got in ahead of me."[51]

In spite of the promise of this sort of activity, Wood managed to carry the election narrowly, aided by the strong Tammany organization, an election split between four parties, and a very strong state-wide showing by the Democrats.[52]

A man with Wood's reputation deserved to be closely watched, and as his term began, observers caught an eyeful. Displaying an astounding amount of duplicity, even for a talented Tammany politician, Wood began moving against civic wrongs and corruption as if he were a pious reformer. In his inaugural address, he proclaimed that it was his intention to end inefficient government, clean the streets, suppress

---

[50] Alexander B. Callow, Jr., *The Tweed Ring* (New York, 1965), 18–21; Leonard Chalmers, "Fernando Wood and Tammany Hall: the First Phase," *The New-York Historical Society Quarterly*, LII (October, 1968), 382.
[51] Callow, *The Tweed Ring*, 18.
[52] [E. Hutchinson], *A Model Mayor* (New York, 1855), 15–16.

crime and violence, and provide economy in the administration of city government. During his first six months in office, it actually appeared that he might accomplish these lofty objectives. He moved to end corruption in the police force, backed the temperance movement by closing saloons on Sundays, cracked down on the operation of brothels, and endorsed the idea of a city university. Laws were enforced as they had not been enforced for fifty years. He even established a complaint book at City Hall in which all citizens could write their grievances so that they could be attended to.[53]

The initial dismay that had greeted Wood's inauguration turned to praise. Important and reputable people throughout the country sought his acquaintance. "The clergy preached about him and prayed for him. The press lauded him. . . . Men who had clamored, before his inauguration, for his incarceration in prison, took him by the hand, confessed their sins, and wished him God speed. . . . Great religious societies passed him votes of thanks . . . To a committee who presented him these compliments he said, 'I am only doing my duty. New York pays enough to be well governed, and she shall be.'" George Templeton Strong could not understand the phenomenon he was witnessing, but was very pleased nonetheless. Summarizing Wood's first two months in office, he wrote, "He is the first mayor, for thirty years at least, who has set himself seriously to the work of giving the civic administration a decent appearance of common honesty."[54]

New York had a new civic hero. On March 15, 1855, in the midst of this quixotic journey in municipal reform, the council reintroduced the issue of the park by again passing its majority committee recommendation to reduce the size of the park. Eight days later, Wood, very much enjoying his new role as leader and spokesman for progressive elements within the city, emphatically vetoed the council's action. "Any proposition having for its aim an interference with the work as originally devised . . . will, in my opinion, jeopardize the success of this most intelligent, philanthropic and patriotic public enterprise."[55]

[53] Chalmers, "Fernando Wood and Tammany Hall," 383–84; also, Allan Nevins and Milton H. Thomas, eds., *The Diary of George Templeton Strong* (4 vols., New York, 1852), II, 217.

[54] Mathew Hale Smith, *Sunshine and Shadow in New York* (Hartford, 1868), 272; Nevins and Thomas, eds., *Diary of George Templeton Strong*, II, 211–12.

[55] For full veto message, see Xavier Donald MacLeod, *Biography of Fernando Wood* (New York, 1856), 307–12.

Politics and the Park [153]

The mayor's veto prevailed without any effort mustered to override it. Indeed, the formidable new mayor, with his strong popular support, was not now a man to be easily opposed or tampered with. The issue of the park's size and location was now finally settled.

Shortly after this episode, cracks began to appear in Wood's carefully constructed image. Approximately six months after his inauguration, some of the worst predictions that had preceded his election began to be realized, and it became clear that his pious behavior had been a temporary façade. During the remainder of his three terms in office, few opportunities for self-aggrandizement eluded him. For a brief period, however, he had won the support of the city's respectable gentry.[56] Among them were many who were strong backers of the park, and who were now grateful to have been the unwitting beneficiaries of part of his fanciful charade. A later evaluation of Wood's motives, cynical but perhaps more accurate, held that he had moved to protect the park to enhance his prospects of later extracting huge sums of graft from the contractors hired to develop and improve it.

The last step involved in the process of acquiring the park was to appraise the value of the land and take possession of it under the powers of eminent domain. For two years, the commissioners of assessment and apportionment had been at work assigning values to the more than 7,500 building lots embraced by the site. They had also estimated the amount of monetary benefit that would be gained by the properties near the park and delineated the territorial limits over which this benefit assessment should be spread. The commissioners' report, submitted on July 2, 1855, had only to be confirmed by a judge of the state supreme court.[57]

[56] Callow, *The Tweed Ring*, 18–19.
[57] [Hutchinson], *A Model Mayor*, 42–43.

This diagram, "First study of design for the Central Park," was presented by Calvert Vaux and Frederick Law Olmsted in 1858 in their report Description of a Plan for the Improvement of the Central Park. "Greensward." THE NEW-YORK HISTORICAL SOCIETY.

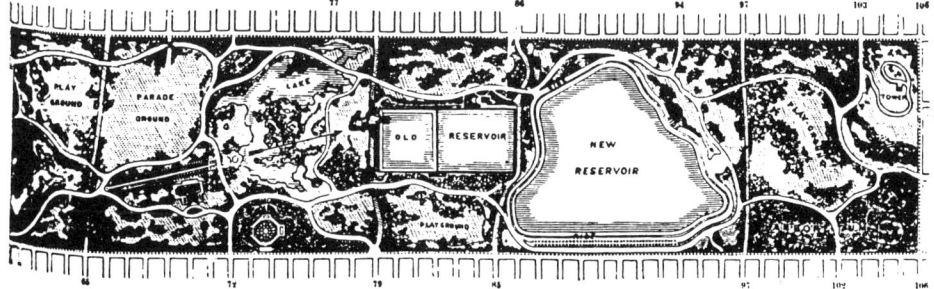

Immediately after the report became public, strong opposition again emerged. A large number of property owners began opposing confirmation, claiming that the amounts of money they would either be offered or assessed were grossly unfair. Indignant over the estimates, they boldly declared that there was no judge in the city who would dare give the necessary approval. Judge Roosevelt, who would normally sit in the district, effectively eliminated himself from the case by publicly announcing his agreement with some of the opposition's claims.[58] Only after the governor reassigned Judge Harris of Albany to help cover the district workload was the matter able to receive a hearing.

More than forty lawyers appeared in opposition to the matter representing various parties who felt aggrieved by the proposed payments that had been listed. The hearings dragged on for days while each presented his case. The hopes of Robert Dillon, the corporation counsel who presented the report for confirmation, dwindled before this well-organized legal onslaught. On the last day, all he could urge in his closing remarks to the judge was, "Sign this report, and old age and prattling childhood will thank you."[59]

On July 5, 1856, Judge Harris signed the report of the commissioners, noting that he had considered all of the major objections presented, but had found them all to be without essential merit. Since less than three percent of the owners of the 7,500 lots in question had appeared to oppose the appraisal, it was the court's feeling that justice had been done and that the city might now proceed with acquiring and constructing the park.[60]

Accordingly, the comptroller submitted a resolution to the common council for the payment of $5,073,433, of which $1,658,395 was to be paid by owners of the land adjacent to the park in view of the prospective benefit which the park's presence would yield to them. The remainder was underwritten by a bond issue of the city at a rate of interest not to exceed seven percent.[61]

Thus, in the summer of 1856, New York was in possession of its park.

[58] Hall, "Central Park in the City of New York," 460–61; Nevins and Thomas, *Diary of George Templeton Strong*, II, 251.
[59] Hall, "Central Park in the City of New York," 461.
[60] Board of Commissioners of Central Park, *First Annual Report*, 103–11.
[61] Durand, *The Finances of the City of New York*, 100. For a general history of the city's use of the benefit assessment as a means of paying for public improvements, see ibid., 58–59; Board of Commissioners of Central Park, *First Annual Report*, 112–13.

nearly twelve years after William Cullen Bryant had first advocated it in the *New York Evening Post*. A great deal of credit for the emergence of the park from this protracted political struggle must certainly be given to the vision, tenacious support, and leadership of individuals such as Bryant, Downing, Kingsland, and even Wood.[62] It should be recognized, nevertheless, that the successful political struggle for the acquisition of the park resulted from a set of fortuitous circumstances. There is no evidence that the primary actors in the movement for the park acted in a highly coordinated or concerted fashion. Rather a host of individuals and organizations were attracted to the issue of the park by a set of diverse motivations. In the aggregate the arguments of each were mutually reinforcing. The result was the knitting together of a coalition of sufficient strength to sway popular opinion and convince public officials of the validity and necessity of a park.

It is equally important to recognize the social context that the struggle for the park had made manifest. Specific arguments and actions of individuals were most often only the reflection of several currents of thought in the larger society. The arguments for the park relating to public health improvements, an emerging urban consciousness and civic pride, and that it would be a device for lessening class antagonisms, drew on progressive ideals aimed at positively reforming the growing city. Conversely, the struggle for the park also benefitted from conservative views. The city's rapid urbanization in the 1840s and 1850s had displaced and forced to distant locations the many private gardens, nearby farms, and extensive woodlands that had just recently been a characteristic part of the urban landscape. Those arguments based on the romantic notion of the curative powers of nature and the park as an urban antidote were a reaction by urbanites to the circumstances that threatened to deprive them of what they had accepted as commonplace. In this light the movement for the park was an effort to restore within the city something that had been lost. It was the ability of the park to simultaneously appeal to both progressive reform ideals and certain conservative impulses that sustained and gave broad-based credence to the park issue as it ran the difficult gantlet of public decision-making.

[62] In 1900, the city commemorated Bryant's formative role when it erected a statue of him and named a small open space on the western side of the present New York Public Library in his honor.

Private Plans for Public Spaces: The Origins of Chicago's Park System, 1850-1875

BY GLEN E. HOLT

"It is singular, that with all her characteristic business energy and forethought, [Chicago] has so far neglected to secure ample grounds for park purposes; but the time has now arrived when it becomes necessary to act...."

Dr. John H. Rauch in Public Parks *(1869)*

WHEREVER ONE GOES in Chicago, the effects of planning are apparent. Whether walking along the lakefront, crossing the river, or driving on the city's streets and expressways, one is surrounded by evidence of efforts to control and shape the natural environment.

Many features of our present-day city may be traced to the magnificent *Plan of Chicago* prepared by Daniel H. Burnham and Edward Bennett for the Commercial Club in 1909. But Burnham and Bennett were by no means the first Chicagoans to address the problems of urban land use. In urging the creation of more and better recreational areas, they followed in the wake of earlier citizens who had already laid the basis for one of the nation's largest and most attractive urban park systems. Although these early park promoters were less formal in their methods than Burnham and Bennett—and certainly less self-conscious about what they were doing—they articulated an approach to urban planning that was to reappear many times in Chicago.

Like the Burnham Plan, which was commissioned and sponsored by private individuals, the parks were created through the efforts of business and civic leaders, physicians, lawyers, and real estate developers who responded to a need that public officials were unwilling or unable to satisfy. Like the members of the Commercial Club, the park advocates hired professional designers who studied the problem, suggested ideas, and formalized their proposals on paper. Once the concept had been developed, the backers waged publicity campaigns and lobbied for the appropriation of public funds. The process is not unfamiliar even today, for as the park planners demonstrated, it often brings results.

༄

As early as 1849, one of the city's leading boosters, real estate man John S. Wright, published a letter in one of the city's newspapers outlining a splendid vision:

I foresee a time, not far distant, when Chicago will need for its fast increasing population a park or parks in each division. Of these parks I have a vision. They are all improved and connected with a wide avenue, extending to and along the lake shore on the north and south, and so surround the city with a magnificent chain of parks and parkways that have not their equals in the world.

Wright's prophecy was no more than a dream in the late 1840s, not only for Chicago but for older American cities as well. Only a few years

---

Glen E. Holt teaches history and urban studies at Washington University, St. Louis. He is co-author of *Chicago: A Historical Guide to the Neighborhoods* just published by the Chicago Historical Society, and of a forthcoming social history of the city to be published by the University of Chicago Press.

Lincoln Park, early 1900s. The designers of Chicago's parks made provisions for a variety of pleasurable activities, including playing fields, walking paths, and benches in their plans. CHS, gift of Lake Bluff Public Library.

earlier, the poet and philosopher, William Cullen Bryant, had begun a public campaign for large urban recreational grounds, urging New York City to purchase outlying lands and transform them into "surpassingly beautiful pleasure-grounds" in advance of the "population of the city . . . sweeping over [these areas] and covering [them] from our reach." Another leading advocate of parks was landscape architect Andrew Jackson Downing, who, comparing New York parks to those in London, concluded, "What are called parks in New York are not even apologies for the thing; they are only squares or paddocks." After a number of influential political figures joined the movement, the city obtained authorization for land acquisition on Manhattan Island above 57th Street. The purchases were completed in 1856, and a year later the park commissioners appointed Frederick Law Olmsted as the first superintendent of the new public grounds.

At the time of his appointment, Olmsted was best known in literary and scientific circles for his *Walks and Talks of an American Farmer in England* (1852) in which he revealed considerable knowledge of scientific agriculture. When Andrew Jackson Downing died in 1852, Olmsted sought out Downing's former partner, Calvert Vaux, and the two men formed what became the foremost landscape design team of its time. Olmsted and Vaux's 1857–58 design for what was then called "Greensward" soon became the basic plan for Central Park.

Inspired by the creation of these great pleasure grounds, other cities sought to emulate New York's example. Within a decade after the publication of the Central Park plan, Baltimore and Philadelphia had established large public grounds and a number of other major cities were considering the idea. Even in Chicago, whose previous record for creating parks had been lackluster at best, prospects were rapidly improving.

Chicago's first public ground, Dearborn Park, had been designated in 1839. Few resources were spent to improve this two-acre plot on

Union Park on the West Side is one of the oldest parks in Chicago, dating from the 1850s. From *Tally Ho! Coaching through Chicago's Parks and Boulevards*, 1889. CHS.

Michigan Avenue between Randolph and Washington, and in 1897 it became the site of the Chicago Public Library. Washington Square, located east of North Clark Street between Delaware and Walton, was dedicated as a public space in 1842 but had little in the way of good design to add to its simple openness. After 1854, the principal park in the city was the 18-acre Union Park on the West Side off Ashland Avenue. Its elegant formal landscaping reflected its setting in a wealthy residential neighborhood. At the time of the Civil War, the remainder of the forty-odd parcels of designated parkland scattered through the north, south, and west divisions were hardly more than ill-shaped vacant lots transferred to the city by developers as they opened their subdivisions.

In fact, the largest parklike spaces to be found in the Chicago area were the handsome private cemeteries being laid out beyond the city limits. Beginning with the founding of Rosehill in 1859, followed by Calvary (1859) and Graceland (1860), these cemeteries were designed to replace the poorly drained, overcrowded City Cemetery on Clark Street which had provoked mounting criticism throughout the 1850s. In 1858, when Dr. John Rauch of Rush Medical College circulated a manuscript in which he related careless burial practices to disease, a number of prominent North Side residents— including George W. Dole, Gurdon Hubbard, and Walter Newberry—urged the city council to close the City Cemetery and move the bodies to another location. The council was more than willing to oblige when groups of developers stepped forward with proposals to landscape and maintain private burial grounds modeled after the "rural cemeteries" becoming fashionable in large cities on the East Coast.

These rural interment places were strikingly different from earlier burial grounds. Instead of formal, crowded rows of sarcophagi, visitors found undulating roadways, colorful gardens, widely spaced crypts and headstones, and heroic statues cast in the likenesses of civic leaders and war heroes. Whereas older cemeteries had been primarily distinguished by architectural monuments, the new ones were embellished parks intended to uplift the spirits of the living.

According to one local journalist, Graceland—laid out by landscape artist H. W. S. Cleveland five miles north of downtown—soon

Parks and Planning

gained a reputation as the most beautiful cemetery in Chicago. Its managers passed specific rules forbidding "the setting up of unsightly headstones and gaudy monuments" in order to preserve the integrity of the landscaping and maintain "the most pleasing park effects so as to produce upon the visitor a sensation of rest and peace." Rosehill, located seven miles northwest of the business district, and Calvary, sited ten miles north along the lake, were even farther removed from the rush of city life.

Thus it is not surprising that, even before these cemeteries were completed, Chicagoans began to use them for recreational purposes. Interlopers on cemetery property became enough of a problem to lead cemetery boards to pass rules restricting entrance. Picnickers were deterred from the beginning, usually by a gateman who confiscated lunch baskets from anyone who dared to eat on the well-kept lawns. One cemetery charged admission to all but those who brought along their burial lot certificates. But despite such regulations, cemetery-going continued to be a popular activity.

This situation obviously lent weight to the arguments of local park advocates, who were becoming increasingly vocal by the late 1850s. It may have been that the cemetery plans stirred interest in the park idea by suggesting how landscaping techniques could be used to enhance the local terrain. The continued growth of the city, both in population and area, contributed to the feeling that action should be taken soon, while there were still open areas to be saved from development. As always, local pride encouraged the belief that Chicagoans could equal, if not outdo, New York's example in any and all matters. And because the city had recently embarked on a plan for a new sanitation system, which limited the amount of public funds available for the purchase of park land, it was clear that private citizens would have to take the initiative in proposing a plan of action.

Some wealthy North Siders—including many veterans of the earlier fight to close the

INTERIOR VIEWS IN ROSEHILL.

Chicago's rural cemeteries were laid out to achieve "the most pleasing park effects." From *Description and Dedication of the Rosehill Cemetery*, 1859. CHS.

City Cemetery—led the way. In 1861 they persuaded the city to designate an eighty-acre tract north of the old cemetery as a public ground. Two years later, these residents obtained state legislation creating a North Parks Board.

The author of this legislation was Ezra B. McCagg, who with his partner, South Sider J. Young Scammon, took time from a busy law practice to work on behalf of a number of important civic projects. "Broad and catholic" in his education and interests, McCagg was a charter member of the Chicago Historical Society, the Chicago Astronomical Society, and the Chicago Academy of Sciences. During the Civil

Parks and Planning

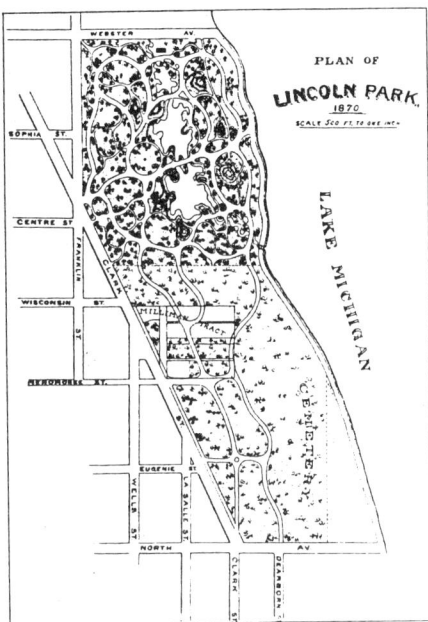

A sixty-acre piece of the City Cemetery, combined with eighty acres to the north, formed the basis of what was designated as Lincoln Park in 1865. From *Report of the Commissioners and a History of Lincoln Park,* 1899. CHS.

War, he served as president of the North Western Sanitary Commission.

McCagg also handled the litigation which made it possible for the North Parks Board to acquire a sixty acre piece of the City Cemetery which, combined with the eighty acres to the north, formed the basis of what was designated as Lincoln Park in 1865. John C. Ure, a local carpenter-turned-landscaper, was hired to lay out the first tract, but continuing litigation, financial problems, and a limited mandate from the state prevented the North Parks Board from creating a fully developed park.

Meanwhile, a group of south suburban residents, primarily representing real estate interests in the towns of South Chicago, Hyde Park, and Lake, united to promote the creation of a large South Side park. By 1866 this group was ready to seek legal authorization for its venture and called upon McCagg to write the legislation. In authoring the bill, McCagg demonstrated his civic leadership once more, for there was bitter rivalry among South Siders, North Siders, West Siders, and suburbanites over nearly every issue involving public improvements.

The leader of the legislative fight for the South Park was land developer Paul Cornell, who in 1856 had founded and laid out the 300-acre railroad suburb of Hyde Park. Cornell hoped that the creation of a park nearby would set off a new burst of land purchasing in Hyde Park, sales having fallen off after an initial wave of land buying in his development there.

Largely through Cornell's efforts as a lobbyist in Springfield, the South Park Bill was approved by the General Assembly in 1867 with the provision that the voters of the three suburban towns of South Chicago, Hyde Park, and Lake, as well as those of a portion of the city's South Side, were to hold a referendum to approve the creation of a common taxing district to support park development. Citizens of the three suburban areas acted favorably, but city voters rejected the measure because they thought the new park would be too far away to do them any good. Further action had to await the meeting of the next legislature.

At this point a new group stepped forward to advocate more open space for the city. In November 1868, the Chicago Academy of Sciences asked Dr. John Rauch to prepare a paper on public parks to be read before its members. Within a couple of months, Rauch published *Public Parks: Their Effects Upon the Moral, Physical and Sanitary Conditions of the Inhabitants of Large Cities; With Special Reference to the City of Chicago.*

Rauch's treatise began with a synoptic but highly readable history of parks from ancient times to the present, from which he concluded

Parks and Planning

Washington Park, 1906. The Olmsted and Vaux plan called for the creation of rustic meadows as well as formal gardens. CHS.

that Chicago had not built parks because its citizens had been too preoccupied with other matters during the city's brief existence. But "the time has now arrived," Rauch asserted, "when it becomes necessary to act, and act in a manner that will not leave her behind, as compared with other cities, in those arts which embellish and render cities attractive as places of abode." In fact, he argued that the matter was of the utmost urgency because parks were essential to public health. The city's morbidity rate, he claimed, was directly related to its climate, which not only contributed to the spread of certain diseases but encouraged residents to overwork. Parks would allow citizens to "enjoy themselves in a rational and healthful manner" and expose them to the "moral influence" of nature, of which those surrounded by the "artificial conditions . . . in cities" were deprived.

Under the united pressure of civic leaders like McCagg, real estate developers like Cornell, and sanitarian reformers like Rauch, the Illinois General Assembly passed bills creating the South, West, and Lincoln Park commissions in February 1869. These agencies, to be administered by commissioners appointed by the governor, were empowered to act as autonomous governments quite separate from the City of Chicago or its suburban towns. The powers given to the commissioners were extensive, allowing them to buy or condemn land with just compensation, to assess and collect taxes in support of park construction and operation, and to borrow millions of dollars so that work could begin immediately.

Since land acquisition was the major expense of the park boards, especially in their early years, the real estate speculators who had been among

Parks and Planning

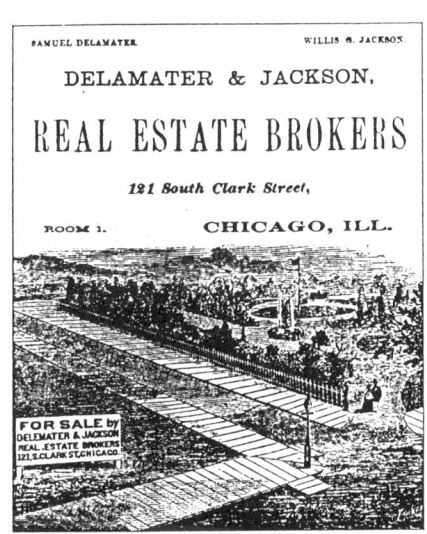

Real estate promoters were among the most active promoters—and among the immediate beneficiaries—of park development. From *The Parks and Property Interests of the City of Chicago*, 1869. CHS.

the chief advocates of a park system turned out to be its chief beneficiaries. In the months following the passage of the park bills, they continued to play a pivotal role.

The vote for creating the park commissions had not been unanimous, and some of the real estate men who advocated open spaces believed that their principal opponents were the unpropertied who were likely to object to improvements that would raise the purchase price of real estate. Even the *Chicago Tribune* expressed doubts when it warned against "withdrawing capital from its legitimate and useful channels to be locked up in park fronts." A number of real estate firms responded by sponsoring publication of an anonymously authored booklet, *The Parks and Property Interests of the City of Chicago* (1869), which attempted to explain in the most conservative terms the benefits to be gained from building parks.

The author claimed that the anticipated rise in real estate prices following park development would be a major benefit, noting that New York's Central Park "had hardly been staked out before the hoped-for rise in the value of the surrounding lots began, and to-day that rise has reached a point beyond the wildest expectation." In Chicago, the author continued, the rise in property values would be so large that any investment for parks would pay for itself in the form of increased taxes to the city.

The pamphlet went on to stress that even those who had no property benefited from access to open space. The poor, readers were told, would "be gainers without a single drawback. Free of expense to them, except for their time, they will be privileged to enjoy in these grounds not only pure air, but the beauties of art and nature, which are nowhere capable of being rendered so impressive as in a first-class urban park." Through exposure to the beautiful landscaping of large parks, the lives of the poor would be enriched and their vision broadened.

Many of those appointed to the new park commissions were men who, like McCagg and Cornell, had worked hard to initiate the park movement and whose stature in the local business community lent credence to the undertaking. Among the members of the South Side board were dry goods merchant Chauncey T. Bowen and George W. Gage, co-owner of the Grand Pacific Hotel. The West Side board included the well-known Chicago lawyer George W. Standford and Henry Greenebaum, a leading member of Chicago's Jewish community; and on the North Side Board were railroad official John B. Turner and police official and politician Joseph Rehm. It was well that men with good reputations were appointed to these offices, for the park commissioners were soon involved in big business dealings. Between the year of their creation and 1900, the Lincoln Park Board expended $8,475,000; the West Park Board, $16,961,000; and the South Park

Parks and Planning

Stereograph of the South Park (later Washington and Jackson parks), 1870–71. Contoured landscaping, shrubbery, and curving roadways were key elements of the Olmsted and Vaux plan. CHS.

Board, $21,120,000—a total of $46,556,000.

The commissioners of the three park boards moved as quickly as these funds became available to build up the recreational grounds under their control. In each case they began by procuring the services of professional designers who would shape their ideas and give them physical form. The Lincoln Park commissioners moved first, hiring Swain Nelson, a Chicago landscaper, to continue and enlarge upon the work begun by Ure several years earlier.

Although money was a limiting factor in all

Parks and Planning

the park systems, the West Park Board in particular suffered from the taint of bid rigging and other forms of corruption. Still, beginning in 1871, the commission had the services of a first-class landscape architect, William LeBaron Jenney. Better known as an architect and engineer, Jenney laid out the basic scheme of the West Park system during the next three years.

The South Park Board had the good fortune to obtain the services of Olmsted and Vaux, who had come to Chicago in 1868 to work on a design for the Riverside Improvement Association. At that time, Olmsted stayed at the home of Ezra McCagg who, despite fervent efforts, was unable to retain the renowned team of Olmsted and Vaux to design Lincoln Park because the North Side board was still involved in litigation with the city over the cemetery tract. Meanwhile Dr. Rauch, who had an even more ambitious plan in mind, wrote Olmsted that he was developing a scheme by which the two partners would be able to design Chicago's entire park system. But the fact that there were three park boards, all outside of the control of city government, doomed this scheme.

Within a few months after being hired by the South Park Board, the partners submitted an elaborate plan for a year-round pleasure ground for all classes of city dwellers. As the partners laid out their design, they attempted to combine the natural beauty of the lakefront site with quiet landscapes variegated with woods, gardens, and knolls. In some areas, one could ramble through rustic meadows and groves, as in the countryside, while others were severely manicured to provide a setting for an architectural feature or scenic vista.

Stylistically the plan featured many of the design elements which the landscapers had developed for Central Park in New York. But because of Chicago's pervasive flatness, the designers gave much more prominence to lagoons, ponds, and streams which would mirror the surroundings and deepen their image to make the whole park appear more lush than it really was. As the designers explained in a letter to the commissioners:

[By creating lagoons] you can have placid and limpid water within these shores that will mirror and double all above it. . . . Thus . . . you can secure a combination of the fresh and healthy nature of the North with the restful, dreamy nature of the South, that would in our judgment be admirably fitted to the general purposes of any park, and which certainly could nowhere be more grateful than in the borders of your city, not only on account of the present intensely-wide-awake character of its people, but because of the special quality of the scenery about Chicago in which flat and treeless prairie and limitless expanse of lake are such prominent characteristics.

The park lands included many playing fields. The South Park, like New York's Central Park, was designed so as to create a system of outdoor recreation spaces in order to "provide all the forms of recreation which the community owes to its members." Olmsted believed that parks should give opportunities for members of the many diverse groups who made up the population of a large city to meet each other. Writing in 1870, he asserted that urbanites would become more "gregarious" and "neighborly" through participation in active sports as well as in those activities which were "favorable to a pleasurable wakefulness of the mind without stimulating exertion," like strolling along a path or sitting quietly on a bench. A good urban park, he suggested, should be conducive to both kinds of relaxation. But, above all, a park should be a relief from the hectic life of the city. "What we want to gain" by park design, he wrote, "is tranquillity and rest for the mind."

During the first decades of their existence, none of Chicago's large parks achieved the ideal that Olmsted envisioned. The Fire of 1871 destroyed the downtown offices of the South Park Commission along with the original Olmsted and Vaux plans, and the Panic of 1873 adversely affected the finances of all the park boards. Even before the panic, however, the

Parks and Planning

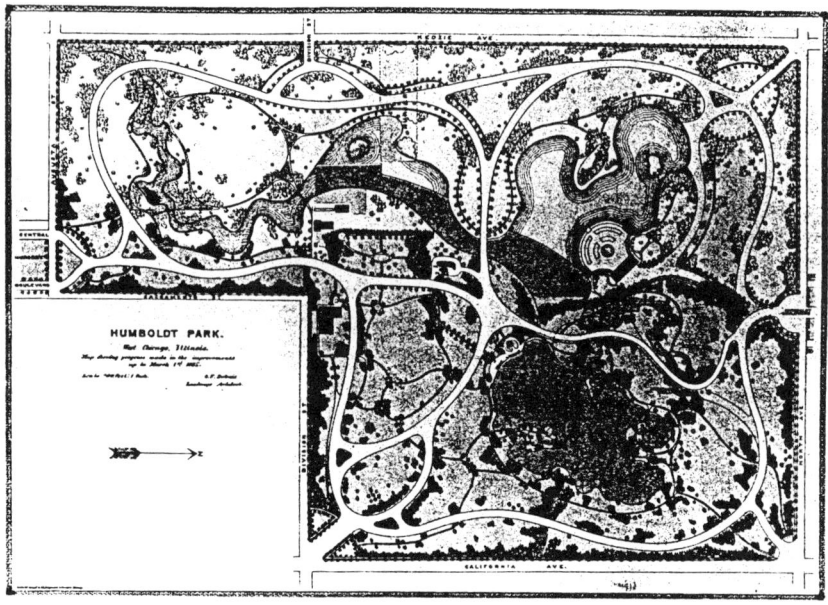

O. F. Dubuis's plan for Humboldt Park on the West Side called for the creation of a 39-acre lake, a miniature waterfall, and a river bubbling out of an artesian well. CHS.

South Park Board had balked at the cost of implementing Olmsted and Vaux's design, and in September 1872 the commissioners hired H. W. S. Cleveland to take over the South Park project with orders to trim the scale and eliminate the larger lakes as well as "the use of statuary, stonework or costly buildings."

Olmsted and Vaux had warned against such tampering when they presented their original plan. "It is of the utmost consequence that the essential ends should be clearly seen before the work is organized," they had written, and be it "five or fifty years hence, and under whatever changes of administration and changes of fashion, these great ruling ends should be pursued with absolute consistency." In the years that followed, the South Park Board compromised this mandate, mutilating parts of the plan beyond recognition but executing other parts so that the original scheme was not wholly lost.

The creation of the three park systems came at a fortuitous time, for during the last three decades of the nineteenth century Chicagoans spread out to occupy new subdivisions, thus decreasing the availability of potential park lands. After 1880, few new park spaces of any size were added to the systems, and by 1909 the city had dropped from second to thirty-second in the amount of park acreage it offered each inhabitant.

Contemporary Chicagoans owe an enormous debt to the small groups of civic leaders, real estate speculators, and sanitarians who worked so diligently to reserve open space for future

182 Chicago History

Parks and Planning

The plan for Humboldt Park took many years to complete. In the meantime the area attracted nature lovers like these artists, who brought umbrellas to provide their own shade. CHS, gift of Mrs. Carl Sonnichsen.

generations. As New York reporter Julian Ralph noted in the early 1890s, "Chicago's park system is truly her crown, its diadem" that "like a courtly hat, sets off the costume of the city." Even more than the size of the parks, it was "the energy which has been expended upon them that causes our wonder."

Ralph's comment would have been even more pointed if he had gone a step further and noted that the inspiration for the system and the energy to execute it had come from groups of private citizens, acting because Chicago's city government was overburdened with other tasks. That tradition continued long after the creation of the three park commissions. The Burnham Plan—the "constitution" of all subsequent Chicago plans—was prepared entirely in the private domain. And although planning is now recognized as a public function administered locally by a number of agencies, Chicago's private planning tradition continues to be a force in civic life. In 1973, for example, the Chicago Central Area Committee, composed of a hundred top businessmen in the city, commissioned the Chicago 21 plan intended to revitalize the downtown.

Frederick Law Olmsted understood the benefits to be gained when private groups of citizens took part in the planning process. While designing the South Park, Olmsted praised Ezra McCagg's efforts on behalf of the park systems. According to the designer, McCagg was one of a growing number of "Chicago men of business" who took time to listen to planning professionals and then raised money to turn visionary ideas into realities.

Chicago History 183

Lincoln Park, early 1900s. Designers of Chicago's parks created lagoons, ponds, and streams which mirrored the surroundings and made them appear more lush than they really were. CHS, gift of Lake Bluff Public Library.

These "civilized men," as Olmsted called them, were responsible for much of the planning that was done in Chicago in the late nineteenth century. The breadth of their vision can still be seen in the parks which surround us today.

Selected Sources

Annual Reports of the Lincoln Park, South Park, and West Park Commissioners, 1871–1900.
City of Chicago. "The Public Parks of Chicago: Their Origin, Former Control and Present Government." *Chicago City Manual* (1914).
City of Chicago. *Report of the Special Park Commission to the City Council of Chicago on the Subject of a Metropolitan Park System* (1904).
Cranz, Galen. "Models for Park Usage: Ideology and the Development of Chicago's Public Parks." Unpublished Ph.D. dissertation, University of Chicago, 1971.
Davenport, F. Garvin. "John Henry Rauch and Public Health in Illinois." *Journal of the Illinois State Historical Society* 50 (Autumn 1957).
Fabos, Julius, Gordon T. Milde, and V. Michael Wienmayr. *Frederick Law Olmsted, Sr., Founder of Landscape Architecture in America*. Amherst: University of Massachusetts Press, 1968.
Olmsted, Frederick Law. "Public Parks and the Enlargement of Towns." *Journal of Social Science* 3 (1870).
Olmsted, Vaux & Co. *Report Accompanying Plan for Laying Out the South Park*. Chicago: Evening Journal, 1871.
Ranney, Victoria Post. *Olmsted in Chicago*. Chicago: The Open Lands Project, 1972.
Reps, John. *The Making of Urban America: A History of City Planning in the United States*. Princeton, N. J.: Princeton University Press, 1965.

Frederick Law Olmsted: Landscape Architecture as Conservative Reform

Geoffrey Blodgett

THE coincidence in 1972 of Frederick Law Olmsted's one hundred and fiftieth birthday with a revival of environmentalist concern over the plight of the city won for America's greatest landscape architect a splash of deserved national attention. But some of his celebrants had trouble locating Olmsted as a participant in the history he lived through. Journalists linked him vaguely with Jeffersonian agrarianism, with the New England village green, and in one instance with Edgar Allan Poe.[1] A serious effort was made to tie the young Olmsted of the 1850s to Fourierite utopian socialism and the aging Olmsted of the 1890s to Edward Bellamy's utopian nationalism.[2] One result of all this was a certain historical deracination of the man. His reputation "took off." Lauded for his long vision, Olmsted became a visionary for the 1970s—a planner who shaped the future by transcending his own environment, casting aside its blinders and inhibitions to bring hope and wisdom to the present. "It is against this American," one breathless sesquicentennial enthusiast concluded, "that we must measure the captains who must now guide spaceship Earth."[3]

Historians know Olmsted from his travels through the antebellum South and his work with the U. S. Sanitary Commission in the Civil War as well as his contributions to park design and urban planning. The several facets

---

Geoffrey Blodgett is professor of history in Oberlin College. The author wishes to acknowledge the support and assistance of the American Council of Learned Societies and the Charles Warren Center, Harvard University.

[1] For the reference to Edgar Allan Poe, see Richard Schickel, "Frederick Law Olmsted, creator of 'The Central Park,' " *New York Times Magazine* (Dec. 31, 1972), 12-13. Among architectural critics, Ada Louise Huxtable has been uncommonly perceptive in treating Olmsted. For example, see Ada Louise Huxtable, "It Isn't Green Cheese," New York *Times,* May 21, 1972.

[2] Albert Fein, *Frederick Law Olmsted and the American Environmental Tradition* (New York, 1972), 8-10, 15-18, 57-61.

[3] Washington *Post,* Jan. 29, 1972.

of his career have merited growing scholarly attention.[4] But Olmsted's experience across the postwar years has yet to be fully understood against the peculiar social and political environment of the Gilded Age.

The purpose of this essay is to fix Olmsted in the group structure of postwar reformers and to appraise the problems he met and the values he wanted to enforce through his professional work. It will try to explain the continuities in Olmsted's social attitudes which spanned his transition from journalism and public administration to the new profession of landscape architecture. These continuities formed the fabric of a profoundly conservative concept of reform. They included a stubborn faith in political and social democracy—provided that democracy remained responsive to the cues of trained and cultivated leadership; a belief that American society urgently needed to fortify itself against the crude and materialistic impulses of popular culture; and a hope that the tensions of a newly urban nation might be moderated by structural arrangements, both political and aesthetic, to foster respect among rival social groups.

Since Olmsted wrote less as he grew older, and what he wrote grew more opaque, his postwar attitudes must be read mostly out of the pattern of friendships, causes, and practical preoccupations which governed his last thirty years of work. Like the careers of his colleagues in conservative reform, his was heavy with both pride and frustration—pride in personal achievement, and frustration at public indifference to his talents and service. One long letter, written in the 1870s to an English-born acquaintance who lived in aristocratic seclusion at Newport, summed up his determination not to be cast aside by popular rebuffs. The American majority had many faults, he confessed. But the worst result of its behavior was the morbid apathy it could inspire among the cultivated few. Olmsted went on to lecture his Newport friend:

You—your class—perceive your superiority in certain respects to the mass of the people but because they think too well of themselves, are too original, self-sufficient, and too much inclined to recklessly busy themselves in matters with which they have no natural concern, and because they have not made arrangements politically and socially, as in England, with special reference to the con-

---

[4] Laura Wood Roper, *FLO: A Biography of Frederick Law Olmsted* (Baltimore, 1973). Earlier studies include Broadus Mitchell, *Frederick Law Olmsted: A Critic of the Old South* (Baltimore, 1924); Arthur M. Schlesinger, "Introduction," Frederick Law Olmsted, *The Cotton Kingdom: A Traveller's Observations on Cotton and Slavery in the American Slave States*, ed. by Arthur M. Schlesinger (New York, 1953), ix-lvi; and William Quentin Maxwell, *Lincoln's Fifth Wheel: The Political History of the United States Sanitary Commission* (New York, 1956). For a discussion of the conservative strain among Olmsted and other members of the Sanitary Commission, see George M. Fredrickson, *The Inner Civil War: Northern Intellectuals and the Crisis of the Union* (New York, 1965), 98-112.

venience with which superior talent, tact and taste may be exercised for the benefit of the community, you assume to yourselves the right to live quiet, scholarly, secluded and selfishly domestic and aesthetic lives.

Olmsted ended with this affirmation:

The difficulties, annoyances and embarrassments which gentlemen and gentlewomen of any talent have to meet in doing their duty with their talent are certainly very great, and talent is not to be exercised here with the pre-ordained quiet, grace and decorum which may be associated with it in a country of thoroughly well-established and congealed civilization. The greater is the need, however, that it should be exercised courageously, resolutely, and perseveringly.[5]

The decade from 1855 to 1865 had brought Olmsted into friendly contact with others of similar conviction. These included the writer George William Curtis, a Staten Island neighbor whom Olmsted had joined in an abortive publishing venture with *Putnam's Magazine* in 1855; Edwin L. Godkin, whom Olmsted befriended soon after the young Englishman's arrival in New York in 1856; Charles Francis Adams, Jr., the young Boston lawyer who entered into correspondence with Olmsted in 1861; Charles Eliot Norton of Cambridge, an admirer of Olmsted's writings on the South who met him through Curtis in 1862; and the editor Samuel Bowles, of Springfield, Massachusetts, whose friendship with Olmsted dated from 1865. These men formed the core of a gentlemanly cosmopolitan élite which tried hard through the postwar years to impose its will on American political and cultural development. With others of like mind—Henry Adams, Edward Atkinson, Jacob D. Cox, David A. Wells, and Horace White—they launched such ventures as the *Nation* and American Social Science Association, tried to force congressional tariff and civil service reform, helped to start the ill-fated Liberal Republican movement of 1872, and strove thereafter to function as a third force in two-party politics.[6]

The fortunes of this group—an aspiring intellectual élite in a nation which did not want an élite and met its overtures with constant scorn—have been the object of lively scholarly contention.[7] In judging the record of genteel reform, historians have tended until recently to focus on its

[5] Frederick Law Olmsted to Katherine P. Wormeley [1870s], Frederick Law Olmsted Papers (Manuscript Division, Library of Congress).
[6] Geoffrey Blodgett, "Reform Thought and the Genteel Tradition," H. Wayne Morgan, ed., *The Gilded Age* (Syracuse, 1970), 55-76.
[7] For a comprehensive critique, see John G. Sproat, *"The Best Men": Liberal Reformers in the Gilded Age* (New York, 1968). See also John M. Dobson, *Politics in the Gilded Age: A New Perspective on Reform* (New York, 1972); John Tomsich, *A Genteel Endeavor: American Culture and Politics in the Gilded Age* (Stanford, 1971); and Stow Persons, *The Decline of American Gentility* (New York, 1973).

role in national elective politics and have neglected its strenuous efforts beyond the rim of party strife to build stable institutional props for a nation confronting fast social change. Olmsted's postwar work in landscape architecture, like Godkin's, Bowles' and Curtis' careers in journalism, Henry Adams' career as novelist and historian, Atkinson's and Wells' careers as economic publicists, Cox's career in academic administration, Norton's career as a teacher of fine arts, and Charles Francis Adams' career in railroad regulation, reflected a common urge to focus professional intelligence on goals of social order and cohesion. Olmsted's parks are among the most durable relics of this urge. Their very longevity allows scholars to assess their meaning across an unusually broad perspective against criteria of functional utility and popular acceptance, criteria which were often the nemesis of his colleagues in conservative reform.

Olmsted's connection with the reformist gentry was not a matter of coincidence or chance. He shared their assumptions about the design of a good society, where hierarchy, deference, and skilled leadership might impose tranquility on a contentious, egalitarian people. He disliked the headstrong ideological fanaticism of both abolitionist extremists and evangelical Protestant sectarians in the 1850s—and these attitudes were pervasive among his new friends.[8] With them he also mistrusted the myopic self-interest of freshly rich merchants and entrenched local politicians. Oppressed by the lack of professional standards among lawyers, businessmen, journalists, and publishers, he struggled to translate the private ethics of the gentlemanly amateur into efficient public conduct.[9] The meanders in his own prewar career reflected not only periodic personal aimlessness but a faith in the potential omnicompetence of well-bred men with broad intellectual horizons. The exhilarating sense of public purpose which the Civil War crisis brought to his friends had been matched in Olmsted's case only by the prior task of creating Central Park, a project he eagerly took up after the collapse of *Putnam's Magazine* in the depression of 1857.[10]

By the time the war broke out, the main outlines of Central Park were essentially complete. Olmsted's departure in 1861 to become executive secretary of the U.S. Sanitary Commission hardly ended his ties to the

[8] For Olmsted's attitude toward abolitionists, see Roper, *FLO*, 84-85. For his antisectarianism, see Olmsted to his father, Aug. 12, 1846, Olmsted to his wife, July 29 [1863], and Olmsted to Charles Loring Brace, Dec. 21, 1873, Olmsted Papers.
[9] Olmsted to Edwin L. Godkin, Feb. 20 [1864?], Edwin L. Godkin Papers (Houghton Library, Harvard University); Olmsted to Horace W. S. Cleveland, Feb. 9, 1881, Olmsted Papers.
[10] Calvert Vaux to Olmsted [1859?], Olmsted to Mariana Van Rensselaer, June 11, 1893, Olmsted Papers. See also Roper, *FLO*, 109-31.

park. It did signal a strong new concern for the politics of national survival. Southern secession, which he called the "dignification of anarchy," stirred him to deep nationalist feelings.[11] Never a believer in laissez-faire, he shared with Curtis, Godkin, and Norton misgivings over the management of the Union war effort. His admiration for "the low, obscure, mysterious strength of the free and unenlightened people" was contingent on a felt need for "large purposes" governed by a "central will and power."[12] While these values endured through the war and beyond, Olmsted was for a long time puzzled how he might help fulfill them.

In the U.S. Sanitary Commission he showed the same combination of managerial talent and impatience toward superiors which marked his career as park superintendent, and by 1863 he had had enough of it. Meanwhile he considered posts as street commissioner in New York and federal commissioner of agriculture in Washington. The alternative of building a private practice in landscape gardening did not seem to promise steady satisfaction.[13] In the summer of 1863 Olmsted and Godkin laid the first, premature plans for the *Nation*, a project to consolidate and elevate the tone of public thought.[14] Two months later he headed for California to seek success in a hopeless mining venture. Friends' bewailed his departure, certain that his talents were needed closer to home. While in California he began "a heavy sort of book" about American civilization which he never finished.[15] A surviving fragment of its outline shows the tenacity of his concern for adequate political organization in a ramshackle society of continental scope: "Administration, science of, defective Tendency to trust to laws & machines Neglect executive—incompetency & recklessness of officials. Diffused responsibility. Short terms. Need of civil service organization—training, promotion." He planned next to write of hopeful symptoms: "How progress to come? Study of wants. Study of modern requirements, of means to them." Among these, significantly, he listed park reform and the design of streets.[16]

Meanwhile a career choice still confronted him. Although the barbarous

---

[11] Reflections dated July 31, 1861, Olmsted Papers.
[12] Mitchell, *Olmsted*, 38; Roper, *FLO*, 69, 93; Olmsted to his half-brother [?], Jan. 28, 1862, Olmsted Papers; Olmsted to Charles Eliot Norton, March 3, 1862, Charles Eliot Norton Papers (Houghton Library, Harvard University).
[13] Olmsted to his father, April 19, 1862, Olmsted Papers.
[14] Godkin to Olmsted, May 9 [1863], untitled prospectus [June 1863], *ibid.*; William M. Armstrong, "The Freedmen's Movement and the Founding of the *Nation*," *Journal of American History*, LIII (March 1967), 708-26.
[15] Olmsted to Godkin, fragment of letter [1864], Godkin Papers. See also Roper, *FLO*, 247-57.
[16] Rough draft of outline [undated], Olmsted Papers.

informality of social relations in California at first put him off, he toyed with the notion of luring Godkin west to help him start a San Francisco newspaper.[17] Meanwhile, Godkin joined Curtis in trying to land for Olmsted the directorship of the Freedman's Bureau in Washington, and Wells included Olmsted among potential colleagues on a special postwar revenue commission.[18] Finally Olmsted decided to come back and join the work of building Brooklyn's Prospect Park. By the summer of 1866 he was happily engrossed in the old tasks. "[M]y enthusiasm and liking for the work is increasing to an inconvenient degree," he told Norton, "so that it elbows all other interests out of my mind."[19] The return to New York had brought him back to the *Nation* as well, and during the troubled early phase of the journal's management he and Norton were Godkin's most faithful aides. But writing had gotten difficult for Olmsted. "I am the slowest and heaviest and sickest dragoon that ever was pushed into the bogs of literature," he complained in 1867. "A single day's writing knocks me up for a week."[20] Without quite realizing it, and in a manner that some of his associates interpreted as retreat, Olmsted had found in landscape architecture rather than in journalism or administration his life's calling. As it worked out, the choice would bring him into more intimate practical contact with the problems of urban democracy than any of his collaborators in conservative reform.

His interest in national party politics flagged. The intolerance of congressional Radicals, and their demand for prompt enfranchisement of the freedmen, disillusioned him with Reconstruction. The Radicals, he feared, were rending the structure and processes of government in a thoughtless, arbitrary drive for quick results. Moreover, under Radical leadership the Republican party was filling with "a raft of mercenaries . . . who don't see beyond their nose in the real work before us."[21] Increasingly he was persuaded that the "real work" lay outside party politics. He remained peripherally involved in the efforts of the cosmopolitan gentry to avert what they regarded as the degeneration of the Republican party and to otherwise shape the course of postwar public life. He was one of the

[17] Olmsted to his wife, Feb. 24 [1865], *ibid.*; Roper, *FLO*, 275, 278.
[18] George W. Curtis to Olmsted, March 30, 1864, Olmsted Papers; Godkin to Olmsted, April 2 [1865], Godkin Papers; David A. Wells to Edward Atkinson, April 6, 1865, Edward Atkinson Papers (Massachusetts Historical Society).
[19] Olmsted to Norton, July 15 [1866], Norton Papers.
[20] Olmsted to Andrew D. White, June 27, 1867, Andrew D. White Papers (University Archives, Cornell University).
[21] Godkin to Norton, Feb. 20, 1866, Godkin Papers; Olmsted to Norton, Sept. 19, 1866, Norton Papers; Olmsted to Thomas H. Clark, Aug. 5, 1889, Olmsted Papers.

founders of the American Social Science Association (ASSA), whose charter stressed the "responsibilities of the gifted and educated classes toward the weak, the witless, and the ignorant," and delivered one of his major papers on urban parks to a Boston meeting of ASSA in 1870.[22] While he did not count himself a "zealous Free Trader," the intrigue and manipulation swirling around the policy of high protection repelled him; and he shared the desire for tariff reform which Wells, Atkinson, and others pursued within ASSA.[23] He was caught up in the preliminaries to the Liberal Republican movement of 1872 and pulled off the route to the Cincinnati convention only after Horace Greeley moved in on it. His contempt for Greeley as the exemplar of erratic popular journalism and reformist quackery was absolute. When others of like mind tried to undo the Cincinnati fiasco by forming yet another ticket, Olmsted was startled to learn he had been nominated for vice-president by a rump convention of his friends. Angered and embarrassed by this climactic absurdity, he disowned the action and wound up supporting Ulysses S. Grant.[24]

Over the next decade Olmsted stayed clear of reform meetings and joked about "the disorganization of which I am a humble member."[25] For him as for his friends, politics was no longer an opportunity but an ugly problem. Clues to his transformation of attitude cropped up in unexpected contexts. By 1874, when he had begun the project of landscaping Capitol Hill in Washington, his preference for centralized and orderly national governance found expression in a wholly aesthetic perception. To his eye the arrangement of federal buildings in Washington was "broken, confused, and unsatisfactory," and he remarked that the physical appearance of Washington was "often alluded to as a standing reproach against [our] system of government. . . ." "In short, the Capitol of the Union manifests nothing so much as disunity. . . . What is wanting

[22] Frank B. Sanborn to Olmsted, Oct. 18, 1866, *ibid.*; Frederick Law Olmsted, "Public Parks and the Enlargement of Towns," S. B. Sutton, ed., *Civilizing American Cities: A Selection of Frederick Law Olmsted's Writings on City Landscapes* (Cambridge, Mass., 1971), 52-99. For ASSA, see L. L. Bernard and Jessie Bernard, *Origins of American Sociology: The Social Science Movement in the United States* (New York, 1943), 527-607; Irwin Unger, *The Greenback Era: A Social and Political History of American Finance, 1865-1879* (Princeton, 1964), 136-39.

[23] Olmsted to Samuel Bowles, May 14, 1872, Olmsted to Fred Kingsbury, Sept. 6, 1893, Olmsted Papers.

[24] Olmsted to Godkin, April 4, 1863, Godkin Papers; Olmsted to Bowles, May 7, 11, 1872, J. M. McKim to Olmsted, June 24, 1872, Olmsted Papers; Joseph Pulitzer to Whitelaw Reid, June 12, 1872, Whitelaw Reid Papers (Manuscript Division, Library of Congress); Roper, *FLO*, 340-41.

[25] Olmsted to William Dorsheimer [1870s], Olmsted Papers.

is a federal bond."[26] His old values had survived, but landscape architecture rather than politics was now his method for promoting them.

The one political issue calculated to fire his reform impulse was civil service reform. The Central Park project had engaged him in fierce feuds over patronage; and by the 1870s he had acquired a fund of experience on the subject unmatched among his friends. The chairmanship of Grant's civil service commission was yet another of the posts urged on him after the war. While he shunned the office, his anxiety about the problem was keen. The spoils system, he believed, had produced a new definition of the word "influence," one which turned honest jobseekers into wrecks of demoralized dependence on the favor of party hacks. Washington, he wrote, was the center "of a system between which and its extremities there is a ceaseless flux and reflux of influence." Ironically, the system created a bond between local and national politics which Olmsted—long an advocate of centralized administrative authority—could only repudiate as a symptom of national decay.[27]

The assassination of James A. Garfield in the summer of 1881 revived Olmsted's functional contact with Curtis, Carl Schurz, and other civil service reformers. Writing to Schurz that "the country is at white heat," and ready to be moved on the issue, he joined the Civil Service Reform Association; and his essay, "The Spoils of the Park," was soon being circulated and read as a reform polemic. After the passage of the Pendleton Act, he hoped the movement would swing its attention to the problems of spoils at the city level.[28] Despite a lifelong aversion to the Democratic party, his admiration for Grover Cleveland (who as governor of New York had responded well to the campaign of Olmsted, Norton, and Henry Hobson Richardson to save Niagara Falls) seems to have aligned

[26] Olmsted to Justin Morrill, Jan. 22, 1874, *ibid.* Henry James, in his story, "The Point of View," conveyed a similar impression of Washington by a European observer of the early 1880s: "No movement, no officials, no authority, no embodiment of the State. . . . You go into the Capitol as you would into a railway station. . . . No functionaries, no doorkeepers, no officers, no uniforms, no badges, no reservations, no authority—nothing but a crowd of shabby people circulating in a labyrinth of spittoons." Henry James, *Lady Barbarina, The Siege of London, An International Episode, And Other Tales* (London, 1922), 525. See also F. O. Matthiessen, ed., *The American Novels and Stories of Henry James* (New York, 1964), 326; Allen Guttmann, *The Conservative Tradition in America* (New York, 1967), 63-64.

[27] Curtis to Charles J. Bonaparte, Oct. 28, 1882, Charles J. Bonaparte Papers (Manuscript Division, Library of Congress); E. B. Elliot to Olmsted, April 16, 1873, Frederick Law Olmsted, "Influence" [1882], Olmsted Papers.

[28] Olmsted to Carl Schurz, July 16, 1881, Carl Schurz Papers (Manuscript Division, Library of Congress); Curtis to Olmsted, July 17, 1881, William Potts to Olmsted, Aug. 26, 1881, Norton to Olmsted, March 4, 16, 1882, Olmsted Papers; Olmsted to Norton, Aug. 14, 1883, Norton Papers.

him with the Mugwump bolters of 1884.[29] But by the mid-1880s the pressures of his professional career precluded further involvement in national politics.

The superb achievements of that career insulated Olmsted from the stigma of genteel failure which dogged his colleagues in conservative reform. Yet his parks may be understood to reflect as accurately as civil service reform or tariff reform or Mugwump journalism a common group desire to counter the headlong popular impulses of the Gilded Age. The urban park, like the well-designed campus or suburb, was in his mind an urgent antidote for the restless habits of the American majority. Because his critique of these habits was so often clothed in an aesthetic rather than political vocabulary, it was less vulnerable to public scorn. He could castigate Andrew D. White, Cornell's president, and Tweed's Peter Sweeny with equal vigor for their shortsighted use of land, and survive with his professional credentials intact. Moreover, the creation of large city park systems was one of the few enterprises of the age around which it proved possible to gather a broad consensus in favor of conscious public planning. Park reform ultimately engaged the support of three important groups—the cosmopolitan gentry, municipal politicians, and businessmen interested in speculative ventures in urban real estate and transit—which were frequently at each others' throats over other issues confronting the city. Also, Olmsted's parks seemed to offer an attractive remedy for the dangerous problem of discontent among the urban masses. In contrast with other reforms put forward by the gentry, they visibly affected the everyday habits of large numbers of people. By providing pleasant and uplifting outlets in the narrow lives of city-dwellers, they promised a measure of social tranquility.

Yet Olmsted was constantly embittered by the public's failure to understand the purpose of his parks or accept his trained expertise. His attitude on this score was as candidly élitist as that of any political Mugwump. His anger focused on the fate of Central Park and the long quarrel over its meaning and use that ended in Olmsted's ouster from the city's park department in 1878 at the insistence of Tammany's Honest John Kelly. From the outset Olmsted had defined the park primarily as a work of art, and its primary benefits remained in his mind mainly visual

[29] For Olmsted's attitudes toward Grover Cleveland, see Isaac G. Perry to Olmsted, Sept. 18, 1883, Olmsted to Brace, Nov. 1, 1884, Henry Hobson Richardson to Olmsted, Feb. 6, 1883, Jan. 20, 1885, and H. W. S. Cleveland to Olmsted, Oct. 4, 1885, Olmsted Papers; Alfred Runte, "Beyond the Spectacular: The Niagara Falls Preservation Campaign," *New-York Historical Society Quarterly*, LVII (Jan. 1973), 30-50.

and psychic. It would bring relief from the constrictions of Manhattan's expanding street grid (most vividly recalled by Edith Wharton, who described the city of her childhood as "this little low-studded rectangular New York . . . , this cramped horizontal gridiron of a town without towers, porticoes, fountains or perspectives, hidebound in its deadly uniformity of mean ugliness . . .").[30] Olmsted wrote at length about the therapeutic value of the urban park in offering escape from the stacked compactions of the commercial city. Frequent release from urban tensions was vital to all urban classes, and Central Park would serve them all. While Olmsted disliked the grandiose park portals proposed by Richard Morris Hunt in the 1860s, the earliest gate names—Merchants', Artisans', Artists', and Scholars'—were consciously intended to symbolize an orderly access to the park by all classes and occupations. (The names of succeeding entries—Women's, Children's, Mariners', Strangers', and so on—pursued this theme.)[31] While in Olmsted's mind the pleasure to be taken from the park was a highly contemplative sort of recreation, he insisted that uncultivated working people could share its subtle refreshment—that rural scenery could impose a calming sense of its own sacredness on the "rough element of the city."[32] As time passed, Olmsted laid increasing stress on the hygienic and sociological benefits of the park. Its open spaces became, in the phrase of the day, the lungs of the city, a resort of cool breezes and cleansing sunlight against the disease-laden miasmic vapors of the inner city.[33] Moreover, the natural simplicity of pastoral landscape would, he hoped, inspire communal feelings among all urban classes, muting resentments over disparities of wealth and fashion. For an untrusting, watchful crowd of urban strangers, the park would restore that "communicativeness" which Olmsted prized as a central American need.[34]

All this was a mighty order for Central Park. Olmsted's insistence on the integrity of the park as a work of art, with all its elements uniting in a single organic design, was doubtless compatible with the several purposes he claimed for it. But more prosaic minds defined its multiple functions in less consistent terms and saw in its vast stretches obvious opportunities

[30] Edith Wharton, *A Backward Glance* (New York, 1934), 55.
[31] Fein, *Frederick Law Olmsted*, 11-13; New York *Evening Post*, July 23, 1880.
[32] Olmsted to Reid, March 2, 1877, Olmsted Papers. See also Roper, *FLO*, 284.
[33] Olmsted lost his first child to cholera-infantum and shared the belief of his generation in the value of fresh sunlight as a preventive to illnesses caused by "miasmatic contagion." Olmsted to George W. Elliot, April 28, 1890, Olmsted Papers.
[34] Frederick Law Olmsted, "Trees in Streets and in Parks," *Sanitarian*, X (Sept. 1882), 513-18; Roper, *FLO*, 253, 318-19.

to fill empty space with fresh projects on popular demand. Olmted took grim satisfaction in cataloging the "variety of purposes, vague and variable," urged for the park over the years: parade grounds for military displays, churches, zoos, race tracks, steeplechase, world's fair, concessions for goat, pony and donkey rides, mineral waters, sailboats, merry-go-rounds and roller-coasters, burial grounds for General Grant and other eminent dead, facilities for skating, curling, croquet, archery, tennis, cricket, and baseball, space for private gardening, fireworks displays, ballon ascensions, dog shows, and exhibitions of fat cattle. The list was unending, and the pressures for intrusion relentless.[35]

The combat between the original concept and later amendments has raged down to the present. Defenders of the park have invoked Olmsted's genius as well as his arguments in the cause of preservation. He remains an awesome if embattled authority. Perhaps his most touching lament is found in "The Spoils of the Park," the testimony of a wounded man over his twenty-year fight to save the park from New York's politicians: "Let it be understood what this meant to me,—the frustration of purposes to which I had for years given all my heart, to which I had devoted my life; the degradation of works in which my pride was centred; the breaking of promises to the future which had been to me as churchly vows."[36]

One can read "The Spoils of the Park" with entire sympathy for Olmsted's troubles and still detect between its lines a struggle over competing goals which is precisely analagous to the strife, waged across the Gilded Age in other arenas, between the cosmopolitan, professional élitism of the Mugwump gentry and the pluralistic impulses of urban democracy under locally elected leaders. In Olmsted's case much of the problem lay in the inherent ambiguity and novelty of Central Park, the first large public park in the New World. Translating an eighteenth-century, aristocratic, European concept of sculptured pastoral space into the American urban vernacular was no easy feat.[37] Central Park was not only a work of art, a gift of rural beauty for the dreary city, but a massive

---

[35] Frederick Law Olmsted, *Frederick Law Olmsted, Landscape Architect, 1822-1903: Forty Years of Landscape Architecture; Being the Professional Papers of Frederick Law Olmsted, Senior*, Frederick Law Olmsted, Jr., and Theodora Kimball, eds. (2 vols., New York, 1928), II, 247-48; Olmsted to Vaux, Nov. 4, 1883, Olmsted Papers.

[36] Frederick Law Olmsted, "The Spoils of the Park," *Frederick Law Olmsted*, II, 117-55. *Ibid.*, II, 137.

[37] For an authoritative discussion of the English and European background of the country park, see Norman T. Newton, *Design on the Land: The Development of Landscape Architecture* (Cambridge, 1971), 207-45.

municipal public works project, and an anticipated center for lively urban recreation. These blurred purposes were built into the city's decision to launch it back in 1857. Conflicting inferences about the park were compounded by contrasting time-spans in men's thoughts about it. The politician habitually construed the park as vacant space to be filled with jobs and structures on a schedule set by the next election, the next audit or appropriation, the next batch of obligations coming due. Whether he was a Tweed man or a Kelly man or a Samuel J. Tilden Democrat, the city official saw the park in relatively short-range terms as a current item on an endless agenda. Olmsted in contrast set his goals for the park well in the future. The long reach of his thought derived in part from his special landscape style, evolved from the English picturesque tradition of Sir Uvedale Price, which aimed for a natural, informal, and untended look to spatial sequences. The appearance of a "finished" Olmsted landscape required decades to mature. The results he wanted lay, in their earliest fulfillment, forty years ahead, when he anticipated that Central Park would lie in the middle of a city population of some two million.[38]

These rival priorities dividing landscape planner from politician sharpened the dispute which pitted Olmsted's personal authority against the pluralistic demands of the city. Landscape architecture was an infant among American professions. Olmsted worried over the complexities of its definition, its lack of popular recognition, and its consequent poverty of sanctions against the sway of democratic "common sense." He was furious about the dilettante image of the profession exploited by his critics, who, he felt, dismissed him as a "silly, heartless, upstart, sophomorical theorist. . . ."[39] The dispute came into focus over issues of labor recruitment, park maintenance, and crime control. Olmsted wanted qualified assistants, trained in their several skills, to guide the work of a diligent labor force, hired at low wages for long hours. Politicians, on the other hand, eyed the labor force in terms of patronage quotas and rewards, tending toward greater indulgence over issues of skills, wages, and hours. Olmsted estimated that the city's park commissioners wasted nine-tenths of their energy on patronage, and he fumed over the large numbers of physical derelicts and deadbeats who wound up on the park rolls. The function of police and maintenance staffs provoked comparable quarrels.

[38] Olmsted, *Frederick Law Olmsted*, II, 139; Olmsted to Gardening Staff [1873], Olmsted to Henry K. Beekman, June 10, 1886, Olmsted Papers; Arthur Spencer, "The Art of Frederick Law Olmsted," *Craftsman*, V (Nov. 1903), 105-12.

[39] Olmsted to W. B. Duncan, Sept. 22, 1870, Olmsted to C. A. Roberts, July 1889, Olmsted Papers; Olmsted, *Frederick Law Olmsted*, II, 131.

Olmsted and his aides wanted to train the keepers' force in the tactics of crowd control to protect the park against "the shock of an untrained public." For politicians the park was municipal space to be policed like the rest of the city against violent, visible, and scandalous crimes. The upshot was that major park thoroughfares were well-guarded while prostitution and petty vandalism thrived in more secluded areas.[40]

Behind all these particular disputes lay a fundamental divergence of attitudes. Olmsted prized the park as an inviolable exemption from the city and as a counterforce against its evils, much as the civil service or tariff reformer idealized his cause as a cure for the corruptions of partisan politics. In contrast the politician, especially in the Tweed era, habitually wove the park into his calculations of local constituents' needs and "projected the city into the park."[41]

Olmsted never satisfactorily reconciled his tranquil, unitary vision of Central Park with the desires of its users. He had special trouble coping with the demands of the active young working-class male. In his writings he repeatedly dwelt on the needs of "town-strained" women, invalid children, busy merchants and their confined wives, and families in search of Sunday relaxation. He offered the park as a surrogate pleasure for city-dwellers who could not escape to the scenic spectacles of mountain and shore favored by the rich. Sharing a widespread conception of the urban lower classes as immobilized by their working environment, he thought of the park as therapy for the plight of trapped and passive people.[42] Like most thoughtful contemporaries of his class, he underestimated the bent for vigorous, organized leisure-time activity among boys and working men, and responded grudgingly to their desire for "manly and blood-tingling recreations," "boisterous fun and rough sports." Eventually, Olmsted built into the design of Riverside Terrace, overlooking the Hudson, certain facilities for these sorts of pastimes, but work on the Riverside project had barely begun when he left the city.[43] Space allocations for such pur-

[40] Olmsted, *Frederick Law Olmsted*, II, 101, 105, 124-36; Olmsted to Henry G. Stebbins, July 30, 1873, Olmsted Papers.

[41] Seymour J. Mandelbaum, *Boss Tweed's New York* (New York, 1965), 74.

[42] Among conservative reformers, Wells was a leading authority on the way the American labor force should spend its time. In the midst of an argument against legislating the eight-hour day, Wells wrote that "it is necessary to keep in view the fact that all men, with the exception of the comparatively few who inherit a competence, are born, as it were, into a condition of natural bondage . . . [t]o the necessity of earning their living by hard and continuous toil." David A. Wells, *Recent Economic Changes: And their Effect on the Production and Distribution of Wealth and the Well-Being of Society* (New York, 1889), 445.

[43] Olmsted to Reid, March 2, 1877, Olmsted to "Dear Sir," Aug. 6, 1885, Olmsted to Paul Dane, Dec. 22, 1890, Olmsted Papers; Roper, *FLO*, 356, 360.

poses remained for him a curiously difficult concession, symptomatic perhaps of his own rural and gentlemanly upbringing as well as his mistrust of lower-class cultural autonomy.

Lower-class political autonomy was also a problem for Olmsted, as it was for his associates in conservative reform. Over the years he reserved some of his choicest epithets for New York City Irish Democrats and their leaders. Ever since the wartime draft riots his thoughts were scarred by alienation from this breed. Periodically in the struggles over Central Park he and his friends tried to muster the city's social élite against the Democrats in the city hall in support of his positions. But the New York élite of the 1870s was a fragmented scattering of fading Knickerbockers and stylish new rich, lacking both cultural continuity and political cohesion. It was hard to mobilize into a metropolitan civic force against the localism of city politicians.[44]

The Tammany press could afford to dismiss Olmsted's backers as "the Miss Nancies of Central Park art," who "babble in the papers and in Society Circles, about aesthetics and architecture, vistas and landscapes, the quiver of a leaf and the proper blendings of light and shade. . . ."[45] Olmsted's friends, for whom such rhetorical sneers were commonplace, tried hard to avert his dismissal from the park in 1878. But their petition of protest, trailing signatures from prominent merchants, bankers, publishers, journalists, artists, and writers, proved useless against the will of Tammany's Kelly.[46] Four years later Theodore Roosevelt, the young scion of the city's élite serving his political apprenticeship in the state assembly, broached a scheme to lure Olmsted back to Central Park on terms which would give him central executive authority free from local political pressures. The proposal echoed Olmsted's own prescription for sane administration with remarkable fidelity. But by then Olmsted had moved his firm to suburban Boston and washed his hands of further dealings with New York.[47]

Another decade would pass before New York cosmopolitans could score a major victory in defense of Central Park. In 1892 Tammany's George Washington Plunkitt nudged through the state legislature a bill authorizing a race-track speedway along the west side of the park. The reaction was swift: facilities for metropolitan communication, reform

[44] Frederic Cople Jaher, "Nineteenth-Century Elites in Boston and New York," *Journal of Social History*, 6 (Fall 1972), 60-65.
[45] New York *Evening Express*, quoted in Olmsted, *Frederick Law Olmsted*, II, 109.
[46] *Ibid.*, 113; Roper, *FLO*, 360-61.
[47] Theodore Roosevelt to Olmsted, March 19, 1882, Olmsted Papers.

mobilization, and "public-interest" lobbying had improved vastly since the 1870s. Led by the City Reform Club (which Roosevelt had organized back in 1882), cosmopolitans mounted a massive publicity campaign against the track, staged a public meeting at Cooper Union, dispatched trainloads of aroused citizens to Albany, and secured repeal within a month. At the Cooper Union rally, a letter from Olmsted had helped fuel the protest. The letter was curiously businesslike and unsentimental, stripped of aesthetic or humanitarian concern. Since the speedtrack was not only immoral but unconstitutional, in his judgment, it would "lessen the security of every man to the enjoyment of his earnings, and tend directly to anarchy."[48] This was Olmsted's last public communication to the city he had served for twenty years.

His work on the Boston park system, to which he gave close attention over the 1880s, is an instructive sequel to his experience in New York. The peculiar topography of Boston combined with its social and political environment to help Olmsted resolve many of the conflicts precipitated over Central Park. He had been in touch with Boston park enthusiasts since his ASSA lecture there in 1870. "Boston is a crooked confused territory," one Bostonian wrote to him; "if we ever get straightened out, it must be in the next or succeeding generations; if we ever have parks, now is the time to secure the lands for the purpose."[49] The incentive for action was the great Back Bay landfill project, which opened up choice new real estate and the promise of suburban development to the west of the city.[50] Gathering taxpayers' support for a park system through this area proved slow work, but just when Olmsted was removed from Central Park, Boston was ready to receive him. Seared by his New York experience, warned about the growing power of Boston's Irish municipal politicians, Olmsted doubted he would fare much better in Boston. "You are dependent on a public which is not only exceedingly ignorant in respect to the concerns with which you are about to deal," he told the chairman of the city's park commission, "but which is always ready to act on superficial views of them with great and dangerous energy."[51] He offered his service as a consultant with careful reserve. By now an established expert in his field, heading a large firm with a national pool

[48] Robert Muccigrosso, "The City Reform Club: A Study in Late Nineteenth-Century Reform," *New-York Historical Society Quarterly*, LII (July 1968), 239, 250; Roper, *FLO*, 434.
[49] James Haughton to Olmsted, Feb. 14, 1870, Olmsted Papers.
[50] Walter Muir Whitehill, *Boston: A Topographical History* (Cambridge, 1959), 141-73.
[51] Olmsted to Charles H. Dalton, May 13, 1878, Olmsted Papers.

of public and private clients, he could insist on administrative arrangements to protect his authority against the political intrusions he expected.

But Boston turned out to be different. The elegant names on the petitions—Martin Brimmer, Henry Winthrop Sargent, Charles R. Codman, Oliver Wendell Holmes, Sr., Richard Henry Dana, Jr., Charles William Eliot, William Endicott, Jr., Leverett Saltonstall—meant far more in the politics of the city than their counterparts in New York. In part because of Boston's slower growth over the century, its upper classes not only enjoyed greater solidarity by family and cultural inheritance, but retained a strong grip on the commercial, professional, and political life of the city. Godkin's remark that "Boston is the only place in America where wealth and the knowledge of how to use it are apt to coincide" seems vindicated by recent systematic analyses of nineteenth-century Brahmin staying power and the strong record of civic responsibility it produced.[52] Olmsted's work in Boston benefited directly from Brahmin patronage. His famous "emerald necklace," winding its way over six miles from the Public Garden across Back Bay and Charlesgate, along the Fenway through Jamaica Pond and the Arnold Arboretum to its climax in Franklin Park, engaged the resources of the city in a remarkable mix of public and private enterprise. The system developed in a pattern of fruitful interaction among wealthy Back Bay and suburban landowners, museums, colleges, and other cultural institutions which migrated to the edges of his park chain. It also enjoyed steady municipal backing.[53]

The caliber of the municipal support startled Olmsted after his bouts with Tammany Hall. His early work on the Fenway—one of the most elaborate technical feats of his career—was barely completed when Boston's first Irish Democratic mayor, Hugh O'Brien, took office in 1885. O'Brien promptly replaced the city's all-Republican park commission with Democrats. The most powerful new member was Patrick Maguire, the rising boss of the city's Democratic party. These ominous events plunged Olmsted into gloom. His fellow landscape architect, Horace Cleveland of

[52] Jaher, "Nineteenth-Century Elites in Boston and New York," 58-68; Paul Goodman, "Ethics and Enterprise: The Values of a Boston Elite, 1800-1860," *American Quarterly*, XVIII (Fall 1966), 437-51.

[53] For a recent study of Olmsted's Boston park system and its impact on the local environment, see Department of Landscape Architecture, Harvard Graduate School of Design, *Olmsted's Park System As Vehicle in Boston* (Cambridge, 1973). See also William Weismantel, "How the Landscape Affects Neighborhood Status: The Conserving and Renewing Influence of Boston's Charles River Basin and Park System," *Landscape Architecture*, LVI (April 1966), 190-94. For Olmsted's relation to the complex origins of the Arnold Arboretum, see S. B. Sutton, *Charles Sprague Sargent and the Arnold Arboretum* (Cambridge, 1970), 52-64.

Chicago, commiserated with him. "It gave me a sickening sensation to read your account . . . ," Cleveland wrote. "It is enough to make the old Bostonians of past generations turn in their graves to think of the city being given over to Irish domination and I cannot but fear that you will suffer discomfort from this last throw of time's whirligig."[54] Olmsted had misjudged both O'Brien and Maguire. O'Brien managed the city's business to the satisfaction of Boston Mugwumps and was soon winning favorable notice in the columns of Godkin's *Nation*. As for Maguire, a tough political professional with substantial real estate interests in suburban Roxbury near the route of Olmsted's park chain, his main political ambition was to bring Boston's Irish Democrats into functional rapport with the party's Yankee élite. His service on the park commission coincided with this aim.[55]

Olmsted's suspicions about the new board were not easily dissolved. "Men less interested in the parks as parks, it would be hard to find," he told Norton, "It will be a study to see how their real interests will be pursued across the Civil Service regulations."[56] By the end of the decade he was ready to confess he had been wrong. Referring to the consequences of the city's "political revolution" of 1885, he acknowledged that his work on the Boston parks had been unimpeded by a single appointment, dismissal, contract, or purchase made for partisan purposes. He knew of no other park department in the country which could match this record. His praise ended with this ultimate accolade: "I do not think that at so early a stage any other park work has come so nearly to be recognized and treated as a work of art."[57] While Boston was hardly free of the turmoil and inefficiencies plaguing urban America, Olmsted's words paid tribute to a singular feature of the city at that time. He had discovered a nineteenth-century political community which had not yet been torn apart by factional strife, class resentment, or ethnic rancor.

There were other satisfactions. The loosely strung, cumulative quality of Olmsted's Boston park system, following topography and residential growth from city to suburb, offered a much less constricted setting for his designs than Central Park. Its development, moreover, coincided with a revolution in the technology of rapid transit—the arrival of the electric

[54] H. W. S. Cleveland to Olmsted, March 12, 1885, Olmsted Papers.
[55] Geoffrey Blodgett, *The Gentle Reformers: Massachusetts Democrats in the Cleveland Era* (Cambridge, 1966), 59-63, 141-45.
[56] Olmsted to Norton, May 2, 1885, Norton Papers.
[57] Frederick Law Olmsted, "Remarks about a Difficulty Peculiar to the Park Department of City Governments," *Fourteenth Annual Report of the Board of Commissioners, Department of Parks, City of Boston* (Boston, 1889), 48-53.

trolley—which drew a greatly enlarged and more mobile clientele to his parks.⁵⁸ Also by the late 1880s Olmsted was able to respond more flexibly to the growing public taste for active recreation which would change the style of American popular culture in the decade ahead. His rationales for Franklin Park, the last of his three major urban parks, rehearsed the arguments for pastoral tranquility to counteract the oppressions of city life—"excessive nervous tension, over-anxiety, hasteful disposition, impatience, irritability"—and noted that the test of the park would be its value to the wives and mothers of the working class, the class which "shortly in the future [will] lead in the affairs of the city." The broad central space of Franklin Park was designed as a scenic country park. But around this rural core Olmsted introduced some ten other segments —space for boys' athletics, tennis courts and ball diamonds, refreshment pergola, musical amphitheater, zoo, deer park, nursery, playground (complete with see-saws and goat carriages), and a carriage promenade to be decorated with statues, bird cages, and water jets.⁵⁹ One has the sense that Franklin Park was somehow Olmsted's Boston response to the popular pressures on Central Park.

Franklin Park was not expected, however, to bear the whole burden of modern activism. Olmsted wanted no men's athletic teams playing there; he wanted labor agitators and other speechmakers barred from its grounds; he wanted schoolchildren trained in dutiful respect to its peaceful influences; and he repeatedly urged that flat land outside the park be set aside for military musters, fireworks, and balloon ascensions. He specified that other facilities for physical activity be located at scattered sites elsewhere in the city.⁶⁰ Most successful of these, in his mind, was the Charlesbank outdoor gymnasium. A letter to the journalist Sylvester Baxter, a chief promoter of his Boston park system, reflects Olmsted's satisfaction at the well-ordered social hierarchy operating at this center. "As far as I can estimate," he wrote, "90% of all who use it are young men of the 'work-

---

⁵⁸ For the impact of rapid transit on Boston urban growth, see Sam B. Warner, Jr., *Streetcar Suburbs: The Process of Growth in Boston, 1870-1900* (Cambridge, 1962). When the Franklin Park Playstead was dedicated in 1889, Henry M. Whitney's West End Railroad Company, then the country's largest rapid transit firm, provided a brass band and free transportation to schoolchildren for the occasion. See Blodgett, *Gentle Reformers*, 122-24.

⁵⁹ Frederick Law Olmsted, "Notes on the Plan of the Franklin Park and Related Matters," pamphlet published by the Boston Park Department (Boston, 1886), 45, 53, 101, 102. For an important view of the change in popular mores which occurred in the 1890s, see John Higham, "The Reorientation of American Culture in the 1890's," [Horace] John Weiss, ed., *The Origins of Modern Consciousness* (Detroit, 1965), 25-48.

⁶⁰ Olmsted and his son to Boston Park Commissioners, Dec. 31, 1888, Olmsted to Dalton, July 29, 1889, Thomas J. Emery to "Boston Parents," June 10, 1889, Olmsted to Thomas L. Livermore, Feb. 4, 1892, Olmsted Papers.

ing class,' factory hands & c. Negroes and Jews in their full proportion. The remaining 10% chiefly clerks, mostly of low degree, about 1% of college men or others coming well dressed and whom you might find at the Athletic Club."[61] The system was working.

In succeeding years, especially during the mayoralty of the young Brahmin Democrat Josiah Quincy, the city would expand its playground and gymnasium program well beyond Olmsted's prescription. And in the early 1890s, under Grover Cleveland's young protégé, Governor William E. Russell of Cambridge, the state created a metropolitan park commission, chaired by Olmsted's old friend Charles Francis Adams, Jr., which supervised a vast elaboration of parkland, boulevards, and beaches through the outer reaches of the city. Two Olmsted disciples, Baxter and the young landscape architect Charles Eliot (son of Harvard's president), were the driving force behind this expansion of Olmsted's Boston work toward the end of the century.[62] As Olmsted's career neared its close, he urged his partners to concentrate their best energies on the completion of the Boston projects. In their potential historical and educational impact they were, he said, "the most important work of our profession now in hand anywhere in the world."[63]

During one of Olmsted's periodic moods of gloomy self-doubt in the early 1880s, his friend Norton told him that he expected too much of the American people if he wanted them to understand him: "You are preaching truths above the comprehension of our generation." Venting his own harsh regard for American culture, Norton added, "You are compelled to throw your pearls before swine, and are fortunate if they do not turn and rend you for not giving them their favorite swill." When Olmsted died in 1903, Norton wrote to Olmsted's son in gentler tones: "Few men have done better service than he, service beneficent not only to his own generation, but to generation after generation in the long future."[64] As it turned out, the years proved kinder to Olmsted's reputation than to his creations.

His major parks, yielding steadily to popular pressures toward redefinition of use and thus of appearance, reached a peak of public acceptance around the time of World War I. Beginning in the 1920s, as the automobile replaced the trolley, exploded the spatial boundaries of the city, and started thinning out the population at its centers, the first small signs

---

[61] Olmsted to Sylvester Baxter, Sept. 2, 1889, *ibid.*
[62] Blodgett, *Gentle Reformers*, 125-26, 250-52.
[63] Olmsted to his partners, Oct. 28, 1893, Olmsted Papers.
[64] Norton to Olmsted, Oct. 23, 1881, Norton to Olmsted's son, Sept. 3, 1903, *ibid.*

of neglect and blight appeared. Americans now took their rural scenery through a car window, and urban carriage boulevards widened into commuter routes, often cutting off parkland from surrounding neighborhoods. A subtle mixture of modern trends—the shift toward commercialized spectator pleasures, the intensified organization of urban play, black and white migration in and out of the city, the relative impoverishment of municipal budgets as the federal welfare state began to deal more directly with individual human needs, the intangible but obvious triumph of city-oriented living styles over rural memories—all diminished the utility and attractions of the large urban park. By the 1960s a much smaller fraction of New Yorkers were using Central Park than a century before, and the desertion of Franklin Park had become a Boston scandal. In the teeth of public indifference, urban planners conferred earnestly to discover safe and vitalizing uses for vacant park space. Twentieth-century sociology and technology had all but overwhelmed Olmsted's planning vision, and the best hope for the survival of his parks seemed to lie in their rediscovery as works of art.[65]

Yet to measure Olmsted's significance by the current condition of his parks would miss the point of his career. He had pioneered a new profession and prodded the idea of the public park well along toward maturity in America.[66] Beyond that, his career forecast the process by which cosmopolitan élites, deprived of grass-roots political power, learned to assert their authority in public life through specific technical expertise in the higher echelons of urban governance. He left reasons for rediscovery beyond his time. As one student of modern urban landscaping put it: "The possibilities of master planning and urban design, by which construction and green space could play a gay and variable counterpoint throughout our communities, are just beginning to make some small impact upon our development thinking, though forecast one hundred years ago by Olmsted."[67] Another specialist added, "We have not shown the ability to design anything much larger than a tot lot which reflects the differences between our way of life and that of Olmsted."[68]

[65] For the best analysis of the impact of the twentieth century on Boston's parks, see *Olmsted's Park System As Vehicle in Boston*. For Central Park, see Ada Louise Huxtable, "Just a Little Love, a Little Care," New York *Times*, Dec. 9, 1973; and Lucinda Franks, "An Oasis of Green in Need of Rescue," *ibid.*, March 22, 1974.
[66] An English observer reported in 1890 that "a veritable rage for park making seems to have seized the American public." Earl of Meath, *Public Parks in America* (London, 1890), 3.
[67] Garrett Eckbo, *Urban Landscape Design* (New York, 1964), 99.
[68] Julia J. Broderick, quoted in *Beauty for America: Proceedings of the White House Conference on Natural Beauty, Washington, D.C., May 24-25, 1965* (Washington, 1965), 531.

Olmsted's way of life, together with many of the values he shared with the genteel reformers of the Gilded Age, disappeared before the nineteenth century was out. His hopes for a measure of social amelioration through projects in landscape architecture, like the hope of the civil service reformer that democratic politics might be purified by an end to spoils, and the hope of the tariff reformer that freer trade would help solve the riddle of domestic economic strife, depended on an all-but-forgotten social vision. Its believers thought that adequate structures of social and political intercourse could be defined for the popular mass by a cultured élite hovering above, to temper and redress the major public grievances of their day. Few of them ever wholly dropped their faith in gradual human improvement under the stewardship of trained talent. But their chosen tactics of improvement—even Olmsted's—only dimly anticipated the wrenching demands of the century ahead.

For all his artistic genius and brooding concern to enrich the quality of urban life by spatial design, Olmsted shared the programmatic inhibitions of his generation. He and his friends imagined that a commonwealth of free and diverse people, contained in an orderly public environment, governed by a benign and sanitary administrative state, was not only desirable but possible. Idealizing a rather static and formal conception of the social relations which ought to govern the American populace, they underestimated the aggressive thrust of American pluralism. The multiplying dislocations and resentments of social inequality and the bold measures required to order a nation of hostile strangers remained beyond their reckoning. Thus they minimized the need for more direct solutions to the problems accumulating in their lifetime. They saw no virtue in strenuous political manipulation, official coercion of private behavior, or closely managed economic change. Their successors in reform discovered otherwise. Meanwhile Olmsted's parks remained as battered monuments to the imagination of their generation at its best, and also to the constraints of their democratic faith.

THE NEW ENGLAND QVARTERLY

JUNE 1976

THE LANDSCAPER'S UTOPIA VERSUS THE CITY: A MISMATCH

ROSS L. MILLER

THE landscape architect was in a unique position at mid-century to influence the planning of the American city. There was a strain, however, in the uneasy partnerships forged between planners and city governments. The nineteenth-century landscape architecture movement was a vestigial part of the apparatus responsible for the meteoric growth of the city. It was vestigial in the sense that landscape architects, committed to an agrarian ideology, enthusiastically cooperated in the development of urban areas that were, in totality, not hospitable to their Jeffersonian notions of the land. Their historical rôle is a dramatic acting out of a conflict implicit in American democracy. Their problem was how to maintain cultural ideas associated with a preurban society in the face of rapid urbanization. But at mid-century it was too late effectively to change the basic social and economic conditions of the American city. The landscape architect thus found himself in the inglorious position of trying to salvage what he thought to be the essence of American democratic life from the philistinism of the commercial city. His solution was to design park lands for the urban centers.

Although parks offered relief from the unrelenting pressures of urban life, the mere redesign of the cityscape was not enough to redirect the main line of urbanization which had made the city less an environment to live in than a place to make money. Often, at their very best, architects like Frederick Law Olmsted could offer only a periodic escape.

> Building can be brought within the business of the park proper only as it will aid escape from buildings. Where building for other purposes begins, there the park ends. The reservoirs and the museum are not a part of the park proper: they are deductions from it. The sub-ways are not deductions, because their effect, on the whole, is to enlarge, not lessen, the opportunities of escape from buildings.[1]

Olmsted was opposed to the very thing his technology helped to augment. The buildings and the businesses they housed provided the city's rationale. Hadn't Olmsted himself argued, in 1856, in response to criticism of New York's Central Park that open lands in the city were to increase significantly the value of contiguous properties? While he was prepared to justify the economic advantages of the acquisition and development of park lands to convince reluctant public officials of the value of his plans, Olmsted never was confused about the actual need for city parks. But he miscalculated the effect that his planning would have on changing basically mercantile assumptions about the direction of an American urban society. Like many of his contemporaries, Olmsted was a half-hearted utopian who in seeking to attack the commercial city, through application of his technology, only made it more efficient.

Horace Cleveland was one of Olmsted's contemporaries who thought that he was effecting serious institutional reform through his scientific management of the landscape. When he wrote in *Landscape Gardening as Applied to the Wants of the West* (1873), he voiced what he felt to be a widely held principle:

> Landscape gardening, or more properly landscape architecture is

[1] Frederick Law Olmsted, "The Spoils of the Park," in Albert Fein, Editor, *Landscape Into Cityscape* (Ithaca, New York, 1968), 395.

the art of arranging land so as to adapt it most conveniently, economically and gracefully, to any of the varied wants of civilization.[2]

Cleveland still believed that environment, not money, was the shaping force in American life. He did not fully recognize urbanization as the kind of total change it was, and regarded it solely within the terms of a demographic problem. If people were leaving the country in ever-growing numbers, out of economic necessity, then it was the job of the landscape planner to bring the rural life along with them.

Cleveland, like Olmsted, was in a good position to feel sympathy for the displaced farmer. Both tried their hands at agricultural experiments: Olmsted at a farm on Staten Island; Cleveland on a large piece of land in Burlington, New Jersey. The interesting point is that neither had to turn to farming for economic reasons, but experimented in agriculture from ideological motivations. Self-consciously, they placed themselves in intimate contact with nature in an effort to re-create that pristine relation which they felt the first American settlers had to the land. It was this belief in the positive spiritual effects of the natural environment that influenced their view of the city and determined their philosophy of planning.

The park offered a compromise to those who had come to see the city as representing all that they hated about the progress of American society. Even persistent urban critics, like the Reverend Henry Bellows, saw park lands liberating the cities, those "pestilential inclosures." Bellows wrote in a popular article that even the new urban dwellers saw fit to extend themselves "to provide the largest and most costly opportunities for the enjoyment of their own leisure, artistic tastes, and rural instincts, is emphatically declared in the history, progress, and manifest destiny of the Central Park."[3] Bellows' new acceptance of the city encouraged Olmsted and Cleveland, for he seemed to confirm their view of the American mid-century

[2] H. W. S. Cleveland, *Landscape Architecture as Applied to the Wants of the West*, Roy Lubove, Editor (Pittsburgh, Penn., 1965), 5.

[3] Henry W. Bellows, "Cities and Parks: With Special Reference to the New York Central Park," *Atlantic Monthly*, VII, 421 (April, 1861).

city which had to meet special cultural demands. While Europe had a long urban history, America urbanized within a matter of decades. Her cities literally grew from gardens. There could be no significant acceptance of urbanization without the *appearance* of serving her "rural instincts." The landscape architecture movement helped to maintain this illusion.

The landscape architect by reclaiming land unfit for profitable development created, in Olmsted's words, greenswards to preserve something of the citizen's former intimacy with nature. At best, the park might make the city disappear. Olmsted wrote:

> Practically, what we most want is a simple, broad, open space of clean greensward, with sufficient play of surface and a sufficient number of trees about it to supply a variety of light and shade. This we want as a central feature. We want depth of wood enough about it not only for comfort in hot weather, *but to completely shut out the cities from our landscapes.* [emphasis mine][4]

The city, though made invisible, would never disappear. However, because landscape architects, unlike common antiurbanites of their day, realized they could not resist the historical trend of urbanization, their environmental planning concentrated on incorporating aspects of the rural landscape within the boundaries of the city. In this way, they felt, one might appear to reestablish the preindustrial balance between town and country. The landscape architect was a sophisticated urban critic who, though he could not, and would not, deny the fact of the American city, tried to control its effect upon a culture that was basically agrarian in ideology. Olmsted saw the park as a *tableau vivant* of the past that was meant to act in a dialectical relationship to urban life—much as the country itself before it was overwhelmed by urbanization. Sometimes this desire to divest the city of its cultural force led the planner to overreach his powers. Olmsted was driven to plan a park for

[4] Frederick Law Olmsted, "Public Parks and the Enlargement of Towns," in S. B. Sutton, Editor, *Civilizing American Cities: A Selection of Frederick Law Olmsted's Writings on City Landscapes* (Cambridge, 1971), 80.

LANDSCAPER'S UTOPIA VERSUS THE CITY 183

Brooklyn that *literally* replanted rural life there. A promenade opening at strategic intervals revealed the pleasing sight:

Of beautiful meadows, over which clusters of level-armed sheltering trees cast broad shadows, and upon which are scattered dainty cows and flocks of black-faced sheep, while men, women, and children are sitting here and there, forming groups in the shade, or moving in and out among the woody points and bays.[5]

The ambitious nature of Olmsted's plan gives an insight into the tone of mid-century landscape planning as a purely metaphoric response to hard economic facts. Merely presenting the proper elements of the village green and common pasture in Prospect Park might be reminiscent of an earlier age, but could not reassert these attractive images as living institutions. Olmsted's careful evocation of them was merely nostalgic and reveals the weaknesses of urban planning that conceived itself as preserving the values of a threatened order. But Olmsted and his contemporaries were caught in a serious dilemma at mid-century. Unplanned urban growth had proceeded for so long that it was almost impossible to offer more than cosmetic solutions to the deepest problems of design. For even when new cities were planned in the West, they followed the grid plan that had been the model for towns since the land surveys of 1785. Therefore, as Horace Cleveland notes in his *Landscape Architecture,* landscape architects were more often planning *around* than actually planning the American city. The grid plan defined the physical restrictions, and the city's elaborate commercial needs provided the economic conditions imposed on the urban planner. The actual extent of urbanization thus made it virtually impossible to achieve the fundamental changes envisioned by the landscape architect.

The degree to which city growth affected the structure of American society is reflected in Adna Weber's pioneering statistical study, *The Growth of Cities in the Nineteenth Century* (1898). His conclusions confirmed the intuitions of the planners. Urbanization progressed at such an accelerated rate that

[5] Sutton, *Civilizing American Cities,* 81.

it seemed more an organic or natural force than a controllable phenomenon, especially within the priorities set by the commercial city.

A glance at some of Weber's findings shows the extent of the problem. Life was clearly in the cities. While in 1800, 210,873 persons resided in six cities; in 1890, 18,284,385 lived in 448. But more important, in 1790 the percentage of city dwellers was 3.35 and in 1890 it had climbed to 29.2. Yet however significant the geometric rise in population was, the corresponding shift from a rural to an urban-based population stood out as the critical component of Weber's demographic portrait.

The landscape architect was sensitive to the dislocating effect of urbanization upon the individual citizen as well as the values upon which the nation was founded. Democracy was not well-suited to the increasing scale of urban society. One could no longer assume the existence of an homogeneous population in which well-meaning groups could reflect the will of an entire citizenry. The American city was less a union than a conglomerate of neighborhoods with competing needs and values. The city life that increasingly had become the major mode of existence was essentially unknown to the country's founders. A solution had to be found that would reestablish an environment more conducive to the proper operation of a republic.

The city park was viewed as the proper place to begin the reconstruction of a way of life lost with urbanization. The formidable Reverend Henry Bellows, representative of the mid-century urban critics, who had once written, the "first murderer was the first city-builder," was able to say of the urban park:

The actual existence of the Central Park in New York,—the most striking evidence of the sovereignty of the people yet afforded in the history of free institutions,—the best answer yet given to the doubts and fears which have frowned on the theory of self-government,—the first grand proof that the people do not mean to give up the advantages and victories of aristocratic governments, in maintaining a popular one, but to engraft the energy, foresight, and liberality of concentrated powers upon democratic ideas, and keep all that has adorned and improved the past, while abandoning what has impaired and disgraced it.[6]

Here is a more ministerial version of Olmsted's invisible city, significant in its selectivity. While the city-builder is "a murderer," the urbanite refreshed by the park is the true democrat. Bellows' bifurcated vision fails to recognize that both the city-building murderer and the urban park-goer became the same person at mid-century. Yet it is precisely this double vision that provides a key to landscape planning. Nineteenth-century landscape architects saw their parks as democratic free states in the midst of commercial empires. And at their finest, these archipelagoes might communicate a democratic spirit seemingly lost somewhere in the transition from a rural to an urban nation. The architect's intent was often vague, but the faith was deeply held that somehow the park, in addition to making the city look better, would improve the city-dweller's behavior. This naïf belief in a controlled environment informed planning throughout the century.

Charles Sargent, Director of the Arnold Arboretum, and editor of the influential *Garden and Forest* (1888-1897), in an 1889 editorial still warned against the further encroachment of the city, as if it were not already an accomplished fact. His evangelical argument for park lands, in the context of Weber's demographic study, was like the Dutch boy with his finger in the dike.

The future of the city parks in this country is by no means secure—nor will it be, until the people generally understand that these parks have a function to fulfill which is quite as distinct as that of churches and schools and libraries, and until it comes to be a general and unquestioned belief that these pleasure grounds are absolutely indispensable to the well-being of those who are subjected to the complex conditions of modern city life.[7]

---

[6] Bellows, *Atlantic Monthly*, VII, 421 (April, 1861).

[7] Charles S. Sargent, "The Proper Use of Public Parks," *Garden and Forest*, II, 458 (Sept. 25, 1889).

Olmsted had made the same point nearly twenty years before in his address, "Public Parks and the Enlargement of Towns" (1870), when he saw the parks replacing the churches as the major ethical influence on American life. There was good evidence to support his claim:

> While most of the grog-shops were effectually closed by the police under the Excise Law on Sunday, the number of visitors was considerably larger than before. There was no similar increase at the churches.[8]

But the idea that the park would express a lost democratic voice was always a part of the landscape architecture movement. Andrew Jackson Downing, the first American landscape architect, based his philosophy of planning on classic notions about the power of environment to affect values. He outlined the ways a plot of land might be expected to affect the society as a whole:

> It is republican in its very idea and tendency. It takes up popular education where the common school and ballot-box leave it, and raises up the working-man to the same level of enjoyment with the man of leisure and accomplishment. The higher social and artistic elements of every man's nature lie dormant within him, and every laborer is a possible gentleman, not by the possession of money or fine clothes—but through the refining influence of intellectual and moral culture... Plant spacious parks in your cities and unloose their gates as wide as the gates of morning to the whole people.[9]

Downing, Olmsted, and Sargent exhibit the same utopian rhetoric. Somehow the parks would accomplish for American society what the culture had failed to do as a whole. But the idea that democracy might survive as islands in a hostile sea was all that the nineteenth-century democrat felt he could offer the drowning urbanite. The problem was that the traditional American values, formulated in the previous century by agrarian republicans, were now cut off from any effective

---

[8] Sutton, *Civilizing American Cities*, 96.
[9] Andrew Jackson Downing, "The New York Park," *Rural Essays*, VIII, 147 (August, 1851).

economic or political mechanism for change. The resulting paradox was that of static cultural notions in conflict with an expanding nation whose only principle seemed to be growth in the name of progress. The landscape architecture movement was in the odd position of imposing the older pastoral values, three-dimensionally, in the form of park lands, upon a basically hostile cityscape. Their planning often seemed vague and strained because it tried to do too much. The landscape architect could easily make the city more livable, but he could not redeem it, or change its basic commercial character. Yet precisely this element of trying to wish away the prevailing economic organization of the city weakens much urban planning. Sargent, in the editorial mentioned above, went on to maintain that the park, unlike the contemporary church, discouraged dangerous class divisions and had a fortunate democratic effect. It, unlike the city proper, was no place for a millionaire.

> But it is for those who have no country seats, and who take no vacations, and for their children, that this delightful picture of rural peace stands ready to furnish rest and healing, both to the mind and body.[10]

The sentiment is utopian only because there is no effective way of implementing it. Although, it is the prevailing sense of the landscape movement that only in sentiment was it able to correct the social ills to which it alluded. Their parks were to be "pictures," or "museums" as Sargent eventually came to see them—to be viewed but never walked upon. Here again was the radical politics of the New England Brahmin who never attached his vision to an active political movement. Sargent, Olmsted, and Downing all displayed the utopian quietism characteristic of the age. Their parks, or more properly the rationale that created them, were almost literal translations of the Unitarian lecture translated and applied to the land. Witness William Ellery Channing:

> With what face can the great cities of Europe and America boast

[10] Sargent, *Garden and Forest*, 457.

of their civilization, when within their limits thousands and ten thousands perish for want of God's freest, most lavish gifts! Can we expect improvement among people who are cut off from nature's common bounties, and want those cheering influences of the elements which even savages enjoy.[11]

Channing's criticism was clear. The urban "savage" was depraved not because of poverty, ill health, or lack of employment, but because he was denied Nature's healing powers. Channing provided an intellectual accommodation to the industrial city that many of his contemporaries were unable to make. Traditionally, the solution had been to remove oneself from the crass and brutish centers. Charles Eliot Norton, for example, left "urban" Cambridge for the Berkshires, protesting there was no longer any hope for him or his kind because industrialization had made Eastern Massachusetts unlivable. His move to Ashfield signified the same elaborate rejection of American culture at mid-century that prompted the expatriation of Henry James some years later. But these were all men who felt that they lacked weapons with which to fight. Retreat suited them temperamentally and favored their art. However, for Channing who shared many of his friends' criticisms of the city, there seemed no reason to retreat. His belief in the spiritual effects of the natural environment was so strong that a city that imposed its own somber reality of mortar, brick, and pavement could not fail to be overcome by a force as simple as a park.

The Transcendentalist imaginative conversion of the concrete into the abstract was a motivating influence upon the New England landscape architects: Olmsted, Downing, Cleveland, Copeland, Eliot, and Baxter. They inherited a habit of mind that read an allegorical or metaphysical meaning into the experience of everyday life. In this way, it was easy for the landscape planner to imagine that he was settling the most complex kinds of historical and cultural problems by redesigning the physical landscape. For at mid-century there was

[11] William Ellery Channing, *Lectures on the Elevation of the Laboring Portion of the Community* (Boston, 1840), 64.

LANDSCAPER'S UTOPIA VERSUS THE CITY

thought to be a strong connection between the environment and political abstractions as vague as "democratic." A park could in this special sense be an actual agent for democracy. So all this rhetoric from Downing to Sargent was finally less metaphoric than part of a corporate or national fiction.

At mid-century both the moral and technical critiques of the city merged. Intellectuals and planners concentrated their attack on the city as a negative environment, and in this way treated a problem of enormous historical consequences as merely an extension of their critique of a materialistic society. Emerson, who once observed that he suffered a "loss of faith on entering cities," viewed the city as the principal challenge to democracy:

We divorce ourselves from nature; we hide ourselves in cities and lose the affecting spectacle of Day and Night which she cheers and instructs her children withal. We pave the earth for miles with stones and forbid the grass. We build street on street all round the horizon and shut out the sky and the wind; false and costly tastes are generated for wise and cheap ones; thousands are poor and cannot see the face of the world; the senses are impaired, and the susceptibility to beauty; and life made vulgar.[12]

Emerson's criticism gave to the landscape planner's work a quality of high seriousness, and along with Channing and others provided a theoretical framework to which architects could refer their vision of planning. Planners now saw the city as a threat to American values because it immured one from the soothing intimacy of Nature. It produced an ideological justification for men committed to planning cities that were neither firetraps nor breeding grounds for disease. Although the transcendentalists' experiments in utopian communities failed, they had in the architects of the landscape movement their chevaliers.

The planner of parks became more than a technician and assumed the burden of having to maintain an idealized notion

[12] Ralph Waldo Emerson, "The Eye and Ear," in Stephen E. Whicher, Robert E. Spiller, Wallace E. Williams, Editors, *The Early Lectures of Ralph Waldo Emerson*, II, 1836-1838, 273 (Cambridge, 1964).

of democracy in the face of the contemporary city. Yet it allowed him more effectively to convince the reluctant municipal authorities of the virtues of park lands, and gave him a sense of purpose that came with thinking himself part of a movement to redeem the urban spaces. The landscape architect's hope was that nature, in the form of a well-managed park, transplanted to the heart of the city, would serve as a vehicle of social change in America as potent as the seventeenth-century country church or the eighteenth-century town. Horace Cleveland took the argument to extraordinary lengths in his advocacy of a municipal park system for St. Paul. Here is part of his remarkable address on June 24, 1872:

> It is a wise expenditure of public money to use it in providing places and means of public entertainment, of a refining and elevating character, which is the nature and should be the ultimate object of every form of art. The love of natural beauty which is instinctive in the human heart lies at the foundation of artistic taste, and is the element which may be relied upon, with most certainty, as a means of attracting and refining even the most degraded. If you doubt it, take in your hand a simple boquet [sic] of flowers and walk with it through the meanest slums of a great city, and see the eager looks which will be cast upon it by those whose appearance gives no token of anything like refinement, and how the ragged, dirty children will run after you, begging a flower; or go with a mission school of those same children for a day's picnic in the country, and witness their delight in getting into the woods and green fields, and you will learn that no greater luxury can be provided for those whose lives are passed in the din and turmoil of the streets than the opportunity to indulge their craving for a glimse [sic] of nature.[13]

Cleveland's speech is quoted at length because it identifies the misplaced optimism of the nineteenth-century landscape planner. His euphoric mood encouraged those who hoped that an agrarian democracy could live, basically unaffected, within the

[13] H. W. S. Cleveland, *Public Parks, Radial Avenues and Boulevards: Outline Plan of a Park System for the City of St. Paul* (1885). Addresses delivered before the Common Council and Chamber of Commerce: June 24, 1872, and June 19, 1885.

structure of a city that radically opposed it, not unlike the hermit crab that remains the same within the different shells he scavenges. Taken to its logical extension, the man with a flower is an ambulatory park. So the park itself, like so much of Transcendental thought is not confined by the limitations of time and space.

At the century's end, Sylvester Baxter, the Boston landscape architect, was still able to echo Cleveland and Olmsted's faith in the livable quality of the American city, if only the urban environment might be redeemed by rural scenes. Baxter maintained in his "The Imaginative Element in Landscape" in *The American Architect and Building News* (1898) that unflagging belief in Nature's powers would locate America's lost Eden in a no less likely place than the city center. Utopian quest for the perfect community had come full circle—those who had forsaken Boston for Brook Farm found themselves back in town again. Baxter urged the appeal of the park:

> This charm lies in the emphasis given to the sense of relief from conditions obtaining in the outside world, tinged with an indifference to cares left behind, much like that which a dweller in Paradise might regard the forsaken scenes of his earthly life.[14]

The city posed an elaborate challenge to the landscape architect. Why retreat if he could bring nature back to man? If civilization's record is, as Levi-Strauss has noted, the transformation of raw to cooked, profane to sacred, silence into noise, disorder into order, wilderness into city—then how much more accomplished would be the society that chose to master these relationships? Man could manipulate his environment more usefully and efficiently once he achieved a natural balance with nature. The landscape architect would not establish the former ecological system that saw man a victim, but would create an environment where neither man nor nature *appeared* to consume each other. Primitive man had shown his mastery over nature by killing the beast; civilized man

[14] Sylvester Baxter, "The Imaginative Element in Landscape," *The American Architect and Building News*, LVIX, 11 (Jan. 8, 1898).

tamed him to meet his needs. In large part, the appeal of the nineteenth-century landscape architecture movement was imperialistic, for through its pretense of relinquishing power over nature, in freeing land from development, it managed to control her more completely.

The landscape architect was at the center of an irreconcilable conflict that threatened nineteenth-century America. It finally was impossible to reconcile the agrarian respect for the land with a commercial society whose economic health depended upon the active exploitation of the landscape. Yet the landscape architect's response to this dilemma, in retrospect, seems particularly satisfying. He managed to embody this larger conflict into the actual terms of his planning. While acting out a primal desire to subdue the land, he succeeded in remaining within the sanctions of the New England gentleman. The concept of the New England village green is reasserted in the American urban park by the nineteenth-century landscape architects. Their planning assumed a horizontality consistent with gradual population growth and unlimited resources of land. However, they were unable to foresee that increased density would force the city to grow vertically within the traditional grid plan despised by sensitive landscape planners. The skyscraper, pioneered in Chicago by William Le Baron Jenney in the 1880's would accommodate the city far more efficiently than open park lands. America's landscape architecture movement was essentially anachronistic and its effect on city planning was never fully realized. In establishing the park as an integral part of the city, the landscape architect was not completely successful in defying the philistine culture around him, but he did create in the park a prominent source of relief from the persistent demands of urban life. His parks succeeded as potent cultural icons, organic statuary, to a more heroic time when the American, more than any other man, appeared to be in harmony with nature.

The lasting significance of the landscape movement's work is that it gave Americans a way to deal with urbanization. Today, a walk in any urban park gives a contemporary sense of

LANDSCAPER'S UTOPIA VERSUS THE CITY

the physical aspects of their accomplishment. The city seems respectfully to have grown around the open land leaving scores of acres unaffected by its colossal presence. This illusion of untouched nature is part of the achievement of the landscape artist. All the graded, excavated, and blasted land was made to look as if a human hand had never touched it. The thrill and triumph of the landscape architect, or just the walker in the park, is that of the truly civilized man, like Thoreau, who knows that he can devour nature but rather chooses to watch his creations, "Cheerfully returning to their wild and primitive state."

The Frederick Law Olmsted Plan for Tacoma

BY NORMAN J. JOHNSTON

On July 3, 1873, the executive committee of the Northern Pacific Railroad Company telegraphed to its West Coast representatives that their recommendation for the location of "Terminal City" on Puget Sound had been approved. By this action the committee made official a decision that had been a source of much uncertainty among the finalists—Tacoma, Seattle, and Mukilteo: Tacoma was to be the Pacific Northwest terminus of the line that was still under construction from Saint Paul westward to Kalama on the Columbia River and thence north to Puget Sound. The minutes of that same meeting also noted that two members of the company's board of directors, Charles B. Wright of Philadelphia and Charlemagne Tower of Pottsville, Pennsylvania, "were appointed Committee to lay out and own Terminal City. . . . The town plan will be made here as soon as topographical map and other data received."[1]

Initial work on the plan was begun under the direction of General James Tilton as chief engineer, who, it was reported, had selected Melbourne, Australia, as his model.[2] The history of speculative town platting as an aspect of 19th-century railroad expansionism is clearly documented as to the preferences in town plans. The Illinois Central Railroad, for example, had a standardized plat, entirely rectangular in outline, in blocks, and in building lots, with equal halving of the plan on either side of the railroad right-of-way. Melbourne (which was laid out in 1837) demonstrates the same worship of regularity, as a description written in 1850 makes clear:

the only skill exhibited in the plan of Melbourne is that involved in the use of square and compasses. Pope's couplet, slightly modified, exactly described Melbourne. . . .
Street answers street, each alley has its brother,
And half the city just reflects the other.[3]

There is no indication why General Tilton went so far afield for his model. Any one of numerous towns and cities in the United States would have served as nicely in reflecting allegiance to the same mechanical inspiration.

The character of Tilton's plan was described in some detail (although without accompanying plan) in the Tacoma *Weekly Pacific Tribune*. There were to be five main avenues,

two of which are diagonal and three parallel to the water front. . . . All five avenues are one hundred feet broad and two of them are about a mile and a quarter long. The object of the diagonal avenues is to permit easy grades of approach from the water to the upper or higher plateaus, and the use of street cars to reach the upper from the lower levels. These avenues are flanked by blocks of lots on either side, the blocks 300 feet in length running 120 feet back to a narrow street forty feet wide, thus avoiding the narrow and filthy alleys which disfigure so many older cities. . . . All other streets are 80 feet wide. . . . A natural mount 315 feet high, elliptical in shape, and occupying about 27 acres . . . is laid out in the midst of the plat or town site, about 1000 feet from the bay. This is proposed as a public park or site for the erection of public buildings. . . . The town, as laid off, also contains two smaller public parks upon high ground, one at each end of the town and a mile apart. . . . It requires

---

[1] Minutes of Board of Directors and Executive Committee, July 10, 1873, Northern Pacific Company Records, Minnesota Historical Society, Saint Paul, Minn. The site for the company's new city was south of an already existing small town, Tacoma City—formerly Commencement City—where local activities and enterprises, including the office of the newspaper, awaited the new town's development (see Figure 3).

[2] Tacoma *Weekly Pacific Tribune*, Aug. 29, 1873. The same interests also published the Tacoma *Daily Pacific Tribune*, the stories from one often appearing verbatim in the other.

[3] James Grant and Geoffrey Serle, *The Melbourne Scene, 1803-1956* (Carlton, Victoria, Australia, 1957), 65.

Norman J. Johnston is associate dean and professor of architecture and urban planning at the University of Washington. An earlier version of this article was read at a meeting of the Northern Pacific Coast Chapter, Society of Architectural Historians, held in Seattle, Oct. 14-15, 1972.

no prophet to predict the certainty of its high density in the near future as the first city of the Republic upon its Pacific waters.[4]

Town planning was paralleled by the establishment of the Tacoma Land Company, authorized by the company's executive committee on July 10, 1873, to handle administration and marketing of the new city's land.

In the meantime, however, and quite unknown to the Tacoma *Pacific Tribune*'s editor, the railroad company's eastern office abruptly changed course and hired Frederick Law Olmsted, the foremost American landscape architect of the 19th century, to plan the new city. On October 6 the *Pacific Tribune* suddenly announced that Tacoma's plan was now "being prepared from the surveys of the Company's Engineers, by the distinguished Engineer and Landscape Gardener, F. Law Olmstead [*sic*], who laid out Central Park in New York City." While the events surrounding this unexpected switch are not known, certain circumstances may explain it. The president's office of the railroad company as well as its land department were in New York City, and it was there that the board of directors and the executive committee met. Given the prominence of Central Park in the city and Olmsted's role as its planner and administrator, it is entirely likely that his name was familiar, at least to the company's New York executives.[5]

More specifically, however, the presence of Frederick Billings on the company's board and executive committee was a likely factor in the selection of Olmsted. In 1863 Olmsted had become the superintendent of the Mariposa Estate, a large California gold-mining operation near Stockton. Billings, then a prominent San Francisco citizen, was the lawyer for one of the estate's principal owners and participated in introducing Olmsted initially to the properties. Although the venture was ill-fated, it led to a number of opportunities for Olmsted under Billings' aegis. Among them was a park plan for San Francisco and in 1866 a plan for the new town of Berkeley, the latter to include a campus for the proposed College of California of which Billings was a trustee. While neither of these plans was realized, Billings did not forget Olmsted. Later, when Billings invested in the Northern Pacific Railroad Company, became a company director, and organized its land department, he supported Olmsted as town planner for Tacoma.[6]

Then there was Charles B. Wright, a vice-president of the company, a member of both the board and the executive committee, and one of those appointed on July 10, 1873, to "lay out and own Terminal City." He was also president of the Tacoma Land Company for developing and marketing the new city. While antecedent connections between Olmsted and Wright are less clear than they are between Billings and Olmsted, it is possible that Wright was more than superficially aware of Olmsted's reputation. As a Philadelphian, he may have been less conscious of Olmsted's work on Central Park than the New York board members were. But he may have known of Olmsted through the latter's association with Fairmount Park in Philadelphia, another great urban park and the most fashionable of that city's establishment monuments.

THE development of Fairmount Park, still the largest city park in the United States, began early in the 19th century. One of the park's original commissioners was Theodore Cuyler, a distinguished Philadelphia lawyer who specialized in corporation law and railroad litigation and was solicitor for the Pennsylvania Railroad Company. Like Cuyler, Charles Wright was also involved in railroad enterprises; one of the lines which Wright served as director became an important part of the Pennsylvania Railroad system during the years when both men were active in the affairs of their respective companies. Moreover, they lived within two blocks of each other in the Rittenhouse Square neighborhood.[7]

We know from existing correspondence that the firm of Olmsted and Vaux (Calvert Vaux was Olmsted's partner) was being considered in 1872 for work by the Fairmount Park Commission. It seems reasonable, therefore, to infer that, in a society as well structured as Philadelphia's, the circles of two such substantial members would inevitably have touched and probably overlapped. Wright undoubtedly was already aware of

---

[4] *Weekly Pacific Tribune*, Oct. 3, 1873.
[5] *Daily Pacific Tribune*, Oct. 6, 1873. Little is known about the switch in Tacoma's city planners, for the Frederick Law Olmsted Papers (deposited in the Library of Congress) are incomplete. The collection contains only fragmentary materials relating to Olmsted's work in the Tacoma plan, including some correspondence and what appears to be some sketches of possible street arrangements. That even the Olmsted office was puzzled by the switch is shown by a 1909 letter from the firm to John Olmsted (F. L. Olmsted's stepson), then visiting Tacoma, inquiring if he could arrange for a photographic copy of the original plan which was supposedly on file in the public library. The younger Olmsted was also asked to get a copy of the report, if there was one. Perhaps further clarification of events may be found in the Northern Pacific Company Records. So far, however, references to Olmsted and the Tacoma plan remain undiscovered.

Olmsted's reputation and thus was prepared to give serious consideration when Billings proposed Olmsted as Tilton's successor.

Billings and Wright, confronted with the tedious mechanics of Tilton's plan, could appreciate its contrasts with the imaginative approaches demonstrated by Olmsted at Berkeley and by his plan (with Vaux) for the railroad suburb of Riverside, Illinois (discussed below). At this stage of development, forceful influence must have been required to persuade the board to replace Tilton with Olmsted. Wright and Billings together would no doubt have provided the necessary clout. In their positions of authority for laying out the terminal city, they swayed the board to their view. Thus on September 19, 1873, Billings telegraphed to Olmsted: "Can you come here Wright wishes to leave this afternoon and wants to see you board decided to employ you."[8]

Olmsted quickly accepted the commission. On September 25 he wrote to Billings and proposed that G. K. Radford, "an experienced sanitary and hydraulic engineer," be associated with him in working on the plan.[9] He stated briefly what he would include in the plan:

> Our undertaking will be to devise an arrangement in which, so far as shall appear from the snaps you furnish us, the difficulties of the site [of the proposed terminal city of the Northern Pacific R.R.] in respect to grade of streets shall be better met than they are in either of the plans you have already had prepared.
>
> The data are insufficient for a determinate plan and the preliminary study which we shall make will, of course, have to be adjusted, after more detailed survey to the minor inequalities of the surface and to any other conditions not exhibited to us at this time.
>
> The plan is to be adapted to ordinary methods of sewerage, water supply and other modern commercial conveniences or if it presents any extraordinary difficulties in these respects, practicable methods of overcoming them are to be devised and indicated.
>
> The charge for the work is to be two thousand dollars....[10]

---

[6] Clarification of Olmsted's relations with Billings was established in Laura Wood Roper's *FLO: A Biography of Frederick Law Olmsted* (Baltimore, 1973).

[7] J. Thomas Scharf and Thompson Westcott, *History of Philadelphia, 1609-1884* (Philadelphia, 1884), II, 1546-47; Henry Hall, ed., *America's Successful Men of Affairs* (New York, 1896), II, 895-96.

[8] Frederick Billings to Olmsted, Sept. 19, 1873 (telegram), Olmsted Papers.

[9] Olmsted to Billings, Sept. 25, 1873, *ibid*. Olmsted's partnership from Central Park days with Calvert Vaux had been terminated in 1872.

[10] *Ibid*. Note also that Olmsted makes reference to two plans already at some level of completion by making inferences as to their quality.

[11] Charles B. Wright to Olmsted, Sept. 27, 1873. Olmsted Papers.

[12] Several sketches among the Olmsted Papers pertain to the Tacoma plan.

The terms were satisfactory to the company, though Wright, as president of the Tacoma Land Company, noted that Olmsted failed to mention the date of "delivery of the Plan. It is of extreme importance that we have it at the earliest day possible, and it was understood that you would

Courtesy of the author

Figure 1. Olmsted sketches for Tacoma

finish it in six weeks when we had our last interview."[11]

The record of subsequent activity leading to Olmsted's plan is fragmentary. His papers include some sketches (Figure 1) which appear to be related to the Tacoma plan.[12] They reaffirm what was already established, however: his unorthodox views about city planning in contrast to those displayed by the Melbourne and presumably Tilton plans. That Olmsted would be unconventional the company's directors surely

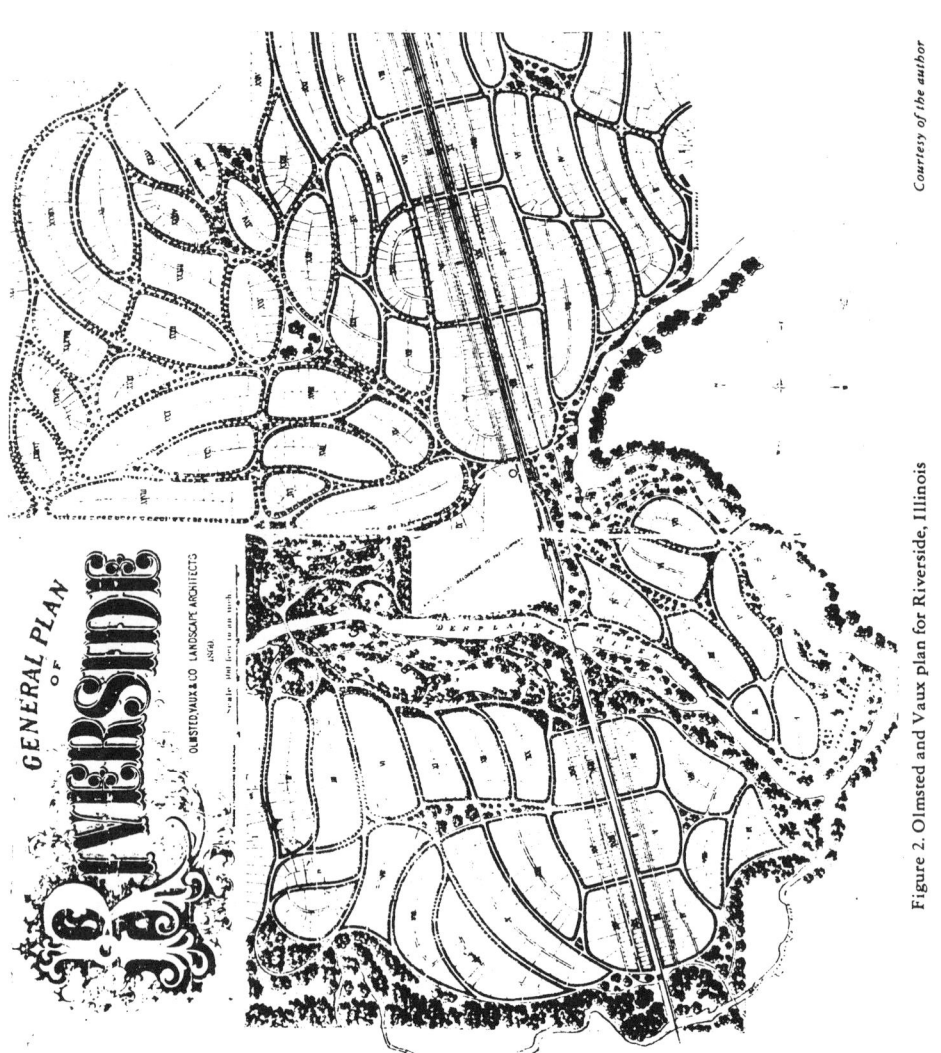

Figure 2. Olmsted and Vaux plan for Riverside, Illinois

knew; his extensive practice developed since the early 1860s fully demonstrated his approach.

Olmsted's unorthodox views were especially evident in his plan for Riverside, another land development, though smaller, for a residential community on the Quincy Railroad west of Chicago (Figure 2). The Olmsted and Vaux plan for Riverside had antecedents in the design for an earlier subdivision, Llewellyn Park in New Jersey. The park designer, Alexander Jackson Davis, had been an early influence on Olmsted and had had previous associations with Vaux. The partners saw in the picturesque naturalness of Llewellyn Park the potential for something other than rigid geometry in community planning.[13]

The design for Riverside, while following the lead of the earlier community, nevertheless had its own individuality. The partners acknowledged the Des Plaines River as a key design determinant, preserving and enhancing the naturalism of its form to become an extended park winding through the area. A framework of slowly sweeping tree-lined streets, irregular residential blocks of building lots, and varied public open spaces completed the design. The only strictly straight lines in the plan were those set by the railroad which cut across the site and connected it to Chicago.

It seems unlikely, therefore, that the board members, in the course of interviewing Olmsted or in checking his professional records, would have been unaware of the approach he could be expected to take in developing a plan for their terminal city. Precedent and extant sketches point clearly toward his efforts to devise a plan that would harmonize the rather special natural conditions of Tacoma's site with provisions for its urban development and his rejection of conventional practices.

THE work must have proceeded quickly, for the plan was completed and delivered to an expectant community late in December. It was a package filled with confusion for an unprepared public (Figure 3). The editor of the *Pacific Tribune*, as a local booster, was more concerned that potential lot purchasers might weary of any further delays in placing land on the market than he was in design niceties. He therefore sounded a cautiously reassuring note, observing that the new plan was "approved by many men of ripe judgment and unquestioned taste, who recognize in it much merit...."[14]

On December 23 the editor reported that the plan had arrived on the previous Sunday and was on display in the company offices:

The new plan differs essentially from the old, and is, as far as we know, unlike that of any other city in the world. Its main features are, briefly described, about as follows:

The ground laid off is on the southern shore of Commencement Bay 1000 acres in extent, and reaching from the Galliher mill pond two and a half miles down the bay to the Tacoma mill pond. A portion of the mudflat is also laid off, for future use. The most peculiar features of the new plan are the varying sizes and shapes of the blocks, and the absence of straight lines and right angles. Every block and every street and avenue is curved. The lots have a uniform frontage of 25 feet, but differ in length, averaging, however, 180 feet. The curvature of the blocks does away with corner lots, and their great length with much of the misery of street crossings, where collisions and accidents always happen, and where mud and dust are invariably the deepest.... The three grand avenues are Pacific, Tacoma and Cliff. Pacific leads up the bank, from the railroad dock, and out into the country; Tacoma is about a mile only in length, intersecting up in town with Pacific avenue, and running down to the beach between the old and new towns; Cliff avenue extends along the brow of the bluff, two miles or more in length.... The first is intended for the business of the town, and for country trade and driving; the second takes past the principal parks; and the third will be magnificent for residences, promenading and driving, as it will be high and sightly, with nothing between it and the water.... There are seven parks laid out, consuming about 100 acres of the ground, and varying from 2 to 30 acres each in extent.... Being of so novel a character, those who have seen the plan hardly know whether or not to admire it, while they are far from prepared to openly condemn it. Time alone will prove its practicability. Certainly, if a large city is ever built there, after that plan, it will be through and through like a park, and have very many important advantages over other cities.[15]

It is likely, however, that another contemporary observer who described the plan as having blocks "shaped like melons, pears and sweet potatoes" more accurately reflected its local reception.[16] Regional reaction also was bemused; the Portland *Bulletin* is reported as being

rather humorous over the new Tacoma town plat, though expressing no disapproval of it, and gets off the following on the subject:

"This wondrous town, as if fully resolved to make itself worthy of its high destiny as the future mart at which the business of two hemispheres is to be transacted, has received a new 'plat,' got up at the East regardless of pains and expense, and sent out all the way to Puget Sound for the delight of terminal lot holders. The 'new plat' as described by the Tacoma newspaper, is a thing brave and grand enough to make the fortune of a town even less pretending than Tacoma. In fact a town with a 'plat' gotten up on such elab-

---

[13] Albert Fein, *Frederick Law Olmsted and the American Environmental Tradition* (New York, 1972), 33.
[14] *Daily Pacific Tribune*, Dec. 23, 27, 1873. Although there was company development activity in the terminal city, sale of land for non-company purposes awaited a plan and identification of lots for public sale.
[15] *Ibid.*, Dec. 23, 1873.
[16] Glenn Chesney Quiett, *They Built the West: An Epic of Rails and Cities* (New York, 1934), 414.

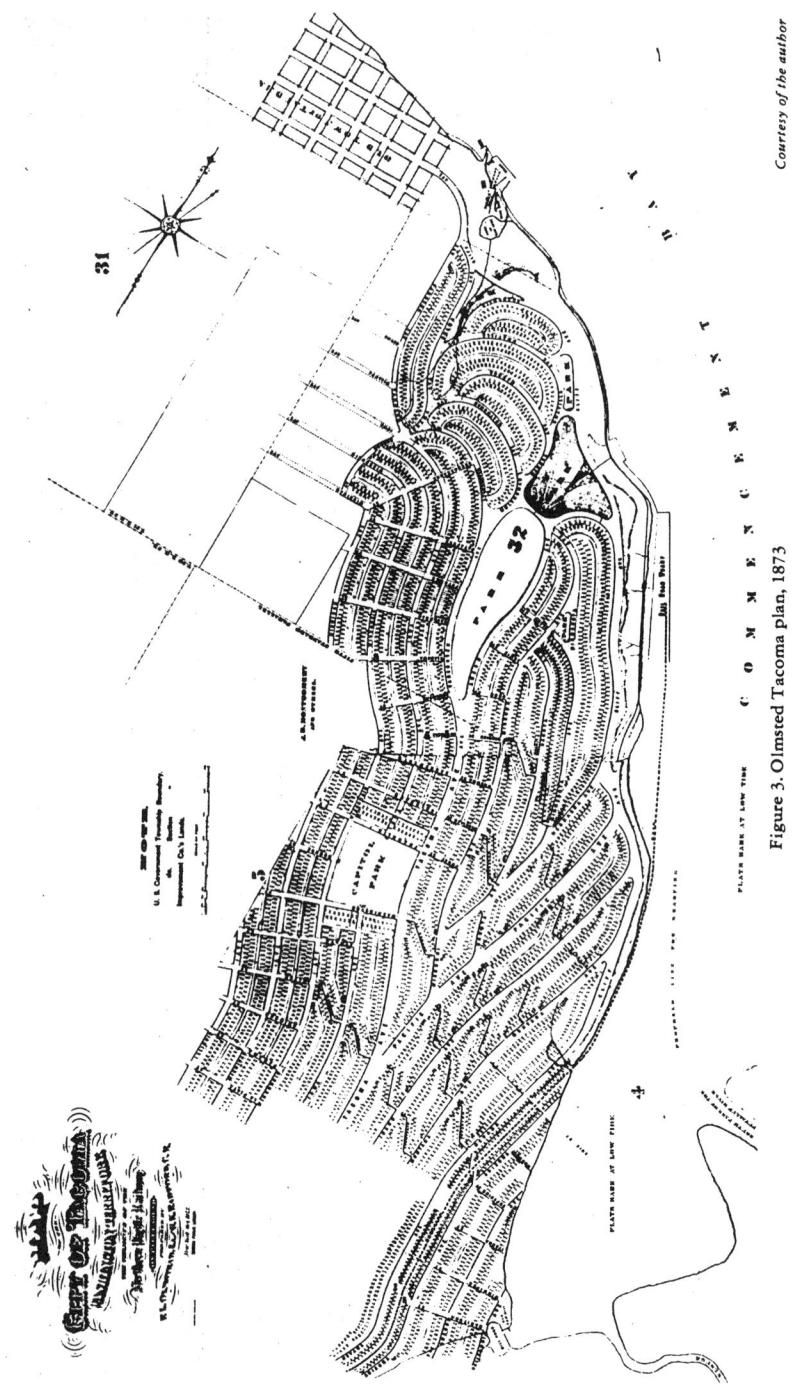

Figure 3. Olmsted Tacoma plan, 1873

orate principles can't possibly require much else to complete its greatness. It is already a city set upon a hill, or two hills, for that matter. We were told at the offstart that the new plan makes Tacoma 'unlike any other city in the world.' It would be ridiculous indeed for such a city to copy after unpretending places like Chicago or San Francisco. Tacoma resolves to have an individuality, and to assert it.

"The city as laid out is already two and a half miles long. There are neither straight lines nor right angles. The curve is the favorite geometrical line at Tacoma. It is supposed to be borrowed from the magnificent movements of the celestial spheres, or other great operations of nature, which abhor right angles and straight lines; and with these movements Tacoma is determined to be in harmony. In consequence, there are no corner lots. . . . Seven great parks are laid out in the city, of different forms and dimensions. The largest, however, is less than half a mile long, which seems to be rather small for the pretensions of so great a place. . . . Tacoma, with her new 'plat,' must be about as perfect as anything can be in this ill-favored world."[17]

CLEARLY some effort to overcome local apprehensions was required. The *Pacific Tribune* tried to reassure the community and investing public, noting that the original plan

sketched for them by Gen. Tilton, though possessing many admirable features, was yet open to criticism and objection. Therefore the most distinguished landscape engineer of the country was consulted, and an entirely new plan was the result. This is approved by many men of ripe judgment and unquestioned taste, who recognize in it much merit; in their view it will make a beautiful city, and is in every respect adapted to the character of the ground. . . .

A consciousness of being right has evidently actuated the managers of the Pacific division of the N.P.R.R. . . . Not only in locating the terminus, but in all their subsequent action, this is evident; and, save by unscrupulous, mendacious, hireling editors and their abettors, none have any fault to find with their course. . . .[18]

In spite of the *Pacific Tribune*'s efforts, no doubt contemporary wisdom continued to be considerably shaken and uncertain in the face of such an idiosyncratic city plan. What precedent did it have in the experience of those for whom it had been prepared? The typical American was almost invariably surrounded both in city and countryside by rigid grid patterns of streets, blocks, lots, and fields, dull enough to the eye but infinitely practical and understandable to a people viewing land primarily as a medium to be bought, parceled out, and sold. Tacoma was simply a local manifestation of a 19th-century surge of westward expansionism and new-town promotion schemes, and the pragmatism of straight lines and right angles must have been

---

[17] *Daily Pacific Tribune*, Dec. 30, 1873.
[18] *Ibid.*, Dec. 27, 1873.
[19] *Ibid.*, Feb. 4, 1874.

sorely missed by Tacomans eager for a plan that would allow them to get on with the central business of selling and buying lots and bringing their town into reality.

The local press made little mention of any such uncertainties over the Olmsted plan. There was, however, a hint of something afoot on January 31, 1874, when the *Pacific Tribune,* in a small item on an inside page, revealed that "In the [company's new] upper town something of a change is in progress, the nature of which we are not yet at liberty to announce. Suffice it to say, however, that it will be a change of improvement, and one highly beneficial to all our townspeople." Four days later the *Pacific Tribune* resolved the uncertainty:

We are now authoritatively empowered to state that the change we alluded to the other day in the railroad townsite plan has been fully consummated, and the Olmstead [*sic*] plan thrown overboard in toto. Captains Smith and Eastwick, with their corps of surveyors, commenced yesterday running new lines, in accordance with the plat last adopted. By that, the town will be laid off in large squares with 50-foot front lots, wide alleys, wider streets, and splendid, great avenues—it being substantially the first plan, with improvements.[19]

The Olmsted plan was thus abandoned for what was essentially a return to the Tilton plan that had been summarily discarded in September when the board hired Olmsted. In fact, the description in the *Pacific Tribune* on March 2, 1874, is simply a repeat of what had first appeared in the October 6, 1873 issue when the editor was still unaware that Olmsted had replaced Tilton as Tacoma's planner.

How the company dealt with Olmsted in releasing him from his contract is not known. No record has so far shown up to cover what must have been a distasteful episode for all parties. Perhaps the very lack of evidence is an index of the disappointments and frustrations which Olmsted's brief experience with the company represented. All concerned seem to have done as much as possible to erase the record of Olmsted's work for Tacoma, leaving only our speculations of what might have been.

Now the effort was to make up for lost time. Throughout March two surveyor crews worked on the upper town, basing their efforts on the new alignments, while Captain Eastwick in the company engineer's office was drawing up the plan and no doubt trying to stay ahead of the crew which was staking it out in the field. The *Pacific Tribune* reported that "Special agent [Theodore] Hosmer has the entire supervision of everything connected with the townsite, and is doing all that he possibly can to improve it, and hurry it into market."[20]

Finally, on April 15, 1874, the sale of lots began, and so began also the processes of development that would translate the plan into the reality of streets, buildings, and human occupancy, creating the forms of the city we know today. Thus Tacoma's 43-day experiment in individuality, in planning matters at least, was a thing of the past, the residue being no more than the original ink-on-linen drawing now held by the Washington State Historical Society in Tacoma. The local residents quickly settled comfortably into a framework of the familiar with a plan conventionally dull, a pattern shared by all Tacoma's sister cities on Puget Sound and in most of America, then and now.

[20] *Daily Pacific Tribune*, March 25, 1874. Theodore Hosmer was resident agent in Washington Territory for the Tacoma Land Company.

THE CITY BEAUTIFUL MOVEMENT
Forgotten Origins and Lost Meanings

JON A. PETERSON
City University of New York

Historians have paid little attention to the quest for the City Beautiful at the opening of the twentieth century. The subject has mainly attracted commentators upon urban and architectural design who have emphasized two themes, the City Beautiful's devotion to classic-Renaissance taste in the building arts—the Boston and New York Public Libraries are noted examples—and its commitment to monumental city planning. The McMillan Plan for Washington, D.C., issued in 1902, epitomizes the latter. An updated version of the then neglected L'Enfant layout, the McMillan Plan made possible the Washington so familiar to tourists today—the vast, tree-lined Mall; the Lincoln and Jefferson Memorials, each terminating grand vistas; and the cluster of classic-style buildings near the U.S. Capitol. The ascendancy of this pattern of taste, observers have repeatedly asserted, derived largely from the Chicago World's Fair of 1893, the famous White City. That spectacle with its great water basin framed by white palaces reminiscent of Ancient Rome and Renaissance Italy dazzled the multitudes, stamped the new style upon the nation, and unveiled the virtues of large-scale civic design.[1]

This paper seeks to open fresh perspectives upon the City Beautiful. That it embraced classic-Renaissance architecture and monumental planning is not questioned. What is claimed is that the City Beautiful had other meanings and origins and that their recovery enables us to recognize the phenomenon as a complex cultural movement involving more than the building arts and urban design. Three concepts are essential to this reconstruction: municipal art, civic improvement, and outdoor art. Each played a vital, if now forgotten, role in launching the movement; each had distinct historical roots predating the Chicago World's Fair; and each began with different constituencies.

The origins and nature of these three causes, their fusion into a movement, and the special flavor they imparted to that outcome represents the main concerns of this inquiry. The formative years of the City Beautiful were 1897 to 1902. In this period the three causes developed national expression. Their leaders recognized each others' common interest in civic beauty, joined forces at major conferences, and blended their once distinct goals. By 1902 local campaigns seemingly mushroomed across the nation—in small towns, medium-sized cities, and metropolitan centers; in the Northeast, Midwest, South, and Far West—and a nationally coordinated promotional strategy crystallized. Pursuit of monumental city plans, though advocated by some architects, did not characterize these years. The local groups that gave the new movement so much of its force commonly pursued piecemeal programs, sometimes favoring big projects but often stressing small, feasible goals.

Municipal art began in New York City in the 1890s. Only recently recognized as a root of the City Beautiful, it included meanings not commonly associated with that slogan, notably a zeal for decorative art and an advocacy of small-scale adornment.[2] Decorative art referred to artistic works, especially sculpture, murals, and stained glass, designed to complement the forecourts, facades, and the public interiors of major buildings. All this required close cooperation between architect, sculptor, and painter and was often known as collaborative or allied art. H. H. Richardson of Boston, the most innovative architect of the Gilded Age, pioneered the concept in the early 1870s and through his famous Trinity Church project instilled the goal in three influential New Yorkers, architects Stanford White and Charles McKim and sculptor Augustus Saint-Gaudens.[3] From 1886 onward the Architectural League of New York, itself constituted as a body of allied artists, staged annual exhibits featuring decorative work.[4] In 1887 McKim advanced the cause dramatically by insisting that murals and sculpture adorn the public library he would design for Boston.[5]

The Chicago World's Fair clearly did not initiate American artists to decorative art, but it gave such work unprecedented recognition. The terraces, rostral columns, and fountain basin of the Court of Honor bristled with sculpture while frescoes enlivened the entryways to the exhibition halls. This lavish fulfillment of what Richardson had begun, albeit in a wholly different setting, lay behind the creation of the Municipal Art Society of New York in March 1893, on the eve of the Fair's opening. Richard M. Hunt, dean of the American architectural profession, builder to the Vanderbilts, and designer of the central edifice of the White City, oversaw the founding. He and the artists who joined him, many just back from Chicago, defined their goal as providing "adequate sculptural and pictorial decorations for the public buildings and parks in the city of New York."[6] They sought, in short, to municipalize decorative art, to convert city government to art patronage.

No one then labeled this aspiration the City Beautiful nor did the Municipal Art Society contemplate city plans. In fact, their modest goals faltered amid the severe mid-1890s depression. Anticipating 2,000 members, the Society claimed only 350 five years later. Announcing it would stage annual contests for decorative works and donate the winning design to the city, it held only one with its own funds, in 1894, for a set of courtroom murals. The organization apparently lacked the resources its original goals required.[7] Elsewhere, its example inspired only one similar society begun in Cincinnati in 1894.[8]

By 1897 as the depression lifted, the New York art establishment—the most sizable in the world this side of Paris and the most influential in the United States—gave every sign of heightened collective confidence, increased assertiveness, and intensified interest in municipal art. In 1893 and 1895 sculptors and then mural painters created national societies based in the city. Each kept a weather eye open for decorative art opportunities. In 1895 the major art societies formed the Fine Arts Federation to secure united action on common issues and loudly protested an official site choice for a major patriotic monument and agitated successfully to include in the new charter for the Greater City of New York a municipal art commission to oversee art acquisitions by the city.[9]

Furthermore, architects in New York and elsewhere during the depression had dreamed of large-scale civic embellishments, though not comprehensive city planning. Design contests among architectural clubs in various cities reflected this new aspiration: in Boston, a competition for the design of Copley Square; in Cleveland, for a public building group; in New York City, for a plaza entry to a terminal passenger station. The Chicago Fair had probably stimulated these essays in public art. It had certainly inspired the Cleveland project as well as Daniel Burnham's personal scheme for a vast Chicago lakefront park, drawn in 1896.[10] From the public's perspective, however, these developments had been off stage; even architectural publications had paid them minimal heed.

Once prosperity returned, the artists' mood shifted. Municipal art in New York from 1897 onward became an aggressive, expansive, much-proclaimed enthusiasm. Decorative art made new conquests and the term "municipal art" expanded to embrace virtually every proposal—small or large—for enhancing the city's appearance. European urban scenes—the great boulevards, plazas, monuments, bridges, and esplanades—familiar to artists from student days and later travel, inspired many recommendations. Municipal art became as broad as the artists' revulsion for New York was wide. They deplored the destruction of colonial houses and the quarrying of the Palisades. They condemned advertising monstrosities, crass sidewalk fixtures, and banal business streets.[11] Less an ideology than an activated urbanity, municipal art was rooted in the jarring contrasts between the artful civic scenes of Europe and the artless cityscapes of America. Its proponents spoke far more often of Paris, Rome, and Florence than of the White City.

With greater enthusiasm came greater visibility. The civic-minded Reform Club of New York aired the artists' views in their new quarterly, *Municipal Affairs,* from 1897 onward. In 1898-1899 The Architectural League of New York staged public discussions of "The Plan of the City," featuring monumental bridge-approach schemes, a seven-mile Hudson River terrace, and other major embellishments.[12] The National Sculpture Society made the deepest popular impression, tapping the exuberant patriotism that closed the century. Waiving professional fees, they erected a stunning, white, sculpture-laden triumphal arch in Madison Square as the visual climax to a stupendous, two-day welcome-home celebration for the Hero of Manila. A spectacular success, the Dewey Arch raised new hopes for a transformed New York.[13]

By 1899 the City Beautiful metaphor symbolized this new enthusiasm. And it was New York artists and art critics who first used the term. They lifted it from the arts and crafts movement in England. In 1896 the Arts and Crafts Exhibition Society of London sponsored five lectures on "the application of the idea of beauty as well as of utility to the organisation and decoration of our greater cities." T. J. Cobden-Sanderson, a book illustrator and friend of William Morris, emphasized the phrase in his introductory talk. Published under the title *Art and Life, and the Building and Decoration of Cities,* the lectures became available in 1897.[14] The new slogan, never before used in municipal art discussion, quickly took hold. By March 1898, Charles R. Lamb, an architect active in New York art circles, was exhorting his city to realize "the dream of the idealist, 'THE CITY BEAUTIFUL.' "[15] *Municipal Affairs* conferred full blessing upon the term in its December 1899 issue, splashing the words across its front cover.

Other events in 1899 revealed the spread of municipal art beyond New York to other major cities. In Cleveland a national convention of architectural clubs, the first of its kind, organized the Architectural League of America. Nearly all members were young professionals. The great excitement of their meeting focused upon the Cleveland Chamber of Commerce and its recent endorsement of a "group plan" for public buildings. Within a year the League had formed a National Committee on Municipal Improvements and Civic Embellishments to encourage public art elsewhere.[16] Meanwhile, in Chicago several dozen artists struggled to organize what would become, in 1901, the Municipal Art League.[17] And in December, the Municipal Art Society of Baltimore, begun earlier in the year, sponsored the first municipal art conference in the United States. Speakers—mainly artists and art critics—came from New York, Boston, Chicago, Philadelphia, Washington, and Rome, Italy.[18]

Municipal art did not yet mean planning. Its implicit ideal of the city as a work of art honored many impulses. Certain architects by 1898-1899 favored large plans, and their thinking pointed toward the scheme for Washington in 1902 and other grand designs celebrated as part of the City Beautiful.[19] Others along with most artists urged more minute changes in the cityscape. Geroge Kriehn, a Chicago art historian, articulated the prevalent view in an address to the Baltimore conference. "Of all modern cities," he said, "Paris, more than any other, deserves the title of 'The City Beautiful.' " But he favored a particularistic approach, not a Haussmannic one. He condemned the inartistic condition of American cities and the "hideous signs and billboards" that disfigured them. He advocated "enforcement of smoke ordinances," the "judicious use of color" to enliven business streets, the display of trees, fountains, and statues in public places, and the creation of splendid civic buildings adorned with murals and massed in groups. "If we take every element of ugliness one by one, and try to root it out," he declared, "the task will not be difficult."[20]

Small-scale, piecemeal projects played an even more dominant role in civic improvement. This second, little known source of the City Beautiful discloses still other meanings and origins of the movement and helps recover the significance of Charles Mulford Robinson as prophet to the cause. Unlike Daniel Burnham, who personified the big side of the City Beautiful, especially its penchant for grand plans, Robinson knew the small side intimately. He became the first to recognize fully the underlying unity of the movement and to provide in his prolific writing a mirror by which the disparate groups could perceive their common identity.

Civic improvement began as a laymen's cause and flourished initially in small to medium-sized cities. The organization that gave it national leadership originated, somewhat improbably, in Springfield, Ohio, a college town and publishing center forty-four miles west of Columbus. D. J. Thomas, a local publisher of floral and pet magazines, had become interested in village improvement societies in 1899 and had printed reports about some in New England, the South Atlantic states, California, and elsewhere in his magazine, *Home and Flowers*. Neither he nor Jessie M. Good, the energetic spinster who wrote the accounts, anticipated their appeal. Letters poured in, many requesting an information center on improvement work and others asking "why not start a national movement for civic beauty?"[21] In response, *Home and Flowers* staged a convention of improvement associations in Springfield, October 10, 1900. Ohioans predominated, but some individuals arrived from St. Paul, Minnesota, Oakland, California, and Pensacola, Florida. Professor Charles Zueblin, a University of Chicago sociologist and skillful popular lecturer, attended as did Frank Chapin Bray of Cleveland, editor of the influential Chautauqua magazine, and Samuel "Golden Rule" Jones, Mayor of Toledo. Together they created the National League of Improvement Associations and resolved to urge "all organizations interested in the permanent improvement and beautifying of American homes, and their surroundings, whether in country, village, or city, to unite with us in membership."[22]

Like the decorative art theme within the City Beautiful, village improvement had roots predating the Chicago World's Fair. As far back as 1848, Andrew Jackson Downing, the preeminent popularizer of English landscape gardening in America, had called upon urbanites who aspired to "country life" to establish "rural improvement" societies for encouraging tree planting and tasteful architecture.[23] Downing's famous books on country houses and their landscaping inspired a succession of works that provided the aesthetic rationale for village improvement in its early years.[24] The first society to fulfill it, the Laurel Hill Association, began in Stockbridge, Massachusetts, in 1853 and became the prototype for all that followed. At the outset Stockbridge was a neglected Berkshire mountain town with rutted streets, treeless roadsides, a tumbledown cemetery, and an unkempt commons. By the 1870s Stockbridge was famous. Its residents walked along neat gravel sidewalks, enjoying the shade and well-kept lawns. The streets, long since regraded and paved, offered quiet rides for the wealthy families who sought summer respite from the city.[25] By 1880 Massachusetts had twenty-eight associations and Connecticut between fifty and sixty, many in country towns anxious to capture the summer trade.[26] Cleanliness, order, and cultural activity as well as picturesque landscape amenities gave substance to the village ideal under these conditions.

In the 1890s the concept spread beyond New England, disseminated in part by articles in *The Atlantic Monthly, Forum,* and other national magazines.[27] Societies begun in Honesdale, Pennsylvania, in 1892, and in Montclair, New Jersey, in 1895, received wide publicity. Women dominated many groups. The Honesdale Improvement Association with 230 members, for example, admitted men only on an honorary basis. Many associations, thus, belonged to state federations of women's clubs through which they kindled further interest. In the South Atlantic states the Seaboard Airline Railroad, running from Portsmouth, Virginia, to Atlanta, Georgia, attempted to organize an improvement society at every stop on its line in the late 1890s with a view to attracting northern industry. By 1900 California had "several dozens" of associations, the greatest concentration outside of New England and many but one or two years old.[28]

The National League of Improvement Associations approached improvement as a crusade. Unsophisticated, wellmannered, and very much in earnest, its founders preached, in their own words, "the gospel of Beauty and the cult of the god sanitation."[29] Jessie Good, the national organizer and unofficial propagandist, captured the zealous enthusiasm of many local groups, especially those led by women, whether in the League or not:

> No task is too great for these associations to undertake. They will direct the digging of anything from a sewer to a flower bed. They will order down your front fences and order up electric lights with equal sangfroid. Water flows at their command. They create sentiment in favor of ornamental back yards and tidy alleys. Indeed, they offer you prizes for the prettiest back yard and neatest alley.[30]

For Charles Zueblin, the second president, how to direct these local energies became the critical issue.

The answer unfolded in 1901-1902: it was to identify improvement effort with the mainstream of Progressive reform. At its second convention in August 1901, the organization renamed itself the American League for Civic Improvement and defined its goals as "the promotion of outdoor art, public beauty, town, village, and neighborhood improvement."[31] By emphasizing "civic improvement" over "village improvement" in its new title, the League aligned itself with the reform ethos of the era or what Zueblin repeatedly called "the new civic spirit."[32] In its second year the League won full support from the Chautauqua institution, which soon showered its members with improvement study-guides.[33] By its third convention in September 1902, the League had created fourteen advisory councils of nationally known experts in such areas as municipal art, municipal reform, social settlements, sanitation, and recreation and championed itself as a "federation of organizations and individuals aiming to promote the higher life of American communities."[34] The implicit goal of building a roof organization for Progressive reform never came to pass, but the League did prosper. By 1902 it had six times as many individual members (232)—many of them important opinion leaders—and three times as many association members (148) as the year before. And it had shifted its headquarters from Springfield to Chicago.[35]

The aesthetic goals of improvement societies, whether in or out of the League, blended images of small-town beauty with order, cleanliness, and moral uplift. A Dayton, Ohio, newspaper captured the vision nicely: "The town which has well kept streets, beautiful parks, attractive home grounds, plenty of fresh air and generally favorable sanitary conditions is the town the moral development and industrial progress of which will always commend it."[36] Dozens of reports for 1902 alone confirm this description. The civic committee of the Nebraska Federation of Women's Clubs, for example, started a "vigorous campaign" for "rest rooms in towns and cities; forestry; vacant lot cultivation; improvement of church exteriors and surroundings; and cemetery improvement." The Society for Beautifying Buffalo, led by a park commissioner, instituted "a crusade against the flaring billboard" then defacing "too many neighborhoods." The Village Improvement Society of Idaho Falls, the second largest club in the state comprising seventy "leading women" of the city, agitated successfully for "fifty rubbish boxes of uniform size, painted white and neatly lettered" and for tree planting on residential streets. In Louisville, Kentucky, the Women's Club "began with the passing of an anti-expectoration ordinance" and then took up the questions of "tree-planting, street wires, the smoke nuisance, vacant lots, signs, and playgrounds."[37]

Civic improvement also spread to metropolitan centers such as Chicago, St. Paul, and Milwaukee. The Civic League of St. Louis won the most acclaim. Begun early in 1902, the League sought to revamp St. Louis in time for the Louisiana Purchase Exposition of 1904. It gained nearly 2,000 members in ten months and in the same period built three public baths in poor neighborhoods, became the watchdog of the billboard and health ordinances, supported a major cross-city boulevard proposal, helped activate a "keep our city clean" campaign, secured appointment of a woman sanitary inspector, encouraged tree planting and children's gardens, and demanded clean water in a city where liquid mud too often ran from the taps. "In short," said Mrs. Louis Marion McCall, an officer in both the Civic League and the American League for Civic Improvement, "there is such an incipient renaissance on in the staid old city of St. Louis as is to be found nowhere outside of the national capital with its stupendous and colossal scheme of beautifying the city of magnificent distances. It touches everything in the city's life."[38] Her comparison was apt, for St. Louis and Washington both exemplified the City Beautiful at that time, St. Louis the project-upon-project approach then dominant and Washington with its comprehensive plan (the McMillan Plan of 1902) the wave of the future.

By the years 1900-1901 a remarkable variety of groups favored some form of aesthetic betterment. Apart from those already noted—municipal art societies, village and civic improvement associations, various architectural and art organizations, the Chautauqua institution, local and state women's clubs—there was one of special importance, the American Park and Outdoor Art Association. Begun in 1897, it championed the third neglected element of the City Beautiful, outdoor art or the cultivation of landscape beauty especially as found in great city parks.

Rooted in the romantic ethos of the pre-Civil War era and given physical expression by Frederick Law Olmsted and other landscape designers from the 1850s onward, outdoor art enjoyed widespread but unorganized and often naive public sympathy by the 1890s. The Association sought to educate, intensify, and focus this support. Its members, numbering 237 by 1900, consisted mainly of landscape architects, park superintendents and commissioners, and highly knowledgeable laymen. Priding themselves as guardians of landscape taste, they met annually in cities with major park systems, partly to draw attention to these great works and to expound the "proper" principles of park development. To advance outdoor art they repeatedly promoted the landscaping of factory grounds, school yards, railroad-station sites, and city streets; attacked the mounting billboard nuisance; and pleaded for state parks and forest preservation. Like others who favored beautification, they emphasized piecemeal, practical projects. Even children's gardens, a favorite objective, fulfilled their purposes, they believed, by nurturing a love of nature and with it hopes for a more beautiful America.[39]

In 1900-1901 the City Beautiful movement completed its gestation. The organizations supporting municipal art, civic improvement, and outdoor art began interacting and sharing ideas as never before. At national conferences landscape enthusiasts entertained speeches on municipal art; civic improvers claimed outdoor art as a formal goal; and municipal art societies supported park development and advertising regulation. The possibility of merging the American Park and Outdoor Art Association with the American League for Civic Improvement arose; fulfilled in 1904, this union produced the American Civic Association.[40] The key national organizations also evolved a common strategy, notably the promotion of an elaborate "model city" exhibit for the St. Louis World's Fair.[41] Through such interchanges and programs, the City Beautiful metaphor ceased to express municipal art enthusiasm alone and became everybody's slogan, as applicable to tree planting as to architectural adornment.[42] This mingling of organizations and ideas gave the City Beautiful its complexity as an ideal and its vitality as a cause. With the process begun, the birth of the new movement could be proclaimed.

The man who wrote the birth certificate was Charles Mulford Robinson. Born April 30, 1869, he had grown up in Rochester, New York, in the historic and sedate Third Ward whose "quaintness" and "village-like" atmosphere he would later celebrate in several small books.[43] Graduated from the University of Rochester in 1891, he became a reporter for the Rochester *Post-Express* and eventually an associate editor. Even dispositioned and optimistic by temperament, he had a gentle wit and engaging personal manner. A lucid and prolific writer, he would bring to the City Beautiful movement an inimitable talent for elucidating its inchoate events. Travels in Europe in 1891 and 1894 aroused his first interest in civic scenes, and in 1899 when *The Atlantic Monthly* published three articles of his on "Improvements in City Life," one discussed "Aesthetic Progress." *Harper's Monthly* liked it and sent Robinson to

Europe to write of comparable developments. From this point onward, Robinson's role as a civic art publicist was set.[44]

Robinson's first major book, *The Improvement of Towns and Cities,* not only appeared amidst the burgeoning City Beautiful movement, it overviewed all the varied endeavors and declared that they represented not many efforts but one. In his preface Robinson listed over 110 societies then active, many of them roof organizations, some of them in England and Belgium, portrayed them as "one brotherhood in the joyous and earnest new crusade for beauty of town and city."[45] He intended his work as a manual for all the groups, seeking to reduce the isolation between each and instill a consciousness of interdependence. Presenting all the goals of the movement in a logical order, he hoped that the entire pattern of activity might be perceived and a harmonious result encouraged.

The City Beautiful for which Robinson spoke was still in its preplanning phase. His book, subtitled "The Practical Basis of Civic Aesthetics," stressed piecemeal projects suited to every known form of betterment effort. The opening chapter discussed the city's site without emphasizing planning. Site-selection principles merited attention, Robinson argued, so that the few locational advantages remaining to cities might be exploited, such as neglected hilltops and waterfronts.[46] Next he outlined ideal street systems, including Vienna's famous ring streets, but he found such models serviceable mainly in suggesting how to mend existing arrangements.[47] Five chapters on street beauty followed, each a civic improver's delight. They touched everything from tree planting and burial of overhead wires to beautification of street fixtures, smoke abatement, and advertising regulation. Another four chapters on the "Aesthetic Phase of Social and Philanthropic Effort" honored outdoor and municipal art, by taking up parkways, parks, ornamental squares, playgrounds, and architectural concepts such as building decoration and historic preservation. Chapters on sculpture, art education, and the methods of securing civic art closed the book.

The prophetic nature of Robinson's work fast became apparent. He had drafted it in 1900 before the cause he proclaimed had attracted general notice. His publisher, G. P. Putnam's Sons, skeptical that a market existed, forced him to meet printing costs. Issued in May 1901, *The Improvement of Towns and Cities* sold immediately and well. In November, Putnam's reprinted it. By 1916 it had passed through eleven editions. Key opinion leaders saw its value and elevated Robinson to the top ranks of City Beautiful organizations. Within a year and a half of publication, Robinson had become recording secretary of the American League for Civic Improvement, acting secretary of the American Park and Outdoor Art Association, and member of the inter-association committee charged with planning the "model city" exhibit for the St. Louis World's Fair.[48] Hailed by Zueblin as "the leading authority in the country," Robinson had written what one improvement official dubbed the "bible of the believers in the city beautiful."[49]

Only after 1901 did the movement which Robinson's book so perfectly mirrored gradually shift toward city planning. In 1902 the McMillan Plan for Washington and a now-forgotten scheme for Harrisburg, Pennsylvania, provided the nation its first usable examples of comprehensive city planning.[50] Robinson, Zueblin, and other City Beautiful spokesmen—even the Chautauqua institution—seized the meaning of these events and thereafter promoted planned civic betterment.[51] Even small towns, Robinson argued in 1902, should seek an expert to "suggest a general scheme" of action. "Instead of having spotty improvements here and here, that have no connection with one another and no permanent character," the advisor would "make every effort count as a step toward the consummation of a harmonious general plan. There will be nothing wasted and nothing duplicated."[52] He emphasized this new perspective in his second major book, *Modern Civic Art,* issued in 1903.[53]

The conversion of the City Beautiful to planning came slowly and never fully succeeded. As late as 1904 only New York and San Francisco had taken steps to secure comprehensive plans.[54]

Thereafter, sustained planning activity commenced, at least a dozen cities acquiring plans in 1905-1908. By the latter date New York, San Francisco, and St. Louis had reports. So did many lesser places: Columbus, Ohio; Columbia and Greenville, South Carolina; Roanoke, Virginia; Denver, Colorado; San Diego and Oakland, California—even distant Honolulu and Manila.[55] By this point the equation of the City Beautiful with city planning had far more truth, but it remained a partial truth. In 1901 nearly 1,000 improvement organizations existed. An inquiry in 1905 counted 2,426 "improvement societies," and impressionistic evidence for 1908 suggests no diminution of activity.[56]

We can now summarize the forgotten origins and lost meanings of the City Beautiful. Contrary to conventional wisdom, the movement began between 1897 and 1902 as interest in municipal art, village and civic improvement, and outdoor art found organized, interconnected expression and gained its best spokesman in Charles Mulford Robinson. Those who have overlooked the small-scale side of the City Beautiful have not merely passed over a curious interest in ornamental lampposts, street trees, public murals, or rubbish cans; they have ignored a pattern of activity sustained by thousands of civic groups across the nation. Unlike commentaries that trace the origins of the City Beautiful to the Chicago World's Fair, this account insists upon additional influences, notably decorative art, concepts of small town beauty, and landscape design ideas. Also emphasized is the movement's congeniality to piecemeal change; only after 1901 did comprehensive city planning become a widely advocated goal.

This altered perspective upon the City Beautiful suggests new judgments of its significance. These can only be sketched. The prosperous middle and upper class elements of towns and cities who gave the movement its force, seized the long-established belief in the morally uplifting value of beauty and placed fresh energies behind it. Exuding the social optimism of the Progressive era, the national spokesmen for the cause repeatedly claimed that beauty would evoke or at least express a regenerated civic life. The prominence of this theme suggests that for many the City Beautiful was the aesthetic expression of turn-of-the-century urban reform. The small-scale side of the movement also helps explain its vitality. A comely park, a clean street, a dignified city hall: these and dozens of other practical goals kept local organizations active and larger dreams alive. They also enabled City Beautiful proponents to blend civic boosterism with reform. A more attractive city, they claimed, would promote tourism, enlarge trade, and generally revitalize the local economy.

Finally, the City Beautiful may also be seen as a never-very-systematic cluster of environmental norms popularized among the middle and upper classes. The standards had been in the making before the Chicago World's Fair as the previous discussion of municipal art, civic improvement, and outdoor art reveals. But not until 1897-1902 had these disparate goals been commonly fused together, celebrated with a slogan, and championed so widely and vigorously. Inspired by the Fair and European civic art as well, this newly constituted demand for beauty, order, and cleanliness may have left more enduring marks than commonly appreciated. Today at the prosperous fringes of American cities sidewalks are straight, utility wires are often buried, advertising signs are confined to commercial areas, civic buildings are attractive by many standards, streets are swept. If not, community sentiment holds that they should be. Many aspects of the City Beautiful persist in zoning codes, subdivision regulations, and local ordinances and, more profoundly, in the culture of suburbia. The movement died long ago, but its legacy may be so commonplace that we have overlooked it.

NOTES

1. The most complete account of the City Beautiful to date is Mel Scott, *American City Planning since 1890* (Berkeley, 1969), 47-109. For critical commentaries, see Lewis Mumford, *Sticks and Stones: A Study of American Architecture and*

Civilization (New York, 1924), 123-151; Thomas Adams, *Outline of Town and City Planning: A Review of Past Efforts and Modern Aims* (New York, 1935), 179-182, 197-205; Robert Averill Walker, *The Planning Function in Urban Government* (Chicago, 1941), 12-16; John Burchard and Albert Bush-Brown, *The Architecture of America: A Social History and Cultural Criticism* (Boston, 1961), 246-250; and Norman Newton, *Design on the Land: The Development of Landscape Architecture* (Cambridge, 1971), 413-426. For a more favorable assessment, see Christopher Tunnard, *The City of Man* (New York, 1953), 303-313; Christopher Tunnard and Henry Hope Reed, *American Skyline: The Growth and Form of Our Cities* (New York, 1953), 136-153; and Christopher Tunnard, *The Modern American City* (Princeton, 1968), 36-66. The only historian to overview the movement is Roy Lubove, *The Progressives and the Slums: Tenement House Reform in New York City, 1890-1917* (New York, 1962), 217-221; and *The Urban Community: Housing and Planning in the Progressive Era* (Englewood Cliffs, 1967), 59. For a case study demonstrating the importance of park promotion to beautification but applying the term City Beautiful partly to the 1870s and 1880s before it came into use, see William H. Wilson, *The City Beautiful Movement in Kansas City* (Columbia, 1964). For the contributions of Daniel H. Burnham to City Beautiful planning, see Thomas S. Hines, *Burnham of Chicago: Architect and Planner* (New York, 1974), 74, 158, 166, 368.

2. For brief sketches of the relationship of municipal art to the City Beautiful, see Scott, *American City Planning*, 43-46; and Harvey A. Kantor, "The City Beautiful in New York," The New-York Historical Society Quarterly, 57 (1973), 149-171.

3. Royal Cortissoz, *John LaFarge: A Memoir and a Study* (Boston, 1911), 152-160; Charles Baldwin, *Stanford White* (New York, 1931), 45-46.

4. The Architectural League of New York, *Officers, Committees, Members, Constitution and By-Laws, 1905-1906* (New York), 3-5.

5. Walter Muir Whitehill, *Boston Public Library: A Centennial History* (Cambridge, 1956), 142, 148-149.

6. Lillie H. French, "Municipal Art," Harper's Weekly, 37 (1893), 371.

7. Ibid.; Edward Hamilton Bell, "Art in Municipal Decoration," ibid., 38 (1894), 401; *Yearbook of the Art Societies of New York, 1898-1899* (New York, 1899), 87-91.

8. The Municipal Art Society of Cincinnati, *Constitution and By-Laws, Adopted on the Thirty-first of May, 1894.*

9. *Yearbook of the Art Societies*, 108-109, 146-148, 155-156; Editorial, *The American Architect and Building News*, 50 (1895), 141; Editorial, ibid., 55 (1897), 25.

10. For examples of contests, see *Catalogue of the Eleventh Annual Exhibition of the Architectural League of New York* (New Rochelle, 1896), 10; "The Society of Beaux-Arts Architects," The American Architect and Building News, 51 (1896), 78-79; "T-Square Club of Philadelphia," ibid., 52 (1896), 39; Herbert B. Briggs, "Cleveland Architectural Club," ibid., 48 (1895), 7. For the genesis of the Cleveland and Chicago-lakefront schemes, see Hines, *Burnham of Chicago*, 159-160, 313-314.

11. Frederick S. Lamb, "Municipal Art," Municipal Affairs, 1 (1897), 674-688. See also entire issue, ibid., 2 (1899).

12. *Yearbook of the Art Societies*, 56, 61, 63-69.

13. Barr Ferree, "The Dewey Arch," The American Architect and Building News, 67 (1900), 11-12, 19-20; "Celebrating a New Era," Harper's Weekly, 43 (1899), 954.

14. Arts and Crafts Exhibition Society, London, *Art and Life, and the Building and Decoration of Cities* (London, 1897), 5, 43.

15. Charles R. Lamb, "Civic Architecture," Municipal Affairs, 2 (1898), 72. Capitalized letters as in the original text.

16. The Architectural League of America, *The Architectural Annual* (Philadelphia, 1900), 52, 118-120, 197-212, 279; "Topics of the Day," Architects' and Builders' Magazine, 1 (1900), 337.

17. Charles Mulford Robinson, "Among the Improvement Clubs," Municipal Journal and Engineer, 12 (1902), 112.

18. George Kriehn, "The Baltimore Conference on Municipal Art," in Architectural League, Architectural Annual, 47.

19. Most architects who promoted the big side of the City Beautiful in 1898-1899 had not yet settled upon the concept of a comprehensive city plan. The Architectural League of New York exemplified the most advanced thinking. One architect-member, Julius F. Harder, voiced the principle of a general plan early in 1898, but when the League discussed "The Plan of the City" in the winter of 1898-1899, its members outlined a series of distinct, large-scale projects, not an integrated program for reshaping New York. Julius F. Harder, "The City's Plan," Municipal Affairs, 2 (1898), 24-25; *Yearbook of the Art Societies*, 63-69.

20. Kriehn, "Baltimore Conference," 47; George Kriehn, "The City Beautiful," *Municipal Affairs*, 3 (1899), 595.

21. "The National League of Improvement Associations: A Short History," in Jessie Good, *The How of Improvement Work* (Springfield, 1901), 44; Benjamin F. Prince, *A Standard History of Springfield and Clark County, Ohio* (Chicago, 1922), 178-179; Clifton M. Nichols, "The Printing and Publishing Interests of Springfield, Ohio, 1800-1900," in Benjamin F. Prince, ed., *The Centennial Celebration of Springfield, Ohio, Held August 4th to 10th, 1901* (Springfield), 224. Nichols reported *Home and Flowers'* circulation as 125,000 for 1901.

22. *Dayton Daily Journal*, Oct. 12, 1900.

23. Andrew Jackson Downing, "On the Improvement of Country Villages" (1849) in George William Curtis, ed., *Rural Essays* (New York, 1869), 229-235.

24. Warren H. Manning, "The History of Village Improvement in the United States," The Craftsman, 5 (1904), 423-432.

25. Nathaniel Hillyer Egleston, *Villages and Village Life with Hints for their Improvement* (New York, 1878), 60-67.

26. Birdsey G. Northrup, "Address of Hon. B. G. Northrup" in The West Ewing Improvement Association, *Proceedings of Anniversary Meeting* (Trenton, 1880), 15; Editorial, The American Architect and Building News, 8 (1880), 278.

27. "The National League . . . : A Short History," 42.

28. Mary Caroline Robbins, "Village Improvement Societies," The Atlantic Monthly, 79 (1897), 217, 221; Birdsey G. Northrup, "The Work of Village Improvement Societies," Forum, 19 (1895), 100-102; and Jessie M. Good, *The Work of Civic Improvement* (Springfield, 1900), 6-10, 16, 20-26.

29. "The National League . . . : A Short History," 42.

30. Good, *Work of Civic Improvement*, 10.

31. "Successful Civic Beauty Rally," *Home and Flowers,* 10 (Sept., 1901), 9.

32. Charles Zueblin, "A Decade of Civic Improvement" in *Nation-Wide Civic Betterment: A Report of the Third Annual Convention of The American League for Civic Improvement* (Chicago, 1903), 14; Charles Zueblin, "The New Civic Spirit," The Chautauquan, 38 (1903), 55-59.

33. For the close relationship of the League and Chautauqua, see "Two Notable Civic Betterment Events," *Home and Flowers,* 12 (1902), 143-145.

34. *Nation-Wide Civic Betterment,* inside front cover. Other advisory councils dealt with arts and crafts, civic church, libraries and museums, parks, public nuisances, preservation of nature, rural improvement, school extension, and village improvement.

35. In August 1901, there were 46 association members and 35 individual members. See "Treasurer's Report," *Home and Flowers,* 10 (Sept., 1901), 9; and membership-fee data in "Plans for a Year of Active Work" in ibid., 10 (Oct., 1901), 12. For September 1902 membership, see *Nation-Wide Civic Betterment,* 97-103. The League also listed 29 firms as commercial members.

36. *Dayton Daily Journal,* May 16, 1901.

37. For Nebraska, see "Beautiful American Cities," *Home and Flowers,* 12 (1902), 33. For Buffalo, see "More Beautiful American Cities," ibid., 11 (1902), 24-25. For Idaho Falls, see "Civic Improvement Progress," ibid., 12 (1902), 60. For Louisville, see *Nation-Wide Civic Betterment,* 3.

38. Mrs. Marion Louise McCall, "What Organization Has Done for St. Louis," in ibid., 50-56; "St. Louis Still Brushing Up," *Home and Flowers,* 13 (1903), 252.

39. The American Park and Outdoor Art Association, Proceedings and Annual Reports (various titles), 1897-1903, and throughout.

40. For examples of interaction, see "Two Notable Civic Betterment Events," 143-146; "An Object Lesson in Modern City Making" in *The Twentieth Century City: Proceedings of the Annual Convention, 1901, of The American League for Civic Improvement* (Springfield, 1901), 68-69; and The American Park and Outdoor Art Association, *Proceedings of the Fourth Annual Meeting Held at the Art Institute, Chicago, Illinois, June 5, 6, and 7, 1900,* 22-24, 26, 84-95.

41. For the beginnings of the "model city" project and of merger talk, see "Successful Civic Beauty Rally," 10. Organizations collaborating on the "model city" were the Municipal Art Society of New York, The American Park and Outdoor Art Association, The American League for Civic Improvement, the National Municipal League, and the American Scenic and Historic Preservation Society; see "Object Lesson in Modern City Making," 68-69.

42. For examples of such usage, see "The City Beautiful, Recent Endeavors toward Civic Improvement," Current Literature, 32 (1902), 418-432; and Charles Mulford Robinson, "Among the Improvement Clubs," Municipal Journal and Engineer, 11 (1901), 267.

43. Charles Mulford Robinson, *Third Ward Traits* (Rochester, 1899), 5-8; *Third-Ward Catechism* (Rochester, 1908).

44. "American Society of Landscape Architects, Minutes on the Life and Services of Charles Mulford Robinson, Associate Member," Landscape Architecture, 9 (1919), 180-189.

45. Charles Mulford Robinson, *The Improvement of Towns and Cities or the Practical Basis of Civic Aesthetics* (New York, 1901), viii-xii.

46. Ibid., 3-17.
47. Ibid., 8, 20-25.
48. "Successful Civic Beauty Rally," 8; "Two Notable Civic Betterment Events," 164; *The Twentieth Century City*, 62, 68.
49. "Inaugural Address of President Charles Zueblin" in ibid., 65; McCall, "What Organization Has Done for St. Louis," 50.
50. For the importance of the Harrisburg scheme, see Charles Zueblin, "Harrisburg Plan of Municipal Improvement," The Chautauquan, 39 (1904), 60-68.
51. "Making Chautauqua a Model," ibid., 37 (1903), 449-462; Zueblin, "Decade of Civic Improvement," 16-17.
52. Charles Mulford Robinson, "What the Smallest Town Should Do," Public Improvements, 7 (1902), 108.
53. Charles Mulford Robinson, *Modern Civic Art or the City Made Beautiful* (New York, 1903), 32-35, 271-286.
54. Charles Mulford Robinson, "New Dreams for Cities," *The Architectural Record*, 12 (1902), 410-421. In 1904 the federal government also arranged for a comprehensive plan for Manila in the Philippines.
55. For a list that includes nearly all plans drawn up in these years, see Theodora Kimball, ed., *Municipal Accomplishment in City Planning and Published City Plan Reports in the United States* (Boston, 1920).
56. "Successful Civic Beauty Rally," 8; "The American Civic Association Convention in Cleveland, O., October 4-6," Park and Cemetery and Landscape Gardening, 15 (1905), 372. For 1908, see Charles Mulford Robinson's monthly column "Civic Improvement" in Charities and The Commons, 20-21 (1908).

South side of the Court of Honor and the Administration Building, World's Columbian Exposition, Chicago, 1893. Photograph from The American Architect and Building News, *November 4, 1893.*

The City Beautiful in New York

By HARVEY A. KANTOR[°]

THE City Beautiful movement was the aesthetic renaissance that changed the appearance of many American cities in the late nineteenth and early twentieth centuries. Inspired principally by the "White City" of the World's Columbian Exposition of 1893 in Chicago, the City Beautiful was characterized by neoclassical architecture, massive buildings, grand avenues, large swaths of greenery, reflecting pools, civic centers, and a unity of design and scale.[1]

It is almost impossible to envision these characteristics of the City Beautiful applied to the cultural and financial colossus of urban America, New York City. Yet there was a significant drive to get a City Beautiful plan adopted for New York. This little-known effort culminated in the New York City Improvement Plan of 1907—the city's first general urban plan since the commissioners' report of 1811 set the gridiron street pattern. Although, undeniably, it failed, the 1907 plan tells a great deal about the City Beautiful movement in general and is essential to understanding the difficulties of physical planning in a vibrant and dynamic city like New York. The 1907 plan was a model of the City Beautiful concept—it was neat, symmetrical, and clean. But this predominantly aesthetic ideal was not relevant to the eco-

---

[°] The author is assistant professor of American urban history at the University of Rhode Island.

[1] Robert Knutson, "The White City: The World's Columbian Exposition of 1893" (Ph.D. diss., Columbia University, 1956). General treatments of the fair may be found in John W. Reps, *The Making of Urban America: A History of City Planning in the United States* (Princeton, 1965), 497–502; Mel Scott, *American City Planning since 1890: A History Commemorating the Fiftieth Anniversary of the American Institute of Planners* (Berkeley, 1969), 31–37; and Henry Steele Commager, *The American Mind: An Interpretation of American Thought and Character since the 1880s* (New Haven, Yale University Press, 1966), 394–97. Good material may also be found in works on the major participants such as Charles Moore, *Daniel H. Burnham: Architect and Planner of Cities* (Boston, 1921); Moore, *The Life and Times of Charles Follen McKim* (Boston, 1929); and Frederick Law Olmsted, Jr., and Theodora Kimball, eds., *Frederick Law Olmsted, Landscape Architect, 1822–1903* (2 vols., New York, 1922–28).

[149]

nomic aggressiveness and social diversity of New York in the first decade of the twentieth century. The lesson of City Beautiful planning in New York was the failure of neophyte urban planners to incorporate active economic and social forces into their set vision of the future.

Immediately following the Chicago World's Fair an interest in civic beautification began to be expressed. A small group of New York artists, architects, and civic leaders formed the nation's first Municipal Art Society to promote decorative amenities for their city.[2] Gradually, however, these pioneers in civic aesthetics began to realize that individual artistic projects donated to the city would mean little unless each item fitted into an overall functional city plan. This evolution in thinking—that civic art and functional planning had to be allied com-

[2] A survey of the Municipal Art Society's origins and early work may be found in Harvey A. Kantor, "Modern Urban Planning in New York City: Origins and Evolution, 1890–1933" (Ph.D. diss., New York University, 1971), 29–58.

Suggestions of the National Sculpture Society: a domed reading room for an elevated railroad station at Herald Square and a water gate at 72nd Street and the Hudson River. From Municipal Affairs, *December 1899.*

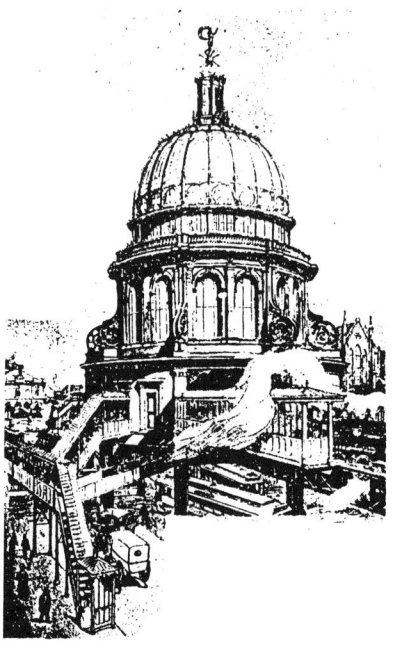

ponents of urban development—was a logical outgrowth of the work done by the Municipal Art Society in the early 1890s.³

The initial stirrings in this local drive for a complete city plan may be seen in the pages of the journal *Municipal Affairs*. This short-lived magazine, begun in 1897 by the Reform Club of New York and influenced by civic art partisans, offered a sympathetic forum for writers interested in better planning in the city. The articles appearing in *Municipal Affairs* mixed the booster spirit so prominent in New York at this time with some of the most original planning ideas of the day. Architect Julius F. Harder, for instance, writing in 1898, predicted that "Civic pride and interest in municipal affairs will in time evolve a logical city plan." Proposing a system of diagonal avenues both to relieve the rigidity of the gridiron and to open up new vistas, Harder was also concerned for the economic welfare of the city. To assure continued supremacy in trade, he believed that New York had to coordinate all of its varied means of transportation with its manufacturing district.⁴ Harder was the first really to express the importance of combining beauty with the city's economy. Sacrificing this balance was the major reason for the later disappointment of the planning activists.

In the December 1899 issue, George Kriehn bolstered the argument for more attention to city planning. He believed that in order to attract a desirable class of residents and to increase the value of real estate, a new effort to plan and beautify the city had to be initiated. More public squares and buildings, more municipal bridge construction, and more artistic street signs and other embellishments were essential to make New York a beautiful city. "Civic patriotism," he wrote, "is an all important factor, and if you add to this the desire to have the very best of its kind, there is no reason why you should not succeed as Florence and Paris have done." In the same issue the National Sculpture Society presented an even more detailed proposal for New York's improvement, but it too focused merely on aesthetics.⁵

---

³ Discussions of the expanding goals of the Municipal Art Society are located in the bulletins of the Municipal Art Society beginning particularly with *Bulletin No. 14* (New York, 1904). See also *Bulletin No. 15* and numbers 18–21 (New York, 1905–6).

⁴ *Reform Club: Officers and Committees, Members, Constitution, By-Laws, Rules* (New York, 1900), 11–12; Julius F. Harder, "The City's Plan," *Municipal Affairs*, II (March 1898), 45, 29.

⁵ George Kriehn, "The City Beautiful," *Municipal Affairs*, III (December 1899), 594–601; "From Battery to Harlem: Suggestions of the National Sculpture Society," ibid., 616–50.

. *The New York Herald,* which had always treated civic art activities warmly, now joined *Municipal Affairs* in publicizing the need for planning. The newspaper ran an extensive feature on "How Can New York Be Made the City Beautiful?" The article was in the form of an interview with George Clausen, president of the Board of Park Commissioners; John De Wolf, landscape architect of the board; Charles R. Lamb, artist and member of the Municipal Art Society; and Niels Gron, a foreign sociologist traveling in the United States. While the three natives extolled the virtues of plans to make New York more attractive, the visitor, Niels Gron, touched on an essential problem in rehabilitating the city:

Before I came to this country, and in all the time I have been here, it never has occurred to me to think of New York as being beautiful. Therefore all this talk of beautifying New York seems strange to me.... We expect of her power and magnificence, but not beauty. If a European came over here and found that New York was beautiful in the same way as the European cities he knew he would be very much disappointed. I do not see how you can make New York beautiful in that way, with the laws and democratic spirit that you have here. The kind of beauty that makes Paris charming can only exist where private rights and personal liberty are or have been trampled on.[6]

Gron identified the major stumbling block in planning or beautifying cities like New York. To remodel, power was essential; and power in a democracy was not concentrated enough. Therefore, the task of wholesale beautification was virtually impossible. The leaders of New York, Gron felt, should realize this and go on to the things they did best.

But such a judgment did not dampen the new enthusiasm for planning. Even those who recognized the difficulties of planning in a democracy expressed optimism that it could be done. *The Outlook* urged New Yorkers to press forward despite some stumbling blocks. "Never before, in the history of New York," the magazine proclaimed, "have so many people been awake to the necessity of planning for the future, and of endeavoring to develop New York on the side of beauty."[7] Now was the time to act.

Work being done in other parts of the country added further im-

[6] *The New York Herald,* April 29, 1900.
[7] "To Make New York Beautiful," *The Outlook,* LXXI (August 23, 1902), 1005–6.

petus. In Cleveland, Kansas City, Baltimore, San Francisco, St. Louis, and Boston, projects were initiated that embodied the City Beautiful concepts. New parkland was added, grand civic centers were planned, boulevards were widened. Public buildings, railroad stations, and monuments were all designed on a massive, harmonious, and classical scale. Nowhere, though, were the guidelines of the Chicago fair follower more successfully than in Washington, D.C. John Reps, in his fine book *Monumental Washington*, attests to the significance of the Washington plan. He states: "the influence exerted on city planning by the Senate Park Commission plan for Washington and its gradual implementation was enormous. The wide and overwhelmingly favorable publicity given to the plan helped to make its chief features known throughout the country."[8]

The New York Times certainly made the capital plan known to its readers. On January 19, 1902, the newspaper published an article on Washington in its magazine section written by the nation's leading architectural critic, Montgomery Schuyler. In an editorial, the *Times* then pressed further for action at home. "A board of experts as competent as those who have revised the plan of Washington would, we are confident, find something worth recommending for the general treatment of New York, as well as innumerable points of detail that could be improved. Not that a busy, roaring town like this can ever become the thing of beauty which the political capital of the Union already in a great degree is. . . . But it can be made immeasurably better looking than it is."[9]

The national planning movement and in particular the national capital plan contributed significantly to the growing local sentiment propelling New Yorkers toward a City Beautiful plan. As the momentum built, the Municipal Art Society began to direct it. On January 31, 1902, it held a dinner meeting to promote the value of city planning. In editorializing about the meeting the *Times* was hopeful that something concrete would now be done. It stated, "The chief of such organizations is the Municipal Art Society, to which New York already

[8] Reps, *Monumental Washington: The Planning and Development of the Capital Center* (Princeton, 1967), 192–93. A good study of a particular city's adoption of City Beautiful planning is William H. Wilson, *The City Beautiful Movement in Kansas City* (Columbia, Mo., 1964).

[9] *The New York Times,* January 19, 1902.

owes so much and may reasonably be expected to owe much more." In 1902 the Municipal Art Society also established a City Plan Committee within its organization and appointed Calvin Tomkins, an expert on docks and transportation facilities, as its chairman.[10]

The Fine Arts Federation joined the Municipal Art Society and *The New York Times* in urging the development of concrete proposals. In early 1902, the federation wrote to Mayor Seth Low suggesting that he consult the Municipal Art Commission on the advisability of employing a commission of experts, as had been done in Washington, to make a study of beautifying the city. Frederick S. Lamb, the secretary of the Municipal Art Society, immediately endorsed the suggestion, believing it "worthy of the enthusiastic support of the entire thinking public." On March 5, 1902, the *Times* published another editorial advocating the establishment of a commission to devise a city plan.[11]

This budding interest in civic development did not go unheeded by the men who held governmental power. Fortunately, Seth Low, mayor of New York in 1902 and 1903, was a sympathetic listener. Low had a long association with the reform elements of the city and was himself a member of the Municipal Art Society. He was receptive to the idea of artistic betterment as a means of inducing civic pride.

Low was further motivated by the active interest in planning of Manhattan Borough President Jacob A. Cantor. Cantor was a lifelong Democratic politician who had been the Democratic leader of the New York State Senate and was then elected borough president on the reform ticket with Seth Low. Cantor was a member of the Municipal Art Society, but it was the demands of his office that virtually forced him to recognize the need for planning. In 1901 an amendment to the city charter had placed all responsibility for public improvements in the office of the borough presidents, a move reflecting the parochial desires of the borough presidents to retain control over works carried out in their own areas. Previously, under the initial 1898 Charter of the Greater City, a board of public improvements had been responsible for coordinating all major projects carried out by the city.[12]

[10] Ibid., February 1, 1902; Municipal Art Society, *Bulletin No. 14*.

[11] *New-York Daily Tribune*, February 10, 1902; *Times*, March 5, 1902.

[12] *Times*, July 3, 1921; *Report of the Charter Revision Commission to the Governor of the State of New York* (New York, 1900), section 383; *The Greater New York Charter* (New York, 1897), section 410.

Therefore, when Cantor assumed office in Manhattan he held responsibility for increased public development. And while he initially was interested only in improvements that would aid his own constituency, he soon widened his vision to a concern for the city as a whole. Perhaps the change in Cantor's thinking came when he was an invited guest at the Municipal Art Society's dinner meeting on January 21, 1902, devoted to planning for more municipal embellishments. The *Times* felt "one of the most hopeful signs of the occasion was the attendance of Mr. Cantor and the interest he took in the subject." The paper also asserted that support of municipal art activities was good politics:

The opposition of Tammany to public art is simply a detail of the opposition of Tammany to civilization in general. . . . If the reform administration succeeds in giving the people of New York object lessons in the value of municipal embellishment, such a success will be of distinct advantage to it when the next municipal election comes around. The powers of the President of Manhattan in this way are considerable. And it is gratifying to have evidence that Mr. Cantor appreciates them and intends to use them.[13]

Cantor first made public his stand on planning in his quarterly report of March 31, 1902. In this he stated a desire for the "benefit of a comprehensive plan" and his belief that the city's development should not "be left to the haphazard conditions which have heretofore existed in the old City of New York." He further expressed to Mayor Low his displeasure with the present condition and pushed for action through planning: "I have noticed a lack of harmony as to the architecture, location, and other features of public improvements, and I believe that if a commission of architects, sculptors, civil engineers and others be appointed, as has been done in the City of Washington, the result of their labors would be very apparent in the general appearance of this city." In a report several months later Cantor considered the propriety of appointing a commission himself to plan for beautifying the borough of Manhattan so that the city's appearance would not be left "to the haphazard conditions which have heretofore existed."[14]

The major newspapers of New York rallied to Cantor's position. The *Tribune* vigorously praised his reports and hoped that a commission

[13] *Times*, February 1, 1902.
[14] *Report of the President of Borough of Manhattan of City of New York* (New York, 1902), 10, 9; *Tribune*, August 18, 1902.

such as he proposed would be appointed immediately. The *Times*, believing it was the striking success of the Washington plan that had induced Cantor to action, congratulated him and said that "to Mr. Cantor belongs the distinction and the credit of having been the first municipal official to propose the preparation of such a comprehensive plan for the improvement of Manhattan."[15]

Mayor Low, late in 1902, was finally moved into action. But instead of appointing a commission empowered to make specific plans immediately, as Cantor had advocated, Low did a curious thing. He merely asked the Municipal Art Society to gather together various groups within the city to prepare a preliminary report on how the disparate interests in New York should work to evolve a united city plan and what the goals of such a plan should be.[16] This slowdown tactic not only eventually cost the mayor the opportunity of appointing the commission that was established, but also ultimately cost the city an effective plan. A sin of omission not commission, it illustrates the general lack of force and drama that in the end doomed the City Beautiful concept in New York.

Nonetheless, the Municipal Art Society followed the wishes of the

[15] *Tribune*, August 19, 1902; *Times*, August 19, 1902.
[16] *Times*, November 30, 1902.

Plan for the treatment of space in front of the Capitol, Washington, D.C. From Harper's Weekly, *February 1, 1902.*

mayor and called the first meeting of the temporary conference on planning on November 29, 1902. They brought together representatives of many of the most important business and professional organizations in New York, who agreed to collate all the ideas and suggestions that had been brought forward by any group in the past fifty years. And, at the initial meeting, they decided upon the general nature of the report they were to make. It was established that "before any scheme for beautification of Greater New York can be successfully carried out the structural and transportation changes must be first determined."[17]

The second and final meeting of this temporary conference was held one week later with William King of the Merchants' Association presiding. Here the individuals contributed recommendations reflecting their particular organizations. Freight terminals, proper treatment of monuments, rearrangement of streets, and new municipal buildings were all discussed as items to be presented in a city plan; and it was left to the Municipal Art Society to draw up the recommendations properly and submit them to the mayor. The *Times* was grateful for the work done by the Municipal Art Society and the temporary conference and urged that with a "good Mayor and good department heads: now is the time!"[18]

Frederick S. Lamb, as secretary of the society, was given the responsibility of presenting the recommendations of the temporary conference to Mayor Low. The report, submitted on January 11, 1903, contained six separate sections, freight traffic, passenger traffic, parks, public buildings, decoration of public buildings, and public monuments. It included specific recommendations of projects that had been proposed at various times during the last fifty years and also set down guidelines as to the areas that should receive the attention of a city planning body. Great freight terminals were deemed a necessity, in addition to expanded facilities for transferring freight from railroads to ships. The plan projected a dock system similar to Liverpool's and stressed the need for tunnels to supplement bridge traffic across the rivers. It was also thought that a system permitting economical and prompt delivery of merchandise was imperative. The report included

[17] Ibid.
[18] Ibid., November 7, December 24, 1902.

recommendations for easing passenger flow and expediting commercial traffic, and it supported the expansion of the rapid transit system, especially underground. Subsidiary streets were also recommended, along with arcades to relieve congestion on the major avenues. Civic centers, more public monuments, an expanded park plan, new waterfront areas, and a parkway system were all listed as desirable projects.[19]

The report of this temporary conference was the first instance in New York City where both beautification and economic development were formally considered in conjunction. A group of widely differing individuals, called into being by a public official, had succeeded in presenting the first comprehensive survey of New York City's present and long-range improvement needs.

Low was impressed with the findings of the temporary conference and expressed his gratitude to the Municipal Art Society for its accomplishment. He now concurred with the suggestion that a formal commission be set up to promote improvements within the guidelines that had been established. But Low's wishes were not carried out by the Board of Aldermen. His failure to seize his chance when he had it now hurt him, as he was increasingly thought of as a "lame duck" mayor. Tammany members of the board succeeded in delaying action at least until after the upcoming mayoral election in the hope that the idea would die out completely or that Tammany forces might get representation in the new group. Members of the Municipal Art Society responded indignantly to the delay of what one felt was "the most important recommendation made for the improvement of New York for the last century."[20]

Meanwhile advocates of planning continued their efforts to gain public support. The *Times* also continued its prodding by again praising Jacob Cantor's work and attacking the intransigence of such aldermen as Timothy P. Sullivan and David S. Stewart. In promoting city

[19] *Tribune*, January 12, 1903. Report published in *Proceedings of the Board of Aldermen of the City of New York* . . . (4 vols., New York, 1903), I, March 31, 1903, 1220–27. Also in "New York the Beautiful," *Public Improvements*, VI (January 1, 1903), 9–11. Frederick S. Lamb discussed the report in "New York City of the Future," *House and Garden*, III (June 1903), 295–309.

[20] Annual Report of the Mayor, *Proceedings of the Board of Aldermen*, I, January 5, 1903, 13; *Tribune*, March 6, 1903.

planning as a basis for rational expansion, the *Times* also wrote: "of course, considerations of this kind could be expected to appeal only to men of a certain degree of enlightenment, and it would be perfectly futile to urge them upon Aldermen Sullivan and Stewart."[21]

On April 27, 1903, the finance committee of the Board of Aldermen was compelled to hold a hearing on the proposed improvement commission, and artists, architects, and friends of planning in general came out in force. Among those present were Frederick Lamb of the Municipal Art Society; John Carrére of the Fine Arts Federation; Henry R. Towne of the Merchants' Association; Nelson Spencer of the Reform Club; Thomas Fulton of the Citizen's Union; and W. M. Aiken, consulting architect to Borough President Cantor, a significant indication of the organizations most active in urging the reform. These proponents of the proposed commission argued that there could be no artistic development of the city without such an agency. It was pointed out that, under the present system of local boards, improvements were of a temporary and local character, and were made without regard to the artistic benefit of the city as a whole. The finance committee sent a favorable recommendation to the Board of Aldermen, but not until December 1, 1903, did they pass a bill establishing a commission to prepare "a comprehensive plan for the beautifying and development of this municipality." Low was now, in fact, a lame duck mayor. Some people urged him to fill the positions on the commission, but he decided to allow the privilege to pass to his successor, George B. McClellan, Jr.[22]

McClellan was a paradoxical figure both in his general politics and in his stand on the improvement commission for New York. Although he came from an upper-class background, his support came from Tammany rather than from the reform groups that had elected Low. In his first term in office he was influenced by the political ties he had with the organization, but he later broke with Tammany; and during his second term he became a completely independent mayor. His interest in planning and beautification was personal rather than political. Tammany men had always expressed either apathy or scorn for beautifica-

[21] *Times*, April 24, 1903.
[22] *Tribune*, April 28, 1903; *Proceedings of the Board of Aldermen*, IV, December 1, 1903, 682; *Times*, January 22, 1904.

tion schemes, but McClellan's lifelong interest in art made him far more sympathetic to the cause. He was a member of several national organizations of artists as well as vice-president of the American Academy in Rome. His historical knowledge and writings on Italy, particularly Venice, no doubt made him amenable to beautification plans for his own city.[23]

On March 12, 1904, McClellan appointed the New York Public Improvement Commission. His appointments to the commission, however, were uninspired, giving rise to the allegation that he did not take its work seriously. Other than Jacob Cantor, who had to be included as a borough president, the only appointee who was a proponent of the legislation creating the commission was the sculptor Daniel Chester French. The rest were personal friends or distinguished citizens with little known concern for planning. For instance, he named Francis Key Pendleton, a prominent New York lawyer, and director of the Guardian Insurance Corporation, whose father had been the vice-presidential running mate of McClellan's father on the Democratic ticket in 1864.[24]

Announcement of the members of the new commission came as a disappointment to those who had worked so hard to make it a reality. Commenting on McClellan's appointments, the *Times* wrote: "The lay members, the amateurs, are not publicly known ever to have given

---

[23] Harold C. Syrett, ed., *The Gentleman and the Tiger: The Autobiography of George B. McClellan, Jr.* (Philadelphia, 1956), 9–39; *Dictionary of American Biography*, supplement two, s.v. "McClellan, George Brinton."

[24] Others appointed in addition to borough presidents Cantor, Louis F. Haffen of the Bronx, J. Edward Swanstrom of Brooklyn, Joseph Cassidy of Queens, and George Cromwell of Richmond were: Daniel S. Lamont, former secretary of war under McKinley; Frank Bailey, vice-president of Title Guarantee and Trust of Brooklyn; Henry S. Thompson, builder and real estate dealer, who had been Manhattan superintendent of buildings under Low; William J. La Roche, former Democratic state senator and owner of a large hardware company; John W. Alexander, artist and member of the National Academy of Design; Harry Payne Whitney, prominent businessman; Whitney Warren, architect; George A. Hearn of Mutual Life Insurance Company; and James A. Wright. Lamont was initially named chairman but became ill and died in 1905. A competent technical staff, which did most of the actual work, was named. It included Nelson P. Lewis, chief engineer of the Board of Estimate, who became secretary of the commission; John A. Bensel, chief engineer of the Department of Docks and Ferries; O. F. Nichols, chief engineer of the Bridge Department; and Samuel Parsons, Jr., landscape architect of the Park Department. *Times*, March 13, and 22, 1904, July 27, 1930; *Tribune*, March 13, 1904.

George B. McClellan, Jr. THE NEW-YORK HISTORICAL SOCIETY.

any attention to the subject nor to have taken any interest in it. The Mayor does not seem to have taken the matter at all seriously, but to have made up the commission, with one exception, on no better principle than that of paying a cheap compliment to personal friends or to citizens of an eminence irrelevant to the particular work in hand."[25]

With the makeup of the commission such that it gave little hope for inspired results and because of the stipulation, imposed by the aldermen, that work be done by the year's end, few thought that anything substantial would come forth from the deliberations. And when, on December 14, 1904, the report was presented, most of the suggestions were necessarily tentative. Yet the commission did endorse a complete and comprehensive plan for Greater New York. Realizing that construction based on the exigencies of the time had caused New

[25] *Times*, March 20, 1904.

York to develop haphazardly, the commission gave hearty approval to the concept of future planning.[26]

In the fifty-four pages of the report (twenty-two pages of analysis, ten pages listing the subjects considered, and twenty-two renderings of projected improvements), the commission made clear the items it felt should be included in such a plan. Some of these had been suggested in the 1903 report of the temporary conference, but most had been developed during the nine months of public and private hearings held by the commission. The major projects listed combined economic and aesthetic considerations. They included: (1) uniform pier construction for the Hudson River to improve the appearance of Chelsea and also to provide greater recreational opportunities; (2) an elevated highway running along the Hudson from the Battery to 72nd Street; (3) more parkland for Manhattan's upper Hudson River area; (4) a dignified entrance and departure point for Richmond residents at the Battery, including new ferry stations and a large monumental column; (5) tree-planting along the center of Delancey Street; (6) a new park to relieve congestion above the subway loop terminal at the Blackwell's Island Bridge; (7) a permanent parade reviewing stand at 25th Street and Fifth Avenue; and (8) preliminary plans for a civic center complex around City Hall. All of these features, it was believed, had to fit "a comprehensive plan for the City's development . . . so designed that all its parts shall be consistent, the one with the other, and form a homogeneous whole."[27]

In presenting the report to the Board of Aldermen, McClellan endorsed its main conclusion — the need for a comprehensive plan, in contrast to the haphazard development that heretofore had prevailed:

The great error of the past from both the material and artistic standpoints, has been that public improvements have been undertaken only to meet the emergency of the moment, and without regard for ultimate needs. Public buildings have been scattered far and wide, erected in impossible locations, and by architects who have had neither training in art nor conception of public necessities. Streets have been opened, bridges built, and money spent at haphazard according to the fancy or whim of changing administrations,

[26] *The Report of the New York City Public Improvement Commission to the Honorable George B. McClellan . . . and to the Honorable Board of Aldermen . . .* (New York, 1905), especially 1–3.
[27] Ibid., 1, 6–22.

The City Beautiful in New York [163]

with far more regard for the interests of the individuals than for the good of the city as a whole.[28]

Reaction to the presentation of the 1904 improvement commission was mild. The *Times* published its story under the headline "Suggest Vast Schemes for Greatest City" and called it "probably the most elaborate and comprehensive plan for city improvement ever laid before the municipal authorities," but that was all. It printed only this one article, on page six, without illustrating the improvements suggested or editorial comment. The *Tribune* was even less enthusiastic. It called the report "interesting" and work of the members "judicious"; but it showed no great interest in the findings. The *Brooklyn Daily Eagle* was more direct in expressing its opinion, contending that "Manhattan matters" had been treated with much more "warmth and detail" and calling the report as a whole "a disappointment."[29]

Although Mayor McClellan did not even mention this first report in his annual message, he had committed himself to seeing the matter through. Hence he asked the members of the commission to stay on

[28] *Message of Hon. George B. McClellan . . . to the Board of Aldermen Transmitting Report of the New York City Improvement Commission* (New York, 1905), 4.

[29] *Times*, January 3, 1905; *Tribune*, January 3, 4, 1905; *Brooklyn Daily Eagle*, January 3, 1905.

Proposal for an elevated roadway on West Street to improve traffic and freight accommodations. From Report of the New York City Improvement Commission *(New York, 1904).*

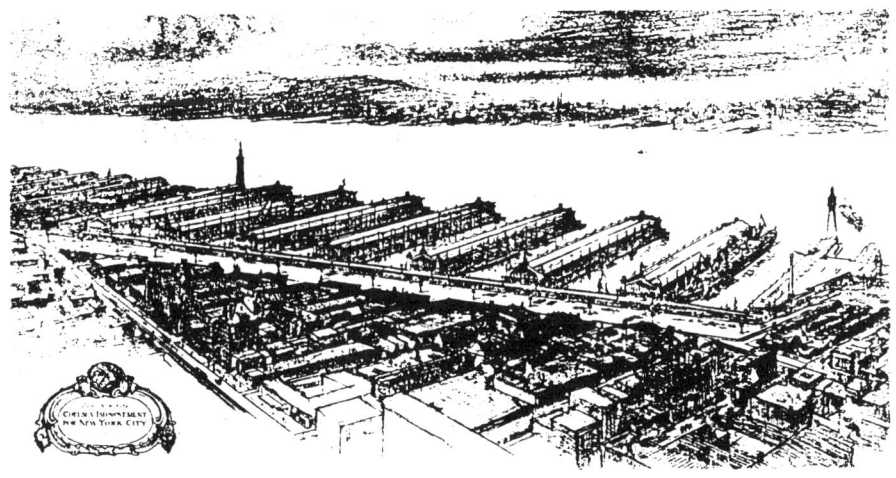

and work toward the preparation of a more complete plan for the city. For two more years, they continued the work of analyzing the needs of the city and selecting appropriate solutions. In January 1907 the commission submitted the first comprehensive report for the future planning of modern New York City.[30]

The 1907 report formed the main contribution of the nation's largest metropolis to the City Beautiful movement. Embodying proposals for grand plazas, increased acres of greenery, and widened vistas at major intersections and bridge entrances, the plan was the embodiment of the City Beautiful concept. It also reflected interest in the basics of an urban plan, such as parks, streets, and highways. The commission asserted that "questions of more or less detail relating to pavements, sidewalks, appropriate house numbers, gas and electric fixtures, manner of indicating the street, locations of statues and monuments commemorating historical events, tree planting, and countless number of other matters," were all "important and essential" if New York were to "take its place as one of the great Metropolitan Cities of the World."[31]

The most impressive argument implicit in the 1907 plan was the need to tie all aspects of Greater New York together. While stressing the importance of retaining the individuality of each separate borough, the point was made that avenues of connection were needed to make access to all parts of the city possible. The Henry Hudson Bridge already was under construction, but the commission recommended connecting upper Manhattan and the Bronx with a new bridge at 297th Street, improving Washington Bridge, and providing a new bridge that would tie Seventh Avenue with the Grand Boulevard and Concourse. A diagonal approach to the terminal at the Blackwell's Island Bridge was suggested as a means of relieving traffic congestion. To give improved access to Manhattan from Brooklyn, a huge circular plaza, eight hundred feet in diameter, was designed to connect the entrances to the Brooklyn and Manhattan bridges. The traffic flowing on and off these bridges would thus radiate out from the circle onto the principal routes of traffic.[32]

[30] *Tribune*, January 3, 1905; *The Report of the New York City Improvement Commission to the Honorable George B. McClellan, Mayor of the City of New York, and to the Honorable Board of Aldermen of the City of New York* (New York, 1907). (Hereafter it will be cited as *1907 Report*.)
[31] *1907 Report*, 7.
[32] Ibid., 11–12, 16, 20.

The systems of avenues connecting the boroughs not only would bring the city closer together, but would also provide an opportunity for extending unbroken ribbons of green park throughout the city by planting trees and shrubs along the avenues. This was one of the most original ideas of the City Beautiful movement, and it already had proven its value in Kansas City.[33] The commission proposed a complete parkway connection from the Bronx parks, down Riverside Drive, across to Central Park, and over the bridges to the park systems of Queens and Brooklyn. Such a pattern would be unrivaled in its extent and variety and would minister "to the needs of the different localities in a way that no other distribution of an equal amount of area could do." The borough of Queens was particularly suitable for such a scheme because of its large amount of undeveloped land. Six detailed maps were presented to show the improved network of park systems the commission proposed. Another major portion of the report dealt with the development of New York's valuable waterfront. The commission proposed that the development of this resource follow a preconceived plan. Both the city and its lessees should agree upon uniform structural standards for all docks and piers, with architectural harmony a constant consideration. They recommended rigid enforcement of the standards, as well as the construction of piers that would give citizens access to the lower waterfront.[34]

The interconnecting street system, the parkway plans, and the uniformity of pier construction were the major proposals of the report, but many other individual projects were recommended. These included the widening of Fifth Avenue and other major arteries, the removal of the wall surrounding Central Park, the reservation of Blackwell's Island as a park, the extension of Riverside Drive, and the proposal that the City Hall be the focal point for a future civic center complex. Most of the projects were accompanied by appropriate illustrations and renderings to show their intended value. These individual projects clearly reflected the dominant aesthetic orientation of the plan and showed the total lack of concern for social benefits that could have been derived from a bolder planning scheme.

[33] Wilson, *City Beautiful Movement in Kansas City*, 89-90, 123-24. See also J. Horace McFarland, "The Growth of City Planning in America," *Charities and The Commons*, XIX (February 1, 1908), 1524.

[34] *1907 Report*, 9, 10, plates I-IV and XXI-XXIII.

The 1907 improvement plan evoked little comment at the time of its presentation. Mayor McClellan, who was busily engaged in his own public works program, had little to say on the subject of planning. *The New York Times* and the *Tribune*, both of which had supported the establishment of a commission, were silent when the final plans were announced. Indeed, the *Times* ran a feature on architectural and engineering events projected for 1907 in New York and made no reference whatsoever to the improvement commission's plans.[35]

But McClellan did get credit for appointing the commission when he was honored on January 28, 1908, by the American Group of the Société des Architectes Diplômés par le Gouvernement, composed of graduates of the Ecole des Beaux-Arts, and given an award "in recognition of the conspicuous service . . . rendered in the cause of civic improvement." Acknowledging his award, McClellan asserted that "it is the city beautiful that compels and retains the love of her people. It is in the city beautiful that civic spirit is at its best." However, despite this avowal, McClellan did little to see that the plans of the improvement commission were ever carried out. Instead of lending his support to the implementation of the plans, the mayor merely allowed the Board of Estimate to file the report in the office of the chief engineer of the board for reference by anyone who contemplated doing anything in the future.[36] City departments, whenever they desired to begin a public works project, consulted the plan for guidelines, but they were not required to follow them, nor was any concerted attempt ever made to implement the plan as a whole. In fact, the widening of Fifth Avenue and several other streets and some pier improvements were the only proposals ever carried out in accordance with the designs laid down in the plan.

Thus, the plan of 1907, launched four years earlier with the enthusiastic support of artists' groups and government figures, when finally unveiled, stirred little excitement and little support. This brief account of its background helps to explain why. The timing of the developments provides one answer. The plan had been subjected to an excessive amount of debate. Three separate groups were asked to deliberate

[35] *Times*, January 6, 1907.
[36] "Award to Hon. Geo. B. McClellan," *The New York Architect*, II (February 1908), [1], [4]; "New York Improvement Commission," *Architectural Record*, XXI (June, 1907), 483–84.

A proposal for widening Fifth Avenue included pedestrian arcades and an overpass at Fifth Avenue and 42nd Street. From Report of the New York City Improvement Commission *(New York, 1907).*

on the topics before any final decisions were reached. Initially conceived in the days when the Washington plan sparked the desire in New Yorkers to prepare one of their own, the plan might have won greater recognition if it had been presented before the momentum of interest was lost. When the final plans were presented most people had lost the enthusiasm that existed when the commission was created. The *Architectural Record* maintained that calling the first temporary conference had been a "tactical mistake" that left the final report "shorn of novelty."[37] If Seth Low had boldly launched a commission in 1902, as many had urged, rather than attempting to build civic group support first, more would probably have been accomplished.

Second was the lack of force behind the report: it was just not dra-

[37] "New York Improvement Commission," 483–84.

matic enough. The 1902 temporary conference had collected the plans various groups had put forth in the previous fifty years; the 1904 report's tentative suggestions were based on these same items; and the 1907 report was, in turn, based on the 1904 plans. Thus when the final plans were announced, Charles Mulford Robinson said, "most found it a twice-told tale—a thing which there is not time for in New York. The commission, in the city where, above all others, public opinion has to be shocked to be aroused, had spent its powder in a salute. It had made a fatal tactical mistake." Robinson believed the plans themselves were not poor ones, but they just did not have the dramatic impact to make them attractive enough.[38]

Frederick Lamb, the former secretary of the Municipal Art Society and the man who had presented the original recommendations for a commission to Low, agreed that this was the plan's primary failing. He expressed his disappointment in an article in 1908 and stated that the shortcomings came "as a result of a definite policy to support only such plans and modifications as may be possible of immediate execution." Lamb believed the plan was thus only "a stepping stone to what must inevitably follow" and that the city needed something "more radical" in terms of projecting future needs.[39]

Third, the composition of the commission helps to explain its lack of greater support. McClellan's selection of his friends for membership on the commission rather than the more ardent supporters of the planning movement reduced the possibility of generating intensive public support. Had Charles Lamb, Frederick Lamb, Arnold Brunner, John DeWitt Warner, John Carrére, or others who had led the drive for the commission been appointed, the product might have been different and greater support inspired. Moreover, apart from this lack of artists' support, McClellan and the commission made no real effort to stir political support either.[40]

But besides the tactical errors committed in setting up and running the commission, the contents of the report itself were responsible for

[38] Charles Mulford Robinson, "'Civic Improvements': A Reply," *Architectural Record*, XXII (August 1907), 118.
[39] Lamb, "New York City Improvement Report," *Charities and The Commons*, XIX (February 1, 1908), 1536.
[40] Herbert Croly, "'Civic Improvements': The Case of New York," *Architectural Record*, XXI (May 1907), 348.

Excavation for the Municipal Building. View looking north from Chambers toward Centre Street, 1909. Photograph from McKim, Mead & White Collection, THE NEW-YORK HISTORICAL SOCIETY.

the lack of excitement. The 1907 plan, because it embodied solely the City Beautiful ideal, did not pay enough attention to the vast economic resources of the city and the way in which these resources could be better developed through planning. Indeed, as Frederick Law Olmsted, Jr., stated, "the esthetic element was clearly over-emphasized."[41] Because financial and economic progress was the dominant thrust of New York's growth and because the 1907 report failed adequately to relate planning and aesthetic improvements to this major aspect of the city's character, it was doomed to failure.

Moreover, the City Beautiful concept did not take into consideration the social needs of the New York community. Nowhere in the entire 1907 report are planning and people related. The schemes were presented as if they were to be constructed in a vacuum rather than in the midst of a bustling and varied population. As Benjamin C. Marsh, a New York lobbyist for reform causes, wrote: "The grouping of public buildings, and the installation of speedways, parks and drives, which affect only moderately the daily lives of the city's toilers, are important; but vastly more so is the securing of decent home conditions of the countless thousands who otherwise can but occasionally escape from their squalid, confining surroundings to view the architectural perfection and to experience the aesthetic delights of the remote improvements."[42] Nowhere in their report did the commission take these social realities into account. Clearly the overemphasis on aesthetic considerations had slighted social concerns.

But Herbert Croly did not believe this was unusual for the City Beautiful approach to planning. In his regular column in the *Architectural Record*, Croly maintained the New York situation was not unique. The failure of New York's plan, rather than representing a temporary setback for the national movement, was instead typical of the inadequacy of City Beautiful planning. New York's case, "the worst failure of all," was nonetheless symptomatic of this generally unrealistic approach to planning. City Beautiful advocates, Croly thought, were deluding themselves if they believed their movement was mak-

---

[41] Olmsted, "The Town-Planning Movement in America," *Annals of the American Academy of Political and Social Sciences*, LI (January 1914), 177.

[42] Benjamin C. Marsh, "City Planning in Justice to the Working Population," *Charities and The Commons*, XIX (February 1, 1908), 1514.

ing any practical headway. The major problem, he believed, was that "the interest of the real estate speculator demands congestion and concentration of business and population, which enormously increases real estate values along particular lines and at particular points, while the interest of the whole people in a beautiful and convenient city demands the distribution of population and business in the most liberal manner and according to an organic plan." Until planning took account of these facts rather than merely attempting to embellish the appearance of the city, no plan for New York would ever become a reality.[43]

All of this was strong criticism for the supporters of urban planning to contemplate. Not only had they encountered particular local political and tactical problems, but the City Beautiful model had provoked little widespread support in New York, and its entire basis had come under attack. Planning advocates had come a long way since the early days of civic art and had accomplished much, but the culmination of their efforts—the 1907 plan—was a failure, and the city continued to grow without plan.

Tremendous public improvements were being constructed—the underground rapid transit system, the new East River bridges, the Pennsylvania terminal, the Municipal Building, new docks, parks, and playgrounds.[44] None of these, however, was being related to a preconceived overall urban plan. New York's impulse toward giantism could not be harnessed by the static conception of the City Beautiful. Those who were concerned about the city's future recognized now that any attempt at planning urban growth in New York required something far more flexible and bold than the plaster models that had stirred their imagination at Chicago's fair in 1893.

[43] Croly, "'Civic Improvements': The Case of New York," 352.
[44] "Changes and Improvements in New York," *The American Architectural and Building News,* LXXIII (July 6, 1901), 1–7.

A Reconsideration of the 1909 "Plan of Chicago"
BY IRA J. BACH

Boulevards, monumental museums, and a scenic lakefront that would set a standard for the City Beautiful— such was Daniel Burnham's dream for Chicago.

THE SCENE IS SET IN 1895. In his offices in downtown Chicago, Daniel Burnham is beginning to plan a beautiful new lakefront for Chicago— a continuous scenic and recreational area festooned with islands, peninsulas, and lagoons.

Successful dreams were not new to the 49-year-old architect. For 22 years the firm of Burnham and Root had designed fine commercial buildings for Chicago. They gave the city its first "skyscraper"—it was ten stories high— and set a trend. Chicago's Monadnock Building, its Rookery, its Western Union Building, and its Rand McNally Building, among others, even now testify to the style and quality of the firm's work. Besides their Chicago work, the partners had erected structures in many places—Bar Harbor, San Francisco, Marquette, and others —even Mexico City.

The two men had been close friends as well as partners for almost 20 years, from their first, difficult years to their recent, highly successful ones. Root, the "inside man," was the chief designer; Burnham was the "outside man," handling the business contacts. Together they were a strong team. Root's love for sculpture, painting, and music also helped shape Burnham's career. It was no accident that Burnham became a great admirer of sculptors Augustus St. Gaudens and Lorado Taft, and of Theodore Thomas, the symphony conductor.

The greatest challenge previously laid before the firm, indeed one of the most important architectural challenges of the century, was the design and construction of the buildings for the Columbian Exposition, held on the shore of Lake Michigan on Chicago's South Side in 1893 to commemorate the four-hundredth anniversary of Columbus' discovery of America. But in 1891, while the great fair was still being planned, gifted John W. Root died, only 42 years old.

The following year, Burnham recruited Charles B. Atwood of New York to fill Root's place as chief designer. Atwood had the same sensitivity in design and planning as Root, and he also loved sculpture, painting, and music. He turned out to be an excellent successor.

To lay out the grounds and the large plan for the Exposition, Frederick L. Olmsted, famed landscape architect, was brought to Chicago. Olmsted belonged to a new breed of city planners. He was a conservationist and an ecologist, a lover of cities when cities were despised. He is responsible for the creation of the large urban park, which he designed with incomparable art and skill for America's large cities, and his work for Chicago can be seen in the shoreline of Jackson Park, once part of the Exposition grounds. His thinking had an enormous influence on Daniel Burnham and on the *Plan of Chicago* which appeared in 1909.

The general scheme of land and water for the Exposition was devised by Olmsted. The arrangement of the terraces, bridges, and landings was planned by Olmsted and his partner, Harry Codman. The size and number of buildings were determined by Olmsted, Codman, and Burnham.

Ira J. Bach, president of the Urban Associates of Chicago, served as Chicago's commissioner of city planning from 1957 to 1965. He is the author of *Chicago on Foot* (Follett, 1969).

132 Chicago History

Frederick Law Olmsted, the creator of America's great city parks, as he looked when he was planning the landscaping of the Columbian Exposition. *Chicago Historical Society*

In the general design of the structures and their placement around a great enclosed body of water, the Columbian Exposition resembled the French Universal Exposition, held in Paris in 1889. The truly exciting aspect of the Chicago design was that it called for filling in seven hundred acres of Lake Michigan. Later, these great fair grounds became an open, green recreational space on the shore of the lake.

Although Burnham, at a testimonial dinner given in his honor in New York on March 25, 1893, gave credit to Olmsted for the design of the Exposition grounds and the new Lake Michigan shoreline, there was still another person who needs mention. James W. Ellsworth, a successful Chicago businessman, was the one who had urged Olmsted to prepare the master plan for the Exposition. And it was this same Ellsworth who later urged Burnham to become interested in planning the city's entire lakefront in the same manner as Jackson Park had been planned.

The idea of creating a vast open and green shoreline by filling in Lake Michigan fired Burnham's imagination and passion. He was determined to make Chicago a "City Beautiful." He soon began to show schematic drawings to almost any civic-minded group in Chicago that would listen to him. This went on for several years—until 1902, to be exact.

In the meantime, Burnham's architectural firm, now D. H. Burnham and Company, had become a large organization with a staff numbered in the hundreds, not unlike some of today's large architectural firms. The firm brought not only prestige to Burnham, but large financial rewards as well.

In spite of his successes, Burnham still had a tremendous urge to undertake large-scale developments and even to remake entire cities. One project of this kind was the 1902 competition to design a new plan for the U.S. Military Academy at West Point. Burnham did not win the competition—the commission went to Cram, Goodhue and Ferguson—but in looking for someone to help him prepare the plan he found a young man named Edward A. Bennett. Bennett had been educated at L'École de Beaux Arts in Paris and was at the time employed in a New York architectural office, but a day spent tramping over the site at West Point with Burnham began a new professional relationship and a lasting friendship.

Burnham had already been commissioned to develop a plan for Washington, D.C., working within the structure of the plan by L'Enfant a century earlier. His plan, completed in 1902, was followed by one for Cleveland in 1903, for San Francisco in 1904, and for the Philippine Island cities of Manila and Bagnio in 1905.

Burnham, as we know, had begun to draw up a plan for a new lakefront for Chicago as early as 1895. But in what Charles W. Norton of the Merchants Club of Chicago described as "those dark years of panic and reaction that followed the World's Fair" nobody would provide financial support for the idea. By 1902, things were

The 1909 Plan

looking up and Norton had become very interested in city planning. He and Frederick A. Delano (uncle of Franklin Delano Roosevelt, 32nd President of the United States) invited Burnham to talk to the Merchants Club about his plan for Washington, D.C. Their ulterior motive was to convince Burnham to make a plan for Chicago. In this they were successful. Burnham accepted the offer, money was raised, and the work began.

The Merchants Club, which had a life of only ten years, was merged into the Commercial Club in 1907, and the Commercial Club then assumed the sponsorship of a plan for Chicago. The agreement was that Burnham and Bennett would be given a free hand in every respect. By 1908, they were ready. Burnham prepared the report; Bennett directed the preparation of the drawings, which were beautifully executed in color by Jules Guerin; and Charles Moore, who later became Burnham's biographer, did the final writing and editing. The whole was bound in a handsome volume and presented to the city of Chicago by the Commercial Club.

The plan had a grand sweep—the entire metropolitan area for a radius of sixty miles. It called for the development of a system of lake-front parks, beaches, yacht harbors, and pleasure-boat piers. The idea, evolved from Olmsted's lagoons, was for a string of green, recreational, offshore islands to bring the city into the lake and vice versa. The islands were to be made of Chicago's abundant supply of waste and fill. A number of interior parks, in scattered locations, were also envisioned, these to be connected by a system of spacious, tree-lined boulevards.

Grant Park was to be the site of three monumental museums, in the Parisian manner. The plan included seven downtown railway passenger terminals, to be connected by subways, and called for the straightening of a portion of the Chicago River for more efficient riverside transportation. Two commercial harbors—one downtown at the mouth of the Chicago River, one at the mouth of the Calumet River—were to be developed. A complete system of street circulation was set forth: boulevard circuits, radial arteries, and a main east-west axis. A new civic center would serve as Chicago's equivalent of the Étoile (star) of Haussman's plan of Paris.

As a matter of fact, Burnham and Bennett were greatly influenced by the enormous civic improvements that had been recently completed in Paris, especially by the broad boulevards and diagonal thoroughfares that Haussman had created there.

A boulevard to connect the north and south sides of the river was planned for what is now Michigan Avenue. The double-decking of Michigan Avenue and Wacker Drive was envisioned, as was the double-decking of the Michigan Avenue bridge. Wacker Drive was to be a free-flowing east-west arterial system that would not interfere with the major north-south traffic on Michigan Avenue.

The park system and traffic arteries were envisioned as extending far beyond the city itself. Large forest preserves were to be acquired, and a system of regional highways formed.

As for political considerations, the rough-spoken, practical-minded mayor of Chicago, Fred Busse, had already been won over to the idealistic adventure begun by the young merchants of the city. In November 1909, he asked the City Council to approve the appointment of a commission to study the Chicago Plan and put it into execution, telling them:

This plan is not to be considered as the embodiment of an artist's dream or the project of theoretical city beautifiers who have lost sight of everyday affairs and who have forgotten the needs and interests of the mass of people. On the contrary, the men who produced the Chicago Plan are all hard-boiled business men. Making Chicago attractive to visitors from all parts of the world will add to Chicago's resources a very great asset, the value of which will be reflected in every piece of real estate within our limit.

And so a Chicago Plan Commission was appointed, headed by Charles H. Wacker,

Chicago Historical Society

The Exposition, looking down the length of the lagoon to the south canal. This wedding of water, land fill, landscaping, and architecture characterized the collaboration of Burnham and Olmsted.

The 1909 Plan

chairman of the Merchants Club's original planning committee. In cooperation with city officials and commercial, transportation, and other interests, it was to work out, step by step, the projects of the great plan, primarily within the corporate limits of the city.

Walter Moody, the Commission's executive director, and Charles Wacker, its chairman, were fervent propagandists. Moody prepared a digest of the Plan and entitled it *Wacker's Manual*. It was one of the first paperback publications of its kind, and it was widely distributed. All the civics classes of the city's school system received it. By the 1920s, the young people who had studied the Plan in their civics classes were voters, and they did not forget what they learned about the advantages of the Plan.

Publication of the *Plan of Chicago* so stimulated the city planning movement that within a few years a hundred American cities had appointed their own planning commissions. By 1920, city plans were the hallmark of almost every large city in the United States.

In 1922, Charles D. Norton and Frederick A. Delano, who had moved to New York, started the movement for a New York Regional Plan, financed by the Russell Sage Foundation. Norton became president and upon his death was succeeded by Delano, who later became one of the moving forces in the establishment of the American Planning and Civic Association and chairman of the National Capital Park and Planning Commission in Washington, D.C. Thus, the spirit of the Chicago Plan permeated city planning throughout the country.

But very few of these plans found even partial fulfillment. This was not to be the case in Chicago, where much that was planned was carried out. Even here, some of Burnham's Plan was never achieved, and much of it took many years.

The attempt to create three huge museums in Grant Park, for example, immediately fell afoul of A. Montgomery Ward. Ward's reputation as an environmentalist began in 1890 when the City Council erected scaffolding in Grant Park to load garbage and street sweepings into railroad cars. The Ward Tower at Michigan and Madison was directly opposite the park, and Ward filed suit to prevent this or any other building project from encroaching on the right of Chicagoans to an unobstructed lakefront. Ward's suit went to the Illinois Supreme Court before it was finally decided in his favor.

Three more legal battles were to follow, each generated by proposals for buildings in the park. One of these involved the Field Museum, for which the will of the late Marshall Field (who died in 1906) would furnish $8 million, provided the City Council could find a suitable site. It was for this reason that Burnham decided to locate the Field Museum in Grant Park.

Despite being labeled "an obstructionist, stubborn and eccentric," and "a public nuisance," Ward persisted in a battle which lasted 20 years and cost him a fortune. He based his suits on the original maps of the area, which showed that the land had been acquired from the federal government and which carried such notations as "Public Ground. Forever to remain vacant of buildings." Ward won every battle he waged for Grant Park.

Only one island was ever built in Lake Michigan—Northerly Island, now the site of Meigs Field. It was hardly a use that Burnham foresaw. However, several peninsulas, such as those at Belmont and Montrose Harbors, have been successfully completed. They, too, were part of the plan.

Freight stations were built instead of the four passenger stations planned west of Twelfth Street. However, the Dearborn and Grand Central stations were built just south of the Loop, and they functioned until 1970. The LaSalle Street Station, which was already in existence at the time of the Plan, is scheduled for removal in 1973. These three and the I.C. terminal have been merged into Union Station. Today there are only two railway terminals in Chicago.

A civic center, planned for what is now the Eisenhower Expressway at Halsted Street, never

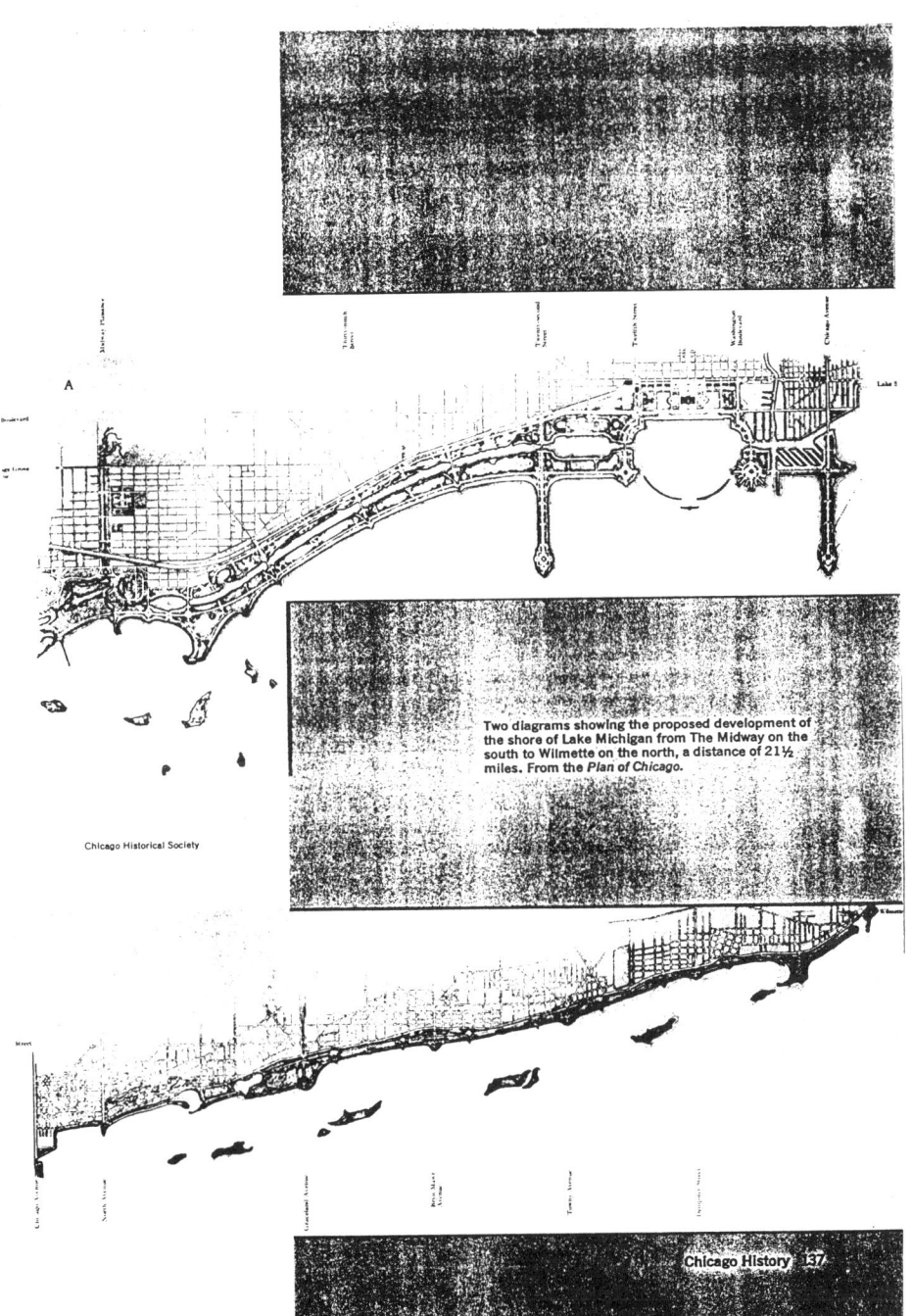

Two diagrams showing the proposed development of the shore of Lake Michigan from The Midway on the south to Wilmette on the north, a distance of 21½ miles. From the *Plan of Chicago*.

Chicago Historical Society

The 1909 Plan

came about. Obviously, with the enormous property investment in the Loop proper, it was next to impossible to move the City Hall, the courts, the county offices and the state offices one mile west and one mile south. A similar plan in 1954, to move the Civic Center to the north bank of the Chicago River and call it the Fort Dearborn Center, also failed—for the same reason. Every Loop property owner fought it tooth and nail.

So much of the 1909 Plan lay outside the city's boundaries that another body besides the city commission, designated by Burnham as the "Metropolitan Commission," was required. But it did not come into being until 1924, when the Chicago Regional Planning Association, a voluntary citizens' organization, was organized. It is interesting that Daniel Burnham, Jr., was one of its leading spirits and its principal backer. This voluntary association was succeeded by the official Northeastern Illinois Planning Commission in 1958—a great lapse of time.

On the positive side, the great sweep of the Lake Michigan shoreline, which evolved from the experience of the Columbian Exposition, is the most stunning success of the Plan. There was also the extension of the Forest Preserve System of Cook County. This system was actually conceived by Dwight H. Perkins, who served his apprenticeship in Burnham's office during the Columbian Exposition. Burnham imaginatively espoused it and made it a major part of his Plan.

The development of a double-decked ring road such as Wacker Drive was an excellent reason for removing the South Water Produce Market from the downtown area. When this congested and dirty marketplace was replaced by Wacker Drive, the central business district benefited enormously. A whole new area for expansion was realized, along with an efficient traffic artery to give it a new advantage. The South Water Market no longer received shipments on the waterfront and could operate more efficiently where it is now, alongside a railroad and an expressway.

Wacker Drive became a reality in the 1920s and was linked to the new Michigan Avenue. The land fill for Northerly Island and Burnham Park also became realities about the same time. They were to be the site of the 1933 Century of Progress Exposition. The plan also created a Congress Street axis on which the alignment of the Eisenhower Expressway followed, necessitating a pass-through portal when the central post office was constructed.

Momentum carried the Chicago Plan Commission along for nearly twenty years. But the Great Depression found Chicago with much left to do, and it was not until the federal government initiated work-relief projects that the Plan could near completion.

The lakefront improvement was one of the largest of these projects. The completion of the Outer Drive Bridge was another. But much remained unfinished. Subsequent plans in 1946 and 1966 updated the *Plan of Chicago*.

How good a plan was it? Lewis Mumford once referred to it as so much "municipal cosmetic," and reading it today, one can see its shortcomings. First, Burnham relied entirely on railroads for intercity movement but, strangely, did not provide for a consolidated railway passenger terminal. Instead, seven downtown stations were planned, two west of the Loop, one on the lakefront at Twelfth Street, and four more, as I have already noted, on Twelfth Street, south of the central business district.

No part of the plan provided for automobile parking. The planning of the railway passenger terminals, recreation areas, civic center, and central business district show no hint of the automobile age which was soon to come. Nevertheless, there was every indication by 1909 that automobiles would soon be a problem to city officials.

Chicago was and is the transportation center of the nation. The railway network was already established. The highway network was to

138 Chicago History

Chicago Historical Society

The Planning Committee of the Commercial Club of Chicago. On the right side of the table: Edward B. Butler, chairman; Daniel H. Burnham; Charles D. Norton; Clyde M. Carr; Edward F. Carry; Edward H. Bennett; John DeLaMater; Charles G. Dawes. On the left: John G. Shedd; Charles H. Thorne; Theodore W. Robinson; Emerson B. Tuttle; John W. Scott; John V. Farwell; Charles H. Wacker.

The 1909 Plan

become a nightmare shortly. It is a pity that Burnham did not foresee this problem.

Already in existence and badly in need of study and consideration by city planners were the slums and blighted areas of Chicago. Burnham and Bennett almost ignored the subject and apparently did not grasp the necessity to plan for their elimination and redevelopment. Burnham devoted only two paragraphs to the subject and his solution was only to recommend a "remorseless enforcement of sanitary regulations." It was Jane Addams, of famed Hull House, who started in 1890 to call attention to the city's slums. Her voice was finally heard, and playgrounds proposed in Burnham's Plan were built in the slums. Still, no effort or plan existed for slum eradication. Jane Addams and other social workers continued their effort for some time—and eventually, with the Great Depression, federal housing funds became available.

Some problems could not have been foreseen, resulting as they did from the enormous changes in technology and science. Although in 1909 the airplane was already a reality, we could not have expected Burnham to anticipate its future impact on cities and their metropolitan areas. Moreover, while voters continued to approve many of the necessary bond issues for implementing the Plan, some popular opposition developed to the widening of commercial streets and boulevards, which was denounced as favoring rich merchants.

In spite of some of the shortcomings to which I have referred, the city was opened up; more areas became accessible; recreational facilities were made available; the lakefront was saved. Burnham inspired Chicagoans to action on a great scale. This was the essence of his contribution.

What was Bennett's contribution to the Chicago Plan, which is almost always referred to as the "Burnham Plan"? Bennett seems to be the forgotten man. How did this come about and why?

For one thing, Daniel Burnham was an outgoing, strong, persuasive, gregarious, pragmatic leader. He was the one who made the contacts, who interested connections, who sold the plan; and he was the senior man, old enough to be Bennett's father. Still, was this sufficient reason?

In my search for answers, I went to see Edward Bennett, Jr., his son, who is also an architect. He suggested I might find some answers in his father's diaries, and generously offered to let me borrow them. I chose those volumes which I felt might be most relevant—the years 1906 through 1909. These were the years during which the plan was being prepared. Bennett's diaries reveal him to be a quiet, unassuming, highly disciplined, technically competent person. One can only guess that he took second place out of respect for his elder partner. Perhaps he had no need for self-aggrandizement; his technical work on the plan might have been satisfaction enough.

On the other hand, Bennett's capacity for leadership cannot be denied. After Burnham's death in 1912 and the dissolution of the firm, Bennett established an office of his own. He took in two partners and called the firm Bennett, Parsons & Frost. As the years passed, Bennett grew in stature and had a very successful career. He died in 1954.

What is most important is that together this pair made a rare team. Each complemented the other.

Acknowledgements: Of considerable value were Thomas Hines' unpublished dissertation, "Daniel Burnham, A Study in Cultural Leadership" (University of Wisconsin, 1970), which I was permitted to read at the Burnham Library of the Art Institute of Chicago; *Plan of Chicago*, with an Introduction by Wilbert Hasbrouch, and Charles Moore's *Daniel Burnham* (both, De Capo Press); and *Planning the Region of Chicago*, by Daniel H. Burnham, Jr., and Robert Kingery (Chicago Regional Planning Association).

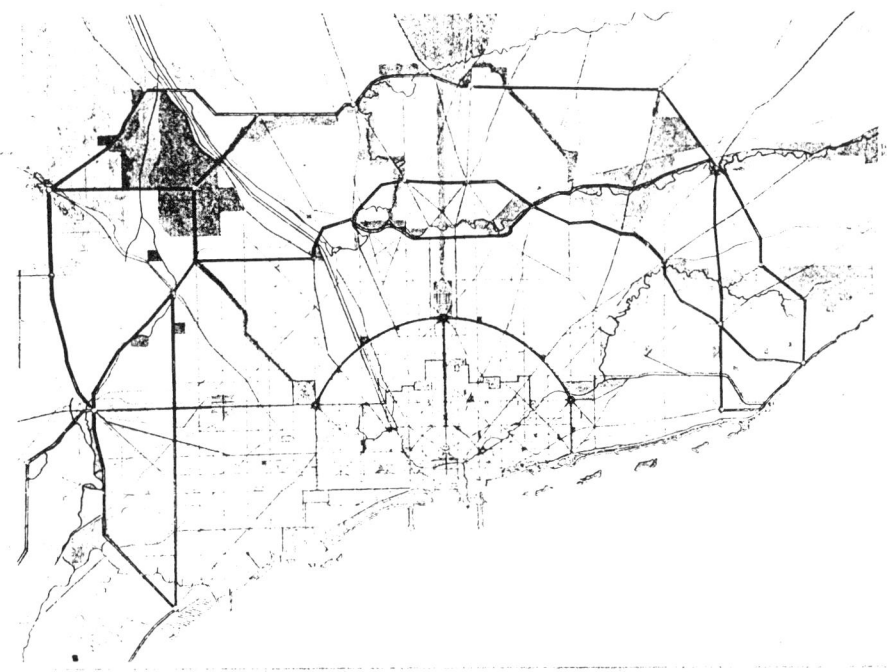

A map of the 1909 Chicago Plan, showing the civic center on Lake Michigan, the improved waterways and lake shore, the complete system of streets and arteries, and the forest preserve system. From *Plan of Chicago*.

Make no Little Plans; They have no magic to stir men's blood and probably themselves will not be realized. Make big plans; aim high in hope and work, remembering that a noble, logical diagram once recorded will never die, but long after we are gone will be a living thing, asserting itself with evergrowing insistency. Remember that our sons and grandsons are going to do things that would stagger us. Let your watchword be order and your beacon, beauty.
— Daniel Burnham

The Commercial-Civic Elite and City Planning in Atlanta, Memphis, and New Orleans in the 1920s

By BLAINE A. BROWNELL

THAT UPPER- AND MIDDLE-CLASS BUSINESS GROUPS HAD HEAVY HANDS in many reform schemes of the early twentieth century and sought to further their own social and economic interests under a mantle of efficiency, economy, and businesslike methods is no longer a new or surprising revelation. It has become, in fact, a prevailing historical orthodoxy. Historians differ, of course, concerning the motives of the groups and precise character of this phenomenon; but whether it be attributed to unmitigated economic self-interest, to a sweeping conservative social view along the lines of "corporate liberalism," or to a "bureaucratic vision" of a "paradise of new-middle-class rationality," its significance can hardly be denied.[1]

The influence of urban business groups in promoting city-manager and city-commission forms of municipal government in the early twentieth century in order to consolidate their interests, expand their power, and ensure efficient urban administration on business principles is one of the more convincing demonstrations of the involvement of social and economic elites in reform activities.[2]

---

[1] James Weinstein, *The Corporate Ideal in the Liberal State: 1900–1918* (Boston, 1968), 3; Robert H. Wiebe, *The Search for Order, 1877–1920* (New York, 1967), 170. Most historians have divided early twentieth-century reform into various elements. Wiebe suggests (p. 176) that the urban reform movement was composed of two major groups: "... one group used the language of the budget, boosterism, and social control, [and] the other talked of economic justice, human opportunities, and rehabilitated democracy." Melvin G. Holli makes a similar distinction between "structural reform" and "social reform" in his *Reform in Detroit: Hazen S. Pingree and Urban Politics* (New York, 1969), 157–81.

[2] See especially James Weinstein, "Organized Business and the City Commission and Manager Movements," *Journal of Southern History*, XXVIII (May 1962), 166–82; Samuel P.

MR. BROWNELL is associate professor of history and urban studies and chairman of the Department of Urban Studies at the University of Alabama in Birmingham. The author is indebted to a grant from the Penrose Fund of the American Philosophical Society and to the Institute of Southern History at the Johns Hopkins University, where he was a senior fellow, 1971–1972.

THE JOURNAL OF SOUTHERN HISTORY
Vol. XLI, No. 3, August 1975

And the search continues for other, similar examples. Strangely, one of the most notable of urban "reform" efforts—certainly, among those which continued into the 1920s—has been all too frequently ignored. Leading commercial and civic groups were, in fact, apparently more prominent and influential in the early attempts to solve urban ills and direct future development through systematic, comprehensive city planning than they were in the revisions of municipal government. In most American cities chambers of commerce, merchants' associations, businessmen's clubs, and other major civic organizations were in the forefront of the city-planning movement, impressing it with their values, goals, and concepts and providing in many cases its initial talent and resources.

The first permanent, official city-planning commission in the United States was established in Hartford, Connecticut, in March 1907. Quickly, cities across the country moved toward planning as a means of alleviating blight, population density, poor transportation, and confusing patterns of land utilization. Many of these functions were not new: building restrictions of various kinds, park projects, and particular arrangements of public structures and streets dated back to the eighteenth and nineteenth centuries. The new element was the *comprehensive* plan, which ideally took virtually every phase of the city's life into account—including railroads, streets, housing, recreation, subdivisions, buildings, and civic art—and which by 1915 had become the fashion. An earlier emphasis on the "city beautiful," stressed by national spokesmen like Charles Mulford Robinson and by local women's groups and focusing on civic art, architecture, and amenities, was rapidly replaced by a concern for the "city efficient," for functionalism rather than aesthetics.

The essential dimensions and style of the modern comprehensive plan were evidenced in the impressive design for Chicago by Daniel Hudson Burnham and Edward Herbert Bennett from 1907 to 1909. Though it included many features of city beautification, such as extensive "pleasure parkways," it also emphasized efficient traffic circulation, a new system of freight handling, the consolidation of railroad facilities, building restrictions to protect property, the necessity for new subdivision regulation, and neighborhood schools. It also dealt with a large metropolitan area rather than simply a group of public buildings or a limited collection of parks. And by 1910 American city planners were highly interested in

---

Hays, "The Politics of Reform in Municipal Government in the Progressive Era," *Pacific Northwest Quarterly*, LV (October 1964), 157–69.

regulating patterns of land use through the adoption of European zoning schemes.³

Typically, local attempts at city planning were initiated by strictly commercial groups like chambers of commerce or by a number of voluntary business and civic bodies. Largely in response to these early efforts, an official or unofficial planning agency was established by the municipal government, its membership composed of unpaid, "public-spirited" citizens and, occasionally, a city-planning expert. After a suitable plan was devised the planning commission and the groups which originally sponsored it sought broad public support through a program of concentrated publicity. Invariably, the arguments advanced in support of city planning included efficiency, economy, businesslike management, functionalism, and an underlying theme of social control. Burnham's Chicago plan, for example, was developed under the auspices of the Commercial Club and, more specifically, with the aid and support of Charles Dyer Norton, an insurance executive, Frederic Adrian Delano, president of the Wabash Railroad, and Charles Henry Wacker, a wealthy merchant. According to one authority the city envisioned in Burnham's plan was "an essentially aristocratic city, pleasing to the merchant princes who participated in its conception but not meeting some of the basic economic and human needs."⁴

Commercial organizations quickly recognized that city planning was "directly connected" with "industrial and commercial work." Savings gained through managerial efficiency and new production techniques could be lost in congested streets and transportation foul-ups; unregulated land use could undermine property values and the security of investments; and inadequate facilities and amenities might not appeal to new industries and workers.⁵ In addition, commercial and civic groups saw in city planning a chance to inspire new enthusiasm, larger memberships, and additional influence in urban affairs for themselves. As a former officer of the Pittsburgh Chamber of Commerce put it, city planning represented "to these leading industrial associations an opportunity to take a new and more commanding place for the benefit of their

---

³ Burnham and Bennett, *Plan of Chicago*, edited by Charles Moore (Chicago, 1909); Benjamin C. Marsh, *An Introduction to City Planning: Democracy's Challenge to the American City* (New York, 1909); Mel Scott, *American City Planning Since 1890* (Berkeley and Los Angeles, 1969), 100–109.

⁴ Scott, *American City Planning*, 101, 108 (quotation); Miriam I. Ross, "A Primer of City Planning Progress and Legislation," *American City*, XXVIII (February 1923), 131–33.

⁵ George B. Ford, "Chambers of Commerce and City Planning," *American City*, X (May 1914), 448–49. Ford was a member of the city planning committee of the Merchants' Association of New York.

communities than has ever before been offered them."[6]

The significance of city planning for urban history, however, goes beyond this important connection between the local planning movement and upper-class economic concerns. It reveals in a particularly coherent way the responses of commercial and civic leaders to a specific historical situation and reflects their concepts of the urban community at a time when the twentieth-century American metropolis was being formed.

This essay concerns city planning in the urban South during the 1920s and focuses on the cities of Atlanta, Memphis, and New Orleans. The major characteristic of these cities as they approached the third decade of the century was growth, whether measured in population or territorial terms. Between 1900 and 1920 the populations of Atlanta, Memphis, and New Orleans grew by 123, 59, and 35 percent, respectively. Memphis more than doubled its land area through annexation in 1899 and expanded by another 59.3 percent in the next twenty years. Likewise, Atlanta's territory grew by 143.6 percent in the same period. By 1920 New Orleans remained the largest city in the region with a population of 387,219, while Atlanta (200,616) had displaced Memphis (162,351) as the second largest urban center in the Southeast.[7]

The 1920s was in some respects a crucial period for many southern cities. The frequent annexations of the late nineteenth and early twentieth centuries had swelled city boundaries and populations and escalated the demands on municipal authorities for streets, water and gas lines, sewers, police and fire protection, and streetcar service. Neighborhoods were uprooted or transformed, industries converged on residential areas, and business coveted desirable properties along heavily traveled thoroughfares. Growth by annexation was not usually "organic," in the parlance of the time, but was by the addition of seemingly indigestible chunks of land and people, some of which were organized into fairly autonomous communities.

This was urban growth on a grand scale, but it was often chaotic and without visible design. Most importantly, perhaps, southern cities were experiencing for the first time a confrontation between a still accelerating trend toward urban centralization and a new and growing capacity for decentralization provided by technological

---

[6] Richard B. Watrous, "The Responsibilities of Commercial Organizations in Furthering the Adoption of City Plans," *American City*, II (May 1910), 229–31; quotation on page 229.

[7] *Fourteenth Census of the United States . . . 1920*, Vol. III: *Population* (Washington, 1922), 222, 399, 970; Roderick D. McKenzie, *The Metropolitan Community* (New York, 1967), 336–38. The city of Birmingham, by contrast, experienced population growth in the same period of 365 percent and an expansion in land area of over 678 percent.

innovations. These contradictory tendencies, embodied in the skyscraper and the motor vehicle, promised unprecedented urban growth and social transformation and inspired attempts by southern urban elites to lay new foundations of social order and to deal, if only indirectly, with some troubling implications of growth and "progress." Members of the commercial-civic elite thus regarded comprehensive city planning as an essential tool to shape and order the twentieth-century metropolis.

The Memphis City Planning Commission pointed specifically to the annexations of 1899, 1909, 1913, 1917, and 1919 as reasons for a coherent program of orderly development. New Orleans commissioners, noting their city's status as the nation's fourth largest in terms of corporate area, complained of the "growing difficulty in the management of this vast territory in providing means for people to get around, in giving them suitable places in which they may live and work."[8]

It was not until the 1920s that a significant number of American urban areas contracted for comprehensive plans, and this was reflected in the South as it was in other regions of the country.[9] In January 1919 the North Carolina General Assembly passed legislation enabling municipalities to establish official planning bodies, and twelve towns and cities did so by 1930.[10] City-planning committees appeared in Atlanta and Memphis in 1920 and in Nashville a year later. In some cases mayors appointed advisory groups even before they received legislative approval. Thus, the first official commission in Nashville was not established until 1925, and legislative enactment followed rather than preceded the appointment of unofficial commissions in Atlanta and Memphis. Knoxville and New Orleans created authorized commissions in 1923, and the Crescent City committee was reorganized in 1927. Charleston established a City Planning and Zoning Commission in 1929. Though Birmingham failed to initiate a comprehensive plan during the decade, the city did create a zoning board and adopted a traffic plan recommended by an outside consultant in 1927.

While very much a part of the national planning trend, the South contained relatively few city-planning committees by the end of the

---

[8] Memphis City Planning Commission, *First Annual Report: City Planning Commission, Memphis, Tennessee, 1921* (Memphis, 1921), 2; New Orleans City Planning and Zoning Commission, *Major Street Report* (New Orleans, 1927), 8.

[9] The best overall survey of modern city planning in the United States is Scott, *American City Planning*; see especially pages 110–269.

[10] Kay Haire Huggins, "City Planning in North Carolina, 1900–1929," *North Carolina Historical Review*, XLVI (Autumn 1969), 391–92. I am grateful to Philip R. Muller for bringing this article to my attention.

decade. The U. S. Department of Commerce reported 786 official planning commissions throughout the country in 1930; but only 71 of these were located in the eleven former Confederate states. Massachusetts, New York, California, Ohio, and Pennsylvania together accounted for 447 city planning commissions, but Texas had only 17 (the largest number for a southern state), and Alabama and Louisiana had but two each. Nevertheless, by the end of the 1920s some 36 towns and cities in the South had enacted zoning ordinances, and Atlanta, Memphis, New Orleans, Knoxville, Mobile, and Charleston, among other regional cities, had active, official planning committees.[11]

In every major southern city commercial and civic organizations, especially chambers of commerce, were highly visible and important in the planning movement. Of the municipalities which formed planning commissions in North Carolina during the decade local chambers of commerce were extremely influential in at least seven. Members of the local elite were prominent in virtually every city-planning effort in the state.[12] Similarly, the Nashville planning committee was partly a product of discussions within the Exchange Club and the Chamber of Commerce, and Knoxville's Board of Commerce could justifiably take credit for the formation of an official planning body and the completion of a comprehensive plan for the city in 1929.[13]

Atlanta entered the twentieth century with a record of growth that was the envy of lesser cities throughout the region. But she also suffered from the accumulated problems attendant upon growth, including a dearth of parks and recreational areas and a maze of streets and railroads in the central business district. A plan initially proposed in 1909 by Haralson Bleckley, president of the Atlanta Architectural Arts League, to construct a downtown civic center and plaza of shops, restaurants, offices, and hotels above the railroad tracks in the city's core absorbed most of the energies of local civic bodies until 1917, when the idea was finally rejected by the State Road Commission.[14]

---

[11] Lester G. Chase, comp., *A Tabulation of City Planning Commissions in the United States* (Washington, 1931), 1-2, 7-39.

[12] Huggins, "City Planning in North Carolina," 389-90, 392-93.

[13] *Nashville This Week*, I (November 9-16, 1925), 5; Nashville City Council Minutes (Office of the Metropolitan Clerk, Nashville, Tenn.), August 18, 1925, XXII, 360-61; *Nashville Review*, III (September 15, 1921), 9; Lyndon E. Abbott and Lee S. Greene, *Municipal Government and Administration in Tennessee* (Knoxville, 1939), 27-28; Knoxville *Journal and Tribune*, March 25, 1920.

[14] Thomas M. Deaton, "Atlanta During the Progressive Era" (unpublished Ph.D. dissertation, University of Georgia, 1969), 405-407; Walter G. Cooper, *Official History of Fulton County* ([Atlanta], 1934), 441; *City Builder* (Atlanta), I (January 1917), 9; V (May 1920), 22-24; Robert R. Otis, "Atlanta's Plan, 1909-1932" (mimeographed diary, Georgia State

Organizations like the Presidents' Club, composed of chief executives of Atlanta's civic groups, continued to discuss the matter, however, and the Chamber of Commerce, with a membership of 2,890 in 1920, did not relax its efforts for city planning. William J. Sayward, who had recently opened his architectural practice in the Gate City, headed a chamber committee devoted to urban planning and housing conditions in 1919 and consistently promoted the formation of an official municipal planning body. In an address to a chamber gathering in December 1919 Mayor James Lee Key asked the members of the organization, "as representing the public and commercial interests of the city," to help achieve a city plan. As a result of this meeting the first full-scale Atlanta city-planning commission was formed early the following year. "This Commission will be composed of men and women who are thoroughly representative of all interests of the city . . . ," the chamber magazine announced. "The job they have been asked to do is just about the biggest and most important that was ever asked of an Atlanta committee."[15]

Composed of twenty-four members—eight appointed by the president of the Chamber of Commerce, eight by the mayor, and eight by the Fulton County Board of Commissioners—the planning committee elected John William Grant, a former alderman and chairman of the city finance committee, as chairman. Louis P. Marquardt, an attorney and labor representative, and Mrs. Samuel Lumpkin, a prominent civic leader, were designated vice-chairmen. Kendall Weisiger, who headed the efficiency department of the Southern Bell Telephone Company, was named secretary. All but Marquardt were appointed to the commission by the original twenty-four members in an obvious effort to secure leadership with extensive ties to the city's civic and political elite. Other members included Mell R. Wilkinson, the permanent head of the Presidents' Club and a former president of the Chamber of Commerce; two other former presidents and several past officers of the chamber; representatives from the three daily papers; the president of the Rotary Club and a member of its Board of Directors; the head of the Georgia Automobile Association; a former president of

---

Library, Atlanta), 1, 4-5. My account differs somewhat from Deaton's, which relies primarily on Franklin M. Garrett, *Atlanta and Environs: A Chronicle of Its People and Events* (3 vols., New York, 1954), II, 684-86.

[15] Cooper, *Official History of Fulton County*, 802-803, 386; *City Builder*, IV (May 1919), 8; *Atlanta Constitution*, January 6, 1920. The chamber's announcement of the commission and Mayor Key's remarks are in *City Builder*, IV (January 1920), 5-6. A good general presentation of business ideology in Atlanta relating to city planning and other subjects is Charles P. Garofalo, "Business Ideas in Atlanta, 1916-1935" (unpublished Ph.D. dissertation, Emory University, 1972).

the Atlanta Real Estate Board; a city alderman; and two women civic leaders. All in all, fifteen of the commissioners were members of the Chamber of Commerce, and the planning body was immediately endorsed by all leading commercial and civic organizations. In its first meeting the new commission elected the mayor, the chairman of the Fulton County Board of Commissioners, and Eugene Robert Black, president of the Chamber of Commerce, as ex officio members. No blacks were appointed to the commission.[16]

Given responsibility for studying problems of housing, schools, street paving, crosstown thoroughfares, the water system, and city traffic, the unofficial commission began its work in an atmosphere of optimism. However, the commission lasted barely six months. Its large membership proved "unwieldy" and "unworkable," it lacked funds to hire consultants, and its meetings apparently suffered from considerable absenteeism. In August 1920 the state legislature approved an official planning commission for Atlanta, and on October 12 Mayor Key appointed six prominent local citizens to the new committee.[17]

Robert R. Otis, builder and manager of the Peachtree Arcade, a large enclosed shopping mall which opened in 1918, and a former president of both the Atlanta Real Estate Board and the Rotary Club, was elected acting chairman of the commission. The appointment of United States Senator Hoke Smith, secretary of the interior under Grover Cleveland and twice governor of Georgia, obviously heightened the potential political influence of the new planning body. Smith's background in local affairs corresponded closely, however, with that of most other members. A lawyer and financier, he had considerable real estate interests in Atlanta, most notably the Piedmont Hotel. He was a member of the Chamber of Commerce, a director of the Fulton National Bank, and a member of the Atlanta School Board after returning to Atlanta in 1921.[18]

Perhaps the most notable member of the commission, and certainly one of Atlanta's most remarkable citizens, was Joel Hurt. Arriving in the city in 1875 at the age of twenty-five, Hurt established a real estate and insurance business, organized and managed the Atlanta Building and Loan Association in 1879, the Atlanta Home Insurance Company in 1882, and the East Atlanta Land

---

[16] *City Builder*, IV (February 1920), 5, 7; Atlanta Chamber of Commerce, *List of Members* (Atlanta, 1918); Atlanta *Journal*, February 11, 14, 1920.

[17] Atlanta *Constitution*, February 10, 1920; *City Builder*, V (February 1921), 23; Otis, "Atlanta's Plan," 6; Garrett, *Atlanta and Environs*, II, 777.

[18] Dudley Glass, ed., *Men of Atlanta* (Atlanta, 1924), pages unnumbered; Garrett, *Atlanta and Environs*, III, 95; Atlanta Chamber of Commerce, *List of Members* (1918).

Company in 1886. A man of seemingly boundless energies and ambition, Hurt has usually been credited with constructing the South's first skyscraper (the Equitable Building) in 1891-1892 and with developing Inman Park, Atlanta's first residential suburb, and Druid Hills, an even more ambitious outlying residential community. His final accomplishment, completed at the time of his death in 1926, was the Hurt Building.[19]

Other members of the commission were Charles A. Wickersham, president of the Atlanta and West Point Railroad and the Western Alabama Railroad; Frank A. Pittman, secretary and treasurer of the Pittman Construction Company and a former municipal building inspector and city councilman; and Fred J. Terry, who, according to one newspaper account, was "prominently identified with the labor interests of the city." In 1921 Robert Harvey Whitten of Cleveland was engaged as a planning consultant to the commission, and a year later Otis began a series of brief newspaper articles to educate the citizenry on the principles of planning and to draw attention to planning efforts in other cities, especially St. Louis, Cleveland, and Detroit.[20]

The membership of Atlanta's major planning committees reveals a pattern consistent with the experience of other large southern cities. Though efforts were made to include prominent female civic leaders and at least one representative of "labor," the majority of commissioners were affiliated with the white, male, commercial-civic elite. Moreover, they were often associated with real estate development, construction, transportation, and banking—endeavors with more then an incidental interest in the physical development of the city. The financial and social connections of the overwhelming majority of commissioners were primarily local and were concentrated both in the central business district and, actually or potentially, in subdivisions on the urban periphery. Urban planning commissions in the South, in other words, drew most heavily on those local individuals and groups who had considerable ex-

---

[19] Garrett, *Atlanta and Environs*, III, 572-73; Elizabeth Anne Mack Lyon, "Frederick Law Olmsted and Joel Hurt: Planning the Environment in Atlanta, 1892-1894" (unpublished paper presented to the Southeast American Studies Conference, Atlanta, April 27-29, 1972), 2-3, 5; Rich Beard, "Hurt's Deserted Village: Atlanta's Inman Park, 1885-1911" (unpublished paper presented to the Southeast American Studies Conference, Atlanta, April 27-29, 1972), 6, 11, 23-24. I am indebted to Dana F. White for providing me with copies of the papers presented at the conference. For an exhaustive survey of commercial buildings in Atlanta, see Elizabeth Anne Mack Lyon, "Business Buildings in Atlanta: A Study in Urban Growth and Form" (unpublished Ph.D. dissertation, Emory University, 1971).

[20] Garrett, *Atlanta and Environs*, III, 127; *Atlanta City Directory, 1920* (Atlanta, 1920); Atlanta *Journal*, October 12, 1920; Raymond W. Torras, "City Planning Commission," Atlanta *Tribune* (August 1929), 36; Otis, "Atlanta's Plan," 17-18.

perience in finance, transportation, and land development and who were most interested in the consequences of a comprehensive urban design. Conflict of interest was never mentioned and probably was never seriously considered; the backgrounds of such men and women were thought to be positive advantages in promoting the urban welfare. Members of the commercial-civic elite certainly considered themselves "public spirited," and it would never have occurred to them that they might not be capable of representing the interests and concerns of the entire city.

The leading commercial and civic groups in Memphis also demonstrated significant interest in city planning by 1919. The Memphis City Club created a number of standing committees to deal with specific aspects of city planning and recommended that various civic groups join to promote the appointment of an official planning commission. The Engineers' Club adopted a resolution on December 1 supporting a comprehensive plan and forwarded it to the City Club for consideration. Such a plan seemed necessary, the resolution concluded, for "relief from increasing street congestion, solution of transportation problems between various portions of the city, prevention of [the] erratic spread of business enterprise, stabilizing of property values and proper co-ordination among the various interests which constitute city life and growth . . . ." City Club committees also met with similar groups from the Lions Club, the Kiwanis Club, the Rotary Club, the Engineers' Club, the Memphis Art Association, the Nineteenth-Century Club (a large women's organization), and the Chamber of Commerce.[21]

In the same year the chamber—which boasted 3,821 members in July and more than thirty standing committees, many of which dealt with aspects of city planning—established an active City Planning Committee of more than twenty members drawn from various civic organizations, thus, in the chamber's view, "making it representative of [the] entire City." Under the leadership of Wassell Randolph, a local attorney and businessman, the chamber committee initiated a number of meetings with the mayor and the city commissioners. Soon thereafter, on March 30, 1920, a nine-member City Planning Commission was established by municipal ordinance. A year later the commission was "constituted" as an official city agency by state law, the original commissioners being reappointed to staggered three-year terms.[22]

[21] City Club of Memphis, *Bulletin*, November 4, 25, December 30, 1919.

[22] Memphis Chamber of Commerce, *Annual Reports, 1919–1920* (Memphis, 1920), 33; Memphis Chamber of Commerce, *Journal*, II (January 1920), 294; III (May 1920), 108; City Club of Memphis, *Bulletin*, February 3, March 2, 1920; Memphis Board of Commissioners Minutes (City Hall, Memphis, Tenn.), Book G, 78.

"It may be said with becoming modesty," Randolph wrote, "that this [Chamber of Commerce City Planning] Committee is the forerunner of the City Planning Commission—that through the activities of this Committee resulting in several conferences with the City Commissioners, the Commissioners were influenced to give the City Planning Movement careful consideration, with the result that the need for a City Planning Commission became a conviction . . . ." The new commission in its first annual report attributed its origins to the election in 1920 of "a new administration of progressive business men" who had been "elected on a business administration platform," and who "drew largely from the civic organizations which had City Planning Committees" in determining the planning commission's membership. Indeed, Randolph was not only chairman of the new commission but also a former president of the City Club and an active member of the Chamber of Commerce Board of Directors. His civic and business activities included management of his father's properties, especially the Bishop Building, and membership on the University of Tennessee Board of Trustees in 1927.[23]

Other commissioners included Charles J. Haase, a real estate and insurance broker, financier, and president of the Home Building and Loan Association; Edward B. LeMaster, a major realtor and developer who helped organize the Memphis Real Estate Board in 1910 and served as its first president; Samuel Evan Ragland, president of the First National City Bank, founder of the Southern Trust Company (a real estate mortgage firm), and former president and largest stockholder in the Memphis *News-Scimitar;* Dan Wolf, owner of a commercial printing company and former labor editor of the Memphis *Commercial Appeal;* and Walk Claridge Jones, a prominent local architect who designed some two dozen of the city's major buildings. The two female commissioners were Mrs. Irby Bennett, a civic leader especially active in the Nineteenth-Century Club and wife of a prominent Memphis broker; and Mrs. Eleanor O'Donnell McCormack, one of the first presidents of the Nineteenth-Century Club, a former county superintendent of schools, president of the Tennessee Federation of Women's Clubs, Red Cross director, law school graduate, wife of a Memphis cotton dealer, and adviser to important figures in state and local govern-

---

[23] Randolph's comment is contained in Memphis Chamber of Commerce, *Annual Reports, 1919-1920*, p. 33; and the origins of local planning are traced in Memphis City Planning Commission, *First Annual Report,* 9. See also the Biographical Files (Memphis Room, Memphis Public Library); and "Memphis, the South's Paris," Memphis Chamber of Commerce, *Journal,* VII (October 1924), 31.

ment. Serving as ex officio members were the city engineer, the chairman of the Park Commission, and two city commissioners whose responsibilities included public utilities and streets. The commission contained eight members of the Chamber of Commerce and five members of the City Club.²⁴

The commission contracted with Harland Bartholomew of St. Louis for a comprehensive city plan in November 1920, and in April of the following year the members created two principal committees, one for streets and traffic and one for zoning. As the Memphis Chamber of Commerce *Journal* explained it, "The phenomenal growth and expansion taking place in Memphis demanded the services of a body of public spirited men to plan for the future, and correct present defects in our past growth."²⁵

In New Orleans the story was very much the same. The Association of Commerce, which claimed a membership of 4,709 in March 1920, appropriated $7,500 for city planning in 1917. Since most planning consultants were involved in war work, however, it was not until 1919 that the organization's Civic Bureau, headed by Charles Allen Favrot, a socially prominent engineer and architect descended from one of Louisiana's oldest families, was able to engage Philadelphia planner Milton Bennett Medary, Jr., to prepare an initial survey and publicize the importance of city planning. Medary's series of fifty-two articles began appearing in the Sunday issues of local papers in August 1919. In addition, the Civic Bureau completed surveys on schools, juvenile delinquency, and business and industrial properties to assist the consultant in his work.²⁶

Finally, in January 1923 the Association's City Planning Committee met with the New Orleans Commission-Council and shortly thereafter submitted an ordinance creating an official municipal planning body. In February the Commission-Council eliminated the ex officio memberships of various city officials (a move which apparently aroused some minor opposition), declared that all members "shall be real property taxpayers" and serve without compensation, and determined that commissioners should be appointed

²⁴ Biographical Files (Memphis Room, Memphis Public Library); Memphis Chamber of Commerce, *Classified List of Members, Business Mens' Club, Chamber of Commerce, 1916-1917* (Memphis, 1917).
²⁵ Harland Bartholomew and Associates, *A Comprehensive City Plan: Memphis, Tennessee* ([Memphis], 1924), 5; Memphis City Planning Commission, *First Annual Report*, 3; Memphis Chamber of Commerce, *Journal*, V (October 1922), 23.
²⁶ New Orleans Association of Commerce, *News Bulletin*, II (October 12, 1920), 10; II (June 21, 1920), 1; II (March 29, 1920), 3; John S. Kendall, *History of New Orleans* (3 vols., Chicago and New York, 1922), II, 790.

primarily from the city's commercial and civic organizations. The ordinance became law in May. The Association of Commerce took credit for most of these developments; it had expended close to $20,000 on city-planning projects and promotions between 1917 and 1923.[27]

As required by the ordinance, thirteen of the twenty members of the New Orleans City Planning and Zoning Commission were appointed as representatives of designated "leading commercial and civic organizations," including the Association of Commerce, the Board of Trade, the Cotton Exchange, the Contractors and Dealers Exchange, the Real Estate Agents Association, the New Orleans Federation of Clubs, the Young Mens' Business Club, and the Central Trades and Labor Council. (The New Orleans Real Estate Board had merged with the Association of Commerce in 1921.) Each of the designated thirteen organizations submitted a list of three names to the mayor, who then forwarded one name to the Commission-Council for approval. The ordinance also provided that seven representatives (including three women) were to be appointed at large. The commission's work was initially funded by contributions from local individuals and interested groups. Favrot was named chairman of the commission, and General Allison Owen, an architect and builder who belonged to most of the city's major civic clubs and served as president of the Association of Commerce in 1927 and 1932, was named vice-chairman. By 1927 the commission had included among its members (who were appointed for staggered five-year terms) fifteen members of the Association of Commerce and a number of engineers, real estate developers, and contractors. Virtually all of the seven commissioners appointed by the mayor were drawn from the city's commercial-civic elite.[28]

The annual reports of the commission provide an unusually rich source of information concerning its growing activities. During the first year it compiled all city ordinances relating to zoning, introduced a zoning enabling act into the state legislature, completed preliminary work on a zoning plan, held nine public hearings and fourteen general meetings, and received a $250 monthly operating allowance from the Commission-Council and an anonymous private gift of almost $2,000. Harland Bartholomew was engaged in

[27] New Orleans Association of Commerce, *News Bulletin*, V (January 16, 1923), 1; V (January 23, 1923), 2; V (February 6, 1923), 1, 8; V (July 24, 1923), 1; New Orleans *Item*, May 2, 4, 1923.

[28] New Orleans Association of Commerce, *News Bulletin*, V (May 8, 1923), 1, 4; New Orleans *Times-Picayune*, May 2, 1923; New Orleans City Planning and Zoning Commission, *Major Street Report* (New Orleans, 1927) 8; New Orleans Association of Commerce, *Red Book of New Orleans* (New Orleans, 1925); Kendall, *History of New Orleans*, II, 1191-93.

1926 to prepare a comprehensive plan, and the city increased its annual appropriation to $20,000. On June 6 the commission was reorganized by the municipal government: its membership was reduced to fifteen, and representatives of various government agencies were appointed. At the same time the city's annual financial support rose to $30,000, largely to cover Bartholomew's fees and expenses, and work proceeded on the preparation of maps and tables for the major street plan.[29]

The second official New Orleans planning commission retained seven members from the original body and added eight commissioners. Favrot and Owen continued as chairman and vice-chairman, respectively. The new commission's membership included two engineers, two architects, a banker, a real estate and mortgage broker specializing in city property, and one woman, the wife of the city purchasing agent. Ten of the commissioners were also members of the Association of Commerce.[30]

Emphasis on the city efficient was attributable not only to the functionalist movement among planners themselves but primarily to the interests and priorities established by their clients. "City planning," the Memphis *Commercial Appeal* observed in 1922, "really is given to making things useful, efficient and convenient." Rather than focusing on civic decoration, "real" city planning dealt with streets, zoning, and "many other things connected with the economy of population in the mass." Perhaps William J. Sayward of Atlanta said it best: "The city beautiful . . . is a very commendable ideal and one which should be assured its place; but we must not forget that the city beautiful must absolutely be founded on the 'city practical;' otherwise, there is no justification for any procedure along this line."[31]

In facing the consequences of rapid urban population and territorial growth established southern commercial and civic interests apparently had become by the 1920s less enamored of the boom-and-bust enthusiasm that vaulted small towns into great metropolises and more concerned with protecting property or consolidating gains in the mature city. This was no little transition; the business and civic groups that had emerged in the late-nineteenth-

---

[29] See mimeographed annual reports of the City Planning and Zoning Commission for July 17, 1923–August 31, 1924; September 1, 1924–June 30, 1925; July 1, 1926–June 6, 1927 (City Archives, New Orleans Public Library).

[30] New Orleans City Planning and Zoning Commission, *Major Street Report*, 5; New Orleans *Times-Picayune*, June 7, 8, 1927; New Orleans Association of Commerce, *Red Book of New Orleans* (1925).

[31] Memphis *Commercial Appeal*, February 18, 1922; Sayward, "City Planning Committee Urges Survey," *City Builder*, IV (January 1920), 12.

century urban South and had formerly gloried in all forms of growth and expansion simply had too much to lose and too little to gain from chaotic development in the early twentieth century. The development of the city and the forces and problems it spawned led to different notions of what the city should be and how its leaders should respond. The 1920s was a period, at least in the urban South, when commercial-civic elements began to look upon rampant growth as a potential problem rather than an invariable panacea, to consider the urban community as more delicate and vulnerable to dislocation and disorder.

This perception was not simply one of narrow economic interest; commercial-civic spokesmen did not, in fact, separate their concerns into social, economic, and political categories. The kind of city they envisioned secured property and facilitated their economic ambitions, but it also appealed to others in the city who were neither socially prominent nor economically prosperous. To attribute the conceptions of the urban community held by this elite solely to economic concerns or to defenses of free-enterprise capitalism would be a grievous error, similar to the defining of general social class interests in purely economic terms. With their faith in efficiency, organization, applied science, and businesslike methods and their interest in retaining a dominant role for themselves in urban society, members of the commercial-civic elite were appalled by the haphazard waste and potential dangers they saw in unregulated growth. At least some of them were disturbed that many municipalities took their basic shape, not from the decisions of enlightened community leaders, but from the meanderings of Indian trails and cow paths: ". . . instead of being laid out by the highest rate of intelligence . . . ," Sayward complained, the modern city "has in most cases been laid out, strange as it may seem, by the most primitive of minds." Commercial-civic spokesmen increasingly began to emphasize not only growth but "the economic value of a well ordered city."[32] Growth retained a hallowed place in the commercial-civic lexicon, but by the 1920s the principal challenge seemed to be to achieve a city that was both stable and expansive.

Matters of street transportation and zoning dominated the planning movement in the urban South, and most of the rest of the country, during the decade.[33] They formed the bulk of those com-

[32] Sayward, "City Planning Committee Urges Survey," 12–13.

[33] A questionnaire sent to the members of the New Orleans Association of Commerce in 1919 elicited a response that accorded higher priority to paving and street improvements than to the addition of new industries. New Orleans Association of Commerce, *News Bulletin*, I (June 16, 1919), 1.

prehensive plans drawn by Harland Bartholomew. Beginning his highly successful career in 1912 as an assistant engineer for the Newark, New Jersey, plan directed by Ernest Payson Goodrich and George Burdett Ford, Bartholomew became the engineer for the City Plan Commission of St. Louis in 1916 and started his private consulting practice three years later. His firm, Harland Bartholomew and Associates, was exceptionally active during the 1920s, completing comprehensive plans for thirty-two cities, including Kansas City, Pittsburgh, Toledo, and—in the South—Memphis, New Orleans, Chattanooga, Knoxville, and Orlando. His Memphis plan of 1924 became the prototype of his later efforts. Housing and "social" concerns were largely eliminated from his plans during the decade according to one writer, "leaving . . . a planning portfolio confined to the more acceptable objectives of the community's physical and functional reordering." Bartholomew later recalled that he "was not at complete liberty to introduce unusual new ideas and concepts in city planning, nor were the city plans produced exclusively my own work. We made a practice of having members of the city plan commissions participate extensively in the preparation of the comprehensive plan." Consequently, "the technical level of most plans was limited to what we could get the members of planning commissions to accept."[34]

The two major documents of the Memphis City Planning Commission prepared by Bartholomew reflected the principal concerns of the commercial-civic elite. A forty-two-page *First Annual Report* issued in 1921 contained a preliminary major-street plan, a transit proposal, and initial zoning studies; and Bartholomew's *Comprehensive City Plan* of 1924 was organized with attention to major streets, transit, transportation, recreation, zoning, and civic art, with the most detailed and extensive portions dealing with streets and zoning. Likewise, the 1922 annual report of the Atlanta City Planning Commission listed zoning as the top priority of

---

[34] Norman J. Johnston, "Harland Bartholomew: His Comprehensive Plans and Science of Planning" (unpublished Ph.D. dissertation, University of Pennsylvania, 1964), 7–24, 98–99, 122, 144, 154–55, 158, 181–82 (quotations on pages 158, 181–82). Johnston also notes (pp. 143, 150) that the commercial and civic influence on early city-planning efforts prevailed among other Bartholomew clients. In Wichita, Kansas, city planning was initiated through the efforts of the Board of Commerce and the Rotary Club, and the first planning studies in Hamilton, Ohio, were subsidized through subscriptions from the Chamber of Commerce. Bartholomew's firm accounted for almost a quarter of all comprehensive plans drawn in the nation in the first six years of the 1920s, and he served as the sixth president of the American City Planning Institute (the forerunner of the American Institute of Planners) from 1927 to 1929.

business, followed closely in importance by a general traffic plan.[35]

The street system was usually designated, as in Memphis, "the fundamental element" of the city plan, the "skeleton or framework of the city structure." A viable street network would include "main arterial thoroughfares" to carry the heaviest loads of motor traffic, "secondary (crosstown) thoroughfares" to funnel traffic into the main arteries, and "minor streets" to serve specific areas. A primary goal was to widen existing streets and construct new links between them. As the Atlanta planners put it, the "central business section of the city should have an approximate rectangular street layout, every street constituting the central portion of a main arterial thoroughfare." Bartholomew in his New Orleans plan emphasized that streets were by no means equal but served diverse and specialized functions. The main emphasis, he suggested, should be placed on the principal arteries. "Almost all metropolitan centers find it necessary," he wrote, "to designate major streets and devise plans for bringing them into coordinated use."[36]

Major-street plans in this period were aimed at increasing efficient traffic flow and vivifying the urban core. The downtown business district would be a "focal point" linking the main traffic arteries. Bartholomew was concerned, for example, that the locus of principal streets in New Orleans was somewhat removed from the central business section. "The aim," he noted, "is to create a series of wide, direct and well paved arteries radiating from this primary objective." Indeed, the planning metaphors of the 1920s were well chosen to reflect the conceptions of the modern metropolis which existed at the time. "The circulation of the urban body must be kept alive. Structural weaknesses in the arterial system, whatever their cause, bring about disorders which affect every phase of city life."[37]

[35] Memphis City Planning Commission, *First Annual Report;* Bartholomew et al., *A Comprehensive City Plan: Memphis;* Atlanta City Planning Committee, *Annual Report . . . 1922* (Atlanta, 1922), 5. As the decade wore on Bartholomew gave greater emphasis to streets and motor-vehicle transportation. The basic framework established in Memphis was retained in his comprehensive plan for Knoxville in 1929, but a chapter on "Parking and Traffic Problems in the Business District" was added. See Johnston, "Harland Bartholomew," 171; Harland Bartholomew and Associates, *A Comprehensive City Plan: Knoxville, Tennessee* ([Knoxville, 1929]).

[36] Memphis City Planning Commission, *First Annual Report,* 11, 19–28; Atlanta City Planning Commission, *Annual Report . . . 1922,* p. 6; New Orleans City Planning and Zoning Commission, *Major Street Report,* 56.

[37] New Orleans City Planning and Zoning Commission, *Major Street Report,* 56. Special street-transportation studies were also completed by outside consultants for Atlanta, Birmingham, Memphis, and New Orleans during the decade. See John A. Beeler, *Report to the City of Atlanta on a Plan for Local Transportation, December, 1924* (Atlanta, 1924); Ross W. Harris, "Traffic Survey on the Vehicular and Street Railway Traffic Situation of Birmingham" (unpublished manuscript, 1927, City Clerk's Office, Birmingham, Ala.);

The ideal street system facilitated travel toward the central city, centralized the patterns of urban mobility, and vitalized the downtown business district. It was also calculated to promote expansion, especially into previously undeveloped areas. Here the contradictory tendencies of the time, centrifugal and centripetal, were resolved in the paved street, which linked the center with the periphery; and the automobile became the means whereby each could reinforce the other. New Orleans planners, for example, were particularly interested in using the major-street system to exploit regions on the urban outskirts as well as "underdeveloped" areas near the city's core. Bartholomew discovered that the principal area of New Orleans contained 28,000 acres of land, of which only 12,000 were sufficiently developed. Of the remainder, 14,000 acres suffered from "incomplete drainage, sewerage and water services." He suggested that initial concern had to be with correcting past faults in the system, but the street plan should look toward the eventual development of these areas, toward a decentralization of population over a larger territory.[38]

Commercial-civic elements seemed to be quite concerned that the expanding populations of their cities and the accompanying commercial and industrial enterprises would simply compound the confusion that large numbers of people and motor vehicles had already created in the central city. It was through a coherent street plan that such consequences were, at least in part, to be avoided. With the eventual adoption of the Memphis plan, the commissioners fully expected in 1921 that "orderly development will have been made certain for the future. The ultimate in city progress, which in January of 1920 was merely discussed, will have become a reality."[39]

Zoning was a fundamental feature of city planning during the 1920s and was usually the first coercive power obtained by local planning bodies. Many communities, in fact, such as Birmingham, adopted a zoning ordinance and created a zoning board in the

---

Memphis Board of Commissioners Minutes, Book G, 46; John A. Beeler, "Report to the Commissioner of Public Utilities, City of New Orleans on the Street Railway Situation, 1923" (unpublished report, City Archives, New Orleans Public Library); Miller McClintock, "The Street Traffic Control Problem of the City of New Orleans" (mimeographed report, 1928, City Archives, New Orleans Public Library).

[38] New Orleans City Planning and Zoning Commission, *Major Street Report*, 36–37.

[39] Memphis City Planning Commission, *First Annual Report*, 10. Bartholomew's comprehensive plan for Des Moines, Iowa, in 1928 reflected a declining emphasis on minor streets and the addition of "by-pass streets." See Johnston, "Harland Bartholomew," 166–67. These would, of course, become especially prominent in the traffic designs of the 1930s and result eventually in the massive circumvential freeways of the interstate highway system of the 1950s and 1960s.

absence of any efforts toward a comprehensive plan. Zoning in the urban South was much more than the preservation of residential districts against the influx of commerce and industry, though this was obviously one of its avowed purposes. It was in a very real sense a principal tool for stabilizing and fashioning the metropolis, for fixing spatial arrangements, protecting investments and property values, easing the blight and confusion of "transitional" and "mixed" areas, segregating the races, and encouraging the orderly expansion and decentralization of the urban population while maintaining the vitality of the downtown business district.

The Memphis zoning law drawn by Bartholomew went into effect in November 1922 without great difficulty. But in New Orleans and Atlanta zoning ordinances were held up in the courts. New Orleans obtained zoning authority in the Louisiana constitution in 1921, but it was not until July 1923 that the city won the first major court test of its powers. Not until 1929, after two years and seven months of public hearings, was Bartholomew's revised statute adopted by the Commission-Council. In Atlanta the first zoning ordinance, passed in April 1922, was successfully challenged in the courts on the ground that it was an illegal interference with private property rights. An amendment to the state constitution was ultimately required to grant zoning authority to Georgia municipalities. Finally, in December 1928 a zoning law based upon the earlier ordinance was approved by the City Council.[40]

Real estate interests initially opposed zoning efforts in some cities, especially Atlanta, but a majority of real estate spokesmen in the urban South praised planning and zoning for guarding land investments. The Memphis City Planning Commission, for example, argued that "Areas now occupied or expected to be occupied for residential purposes . . . should most certainly be given the protection essential to their permanency of development through exclusion of industrial or commercial intrusions." The social and economic chaos of changing neighborhoods and the uncertainty of unregulated development were to be avoided if at all possible. And those members of the commercial-civic elite who sat on city-planning commissions were not loath to contemplate some restrictions on the prerogatives of private property, nor were many of

[40] New Orleans City Planning and Zoning Commission, "Handbook to the Comprehensive Zone Laws for New Orleans, Louisiana" (mimeographed volume, 1929, City Archives, New Orleans Public Library), Chap. IV, 3–4, 7–8; New Orleans City Planning and Zoning Commission, "Report on Factors Involved in Carrying out the City Plan," 29; Bartholomew *et al.*, *A Comprehensive City Plan: Memphis*, 117–21, 127; Wassell Randolph, "Municipal Zoning: Proposed Ordinance," Memphis Chamber of Commerce, *Journal*, V (May 1922), 37–38; Garrett, *Atlanta and Environs*, II, 839; Robert Whitten, "Atlanta Adopts Zoning," *American City*, XXVI (June, 1922), 541–42; Atlanta *Constitution*, December 22, 1928.

those voluntary groups which provided the initial impetus for planning. As Randolph observed, the "modern view" of city planning "is that the public can control the private use of realty as to prevent an owner making a use of his lot which will depreciate the value of his neighbors' lots." Zoning might "interfere with the plans of individuals," the Memphis Chamber of Commerce *Journal* commented in 1922, "the same as other phases of city planning will temporarily discommode some of the people whose property is affected. But this is the cost of progress, and today's loss, in any program of permanent improvement, is compensated by tomorrow's gain." City planning was likened to the process in "every large industry" of "logically planning the arrangement of its plant and equipment . . . ," and zoning was "merely the common sense application of this same universal principle of orderly arrangement to the development of our city."[41]

The Memphis plan zoned older residential areas on the edges of commercial and industrial regions for both single-family dwellings and apartments in order to "fix the character of these transitional districts." These intermediate areas could also serve as buffer zones between heavily business sections and the low-density residential regions at some distance from the urban core. The idea was to "give stability and character, as well as encouragement, to the proper development of the city."[42]

Spatial stability in the South also meant racial segregation. Like most American cities southern urban areas reflected informal patterns of spatial separation along racial lines. Randolph observed that most black neighborhoods in Memphis were found "in the lower ground bordering on the drainage courses." The rule "is that the colored population is found exclusively in the cheaper, less desirable sections of the city. Thus, we have a sort of natural zoning of the races."[43] However, these informal boundaries had a tendency to float with the tides of urban growth and change.

[41] Memphis City Planning Commission, *First Annual Report*, 15-16; Randolph, "Municipal Zoning; Proposed Ordinance," 37; Memphis Chamber of Commerce, *Journal*, V (August 1922), 51; (September 1922), 27; Johnston, "Harland Bartholomew," 163-64, 199. Also see Huggins, "City Planning in North Carolina," 392. Johnston maintains (p. 158) that by the time of the 1924 Memphis plan, "the whole idea-concept of community over private right as expressed by Bartholomew's earlier reports is obscured." Johnston is misled here by his reliance on Frederick Lewis Allen's portrait of the decade, for such an "idea-concept" is indeed found, even in southern business publications and in Bartholomew's plans for southern cities. The point is that the reordering and structuring of the city, the prevalence of community over private rights, was made to conform to commercial-civic interests, concerns, and priorities.

[42] Bartholomew *et al.*, *A Comprehensive City Plan: Memphis*, 123 (first quotation); Memphis City Planning Commission, *First Annual Report*, 16 (second quotation).

[43] Memphis City Planning Commission, *First Annual Report*, 7. For information on infor-

The first zoning law in Atlanta changed informal Jim Crow arrangements into a formal pattern of residential segregation. Residential areas were divided into white, black, and undetermined zones, while black servants' quarters in white neighborhoods and white property ownership in black sections were legally sanctioned. The plan, devised by Robert Whitten, was, according to *Survey* magazine, "the first to embody in an outspoken form segregation along the line of social composition of the population" and constituted a potential precedent for separating immigrants and other ethnic groups in northern and western cities.[44] Whitten defended the concept on the grounds that it was neither undemocratic nor antisocial. The creation of "colored districts" provided "adequate areas for the growth of the colored population" and encouraged blacks to develop "a more intelligent and responsible citizenship." Separation lessened the possibility of race riots and social upheaval, he claimed, and stabilized property values in transitional racial areas. "Hundreds of acres of land were left undeveloped or poorly developed in various parts of the city," he observed, "because of uncertainty...." Whitten also repeated a maxim of most planners of the time: "... wherever you have a neighborhood made up of people largely in the same economic status, you have a neighborhood where there is most independence of thought and action and the most intelligent interest in the neighborhood, city, state and national affairs."[45]

Zoning had been recognized for some time as a tool for fixing existing spatial arrangements, but it was not an arbitrary imposition of a static pattern. It was also a method for promoting urban expansion, of extending the city into surrounding territory and encouraging economic development. Height restrictions discouraged the rise of skyscrapers since, according to the planning theory of the time, such structures were "uneconomical" and "injurious to the community." By limiting building heights population density would be

---

mal and statutory residential segregation in Birmingham, see Carl V. Harris, "Reforms in Government Control of Negroes in Birmingham, Alabama, 1890-1920," *Journal of Southern History*, XXXVIII (November 1972), 571; *Zoning Ordinance of Birmingham, Alabama* (Birmingham, 1926), 12-15; *Birmingham News*, June 15, 1926; Blaine A. Brownell, "Birmingham, Alabama: New South City in the 1920s," *Journal of Southern History*, XXXVIII (February 1972), 29.

[44] "The Atlanta Zoning Plan," *Survey*, XLVIII (April 22, 1922), 114-15. Separation of population groups by zoning was not unprecedented before the 1920s. California municipalities employed crude zone districts to segregate Chinese immigrants in the 1880s. See Sam B. Warner, Jr., *The Urban Wilderness: A History of the American City* (New York and other cities, 1972), 28-29.

[45] Robert Whitten, letter to the editor, *Survey*, XLVIII (June 15, 1922), 418-19. According to the Atlanta City Planning Commission's *Annual Report ... 1922*, p. 4, residential segregation was adopted for "the promotion of public peace, order, safety and general welfare...."

lessened and urban residents dispersed over a larger area. Planning committees also sought through subdivision ordinances to direct the development of the city into peripheral sections, even beyond the municipal limits. In his Memphis plan Bartholomew wrote that "the primary purpose of city planning and zoning is to regulate and distribute the population of a city for the protection of health, safety and general welfare...." Planners in New Orleans were particularly anxious to populate those regions of the city which had only recently been rendered habitable by sewer and drainage improvements, and Atlanta planners devised their zoning ordinance to promote "the spreading out of the population" and prevent "excessive over-crowding in the tenement house areas...." In addition, sizable tracts were allocated for industry, and the major thoroughfares were zoned for commercial use, creating a ribbon pattern of business expansion throughout the city.[46]

The preparations involved in the Memphis zoning plan were fairly typical: an extensive survey of existing tendencies in land use was followed by the drawing of use, height, density, and land-value maps, as well as other specific studies. The emphasis, as one newspaper said of the New Orleans plan, was on "dividing the city into the zones with as little change as possible and with an eye to the natural growth of each activity." Order was the key word, though its substance was often attempted through the preservation of older patterns of land utilization. Thus, traditional habits of mixed land use in New Orleans were reflected in a plan that resembled less a streamlining than a crazy quilt of various zones. The extensive area south of the business district in Memphis, containing railyards, terminals, factories, and warehouses, was designated industrial and unrestricted; large blocks in the downtown area and along the major streets were zoned commercial; and most of the areas two to four miles outside the central section were set aside for residential use, primarily single-family dwellings. The heights of buildings tapered off abruptly the farther one moved away from the business district. This was essentially, of course, the land pattern of the twentieth-century metropolis, which zoning plans fully accepted and encouraged. As far as the planning commissioners were con-

---

[46] Bartholomew et al., *A Comprehensive City Plan: Memphis*, 124, 126; New Orleans City Planning and Zoning Commission, "Handbook to the Comprehensive Zone Laws," Chap. II, 2; New Orleans City Planning and Zoning Commission, *Major Street Report*, 34; Atlanta City Planning Commission, *Annual Report . . . 1922*, p. 4; Johnston, "Harland Bartholomew," 163–64. Johnston writes that securing approval for any type of zoning during the 1920s meant "buying off the business interests and the boosterism of their confident expectations of the times."

cerned, the city was endangered by such patterns only when they were uncontrolled and without direction.[47]

Comprehensive city planning obviously involved more than major streets and zoning, though these elements received by far the greatest emphasis. Recreational areas were exceptionally sparse in Atlanta and also to some extent in Memphis and New Orleans. Intensive land use in downtown New Orleans placed most parks in areas of low population density, thus underlining the advantages of urban decentralization. In Memphis, Bartholomew proposed a number of community centers, playgrounds, and small neighborhood parks and planned a major downtown park on "The Island," a small strip of land directly across the Wolf River from the central business district. Boulevards and scenic parkways were also included in his overall scheme. The riverfront areas in both Memphis and New Orleans, which were choked with railroad tracks, warehouses, and shipping docks, also received the planner's attention. Bartholomew's most ambitious vision, perhaps, entailed a totally renovated Memphis waterfront, with modified Greek temples at the river's edge rising dramatically to what has been described as "an acropolis effect on the bluffs." Some features of the city-beautiful emphasis were also retained, with plans in New Orleans for additional trees and monuments, the preservation of the Vieux Carré, and the elimination of billboards, sidewalk obstructions, and overhead electrical wires.[48]

Significantly, few of these proposals were ever acted upon. A successful Vieux Carré Commission was organized in New Orleans to protect the architectural character of the French Quarter, but such protection obviously had important economic as well as aesthetic advantages. Action came almost solely with respect to streets and zoning. Matters of housing, particularly for lower-income groups, were virtually ignored, even though dwelling shortages plagued most regional cities in the first years of the decade. The solutions offered for this problem were along the lines of increased mortgage capital and additional private construction. Parks and street improvements were concentrated in the central business district and

[47] Bartholomew et al., *A Comprehensive City Plan: Memphis*, 118-19, 116; New Orleans *Item*, July 17, 1923; New Orleans City Planning and Zoning Commission, "Handbook to the Comprehensive Zone Laws," Chap. V, 29; Randolph, "Municipal Zoning; Proposed Ordinance," 37-38.

[48] New Orleans City Planning and Zoning Commission, *Major Street Report*, 45, 40; Bartholomew et al., *A Comprehensive City Plan: Memphis*, 93-115, 132-33; Virginia Phillips, "Rowlett Paine, Mayor of Memphis, 1920-1924," West Tennessee Historical Society, *Papers*, XIII (1959), 103 (quotation); New Orleans City Planning and Zoning Commission, "The Plan for Civic Art" (mimeographed report, April 8, 1931, City Archives, New Orleans Public Library), 31.

in white neighborhoods, ignoring many crucial needs of the significant black populations in these cities. Finally, in the press of their more immediate concerns, southern city-planning commissions never seriously considered plans for schools, waterworks, and other important municipal facilities, though a series of bond issues in Atlanta, Memphis, and New Orleans generally recommended the expansion of such services. Planning commissions did, however, make recommendations on street-railway routing.

The city planning adopted with such alacrity by the urban commercial-civic elite was hardly an unqualified success. It was fraught with problems and difficulties that deepened during the 1920s and into the depression years. Municipal governments and state legislatures were often reluctant to grant power or autonomy to city-planning bodies, and the advocates of city planning were themselves soon caught up in the policy wrangles which accompanied ambitious schemes of this sort.

City-planning commissions were usually empowered to survey urban conditions, draw up plans and recommend ordinances, review street projects and land subdivisions, and in some cases act as review boards on the zoning statutes. The Atlanta commission's authority extended to an area six miles beyond the city limits. The actions of the commissions, however, were completely subject to the approval of the municipal governments, without which none of their decisions had the force of law. Bartholomew noted in his Memphis plan that without politically astute leadership on the planning commission neither the general public nor elected officials would abide by the substance of the comprehensive design. Similarly, the New Orleans commission warned that without "general acquiescence" in planning policies "individual and local interests will gradually bring about changes and amendments for selfish reasons until the entire scheme has been vitiated." And this, of course, was "the very sort of practice that has brought American cities to their present state of physical deficiencies." To preclude this possibility the commission recommended the formation of voluntary citizens' committees to support actively and publicly the comprehensive plan and its enforcement.[49]

Atlanta never adopted a comprehensive plan during the decade, though local planning advocates did achieve a zoning ordinance and a new street-numbering system. In a letter to the mayor in late

---

[49] See Bartholomew et al., *A Comprehensive City Plan: Memphis*, 137–39; *The Charter and Ordinances of the City of Atlanta. Code of 1924* (Atlanta, 1924), 132–33; New Orleans City Planning and Zoning Commission, "Report on the Factors Involved in Carrying out the City Plan," 26–27.

1931 Robert Otis complained that Atlanta, "in the absence of sustained effort, fixed policy and sufficient funds, is still without a definite Plan for its growth." Bartholomew lamented in 1939 that the Gate City lagged twenty years behind other urban areas in the progress of its planning efforts. Planning commissions complained constantly of inadequate funding, public misunderstanding, and the intransigence of public officials. Carrying out the major features of the street plans, and especially the time-consuming and politically delicate enforcement of zoning laws, drained many planning bodies of their energies and prevented a genuinely comprehensive approach to urban ills. From the beginning Atlanta's commission "became immersed in zoning matters," according to Otis, "which forced a separation of the two into distinct boards." Long-range planning gave way, in other words, to immediate, piecemeal changes. Even in Memphis, where Bartholomew completed a major revision of his plan in 1940, many provisions were left unfulfilled. A newspaper study in 1947 found fifteen of the city's streets significantly improved as Bartholomew recommended, but twenty others were virtually unimproved, and thoroughfares that ran east and west had received more attention than those which ran north and south. The formation of city-planning commissions had been heralded throughout the urban South, at least among spokesmen for the commercial-civic elite, as ushering in a "new epoch" in city development, but these expectations were not to be fulfilled during the 1920s.[50]

One principal reason for the sudden collapse of many local planning activities at the end of the decade was, of course, the arrival of economic depression. Bartholomew's contract with the New Orleans commission was terminated in January 1930, and a year later the commission's annual budget was reduced from $20,000 to $7,500. The Commission-Council appropriated $6,000 in 1934 for printing the zone handbook and planning surveys, but this was never done. Likewise, the Atlanta commission's 1931 proposal for the extension and widening of over seventy streets at an estimated cost of $3,600,000 came at a most inopportune time.[51]

Though city planning during the 1920s was not entirely successful, it did reveal in its expressed purposes and policies the aspirations and concerns of the commercial-civic elite who fashioned and

[50] Otis, "Atlanta's Plan," 19, 20; Garrett, *Atlanta and Environs*, II, 820; Atlanta *Constitution*, December 13, 1939; Memphis *Press-Scimitar*, October 6, 1947; New Orleans *Times-Picayune*, June 22, 1923.

[51] See mimeographed annual reports of the New Orleans City Planning and Zoning Commission (City Archives, New Orleans Public Library), for 1930, 1931, and 1933; Otis, "Atlanta's Plan," 24-25.

supported it. Cities, "like all living organisms," Bartholomew wrote in the Memphis plan, "must either progress or decay." This familiar maxim of urban boosterism, linking progress and population growth, was very much alive in large southern cities, but the members of city-planning commissions were also apprehensive lest unregulated growth, given the complexities of the modern metropolis, lead ultimately to deterioration. Unless cities provided adequate facilities for traffic, education, recreation, and public health, the Atlanta *Journal* feared, "its very progress will become a penalty. Material expansion is worthwhile only to the extent that it is accompanied by inner civic advancement."[52]

Unbridled individualism was equated in planning reports with anarchy, and a state of "disorderly development" that may have been tolerable in the early stages of a city's life became unacceptable in the mature metropolis. Atlanta's "pioneering days are over," Sayward wrote, "its future is assured and its continued commercial supremacy cannot be doubted. This is the time for Atlanta, as it has been for all progressive cities, to take stock of herself with particular regard to those values which exist beyond the mere supply of bread and butter for our stomachs or clothes for our backs." Earlier necessities had dictated a chaotic urban arrangement that had "not kept pace with our commercial progress." All of which somehow led Sayward to the question: "Shall we permit ourselves to go down in history as a nation of traders simply like the Phoenicians or the Carthaginians, or shall we aspire to something like the measures of Athens and Rome?" References to antiquity aside, the principal concerns of commercial-civic spokesmen and their planners in the 1920s were precisely those of bread and butter and social order. They had come to believe, as Bartholomew wrote in his Memphis plan, that "Uncontrolled growth invites chaos and economic disaster."[53]

Planning commissions in Atlanta, Memphis, and New Orleans sought to achieve both stability and expansion, attract new industry and populations, ensure property values, curtail threats to the established order (whether social discontent or chaotic growth), and continue control of urban affairs in the hands of the commercial-civic elite. All this could presumably be achieved through the application of scientific expertise and businesslike methods under the

---

[52] Bartholomew et al., *A Comprehensive City Plan: Memphis*, 137; *Atlanta Journal*, February 13, 1920.

[53] New Orleans City Planning and Zoning Commission, "Handbook to the Comprehensive Zone Laws," Chap. I, 2; comment by Sayward, *City Builder*, III (May 1918), 13; Bartholomew et al., *A Comprehensive City Plan: Memphis*, 6.

aegis of enlightened local civic leadership. City-planning commissions were thus called upon, like voluntary commercial and civic groups, "to correlate and to harmonize the various interests of the city"—as the Atlanta *Constitution* put it—"and to bring them together in a working whole in pursuit of a definite general plan, concurred in by all, whereby to bring the city up to the required standard of efficiency in all of its departments and activities."[54]

In assessing the historical significance of city planning, at least in three southern cities during the 1920s, several points seem obvious. First, local planning efforts were dominated throughout the decade, not by housing reformers or academicians or even by professional planners, but by the commercial-civic elite. Spokesmen for business groups and voluntary civic associations regarded urban planning as a logical extension of the philosophy and methods employed in running large, complex, corporate economic enterprises, and they tended to emphasize notions of efficiency, economic growth, and social order. Secondly, commercial-civic spokesmen readily acknowledged the need to restrict private property rights in the public interest. They pointed specifically to the chaos proceeding from unregulated land use and equated it with a state of virtual anarchy. But if they were willing to limit the *rights* of property, it was primarily for the purpose of enlarging the *security* of property in a rapidly changing urban environment. Property was not only a source of income and social status but a major bulwark of social stability and economic order. Clearly implied in all their statements and policies was the proviso that the "public interest" was best determined and advanced by persons like themselves, by those with a significant and tangible stake in the city. Thirdly, commercial-civic elements were eager to engage municipal governments in the planning movement. They believed that without statutory authority and the approval of local government city planning would be severely limited in its impact. Thus, commercial and civic groups began their initiatives for planning by promoting the idea of official commissions operating as agencies of municipal government. Rather than looking upon this as a threat to the private sector, they supported a useful partnership between city government and local economic interests and civic leadership as necessary to carry out the purposes of city planning.

Finally, plans concerning the physical development of the city, which commercial-civic representatives helped to fashion, contained elements of social control. These elements derived from a

---

[54] Atlanta *Constitution*, February 10, 1920.

general perception of the urban situation and the notion that the efficient and orderly functioning of the physical city would significantly reinforce social order. The stability of property values, the racial segregation of residential areas, the improvement of local transportation, and the provision of recreational facilities were obviously calculated in part to remove sources of urban discontent and cope with some of the troubling consequences of "progress." The concept of social control as a motive is, of course, subject to abuse just as other themes and interpretive rubrics are susceptible of distortion. But members of the commercial-civic elite were obviously not interested in radical alterations of the existing order, and the plans they approved were deemed desirable precisely because they promised to secure the fruits of that order and revitalize it.

One question remains to be answered: If commercial and civic groups which included some of the most influential local citizens uniformly supported the idea of city planning, why did city-planning commissions not accomplish considerably more than they did during the 1920s? Some of the answers to this query are rooted in fact, others in conjecture. For one thing, members of the commercial-civic elite were hardly disinterested. City planning was fine, but when it came to specific policies individual property owners were likely to appeal a zoning ruling that did not suit them. Municipal governments were equally likely, if one can believe the complaints of many planning commissioners, to grant exceptions to the zoning law. City planning and zoning thus tended to break down at their most vulnerable level—the widening of a specific street, the zoning of a particular block. To know the full story would entail monumental labors in obscure and incomplete records, but it is reasonable to assume on the basis of known facts that the problem existed.

Planning advocates complained most often about a lack of funds, even in those cities where comprehensive plans were subsidized out of city treasuries. Municipal authorities were reluctant to devote large amounts of scarce resources in a total commitment to city planning, especially when public approval of bond issues for expanded city facilities was difficult to obtain. Furthermore, city planning never enjoyed a ground swell of popular support. Its advocates among the commercial-civic elite were legion, and virtually no citizens or group opposed it, yet it never assumed the status of a major issue and was rarely submitted to a public referendum. The massive publicity drives launched in its behalf and the hearings held on zoning provisions stirred some public interest, to be sure;

but a continuing commitment to planning required, as the planning advocates themselves admitted, a fairly significant degree of popular enthusiasm. Planning commissions accomplished enough in the urban South during the 1920s to warrant continued commercial-civic support, but their functions were far too complex to engender general public enthusiasm, and their achievements were not so grand as to justify the huge outlay of resources that might have produced more impressive results.

Perhaps the principal burden under which these city-planning commissions operated during the decade was simply the weight of the work itself as well as the limits of time, energy, and, to some degree, of financial support. The tasks which these commissions and their advocates set for city planning were simply too enormous and the expectations too great; and just as some initial successes were achieved the depression diverted public attention and resources elsewhere.

Many reform efforts of the early twentieth century were fundamentally elitist; they were calculated to preserve the existing order and often ignored the concerns of the great masses of people who would feel their impact most directly. (On the other hand, many such reform attempts failed because they were not supported by coalitions of varied interest groups.) Charges of elitism have been leveled with considerable accuracy at city planning. Later generations have been especially appalled by the emphasis during the "business decade" on streets, zoning, and efficiency and by the neglect of housing, unemployment, poverty, and human needs. Certainly, city planning in the urban South rested on commercial-civic conceptions of the urban community that were narrow and simplistic: the city, after all, was not a business corporation. The planning movement also failed to confront fully the issue of growth, continuing to harbor the notions that growth was an essential measure of urban success and that the city which failed to expand would surely die.

Criticisms of commercial-civic purposes, priorities, and economic policies have not, however, always extended to the *methods* of planning employed during the 1920s. The advocates of city planning held some terribly easy assumptions concerning the curative powers of skilled municipal management. Their belief that technology and improved communications and physical facilities, if properly arranged and directed, could maintain urban unity and allow continued growth without serious problems simply ignored the complex patterns of human life upon which technology was to be superimposed. Social and economic order, and the future of the city, depended on far more than matters of street layout, zoning, and additional facilities. No matter how often the planners resorted to the organic metaphor, one suspects that their principal conception of the city in this first decade of the automotive age was decidedly mechanistic.

City planning was an idea whose time had come by the 1920s, but as a tool of social control or of radical urban renovation it required considerable sharpening. Some of the classic planning problems and dilemmas of the twentieth century appeared at the beginning: Who should fashion the plans, and in whose interests? What is the nature of the urban community, and which of its features should be preserved? What is the potential of technology, and how can its impact on the complex urban fabric be anticipated and controlled? Should the function of planning be rooted in the neighborhood, the municipality, the metropolitan area, or the region? The art and science of planning have become immensely more sophisticated in concept and method since the 1920s, but many of the lessons of that decade apparently have yet to be learned.

MARK B. LAPPING

Radburn:
Planning The American Community

"The formation of the Regional Planning Association of America (RPAA) in 1923 signified," historian Roy Lubove has asserted, "a sharp break with traditional housing and planning objectives in the United States." Instead of supporting ventures of a speculative nature in the area of housing and community development, the RPAA sought to promote new, planned environments in harmony with man's social, psychological and biological needs. Never really an organization in the strict sense of the word, the RPAA was "little more than a circle of friends held together by a broad conception of planning."[1] Composed of planner-architects Clarence Stein, Henry Wright and Frederick Lee Ackerman, conservationist and regionalist Benton MacKaye, urban critics Lewis Mumford and Charles Whitacker, realtor Alexander Bing, economist Stuart Chase and housing specialist Catherine Bauer, the RPAA also attracted such environmental thinkers and reformers as Tracy Auger, Clarence Perry, Robert Bruere, Herbert Emmerich, Charles Ascher and Harold Buttenheim.

Utilizing the tools and insights of the European planning tradition, which included strains of utopianism, socialism, urban decentralization and the Garden City movement, and the basic premises of contemporary regionalists, such as Patrick Geddes, the RPAA experimented with alternatives to unplanned settlement and development. In place of "blighted cities," which Clarence Stein also

---

1. Roy Lubove, *Community Planning in the 1920's: The Contribution of the Regional Planning Association of America* (Pittsburgh, 1963), 1; Benton MacKaye, "The RPAA: A Reminiscence," in Clarence Stein Mss, soon to be deposited at Cornell University; Mel Scott, *American City Planning Since 1890* (Berkeley, 1969), 223.

Mr. Lapping, Associate Director of the Environmental Program, The University of Vermont, was aided in the preparation of this article by a grant from the New Jersey Historical Commission.

85

referred to as "Dinosaur Cities," and the isolation and squalor of incompletely and poorly developed rural areas, the RPAA sought to create a viable "middle landscape" whose dimensions and qualities found their articulation in the RPAA's most important and daring venture, the plan for the new town of Radburn, New Jersey.[2]

Conceived as a "town for the motor age," Radburn was a community rooted in the social as well as physical theories of the RPAA. Even though the town as planned and conceived never fully developed—only part of the original plan was implemented before the Great Depression bankrupted the project—the "Radburn Idea" remains a testament to the RPAA's special brand of creative environmental innovation and synthesis. As with the RPAA which founded Radburn, the plans and concepts embodied in the new town were the results of a group effort. While planner-designers Wright and Stein and theorists MacKaye and Mumford figure pre-eminently in the experiment, the RPAA as a whole must be credited with the success of the project. For as Mumford has concluded, "ultimately, it was out of this group as whole, rather than simply out of those most directly responsible, that some of its best products came forth... the Radburn plan itself."[3]

Radburn was, as planner Stein noted, "a revolution in town planning." However, while the total plan was a major innovation in community and environmental design, "none of the elements that made up the Radburn idea was completely new." Rather, the parts which composed the whole were largely derived from much that went before in the development of town planning theory, and the ideas of the RPAA helped further to modify and define the use of such elements. At bottom, Radburn was the result of a brilliant synthesis of equally brilliant and seminal concepts which, before the RPAA organized them into a systematic plan, remained largely isolated one from the other and somewhat marginal to the problem of creating total living environments. The result was a plan which "revolutionized the planning of residential areas,"

---

2. Clarence Stein, "Our Blighted Cities," *The American Architect and Engineer,* CXIV (Aug., 1933); Clarence Stein, Dinosaur Cities," *The Survey Graphic,* 54 (May 1, 1925), 134-38; Leo Marx, *The Machine in the Garden: Technology and the Pastoral Ideal in America* (New York, 1964); Mark B. Lapping, "The Middle Landscape and American Urban Theory," (Ph. D. diss., Emory U., 1972).

3. Clarence Stein, "Radburn and the Radburn Idea," unpublished ms., Stein Mss; Lewis Mumford, *The City in History* (New York, 1961), 51; Albert Mayer, *The Urgent Future: People, Housing, City and Region* (New York, 1967), 78, 81n; Anthony Bailey, "Radburn Revisited,"*The Regional Planning News,* 76 (Dec., 1964), 1; Henry Wright, "The Autobiography of Another Idea," *Western Architect,* 39 (Sept., 1930), n.p.; Clarence Stein, *Toward New Towns For America* (Cambridge, 1966), 37; Lewis Mumford, "Restored Circulation, Renewed Life," *From the Ground Up* (New York, 1956), 224; Lubove, 67; Lewis Mumford, "Introduction" to Stein, *New Towns,* 15.

and, in the opinion of one of America's foremost planning critics, and a sometimes bitter opponent of RPAA ideas, Thomas Adams, it was "the most forward step in town planning in America."[4]

Though the members of the RPAA generally held similar ideas and values, and accepted the many insights of the European planning tradition, the Garden City movement and the dictates of environmental theorist Patrick Geddes, there still remained the problem, as in any planning process, of organizing and integrating ideas and values into a systematic operation which could be implemented. To this end the RPAA held discussions on the "problems connected with a Garden City" at the Hudson Guild Farm in Netcong, New Jersey through the year of 1927, in an effort to arrive at a concrete course of action.[5]

The most pressing issues which faced the group at the meetings included the matters of the settlement's projected size, land ownership and community government, the economic basis of the community and the class composition of the town. Because of the complexity of these issues and the very nature of new town development, the RPAA took cautious steps in these discussions and this perhaps explains why few unanimous views were expressed during the meetings.[6] Indeed, the RPAA discussions were extremely fluid, but some important views, which found at least consensus support, were expressed.

On the matter of size limitation, it was generally agreed that a population of 50,000 was desirable and that a population above that maximum limit would, as Stein maintained, "complicate and heighten the costs of city life." Henry Wright likewise maintained that if the town's population went beyond 50,000 a "complete system of transportation would have to be installed; and this would be an expense out of proportion to anything that might be gained by increasing the size of the city." Moreover, member Russell Black asserted that modern technology reduced the need for the new city to be entirely self-sufficient and that some institutions, such as a modern comprehensive hospital, could be developed in an area which would benefit the region as a whole, for new transportation systems would provide access to more people than would be possible if the hospital were located merely to meet the needs of the new city. This discussion demonstrated the extent to which the RPAA fully accepted the concept of population limitation so fully articulated by Geddes in his analysis of the problems of overcrowding and city life. The notion that cities diminish in their relative effectiveness to provide good and humane en-

---

4. Stein, "Radburn Idea," 11; *Planning Standards: A Draft Copy* (Dept. of City and Regional Planning, Pratt Institute), 30; Scott, 264.
5. Mumford's minutes of these informal discussion, presided over by Stein, are in the Stein Mss. Hereafter cited as "Minutes."
6. Lubove, 64.

vironments in relation to a rising population base was fully accepted by the RPAA and became a theme which runs throughout the Radburn project. Then, too, Black's point that new cities need not be self-sufficient but rather should be regionally oriented continued Geddes' thoughts on cities and reiterated Benton MacKaye's strong regionalist approach to planning. MacKaye, more than any other member of the group, with the possible exception of Mumford, understood Geddes' regionalist imperative and devoted much of his time and energy to the cause of conservation and regional approaches to planning.[7]

Of the discussions on life-support systems for the new city, those on the nature of the local economy and government were most crucial. Here again a consensus was achieved. The participants all agreed that Radburn had to contain its own industrial and commercial basis, lest it become a mere suburban appendage to another city. Moreover, the discussants realized that only certain industries should be encouraged to develop in the community. The criterion for such development was both clear and simple; only those industries which had a wage scale "adequate to the garden city standard of living" would be established in Radburn.[8] This translated as those industries and corporations which could provide a basis for middle-class community composition. Clarence Stein put the matter clearly when he argued that:

> If the poorly paid workers are admitted to the garden city, the industry that used them would either have to subsidize these worker's houses or advance their wages; there was no other way of providing them with the barest minimum of good houses unless the garden city duplicated the very conditions that it existed to escape from.

Moreover, Lewis Mumford argued, unless industries which could support middle-class life-styles and patterns came to Radburn, the new town would "have a shanty-town slum on its outskirts" and this would spell the failure of the entire community planning effort. The members of the RPAA were aware that their experiment in community planning with a middle-class bias could not solve all of society's problems, though the development of a more humane political economy appeared to them a pressing problem, and thus they limited their experimentation on this level. They believed that the town could not be integrated on all class and strata levels, and their overriding concern still revolved around the establishment of a planned new community. As Clarence Stein

---

7. "Minutes," Oct. 8-9, 1927. Lubove attributes the comments to Henry Wright, but a careful reading suggests that Black made the points. See also Benton MacKaye, *The New Exploration: A Philosophy of Regional Planning* (New York, 1928).

8. "Minutes," 3.

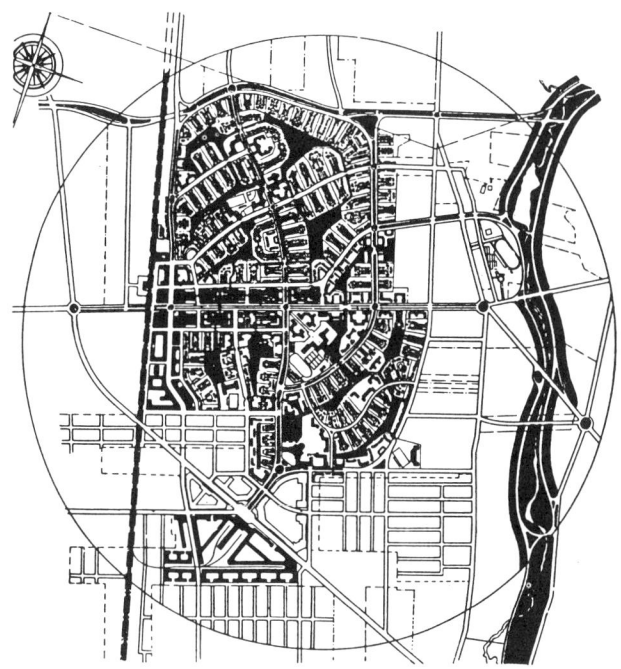

Plan for the town of Radburn.

saw it, the objective was to develop the type of community evolved in Rochester rather than in Buffalo, for in "one city decent houses could be built for a majority of the workers, in the second city there were large tracts of slums." Indeed, this comparison accurately expressed the concern of the RPAA. They saw Buffalo as a polluted, culturally deprived, festering metropolis which attracted unskilled and semi-skilled workers who could offer little to building the sort of community which the RPAA saw as vital. Rochester, on the other hand, had a progressive and aggressive business community which provided civic and cultural leadership for the entire city. Moreover, Rochester's industrial base, as the RPAA saw it, attracted skilled workers who had the economic ability to afford decent housing and life-styles which reinforced property ownership and the desire to maintain it. That these generalizations were oversimplifications and largely mythic is of little consequence. For what is important is the fact that the RPAA acted on the basis of these perceptions and thus fostered the development of a middle-class community in Radburn.[9]

The discussion of local economic considerations also turned to an evaluation

---

9. "Minutes," 3.

of unions. Mumford maintained that "an open shop town would confirm unionists in the soundness of their position in opposing decentralization; and that in such a case the whole movement of decentralization would get a black eye." Geddes Smith suggested that a company town would also be fought by unions, but suggested too that a community with a full range of industries would be beneficial to all Radburn residents, not solely those who were unionized. This point was further supported by Stein and Edith Wood, both of whom reported that Letchworth, Ebenezer Howard's first Garden City in Great Britain, contained sixty industries and that such an economically mixed local structure was beneficial to all members of the community. Thus, the consensus of the group supported the vision of a locally established economy which would provide a large variety of jobs and employment, but only of the kind which could support middle-class residents.[10]

A lively debate developed when discussants turned to a consideration of Radburn's governmental structure. Any analysis of the matter had as its immediate point of reference the RPAA's first experiment in community planning, Sunnyside Gardens in Long Island, New York, in 1924-27. Sunnyside was developed by the RPAA through its development and realty arm, the City Housing Corporation under the direction of realtor Alexander Bing. It was constructed on a seventy-acre tract which was dissected by a gridiron street pattern which divided the land into many rectangular blocks. Though the RPAA sought to change this physical system and evolve beyond the traditional gridiron, they were unsuccessful because of New York City's laws and hence had to make do with a pattern which ultimately worked against many of the objectives of the plan, which were "to produce good homes at as low a price as possible...." Nonetheless, Sunnyside was a good laboratory and the lessons learned from it aided the RPAA in planning Radburn. Sunnyside's governmental system revolved around the individual block organizations, or block trusts, and the Sunnyside Community Association. Initially the members of the RPAA thought that participants in the block trusts would be too lax in their responsibilities, but experience indicated that "if anything, they had proved too vigilant." This vigilance retarded the over-all workings of the community and the Community Association, for each block trust carved out its own area of control and relinquished power only grudgingly. When evaluating the governmental experience and its relevance for the projected new town, Herbert Emmerich concluded that it demonstrated "the inadvisability of releasing some of the community's functions at once to the community," for all too often the trustees, who "administered the central open area and who passed upon changes insisted

---

10. "Minutes," 3.

by the owners... created a certain amount of friction and delay."[11]

Emmerich's observations were countered by both Charles Ascher and John Elliot. They maintained that even though "they were unable to manage the affairs of the court with as much dispatch as if those things passed through a single responsible person," the trusts still had "given the residents of the community a feeling of responsibility" and the "share of self-government created in those matters relieved the Corporation from the irritation caused by interferences which were doubly irritating when undertaken by people over whose nomination the community had no control." Ascher summed up his appraisal of the governing process by noting that it was adding to "the knowledge of what functions were and could be performed by the community" and that this had a greater meaning than efficiency in policy making. Emmerich admitted that his point of viem had been modified and that he could see that "the immediate sacrifice of efficiency might be made up for by the increasing knowledge and practice of government." Hence, a consensus was finally achieved and while it was recognized that the process of self-government in Sunnyside Gardens had created certain problems, its assets outweighed its liabilities. The principle of self-regulation was reaffirmed and Radburn would be administered through the Radburn Association under guidelines outlined by the RPAA in much the same manner that the block trusts and the SCA operated in Sunnyside. In committing itself to self-government at the expense of administrative efficiency, the RPAA was setting itself against a traditional pattern in American community planning wherein efficiency was all important and little else was of much concern.[12]

In any consideration of the town's governmental mechanism, attention had to be paid to the matter of the control and administration of the land and other real property. Henry Wright suggested that a well-planned physical lay-out reinforced by zoning codes and ordinances would be more than sufficient to control land use in the community. Charles Ascher argued, on the other hand, that zoning codes were too often easily circumvented and that the City Housing Corporation owed it to prospective residents of Radburn to protect them by all means possible against speculative activities. He proposed a rigid deed system "embodying what usually goes into a municipal charter of government." Such a document should be developed by the town's parent institution, the City Housing Corporation, and would have to meet with the approval of Radburn's residents or else they would not choose to reside in such a community. A compromise of these two positions was put foward by Stein and Harold Butten-

---

11. Lubove, 58; Stein, *New Towns,* 22; "Minutes," 4.
12. "Minutes," 5. On the ethic of efficiency and its effects, see Robert Wiebe, *"The Search for Order: 1877-1920* (New York, 1967).

heim. They suggested that zoning codes could be effective as a means of land-use control if the lease or deed left ultimate authority in the hands of the citizen group, the Radburn Association. It was understood by the planners that the Radburn Association would work for the "advantage of the whole community since the community developed it and ran the organization as it saw fit."[13]

If these are but a few of the directions in which the planners sought to move, they were of a precise nature. The more general goals suggest something of the utopian quality of such new town endeavors. Above all else, Radburn was seen as the fruition of years of publicity and agitation for a garden city as first articulated in the writings of Ebenezer Howard. While planner Stein thought of Radburn as a "new form of city," his co-worker Henry Wright saw the need to move beyond Howard's early formulations by suggesting that vast changes in the technology of urban life, such as the rise of automobile transportation, now required that Radburn "had to meet a new set of conditions" which made many of Howard's ideas obsolete. Nonetheless, Radburn was designed essentially within the Garden City tradition.[14]

If the automobile became a new element in the planning process, it was also the crucial one, as the RPAA saw it. This is not to suggest that the members of the group thought well of the car. On the contrary, the automobile presented itself both as the epitome of man's privatistic instincts and as the major force causing the destruction of the environment. Yet, the RPAA realistically assessed the role of the car in American society and came to the determination that only through planning with the automobile in mind could it be controlled. Hence, in describing the manner in which the group related to this artifact of urban civilization, and its negative externalities, one can discover both the general planning schemes of the RPAA and the social goals it sought to implement through the new town.

According to Stein, planning Radburn involved answering the question, "How can we live happily, safely and graciously in the motor age, with minimum danger from, but the maximum use of, autos?" As the RPAA saw it, traditional city development had never really confronted this problem. Rather, it created and intensified the problem by combining the worst possible physical elements of design: streets were "through streets" with no functional differentiation; pedestrians and machines "collided about every 250 feet;" houses and their views faced on to the roads; automobile movement was too slow; streets occupied too much land; trips to commercial, educational and cultural facilities were too often "dangerous, annoying and nerve-wracking: because of the

---

13. "Minutes," 6.
14. Stein, "Radburn Idea," 3; Wright, 3.

constant confrontation between man and the machine." These problems led to the conclusion that early urban development and planning was never really geared to a mode of rapid transit like the automobile and that the existence of this new urban element made existing cities both dangerous and anachronistic in the context of planning and design for human use and utility. The point was to develop urban patterns which would mediate between man and machine, between nature and civilization, and follow up on Aristotle's recommendation that a "city should be built to give its inhabitants security and happiness." In an effort to achieve this definition of urbanity, the RPAA was again forced to analyze goals and objectives in light of the realities previously described.[15]

The analysis shifted from the macro—the town—to the micro—the neighborhood—in an effort to gain a different perspective for determining just how planning must relate to the automobile. What eventually evolved was a well-defined "neighborhood concept" which owed much to the early work of RPAA advisor Clarence Perry, who introduced the neighborhood unit concept into the lexicon of modern planning. Perry's ideal of community organization and planning along neighborhood lines grew out of his experiences as a resident of Forest Hills Gardens, New York, a project of the Russell Sage Foundation. As planning historian John Reps has asserted, by living in Forest Hills Gardens, Perry "obtained much of his practical knowledge of group interaction within a unified composition of spaces and buildings:" the elementary school, which defined the outer limits and boundaries of the neighborhood through its restricted enrollment numbers; parks and playgrounds and "open spaces" which would comprise approximately 10 per cent of the total land mass; commercial establishments serving daily needs grouped together and located on the periphery of the neighborhood; and, a street system which brought about the "deflection of all through traffic ... clearly set off (from) the neighborhood."[16]

With the neighborhood as the basic element in the total town plan, Perry believed a more harmonious life with a true "sense of community" could be experienced. The RPAA concurred with this perception, and Stein went so far as to state that "at Radburn, the neighborhood idea formed the basis of the town plan." If the neighborhood was the physical element around which all else revolved, then it was the family unit, and particularly the family with a young child, which became the basic social unit within the Radburn plan. Indeed, it can be suggested that Radburn was really planned almost solely with the child and his interests and needs in mind. In this sense, the automobile

---
15. Stein, "Radburn Idea," 2; Stein *New Towns,* 41.
16. John Reps, *The Making of Urban America: A History of City Planning in the United States* (Princeton, 1965), 525; James Dahir, *The Neighborhood Unit Plan and Its Spread and Acceptance* (New York, 1947), 16.

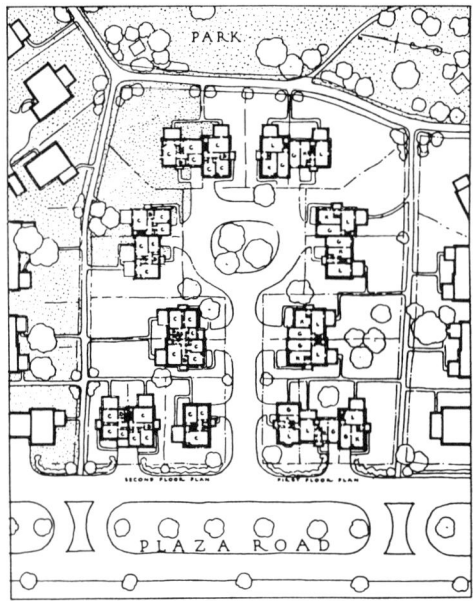

Plan of one of the cul-de-sacs at Radburn.

was seen as an intruder against which the planners had to create an environment which would protect the child. Seen in this light, Radburn follows in a long tradition of utopian planning efforts which consistently attempted to protect people against incursions from the outside "wicked world." In the context of Radburn, the automobile was the "wicked world" but it could not be ignored; it had to be contained and utilized in such a manner as to limit its direct impact on everyday life in the community. It may indeed be concluded that Radburn was something of a "kid's town", for as Stein once noted, "Radburn is above all else a town for children."[17]

To develop a community which could integrate the use of the automobile with the safety demanded for children, certain planning devices were utilized: the superblock with its special circulation systems; the segregation of pedestrian and vehicular traffic; interior open spaces and park lands occupying the marrow of the superblock; and houses turned away from the road and the flow of traffic and toward the park instead. Each of these specific elements had been utilized in other historical contexts and experiments, but the integration and

---

17. Stein, "Radburn Idea," 24; Stein, *New Towns,* 51. The term "sense of community" is most difficult to define, but one sociologist, who discovered ninety-four different definitions of the term, also found that sixty-nine of them stressed three elements: existence of social interaction, commonality of cultural and social ties, and commonality of spatial location and proximity. G. Hillery, "Definitions of Community: Areas of Agreement," *Rural Sociology* 20 (1955), 11-123.

synthesis of these formed the "Radburn Idea."

The superblock—10 to 15 times as large as the characteristic city block (about 1000' X 2000', as compared with 200' X 600')—restricted the use of the automobile. The car ran around the block rather than through or across it. Buildings of both a community and residential nature did not front on the peripheral street which circumscribed the superblock. Instead, edifices were designed to be built into the superblock connected with the peripheral streets by service roads which ultimately ended in "dead ends" or cul-de-sacs.[18]

The superblock had its origins in the Garden City movement. Stein and Wright studied their use in the two leading experiments of this type, Letchworth and Welsyn in Great Britain. Superblocks, as Wright saw them, "reduced the number of traffic streets and intersections, place a large majority of houses on quiet closed-end lanes" and produced the possibility of developing a truly segregated vehicular and pedestrian traffic system. Stein has suggested that the Dutch had developed a modified superblock in Manhattan when they first established New Amsterdam, but asserted that it was Ebenezer Howard who made the superblock a permanent element in the lexicon of modern planning.[19]

The superblock also implied a new and different system of vehicular circulation. The RPAA developed the use of specialized roads both as a response to the needs of the community and also as a reaction against the traditional checkerboard or grid pattern. The peripheral road which circumscribed the superblock was termed a "secondary collector road" which would be a feeder into a wider and potentially quicker avenue or highway system. The collector road itself received traffic from the dead-ends or cul-de-sacs which were the most basic vehicular paths into the community. Hence, distinctions were made between paths for service, parking and collections—the cul-de-sacs; paths for the collection of vehicles—the peripheral circumscribed roads; and paths for the rapid movement of traffic from one section to another—the highways or avenues.

These distinctions in a circulation system and particularly the development of the latter type of road also reflected another concern of the RPAA in town planning: the "townless highway" and its close relation, the "highwayless town." First articulated by RPAA member Benton MacKaye, the "townless highway" was a major vehicular artery which could move its cargo quickly and safely because it did not travel through cities but rather around the communities, bypassing them entirely. As Lewis Mumford put it:

> Highway planners have yet to realize that these arteries must not be thrust

---

18. Stein, "Radburn Idea," 6.
19. Stein, "Radburn Idea," 12; *New Towns,* 44; Wright, 5.

into the delicate tissue of our cities; the blood they circulate must rather enter through an elaborate network of minor blood vessels and capillaries.[20]

While this biological metaphor once again suggests an organic interpretation of community life and structure first derived from Geddes, it also demonstrates the reasons why streets in Radburn had different functions in the very first place; no two roads served the same exact function and the idea was, at all times, to make the best out of a bad situation—keep the automobile where it will do the least harm but serve the greatest social utility. Hence, roads were to be developed which would take advantage of the high speeds the automobile could attain, but those roads closest to where the family resided were modified and down-graded to meet the potentialities and habits of man rather than the machine.

The development of special circulation systems led logically to a consideration of the specific relationship between the pedestrian and the machine. Once again, the emphasis was placed on protecting and insulating man from the automobile, and the result was a system of near absolute segregation of one element from the other. Stein pointed to the designs of Frederick Law Olmsted and Calvert Vaux from New York City's Central Park as a precedent for the segregation of such traffic.[21]

The RPAA sought to reproduce this classic planning solution. The segregation of traffic along specifically defined roads implied a system of paths for pedestrian use which would by-pass the automobile paths. This pedestrian traffic system in Radburn was tied-up with the open spaces and park system, which composed the heart or marrow of the superblock's land mass. Footpaths leading from individual homes joined into a system of paths which took the pedestrian through the core of the superblock onto overpasses or to underpasses which by-passed the automobile paths completely. In turn, these paths led to schools, commercial establishments and other community structures and components. A child could leave home and walk to school bouncing a ball without once having to stop for an automobile—and of course this is precisely what the planners had in mind! The open spaces were conceived as the backbone of

---

20. Benton MacKaye, "The Townless Highway," *New Republic* (Mar. 30, 1930): Benton MacKaye and Lewis Mumford, "Townless Highways for the Motorist: A Proposal for the Automobile Age," *Harper's* 163 (Aug., 1931), 347-356; Lewis Mumford, *The Highway and the City* (New York, 1964), 246.

21. Stein, "Radburn Idea," 14; Stein, *New Towns,* 44. Lubove, 137, cites an interview with Stein to deny that Radburn was directly inspired by Central Park. Stein, in an interview with the present author on June 6, 1970, confirmed that Central Park was a definite influence in this phase of planning Radburn. But Charles Ascher, interviewed by the author on May 16, 1973, supported Lubove's view.

the superblock and the planners hoped that these areas would provide the main recreational sites for the new town. Stein saw these parks as the core of this middle landscape plan:

> He [the pedestrian] may stroll quietly across the green. He passes children at play or on the way to school. He glimpses gay crowds around the swimming pool or walking there in bathing suits. He sees elderly folks taking in the sun or shaded by trees that have been there twenty years or more. It is a peaceful escape from the hazards of the motor age.

Stein described the inner park as "the heart of the superblock... a community park running the length of the superblock. This green center is like a lake surrounded by bays which consist of private gardens, separated by tree lined paths."[22]

The continuity of the green open spaces was further enhanced by homes which fronted on the interior park instead of the more traditionally sited homes which fronted on the street and faced the moving traffic. The precedent for houses thus turned around, and with two entrances, came from Henry Wright's experiences as a young student traveling in Europe.

> In 1902, as an impressionable youth just out of architectural school . . . at Waterford . . . Ireland, . . . I passed through an archway in a blank house wall on the street to a beautiful villa fronting upon spacious gardens. That archway was a passage to new ideas which have struggled up through the years: I learned then that the comforts and privacy of family life are . . . to be found . . . in a house that judiciously relates living space and open space, the open space . . . being capable of enjoyment by many as well as by few . . . [23]

To be sure, each house in Radburn was planned to have an entrance on the cul-de-sac as well as on the park, but the living room and as many bedrooms as possible—the essential "living" rooms as the RPAA saw it—were to have vistas of the green areas. The concept of the "good life" had meaning for the RPAA only within the context of open spaces and green areas which implied serenity, peace, and strong community and familial ties. The plan for Radburn, accordingly, attempted to provide the sense of community, togetherness, convenience and culture that properly planned cities generated. In this sense, Radburn was a true expression of the middle landscape ideal, wherein a rural physical setting had grafted on to it the necessary amenities and conditions of

---

22. Stein, "Radburn Idea," 6-7.
23. Wright, 3; Stein, "Radburn Idea," 16; Stein, *New Towns,* 48.

life cities provided.[24]

Planning critic and historian Thomas Reiner, in his *The Place of the Ideal Community in Urban Planning,* has asserted that ideal communities can be of two sorts: a "design can either serve to support an existing social order or it may urge a radical departure." A departure upon the pioneering social analysis of Karl Mannheim, Reiner's work has considerable relevance here. If we can conceive of Radburn as an "ideal community," and certainly the RPAA thought of it in these terms as the group proceeded to move through the planning process, it becomes apparent that Radburn was a traditional response to an old and now familiar set of problems all revolving around the issues of decent housing and stable community. Of this type of plan, Reiner writes that it is

> a solution within the framework of the currently expressed goals of the residents. The ideal community in this instance is a reordering, a tidying up . . . No fundamental societal innovations are suggested. The design calls for an ordered replacement of the chaos characterizing the landuse distribution in urban areas along lines suggested by successful, stable, suburban home districts.[25]

Seen in this light, Radburn was a rather traditional conceptualization of the ideal community. The very traditionalism of the town is best expressed in two elements: housing patterns and community organization. The predominant housing of the town was the single family, private and detached dwelling. In this regard, Radburn tends to perpetuate what has become a consistent American pattern-private and individual as opposed to corporate and communal. The private, single-family home was the natural housing component plan which valued the traditional nuclear family as the organic keystone of culture.

The organization and structure of community life as anticipated by the RPAA differed little from the more normative behavior encountered in then contemporary American suburbs. Friendships and relationships were based upon the elements of propinquity and homogeneity. And it is in this area that the planner has his greatest effect, for

> the architect who builds a house or designs a site plan, who decided where the roads will and will not go, and who decided which directions the houses will face and how close together they will be, also is, to a large extent, deciding the

---

24. See Stein's heavy use of this imagery throughout *New Towns.*
25. Thomas Reiner, *The Place of the Ideal Community in Urban Planning* (Philadelphia, 1962), 20.

pattern of social life among the people who will live in these houses.[26]

Propinquity, or the proximity between one person and another along a spatial plane, leads to visual contact between people and this may result in face-to-face contact. As a result, propinquity may be the first step in the development of friendships and social life. As sociologist Herbert Gans writes:

> Propinquity not only initiates relationships, but it also plays an important role in maintaining the less intensive ones, for the mere fact of living together encourages neighbors to make sure that the relationship between them remains positive. Propinquity cannot determine the intensity of the relationship, however; this is a function of the characteristics of the people involved.[27]

Hence, propinquity, which is a direct result of the site or plan, may largely determine the quality, but not necessarily the intensity, of social life in a community. In the case of Radburn, propinquity was built into the plan. While people are discouraged from developing a propinquitous relationship based upon the reality of the automobile, they are encouraged by the plan to have a large degree of face-to-face contact in community facilities, on the pedestrian paths and in the park or open spaces of the community. But as Gans further points out, propinquity alone cannot create a social relationship of any intensity. For this to happen, people must realize, or they must strive to create, a homogeneity among themselves. In this sense, homogeneity need not be related specifically to race, economic background or occupation, but rather it is a mosaic in which background, class, life-style and child-rearing practices can serve as roots of a community.

The need for commonalities or homogeneities is greatest, Gans asserts, among

> neighbors with children of equal age and among immediately adjacent neighbors. Children, especially young ones, choose playmates on a purely propinquitous basis. Thus, positive relations among neighbors with children of similar age are best maintained if the neighbors are comparatively homogeneous with respect to child-rearing methods.

Radburn, because it was designed as a child-oriented community, relied upon

---

26. Festinger, Schachter and Black, *Social Pressures in Informal Groups* (New York, 1960), 160.
27. Herbert Gans, "Planning and Social Life," *Journal of the American Institute of Planners,* XXVII:2 (May, 1961), reprinted in Gutman and Popence, *Neighborhood, City and Metropolis* (New York, 1970), 747.

a social life developed out of the homogeneity of such people. In this regard, Radburn did not break with old, established patterns of community organization, since it sought to bring people together who had such interests and commonalities. This was further insured by the fact that the plan and the community were very much child-oriented. As Gans further suggests,

> My observations suggest that in the new suburbs, values with respect to child-rearing, leisure-time interests, taste levels, general cultural preferences, and temperament seem to be most important in judging compatibility or incompatibility.[28]

In the Radburn plan, such a compatibility was insured by the plan itself for it forced propinquity and also helped to insure that the homogeneity necessary would be created by people with similar backgrounds, life-styles and child-rearing philosophies, since it was middle class in its orientation, local economic bases, housing possibilities and amenities. The RPAA was keenly aware of the implications of such planning policies and designs. The town was to reflect the needs and interests of middle-class people, as the RPAA defined "middle-class." This meant structuring social life in such ways that middle-class levels of taste, aspiration and modes of living would be the paramount consideration of the community. That the RPAA thought all middle-class people acted alike and believed in the same values suggests the parochialism of the group and the dominant traditions and theories of planning and design then in circulation.

Radburn's importance as a model for future town planning can be witnessed throughout the world. The British new towns policies of the post-war era, the Scandinavian experiments in satellite community development, including Finland's justly famous town of Tapiola, the urban growth and development strategies of India, the Soviet new city programs and Japan's decentralist policies now being drafted all bear the imprint of Radburn. In the United States, two generations of planners have read the books and studied the plans of the RPAA, but surprisingly few such new towns as Radburn have been created here. Yet thousands of suburban tracts all across the nation bear some resemblance to Radburn. Perhaps the RPAA members would feel uncomfortable knowing this but as this essay has attempted to suggest, Radburn was consistent with the needs and articulated values of those millions of Americans who have come to constitute the middle-class "housing market." Perhaps the real importance of Radburn rests in its ability to become the synthesis of the obvious and the desirable. And this, as planners know, is rarely achieved.

---

28. Gans, 749. See his analysis in *The Levittowners* (New York, 1967), which stems from his residence in Levittown, N. J.

HISTORICAL BIOGRAPHY

Rexford Guy Tugwell:
Initiator of America's Greenbelt New Towns, 1935 to 1936

David Myhra

Between 1935 and 1936, the United States Department of Agriculture (USDA) initiated a public housing program that resulted in the construction of planned new communities called Greenbelt Towns. The prime mover behind this effort was Rexford Tugwell. The significance of this idea was his advanced concept of resettling the rural poor in planned towns at the edge of urban areas. Tugwell recognized, earlier perhaps than many of his colleagues, the "push-pull" tendencies emerging in American society in the 1930s. Arguing that urban growth was inevitable, Tugwell's Greenbelt concept was to demonstrate how housing could be surrounded with a more pleasing environment in order to accommodate the expanding rural to urban migration. In less than two years Tugwell's Resettlement Administration planned and constructed three new communities and litigated a fourth. By all standards, these accomplishments demonstrate an unprecedented speed record for action by a bureaucracy.

BACKGROUND OF THE IDEA

Urban planning literature becomes cloudy when describing the ideological origins of America's Greenbelt New Towns of the 1930s, the first completely planned communities to be built in this country. Available material is full of references to Ebenezer Howard and his English Garden City Movement.[1] However, a closer examination indicates that these towns originated largely through the effort and persistence of one man in Franklin D. Roosevelt's Administration, Rexford Guy Tugwell. The Greenbelt New Town program was Tugwell's idea;[2] it was an extension of his land use programs which he envisioned as correctives to the problems of rural poverty facing millions of farm families during the "Great Depression" in the 1930s.[3]

Tugwell was not an urban planner, but an agricultural economist, on the faculty of Columbia University. He was invited to become an economic advisor to Roosevelt during his presidential campaign of 1932, becoming one of the original members of FDR's "brain trust" and later, Undersecretary of Agriculture. One of Tugwell's prime functions was as Roosevelt's "idea man." Referring to the problems of the nation, Tugwell noted in his Diary, "Whatever the situation we were in, I tried to think of ways out. I took literally dozens of these [ideas] to the President, sometimes after consultation with others, sometimes after going to the length of drafting a memorandum, and sometimes just as a suggestion to catch his mind as it worked on a problem." One such idea that Tugwell presented to Roosevelt was his Resettlement concept. This hoped to establish a comprehensive program of action to alleviate the socioeconomic problems then confronting the American farm population.

The very heart of the Resettlement conception was the simultaneous attack on the wastage of people and

---

David Myhra, Associate AIP, is presently Senior Scientist for Westinghouse Electric Corporation's Environmental Systems Department, Pittsburgh, Pennsylvania. His primary areas of interest are the planning and siting of large-scale electrical generating stations. He holds a B.S. and M.S. in economics, and is a Ph.D. candidate in Urban Planning at Princeton University. Previous articles by Mr. Myhra have appeared in publications such as the *Journal of Urban Law, Park Practice Trends,* and *Public Utilities Fortnightly.*

the inefficient use of resources. Resettlement undertook to remedy all this. It meant to assist the families in the worst situations to find new and more economic farms or to locate elsewhere in other occupations with a prospect of work and income (Tugwell, 1959, p. 160).

THE PLIGHT OF AMERICAN FARMERS

In the 1930s, American farmers were in trouble. Soil erosion, labor displaced by mechanization, over-production in the early 1920s, and changing food consumption patterns were causing widely ranging difficulties for most farmers and farm families.[4] Millions were on direct relief and thousands were flocking into urban areas in search of jobs and housing. The cities were not able to accommodate them because of their own lack of housing.

Something had to be done in order to ameliorate these problems. What resulted grew not only out of an altruistic attitude, but also from the belief that rural America was on the verge of a revolution (Lowi, 1969, p. 290). Steps had to be taken, and Tugwell believed that these steps had to occur in the city (Mann, 1952). The city became for Tugwell the corrective for the amelioration of rural poverty problems (Tugwell, 1959, p. 160).

TUGWELL THE ECONOMIST

Tugwell entered governmental service with extensive experience in college teaching and holding a Ph.D in economics from the University of Pennsylvania. His economic theories may be described as Institutional, a concept which prevailed at the beginning of the twentieth century. Through such men as Thorstein Veblen and Simon N. Patten, economic thinking underwent its great reformation. The economic heterodoxy that permeated American thinking was in sharp contrast to that which had prevailed before the turn of the century. There came into being a greater empiricism, a more rational outlook, and a more practical application. When closing the gap between economic theory and practical application, heterodox economists such as Tugwell provided a significant challenge to what had been know as economic orthodoxy (Mann, 1952).

Veblen, Simon and, later, Tugwell found their strength in the fact that their theorizing was relevant to the problems facing the American economy. By adopting a pragmatic outlook and relying upon cultural sciences for support, institutional economists presented a body of doctrine which had the welfare of the public as its goal, to be accomplished through social reform and an experimental approach.

> In the strictest sense, the Resettlement Administration is not in the housing field at all. It is building houses, true, but its considerations go beyond the fact, important as that fact is, that millions of Americans need new homes if a minimum standard of decency is to be attained. What the Resettlement Administration is trying to do is to put houses and land and people together in such a way that props under our economic and social structure will be permanently strengthened (Tugwell, 1936, p. 28).

Tugwell's interpretation of economic development involved a consideration of what he described as cultural equilibrium. The economic process was one in which there was movement (push-pull) from one cultural equilibrium to another. He found that American institutions such as farming were reaching a new equilibrium. Consequently, maladjustments were witnessed, which had to be harnessed in order to obtain the maximum welfare. Tugwell believed, as did many of the "institutionalists," that man had to shape institutions rather than men so that both undesirable or antisocial impulses and economic activities would be corrected. This attitude stemmed from the belief that basic human drives were too strong to be channeled by police methods. Thus the desire to change institutions rather than men was accompanied by a belief in democracy and planning (Sternsher, 1964, p. 15).

Tugwell as an "institutionalist" believed that man had to respond to changing social and economic conditions through planning. There was no choice. He believed that men could assure progress by designing social mechanisms to meet specific needs, emphasizing experimentation as the technique of planning. But at the same time he rejected the dogmas of Marx and classical liberalism. Tugwell maintained that effective social policies had to be dictated by contemporary resources, techniques, and circumstances; that they had to be tuned to the times rather than to an imaginary environment in some Utopia (Sternsher, 1964, p. 15).

As an economist, Tugwell reached the crest of importance in 1932, when he was called by Franklin Roosevelt into the services of the New Deal. Tugwell had many novel ideas about economics and its application to the difficulties confronting rural America at that time. In fact, many of his economic theories are still in opposition to current "growth pole" economic thoughts regarding regional and rural development. In this context, regional development or rural development, broadly defined, is a nationwide effort to develop the resources of rural areas in order to improve economic, educational and cultural conditions for those who wish to live there.

However, if people remain on scattered settlements of thinly populated cities and towns, requirements for economic and social investments are created that tend to be uneconomical. Tugwell's belief is that those who argued in 1935, as well as those who argue now in 1974, that rural development is a viable corrective to rural poverty are failing to be pragmatic. In other words, they are failing to accept rural decline as inevitable in the face of increasing technology. Small communities and towns, even if grouped together under the "growth pole" concept, require centralized sewerage and water systems, education, police and fire protection, roads and highways, and so on. Tugwell's response says in essence, "Wouldn't it be better to capitalize on our already existing social and economic investments in the larger cities, and construct examples of how housing might be surrounded by a more pleasing environment?" Tugwell's ideas were manifested in the Greenbelt New Town program.

THE GREENBELT NEW TOWN PROGRAM

America's Greenbelt New Town program officially began on April 30, 1935, when President Franklin D. Roosevelt signed Executive Order No. 7027, creating the Resettlement Administration, with Dr. Rexford Guy Tugwell as its Director (Rosenman, 1950). This agency came under the auspices of the Department of Agriculture where Tugwell had served as Undersecretary since 1933. Funding was provided through the Emergency Relief Appropriations Act of 1935 (Emergency Relief Appropriations Act of 1935, U.S. Statutes at Large). However, the entire construction was halted a mere eighteen months later on May 18, 1936, when this Act was declared unconstitutional (Franklin Township v. Tugwell). After 1936, the Federal Government maintained what had been completed, finally selling its interest in 1955 to private developers. However, during its brief eighteen-month existence, Tugwell's staff of architects, city planners, and engineers, many of them America's foremost authorities, managed to plan and construct three new towns and litigate a fourth, setting an excellent speed record for action by a government bureaucracy.

PROBLEM OF DISPLACED FARM WORKERS

Rexford Tugwell had initially joined Franklin Roosevelt's campaign staff as an agricultural economist in 1932, later becoming Undersecretary of Agriculture. In his position as Undersecretary, Tugwell was pushing the United States Department of Agriculture into land reform and soil conservation programs in an effort to improve economic conditions on American farms.

He recognized, perhaps earlier than his colleagues that farming as an institution was changing because technology was increasing the yield. This resulted in a displacement of surplus farm workers. These displaced rural people had few options open to them except migration into the cities, seeking work. The farmer, in particular, had been affected by the "Great Depression" of the thirties, with more than five million families living in quiet desperation, dependent at one time or another on local, state, or federal relief (Tugwell, 1959). A large number of farm families were living on land so poorly adapted to farming that they could no longer subsist from it. Other families whose land was more productive had been severely handicapped by excessive financial burdens through overproduction, when strong European markets for grains disappeared after the First World War. Uneconomical methods of farm management and inadequate farming equipment were also contributing factors, together with soil erosion. When grouped together, these facts made the American farmer suffer more during the depression than perhaps any other socioeconomic group, except for the Negroes.

None of these conditions were new. They had been developing over a period of decades, becoming intensified in the late 1920s and early 1930s. As early as 1900, people were becoming concerned over the way the land had been mistreated in the rush for increased yield. Reckless deforestation practices by "lumber barons," for example, prompted Theodore Roosevelt and Gifford Pinchot to establish a National Conservation and Forest Service to save what then remained of our once boundless timberlands. But the immense demands of many European countries for foodstuffs during the First World War checked the young policy of conservation and, in fact, reversed it. "We were told that wheat would win the war"; as a result, the prairies were ploughed up far beyond the limits of economic productivity in order to take advantage of abnormally high wheat prices abroad (Tugwell, 1935, p. 3).

After the war, attempts were made to check the results of overpricing, overfarming, deforestation, and soil exhaustion, although very little was achieved. All through the 1920s, as most European countries became agriculturally self-sufficient, American farmers were suffering from overproduction and low prices. In addition, a new dimension to the growing farm problems was becoming evident when, as early as 1931 and 1932, dust storms began to blow away the top soil in western Kansas and eastern Colorado. Year by year the area affected by these storms increased until the great drought of 1934 threatened to make a large section of inland America into desert land. Nebraska, Kansas, Wyoming, New Mexico, Colorado, Texas, Oklahoma, and even the Dakotas, Iowa, and Minnesota were affected by this drought. Feed crops withered, water sources dried up, starving cattle slowly died, and farm families departed by the thousands for the cities, seeking housing and employment. To Tugwell, this was not a temporary trend, but a fundamental socioeconomic change that could be expected to continue. Tugwell felt that a radical reorganization of agriculture along industrial lines was in process. Even the demand for products was changing. The American diet, for example, was evolving from starch to protein, the development of synthetic fibers was lessening the demand for cotton, and farms were being mechanized. All these factors led to the same conclusion: the release of large numbers of farmers and farm laborers from their jobs, homes, and means of livelihood (Tugwell, July 1936, p. 38).

Two major problems confronted the New Deal administration. One had to do with the need for an extensive land reclamation program. The other had to do with the displaced farm family. The first problem was by far the more easily corrected. Farm lands damaged by ignorant, shortsighted, or wasteful methods of farming could be improved by better methods or techniques. Exhausted soil could be checked by the use of chemical fertilizers, rotation of crops, and other methods of scientific agriculture. But the task of resettling farm refugees was another matter. Most of the displaced farm families were seeking employment and housing in the larger cities. Tugwell felt conditions there were no better because a lack of imaginative city planning was creating problems equally as grave as those found in rural areas (Conkin, 1959, p. 153).

TUGWELL OPPOSES ROOSEVELT'S "BACK TO THE LAND" CONCEPT

However, there was a considerable difference of opinion as to the best methods for relieving this situation. Roosevelt felt that rural poverty was correctable at the source, through better farm management and rural subsistence homes. He believed vast areas of American cities should be razed (slum clearance, he called it), and the people released to rural homesteads, a "back to the land" movement.[5] Tugwell, on the contrary, felt that this would not correct the problems inherent in the farm situation. Although he was concerned about existing urban problems such as the lack of housing, his priority lay with the rural people whom he felt had been neglected for too long. Poor land makes for poor people, Tugwell believed, so it was necessary either to find these poor people better land and teach them to work it profitably, or to relocate those who could not continue to farm close to employment opportunities in the cities.

Tugwell's correctives to rural poverty were just the oppo-

GREENHILL, OHIO *The second Greenbelt New Town built is located twelve miles north of Cincinnati's CBD. The tract contains 5,930 acres and was initially designed to accommodate 1,000 homes and necessary facilities.*

site of what FDR envisioned. Roosevelt would not or could not recognize the forces that were pushing the population off the farms and into the cities. Tugwell did; consequently he felt that urban areas had to be prepared to absorb very large numbers of people from the farms, and he believed very strongly that rural poverty could only be corrected in the city (Tugwell, 1935). These correctives would be industrial employment and the growing opportunities in the service industries. Industrialization in rural areas as an alternative was unacceptable because it was too slow and uncertain as a definite process, as well as inefficient and uneconomical for business itself. Besides, Tugwell felt that industry could not be encouraged to locate in rural areas. Rural industrialization simply was not a viable alternative.

The correct approach toward the elimination of rural poverty, Tugwell believed, lay in the creation of new urban resettlement projects (new towns) that would house the displaced farm family while the father, or head of the household, could obtain employment in nearby industry.

In this regard Tugwell differed from Ebenezer Howard. Although both men believed that the city was basically unfit for human habitation, each proposed different solutions. Tugwell saw uncontrolled urban growth and a lack of planning as part of the problem (Conkin, 1959). This situation could easily be corrected, he believed, through demonstration projects in suburban settings, physically illustrating how urban growth could be developed if a conscientious effort was made to surround housing with a more pleasing environment. Howard, on the other hand, believed urban form could be made more livable only if city dwellers were removed entirely and located in rural, self-sufficient garden cities. Tugwell didn't agree with so drastic a measure. He believed in the city and was confident of its continued growth and development. However, the laissez faire attitudes in handling urban growth would continue to create distress because of the impact of advancing technology on farming and farm workers.

Franklin Roosevelt, however, remained an ardent admirer of the pastoral life. He was absorbed with land, forests, and waters, in his continued search for a better design for national living. "Utopia," Schlesinger wrote, "still presented itself to him in the cherished image of Hyde Park . . . tranquility in the midst of rich meadows and farmlands, deep forests, and a splendid flowing river" (Schlesinger, 1958, p. 319). In the 1920s FDR had discussed the possibility of keeping people on the land by combining farming with part-time local industry. As Governor of New York, he had talked of redressing the population balance between city and countryside, "taking industry from crowded urban centers to airy villages, and giving scrawny kids from the slums opportunity for sun and growth in the country" (Schlesinger, 1958, p. 319). "I want to destroy all this," he once said of cities, "this is no way for people to live. I want to get them out on the ground with clean sunshine and air around them, and a garden to dig in. Spread out the cities, space the factories out, give people a chance to live" (Schlesinger, 1958, p. 364).

To FDR, the Great Depression and the Presidency provided new opportunities to move toward a balanced civilization. Against the backdrop of drought and dust, Roosevelt

HIGHLIGHTS OF THE PROGRAM

In capsule form, these are the highlights of the Greenbelt New Town program:

February 1935	Tugwell suggested his concept of Greenbelt New Towns to President Roosevelt.
March 1935	FDR gave Tugwell permission to begin staffing and formulating plans.
April 1935	FDR signed Executive Order #7027, creating the Resettlement Administration within the United States Department of Agriculture, with Tugwell as Director, to build the Greenbelt New Towns.
May 1935	Tugwell's initial staff began studying 100 cities in the United States as potential sites for new planned communities.
July 1935	Tugwell pared the list to twenty-five possible sites.
September 1935	FDR approved eight cities for Greenbelt New Towns and allocated $68 million for their construction. Tugwell actually received only $31 million and the number of New Towns was further reduced to five. They included sites at St. Louis, Cincinnati, Milwaukee, Washington, D.C. and New Brunswick, N.J. Plans for the proposed Greenbelt New Town in St. Louis were dropped after disagreement with the St. Louis Plans Commission.
October 1935	Construction began on three of the four Greenbelt sites: Washington, D.C., Milwaukee, and Cincinnati. The New Jersey site experienced delays due to opposition.
December 1935	Franklin Township (New Brunswick, New Jersey) prepared for a legal battle in its efforts to stop the Greenbelt New Town project, asking the Federal District Court in Newark to issue an injunction restraining the Resettlement Administration from proceeding with construction. The Court refused to do so.
January 1936	Franklin Township hired Dean Acheson as counsel and reinitiated their suit in the Supreme Court of the District of Columbia against Rexford Tugwell. Franklin Township's objections were again overruled.
February 1936	Dean Acheson appealed the decision.
May 1936	The United States District Court of Appeals for the District of Columbia handed down a decision prohibiting the construction of the fourth Greenbelt New Town in New Jersey. The other three New Towns were unaffected. In addition, however, the Court of Appeals ruled that the Greenbelt program's funding source, the Emergency Relief Appropriations Act of 1935, represented unconstitutional delegation of legislative power to the President; therefore the entire Act was unconstitutional. All monies for the Greenbelt New Towns program ran out.
June 1936	Plans to appeal the decision to the Supreme Court of the United States were abandoned. Plans for Greenbrook, New Jersey, were also abandoned, and the other three Greenbelt New Towns were finished as far as possible with monies already appropriated. Tugwell became increasingly harassed by Congressional leaders who wanted his resignation.
December 1936	Tugwell resigned, hoping then that Congress would leave the Resettlement Administration alone to finish its work. However, the entire organization was dismantled, being absorbed by other federal agencies. The United States Government retained ownership and managed all three existing New Towns.
January 1955	The Federal Government sold its Greenbelt New Town interest to private developers, ending Tugwell's initial effort to surround urban housing with a more pleasing environment.

hoped to awaken in the American people a sense of urgency about their ultimate basis in nature.

Tugwell could not accept this concept. He felt that the meaning of wilderness had been confused by a strange sort of romanticism which had its roots in the writings of Rousseau, Chateaubriand, and other French writers just before the outbreak of the French Revolution—men who were fascinated by the idea of "back to nature." In the 1920s and 1930s tales and verses abounded, setting forth the triumphs of man in rural areas. The writings of Jack London, the tales of Stewart E. White, and the verse of Robert W. Service all spoke of situations in which the rural life cured men of their weaknesses. On a more sophisticated level and with greater literary skill, Rudyard Kipling romanticized the prophylactic qualities of nature. As a result, FDR and other "back to the land" advocates revived the theory that American pioneers and existing farmers drew strength from the land (Roosevelt, 1970).

Tugwell questioned this concept of the spiritual influence of the land. It may have been true that the westward trek was epic and that the men, and particularly the women, who crossed much of the continent on foot were a tough breed. But they won not because the land and nature had given them spiritual strength, but because they had overcome the wilderness. Their physical endurance was fortified by the vast amount of labor they had to perform in order to survive and not because of imaginary forces supposedly spawned by rural living. Instead of inspiring them, the wilderness actually embittered them. They were at the mercy of the seasons and of the weather, they endured thirst and hunger, and many of the weak died (Roosevelt, 1970).

Tugwell strongly believed that rural life was bleak and irrational. For the more competent farmers with equity in substantial acreages and with able-bodied sons, the farm was a beneficial institution (Baldwin, 1968, p. 87). But for the chronically insecure small farmers, it often became a trap. To Tugwell there was no romance in agriculture and rural life and, in 1930, he painted the following picture:

> A farm is an area of vicious, ill-tempered soil with not a very good house, inadequate barns, makeshift machinery, happenstance stock, tired, overworked men and women ... and all the pests and bucolic plagues that nature has evolved ... a place where ugly, brooding monotony that haunts by day and night, unseats the mind (Tugwell, et al., 1930, p. 85).

In particular, he fundamentally disapproved of the whole rural homestead approach. The family farm seemed to him to be as much a monument of the primitive past as was the small business; both were structured defects in an economy committed to large-scale units. Tugwell felt that this "back to the land" ideology went against technology, and to do that was to go against history. If the family farm or the rural homestead had a role, it was at best peripheral, exacting a far higher economic cost than social value justified (Schlesinger, 1958, p. 369). "I am inclined to believe," he wrote in 1933, "that such settlements will function merely as small eddies of retreat for exceptional persons and that the greater part of our population will prefer to live and work in the more active and vigorous mainstream of a highly complex civilization" (Schlesinger, 1958, p. 369).

THE CITY AS CORRECTIVE

The correct approach to mitigate rural poverty, he felt, was in the cities. The cities themselves could also benefit, for here was a rare opportunity for almost limitless experimentation in land use planning, community planning, massive rural conservation programs, and a better life for exhausted people. But the opportunity for the concurrent correction of rural poverty and urban problems was not being taken advantage of. In addition, Tugwell in his position as Undersecretary of Agriculture was becoming disappointed. His private hopes for awakening the conservative USDA to the needs of the marginal farmer were not materializing (Baldwin, 1968, p. 88).

STEPS TOWARD CREATION OF RESETTLEMENT ADMINISTRATION

By 1935, business was showing signs of improvement, and the older members of Congress were beginning to question many of the recovery methods used by Roosevelt to stimulate the depressed American economy. Many felt that some of FDR's programs were too socialistic and radical. Tugwell realized that if socioeconomic improvement was to occur, it was necessary to take action immediately. But a close inspection of the USDA revealed that agencies dealing with land and poverty programs were working independently of, and often competing with, one another. Tugwell felt that a program consolidation under one agency was necessary to implement improvement of rural poverty conditions, thus permitting a better use of the land. FDR knew this also, for both had discussed a centralization of these programs, but, due to administration difficulties and interagency rivalries, reorganization had not been accomplished. In early 1935, Tugwell decided that there was little he could accomplish without this reorganization, and began to consider leaving the USDA (Baldwin, 1968, p. 88).

On February 18, 1935, Tugwell suggested in conversation with FDR that he wanted to resign his position. FDR refused to consider such a move; in fact, Tugwell wrote in his Diary, "He regarded me as a distinct political asset ... he had no intention of letting me go at all." During the days that followed, he and FDR discussed several courses to follow. FDR's intention was the implementation of "new" policies outlined in his State of the Union message of January 4, 1935. These included three types of security: livelihood, hazards of life, and housing. The type of housing reform FDR advocated was a form of slum clearance. Tugwell, however, was not in agreement because, in his opinion, FDR's plan would not go far enough in correcting the problems of the rural poor.[6] Still dissatisfied, Tugwell again discussed possible resignation with FDR, who then suggested that he consider other approaches regarding the slum clearance issue and work out possible solutions. On March 3, he again talked with Roosevelt:

> FDR let me off slum clearance, though he laughed at me for not wanting to do it. I talked to him about satellite cities as an alternative and it interested him greatly. My idea is to go just outside centers of population, pick up cheap land, build a whole community and entice people into it. Then go back into cities and tear down slums and make parks of them. I could do this with good heart and he now wants me to (Diary, March 3, 1935).

Four days after Tugwell had spoken with Roosevelt about his "satellite cities" plan, he reported, "I submitted my charts and plans to FDR and he approved completely, giving me permission to get the things organized" (Diary, March 7, 1935). His attitude was reminiscent of a piece he had written twenty years earlier for the Intercollegiate Magazine while a sophomore at the University of Pennsylvania —a piece which would provide a great deal of pleasure for his critics in the years to come.

> I am strong
> I am well made
> I am muscled and lean and nervous
> I am frank and sure and incisive.
>
> I bend the forces untameable;
> I harness the power irresistible—
> All this I do; but I shall do more.
>
> I am sick of a nation's stenches,
> I am sick of propertied czars ...
> I have dreamed my great dream of their passing.
> I have gathered my tools and my charts;

GREENDALE, WISCONSIN The third Greenbelt New Town is located eight miles southwest of Milwaukee. The tract comprises 3,410 acres and contained initially 750 homes, commercial area, and facilities.

My plans are fashioned and practical;
I shall roll up my sleeves . . . make America over
(Bolles, 1936, p. 77).

THE AUTOMOBILE AND GREENBELT

Literature is replete with statements that the men who designed and laid out the Greenbelt towns drew on a rich international heritage of town planning theory and practice (Arnold, 1971, p. 3). Particular reference has been made to Ebenezer Howard and his Garden City movement. However, there is little evidence to suggest that Tugwell was influenced by Howard to any great extent. According to John Lansill, Tugwell's Director of the Suburban Resettlement Administration, both men were highly influenced by other American planned communities during this period, communities associated with the introduction of the automobile in the 1920s (Lansill, 1972).[7] As Mel Scott notes, after 1920 people began to buy automobiles by the millions, 2.3 million in 1922 and more than 3.0 million annually from 1923 through 1926. In 1927 sales went to 3.8 million and reached 4.5 million in the climatic year of 1929 (Scott, 1971, p. 186). The sheer number of automobiles contributed enormously to environmental and financial stress. Many problems were created, among them a demand for better streets and roads, and for better paving and wider streets on the part of the merchants, who complained that the existing streets were choked with traffic. An additional strain was placed on municipal treasuries which had to purchase expensive traffic and road maintenance equipment. The boom in automobiles had a very grim aspect also; by 1925, traffic accidents were claiming approximately twenty-four thousand lives annually.

According to Scott, the incidence of fatalities and injuries caused by the automobile was the factor which prompted some of the most constructive endeavors of the times and did much to stimulate interest in city and town planning (Scott, 1971, p. 188). In the 1920s, developer William Harmon stated that all his future housing plans would include their own recreational sites because automobile traffic had made streets literally death traps for children and pedestrians. Clarence Perry was designing residential areas that would be free from noise, fumes, and the hazards of automobiles. Radburn, a typical example of what Perry had in mind, was described as "a city for the motor age." It had superblocks of thirty to fifty acres in which there were interior parks where children could play without fear of falling beneath the wheels of cars. A host of other housing developments throughout America in the 1920s and 1930s were designed to restrict the use of the automobile and make the environment safer. Among these were Shaker Heights in Cleveland, designed by the Van Sweringen brothers; Torrance, California, designed by J. S. Torrance; and the Country Club District of Kansas City, designed by Jesse Nichols. The Van Sweringens employed many of the features of suburban residential development later to be used in planning the typical Greenbelt New Town: abandonment of the traditional gridiron and substitution of curving and semi-elliptical roads leading from main automobile boulevards, the preservation of natural park areas throughout, and strict architectural requirements (Glaab and Brown, 1967, p. 283).

For these reasons, Lansill maintained that the Greenbelt New Town program initiated by Rexford Tugwell owed few direct intellectual debts to Howard, instead drawing heavily on the newly created American school of thought concerning urban development. Walt Creese notes that

> an exercise can be prepared to show that the United States, with its rapid growth in the nineteenth century and its receptivity to novel schemes, contributed substantially to the impetus of the garden city movement. It would require only a little chauvinism to persuade us that most of the basic premises of the garden city movement in England originated here in the United States (Creese, 1966, p. 1).

EARLY GREENBELT DESIGNS

For Beltsville, Maryland, Tugwell originally envisioned a group of skyscrapers fifty or sixty stories high, cruciform in plan and very widely spaced, containing housing, administrative, and commercial space. These designs were greatly influenced by Le Corbusier's Ville Contemporaine, the city designed for three million inhabitants which was displayed at the Paris Exhibition of 1922. Le Corbusier's city was surrounded by a "green belt" several miles wide, permanently isolating and protecting it; industrial districts were situated to the east, with farms and a sports arena to the northwest. The optimum population of three million was not to be exceeded; additional new cities would be built to accommodate the excess. With the possible exception of Tony Garnier's Plan for an Ideal City of thirty-five thousand (1901-1904), Le Corbusier's Ville Contemporaine was the first really contemporary vision for a new metropolis: an imaginative exercise in ideal city planning, bringing into play all the then known and anticipated technological advances and building forms (Anthony, 1967, p. 281).

However, John Lansill, Tugwell's friend since their days as students at the University of Pennsylvania, was appalled by Le Corbusier's design. Lansill, upon graduation from the Wharton School of Finance, had entered a Wall Street brokerage house and had lived and worked among the concrete canyons of Manhattan. It was an architectural form he never enjoyed, and he thought the idea of purposefully designing a city from the beginning and constructing it in this manner was insane. Lansill was able to convince Tugwell to abandon Le Corbusier's Ville Contemporaine idea in favor of single and multi family housing units.

The first fruits of the Greenbelt New Town program were not altogether encouraging. "One of the major problems in getting the program started was the difficulty of getting together a staff capable of handling a huge building problem" (Lansill, 1972). To its distress, the Resettlement Administration was handicapped by the nationwide ignorance about housing. In addition, it appeared that Tugwell had a bias against architects and town planners (Lansill, 1972). Part of the reason stemmed from the experiences of the Public Works Administration (PWA) in its attempts to construct low-cost housing in urban areas, in conjunction with minor slum clearance programs. PWA had found that most American architects and town planners had conceptual difficulties in attempting to design reasonable low-income housing within the constraints established by budgets and land use requirements.[8] Tugwell also believed that architects and town planners were too utopian and idealistic. Consequently, the Resettlement Administration did not immediately turn to city planners or designers for advice, but rather to its own engineering staff which had considerable experience in designing many rural low-income subsistence homestead projects (Arnold, 1971, p. 47).

The first design for Greenbelt, Maryland, represented a typical subdivision of the period, calling for a grid land use plan with over sixty miles of streets. This might have been the model for all the succeeding Greenbelt New Towns if it had not been for Warren Vinton. Vinton was the chief economist of the Resettlement Administration and he had mentioned the Greenbelt design to a group of friends, several of whom were architects. Sketching out the plans as he remembered them, Vinton was persuaded that the engineers had produced an undistinguished, unimaginative design for a housing project of Greenbelt's magnitude (Baldwin, 1972). John Lansill was later approached about the inadequacies of the design and with Tracy Augur, Tennessee Valley Authority's chief town planner, they agreed to approach Tugwell with the recommendation that all the engineers be replaced with professional town planners. Tugwell, though reluctant, allowed the change to take place. The engineering staff was dispersed, and a separate planning and architectural team was designed for each of the four Greenbelt towns (Lansill, 1972). (See chart 1.)

PLANNING THE FOUR TOWNS

The planning of the four towns intentionally reflects four different approaches to the problem. Setting up four parallel, vertical organizations may seem, on superficial view, extravagant in its duplication and cumbersome in procedure. However, John Lansill felt that as the head of a new type of venture and as a layman dependent on the technicans to carry out the program, he could not afford to rely on any one theory of design procedure. Moreover, the projects were in four widely differing localities; local laws, prejudices, habits, and wants would all have to be considered. After an abortive start with the in-house architectural engineers, Lansill felt that the time for standardization was not yet here. Because the whole venture was in the nature of an experiment, the more talent that could be enrolled, the better the chances for success.

According to Arnold (1971, p. 83). The Resettlement Administration could have stayed with the dull, unimaginative designs put forth by the initial engineering group. It could have met its primary responsibility by merely constructing a large number of simple dwellings. But the receptivity of Tugwell and Lansill to design criticism was unusual; as a result the enthusiasms of the planners and architects in the Resettlement Administration became widespread. They were inspired, said Lansill, by the standard set by Tugwell to create a demonstrable example and set it before the American people (Lansill, 1972). As the project evolved they became increasingly convinced that they were involved in one of the most significant American experiments in city building the nation had ever seen. Will Alexander says, "The young architects felt sure that this Resettlement Administration was going to revolutionize the concept of urban built form" (Arnold, 1971,

p. 50). Marquis Childs recalled the enthusiasms of the planners who kept the lights burning far into the night, and said, "They thought they were planning a new world" (Arnold, 1971, p. 50).

No one within the Resettlement Administration posed his own ideas on the planning staff. Therefore, each separate team worked independently of the other town planning staffs. This was necessary because each town site was different in topography, population, economy, and legal structure. Each planning staff had three departments: town planning, architecture, and engineering. Subsections were established to plan electrical, heating, utilities, and landscaping. The planning staff was headed by one or two men designated as chief town planner, chief architect, or chief engineer, but the group was collectively responsible for the whole project.

The Greenbelt town plan included a sweeping crescent-shaped town along a beautifully wooded ridge with the open end of the crescent facing prevailing summer breezes. Greenhills was built along the crest of a number of small ridges cut by ravines and resulted in a somewhat irregular town pattern. Greendale is laid out on very gently rolling land, and the tract is cut in by a small creek running through its very center. Greenbrook would have been built on nearly flat terrain.

Low residential density was considered desirable for all the towns. In the residential area of Greendale there were approximately 5 families per acre. At Greenhills, there were 8.5 families per acre and at Greenbelt, 4 families per acre.

At Greenbrook and Greenbelt the curvilinear streets were designed to form superblocks which were intended to form a physical basis for the development of neighborhoods, as had been done at Radburn and several other new towns. The Greendale planners rejected the superblock as well as curvilinear streets. Elbert Peets, the town planner, was attracted to traditional architectural styles, particularly that of colonial Williamsburg. Peets later said, "It was not quite an accident that in its skeleton organization the plan of Greendale is much like the plan of Williamsburg" (Arnold, 1971, p. 94).

The exterior design of the buildings for all three of the Greenbelt towns is generally considered disappointing. Henry Churchill, an advisor, called the exteriors "competent and undistinguished." There was no conscious effort to follow any set precedent in the design of the buildings and if one had to label the style, it could be called "functional" or "contemporary" (Arnold, 1971, p. 102). Basically, Greenbelt's architecture is an example of what the designers of the 1930s regarded as the "New Tradition" (now called the International Style in architecture), a reaction against the ornamentation and sentimental traditionalism of Victorian styles which held their own in the United States up to and including the 1920s. Greendale, from the aesthetic point of view, is considered to be the most interesting. Peets, the head architect, patterned his houses on the American colonial pattern, close to the street with small fenced yards on the side and rear. Nevertheless, each group of planners for the Greenbelt towns showed remarkable imagination and thoroughness in the face of great pressures during the depression days of the mid-1930s and with a back-breaking schedule to achieve these accomplishments in a period of one and one-half years.

GREENBELT OPPOSITION AND THE COURTS

It was no secret that the Greenbelt New Town program was pioneering a new pattern of rural-urban industrial life. However, not everyone appreciated the pioneer spirit of Tugwell and the Greenbelt town planners. When the plans for the fourth new town, Greenbrook, were announced, this lack of appreciation appeared in the form of a legal challenge.

Greenbrook was to have been the largest of the Greenbelt

Chart 1 *Greenbelt New Town Organizational Structure*

	Henry C. Wallace	Secretary, Department of Agriculture		
	Rexford Guy Tugwell	Director, Resettlement Administration		
	John Scott Lansill	Director, Suburban Resettlement		
	Henry Wright	General Consultant		
	Clarence S. Stein	Architectural Consultant		
	Tracy Augur	Regional Consultant		
	Earle Draper	Policy Formation		
	Catherine Bauer	Special Consultant		
	Russell Bloch	Special Consultant		
	Tilford Dudley	Land Acquisition		
	Reid W. Diggs	Budget & Finance		
	Warren S. Vinton	Social & Economic Research		
	Frederich Bigger — Chief of Planning			

Section	Greenbelt	Greenhills	Greendale	Greenbrook
Architects	Reginald S. Wadsworth Douglas D. Ellington	Roland A. Wank G. Frank Condner	Harry A. Bentley Walter G. Thomas	Albert Mayer Henry S. Churchill
Planners	Hale Walker	Justin Hartzog William A. Strong	Elbert Peets Jacob Crane	Henry Wright Allen Kanstra
Engineers	Harold B. Bursley	William T. Powell	Walter E. Kroening Charlton D. Putnam	Ralph Eberlin
Regional Coordinator	William Richards	Albert Miller	Fred L. Naumer	Isaac McBride

projects, containing over twenty thousand people. Its location was between New Brunswick and Princeton, New Jersey. By a three-to-one decision in the United States Court of Appeals in the District of Columbia on May 18, 1936, the Resettlement Administration was enjoined from proceeding with its construction. In arguing the case before the court, Dean Acheson, counsel for the Township, pleaded that this new town would cause something of a revolution in the character of the Township, changing it from rural to urban in nature almost overnight and adding to the cost of local government without supplying a compensating source of revenue. Another factor was that Greenbrook was designed to accommodate twenty thousand people, and many residents within the Township feared that existing property values would drop if a United States government-subsidized new town were constructed. The Township had other than monetary interests in the Greenbrook case; by forcing an unwanted development upon it by the Federal Government, it was argued, the Township would be in danger of losing its home rule (The United States Law Week, 1936, p. 6).

In a lengthy opinion, the Court also held that the provision of the Emergency Relief Appropriations Act of 1935, pursuant to which the Resettlement Administration was created, constituted an invalid delegation to the President of the Congressional power to legislate because (Minutes of the United States Court of Appeals for the District of Columbia, 1936):

1. There was no adequate definition of the subject;
2. There was nothing in the Act directly prescribing the powers and duties of the President with respect to housing; and
3. The declaration of purpose was too vague.

Ordinarily Congress may lay down policies and establish standards, leaving it to the appropriate government agencies to make subordinate rules within prescribed limits, to fill in details, and to determine the facts to which the policies declared by the legislature apply. Under this Act, the Court declared that no policies or standards were laid down, and the President was improperly free to decide when, where, and how housing projects could be established (Robbins, 1936, p. 5).

This objection could have been cured by amendment to the original Act or by new legislation. However, the Court went further and held that the Federal Government had no power to engage directly in housing activities for two reasons:

1. That such activities are not within the scope of the powers granted to Congress, because housing projects "have no connections with the general welfare"; and
2. That such activities are reserved for action by the states alone. Therefore, legislation by Congress for that purpose is forbidden (Minutes, 1936).

Although the Circuit Court's decision seemed to doom the entire Resettlement program, the United States Attorney General announced that the decision would be limited to the New Jersey project, Greenbrook. An appeal to the Supreme Court was dropped, and the other projects which remained unchallenged were pushed toward completion with the funds already allocated to them. However, new projects could not be initiated because the Emergency Relief Appropriations Act which provided the funds to build the new towns had also been declared unconstitutional (Minutes, 1936). For all practical purposes, the Circuit Court's decision brought to a halt America's first large-scale attempt to integrate all the factors that go into making a balanced community—towns planned from the beginning according to a definite conception of purpose and overall balance.

OPPOSITION TO RESETTLEMENT

As Lash noted, both Eleanor and Franklin Roosevelt supported the Resettlement Greenbelt project. But even this support was not enough. By 1936, the mood of the country, and especially that of Congress, was growing hostile to the whole idea of publicly planned communities. The political environment had become unfriendly to such social experimentation and to such reformers as Tugwell who wanted to "make America over" (Lash, 1972, p. 413).

Eleanor Roosevelt, a strong supporter of the rural subsistence homesteads, felt saddened about the opposition to the Resettlement project. "'If experiments like Resettlement are not justified," she said, "we must go along the beaten path and be contented with the same type of living which has driven people out of rural districts in the past and into the cities where they have become equally unhappy under present industrial conditions" (Lash, 1972, p. 417).

However, the lessons of the Greenbelt new towns went unappreciated. Instead of a planned approach to the related problems of the flight from the farms, urban congestion, and industrial decentralization, the outcome was left to the unchecked operation of social and economic forces that had produced the crisis of the cities in the first place (Lash, 1972, p. 417).

Tugwell had hoped to construct a good many projects; at a press conference he once remarked that we need three thousand new towns instead of the three being planned. But the entire Administration came under such fierce attack that the program was limited to three, which were never completed, and were later disposed of by the government to speculators. Tugwell thought the attack stemmed from the belief that the Resettlement Administration was doing something for those who had done nothing to deserve it: an administration of extravagant do-gooders (Tugwell, 1959, p. 163).

PLANNING

Another source of conflict between Congress and the Resettlement Administration was the stress placed on planning, especially the idea of land use control, and the retiring of land no longer suitable for agricultural use. Congress met this idea with "complete scorn." "They let us know that this was a fancy idea devised by intellectuals, therefore, it was wholly impractical; and they refused to have anything to do with it," Tugwell wrote (1959, p. 161).

Critics may have disagreed about Tugwell's ideological commitments but on one point there was agreement, that he was basically an iconoclast (Baldwin, 1968, p. 88). Hostile to the traditional laissez faire attitude with its tendency toward anarchy, Tugwell saw national salvation lying not simply in productive efficiency, technological innovation, and improving the market mechanism, but also in growth guided by public planning and control.

Although he did not expect ideality to be just around the corner, Tugwell knew that planning implied a revolution, with new attitudes, new disciplines, revised legal structures, unaccustomed limitations on freedom, and an end to privatism (Conkin, 1959, p. 151). He felt that people were generally opposed to planning; that there were strong emotional and physical investments in the status quo; that the effectuation of planning required change in institutions, a realignment of vested interests, and the displacement of people; and that planning involved conclusions and commitments with respect to an indefinite future (Tugwell, 1947). He had realized that it was perhaps more difficult to plan than not to plan, seemingly easier to wait until the situation was self-evident and decisions were forced upon him. He felt that these were limitations to be overcome rather than reasons not to proceed. When Tugwell looked around him, he saw trends in society which suggested that there were no alternatives to increased planning, the growing technological and organizational complexity of business and government, population growth and migration patterns, the continued specialization of labor, and the foreseeable exhaustion of many of the natural energy sources on which the nation relied.

To Tugwell his Greenbelt towns represented a pioneer effort. Through them he hoped to weave a new pattern of rural-industrial life, a method of land use in which the old, wasteful practices never had a chance to get started.

> I really would like to conserve all those things which I grew up to respect or love and not see them destroyed.

I grew up in an American small town and I've never forgotten it. No one was very rich there, but no one was very poor either. I can't make this Park Avenue country club life seem right, along with slums and breadlines, ballyhoo, speculation; I can't make this fit into my picture of American institutions.

I'm for decentralization, for simplicity of life, along with a recognition of the complexity of industrial and scientific civilization. It seems to me that electricity, vacuum tubes, Diesel engines and all those other things ought to make it possible for us to approximate that "no riches–no poverty" kind of life in which I grew up (Lord, 1947, p. 360).

CONGRESS KILLS RESETTLEMENT ADMINISTRATION

But young intellectuals such as Tugwell who influenced the President and who disregarded traditional political methods were bound to arouse a mounting resentment and rebellion on the part of Congress. Their lack of a definite mandate and their lack of political experience proved to be a decided weakness.

Tugwell wrote, "We were a Presidential protégé; and we were among the first to suffer from the inevitable upsurge of antipresidential emotions following his great second term victory" (Tugwell, 1959, p. 163). He felt that Congress as an institution could not tolerate its being outshone by the President. When the 1936 election was over, Congress was in a mood to assert its prerogatives, and the Resettlement Administration was one of the first programs to be eliminated.

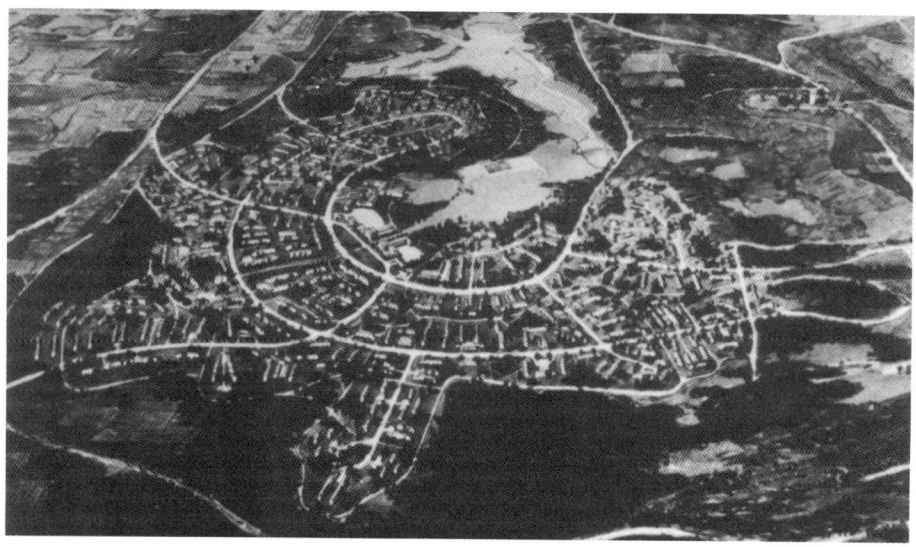

GREENBELT, MARYLAND   The first of the Greenbelt New Towns is located ten miles from the center of Washington, D.C. near Andrews Air Force Base. The tract contained 5,400 acres and initially contained one thousand homes.

On December 31, 1936, Tugwell resigned his position as the head of the Resettlement Administration. His organization was under attack from several sides and he felt that if he left then, the legislators might be content with his resignation and leave the Administration alone to do its work. But he was mistaken. In fact, it was completely dissolved. Twenty-three years later he had this to say to younger successors in governmental service:

> If you feel impelled to organize a constructive attack on social ills, be sure that you are riding a drift of support likely to register at the source of funds. In other words, the Congress must have a bad conscience too.
>
> Be sure that those who will be benefited will be able to, and will, register their support whenever the struggles for your continuance occur.
>
> My final advice to those who are thus moved by injustices and human needs, and who think they perceive better possibilities through social organization, is to go ahead. Fail as gloriously as some of your predecessors have. If you do not succeed in bringing about any permanent change, you may at least have stirred some slow consciences so that in time they will give support to action. And you will have the satisfaction, which is not to be discounted, of having annoyed a good many miscreants who had it coming to them (Tugwell, 1959, p. 164).

CONCLUSION

The three completed Greenbelt new towns represent the Federal Government's initial efforts in building new towns in America. They were not the garden cities of Ebenezer Howard, economically complete, but satellite suburbs, made possible for the first time because of the universal and economical availability of the automobile. Howard's garden cities may be thought of as being escapist, reflecting a desire to leave London entirely. Tugwell, on the other hand, believed existing cities could be made more livable but he was dismayed by their deficiencies, which were due to a lack of order, management, and control. In addition, with technology displacing farm workers and releasing them to industrial employment in the cities, Tugwell believed that urban growth and development had to be controlled, not stopped or abandoned, but guided and regulated through planning. The Greenbelt new towns would demonstrate this belief. However, Tugwell's demonstration of more orderly growth, his efforts to surround housing with a more pleasing environment went unappreciated and ultimately were rejected. It was simply a road not taken. In the late 1940s or early 1950s, Tugwell wrote:

> I am, after all these years, still bitter about the disappearance of the Resettlement Administration and still harbor, in spite of myself, a good deal of stubborn resentment. No one paid any penalty for killing Resettlement. But I still believe that something like it must be done for the sake of the people and the land. I hope in its next incarnation it will meet with greater success (Diary, section 7, p. 34).

Acknowledgements

The author would like to express his appreciation to the JAIP reviewers and to Dr. Virginia Yans-McLaughlin of the City College of The City University of New York for their helpful comments and suggestions in the preparation of this manuscript.

NOTES

1 See, for example, Glaab and Brown, 1967, p. 303, and also Stein, 1957, pp. 120 and 130.
2 Tugwell writes: "The idea for this agency was my own, and I was made its administrator. President Roosevelt was, however, immediately interested because it touched matters he cared about a great deal" (Tugwell, 1959, p. 159).
3 Tugwell notes: "The conception of suburban resettlement came less from the garden city of England than from some studies of our own population movements which showed steady growth in the periphery of the cities...in other words [Greenbelt] accepted a trend instead of trying to reverse it" (Tugwell, 1937, p. 43) and Lash writes: "Tugwell's emphasis as resettlement administrator was on land reform. His program sought to 'take poor people off poor land and resettle them where good land, good organization and good advice might rehabilitate them.' In addition, he promoted the brilliant concept of the Greenbelt towns, garden communities built in wooded areas adjacent to industrial areas" (Lash, 1972, p. 413).
4 For one of the best descriptions of the plight of the American farmer during the Depression, see John Steinbeck's *The Grapes of Wrath*.
5 See Roosevelt's article about the benefits of rural life as opposed to urban living (Roosevelt, 1931), and also Slicker's descriptions of Roosevelt's "back to the land" concepts (Slicker, 1959).
6 Tugwell did not embrace slum clearance as did FDR. Tugwell felt that garden cities offered a better environment "for living and working" than did seeking to rebuild existing cities. "Slum clearance has to fight a good many entrenched interests; and its land costs are too high ever to protect the rights of children or ever to provide recreation for adults. Cities will not develop such projects as these; they will probably oppose them" (Tugwell, 1937, p. 43).
  Albert M. Miller's view was similar: "When an effort is made to rebuild bad areas in a city, with new housing, we are confronted with a confused background of extravagant municipal procedure, and often with mythical land values, transportation companies in receivership, defaulting of municipal debt interest and all the rest of the confusion which businessmen of the communities have allowed to grow up around them" (Speech, 1936, p. 15).
7 According to Peets: "The program, the skeleton of ideas and facts, on which Greenbelt is being planned is something like this: Automotive transportation makes it possible for men to live a considerable distance from their work; pure air, rural surroundings, and contact with the ground, are physically and psychically good; life is better in a small town where social cooperation is possible; by eliminating inflated land values, by appropriate planning, by large-scale construction, and by taking advantage of every reasonable means for reducing living costs" (Peets, 1937, p. 409).
8 For examples of these difficulties, see Hackett, 1935, pp. 1 and 4; Stein, 1957, p. 120; and Arnold, 1971, p. 88.

REFERENCES

Anthony, Harry A. (1967) "LeCorbusier: His Ideas for Cities," *American Institute of Architectural Journal*, September.
Arnold, Joseph (1971) *New Deal In The Suburbs*. Columbus,

Ohio: Ohio State University.

Baldwin, C. B. (1972) Interview, August.

Baldwin, Sidney (1968) *Poverty and Politics*. Chapel Hill, N.C.: University of North Carolina Press.

Bolles, Blair (1936) "The Sweetheart of the Regimenters," *American Mercury*, September.

Conkin, Paul (1959) *Tomorrow A New World*. Ithaca, New York: Cornell University Press.

Creese, Walter L. (1966) *The Search For Environment: The Garden City: Before and After*. New Haven: Yale University Press.

Emergency Relief Appropriations Act of 1935, U.S. Statutes at Large, vol. 49, p. 115.

Franklin Township v. Tugwell, 85F (App., D.C.) 208 (1936).

Glaab, Charles N. and A. Theodore Brown (1967) *A History of Urban America*. London: Macmillan.

Hackett, Horatio B. (1935) "Problems and Policies of the Housing Division of P.W.A.," *Housing Officials Yearbook*. Washington, D.C.: National Association of Housing.

Lansill, John S. (1972) Interview, June.

Lash, Joseph P. (1972) *Eleanor and Franklin*. New York: W. W. Norton.

Lord, Russell (1947) *The Wallaces of Iowa*. Boston: Houghton Mifflin.

Lowi, Theodore J. (1969) *The End of Liberalism*. New York: W. W. Norton.

Mann, Maurice (1952) "Rexford Guy Tugwell, Institutional Economist," master's thesis, Department of Economics, Boston University.

Miller, Albert L. (1936) Resettlement Administration, Speech before the Citizen's Committee on Slum Clearance and Low Rent Housing, Cincinnati, June 24.

Minutes of United States Court of Appeals For The District of Columbia #6619, "The Township of Franklin v. Rexford Tugwell," May 18, 1936.

Peets, Elbert (1937) "Greendale," in *City Planning-Housing*, edited by Werner Hegemann. New York: Architectural Book Publishing.

Robbins, Ira (1936) "Resettlement Administration Only Partially Unsettled," *American City*, June.

Roosevelt, Franklin D. (1931) "Back To The Land," *The Review of Reviews*, October.

Roosevelt, Nicholas (1970) *Conservation: Now or Never*. New York: Dodd, Mead.

Rosenman, Samuel I. (1950) *The Public Papers and Addresses of Franklin D. Roosevelt*. 13 volumes, New York: Random House.

Schlesinger, Jr., Arthur M. (1958) *The Coming of the New Deal*. Boston: Houghton Mifflin.

Scott, Mel (1971) *American City Planning*. Berkeley, Calif.: University of California Press.

Slichter, Gertrude A. (1959) "Franklin D. Roosevelt's Farm Policy As Governor of New York State, 1928-1932," *Agricultural History*, October.

Stein, Clarence S. (1957) *Toward New Towns For America*. New York: Reinhold.

Steinbeck, John (1939) *The Grapes of Wrath*. New York: The Viking Press.

Sternsher, Bernard (1964) *Rexford Tugwell and the New Deal*. New Brunswick: Rutgers University Press.

Tugwell, Rexford Guy, et al. (1930) *American Economic Life and The Means of Its Improvement*. New York: Harcourt, Brace.

Tugwell, Rexford Guy, "Diary Notes," manuscript, FDR Library, Hyde Park, New York.

―――― (1935) "No More Frontiers," *Today*, June 22.

―――― (1936) "Down To Earth," *Current History*, July.

―――― (1936) "Housing Activities and Plans of the Resettlement Administration," *Housing Officials Yearbook*, March. Washington, D.C.: National Association of Housing.

―――― (1937) "The Meaning of the Greenbelt Towns," *The New Republic*, February 17.

―――― (1947) *The Stricken Land*. New York: Doubleday.

―――― (1959) "The Resettlement Idea," *Agricultural History*, October.

The United States Law Week (1936) "Resettlement Administration—Constitutionally Injunction," May 19.

Photograph on page 176 used with the permission of *Center* Magazine

Frank Lloyd Wright and the American City: The Broadacres Debate

Stephen Grabow

Frank Lloyd Wright's principal attempt at urban planning—Broadacre City—constitutes an enigma. On one hand it has often been dismissed as an example of impractical utopianism; but on the other hand it seems to have foreshadowed forty years of suburbanization in the United States. To account for the paradox, several attempts to reassess the significance of Broadacre City have appeared in the last two decades. Combined with the original reactions to Wright's proposal in the thirties and forties, these discussions provide a timely debate which, upon examination, reveals part of the sociology of knowledge in architecture and planning. The first part of this article briefly summarizes Wright's proposal, including the philosophical background of Broadacre City, the spatial influences, and the reinforcement and support at the time of its publication. The second part analyzes the ensuing debate over questions of procedure and content between 1933 and the present. And the third part examines the disagreement in terms of the professional and philosophical orientations of the critics.

In 1962, a forum held by Resources for the Future concluded that the classical city of urban history—the dense concentration of people around a civic nucleus—was not a satisfactory pattern of settlement for a postindustrial society (Wingo 1966). The one urban historian who charted this inevitability, E. A. Gutkind (1962), was largely ignored by architects and planners for one very obvious reason: it was difficult to imagine an urban culture without cities.[1]

Only recently have we been able to understand that the collapse and decentralization of big, industrial cities and the phenomenal growth and attraction of suburbs, small towns, and spread-out, relatively low-density, auto-age cities like Los Angeles, Phoenix, and Houston are part of a continuing process of urbanization rather than some terminal state. The revolution in transportation and communications technologies, the emphasis on informational flows over material flows, the cultural diffusion of urban life, and other characteristics of postindustrialization are what undermine the historical advantages of central location and give rise to a more diffused pattern. Metaphors of a new image of the city—Lewis Mumford's "invisible grid," Marshall McLuhan's "global village," and Melvin Webber's "community without propinquity"—attempt to capture the aspatial dimension of such decentralization. Frank Lloyd Wright's principal attempt at urban planning was to anticipate (although in his own inimitable way) these developments.[2]

Stephen Grabow is a faculty member in urban planning and director of graduate studies in architecture and urban design at the University of Kansas. He studied at the University of Michigan, Pratt Institute, the University of California at Berkeley, and holds a Ph.D. in urban planning from the University of Washington. He is currently a visiting fellow at the Center for Environmental Structure at Berkeley.

APRIL 1977

The Broadacres proposal

In 1932, Wright published his proposal for the impending decentralization of urban society into a settlement pattern that, in his own words, was to be "everywhere or nowhere." He called it Broadacre City. In 1935, a model of a typical section of what this city might look like was exhibited at Rockefeller Center in New York and, on tour, around the United States and Europe.

The plan of Broadacre City was a schematic representation of a relatively low-density, continuous urban area in which previously centralized city functions would be decentralized along a linear transportation and communications system. Although there was some mixing of these functions, similar uses of land were grouped together in five large sections (actually continuous ribbons of urban development) parallel to a superhighway and regional rail system.

The section closest to and adjacent to the transportation spine (1 on Figure 1) contained industrial and mercantile land uses of small factories and roadside markets. The next zone (2) was for agricultural uses, principally community-owned small farms. The third and largest section (3) was residential, mainly homesteads of one acre and larger interspersed with elementary schools and (occasionally) higher density housing. The next zone (4) was civic and cultural, including sports facilities, clinics, county government and services, theaters, and institutions of higher education. Finally, the development petered out in a zone of recreational uses (5)—almost a green belt—interspersed with larger (and more expensive) homes.

The main residential zone was a mile wide and of indefinite length. (One can imagine this paralleling the interstate highway system). The entire strip of development, between the transportation spine and the green belt, was not more than two miles wide at any point. The model represented a prototypical four square mile section of this strip of continuous urban development. It was to accommodate 1,400 families at an overall density of nearly two acres per family, although about one-third of the area was devoted to nonresidential land uses.

The preconditions necessary for this plan to be realized included a vast national transportation and communications system, economic and industrial decentralization, an expansion of the role of county governments, and land ownership of at least one acre for every American family. These preconditions, in turn, stemmed from a unique (and idiosyncratic) synthesis of social and political philosophies that Wright believed to be appropriate to America, not only in the context of decentralized urbanization, but also as the American way of life. In four more publications, between 1938 and 1958, he was to articulate this synthesis without substantially changing the original proposal.

Intellectual and physical background

Lionel March (1970) points out that many (if not all) of Wright's views came from some of the most notable intellectuals and practicing politicians of his day. Mainly social reformers, progressives, and liberals, they had one thing in common: they were all, according to Richard Pells's analysis of the period, "radical innovators with profoundly conservative goals" (1973, p. 3). The easy (and sometimes superficial) blending of political theory and empirical reality into seemingly workable plans characterized their peculiarly utilitarian and pragmatic philosophy. They insisted that all theory had to be related to the surrounding environment and that social change was possible only through personal involvement in that environment rather than from a more dispassionate analytic approach.

From William James and John Dewey came the notion that democracy was a continuing process, not a form, and that social institutions should be structured

Frank Lloyd Wright

Division of Special Collections Spencer Research Library, University of Kansas.

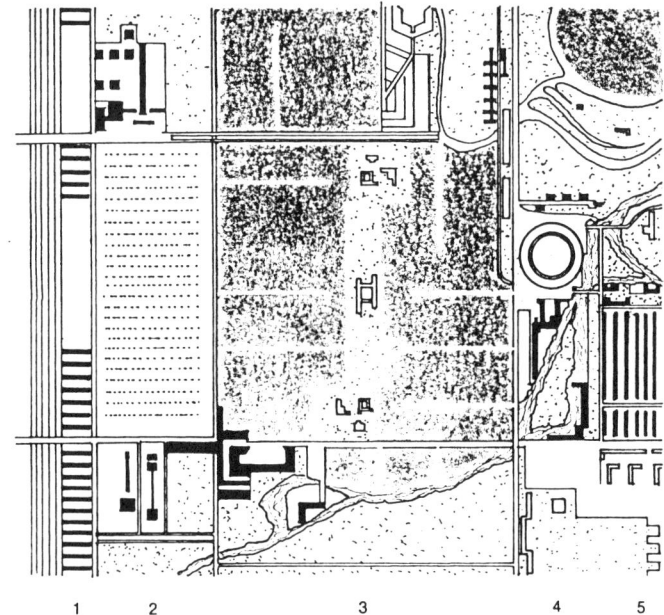

Figure 1.
Five sections were defined in Wright's plan.

Source: Thomas Reiner, The Place of the Ideal Community in Urban Planning. Courtesy of University of Pennsylvania Press.

insofar as they served individual growth through science and communications. (We shall see how this notion backfired on Wright when he translated it literally into a settlement pattern that was perceived by many as formless and unstructured). According to sociologists Jane Addams, Edward Ross, and Richard Ely, big city government and monopoly capital were corrupting these ideals. In the economic sphere, an attack on the conflicting interests in big business, banking, the credit system, and land investments was made by Charles Beard and Thorsten Veblen. Proposals for land and tax reform including a single tax on land, industrial coownership and nationalization, social credit, and "free money" were advanced and supported by most progressive economists, including John Maynard Keynes. In the political sphere, the Wisconsin Progressive party platform of 1934 favored home and land ownership for every American; public ownership of all utilities, including transportation and communications; free education and health care; agricultural and food cooperatives; and the nationalization of banking and lending institutions. Almost all these proposals appeared in Broadacre City.

A combination of the decentralism of Edward Bellamy, Peter Kropotkin, and William Morris, the transcendentalism of Emerson, Thoreau, and Whitman, the land tenure and homesteading notions of John Ruskin and Ralph Borsodi, and the agrarianism of Jefferson as well as his belief in a culture without cities—these views, as interpreted by Wright, formed the philosophical background of Broadacres. And, as March points out, most of what Wright had to say about society, about economics, about industry, and about education can be traced to the work, writings, and actions of these people. As such, they constituted a kind of smorgasbord of progressive opinion expressed in public debate during the era of the Depression in the United States. It was a time in American intellectual history when attention was focused on proposals for recovery and reform, and especially in the architectural and planning professions, large-scale dreaming was fashionable. For Frank Lloyd Wright it was a chance to give architectural form to progressive social goals. This was the hallmark of pragmatic philosophy, to relate theory to the surrounding environment, and Wright took it literally. To physically shape his own proposal he looked to forces which were already shaping the built environment.

In its physical content, Broadacre City was influenced by Wright's experiences in Chicago, Los Angeles, and the Arizona desert (Banham 1969, March 1970, Sergeant 1976). Upon his arrival there in 1887, Chicago was the largest city in the United States and the fastest growing. It had the highest level of individual mobility, the most dispersed industry, the lowest gross population density, and an impressive open space system of parks and boulevards. (Its motto was *urbs in horto*.) In southern California Wright saw the Pacific Electric Railroad network of the twenties and the birth of large-scale automobilization in the "miracle mile" of Wilshire Boulevard. And in the Arizona desert between 1927 and 1929 he experienced firsthand the vast horizontality of the American landscape. It was there, notes Reyner Banham enthusiastically, "that Wright was ultimately to achieve freedom in planning: freedom from axial symmetry, from right angles, and from centralized spaces" (1969, p. 513).

Around the same time, and in the decade immediately following the publication of Broadacre City, Wright's proposal was reinforced by reports to President Hoover's Research Committee on Social Trends regarding decentralization, automobilization, communications, central city decline, and the emergence of spread supercities.[3] In 1935 the National Resource Planning Board recommended ways to encourage industrial and related residential decentralization into the countryside. And in 1944 the Government Committee to Investigate Industrial Centralization lent a moral note to all this speculation by acknowledging a so-called link between centralization and totalitarianism and decentralization and freedom.[4]

Perhaps the strongest support was a petition sent to Washington, D.C., in 1943 urging the Roosevelt Administration to adopt in principle the concept of Broadacre City and to authorize Wright to develop it in practice. The petition was signed by sixty-four important sympathizers, including John Dewey, Albert Einstein, Archibald MacLeish, Nelson Rockefeller, and Robert Moses. Roosevelt, however, had learned a bitter lesson unsuccessfully promoting Rexford Tugwell's greenbelt new towns in the 1930s; and although Wright's proposal appeared closer to his own antiurban sentiments than Tugwell's, nothing came of the petition (Myhra 1974). During the next two decades Broadacre City was to lapse into near oblivion as a result of severe criticism. Norris Kelly Smith's assessment summarized the sentiment:

> To the practical politician and the ordinary citizen Broadacres has meant less than nothing. Judged by the pragmatic standards of the everyday world, it is so irrelevant that it has simply been ignored—for the realization of Broadacre City would require the abrogation of the Constitution of the United States, the elimination of thousands of governmental bodies from the make-up of the state, the confiscation of all lands by right of eminent domain but without compensation, the demolition of all cities and therewith the obliteration of every evidence of the country's history, the rehousing of the entire population, the retraining of millions of persons so as to enable them to be self-sustaining farmers, and other difficulties too numerous to mention. As a practical program it does not even deserve discussion (1966, pp. 153–54).

In examining the record, however, several facts stand out which temper Smith's conclusion and direct attention to a reexamination of the debate. First, out of 100 books on urban planning, urbanism, urban design, or urbanization (excluding those specifically about Frank Lloyd Wright), 34 mention or discuss Broadacre City—roughly one-third of the book literature.[5] Second, eighteen journal articles or reviews between 1933 and 1972 specifically address the proposal. And third, five serious attempts have been made in recent years to reassess its significance. Most of this debate centers either on questions of procedure or on the social and physical content of Wright's plan.

The debate on procedure

In terms of procedure, Wright was applauded for continuing the utopian tradition of planning into the twentieth century, and most of the support he received on this point was essentially support for the value of utopias and the worthiness of an ideal search for order between nature, science, design, democracy, and man (Riesman 1947, Feiss 1959, March 1970, Sergeant 1976). With Wright, the visionary's argument found a dramatic and radical expression (Blake 1964, Reissman 1964). He appeared to expose the then sacred cows of bureaucratic planning—land values, railroad and industrial investments, and insurance and banking interests; he made unattainable visions seem possible; and he furnished material for thought by opening new vistas of speculation in what is now called *futuristics* (Duffus 1938, Thabit 1959, March 1970).

As "social architecture," the principal contribution of Wright's proposal was seen in its repeated insistence on the relationship between the city and the society that produced it (Reissman 1964). Broadacre City was an example of anticipating and following social trends (in Wright's case, decentralization), attempting to project their environmental consequences, and giving them a rational and coherent form (March 1970). And because of the relatively straightforward link between clearly stated assumptions and the physical form of the urban environment, it was viewed as a paradigm of urban design and a model for architects and planners to follow (Weinberg 1961, Reiner 1968). As an ideal urban community, Broadacre City was considered more comprehensive than most in its discussion of planned-for life styles (Reiner 1968).

On the negative side, Wright's utopian formulation

was considered naïve and simplistic by critics who felt he had ignored the dynamic complexity of urban life (Kantorowich 1941, Mumford 1956, Jones 1966). Some maintained it was too private a dream—a personal vision of life imposed at large (Goodman and Goodman 1942, Collins 1970, Twombly 1973). Some even suggested that Broadacre City was just a self-righteous advertisement for Wright's own designs and a display of individual examples of his domestic architecture (Goodman and Goodman 1942, Smith 1966, Reiner 1968, Collins 1970).

Even so, the familiar doctrine of innocence (small-town democracy), original sin (big cities), and redemption (Broadacres) could not be considered legitimate grounds to insist that the city be re-created (Schapiro 1938, Reissman 1964, Twombly 1973). Such a formulation was too sweeping and therefore unable to respond with equal concern to all the differing elements of existing cities. It ignored the possibility of partial, piecemeal, or incremental remedies (*Architectural Forum* 1945, Feiss 1959, Thabit 1959). In short, it would be a gross oversimplification to believe that a physical relocation of the population (even with the social and economic changes proposed by Wright) could solve the functional problems of democracy in a rapidly industrializing society.

What supporters called "social architecture," critics dismissed as "architectural determinism"—the fallacy of assuming a perfect form exists which solves all problems (Banham 1969, Ehrman 1971). Social being is not simply an architectural problem nor is architectural design a universal panacea (Schapiro 1938, Kantorowich 1941, Dyckman 1961, Churchill 1970). In fact, rather than its being a model of urban design, some critics believed Wright's approach was decidedly unprofessional: he had evolved outside the mainstream of modern planning thought and gave little concern for the work of other planners or recognition of other ideal community prototypes (Feiss 1959, Reiner 1968, Collins 1970).[6] Consequently, the plan itself seemed to preclude implementation.

On the question of procedure, then, it would seem that Wright had overstated his case. He had approached planning in the same way he approached architecture—as an artistic problem whose solution would come from the creative act of a personal synthesis. But as Martin Meyerson (1961) observed, such an approach usually results in caricature. Planning is essentially an intellectual task, the greatest contributions coming from analysis rather than through the development of normative imagery. The artist is more concerned with vision; and although, as David Riesman (1947) points out, it takes more courage to deal with what might be than with what is, and it is more difficult to pose great alternatives than to choose among lesser evils, this concern does not have a comfortable role in modern planning practice (Reiner 1968). Wright himself seemed aware of the problem. He cautioned against taking the model of Broadacre City too literally:

> A certain symbolism has been used throughout. It is the artist's way of presenting his subject. . . . The artist, the "dreamer," supplies an element which the scientist, the "expert," the statistician, cannot supply; and that element is *vision* (1940, pp. 27–28).

But even in accepting the visionary aspect of Wright's approach, there is still the problem of Broadacres being too personal a vision to be imposed at large. This is an interesting critique. It suggests that there is a threshold of personal values over which planners' recommendations should not cross. But when is a proposal too personal? Some critics suggested that in Broadacre City Wright had imposed his own life on society. By this we could assume Wright wanted society to live as he was living (or wanted to live). It may even be possible that he saw an expanded highway system, roadside markets, one-acre plots of land, electrification of industry and services, a noncash economy, and all the other economic reforms necessary to bring about Broadacres as facilitating his own life style. But this was unlikely. A description of his life obtained from any of the biographies suggests that, while these proposals might have been nice for him, Frank Lloyd Wright would probably not have been happy in Broadacre City. If he had really designed a personal Utopia it would probably have been no different than the world he moved about in, with the single exception that society would be more tolerant of his idiosyncracies.

He was practicing too public an art to confuse himself with his clients, and it is more than likely that he was acting professionally in piecing together the elements of Broadacre City. Still, there is no getting around the fact that utopian formulation has this characteristic of one person telling the rest of the world how to live. Yet this is precisely what all planners do; the difference is a matter of degree.

Process oriented recommendations which are disjointed, incremental, short term, or constrained by economic and political realities have no less a conviction of being the best course of action than do more sweeping, comprehensive, or utopian proposals. And it is a mistake to assume that the smaller and more constrained the scale of decision making, the less personal the decision. The more likely distinction is that, as the comprehensiveness of the scale increases, the functional rationality, feasibility, and precision of decision making decreases. Planning at this scale is apt to involve intuition, leaps of faith, and a great deal of guesswork. "Yet without great plans," claims

Riesman, "it is hard and often self-defeating to make little ones" (1947, p. 173). To suggest that so-called small-scale, everyday planning does not involve personal conviction is to demean scores of professional planners who, although they believe in what they are doing, struggle behind a mask of objectivity. And at the level of theory, it only serves to reinforce the dialectical opposition between *ideology* and *utopia*.

If, on the other hand, utopian formulation was regarded as a method for testing innovation in planning, a "process for clarifying policy" as Meyerson puts it, then proposals like Broadacre City could be extremely useful in posing potentially desirable ends and then in testing these ends with a logical model. This is precisely the approach taken by Catherine Bauer Wurster (1966) in her model for analyzing the form and structure of future urban complexes where (although disapproving of Broadacre City) Wright's proposal is considered one of several metropolitan alternatives.

It is very unlikely, however, that Wright was interested in either the predictive modeling of different sets of principles or the normative modeling of different reactions to probable futures. His style, perhaps more than anything, succeeded in turning professional attention away from the procedural utility of his plan. Couched in neo-Biblical, neo-Whitmanesque jargon, his turgid prose rivals the most romantic of nineteenth century German idealists (Schapiro 1938, White and White 1962). Full of personal cliches, verbiage, polemics, and repetition, the impact of emotion seems more to cloud the issues than convince the reader (Zucker 1946, Feiss 1959, Collins 1970). For those architects and planners who were seriously interested in the social and physical content of Broadacre City, Wright's presentation required a suspension of disbelief.

The debate on content

In terms of content, Wright was praised for his understanding of the effects of automobiles on urban growth patterns and of the importance of planning an urban pattern that takes the private car into account (Hilberseimer 1944, Jencks 1963, Barnett 1972). Broadacre City appeared to be an accurate statement of the horizontal, automotive expression of life, a lucid presentation of the desirability of low-density living, and an alternate vision to the sheer fixity and abstractness of the high-density urban design proposals emanating from the so-called international school of architecture and urbanism (Blake 1964, Reiner 1968, Banham 1969).[7] This vision was a uniquely American expression of Wright's own agrarian roots and lifelong interest in the relationship between soil, building, and people. The result was perceived by many as a liberation of urban space through modification of the traditional gridiron, a unity of town and country, and a highly practical land use, transportation, and communications pattern which could (with some modifications) increase flexibility, personal comfort, and accessibility (Hilberseimer 1944, Gallion and Eisner 1950, Lynch 1961, Sergeant 1976).

Furthermore, the proposal was realistic. The argument for Broadacre City exudes the desperate hopes of the Depression-wracked thirties and the proposals for family self-sufficiency that were in line with government thinking at that time (Banham 1969, Collins 1970). It also provides a focus for people's irritation with big cities, not only in the thirties, but also in the sixties and seventies (Weinberg 1961, Twombly 1973, Sergeant 1976). As Mel Scott (1969) observed, it was not only more realistic than the European tower-city utopias of the 1920s, but actually quite close to the desires of many Americans, a point which undermines the claim that Wright's proposal was too personal, too idiosyncratic.

In fact, Broadacre City turned out to be one of the most prophetic of all ideal communities in planning literature—an accurate vision of the standard package into which the metropolitan periphery would be subdivided in ideal post-Depression suburbia (Banham 1969, Scully 1969, Sergeant 1976). By concerning himself with many of the problems of the future metropolis, Wright foreshadowed a number of poly-nucleated, auto-age urban patterns that have actually evolved, although without the rational, ordered form proposed in Broadacre City (White and White 1962, Reiner 1968, Frampton 1970, Barnett 1972, Twombly 1973).

But on the negative side, Wright's horizontal liberation of space was perceived by many to be as amorphous as any vast and dreadful suburb (Feiss 1959), a sort of "endless Roadtown" (Bauer 1933), lacking any "plastic interest" whatsoever (Goodman and Goodman 1942, Lynch 1961, Frampton 1970). There seemed to be no articulation of land use distribution, no differentiation of functions, just a uniform physical pattern (Dyckman 1961, Reiner 1968). Its afocal internal structure created a puzzling morphology. This just was not what one expected a city to look like (Goodman and Goodman 1947, Collins 1970). As Frederick Gutheim put it, "Broadacre City was essentially a prairie strewn with factories and other centers, linked by a web of superhighways" (1966, p. 120).

When analyzed by contemporary standards, the transportation system seemed impractical: the vast highways were incompatible with the proposed density levels (Reiner 1968); the multilevel intersections were complicated and inadequate (Blake 1964); there was too much reliance on one mode (the automobile)—a gasoline shortage would be disastrous

(Reiner 1968); and the distances were too long—such a plan would be practical only if the time and cost of travel were reduced essentially to zero (Bauer 1933, Mumford 1956, Lynch 1961, Blumenfeld 1967).

As far as the prophetic quality of Broadacre City was concerned, critics were quick to point out that a suburban settlement pattern was not a city. It didn't promise much excitement, novelty, or culture and would certainly not work for those who liked the density and tempo of big cities (Goodman and Goodman 1947, Mumford 1956, Rosenau 1959, Thabit 1959). To some, this "subdivision plat for a middle class suburb in utopia" was an illusion—the ancient American myth of the small town, a picturesque secessionism (Tunnard and Reed 1956, Feiss 1959). As Lewis Mumford and Morton and Lucia White put it, this was an "anti-city."

The strongest critique, however, was leveled against major contradictions in the social and political philosophy underlying the so-called realistic qualities of Broadacres. For example, the core of Wright's argument (as outlined in 1932) was really a one-hundred-year-old critique of bourgeois society (made by both the political left and right), yet Broadacre City represented an undeniably bourgeois concept of pleasant and spacious living (Churchill 1933, Schapiro 1938, Tofuri 1976). Furthermore, in attempting to bring the city to the country, it appeared that he was indiscriminately mixing urban and rural concepts without understanding these terms sociologically and certainly without understanding their historical significance in any theory of urbanization (Bauer 1933). This was just the sort of architectural determinism planners were to become increasingly skeptical of by mid century.

Wright's concept of a competitive socialism was too full of holes. Critics were quick to point out his avoidance of questions of class and power and his indifference to property relations and the state (Schapiro 1938, Goodman and Goodman 1942, Riesman 1947). His assumption of the abolition of rents and the relinquishment of power and control by industry, all without struggle, betrayed an ignorance of the history of social and political change (Goodman and Goodman 1942, 1947, Thabit 1959). His notion of social credit was incompatible with the noncash (Borsodian) economy he envisioned, and his presentation of industrial reforms was ignorant of existing facts and conditions (Goodman and Goodman 1947). It appeared that he was simply uninformed.

He opposed class stratification yet incorporated an upper-income zone into the residential plan (Bauer 1933, Goodman and Goodman 1942, Rosenau 1959). In fact, the overall treatment of the residents of Broadacre City seems to defy the very individualism for which Wright argued. For one, there is an extremely limited range of living styles—it "leveled" quality; for another, there is a kind of herd instinct implied in the mass use of automobiles (Mumford 1956, Lynch 1961, Weinberg 1961, Reiner 1968). Wright, however, seemed to anticipate this last reaction. He was aware of the fact that the visual pattern of Broadacres suggested standardization and repetition. To get around this he distinguished between physical appearance and social content.

Broadacres rejects the idea that balance and rhythm are directly related to the ideal of freedom which Broadacres desires to preserve. Standardization and repetition are not in themselves unbeautiful—witness a colonnade. Nor are they undesireable [sic] until they enter the domain where human life and individuality should be alive and working, for there they stultify both life and individuality. The degree to which both standardization and repetition may be allowed to enter the life-concerns . . . depends upon the degree to which human individuality is already absent or be willing to be sacrificed (1940, p. 22).

Much as Herbert Gans was to defend suburban life in *The Levittowners* (1967), Wright seems to be saying that you can't tell a book by its cover. Of his own proposal he found it necessary to caution that "there is more between the lines than appears in the lines" (1940, p. 18). While this may not satisfy most critics, it does raise the question of whether or not there is any kind of link at all between design and behavior.

However, those critics who do believe that there are social implications in design saw in Broadacres an atomization of the population into spread-out residential units that would preclude any sense of social grouping, neighborhood, or community (Bauer 1933, Mumford 1956, Rosenau 1959, Reiner 1968). Rather than heightening political identity (as hoped in reports to the Hoover Committee), such a pattern would more likely create conditions suitable for totalitarianism (Kantorowich 1941, Mumford 1956, Lynch 1961, White and White 1962).[8] This characteristic, combined with Wright's reliance on the county architect as a kind of benevolent police power—the equivalent of B. F. Skinner's notorious Fraser in *Walden Two*—betrayed an authoritarian streak in the entire proposal (Goodman and Goodman 1942, *Architectural Forum* 1945, Smith 1966, Twombly 1973). It is undoubtedly this combination which led one critic to call Wright a "fascist" (Schapiro 1938) and another an "architectural megalomaniac" (Kantorowich 1941).

Conclusions

Among the thirty-seven critics whose views on Broadacre City have been published, including those by theorists and historians, there is equal representation from both architectural and planning orientations. The architects are evenly divided between positive and negative reactions to Wright's proposal. The planners have a bit more consensus. Fully three quarters of their reactions are negative.

But after eliminating the cursory, superficial, or passing remarks and concentrating on the detailed analyses of Broadacre City, only sixteen critiques remain. Of these, only four contain positive reactions.[9] The remaining twelve critics, mostly planners, are opposed.[10] The debate suggests, however, that the significant distinction is not professional orientation. Rather, the focus of disagreement is on content, not procedure.

At stake are two fundamentally different images and conceptions of both the city and urban society that need reconciliation. On one hand there is the classical city—the dense concentration of people, buildings, and activities around a civic nucleus; on the other, there is a loosely knit, weakly centered, low-density urban region spread over a wide hinterland. The proponents of the former pattern have five thousand years of urban history on their side. Athens, Rome, Vienna, London, Paris, and New York all testify to the validity of equating urbanity with place, community with propinquity. It is not surprising to find that most of these critics believe in some form of urban renewal and central city reconstruction. In terms of chronology, their positions on Broadacre City were all written before 1969.

The new pattern has a shorter and shakier record. Los Angeles, Phoenix, Denver, Houston, and a nationally increasing trend toward suburbanization (*Time* 1976, *U.S. News & World Report* 1976) show up as signposts of the revolution in transportation and communications technologies, the "global village," and the possibility of "community without propinquity." Critics in this camp have a distinctly different attitude toward cities. Their positions on Broadacre City all appeared after 1969. This is perhaps the critical variable. By the late sixties, disenchantment with urban renewal, model cities, and OEO programs had set in. Following a series of urban riots, there was a growing cynicism toward liberal reform in cities. In planning theory the existing paradigm was breaking down. It was a period characterized by a search for alternative models and a new attitude toward the physical environment (Grabow and Heskin 1973). The "green revolution," the back-to-the-land movement, and the emergence of ecology as a serious discipline all contributed to this change in attitude and the need to bring questions of physical planning and urban design back into modern planning practice.

The history of architecture and urban planning, both as professions and as bodies of knowledge, is closely tied to the evolution of the classical city. Our understanding of the new patterns of urbanization is sketchy at best. Only a handful of architects and planners appear to have accepted these patterns in order to bring them under some measure of control (Lynch 1961, 1965, 1975, Gutkind 1962, Stein 1964, Friedmann and Miller 1965, Webber 1966, Wingo 1966). It was characteristic of Wright to adopt an iconoclastic attitude toward the classical city; it was the same attitude he had so successfully developed toward architecture. Although the difference in his achievement underscores the differences (and even antagonisms) between architecture and planning, we can forgive him for approaching the problem with old tools.

Only recently have urban designers attempted to evolve new concepts of order for the new patterns of urbanization. To Jesse Reichek (1961), for example, the design concepts of the classical city reflect a stage through which the city has already passed, yet they dominate the current state of the art. In his analysis, many of the signs that are frequently mistaken for "urban chaos" are instead the marks of emerging new forms, new kinds of order that reflect the increasingly pluralistic and afocal structure of changing social relationships. Reichek is a painter, yet his views about cities are reinforced by a new school of urban designers who rely heavily on experimental data from cognitive psychology (Vigier 1965).

According to Denise Scott Brown (1969), for example, this order can evolve out of a nonjudgmental attitude toward suburbs, parking lots, billboards, gasoline stations, and all the paraphernalia of so-called strip development. Forty years after Wright learned this lesson from Chicago, Los Angeles, and the Arizona desert, a new generation of architects and planners is "learning from Las Vegas" (Brown and Venturi 1972).[11]

The resistance of many of Wright's critics to the new, postindustrial patterns of urbanization and suburbanization is unsupportable precisely because it places them squarely in the utopian and authoritarian posture of which he was accused. Somewhere, Paul Tillich once said, "It is the spirit of Utopia which conquers Utopia." Is the five-thousand-year-old equation of cities and civilization any less utopian than a plastic arcadia in suburbia?

> Horizontality was Wright's response not only to the earth and the things that grew out of it, but also to the great spaces of America. . . . For this, after all, was the chief characteristic of the New World: space, freedom to move about, an ever expanding frontier. From Walt Whitman to Jack Kerouac, the recurring American theme is the open road, the man on the move, the limitless spaces, especially of the Middle West (Blake 1964, pp. 36–37).

Even within the constraints of an ecological conscience, the "open road" and the American home calling at long range on an advanced industrial technology with which it is invisibly connected meet in Broadacre City with the spatial continuities of a Jackson Pollock painting. For all its weaknesses, that meeting has rarely been attempted and hardly surpassed.

Because of the undeniable flaws in both procedure and content, it is tempting to dismiss Broadacre City along with so many misadventures in urban planning. Yet because of its timeliness and prophetic qualities, it is equally tempting to praise it as an inspiring vision of postindustrial urbanization. Nevertheless, careful examination of the debate precludes the luxury of a simple verdict. In retrospect, neither position is intellectually defensible. The significance of Broadacre City, like so many entries in the sociology of knowledge, is in the questions it raises rather than in the answers it gives.

Perhaps the most important question which grows out of the debate is whether or not it is possible to accommodate the social and political advantages of spatial agglomeration within a far-reaching decentralization of urban settlement patterns. There is little evidence to suggest that this question can be answered within the narrow confines of the professional definitions of urban design. Because the problem cuts across the traditional boundaries of knowledge and expertise, a different generation of architects and planners will have to succeed where both Wright and his critics have failed.

Author's Note

Support for this project was generously provided by a grant from the faculty research fund of the University of Kansas. In addition, the author gratefully acknowledges the assistance and cooperation of Curtis Besinger, Forrest Berghorn, James Mayo, Morton and Lucia White, and Frances Hebenstreit, research assistant and graduate student in urban planning at the University of Kansas.

Notes

1. Although he disavowed Wright's social conservatism, Gutkind himself acknowledged that, in its physical conception, Broadacre City came very close to his own proposals for decentralization (Grabow 1975).
2. An earlier effort, although on a much smaller scale, was Wright's submission in 1913 for a Chicago competition to explore alternate designs of subdivision layouts on a standard section of the mile square gridiron (Martin and March 1972); cf., Alfred B. Yeomans, *City Residential Land Development* (University of Chicago Press, 1916).
3. Malcolm A. Wiley, *Communications Agencies and Social Life*; R. C. McKenzie, *Metropolitan Community*; and J. H. Kolb, *Rural Life*.
4. This is a fuzzy issue and both Wright and his critics are guilty of mixing up demography with political theory. Wright actually favored the centralization of government (1940, p. 30) yet was attacked for his proposed decentralization of population.
5. The books were randomly chosen from a list of all Dewey decimal entries under those subjects. When a book specifically about Wright appeared it was rejected and another selected until 100 entries were collected. The sample thus obtained represented more than 50 percent of the urban collection at the University of Kansas.
6. For example, the proposals of Arthur Comey, Benton MacKaye, John Nolen, Henry Wright and Clarence Stein, Lewis Mumford, and others (Hancock 1967).
7. The reference is to Le Corbusier and his *Ville Radieuse* (1922) which is often contrasted with Broadacre City as polar opposites. However, Scully (1969) notes that some of Wright's own drawings for Broadacres, published in 1934, show striking similarities to some of those for the *Ville Radieuse* and prefigure Corbusier's *Ville Lineaire* (1942). This meshes with Collins's (1970) observation that Broadacres is essentially a linear city.
8. A disclaimer by Wright (1940, p. 9) indicates he at least anticipated and thought about the problem, although it does not dispose of the charge.
9. Reyner Banham (1969), Lionel March (1970), Jonathan Barnett (1972), and John Sergeant (1976).
10. Catherine Bauer (1933), Meyer Schapiro (1938), Roy Kantorowich (1941), Paul and Percival Goodman (1942, 1947), Lewis Mumford (1956), Carl Feiss (1959), Walter Thabit (1959), Kevin Lynch (1961), Morton and Lucia White (1962), Norris Kelly Smith (1966), Thomas Reiner (1968), and George Collins (1970).
11. In 1932 Wright wrote, "[In] the roadside service stations, the distributing centers, in embryo, of the future are appearing. In the gasoline service stations may be seen the beginning of an important advance agent of decentralization by way of distribution and also the beginning of the establishment of the Broadacre City" (p. 69).

References

Architectural Forum. 1945. Review of *When democracy builds*. 87, July: 156.
Banham, Reyner. 1969. The wilderness years of Frank Lloyd Wright. *Royal Institute of British Architects Journal* 76, December: 512–18.
Barnett, Jonathan. 1972. Rethinking Wright. *Architectural Forum* 136, June: 42–47.
Bauer (Wurster), Catherine. 1933. Review of *The disappearing city*. *The Nation* 136, January: 99–100.
Blake, Peter. 1964. *Frank Lloyd Wright*. Baltimore: Penguin.
Blumenfeld, Hans. 1967. *The modern metropolis*. Cambridge, Mass.: MIT Press.
Brown, Denise Scott. 1969. On pop art, permissiveness, and planning. *Journal of the American Institute of Planners* 35, May: 184–86.
———. 1976. On architectural formalism and social concern: a discourse for social planners and radical chic architects. *Oppositions* 5, summer: 99–112.
Brown, Denise Scott, and Venturi, Robert. 1972. *Learning from Las Vegas*. Cambridge, Mass.: MIT Press.
Churchill, Henry. 1933. Review of *The disappearing city*. *Architectural Record* 73, January: 12–14.
———. 1970. The social implications of the skyscraper. In *Four great makers of modern architecture*. New York: Da Capo.
Collins, George. 1970. Broadacre City: Wright's utopia reconsidered. In *Four great makers of modern architecture*. New York: Da Capo.
Dos Passos, John. 1936. Grand old man. *New Republic* 87, 3 June: 93–95.

Duffus, R. L. 1938. Frank Lloyd Wright's way to a better world. *New York Times Book Review* 2 January: 2.

Dyckman, John. 1961. The changing uses of the city. In *The future metropolis*, ed. Lloyd Rodwin. New York: George Braziller.

Ehrman, Jacques. 1971. Live in utopia? *Perspecta: The Yale Architectural Journal* 13/14: 209–218.

Feiss, Carl. 1959. Broadacre City revisited. *Progressive Architecture* 60, July: 181.

Frampton, Kenneth. 1970. Labour, work, and architecture. In *Meaning in architecture*, ed. Charles Jencks. New York: George Braziller.

Friedmann, John, and Miller, John. 1965. The urban field. *Journal of the American Institute of Planners* 31, November: 312–20.

Gallion, Arthur, and Eisner, Simon. 1950. *The urban pattern.* Princeton: Nostrand.

Gans, Herbert. 1967. *The Levittowners.* New York: Vintage Books, Random House.

Goodman, Paul, and Goodman, Percival. 1942. Frank Lloyd Wright on architecture. *Kenyon Review* 41, winter: 7–28.

———. 1947. *Communitas.* New York: Vintage.

Grabow, Stephen. 1975. E. A. Gutkind: the outsider in retrospect. *Journal of the American Institute of Planners* 41, May: 200–212.

Grabow, Stephen, and Heskin, Allan. 1973. Foundations for a radical concept of planning. *Journal of the American Institute of Planners* 39, March: 106–114.

Gutheim, Frederick. 1966. Urban space and urban design. In *Cities and space*, ed. Lowdon Wingo. Baltimore: Johns Hopkins Press.

Gutkind, E. A. 1962. *The twilight of cities.* New York: Free Press.

Hancock, John. 1967. Planners in the changing American city, 1900–1940. *Journal of the American Institute of Planners* 33, September: 290–304.

Hilberseimer, Ludwig. 1944. *The new city.* Chicago: Paul Theobald.

Jencks, Charles. 1963. *Modern movements in architecture.* New York: Doubleday.

Jones, Barclay. 1966. Design from knowledge, not belief. In *The architect and the city*, ed. Marcus Whiffen. Cambridge, Mass.: MIT Press.

Kantorowich, Roy. 1941. Architectural utopias: the city planning theories of Frank Lloyd Wright and Le Corbusier. *Task* 2, 1: 30–35.

Lynch, Kevin. 1961. The pattern of the metropolis. In *The future metropolis*, ed. Lloyd Rodwin. New York: George Braziller.

———. 1965. The city as environment. In *Cities.* New York: Scientific American.

———. 1966. The possible city. In *Environment and policy*, ed. William Ewald. Bloomington: Indiana University.

———. 1975. Grounds for utopia. In *Responding to social change*, ed. Basil Honikman. Stroudsburg, Pa.: Dowden, Hutchinson, and Ross.

March, Lionel. 1970. *Frank Lloyd Wright: an architect in search of democracy; three broadcasts.* On BBC Radio, third program.

March, Lionel, and Martin, Leslie. 1972. *Urban space and structures.* Cambridge, Eng.: Cambridge University Press.

Meyerson, Martin. 1961. Utopian traditions and the planning of cities. In *The future metropolis*, ed. Lloyd Rodwin. New York: George Braziller.

Mumford, Lewis. 1956. *The urban prospect.* New York: Harcourt, Brace, and World.

Myhra, David. 1974. Rexford Guy Tugwell: initiator of America's greenbelt new towns, 1935–1936. *Journal of the American Institute of Planners* 40, May: 176–88.

Pells, Richard. 1973. *Radical visions and American dreams.* New York: Harper and Row.

Reichek, Jesse. 1961. On the design of cities. *Journal of the American Institute of Planners* 27, May: 141–43.

Reiner, Thomas. 1968. *The place of the ideal community in urban planning.* Philadelphia: University of Pennsylvania.

Reissman, Leonard. 1964. *The urban process.* New York: Free Press.

Riesman, David. 1947. Some observations on community plans and utopia. *Yale Law Journal* 57, November: 173–200.

Rosenau, Helen. 1959. *The ideal city in its architectural evolution.* London: Routledge and Kegan Paul.

Schapiro, Meyer. 1938. Architect's utopia. *Partisan Review* 4, March: 42–47.

Scott, Mel. 1969. *American city planning since 1890.* Berkeley: University of California.

Scully, Vincent. 1969. *Frank Lloyd Wright.* New York: George Braziller.

Sergeant, John. 1976. *Frank Lloyd Wright's usonian houses.* New York: Whitney Library of Design.

Smith, Norris Kelly. 1966. *Frank Lloyd Wright.* Englewood Cliffs, N.J.: Prentice-Hall.

Stein, Clarence. 1964. A regional pattern for dispersal. *Architectural Record* 104, September: 205–6.

Thabit, Walter. 1959. Review of *The living city. Journal of the American Institute of Planners* 25, August: 163–64.

Time. 1976. Americans on the move. 15 March: 54–64.

Tofuri, Manfredo. 1976. *Architecture and utopia.* Cambridge, Mass.: MIT Press.

Tunnard, Christopher, and Reed, Henry. 1956. *American skyline.* New York: Mentor.

Twombly, Robert. 1973. *Frank Lloyd Wright.* New York: Harper and Row.

U.S. News & World Report. 1976. Are all big cities doomed? 5 April: 49–64.

Vigier, Francois. 1965. An experimental approach to urban design. *Journal of the American Institute of Planners* 31, February: 21–31.

Webber, Melvin. 1966. Order in diversity: community without propinquity. In *Cities and space*, ed. Lowdon Wingo. Baltimore: Johns Hopkins.

Weinberg, Robert. 1961. Review of *The living city. Journal of the American Institute of Planners* 27, November: 352–54.

White, Morton, and White, Lucia. 1962. *The intellectual versus the city: from Thomas Jefferson to Frank Lloyd Wright.* Cambridge, Mass.: Harvard University.

Wingo, Lowdon, ed. 1966. *Cities and space.* Baltimore: Johns Hopkins.

Wright, Frank Lloyd. 1932. *The disappearing city.* New York: Wm. Farquhur Payson.

———. 1940. The new frontier: Broadacre City. *Taliesin* 1, October: entire issue.

———. 1945. *When democracy builds.* Chicago: University of Chicago.

———. 1958. *The living city.* New York: Horizon Press.

Wright, Frank Lloyd, and Brownell, Baker. 1938. *Architecture and modern life.* New York: Harper.

Wurster, Catherine (Bauer). 1966. The form and structure of the future urban complex. In *Cities and space*, ed. Lowdon Wingo. Baltimore: Johns Hopkins.

Zucker, Paul. 1946. Review of *When democracy builds. Journal of Aesthetics and Art Criticism* 4, March: 195–96.

CITY PLANNERS AND URBAN TRANSPORTATION
The American Response, 1900-1940

MARK FOSTER
University of Colorado

INTRODUCTION

American city planners are deeply divided regarding both the root causes of and potential cures for our urban crisis. Among them, few issues generate more intense debate than the future of urban transportation. Nearly every urbanite is aware of how difficult and time consuming it is to move about in most American cities. Today the big question is whether urban transportation problems can best be solved by public or private means. Many persons urge cities to build new public transportation systems or refurbish old ones. Yet, some cities which have taken such steps have discovered that it is difficult to provide public transportation serving the needs of more than a fraction of metropolitan-area residents. Clearly, there are no quick and easy solutions to America's urban transportation needs.

In recent years it has become fashionable to blame the automobile for America's urban transportation mess. Critics as disparate as John Keats, Ronald Buel, and Lewis Mumford have scored the automobile's shortcomings. Keats criticized the American male's penchant for conspicuous consumption, which made the "fake-jewelry" chromed, tail-finned gas-guzzler "demonstrably more important to us than our human wives, our children, jobs, and even our food."¹ Buel suggested that the automobile dehumanized the typical urban dweller. Isolated in his private capsule from casual contacts with other people, the freeway driver vented his most antisocial, even violent tendencies.² Perhaps no critic matched the articulateness of Mumford, who categorically charged that the automobile and its proponents ruined the twentieth-century urban form. In particular, Mumford indicted them for encouraging suburban sprawl, which brought highly inefficient and wasteful use of space. He noted in 1961 "that the drift to the outer ring has become a mass movement," destroying both urban and rural environments and creating "[nothing] but a dreary substitute, devoid of human form and even more devoid of the original suburban values."³ In Mumford's view, the automobile industry and the oil companies formed a powerful cabal, whose artful propaganda "hypnotized" responsible city officials and induced them to "dismantle all the varied forms of transportation necessary to a good system."⁴ No less culpable in the decline of public transportation were those feckless city planners who should have known better. As Mumford put it.

> By allowing mass transportation to deteriorate and by building expressways out of the city and parking garages within, in order to encourage the maximum use of the private car, our highway engineers and city planners have helped destroy the living tissue of the city and to limit the possibilities of creating a larger urban organism on a regional scale.⁵

Mumford perceived the planners' compliance in almost conspiratorial terms.

Amidst the present debate over future rapid transit systems and air pollution cures, along with concern over soaring fuel costs and fears of OPEC fuel boycotts, dispassionate analysis and quiet reasoning are rare. Two factors account for this. First, many contemporary analyses of American urban transportation search for culprits. Second, few accounts focus upon the interplay of diverse forces prior to World War II which led to the triumph of the automobile in both city and country and the concomitant decline of public transportation. Thus, a vital historical dimension is missing.

This essay suggests that between 1900 and 1940 the problems and prospects of urban transportation were bafflingly complex; there were neither heroes nor villains. Certainly there is little evidence of any organized conspiracy to destroy public transportation in American cities. Several factors explain the automobile's triumph. When the motorized vehicle first appeared around the turn of the century, few perceived its potential effect upon either traffic or future urban development. Until at least the mid-1920s, the vast majority of trolley company officials did not consider it a serious competitor, at least within the cities. Traction officials consistently underrated automobile competition; as late as 1940, many insisted that the privately owned vehicle would never absorb the bulk of trolley patrons. Equally important, city officials and urban planners failed to develop anything approaching a consensus over what constituted an ideal urban form. They were not only divided over whether to encourage centralization or decentralization, but over what factors actually influenced urban growth in any given direction. Many planners, particularly those urging decentralization, perceived the automobile as an ally in promoting suburban development.[6] During the early decades of the automobile's rapid ascendancy, planning forces in most American cities were preoccupied with gaining some degree of public acceptance, official recognition, and minimal funding. Finally, planners were confronted with myriad challenges and distractions other than those directly involving urban transportation: zoning codes, annexation problems, etc. They simply did not have the resources, time, or experience to probe all facets of the challenge of the automobile. That planners failed to consider the full environmental impact of a major technological advancement and were no more farsighted than businessmen and public officials is hardly surprising. Hindsight facilitates casting stones; yet a sympathetic understanding of the extremely difficult conditions and choices faced by pre-World War II urban planners should sober the most caustic critic.

TURN-OF-THE-CENTURY URBAN TRANSPORTATION

At the turn of the century the electric trolley dominated urban transportation. Perfected by Frank J. Sprague and successfully introduced in Richmond, Virginia in 1887, electric cars replaced horse-drawn and cable cars almost overnight. By 1895 more than 850 towns and cities had installed street railways, and competition between rival syndicates for prized franchises prevailed in many others. By World War I, nearly every American city over 25,000 boasted electric lines, and the ubiquitous streetcar transported 14.5 billion passengers in 1917.[7]

Small wonder, then, that when the horseless carriage first appeared on city streets in the 1890s, nearly everybody viewed the new invention with amused tolerance. The 8,000 registered motor vehicles in 1900 posed no apparent threat to the trolley. Many perceived the automobile as a toy, a plaything for the rich.[8] By 1910, however, there were nearly 500,000 motorized vehicles on the road, and the public began to take them seriously.

Most early discussions of the automobile emphasized its potential for solving urban problems, not creating them. This positive theme permeated both popular and professional journals. Prior to World War I, a frequently voiced belief was that the automobile would improve public health and lower street maintenance costs by removing horse-drawn vehicles from downtown streets. Less manure in the streets would mean fewer house and stable flies, which, in turn, would bring greater comfort and enjoyment of life to urban dwellers.[9] Similarly, street maintenance costs would be lowered by eliminating the need for collection of manure. In addition, urban observers reasoned that since trucks could haul four times as much produce as horse-drawn vehicles per square foot of street space occupied, existing streets would suffice for some time to come. The editor of the *Municipal Engineer* dismissed the notion that increased automobile use would force city administrations to rebuild urban areas at massive public cost. The automobile's superior speed would "make the few yards greater to get 'round the rectangular blocks unimportant." The speed of the motor vehicle neutralized, or eliminated the need for diagonal streets between even contiguous suburbs and central business districts; thus, "even much heavier travel [was] not likely to demand greater expenditures for easier methods of communication." Ironically, the very same editor suggested that municipal administrators' adoption of the automobile and motor trucks for public work facilitated the creation of larger, more efficient service districts. Employment of automobiles by public officials would, it seemed, "impress [upon the public] the importance of good boulevards and extensions of present boulevard systems."[10] The implication was clear: the stimulus provided by the automobile would create splendid new streets at inconsequential costs.

Such euphoric thought by the editor of an important engineering journal is less important than the general lack of prescience regarding future urban transportation trends.[11] As interurban electric railways, steam railroads, and the automobile combined to encourage suburban expansion in the late nineteenth and early twentieth centuries, almost nobody perceived the growing complexities of urban transportation. Most observers were still thinking in terms of single transportation companies and individual means of movement, rather than comprehensive, coordinated transit networks. Although municipal ownership of trolley lines had been effected in a few cities by 1900, private ownership remained the rule. Once city councils awarded long-term franchises, they had few levers by which to persuade trolley companies to act in the "public interest."

TURN-OF-THE-CENTURY URBAN PLANNING

Even the most conscientious efforts by city officials to insure adequate urban transportation were hampered by lack of competent, or disinterested advice. At the turn of the century, city planning was in its infancy.[12] The "City Beautiful" forces designed aesthetically pleasing and enormously expensive civic centers and boulevard systems. By 1910, however, a reaction set in, as voices urging scientific planning for the "City Practical" began to surface. George B. Ford, a bulwark of the early planning movement, spoke for some of his peers in 1912:

> The City Beautiful is a most desirable object, for we do crave beauty; but can we with equanimity stand by and help the city spend its money on these frills and furbelows when only a step away the hideous slum, reeking with filth and disease, rotten with crime, is sapping the very life-blood of the city?[13]

Unfortunately, at a time when city planners were few in number, poorly financed, and armed with little political clout, such expressions of social conscience were comparatively rare even among advocates of the "City Practical." Urban reformers in general were overwhelmed by the problems of the early twentieth-century American city. Intelligent reformers realized that in order to exert any impact at all, they would have to limit their commitments. Ford spoke for perhaps a majority of planners when he urged them to focus their attention upon less grandiose, more mundane matters. In addition to growing numbers of automobiles, they had to contend with a host of other problems, including annexation and zoning.[14] Nevertheless, for a variety of reasons, transportation and streets were primary concerns of planners in the decades preceding World War I.

In urban transportation alone the challenges to planners were formidable. Prior to World War I, they failed almost to a man to anticipate the full implications of the potential impact of the automobile upon the city. Nearly all of them shared the view that the electric trolley would serve the transportation needs of most city dwellers in the foreseeable future. The only significant area of disagreement was whether or not lines of transportation should be separated along more than one horizontal plane. George S. Webster, Philadelphia's Chief Engineer, argued that "it is essential to plan in all our large cities to carry the thousands of people, who daily congregate for business or pleasure, over railways constructed either above or below the street surface."[15] But George E. Hooker of Chicago informed listeners at the Second National Conference on City Planning in 1910 that elevated lines were noisy, ugly, and a general "nuisance," while subways were overly expensive and "objectionable from many standpoints."[16]

Only a few city planners seriously assessed the potential impact of the automobile upon the city prior to World War I. Yet even these individuals underestimated the complexities of the issue, and emphasized the auto's prospective virtues rather than its drawbacks. Nobody associated with the early planning movement defended the motor vehicle more energetically than Nelson P. Lewis, Chief Engineer for New York's Board of Estimate. According to Lewis, the automobile exerted a positive influence upon the city for a variety of reasons. By discouraging further centralization it would diffuse land values and "stabilize" real estate. Intelligent policing of traffic flow and regulation of vehicle size would "permit a much greater volume of traffic to be accommodated with safety on the same street." In addition, more extensive use of the private car would "result in a better knowledge on the part of the citizen of his city and its environment."[17] Rather than exacerbate congestion, the automobile would, in Lewis's view, reduce it. By 1915 increased numbers of motor vehicles had encouraged city governments to vastly improve city streets. Lewis told listeners at the planners' annual convention that year that:

> With better paving the traffic is becoming more diffused. The driver of the motor car naturally selects the more attractive streets. The more attention that is given to street details, the better the character of the buildings fronting upon the streets, the more general the introduction of trees and shrubbery—all of which are receiving the attention of progressive real estate developers and those engaged in city planning work—the less will be the concentration of motor car pleasure traffic on certain streets.[18]

This optimistic view received immediate support from C. M. Talbert of St. Louis: "Fortunately, this increased number of vehicles is gradual, if rapid . . . and as stated before by Mr. Lewis, a great many of the problems will solve themselves."[19]

Such euphoric, simplistic assessments of the automobile's impact upon the city did not go unchallenged. Ernest P. Goodrich, Consulting Engineer from New York, for instance, disagreed that the automobile would decrease traffic congestion.[20] Perhaps the most sobering cautionary remark came from a German planner, Berlin's Werner Hegemann, who charged that the automobile divided American city dwellers into two classes: the "barons," riding automobiles, and the "common people," dependent upon public transportation. He pointed out that as the wealthier and more influential upper classes adopted the automobile, they would lose the incentive to fight for public transportation. "The permitting of class distinctions has dangerous results. . . . It . . . means the sanctioning of straphanging for the less fortunate, but rather more numerous "lower" half. It also means that the autoless masses may be kept back inside the area profitably served by the street cars."[21]

Despite the issues raised at this and other meetings of American planners, most members of the profession assumed a laissez-faire attitude toward the automobile. They generally perceived the automobile as a pleasure vehicle, irrelevant to most American urbanites' daily transportation needs. This common view was reinforced by the casual attitude trolley company officials took toward the new invention.

TROLLEY OFFICIALS' VIEWS ON URBAN TRANSPORTATION

The three decades between 1887 and 1917 were the golden age of the electric trolley. Traction companies experienced nearly uninterrupted success. Electric street cars almost completely replaced horse-drawn and cable cars. With 14.5 billion patrons in 1917, electric trolleys dominated urban transportation.[22]

Small wonder, then, that prior to World War I most trolley company spokesmen considered the automobile little more than a nuisance. In 1900, Cleveland Moffett, a prolific playwright, had the prescience to anticipate the conflict between the two forms of transportation: "Indeed the greatness of the automobile lies chiefly in the future, as the greatness of the bicycle is drifting into the past. But the newer product has come to stay . . . Trolley lines are wondering if automobile busses and coaches are destined to war against them, as they warred against the railroads."[23] If trolley officials worried about the motor car, they camouflaged their concern beautifully behind bland masks of public indifference. The industry's quasi-official publication, *Electric Railway Journal*, almost totally ignored the automobile. Its confident editorials assumed that the trolleys would dominate urban transportation in the foreseeable future.

Not until the second decade of the twentieth century did this optimism show cracks. Shortly before World War I, independently owned motor buses and "jitneys" began competing for trolley patrons in a number of cities. Besides clogging streets, particularly in downtown areas, they often paralleled local trolley companies' most profitable routes. In 1914, the *Electric Railway Journal* fretted that independent bus lines in Dallas had drained off one-third of the trolley patrons. The journal charged that the jitneys were "noisy, dangerous to pedestrians, and extremely destructive to the pavement."[24] Yet, trolley officials hoped to turn this challenge to their advantage. Two years later, an *Electric Railway Journal* editorial suggested that if trolley companies could take over the independent bus lines, all would be well:

> The [journal] does not believe that auto buses will ever replace the electric car operating on rails. . . . When a suburban district needs transportation facilities but cannot offer enough traffic to warrant extension of the electric railway system, it would seem wise for the traction company to consider establishing an auto bus feeder service to that district and so hold the trade until an extension is warranted.[25]

Thus the trolley companies would try to beat the independent bus lines at their own game.

Other storm clouds loomed larger. World War I adversely affected the American economy by sparking a severe inflationary spiral.[26] Unfortunately, trolley companies in many cities were committed by long-term contracts to fixed fares, usually a nickel. As a variety of factors stimulated urban expansion, they found themselves providing more service over longer routes for the same fixed fare. Delos Wilcox, a nationally renowned transportation expert, pointed out that automobile competition was forcing many traction companies, originally created to provide quick profits for organizers, to provide better service. In addition, he noted, since inflation was driving up capital construction costs, some sort of public subsidies for trolley lines might be required.[27] Perhaps even more worrisome for the long run was the industry's often negative public image. In many American cities, "reform" candidates, in response to the alleged "public be damned" attitude of electric railway officials, had pushed for municipal ownership of local lines for some years. In the early twentieth century, trolley officials had been forced to deal not merely with idealistic theorists, but also with tough, hard-headed politicians, such as Hazen Pingree of Detroit and Tom Johnson of Cleveland, advocating public ownership of trolley lines. Frederick C. Howe conveyed a sense of the "reformers'" hostility toward privately owned utilities when he wrote in 1912 that "the private monopolies which supply transportation, light, heat, and power are another cause of poverty. They collect such tribute as a corrupt alliance with the city sanctions."[28] As World War I approached, traction industry publications began to express some pessimism. In 1916, William J. Clark, Manager of General Electric's Traction Department, stated that "in the present state of the railway industry, discouraging features stand out more conspicuously than do those which are cheering."[29] Though the trolley ruled city streets in the second decade of the twentieth century, the foundation of its empire had begun to show dangerous fissures.

During the 1920s, traction companies could no longer ignore the automobile. Between 1917 and 1929, the number of automobiles multiplied five-fold; in the latter year, their number exceeded 23 million. Yet, if the 1920s were halcyon days for the automobile, the trolley companies also appeared to share in the general prosperity. Between 1917 and 1923, electric railways added more than one billion patrons, and in 1923, they transported 15.7 billion riders, an all-time high. Patronage declined slightly during the later 1920s—in 1929, it was down to 14.4 billion—but the drop was gradual.[30] Thus, while hindsight reveals the shortsightedness of trolley officials during the 1920s, ridership figures seemed to provide a basis for their optimism.

During the 1920s, company spokesmen maintained their belief that only electric railways could fully serve the transportation needs of America's urban masses. In 1923, C. D. Emmons, President of Baltimore's street lines, categorically stated that "it is well recognized that no form of transportation has yet been devised that can take the place of . . . the electric railways for mass transportation."[31] In 1929, a writer for the *Electric Railway Journal* pointed out that automobile trips of five miles, exclusive of parking costs, were about seven times as expensive as the same trip made by trolley. He insisted that "unquestionably the majority of people prefer to live within reach of public transit facilities. The ownership of an automobile by the family does not fully satisfy the daily transport demands of its different members."[32] Clearly most transit officials thought in linear, concrete terms: higher rates of speed, modern equipment, and inexpensive fares would overcome any short-term difficulties.[33]

Even the most ardent trolley boosters probably did not accept such puffery at face value. In an uncommonly introspective 1924 editorial, the *Electric Railway Journal* summed up a public relations dilemma faced by traction companies: rosy, cheerful accounts of the industry's health would stimulate public demands for lower fares; on the other hand, pleas of poverty in order to effect more equitable fare and taxation schedules would jeopardize the industry's financial standing.[34]

Yet during the 1920s, there were apparently sound reasons for transit industry expectations of continued prosperity. Although the automobile constituted a competitive mode of transportation, it had also increased the "riding habit" of urban Americans. By the 1920s, fewer people were willing to sit at home when they could be out and about in their cities. Transit companies benefited significantly from the fallout. The *Electric Railway Journal* noted that between 1902 and 1922, per capita ridership in cities boasting electric trolleys nearly tripled.[35] Traction company officials were also confident that they could ally the trolley with the motor bus, which had been dramatically improved in design, speed, and comfort. The motor bus would provide electric railways with the flexibility to compete with privately owned automobiles, particularly in low-density suburban areas.[36]

Unfortunately, much of their optimism was based upon unsound reasoning. Electric railway spokesmen, for instance, often held that automobiles had reached the peak of their influence in the mid-1920s. In their view, severe automobile congestion in the central districts robbed the automobile of its major selling points: convenience and speed.[37] A typical *Electric Traction* editorial in 1925 wishfully stated that "the congestion of automobiles, the many resulting accidents, the limited parking spaces, and the greater expense of operating already is driving more and more people to the street car, the elevated, and the big bus with a regular operating schedule."[38] Traction representatives took comfort in soothing statements from the business community about the importance of the trolley in urban transportation. Even the automobile industry repeated this theme. In a 1923 speech before a gathering of traction officials, for instance, Albert Reeves, General Manager of the National Automobile Chamber of Commerce, allowed that "few will deny that the trolley supplies the best form of mass transportation."[39] Guy E. Tripp, Chairman of the Board for Westinghouse, endorsed this view: "Nothing has yet appeared which equals the trolley car for servicing great numbers of people at low cost."[40] Perhaps such blandishments dulled sensitivities of many traction officials to rapidly changing realities in urban transportation.

THE PLANNED RESPONSE

City planners, with their attention riveted upon the dynamics of urban change, are among those groups that could have been expected to perceive the importance of the automobile to the urban transportation network. However, even they often missed the obvious. Part of the reason may have been their lack of funding, political influence, and public support, forcing city planners in the 1920s to focus primarily upon questions of survival and professional recognition. Even in the largest cities, planning agencies were in the earliest stages of development. While urban transportation problems became daily more critical, planners were still trying to unravel bureaucratic mazes at city hall. Historian Mel Scott suggested that they were extremely fearful of being labeled visionaries by politicians, businessmen, and civic leaders. Planners generally avoided the luxury of "adventuresomeness" in thought "because the materialism of the times was inimical to philosophic probing" and because the rapidity of urban growth demanded "practical plans and immediate decisions."[41]

Planners generally possessed little consciousness of either the precarious future of street railways or the full implications of the automobile's triumph upon future urban development. Most experts assumed the indispensability of the electric trolley, hopefully integrated into a comprehensive public transit system. At the 1922 national planning conference, Daniel Turner, transportation consultant from New York, informed his distinguished audience that "in a modern city, street railways are as essential as the homes of the people and the buildings in which they work. In all of their social and economic activities the people are dependent upon their street railway service."[42] Significantly, at a round table discussion among leading planners following Turner's paper, not a single individual challenged the electric trolley's central place in urban transportation or even mentioned the automobile as a serious competitor! At the following year's national conference, George A. Damon, regional planner from Los Angeles, reinforced this trend in transportation thought: "It is hard to conceive of any traffic agency which will have more influence on the activity and corresponding prosperity of the entire district than a well designed rapid transit system."[43]

Yet, while planners maintained their belief in the necessity of the trolley, they did not ignore the automobile's impact upon patterns of urbanization during the 1920s. Those who did discuss the automobile generally emphasized its positive features. Although some persisted in their view that the automobile was still primarily a pleasure vehicle, others were aware of its larger place in urban transportation. Cincinnati planner H. F. Shipley summed up the latter viewpoint when he wrote in 1923:

> We now think in terms of the motor car almost to the exclusion of horse-drawn vehicles. Journeys which were rarely attempted and which when attempted were a matter of hours are now a matter of minutes and are undertaken with little or no compunction. Thousands who use the motor car are now familiar with all parts of the city and interested in the proper layout and construction of good roads everywhere.

Emphasizing the idea that the motor car "has now become the business and social necessity of the average citizen," not merely the rich, Shipley concluded, "Our outlook on life has been immensely broadened by the motor car and this must and will profoundly affect our view of City Planning."[44]

Unfortunately, most city planning commissions during the 1920s were so pressured by organizational difficulties and other responsibilities that few planners had the time to conceptualize, or the authority to implement comprehensive responses to growing transportation problems. A 1924 survey revealed that less than 20% of cities with planning staffs had taken the first steps toward formulating a major street plan.[45] Traffic experts in most cities spent their time providing small-scale cures to immediate crises; their efforts usually provided palliatives rather than cures.

Many of the day-to-day activities of the planners involved helping cities adjust to the automobile, particularly in central business districts. They differed, however, in their view of what caused CBD traffic congestion. Many blamed the automobile and the practice of parking on downtown streets while others blamed subways, elevated railways, and poorly conceived skyscrapers.[46] In many American cities, the role of the planner was scarcely distinguishable from that of the street and highway engineer, and in some the two functions were merged into single departments. Traffic experts immersed themselves in the routine tasks of designing grade-crossing separations, street-widening projects, experimenting with synchronized traffic signals, negotiating downtown parking limitations with local merchants, and wheedling next year's appropriation from tight-fisted city councils.

Nevertheless, a few planners thought of traffic relief in grandiose terms. From the modern perspective, some of their proposals appear fantastic. One planner scientifically "proved" that the most effective means of easing traffic flow in congested districts was to rebuild entire areas in identical, hexagonal blocks; he offered no clue as to who would finance such projects.[47] Other ideas may have been inspired by science fiction writer Jules Verne. Though several practical double-decked street systems actually appeared, most notably Chicago's Wacker Drive, enthusiasts imagined far more elaborate schemes. Proposals and drawings for triple, quadruple, even six-layered downtown street projects were common during the 1920s.[48] San Francisco planner Stephen Child's proposal for elimination of downtown traffic jams was equally startling. Rather than controlling motor vehicle traffic in congested areas, he urged the elimination of all buses and trolleys.[49] This profusion of hastily devised proposals caused Lewis Mumford to complain that "the multiple-decked highways and ariel perspectives that lazy imaginations conjure up" would only increase congestion.[50]

Perhaps no single individual perceived—or stated—the planners' dilemma in clearer terms than Alvan Macauley, President of Packard Motor Company:

> It seems, in many ways, unfortunate that cities in this country became interested in city planning when they did—a little too early—a few years before the traffic problem became acute. If the interest in city planning had arisen simultaneously with the pressure of traffic congestion, the whole city planning movement would have been more powerful and more effective. Its inspiration would have been the city practical rather than the city beautiful. And if it had not been that traffic regulation by policing was so simple and apparently successful in the earlier stages of the traffic problem, it would have been realized sooner that regulation is only a temporary palliative, not a cure.[51]

Clearly, during the 1920s planners had a difficult time striking a healthy balance between inspirational visions and pragmatic responses to real problems.

A root cause of American planners' difficulties during the decade was their failure to achieve a consensus regarding future patterns of desirable urban growth. The big debate focused on whether they should promote or discourage decentralization, although the issue was often poorly defined.

One group of important planners and their powerful allies endorsed decentralization. George A. Damon believed that planners should encourage "great living districts," made up of comparatively small centers of population and industry. Instead of producing tremendous land values at congested centers, their efforts "should be directed toward spreading out those values over a large, contiguous district."[52] In 1920, Harland Bartholomew, an influential consultant from St. Louis, urged decentralization in unequivocal terms. He informed the national planning conference delegates that not only was it imperative to overcome existing congestion, "but it is equally important to avoid congested conditions in cities in which they have not yet developed. We should decentralize and spread our values over a larger area and *automatically* by this distribution of business and traffic *solve* the traffic problem" [emphasis mine].[53] Jesse C. Nichols, internationally renowned developer of the Country Club District in Kansas City, pointed out that creation of outlying shopping centers "denotes progress and growth in our cities."[54] This was no small consideration, particularly during the 1920s.

Some planners, however, criticized decentralization because of the damage it would do to central districts. Robert H. Whitten, a Boston consultant, noted that "the remedy to many seems to be obvious—distribute business and industry over a wider area." But Whitten argued that those who supported decentralization generally urged termination of expenditures on rapid transit and opposed street improvements in the central districts. This was short-sighted, in Whitten's view: "While a certain amount of decentralization might be desirable, there must be some way to bring this about without strangling the patient."[55]

Another thorny issue in the debate among planners was whether rapid transit promoted or retarded decentralization. John P. Fox of Boston argued that cities should build rapid transit lines in order to distribute business and relieve congestion. "All over the world the larger cities are in need of the powerful influence of rapid transit lines to decentralize business and direct future growth."[56] Robert Whitten agreed that the flat fare system of electric lines led to the dispersal of people and industry, but argued that this was costly for cities. "Sprawling development," he noted, required "more miles of track, water, gas pipe, electric wiring, sewers, paving, etc., thus increasing the cost of supplying the city with necessary utilities."[57]

A number of planners were slowly converted to the view that while rapid transit might aid central districts by reducing street congestion in the short run, its long-term impact would be just the opposite. In 1913, Edward M. Bassett, one of the founders of the modern city planning movement, had observed at that year's national planning conference that radial transit lines would maintain the centralized city and prevent congestion. While permitting suburbanization, they would preserve the central district as the hub of commercial activity. As Bassett put it, "Rapid transit is the only thing that will bring low rent and sunny homes to the working people in the great cities."[58] But a year later, in 1914, addressing the same gathering, Bassett did an abrupt about-face, pointing out that "bringing everything to a single center, like the Loop District in Chicago, is one of the greatest mistakes that a city can make. It produces congestion instead of distribution."[59]

By the First World War, it was evident to all that surface cars on downtown streets added to congestion. Up to that point, most planners had agreed that placing rapid transit lines either above or below streets would solve CBD traffic problems. However, during the 1920s some influential planners not only followed Bassett's lead in suspecting that radial lines exacerbated congestion, but they added subways and elevateds to their list of factors effecting that result. In their view, subways were simply part of a vicious circle. They noted that as central districts grew increasingly congested, downtown business interests rallied behind bond issues for transit facilities above or below streets. Easy access to central districts brought more people downtown, increased property values, and stimulated skyscraper development. Central areas of fixed, limited size soon became even more jammed by people and competing forms of traffic than before, which, in turn, stimulated additional demands for expensive new elevateds or subways along parallel routes.[60] Admittedly, trolleys on downtown streets were hopelessly inefficient because of their frequent stops and the fact that passengers usually were required to get on and off in the middle of the street. According to Arthur S. Tuttle of New York, "Street cars in a crowded street add greatly to congestion and little to the solution of the passenger transportation problem."[61] However, Detroit consultant T. Glenn Phillips spoke for many fellow traffic experts when he charged that "the method of relieving traffic by substituting subways for surface transit has already proved a boomerang and will continue to do so."[62]

During the 1920s, the increased congestion in downtown areas often seemed to present unsolvable problems. Though planners disagreed whether the automobile was the primary cause, all agreed that it contributed heavily. On the other hand, many experts perceived the automobile as a positive benefit to the city; by facilitating the development of suburban shopping centers, it could help relieve downtown areas of their worst congestion. Unquestionably, the automobile presented both problems and opportunities to planners. During the 1920s, John Nolen, Clarence Stein, and Henry Wright initiated new town "garden suburb" experiments near some of America's older eastern cities as a means to reduce urban crowding.[63] By the late 1920s, it was evident to all traffic experts that America had entered the motor age; by 1929, most had learned to live with the automobile, even though all did not accept it uncritically.

STREET RAILWAY INDUSTRY RESPONSE: THE 1930s

The Great Depression wrought significant changes in urban transportation. While the automobile industry suffered, the street railway industry suffered even more. Thus, by 1940 the automobile was in a stronger position vis-à-vis the trolley than eleven years earlier. In 1929 electric railways carried 14.4 billion passengers; by 1932 the number plummeted to 9.9 billion. While most industries revived after 1932, electric railways failed to share in the gradual recovery. By 1940, trolley passengers declined to 8.3 billion. While these losses were partly offset by increases in bus patronage, total public transit patronage still dropped from almost 17 billion riders in 1929 to 13.1 billion in 1940.[64] The automobile industry also experienced hard times; sales shrank from a peak of 4.5 million in 1929 to a mere 1.1 million in 1932, and auto registrations dropped from 23.1 million to 20.9 million. The crucial difference between the two industries was that by 1940 the automobile industry was well along the road to recovery. In that year auto sales nearly returned to their 1929 level, with 3.7 million units sold. With increased numbers of second hand automobiles on the road, total registrations in 1940 exceeded the 1929 figure by 4.5 million.[65]

Despite this seemingly incontrovertible evidence that American urbanites preferred the automobile to the trolley, many traction industry spokesmen maintained a surprising degree of optimism. In the early months of the Depression, the decline in transit patronage was gradual; some officials believed that the industry's relatively slow decline compared to those of other businesses proved that trolleys were indispensable.[66] Others opined that during hard times, the electric railway's low cost would place it at an advantage in competition with the more expensively operated automobile.[67] The *Electric Railway Journal*, brandishing incomplete statistics from a few large cities, insisted early in 1932 that the trend was toward increased use of public transportation.[68] An editorial suggested that demographic projections favored electric trolleys; by 1965, the country's population would be 70% urban, providing a massive number of new trolley users.[69] Traction officials also took considerable comfort in the temporary decline in the number of automobile registrations. One transit company president expressed the view that "existing cars have . . . exerted their full effect upon our traffic. Perhaps . . . we may reasonably hope to regain some of our traffic."[70] *Electric Traction* reinforced such wishful thinking when it editorialized, "As a temporary expedient in sparsely populated areas, the private automobile may start new communities, but organized transportation is becoming every day a more dominant force in shaping the character of the future city."[71] A 1939 editorial in the *Transit Journal* noted that of 376 cities with more than 25,000, only seven were without transit service, "virtually the same number that were without service 25 years ago." The editor further claimed that "regardless of whether the American public owns 1,000,000 or 20,000,000 private automobiles, transit remains an essential public service."[72] Even in 1940, when ridership reached its nadir, trolley officials could still find cause for cheer. For once a traction magazine correctly anticipated a major trend. As industry geared up for wartime production after the fall of France, *Bus Transportation* envisioned doubled and triple shifts in plants. "That means a constant increase in riding habit for the bus companies."[73] The editorial suggested that other forms of public transit might also experience a revival.

Despite the transit industry's brave front during the 1930s, less than sanguine articles and editorials regarding the future of public transportation even appeared in the transit magazines. Some realistic traction company officials, unimpressed by short-run statistics, worried about declining patronage during the Depression. It would be nice indeed for the industry if, in fact, the Depression drove the "working man" from his flivver to the trolley. Unfortunately, the "working man" was most susceptible to unemployment. Those without jobs obviously had less need for trolley service. Those who kept their jobs usually kept their automobiles too; they scrimped and saved elsewhere. Thus, the hoped for increases in patronage did not occur.[74] Transit officials also noted that hard times made it difficult for street railways to provide decent service; they had to "make do" with rough rails, decrepit and dirty coaches, and less frequent service. Samuel Riddle, president of the national trolley officials' association, warned in 1930 that "we are challenged today by more private automobiles than ever before. The result is [that] our service is made less attractive to our patrons because we are uable to attain the highest rates of speed possible through the use of modern equipment."[75]

A few trolley company spokesmen inveighed against the complacency of their peers. A New Yorker with a sense of humor predicted hard times ahead for the electric railways:

> It is possible to take a healthy frog, so I am told, set him in a pan of water at room temperature, increase the temperature of the water very slowly until it reaches the boiling point, and Mr. Frog will not jump out. Unaware that any change is taking place, he is gradually lulled into peaceful unconsciousness.[76]

The writer clearly implied that the automobile industry was boiling the trolley business alive. Perceptive electric railway officials understood the appeal of the automobile, even if they were not sure how to combat it. A New Orleans transit executive pointed out that the automobile not only fostered the American spirit of individualism, but provided other tangible advantages. The family deciding upon an excursion had neither to wait nor walk. Just as important, the entire family could be transported at "no incremental cost, as is necessary when individual fares are required." He pointed out that in many important respects, the automobile provided "a character of service of greater utility than that which can be offered by the street cars."[77]

During the 1930s, pessimistic trolley officials vacillated between blaming themselves and the automobile industry for their troubles. In 1931, the editor of *Electric Traction* stated that "the time has passed when the electric railway industry can lay the blame for its troubles to automobile competition, the radio, and other outside interests." A prerequisite to health in the trolley business was for its leaders to stop "talking defeatism."[78] Public transit interests, on occasion, voiced grudging admiration for the auto industry. After noting that "of all the business interests in the country, automobile manufacturing has shown the best self-recuperative powers," a 1934 editorial admitted that "without any government financing, the automobile industry has lifted itself out of the depression by sheer force of good salesmanship."[79] On the other occasions, however, trolley officials attributed the decline of their industry to the insidious machinations of auto interests. A 1937 article charged that "well-organized groups" had combined in an effort to "unpopularize" street cars and drive them off congested downtown streets.

> This is especially true of the group composed of automobile owners. They have their own local automobile clubs which are units of similar state and national organizations—all highly efficient at the job of voicing loud and lengthy protests against any remedies which encroach on what the automobilist conceives to be his rights.[80]

At times, public transportation interests found themselves simply overwhelmed by the automobile's popularity. One editorial told of a local transit company donating free rides to a WPA construction site. Less than half the workers accepted the offer; the rest came by automobile. The writer lamented that "even though on relief the workers found money to buy gas and oil for their private automobiles."[81]

Some of the frustration felt by the street railway officials probably was a result of heavy increases in expenditures for public works, particularly streets and highways. At the outset of the Depression, several municipal experts advised cities to take advantage of low interest rates and sell bonds for needed improvements. Money might never again be so "cheap."[82] Auto interests argued that road building was one of the most efficient and humane ways to combat hard times. Chief of the U.S. Chamber of Commerce's Automotive Division A. W. Childs wrote that "with more than 50 percent of the road building dollar going directly to labor, and something like 25 percent more going indirectly, by way of production machinery and materials, the *immediate* result of larger road building programs would be a rapid increase in employment."[83] Better roads and streets would mean more automobile sales, more jobs; and private business would follow the public sector, increasing its capital flow. Clearly, trolley interests feared the specter of public subsidies for their chief competitor; few influential voices urged funding for refurbishing old street cars or repairing deteriorated road beds. In 1931, Thomas F.

Fitzgerald, a Pittsburgh traction official, urged a reversal of "official" government policy, since street cars were still the "most efficient and economical vehicle for movement of large masses of traffic."[84]

PLANNERS AND URBAN TRANSPORTATION: THE 1930s

The state of flux in transportation thought among a variety of interest groups unquestionably influenced urban planners during the 1930s. Their thinking continued to reflect uncertainty, and the lack of either consensus or coherent direction. Some insisted that the automobile would never replace public transportation. A 1931 study by the Denver Planning Commission concluded that:

> While there is much discussion at the present time and some opinion that mass transportation has been superseded by private automobiles and will eventually be done away with, this does not seem to the commission to be well founded. Casual scrutiny of conditions in Denver and other American cities indicates that mass transportation is a vital necessity and wisdom requires that cities plan for the most efficient transit service possible.[85]

Saco R. De Boer of the Denver commission flatly concluded that "mass transportation is an absolute necessity and therefore will continue to exist."[86] Other traffic experts around the country stressed the idea that planning emphasizing the automobile ignored the needs of the masses and was therefore elitist. Walter Blucher of the American City Planning Institute spoke for some of his peers when he wrote in 1936 that the street car "camel" cannot for very long compete with the automobile if mass transportation is to decrease." He pointed out that abandoning street car lines "does not inconvenience the automobile owner but it does cause an inconvenience to the person who is really not able to pay for expensive transportation."[87]

On the other hand, during the 1930s more and more traffic experts gave up on rapid transit—if indeed they had ever been "sold" on it—and predicted that future planning must emphasize "rebuilding" cities to accommodate the automobile. Some planners were exuberant about the possibilities. Theron Howser of Portland, Oregon, claimed in 1934, "if the entire ground area of the business portion of our cities were to be given up to the exclusive use of the automobile, the resulting increase in safety, convenience, and comfort would be so great that it would cause the greatest period of building activity ever witnessed in America."[88] Miller McClintock, head of Harvard University's Traffic Bureau, sounded a more resigned note when he wrote in 1930 that "We have given up any hope, in most cities, of obtaining any open area in the heart of the central district [for parks]." Suggestive of changing perceptions of many planners since the "City Beautiful" days, he continued, "May we not be able to demolish all of the buildings on entire blocks, use the land not for parks, but for open and improved parking areas, with as much benefit from light and air as if they were parks and yet make them pay their way as sound business ventures?"[89] Several years later, while admitting that public transportation might still have a place, he insisted that "Primarily, however, the internal and external transportation of the city of tomorrow is automotive." He downplayed any future difficulties which exclusive reliance upon the automobile might create: "The planners and engineers of today now recognize the full implications of the automotive revolution and their present works give hope for a speedy elemination of many present day maladjustments."[90] The same Denver planning group which had emphasized the centrality of the street car in 1931 suggested nine years later that trolleys be removed from major streets "because [they] delay the faster vehicular traffic."[91]

One issue which all traffic experts agreed upon by the 1930s was that the automobile promoted decentralization. While they remained divided over whether future planning should pursue a policy of decentralization or centralization, proponents of the former view dominated planning thought. John Ihlder of Washington praised the automobile's effectiveness in promoting decentralization, particularly suburban development: "The private passenger automobile is the best form of transportation now available. The result of suburban development will be the largest amount of land per person for which we can find effective use. The result will be economy in development and operation, and conditions which will be wholesome from both the medical and the social points of view."[92] Cincinnati's Myron Downs endorsed Ihlder's view: "It now seems practical to plan and zone for complete satellite communities throughout the larger metropolitan areas, thereby reducing the existing rush-hour burden on our highways."[93] Walden E. Sweet of Denver argued that the "almost unlimited space" of western cities provided them ideal settings for decentralization: "The ideal of spaciousness has been pursued. To avoid the evils of congestion and overcrowding . . . Denver has aspired to spread widely rather than reach high."[94] Finally, in 1940, with American participation in World War II imminent, some experts argued that decentralized cities would be far less vulnerable to air bombardment than such congested cities as Rotterdam and London.[95]

Amidst such widespread enthusiasm there remained planners who urged caution, or who vehemently opposed burgeoning urban sprawl. Harland Bartholomew, who had lent his influential voice to prodecentralization forces in 1920, performed an about-face in 1932. In an address at that year's national planning conference, he maintained that "decentralization in practice appears to mean . . . moving the population from the centers of the city to the outskirts, and disturbing stores and shops more or less indiscriminately throughout the whole urban area." Hinting at potential problems which automobile-oriented traffic experts might confront in the future, he continued, "I maintain that decentralization, as now practiced, is economically unsound, more or less destructive in fundamental character and may ultimately produce social disadvantages as great as those now found in the centralized city."[96] Suggesting disagreement within planning staffs in western, as well as eastern cities, L. F. Eppich of Denver charged that "the most sinister disease that has affected the stability and the welfare of large American cities [is the] decentralization of urban populations and activities."[97] Finally, even Miller McClintock, the same expert who advocated tearing down entire blocks in central districts to build parking lots, ventured the opinion that "confronted with the seemingly insuperable difficulties, recourse is too frequently found in arguments for decentralization rather than a bold planning suited to the necessity."[98]

From the foregoing, it appears that traffic experts of the 1930s were far less certain than their turn of the century predecessors of what constituted the cityscape of the future. In 1900, the "City Beautiful" ideal reigned supreme, and the planners' choices for physical planning appeared simple. By the 1930s, there were many more confusing options. Some local experts considered themselves little more than traffic engineers, hired to solve immediate, mundane problems of traffic congestion.[99] Operating with very limited budgets, they emphasized the idea that city and regional planning objectives must not be overly ambitious. As L. Deming Tilton of southern California noted, "Many city planning commissions have discovered [that] the proposals which call for large expenditures get fire-whistle headlines, but the quiet, money-saving preventive work which goes on from day to day does not recieve a measure of acclaim in proportion to its importance."[100]

Practical men, the "traffic engineers," had little patience with idealists who envisioned cities of twenty or thirty years in the future, such as Norman Bel Geddes's Futurama, presented at the New York World's Fair in 1939. Though most traffic experts agreed that the city of "tomorrow" must be reshaped in the face of new technology, how far away was "tomorrow?" Should they prepare for the city one year, ten years, or fifty years hence? One sober-minded group of experts asked, "And in the interim, what of the city—shall it adopt the traffic plan of the city of tomorrow and hope to grow up to it, or shall it continue to be planned or readjusted to meet gradually changing needs and conditions?"[101]

CONCLUSION

Hindsight might suggest that the magnitude of the automobile's triumph in urban transportation was, or should have been apparent long before 1940. The facts of the situation are, however, less clear. Urban planners alone should not bear the blame for the passing of the electric trolley, whose fate was largely determined before 1940. Relatively few actually lamented its decay at the time. Struggling for professional recognition, funding, and authority, city planning staffs were too beleaguered by conflicting demands upon their time and energy to give undivided attention to urban transportation. Too many planners, perhaps naively, accepted the assurances of trolley officials that public transportation was an indestructible necessity. Why should they not have believed such boasts? Certainly the electric railways had ruled the streets in the early twentieth century. Should automobile manufacturers be faulted for aggressively marketing the ingenious new invention? They were following what the vast majority of public opinion considered the "American way." The dynamics of urban transportation changed so rapidly between 1900 and 1940 that it is nearly inconceivable how the predominant place of the electric trolley could have remained unchallenged or how urban planners could have enabled cities to avoid midcentury transportation chaos. Yet we are all poorer for the rapid decline of public transportation in our cities—the roots of which were evident before World War II.

NOTES

1. John Keats, *The Insolent Chariots* (Philadelphia, 1958), 12-13.
2. Ronald A. Buel, *Dead End: The Automobile in Mass Transportation* (Englewood Cliffs, NJ, 1972), 4. Other writers have emphasized the notion that early twentieth-century Americans perceived this "privatization" of the commuting experience as a foremost advantage of the automobile over public transportation. See Glen E. Holt, "The Changing Perception of Urban Pathology: An Essay on the Development of Mass Transit in the U.S.," in Kenneth T. Jackson and Stanley K. Schultz, eds. *Cities in American History* (New York, 1972), 324-343.
3. Lewis Mumford, *The City in History: Its Origins, Its Transformation, and Its Prospects* (New York, 1961), 506.
4. Ibid., 508.
5. Ibid., 510.
6. A large number of scholarly works dealt with the suburbanization of the 1920s and the influence of the automobile in promoting it. See, for example, Harlan P. Douglass, *The Suburban Trend* (New York, 1925); James J. Flink, *The Car Culture* (Cambridge,

MA, 1975); Kenneth T. Jackson, "The Crabgrass Frontier: 150 Years of Suburban Growth," in Raymond Mohl and James F. Richardson, eds., *The Urban Experience: Themes in American History* (Belmont, CA, 1973), 196-221; Sam B. Warner, Jr., *The Urban Wilderness: A History of the American City* (New York, 1972); Blaine A. Brownell, *The Urban Ethos in the South, 1920-1930* (Baton Rouge, 1975).

7. Charles N. Glaab and A. Theodore Brown, *A History of Urban America* (New York, 1976), 143-144; *Historical Statistics of the United States: Colonial Times to 1970*, (Washington, DC, 1975), 2: 721.

8. The social history of the automobile has been probed in depth by several writers and will not be covered here. A logical starting point is John B. Rae, *The Road and Car in American Life* (Boston, 1971).

9. "Motor Trucks Relieve Traffic Congestion," *Municipal Engineering* 43 (October 1912), 259; P. G. Heinemann, "The Automobile and Public Health," *Popular Science Monthly* 84 (March 1914), 284-289; "Clean Streets and Motor Traffic," *Literary Digest* 49 (September 3, 1914), 413; W. Hutchinson, "Influence of the Motor Truck in Relieving Traffic Congestion," *The American City* 8 (May 1913), 561-562.

10. "Making and Correcting City Plans," *Municipal Engineering* 43 (September 1912), 171; "Effect of the Automobile Upon Street Improvements," *Municipal Engineering* 43 (September 1912), 236.

11. James J. Flink discusses this concept in "Three Stages of Automobile Consciousness," *American Quarterly* 24 (October 1972), 451-473.

12. The standard history of the planning movement is Mel Scott, *American City Planning Since 1890* (Berkeley, 1969). The early history of planning is well covered in this and other sources; thus, I shall only touch upon it.

13. George B. Ford, "Digging Deeper Into City Planning," *The American City* 6 (February 1912), 559, 562.

14. See, for example, Frederick L. Olmsted, "The Basic Principles of City Planning," *The American City* 3 (August 1910), 67-72.

15. George S. Webster, "Subsurface Structures," *Proceedings of the 3rd National Conference on City Planning* (Philadelphia, May 15-17, 1911), 216.

16. George E. Hooker, "Congestion: Its Causes in Chicago," *Proceedings of the 2nd National Conference on City Planning* (Rochester, NY, May 2-4, 1910), 49.

17. Nelson P. Lewis, "The Automobile and the City Plan," *Proceedings of the 8th National Conference on City Planning* (Cleveland, June 5-7, 1915), 54-55.

18. Ibid., 41.

19. Ibid., 71.

20. Ibid., 75.

21. Ibid., 77.

22. The rise and triumph of the trolley are well explained in George W. Hilton and John F. Due, *The Electric Railways in America* (Palo Alto, CA, 1960).

23. Cleveland Moffett, "Automobiles for the Average Man," *Review of Reviews* 21 (June 1900), 710.

24. *Electric Railway Journal* 43 (May 30, 1914), 1207.

25. Ibid. 48 (August 19, 1916), 300.

26. The cost of living in the U.S. doubled between 1914 and 1920.

27. Delos F. Wilcox, "Problems of Reconstruction With Respect to Urban Transportation," *The American City* 19 (December 1918), 443. As evidence of the seriousness of the transportation "crisis," the same observer had been unalterably opposed to public subsidies just five years earlier. *The American City* 9 (July 1913), 2.

28. Frederick C. Howe, "The City as a Socializing Agency," *American Journal of Sociology* 17 (March 1912), 597. Progressives' attitudes toward the trolley are also explored by Clay McShane, "American Cities and the Coming of the Automobile, 1870-1910," (Ph.D. dissertation, University of Wisconsin—Madison, 1975), 47, 128, 193.

29. William J. Clark, "A Thought on the Railway Industry," *Electric Traction* 12 (September 1916), 663.

30. *Historical Statistics of the U.S.*, Vol. 2, 721.

31. "Coordinating Motor Bus and Electric Railway," *Bus Transportation* 2 (May 1923), 288.

32. Joseph P. Hallihan, "Relation of Rapid Transit to Community Development," *Electric Railway Journal* 73 (September 14, 1929), 912.

33. Edward Dana, "Answering a Growing Need for Adequate Rapid Transit," *Electric Railway Journal* 74 (June 1930), 391.

34. *Electric Railway Journal* 64 (July 5, 1924), 3.

35. George H. Davis, "Coordinated Operation of Street Cars and Buses Urged," *Electric Railway Journal* 61 (June 23, 1923), 1035. Davis cited the figure of 620 rides per capita in 1902 and 1,623 in 1922. These figures are not only misleading, but they are far too high. Certain trolley companies apparently computed per capita ridership using only central city population figures for their bases. By the 1920s, the suburban explosion provided large numbers of patrons who still used trolleys but were not included in the per capita ridership computations.

36. This was a repetitive theme in transit journals during the 1920s. See, for example, *Bus Transportation* (August 1923), 388; "Growing Pains of the Automobile Industry," *Electric Traction* 23 (December 1926), 656.

37. Significantly, electric railway officials perceived urban transportation through rose-tinted glasses and focused virtually all of their attention upon the central districts. In their comparisons of the efficiency of automobiles versus street cars, they invariably contrasted the cost and convenience of trips via each mode from outlying areas directly to the central districts. They appeared to ignore, if they realized, that the private car encouraged a new pattern of travel which was cross-town or lateral and which discouraged travel to increasingly congested central districts. Seldom, if ever, did their offical publications acknowledge the fact that, particularly during the 1920s, downtown business frequently either relocated or opened branches in suburban areas, in order to compete for automobile-oriented customers. That trolley officials recognized this business trend is certain; conversion to bus lines during the 1920s and 1930s makes such a conclusion inescapable. Yet their quasi-official publications never confronted the implications of this trend directly. Nevertheless, trolley officials were not alone in believing automobiles might "saturate" available space during the 1920s. See, for example, "Saturation: A Highway Problem," *Concrete Highway Magazine* 8 (December 1924), 278-279.

38. "Street Cars Coming Back," *Electric Traction* 21 (October 1925), 522.

39. Albert Reeves, "Does Rubber Endanger the Rails?" *Bus Transportation* 2 (November 1923), 527.

40. Guy E. Tripp, "Mass Transportation Must Be Classified and Segregated," *Bus Transportation* 4 (March 1925), 144. Tripp's judgment was not wholly impartial, as Westinghouse supplied a significant portion of the electric railway equipment.

41. Scott, *American City Planning Since 1890*, 251-252.

42. Daniel Turner, "The Fundamentals of Transit Planning for Cities," *Proceedings of the 14th National Conference on City Planning* (Springfield, MA June 5-7, 1922), 104.

43. George A. Damon, "Inter and Intra Urban Transit and Traffice as a Regional Planning Problem," *Proceedings of the 15th National Conference on City Planning* (Baltimore, April 30, May 1-2, 1923), 47.

44. H. F. Shipley, "Cincinnati's Highway System and the City Plan," *Proceedings of the 12th National Conference on City Planning* (Cincinnati, April 19-22, 1920), 51.

45. *Public Works* 55 (June 1924), 181.

46. C. E. Grunsky, "City Planning in Small Cities," *Proceedings of the American Society of Civil Engineers* 55 (April 25, 1929), 1437.

47. Noulan Cauchon, "City Planning and Traffic Congestion," *Roads and Streets* 66 (July 1926), 21.

48. Henry W. Corbett, "Different Levels for Foot, Wheel, and Rail," *The American City* 31 (July 1924), 2-6; John A. Harriss, "And This?" *The American City* 26 (June 1927), 803-805.

49. Stephen Child, "Restricted Traffic District Proposed," *The American City* 36 (April 1927), 507-510.

50. Lewis Mumford, "The Next Twenty Years in City Planning," *Planning Problems of Town, City, and Region: Papers and Discussions,* National Conference on City Planning (Washington, DC, May 9-11, 1927), 56.

51. Alvan Macauley, "Adapting the City to the Automobile," *Public Works* 55 (September 1924), 285.

52. George A. Damon, "Relation of the Motor Bus to Other Methods of Transportation," *Proceedings of the 16th National Conference on City Planning* (Los Angeles, April 7-10, 1924), 80.

53. Harland Bartholomew, "The Urban Auto Problem," *Proceedings of the 12th National Conference on City Planning* (Cincinnati, April 19-22, 1920), 99.

54. Jessee C. Nichols, "The Development of Outlying Shopping Centers," *Proceedings of the 21st National Conference on City Planning* (Buffalo and Niagara Falls, May 20-23, 1929), 16.

55. Robert H. Whitten, "Some Limitations," *City Planning* 4 (April 1928), 81. See also, Harland Bartholomew, "A Program to Prevent Economic Disintegration in American Cities," *Planning Problems of Town, City, and Region: Papers and Discussions, Proceedings of the 24th National Conference on City Planning* (Pittsburgh, November 14-16, 1932), 3.

56. James P. Fox, "Subsurface Terminals For Street Cars Open to Criticism," *The American City* 21 (November 1919), 421-422.

57. *Electric Railway Journal* 54 (November 1919), 831.

58. Edward M. Bassett, *Proceedings of the 5th National Conference on City Planning* (Chicago, May 5-7, 1913), 126.

59. Bassett, *Proceedings of the 6th National Conference on City Planning* (Toronto, May 25-27, 1914), 235.

60. See Benjamin A. Haldeman, "Main Thoroughfares and Street Railways," in John Nolen, ed., *City Planning* (New York, 1929), 279-313; Daniel L. Turner, "The Fundamentals of Transit Planning," *Proceedings of the 14th National Conference on City Planning* (Springfield, MA, June 5-7, 1922), 112.

61. Arthur S. Tuttle, "Traffic and City Streets," *Public Works* 55 (February 1924), 45.

62. T. Glenn Phillips, "The Influence of Zoning on the Design of City Streets," *Proceedings of the American Society of Civil Engineers* 51 (February 1925), 225.

63. Roy Lubove, *Community Planning in the 1920s* (Pittsburgh, 1963), 107-127.
64. *Historical Statistics of the U.S.*, Vol. 2, 721.
65. Ibid., 716.
66. Paul H. Shoup, "Cooperation Essential to Meet 1930s Challenge to Transportation," *Electric Railway Journal* 74 (July 1930), 431.
67. Hawley S. Simpson, "The Economics of City Traffic and Transportation," *The American City* 44 (February 1931), 138.
68. *Electric Railway Journal* 74 (March 1930), 125.
69. "The Growing Need for Public Transportation," *Electric Railway Journal* 74 (May 1930), 247. This editorial was characteristic of the journal's lack of deep analysis. It simply failed to point out that most of the recent urban population growth had occurred in the outlying areas—the very areas which the trolley companies determined were unprofitable.
70. A. J. Lundberg, "Transit Prospects Brighten," *Transit Journal* 77 (October 10, 1933), 375.
71. "Catching Up," *Electric Traction* 26 (November 1930), 573.
72. "Trends in Transit Riding," *Transit Journal* 83 (January/December 1939), 42.
73. "The Bus Job in the Armament Program," *Bus Transportation* 19 (July 1940), 320. The editorial was right. Between 1940 and 1945 bus ridership increased from 4.2 billion to 9.9 billion, while trolley patronage increased from 8.3 to 12.1 billion. After World War II, bus ridership climbed to a peak of 10.7 billion in 1948; then it begain a long slide. In 1970, it was down to 5 billion. Trolley ridership plunged immediately following the war. By 1950, trolley ridership was 6.1 billion, or half of its 1945 peak. By 1970 it was a mere 2.1 billion passengers. *Historical Statistics of the U.S.*, Vol. 2, 721.
74. "Recaptured Auto Patronage," *Transit Journal* 76 (September 1932), 369; A. B. Patterson, "The Private Automobile and its Effect Upon Mass Transportation," *Electric Traction and Bus Journal* 29 (September 1933), 279.
75. "Industry's Fundamental Problems," *Electric Railway Journal* 74 (July 1930), 459.
76. William G. Reilly, "Measuring the Market for Mass Transportation," *Transit Journal* 76 (February 1932), 64.
77. A. B. Patterson, "The Private Automobile," 278. Yet even this perceptive trolley official failed to point out the increasingly important virtue of the automobile's flexibility for the casual shopper. Without paying separate fares, the automobilist could run several errands in separate parts of the city. For example, the worker might wish to make several stops on the way home from work.
78. "Look Within," *Electric Traction* 27 (August 1931), 373.
79. "Automobile Versus Street Car," *Electric Traction and Bus Journal* 30 (February 1934), 36.
80. "Traffic Congestion: Its Cause and its Cure," *Mass Transportation* 33 (November 1937), 359.
81. "Tough Going," *Mass Transportation* 33 (August 1937), 227.
82. Editorial, *The American City* 41 (November 1929), 5.
83. A. W. Childs, "More Road Building Urged to Stimulate Return to Prosperity," *The American City* 44 (January 1931), 94. See also, George C. Dillman, "Road Building as an Agency of Employment," *The American City* 47 (December 1932), 75-76.
84. Thomas Fitzgerald, "Mass Transportation on the City Streets," *Planning Problems of Town, City, and Region: Papers and Discussions at the 23rd National Conference on City Planning* (Rochester, NY, June 22-24, 1931), 25. At the same time, however,

official publications of the American Automobile Association voiced loud, frequent complaints against state legislatures' diversion of gasoline taxes from road construction to relief and other public expenditures during the 1930s.

85. "Extensions of Street Car Lines to Fully Cover City in Years to Come is Basis of New Planning Commission Study," *Denver Planning* 4 (November 1939), 5.

86. Clarence De Boer, "Mass Transportation in Denver," *American Planning and Civic Annual* (Washington, DC, 1932), 198.

87. Walter H. Blucher, "The Economics of the Parking Lot," *The Planners' Journal* 2 (September-October 1936), 119.

88. Theron P. Howser, "A Plan for a City Built to Fit The Automobile," *The American City* 49 (September, 1934), 57.

89. Miller McClintock, "The Better Use of City Streets With Special Reference to Parking On and Off the Street," *Planning Problems of Town, City, and Region: Papers and Discussions at the 22nd National Conference on City Planning* (Denver, June 23-26, 1930), 50.

90. McClintock, "Of Things to Come," in Harlean James, ed., *American Planning and Civic Annual* (Harrisburg, PA, 1937), 385-387.

91. *Denver Planning Primer*, Vol. 6 (Denver, 1940), 43.

92. John Ihlder, "Population Density and Distribution in Urban Areas," *The Planners' Journal* 1 (May-June 1935), 5. Unfortunately, Ihlder did not elaborate on such terms as "economy in development" and "effective use."

93. Myron Downs, "The Case for New Towns," *The Planners' Journal* 5 (March-April 1939), 43-44.

94. Walden E. Sweet, "The Denver City Plan," *Western City* 1 (May 1930), 46.

95. See, for example, "Vulnerability of Congested Populations," *The American City* 55 (August 1940), 55.

96. Harland Bartholomew, "A Program to Prevent Economic Disintegration in American Cities," *Planning Problems of Town, City, and Region: Presented at the 24th National Conference on City Planning* (Pittsburgh, November 1932), 3.

97. L. F. Eppich, "The Problems of Decentralization and Disintegration in Cities," *The Denver Plan*, Vol. 7 (Denver, 1941), 5.

98. Miller McClintock, "Preventive and Palliative Measures for Street Traffic Relief," *City Planning* 6 (April 1930), 99.

99. George E. Hamlin, "Report of Committee on Highway Research Board," *National Research Council: Proceedings of the 9th Annual Meeting of the Highway Research Board* (Baltimore, 1930), 87.

100. L. Deming Tilton, "Preventive Planning," *City Planning* 7 (October 1931), 235.

101. I. S. Shattuck et al., "Traffic Studies in Relation to City Planning," in James, ed. *American Planning and Civic Annual*, 205.

Historic Planning and Redevelopment in Minneapolis

David R. Goldfield

The redevelopment process in Minneapolis involves an attempt to recreate the positive aspects of life that existed in the nineteenth-century city, an era when the city was a dynamic and positive environment. Redevelopment has focused on recovering the importance of downtown, restoring the industrial base lost to the suburbs and revitalizing neighborhood life—all characteristic aspects of the historic city. The city's public planning efforts, well documented by Altshuler and others, have involved significant cooperation among city agencies and private organizations. This paper will focus on the role of the private sector in this partnership to encourage redevelopment.

Nicollet Mall and the industrial development program are two of the major accomplishments of the recovery efforts. Where success has eluded the city, as in the Cedar-Riverside neighborhood revitalization project, more attention to the historic and social needs of residents might contribute to fulfillment of project goals. The Minneapolis recovery effort has demonstrated the benefits of a civic-conscious business elite, a local government willing to innovate with and for private enterprise, a desire in both public and private sectors for quality planning, and the presence of historical perspective in the planning process.

The decline of the American city has a familiar scenario. A decreasing tax base, inflation, and growing demands for services have placed severe burdens on already hardpressed cities. Services such as health delivery, garbage collection, and police protection are, as a result, haphazard and at times inhumane. The questionable quality of drinking water, the dying rivers, the moribund railroad lines, the declining downtowns, the disappearing open space, the triumph of the auto over man and common sense, and the decay of neighborhood institutions have cast a pall over the American city. Writers have already drawn the shroud over urban civilization and buried it with varying degrees of lamentation befitting a fallen giant.

Yet there are indications that reports on the demise of the city may be premature. Several cities across the country are struggling against the enveloping paralysis and are restoring some of the preeminence that the city enjoyed in the nineteenth century. The key to this nascent resurrection is a conscious attempt to recreate the positive features of urban life from that earlier era. Specifically, cities are attempting to:

1. Rehabilitate the downtown and restore its economic, cultural, and residential importance

---

David R. Goldfield, an AIP affiliate member, is assistant professor, Division of Environmental and Urban Systems, at the Virginia Polytechnic Institute and State University. He earned his doctorate in urban history from the University of Maryland in 1970.

2. Restore the city's economic base lost to the suburbs
3. Revitalize neighborhood structures and life

Minneapolis serves as an example of the possibilities and problems involved in applying the usable past to modern planning practices.

Recovery of Minneapolis

Like so many other cities across the country, Minneapolis owes its existence to its strategic location on a river. The city is at the head of Mississippi River navigation. Real estate developers, excited over the town's potential as a lumber center, laid out a traditional gridiron street pattern in 1857 to facilitate the sale of lots. By 1872, the city expanded to 12½ square miles. Flour milling was beginning to challenge lumber as the city's prime industry. In 1881, the mills of John and Charles Pillsbury were producing over 15 million barrels of flour annually. Soon, the Great Northern Railroad complemented the fine river access of the city by erecting a depot along the riverfront.

Hardworking Scandinavian and Eastern European immigrants joined a growing populace to provide the sinews for progress. Their ethnic neighborhoods added a cosmopolitan atmosphere to the old frontier settlement. With an economic base firmly established by 1900 and with effective transportation links, the growth and prosperity of the "Mill City" seemed assured.

By the 1950s, however, the same malaise that was striking other American cities began to affect Minneapolis. The waterfront area had become a refuge for rats; rust was the only presence on the railroad tracks. Auto traffic clogged and polluted downtown. The recently opened Southdale Mall in suburban Edina challenged downtown business prosperity. The old ethnic neighborhoods were in decay and depopulation; industrial flight threatened the city's economic base. It was a sad but familiar urban story. The city, however, still possessed some valuable resources, and these elements attacked the problems besetting their urban environment.

Rehabilitation of downtown—Nicollet Mall

In the tradition of the nineteenth-century city, local entrepreneurs organized to attack the nemeses of the metropolis. Their attention focused on downtown, the historic center of urban life. Businessmen, responding specifically to the exodus of General Mills to the suburbs, formed the Downtown Council in 1955. The following year, the council and city planners formulated a strategy to revive downtown and restore it to its historic function as the economic and cultural nexus of the region (Downtown Council 1974; MPDD 1973). The council hired Barton-Aschman Associates to develop a plan to encompass those objectives. The consulting firm presented the council with five alternative proposals; the business leaders chose the mall and transitway solution in 1960 (Aschman 1971).

The transportation feature of the mall and transitway alternative was the major consideration in the council's choice. Just as turn-of-the-century trolley tracks converged on downtown, so the plan called for bus routes from every Minneapolis neighborhood to culminate at the retail district. The plan proposed the creation of a mall along an eight-block stretch of the city's major commercial thoroughfare, Nicollet Avenue. The mall would be closed to all vehicles except for buses and taxicabs. The proposal relegated the auto—the major downtown polluter and congestor—to the periphery of the mall. Multilevel parking ramps on the mall's fringes would conserve land and provide shelter during inclement weather (Aschman 1971, p. 4).

In order to transport shoppers, visitors, and theatergoers from the mall's outskirts to the various downtown attractions, Barton-Aschman suggested a unique solution that returned downtown to its nineteenth-century pedestrian character. A system of skyways connecting the second level of buildings would extend from the parking ramps to establishments throughout the mall area. The glass-enclosed skyways would keep the pedestrian cool during the summer and warm during the city's long winter months. They also separate pedestrians from the vehicle level. Further, the skyway plan added to the downtown show by providing for art displays and fashion shows along the bridges. The "walking city" with its variety was returning (MPDD 1973) (see Figure 1).

With the problem of pedestrian and vehicular access solved to some degree, the restoration of the diversity and visual excitement of the nineteenth-century downtown presented greater planning difficulties. The gridiron street pattern was a major contributor to sensory underload with its monotonous vistas. The Downtown Council retained landscape architect Lawrence Halprin to transform Nicollet Avenue into a street for people. Halprin took his inspiration from the medieval city with its irregular street system offering the perambulator sharply contrasting vistas and surprises at every wind in the roadway. Its four traffic lanes were cut to two in order to maximize the pedestrian aspect of the mall (Aschman 1971, p. 5).

The success of the plan elements depended, of course, on adequate funding. The creation of the mall, excluding the skyway system, ran close to $4 million—an investment that transcended the financial capabilities of the Downtown Council. Financing the project indicated not only the resourcefulness of the council, but also the efficacy of close public-private interaction—a relationship that has characterized most recovery programs in Minne-

.apolis. The construction cost of $3.8 million was financed as follows:

Urban mass transportation grant (federal): $512,000
Urban beautification grant (federal): $483,000
City bond issue: $2,751,785
Total: $3,746,785

The line score, though, revealed only a portion of the financial story. First, only $1.3 million of the cost was visible above ground. Utilities occupied the entire space under Nicollet Avenue's eighty-foot right-of-way. The private companies, in a display of civic consciousness that is characteristic of the business community in Minneapolis, agreed to inspect their systems and to rework them to conform to the above-ground construction. The city undertook extensive replacement of the water system to accommodate fountains and plants that would adorn the new mall. Fire hydrants were relocated as the sidewalk expanded; this required further adjustments underground. Finally, the city installed a new system of traffic signalization. Electrical circuitry was expanded to service the infrared radiation system that heated the sixteen bus shelters along the eight blocks of the

Figure 1

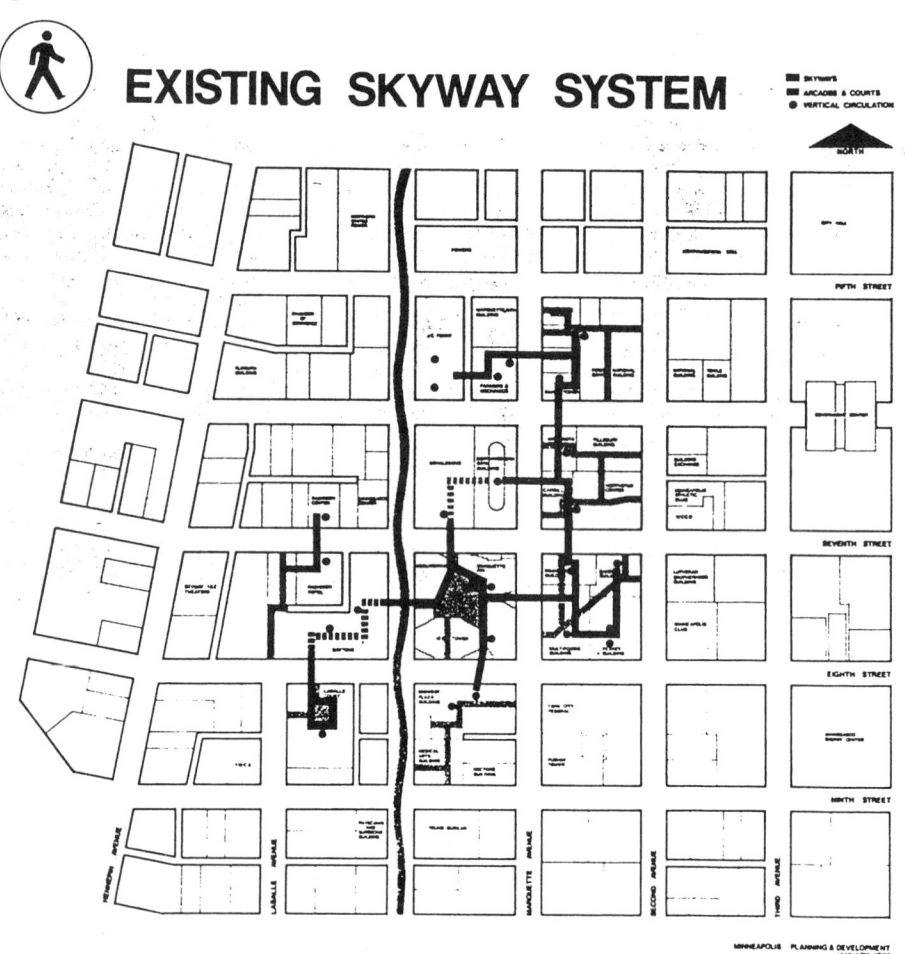

mall. Separate controls for snow-melting grids were embedded in the sidewalks to provide secure footing for the pedestrians (MPDD 1973).

Perhaps the most interesting aspect of the utilities reconstruction was the method the city employed to finance the alterations. Issuing city bonds was not, of course, a unique remedy. The manner of amortizing the bonds, however, was. The city employed a benefit assessment tax to ensure that the burden of paying for the mall would not fall on all of the citizens. Under the plan, the city created two benefit zones—on the mall and off the mall—covering an eighteen-block area. Each zone included sectors providing for 100 percent, 100–75 percent, 75–50 percent, and 50 percent allocations of cost so that properties in the heart of the mall would bear the greatest construction and maintenance expenses. The benefit assessment, in keeping with the restoration theme of the mall, was a common funding method in nineteenth-century cities when local government lacked sufficient resources to undertake massive street-paving and repairing programs (Aschman 1971, p. 5).[1]

Since Nicollet Mall opened in November 1967, the benefit assessment has proved a worthwhile investment for the mall-area entrepreneurs. Businesses reported a 14 percent increase in volume through 1973. The source of the mall's clientele is further cause for optimism about the future vigor of downtown Minneapolis. Over 56 percent of the mall's sales are to families residing more than five miles from downtown. This figure not only signifies that downtown has become, once again, an attraction to people outside the immediate area, but that Nicollet Mall is rivaling the suburban shopping center. Indeed, in a recent assessment of the mall's drawing power, the Downtown Council claimed that the proliferation of suburban malls has impacted those malls more than downtown which offers shoppers a unique experience in addition to a wider variety of merchandise (Downtown Council 1974, pp. 68–72).

The business renaissance in the mall area has helped a struggling mass transit system. The refined routing system and the exclusive busway helped to increase ridership by 8 percent in the downtown area during the past year. In addition, the city added a fleet of minibuses to the mall transportation system. The QT system, as it is called, runs on six-minute schedules and offers rides throughout downtown for ten cents. Last year the minibuses transported over one million passengers. This, in addition to the 8 percent increase in conventional mass transit, indicates the resurgence of public transportation in downtown (Downtown Council 1974, p. 52).

The skyway system remains the backbone of the mall's unique transit system and has played a significant role in enhancing the distinctiveness of downtown. Seventy-six skyways connecting sixty-four city blocks are planned for 1985. At present, there are eleven skyways, all built with private capital. If the system is to be completed, a source of public funding must be tapped. The bridge portion of the skyway costs $100,000 to $300,000, while renovation of building interiors to accommodate the structure runs upwards from $150,000.

The city, in conjunction with the council, is exploring the possibility of levying a benefit assessment tax to finance the completion of the skyway system. The best argument in favor of funding the network is use. On an average winter day, 20,000 people travel the skyway routes. When multilevel parking facilities on the periphery of the mall are completed to connect with the skyways, there will be twice that number using the system. Already, second-floor rents have risen to first-floor levels with no diminution in first-floor business. The system, even though it is incomplete, has proven comfortable for pedestrians and profitable for businessmen (MPDD 1973).

When Nicollet Mall opened in 1967, the Downtown Council was rightfully proud of its accomplishment. The mall, however, could only be a beginning in the long process of restoring downtown and in rejuvenating the entire city. Two major problems remained. First, the desertion of local industry for the suburbs was steadily eroding the city's economic base. Second, the city's most important resource—its people—were finding the suburbs equally attractive, especially in view of the physical decline of the city's residential neighborhoods.

Restoring the industrial base

The erosion of the city's industrial base became chronic during the 1960s. Between 1962 and 1970, 176 industries left Minneapolis with as many as 33 firms leaving during 1967, the year Nicollet Mall opened. The industries moved to the suburbs, especially Bloomington, Golden Valley, and Edina. The companies left behind 180 acres of land, 11,000 jobs, or 4 percent of the city's work force and $1,666,000 in annual property taxes (MIDC 1973, pp. 1–10). It was evident that the era when industry and city were synonymous had passed rudely by (see Figure 2).

The reasons that company spokesmen offered for leaving Minneapolis revealed a number of deficiencies in the urban environment. The Minneapolis Industrial Development Commission (MIDC), a creation of the city council, conducted a survey of firms that had left the city between 1962 and 1970. The study indicated that the lack of space for expansion was the most common complaint of migrating companies.

The absence of local government cooperation was a second major problem encountered by migrating firms. One executive cited the "apparent disinterest of city government in its small industries, with the

Figure 2. Industrial migration

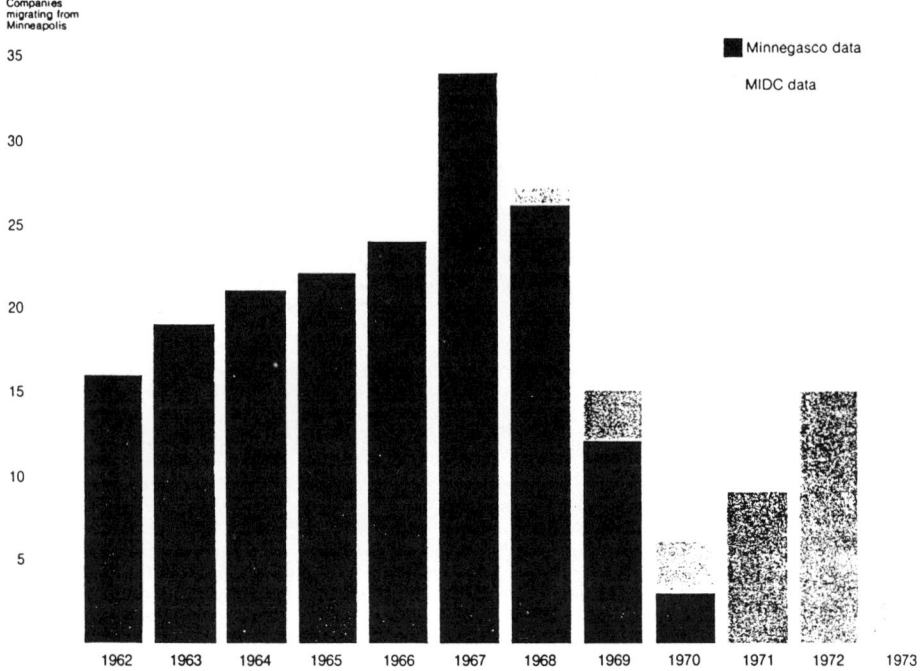

exception of the city assessor, fire inspector, and ticket sellers for the police/firemen's ball" (MIDC 1973, pp. 5–10). Several industrialists maintained that except for an occasional alderman the response at city hall was limited and generally ineffective.

When the MIDC began operations in 1968 it announced two interrelated goals: to halt the migration of industry from the city and to develop long-range policies to maintain and to increase the city's industrial base. To date, the commission's objectives have been only partially fulfilled. Between 1967 and 1970, the number of firms leaving Minneapolis declined, with only six migrating to the suburbs in the latter year. Between 1971 and 1973, the number increased; 1974 showed a decrease.

Apparently, MIDC policies have had only a slight impact, the key variable being the condition of the economy. In short, it is not that fewer expanding firms have decided to leave the city during the past year, but rather that fewer companies have desired to expand. Surveys conducted after 1970 demonstrate that the availability and low cost of land are still the major factors influencing migration. A positive note was that the complaints about uncooperative city officials dropped significantly as a reason for moving. On the other hand, the congested traffic situation around industrial sites caused increasing disruptions to deliveries and to employee access (MIDC 1973, pp. 12–24).

Since 1972, the MIDC has concentrated on securing land for expansion and subsidizing industrialization through various financial devices. The commission received a local appropriation of $400,000 to institute a land reserve program. Land purchased from this fund generated immediate dividends to the city. The Gresen Manufacturing Company constructed a research facility on one of the MIDC sites. Over the next few years, the company expects to hire more than 1,200 employees. The second major development in 1972 was the issuance, for the first time, of municipal industrial development bonds to finance the expansion of a plastics firm specializing in erosion control (MIDC 1972, pp. 9–14).

Industrial development bonds are probably the most effective financial weapon cities can marshal in defending their industrial base. A city may issue up to $5 million worth of the taxfree bonds—more if the particular industry is engaged in air and/or water pollution control. The development bonds differ from general obligation bonds in that the city does not pledge its credit. This means that local government cannot assess property owners to pay the principal and interest. The bonds finance land acquisitions, an expanding or relocating company's construction and equipment costs, and legal and consulting fees. The company occupies its new location as a lessee. The rents received by the city amortize the bond issue. After a stated period of time (usually twenty years), the firm may exercise its option to buy the property from the city at a nominal fee.

Since the interest on the bonds is anywhere from ½ to 2 percent lower than the commercial lending rate, the financial advantages to the company are obvious. If the land is leased, the business may depreciate the building as if it owned it. In event of default, which has never occurred, the city may take possession of the plant or re-lease it. The city, through the development bonds, is able to compete on a more equal footing with suburban communities that are able to offer cheaper land (Minnesota DED 1974).

The MIDC has supported another financial mechanism—the tax increment—to assemble large parcels of land for the purposes of creating industrial parks. Suburbs have long recognized the aesthetics and convenience of such land use. The city, which eagerly adopted the suburban mall concept for its downtown, is developing six industrial parks. The features of contemporary suburban life have proved effective tools for recreating the historic city. The tax increment enables the city to issue general obligation bonds to purchase land and sell it to a private developer at a "written down" price. The "subsidy" allows the city to compete with the suburbs for industrial sites. The differences between the city's purchase and selling prices, plus public improvements like roads and utilities are paid off through the increased taxes (tax increment) on the redeveloped property (MIDC 1973, p. 6).

Besides assembling land, the MIDC is working to broaden the city's economic base. One of the major attractions of the nineteenth-century metropolis was the existence of a large and diverse labor pool. The MIDC supports a vocational training program to meet demands created by new technologies or expanding industries. The Mississippi River, the source of the city's early economic base, is assuming greater importance in MIDC plans in response to rising energy costs. Since barge transportation uses much less energy than any other transportation means, the commission is directing the development of the Municipal Harbor Terminal. It has already installed a granular handling device to facilitate the efficient transfer of bulky commodities from a revived rail freight system to a barge. As truck and auto transportation costs increase, companies located in low-density suburbs might have greater difficulty attracting labor and keeping up with increased costs of moving supplies and manufactured goods. The city hopes to turn the energy problem into an energy advantage (MIDC 1973, pp. 8–12).

Revitalizing the neighborhood

In the attempt to restore the attributes of the historic city, there is no greater challenge for planners than the task of creating a neighborhood. The major difficulty with planning neighborhoods is that historic neighborhoods were not planned, they just happened. Minneapolis' major attempt at neighborhood reconstruction—Cedar-Riverside—demonstrates both the possibilities and the difficulties involved in the recreation process. A century ago, Cedar-Riverside was a growing Scandinavian and Eastern European neighborhood. Its community institutions bore the stamp of its neighborhoods across a thriving urban America.

By 1910, Cedar-Riverside, bordering on the river and a half-mile from downtown, included 20,000 inhabitants. The history of the community thereafter was a recapitulation of the decay of similar neighborhoods elsewhere. The area's economic base—the lumber industry—declined, sons and daughters of immigrants left, and the elderly remained interspersed with lumberjacks, prostitutes, and winos. Cedar Avenue, once the heart of the ethnic community, became derisively known as Snoose Boulevard after the Swedish word for tobacco juice that splattered its sidewalks. By 1960, the population had declined to 4,000 (Fischer 1973).

In what has become a characteristic theme in the recovery of Minneapolis, private initiative began to transform a deteriorating neighborhood into what hopefully would become a model community. Gloria Segal sought a small real estate investment in the city in 1962. Land in Cedar-Riverside was relatively inexpensive, and her immigrant uncle once operated a store there. Sentiment, and financial advice from Keith Heller, a tax expert and professor at the University of Minnesota, convinced Ms. Segal that here was a sound investment. She held some hope for at least the partial redemption of the neighborhood since the University of Minnesota began locating its West Bank campus in the community in 1959. The Segal-Heller investment team looked forward to erecting a small apartment building 'for students, university employees, and staff members of nearby St. Mary's Hospital.

Ralph Rapson, an architect and a friend of both Segal and Heller, was the catalyst who transformed a routine real estate operation into a major recovery project. In 1963 he suggested that, since land was cheap and available, why not plan a larger development. Accordingly, Segal and Heller continued to purchase property in the southwest sector of the neighborhood. In 1965 they formed the Cedar Village Associates and decided to begin planning operations. Imitating the success of the Downtown Council in forming a unique multidisciplinary planning team, the associates hired Barton-Aschman and Lawrence Halprin, the two major figures in the Nicollet Mall project. In 1968, the city designated the entire area for urban renewal and developed a renewal plan in conjunction with the private consortium. From a small apartment building, the project had grown to include the entire community (Cedar-Riverside Associates 1973, pp. 5-8).

Cedar-Riverside is a significant departure from traditional urban renewal projects from two standpoints. First, the private input is overwhelming. Second, the planning team proposed a unique plan that incorporated many aspects of the historic neighborhood. The plan called for high density—a major characteristic of the discrete turn-of-the-century neighborhoods. High-density residential development seemed the optimal land use plan for a number of reasons. The institutions in the neighborhood, including the university, Augsburg College, and St. Mary's Hospital, required numerous housing units. A major objective of the planning team was to combine the working and living experience within the neighborhood as historic communities had functioned.

High density was also necessary because of existing land use. Two freeways had circumscribed the original neighborhood—a typical, though unfortunate, occurrence in the modern city—and nearly 250 acres were given over to institutions, commercial sites, and Mississippi riverfront parkland. This left barely 100 acres for residential development. The projected population of 30,000 by 1990 surpasses the density per acre of the more congested sections of Manhattan. Finally, the developers believed that high density would facilitate social interaction and conserve land for recreational and cultural activities (Cedar-Riverside Associates 1972, introduction) (see Figure 3).

Figure 3

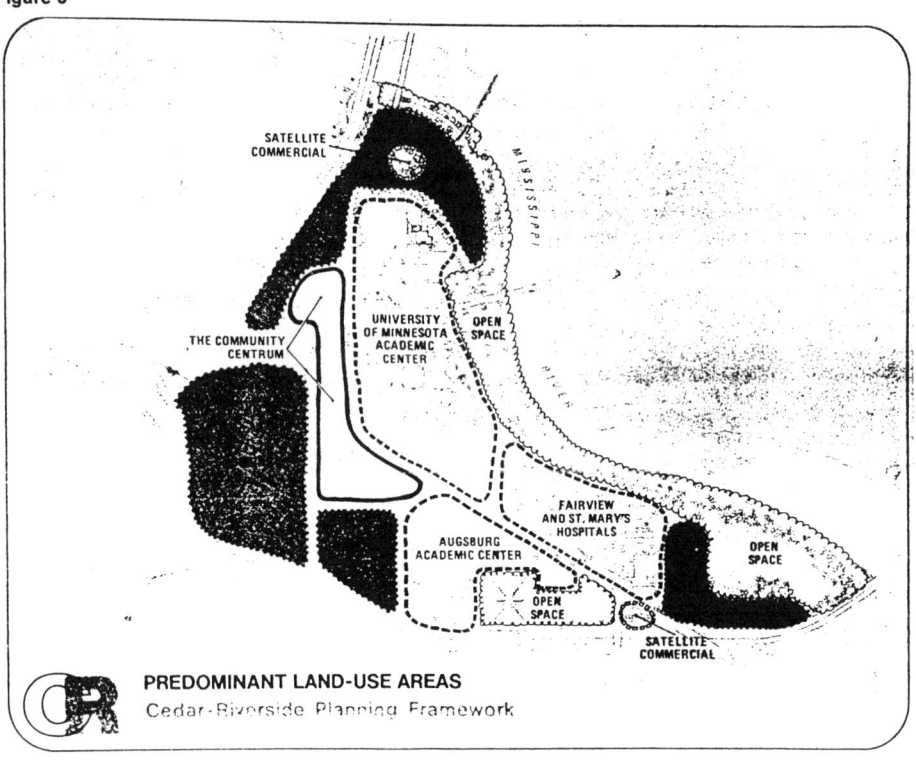

PREDOMINANT LAND-USE AREAS
Cedar-Riverside Planning Framework

High density facilitated the recreation of another aspect of the historic neighborhood: diversity. The plan ensured population diversity by mixing residents of widely varying incomes in their apartment dwellings. Nothing distinguished which unit is subsidized and which unit is renting at the private market value. The Minneapolis Housing and Redevelopment Authority would choose which units to subsidize. There would be no segregation as to building or floor. The plan encouraged cultural diversity by proposing sculpture blocks for local talent, open spaces for art shows and displays, and the erection of artists' lofts and studios to facilitate the creative process (Fischer 1973, p. 14).

The associates did not sacrifice the old neighborhood for the sake of diversity in the new. Dania Hall, the focus of social activities for the late nineteenth-century Scandinavian community, remained the center of attention in the new version of Cedar-Riverside as part of a multipurpose facility called the Centrum. The hall includes a theater and a ballroom. Nearby, a nineteenth-century firehouse is serving as the neighborhood's new social center. Since its rehabilitation in 1973, four weddings have taken place there. The Centrum itself incorporates the major shopping facilities of the neighborhood, though there will be convenience stores throughout the community to avoid segregated functions that destroyed the continuity of historic neighborhoods (Cedar-Riverside Associates 1974; MPDD 1973).

The plan also incorporates principles that have worked in other Minneapolis recovery projects. The automobile, whose accoutrements helped to emasculate the neighborhood, has been relegated to subterranean parking areas in what it is hoped will be a permanent exile. Grade-separated walkways over existing roadways, the closing off of numerous streets (both courtesy of the city), and the partial or complete covering of arterial walkways signal the rebirth of pedestrian travel and the walking neighborhood.

Cedar-Riverside had benefited from several funding sources in the process of implementing its projects. The associates have sunk $25 million of private capital into the project. The scale which the project assumed after 1968, though, obviously outran the financial capabilities of Ms. Segal and her team. Since 1968, the city has worked closely with the associates in funding the project. The city is upgrading Cedar Avenue by adding plantings, furnishings, and ornamental sidewalks. Owners of business property along the avenue, encouraged by city activity and the future of the community, are renovating their own structures. The city Housing and Redevelopment Authority has overseen the public utilities and street improvement work, as well as landscaping plazas and pedestrian bridges that traverse major arteries. Finally, the federal open space program will help to finance a recreational facility on the portion of Cedar-Riverside fronting the river (Cedar-Riverside Associates 1972, pp. 3, 15, 20).

The role of the federal government as a financial partner has increased dramatically since 1968, though there is some uncertainty at present as to the future of federal funding on the project. Under the various sections of urban renewal there are 117 units of low-income housing, 552 federally-subsidized moderate-income housing (FHA 236 program), 408 market rent units (FHA 236b program), and 222 semi-luxury units (FHA 220 deluxe program). The funds are channeled through the city's Housing Authority. The project received a significant financial boost in late 1971 when the federal government designated Cedar-Riverside as its first new-town-in-town project under the New Communities Program. This allowed the associates to issue $24 million in federally guaranteed bonds to implement their plans. In addition, the city became eligible for supplementary loans and grants up to 20 percent of facility costs. In all, about one-half of the housing units for Cedar-Riverside will receive some form of federal financial support (Cedar-Riverside Associates 1973, pp. 3, 14).

The funding and the intergovernmental cooperation have been instrumental in allowing the associates to transform their plans from the drawing board to reality. The first stage of development (there are five altogether)—Cedar Square West—is finished. The "neighborhood" includes more than twenty styles and sizes of apartment dwellings, from four to forty stories, in keeping with the planners' emphasis on design diversity. The rents vary from $41 to $550 a month in the same building. The rents for the non-subsidized units are slightly higher than the metropolitan average—$240 for a two-bedroom compared with $210 for the rest of the area. There is an 850-car garage underneath the Cedar Square West plaza. Federal funds are supplying trees, grass, furniture, and banners. The associates contributed $135,000 to help finance the plaza (MPDD 1973; *Minneapolis Tribune* 1973, pp. 2–26).

Cedar-Riverside Associates have been handling the delicate task of relocation during stage 1. Early urban renewal projects generally minimized the social costs of relocation. The federal Uniform Relocation and Real Property Acquisition Act of 1970, however, required the funded agency to offer financial aid and standard housing facilities to relocatees. Relocation in Cedar-Riverside has been, in contrast to earlier renewal efforts, a private affair. Demolition has been kept at a minimum in keeping with the project's policies of preserving old structures and maintaining the historic character of the neighborhood.

Further, although the associates acquired the right to condemn property in 1968, they have preferred to work according to the willing-buyer/willing-seller principle. When difficulty arises, the associates attempt a compromise. The relatively slow timetable of the project (twenty years) ensures that acceptable dwellings will be available to those who must relocate. Almost all affected residents have been relocated within the neighborhood at no increase in rent. The creation of a new community no longer signifies the destruction of the old. There was a precious social fabric in the historic neighborhood; although frayed, it should be allowed to enrich the recovery process.

Despite the associates' admirable record in the relocation process, some established residents and institutions in the community have voiced strong opposition to what they perceived to be an invasion rather than a resurrection. Part of the difficulty arose from the associates' imposition of a middle-class morality that was incongruous to some of the features of the old community. Associates' spokesmen point proudly to the number of bars that have closed since the project began. Older residents, however, reminisce about the comraderie that pervaded these establishments. While some of this is nostalgia, the loss of community contact points should not be an occasion for rejoice. The associates have moved swiftly and strongly against tenants whom they consider undesirable. The Electric Fetus, for example, was a record shop that displayed nude (simulated) posters of then-President and Mrs. Nixon in 1969. In another publicity stunt, the Fetus promised a free record to anyone who disrobed in the store. The Fetus gave away forty records under the offer before the associates canceled their lease and paid for their moving expenses out of the neighborhood (*Minneapolis Tribune* 1973).

If a community is to be truly diverse and provide residents with choice—the major attraction of urban living—such activities should be allowed to continue. If community residents decide, however, that such activities are, in fact, inimical to community life as they perceive it, then sheer economics will force these enterprises from the neighborhood. In short, such decisions should be reserved for the residents, not for the planners. Planning represents an imposition of sorts in any case. That imposition or control should be maintained in a low profile. As English geographer Peter Hall asserted: "The planner cannot and should not prescribe any ideal pattern of social life; he should merely see that the opportunity for maximum choice is given" (Hall 1975, p. 171). Otherwise, planners court certain opposition.

The certain opposition to Cedar-Riverside originated among older residents and young counter culturists headquartered in the New Riverside Café. The café and the associates have clashed repeatedly during the past few years over community objectives. Early last year, the opposition coalesced into the Environmental Defense Fund, which filed a suit against the associates, the city Housing and Redevelopment Authority, and HUD. The brief contended that the environmental impact statement filed with HUD was incomplete and inaccurate. Specifically, the plaintiffs were concerned about the impact of high-density development on their property and lifestyle (Jacobson 1975).

Whatever the outcome of the suit there will be several changes in the project. First, and most immediate, the financial viability of the project has been threatened. There has been no work on the plans for more than a year. In the meantime the associates have been encumbered by holding costs of several million dollars which are unrecoverable.

Accordingly, the associates have asked the city to assume a greater role in development. The city will exercise a greater input in future planning decisions as an investor and a manager. Lower densities and even greater emphasis on rehabilitation rather than renewal will result from the city's participation (Anderson 1975, Jacobson 1975).

The loss of the high-density component will be a severe setback to a major objective of neighborhood restoration. There could be a compromise, though, that would actually improve upon the original plan. High-rise structures were the major environmental threats cited in the legal action. High rise and high density, however, are not necessarily synonymous. High density in the historic neighborhood community was not achieved through vertical imperialism. Structures rarely went beyond five or six stories. Lower structures, of course, mean less open space, but this is not so much an unfavorable trade-off as it might seem.

Historic neighborhoods created their own open spaces and this in fact might be preferable to pre-planned open spaces which sometimes do not become places for social interaction. Further, decreasing building size would not necessarily result in a density loss. In New York City, for example, public high-rise housing averages 250 people per acre; remodeled brownstone areas run from 180 to 350 people per acre (Whyte 1972).

In short, while Cedar-Riverside must change, it could seize the opportunity to turn what must be a disappointment to the associates into a positive contribution to neighborhood recovery. In any case, it is important that neither the associates, the city, nor HUD abandon the project. It has been a unique endeavor in public-private cooperation that could, in future years, serve as an important inspiration to recovery projects (Whyte 1968).

Model for recreating the historic city

Minneapolis is a case study but by no means the only example of the recovery of the American city. Programs to increase the tax base, restore diversity, and attract people exist in most moderate and large-size cities today. Although the Minneapolis projects—the recovery of downtown, the restoration of an industrial base, and the regeneration of neighborhood life—are not unique, the success of most of these efforts at recovering the city result from a set of factors that might prove beneficial if incorporated in similar efforts elsewhere.

Role of the private sector

The initiative of the private sector has been the most obvious asset of the Minneapolis recovery. Nicollet Mall, the project which began the renaissance, was a conception of downtown businessmen. Local entrepreneurs not only contributed ideas and organization to the mall effort, but money as well in the form of benefit assessments and the skyway system. Although the industrial development program is primarily a city operation, it was local business leaders who sounded the alarm over the city's declining industrial base. For six years, as Cedar-Riverside evolved, it was primarily a private enterprise. In retrospect it was a larger task than the private sector could accomplish—land acquisition, comprehensive planning, and relocation. Nevertheless, whatever Cedar-Riverside becomes, its debt to private enterprise is considerable.

For the city's private entrepreneurs, Minneapolis redevelopment represented a coordination of social and historic priorities with economic motives. The resurgence of downtown, the growing industrial tax base, and the repopulation of a historic residential neighborhood have proved beneficial for local businessmen. The difficulties involved in the Cedar-Riverside project did not result from the primacy of economic considerations, but rather from the particular social and historical visions of the associates and their consultants.

Finally, while urban redevelopment is good business, it would be inaccurate to assume that economic motives solely are the guiding forces behind the private input into recovery efforts. The time and talent volunteered by such groups as the Downtown Council and the utilities companies indicate a civic pride that is reminiscent of the nineteenth-century metropolis. While private enterprise, has over the years, contributed to the present pessimistic urban condition, their value as catalysts for urban redevelopment should not be overlooked.

Public-private cooperation

Minneapolis leaders, especially in the past decade, have nurtured the civic consciousness of local businessmen. Redevelopment strategies in other cities should include programs to enroll, solicit, and consult with the local business community. The Minneapolis study has demonstrated that urban recovery is profitable. Where such organizations as the Downtown Council do not exist, local officials can encourage similar groups by forming a businessmen's committee to channel the views of the entrepreneurs into the redevelopment process on a regular basis.

Minneapolis officials have not only followed the lead of the organized business community but have been innovative in their own right. Financial mechanisms such as the benefit assessment and the tax increment have increased capital flow without placing greater burdens on taxpayers. The state has also proved to be a cooperative partner in the endeavor. From financing industrial redevelopment to landmark preservation, state enabling legislation has blended well with the designs of city business and political leaders. The legislature also created the Metropolitan Council which has lent regional sanction to Minneapolis recovery efforts. Finally, federal programs have aided recovery programs of both private and public sectors at crucial moments.

Quality of planning

In the early stages of Nicollet Mall planning, the Downtown Council expressed the desire that the project be a first-class operation or not happen at all. The mall and transitway plan presented by Barton-Aschman was, by no means, the least expensive or the easiest alternative to implement. It would have been cheaper in terms of money and time to apply some cosmetic changes to the area and leave it at that.

Fortunately, the council and the city chose a broader approach, and the mall project has served as an admirable precedent for future recovery projects. The Downtown Council also established the efficacy of the multidisciplinary approach to planning. The planning team has been effective in getting input from different perspectives. The era when the planner merely concerned himself or herself with the physical dimensions of the project is gone. Minneapolis has been fortunate in the selection of its planning teams as well. Ms. Segal even borrowed Heikki von Hertzen from Tapiola in Finland. Quality, in short, has traditionally outweighed penny-pinching, and the results have proven the worth of this philosophy.

The proclivity of public and private participants to focus on relatively small projects has ensured the greater probability of quality planning. Creating Nicollet Mall and establishing industrial parks indicate the benefits of spot developments that focus all the intensity and expertise of comprehensive planning into a small area with only one or two objectives in mind.[2]

The troubles of Cedar-Riverside stemmed, in part, from its comprehensiveness. Unless all parts of a comprehensive plan are developed simultaneously, which is clearly impossible, the development of one part of the plan often changes the nature of other portions to a degree different from the original plan. The city has a comprehensive plan—Metro Center '85—which revised the 1958–60 plan. The latter plan, although it anticipated redevelopment projects like the mall and river improvements, was formulated prior to the completion of the piecemeal projects (Altshuler 1965).

Historical perspective

The recovery of the city involves the restoration of the attributes of the historic metropolis. No one is suggesting the exact replication of the nineteenth-century city. In terms of air and water pollution, cities are striving to make their natural environment considerably cleaner than the besooted cities of yesteryear. Poverty was more abject, disease was a constant companion, industry crowded open spaces, and plumbing was invariably outdoors in the city of a century ago.

The historic metropolis, however, possessed certain positive aspects that were worthy of recreation. The planning process should proceed with these factors uppermost in mind because they helped to transform the city into an exciting and prosperous environment. Mass transit, pedestrian travel, industry, neighborhood cohesion, high density, an enterprising commercial elite, culture, education, security, a sense of place and, above all, choice, flourished in the historic city. The Minneapolis recovery projects aim at the restoration of these historic attributes.

Historical methodology should enter the planning process in a more specific manner, as the Minneapolis neighborhood recovery projects demonstrate. Cedar-Riverside represented a fine example of the necessity of learning the historic roots of a community. The associates took care to preserve the Scandinavian flavor of the neighborhood, restoring such old structures as Dania Hall and the firehouse and making them part of the new plan.

Careful research into land use patterns, socio-economic status, age composition, and social institutions of the historic immigrant neighborhood would have provided the associates with an even better understanding of the mechanisms of neighborhood life. They might have discovered, for example, that taverns were not a community blight but important contact points for the neighborhood residents. They also might have found a high mixture of functions and the absence of physical barriers that would question the advisability of creating distinctive subneighborhoods.

Finally, the associates could have discerned a relatively large young, single, and transient population—characteristic of immigrant communities. This would have reinforced the associates' emphasis on providing services for the same demographic base that the planners hope to attract to Cedar-Riverside today. While no historic analysis should bind present planning, a restructuring of some of the major patterns of historic neighborhoods will facilitate a recreation of the social interaction and excitement of community life.

The city should be an educational experience in the broadest sense. Diversity is its most effective teaching tool. If the planner's task is to offer the public something "above and beyond what is commonplace and accepted," the historic city affords the planner a model of variety and excitement. The application of the usable past to the planning process will provide a fitting beginning for the next 200 years of American urban life (Hall 1975).

Notes

1. Benefit assessment, in this context, refers to levies for specific improvement projects that benefit only a small portion of the urban population.
2. In this context, comprehensive planning refers to planning a large area with multiple design and planning components and objectives over a period of more than five years.

References

Altshuler, Alan A. 1965. *The city planning process*. Ithaca: Cornell University Press.
Anderson, Larry, supervisor of project development, Cedar-Riverside Associates. Interview, March 10, 1975.
Aschman, Frederick T. 1971. Nicollet Mall: civic cooperation to preserve downtown's vitality. *Planner's Notebook* 1: 1–8.
Cedar-Riverside Associates. 1972. *Proposed development programs, 1972–1975*. Minneapolis.
———. 1973. *Cedar-Riverside new community; narrative description*. Minneapolis.
———. 1974. *Cedar-Riverside planning framework*, Minneapolis.
Downtown Council of Minneapolis. 1974. *Nicollet Mall*. Minneapolis.
Fischer, John. 1973. The possibly glorious dream of Mrs. Gloria M. Segal. *Harper's Magazine* 247: 14–19.
Hall, Peter. 1975. The urban culture and the suburban culture. In *I came to the city*, edited by Michael E. Eliot Hurst. Boston: Houghton Mifflin.
Jacobson, Donald A. vice-president of planning and development, Cedar-Riverside Associates. Letters to the author, February 28, March 18, October 7, 1975.
Minneapolis Industrial Development Commission. 1972. *Annual report*. Minneapolis.
———. May 1, 1972. Guidelines for rating municipal bond issues.
———. 1973. *Annual report*. Minneapolis.
———. 1973. *Industrial migration study, 1962–1973*. Minneapolis.
Minneapolis Planning and Development Department. 1973. Nicollet Mall. *Minneapolis Today* spring.
———. 1973. Skyway system. *Minneapolis Today*, spring.
———. 1973. Cedar-Riverside. *Minneapolis Today*, spring.
Minneapolis Tribune. The old west bank—and the new. *Picture Magazine* 9 December 1973: 2–26.
Minnesota Department of Economic Development. 1974. *Municipal industrial development bonds*. Minneapolis: State of Minnesota.
Whyte, William H. 1968. *The last landscape*, New York: Garden City.
———. 1972. The case for crowding. In *North American suburbs*, edited by John Kramer. Berkeley: Glendessary Press.

Urban Planning As Policy Analysis: Management of Urban Change

Dennis A. Rondinelli

Current approaches to and methods of urban planning are inadequate for effective urban policy analysis. Planners emerging from existing planning education programs have not been provided with the skills, knowledge, and experience required to plan for and guide urban change. Policy planning is a complex process of analyzing, intervening in, and managing the political conflict that is inextricably related to urban change. Research is needed into the structure of public policymaking, characteristics of urban policy formulation and implementation, strategies of intervention, processes of policymaking interaction, and techniques of change-program management. New methods, techniques, and concepts of planning must be developed. If planners are to be effective policy analysts and change managers, they must receive cognitive inputs and skills for dealing with a complex policymaking system that are not now incorporated in urban and regional planning education curricula.

The American planning profession is undergoing a traumatic transformation. Despite the expenditure of millions of dollars over the past fifty years to produce a myriad of master plans for urban development, few cities in the United States have been developed or substantially redeveloped in accordance with a comprehensive plan. Large-scale policies designed to ameliorate major urban social and economic problems have been either ineffective or perverse (Banfield, 1970). Attempts to require comprehensive planning in federal housing, transportation, regional economic development, antipoverty, and community development programs have not succeeded. Academic curricula dedicated to teaching plan-making are questioned and repudiated by a sizable element of the profession and its critics. The "noiseless secession from the comprehensive plan" (Perin, 1967) is forcing planners to redefine their goals and objectives and to search for new roles and functions. Alternatives range from national environmental and physical planning, through a wide variety of social, economic, and technical planning specialities, to neighborhood and minority group advocacy. Concepts, styles, and methodologies run an equally broad gamut (Bolan, 1967).

A consensus is developing within one wing of the profession that planners can perform an important role as urban policy analysts. With the increasing complexity of urban decisionmaking, political leaders and urban administrators are demanding from planners pragmatic assistance with policy formulation and implementation. The cities "want advice on how to choose the right goals and the most effective policies for every function of government," claims Gans (1970:224), "and similar advice is being sought by all institutions and groups who seek to frame their goals and policies in a deliberate manner from federal agencies, civic groups and protest organizations to corporations and semipublic institutions."

Underlying the pressures to transform planning into

Dennis A. Rondinelli is a member of the faculty of the Graduate School of Management, Vanderbilt University. He received his Ph.D. in City and Regional Planning at Cornell University and taught policy analysis, urban planning, and administration at the University of Wisconsin—Milwaukee. During 1970–1971, he was Deputy Chief of the Village Self-Development program, CORDS, USMAC, in Vietnam.

a policy science is a widely held assumption that planners can bring order and rationality to urban policymaking. Friedmann (1969:316) challenges the profession "to undertake the courageous and systematic evaluation of societal performance and to identify the strategic points for massive innovation in the guidance of the system." Bolan (1969) argues that planners, operating within the behavioral parameters of the community decisionmaking process, must adapt their functions to the procedural steps of urban policymaking: structuring and defining proposals, identifying the properties of alternatives, structuring the decision field, and engaging in and implementing decisions. New demands are made on the form and content of planning education. New missions will be required, predicts Altshuler (1970:186), "the purpose of which will be to provide men who have emerged as potentially important decisionmakers with some broad planning perspectives and a capacity for systematic analysis of policy options."

Unlike traditional comprehensive planning that sought to devise a long-range ideal end state for urban development in the framework of a synoptic master plan, policy planning seeks to deal with pressing problems of urban life by influencing the substance and direction of on-going public decisionmaking. Policy planning is action-oriented. It attempts intervention rather than mere prescription. Policy planning is concerned with making an incremental impact on national as well as local policies affecting the quality of urban services and the rate and distribution of urban growth. It involves the organization and evaluation of the programs as well as policy design. Urban policy planning is the management of urban change.

While much has been written about the need for innovation and experimentation to overcome critical urban problems, neither planners nor public administrators have, as Hyman (1971:365) notes, answered the question of who "is competent to plan and direct the revisions necessitated. . . . There appears to be little understanding that a nation in flux requires administrators trained to deal with change." Little evidence exists that planning curricula impart the skills and knowledge needed to analyze policy alternatives, provide training and experience in techniques of intervention in the policymaking process, or generate relevant research into mechanisms of policy formulation and implementation. Few planning education programs focus on the nature of policy innovation, mobilization and utilization of policy-influencing resources, or the management of political conflict necessary to achieve social change in urban areas.

Recent evaluations of the past decade's experience with federal urban and regional development policy not only add empirical evidence to theoretical criticisms of traditional comprehensive planning but may also assist planners to avoid the pitfalls of venturing into the uncharted field of policy planning. The New Frontier—Great Society decade produced the largest quantity of policies designed to ameliorate urban and regional development problems since the New Deal. But careful evaluations of the processes by which these policies emerged reveals the complex interrelationships and narrow parameters within which policy planners must work. This paper aims to characterize, through a series of empirically supported propositions, the nature of urban policymaking and to outline implications for educating planners in analyzing, intervening, and managing policy for urban change.

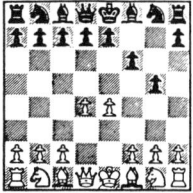

CHARACTERISTICS OF URBAN POLICYMAKING

♟ *Proposition I*

Policymaking is an inherently political rather than a deliberative process. Policy is made through sociopolitical processes—resolution of conflict among groups with divergent interests—rather than by intellectual and deliberative choice (Banfield, 1961; Bauer, Pool and Dexter, 1963; Bauer and Gergen, 1968; Braybrooke and Lindblom, 1963). As a process of political interaction, policy evolves from a process of interorganizational conflict over a wide variety of values, criteria, ends, means, and interpretations of rationality. It is a generator as well as a product of conflict, evolving through a process of "social weighting" that rarely can be comprehensively planned or centrally guided. Groups seeking particular goals or allocations of resources induce response from other groups that stand to gain or lose from enactment of the policy proposals. Through political interaction and social adjustment, the decisions and priorities of the participants in policymaking are ratified, altered, compromised, or rejected (Lindblom,

1959). In some cases, as Bachrach and Baratz (1970) note in their study of antipoverty programs in Baltimore, policies evolve from a history of actions that restrict the choice of alternatives and the margin of acceptable change. Policy can be made through "nondecisions" by the unchallenged drift of events or by deliberate attempts to repress conflict. It may evolve indirectly, generated by unanticipated results of previous decisions. Indeed, policymaking often transcends deliberative problem solving; as a process of political interaction, it is more complex and distinctly different from individual decisionmaking.

☒ *Proposition 2*

Policy is formulated and implemented through highly fragmented and multinucleated structures of semi-independent groups and organizations in both the publice and private sectors, and through a complex system of formal and informal delegation of responsibility and control. If Great Society policymaking taught one lesson, it is the difficulty of controlling either the evolution of policy proposals through legislative enactment or the implementation of policy through administrative management. Power resources are fragmented and widely dispersed. Points of leverage are multiple and decentralized. Policy is formulated and implemented by a multitude of organizations with highly specialized personnel, information, technical expertise, analytical skills, and influence resources. Each group pursues its own perceptions of its interests and its own conception of the public interest. A potentially large number of them gain veto or delaying power over enactment of urban policy proposals and carve out domains or spheres of influence over program implementation. The history of the Model Cities program, antipoverty legislation (Donovan, 1967), the Area Redevelopment Act (Levitan, 1964), the Public Works and Economic Development Act (Rondinelli, 1969), the Appalachian Regional Development program, and Federal Highway assistance (Morehouse, 1969; Levin and Abend, 1971) document the complex interaction of groups at all stages of policy formulation.

Once enacted, policies must be implemented through a highly decentralized governmental structure (Grodzins, 1966). Discretionary authority, regulatory control, allocational responsibility, and approval powers are fragmented through systems of interagency, intergovernmental, and intersectoral delegation. At the federal level, for example, when the Economic Development Administration provides business loans to private firms in economically depressed areas, it must submit the applications to the Small Business Administration for clearance. SBA reviews the proposals and performs credit investigations and market feasibility studies. EDA has little control over the time SBA takes to review the applications, the criteria it uses in the review process, or the people making decisions. EDA supplementary technical assistance programs, moreover, are related to programs administered by other federal agencies. Congress decreed in EDA's enabling legislation that grant proposals dealing with specialized aspects of area development must be reviewed by the Department of Labor's Manpower Training Development Office, the Community Facilities Administration of the Department of Housing and Urban Development, the Farmer's Home Administration in the Department of Agriculture, health facilities program agencies within the Department of Health, Education and Welfare, and the Bureau of the Budget.

Regional development policy is implemented through a quagmire of intergovernmental hybrids. In the Appalachian Regional Commission, for instance, administrative power is shared among a federal co-chairman appointed by the President, the governors of twelve states, and an executive staff responsible to the commission as a corporate body. Substantial influence over decisions is delegated to state government agencies and semi-independent local development district corporations. In Pennsylvania, responsibility for implementation of Appalachian Regional Development policy is delegated by the Governor to the Commonwealth's Department of Commerce, which redelegates planning, clearance, allocation, and review powers to more than a dozen specialized agencies, departments, and commissions over which the Department of Commerce exercises little direct control (Commonwealth of Pennsylvania, 1967).

The reticulated pattern of delegation and fragmentation of power extends beyond government into the private sector. The policy boards of the Model Cities, antipoverty, and Economic Development District agencies are composed of local special interest groups, neighborhood target groups, business and labor representatives, civic and service organizations, as well as local, state, and other government officials. In the traditional sense of administrative responsibility, federal departments providing urban development assistance cannot be held accountable for the outcomes of policies they are assigned to implement. They must rely increasingly on state and local government officials to define local problems, formulate appropriate policy responses, and interpret and implement federal guidelines. Administrative accountability in the Model Cities program, for instance, is shifted almost entirely by formal contracts from HUD to local government agencies. "We are spelling out in clear terms," notes Secertary Romney, "that local government officials must exercise final control and responsibility for the content and administration of a local Model Cities program" (U.S. Congress, 1969). Lines of power and responsibility are intertwined by interdepartmental agreements, delegate agency mandates, and intergovernmental contracts, most of which are nearly impossible to enforce formally and have little legal standing. Enforcement comes through informal pressure and manipulation. The ability to guide, let alone comprehensively plan, national development policies, is highly complicated and narrowly constrained by delegation.

Proposition 3

Policy problems are complex, amorphous, and difficult to define concisely. Urban policy planning is limited, moreover, by political parameters on defining the problem. Problems become the focus of policymaking to the extent that specialized groups and coalitions can bring public attention to them. Few issues are defined in the same way by all who participate in the policymaking process. Each interested organization places a different emphasis on a different component of the problem or defines the whole problem in terms of a part. Interest groups proposing legislation to assist urban depressed areas in the 1960s, for example, saw the problem as one of high unemployment, declining physical plant, changing technological and economic advantages, and obsolete infrastructure in industrial communities. A strong coalition of southern congressmen, who significantly amended the original policy proposals, viewed the problem as underemployment, inability of rural areas to mobilize resources, outmigration of unskilled labor from rural areas to urban centers, and failure to exploit natural resources in agricultural areas. The Appalachian governors saw it as multistate competitive disadvantage. The Department of Labor defined it in terms of the need for massive manpower retraining. Social welfare groups were sure that the crux of the problem was racial injustice, discrimination, lack of educational opportunities, and the need for both "black capitalism" and economic development of center city ghettos. Each group mobilized support for its own definition of the problem. (Rondinelli, 1969).

Proposition 4

Problem perception, policy response and program implementation are characterized by long lead and lag times. Comprehensive analysis and coordinated control of policy implementation are constrained, further, by the long lag and lead times inherent in political interaction. Lags develop between emergence of a problem and public recognition. Acknowledgment of a problem's existence does not assure allocations of public resources for its solution. A lag exists until proponents can mobilize a coalition of support, resolve conflicts with opponents, and gain consensus on appropriate policy responses. The ARA, Public Works and Economic Development, and Appalachian Regional Development acts of the 1960s were policies designed to ameliorate problems of urban and regional economic decline that first arose prior to the 1930s depression. Lags exist, moreover, between the proposal of policies and their legislative enactment. The initial proposal for creation of ARA was made in late 1954; the bill creating the agency was not signed into law until 1961. Although proposals for an Appalachian Regional assistance program first appeared in the mid-1950s, the Appalachian Regional Commission was not created until a decade later. Many components of the Economic Opportunity Act of 1964 were initially introduced during the New Deal. Furthermore, long leads occur between organization of the programs and identification and evaluation of their effects. Thirty years were required to recognize publicly the failure of New Deal social welfare policies. Conditions under which programs were formulated change during both lag and lead times. Perceptions and definitions of the problem, personalities, and motivations of participants change; the strength of demands and support of sponsoring and opposing interest groups shift. The problem itself may be partially or totally displaced from public attention.

Proposition 5

Systematic analysis and evaluation are complicated by the difficulty of determining real policy output. Dror's (1968) distinction between the nominal output of a program (reports, projects, rules, trained manpower, and so forth) and the real output (substantive effects of policies on conditions they were designed to correct) has significance for policy planning. The experience of ARA, EDA, OEO, and Model Cities is one of extreme difficulty in identifying and measuring real policy outputs. By the end of its first year in operation, EDA found it had no way of proving that its activities were responsible for bettering conditions in areas where unemployment rates fell below 6 percent, the termination level for EDA assistance (Rauner, 1967). In order to justify its program to Congress and the Bureau of the Budget, EDA was forced to adopt a "worst first" strategy. Investments were concentrated in areas with the highest rates of unemployment and lowest family incomes—those least likely to be affected by national economic growth. Only in this way could EDA isolate the influence of its program on regional recovery. But the "worst first" strategy raised claims by other federal agencies that EDA's policies obstructed their own plans. The co-chairman of the Appalachian Regional Commission testified to Congress of the difficulties encountered by EDA's plans for development of the most hopeless regions, while the Appalachian Commission was attempting to concentrate resources in the areas of highest growth potential (U.S. Congress, 1967b). Systematic analysis and quantitative evaluation yielded to political and social subjectivity: "Ultimately a value judgment is required to decide whether one unemployed person in Lowville, New York, is equivalent to one low-income family in Wolf, Kentucky," argues a former EDA assistant administrator. "In the same view determining how much of EDA's program appropriation should be assigned to each of its seven program sets is properly a matter of administrative judgment. No mathematical computations or maximizing formula can solve this problem (Rauner, 1967).

Proposition 6

Facts, information, and statistics used to analyze policy alternatives are subjectively interpreted through preconceived specialized interests. Even if "objective" indicators of "optimal" courses of action could be determined, the data would not be treated objectively. Not only the substance of policy but facts and statistics also become the subject of debate and conflict. Quantitative data are rarely interpreted by participants independently of their role perceptions, subjective expectations, preconceived interests, and ideological predispositions. Congressional hearings on regional economic development legislation reveal that neither supporting nor opposing policy analysts allowed facts to complicate the preconceived logic of their arguments. Experts provided congressional committees with analysis yielding diametrically opposed conclusions. Some used the same set of data to support different arguments before different committees. Provisions to prohibit industrial piracy—subsidies that would induce industries to move from one urban area to another—were written into ARA, EDA, and Appalachian bills largely because of the "evidence" presented by national business lobbies that opposed passage of the legislation. "Is it not ironic that the same witnesses who tell us that this legislation is bad because it will be so effective that it will lead to pirating are invariably the same witnesses who tell us that this legislation is bad because it will not help the depressed areas at all?" asked Pennsylvania Representative William W. Scranton at a Congressional hearing on the EDA bill. "These arguments, frequently offered by the same witnesses, are not even consistent" (*Congressional Record*, 1961). A favorite tactic of congressional committee members themselves is to invite policy analysts and experts who will present evidence favorable to their own predisposition toward a policy proposal.

 Proposition 7

The number of possible alternatives for ameliorating policy problems is indeterminate. Alternatives evolve through processes of political interaction. Traditional planning theory requires systematic evaluation of alternatives in order to make optimal choices. Gans (1970:223) defines planning as a "method and process of decisionmaking that proposes or identifies goals (or ends) and determines effective policies (or means)—those which can be shown analytically to achieve the goals while minimizing undesirable financial, social, and other consequences." Yet, in reality, the choice of alternative means is dictated by the possibilities evolving from political interaction rather than from deliberative, a priori, design and analysis. Alternatives are gradually invented out of compromises among participants with different perceptions of the problem, interests, and criteria. Acceptance of one alternative—optimal to one set of interests—need not result in the rejection of others. Mutual adjustments result in creation of new courses of action from combinations of existing alternatives (Diesing, 1955). A priori delineation and evaluation of alternatives is complicated, moreover, by the fact that groups participating in policymaking rarely perceive their goals clearly or define their objectives explicitly. Goal formation is often situational, that is, dependent on expectations of what can actually be achieved under given political conditions at a particular point in time. As expectations change, goals are altered. In most cases, the end-means chain of which Gans and others speak is not a chain at all. Goals may be instrumental rather than terminal. Ends become means: Attainment of one set of goals may merely pave the way to pursue another set. Thus, the number of possible permutations and combinations of feasible or potentially feasible alternatives can be enormous. The alternatives given priority depend in part on the groups drawn into policymaking conflicts and on the strength of their influence.

Evaluation and choice are twice confounded by substantive and political spillovers. Initial policy conflicts often expand into intricate extended networks of secondary conflicts over values, ideology, and socioeconomic and political costs and benefits. Spillovers occur from and to related policy problems. Participants in policymaking often come into conflict over questions that have little to do with the substantive content of the problem. They become enmeshed in arguments involving personal political ambitions, personal and organizational prestige, control over funds and other resources, and philosophical doctrine.

Finally, political parameters may make consideration of a wide range of alternatives impossible, limiting evaluation to a restricted set or to only one. The running conflict over delegation of functions and authority in the ARA, EDA, and OEO programs strongly reflected the power of the Budget Bureau to restrict consideration of other forms of organization. Senator Paul Douglas and his associates on the Banking and Currency Committee, for instance, favored creation of independent regional development assistance agencies capable of performing their own planning and operational functions. But the Budget Bureau and some specialized federal departments insisted on delegation of ARA and EDA powers. The intensity with which the Bureau of the Budget fought for delegation foreclosed the possibility of dispassionate, objective analysis and choice of the optimal alternative. "I originally favored a single agency operation," Douglas recalls, "but I was overruled by the bureaucracy downtown in the Budget Bureau, and my head was so bloody after that encounter that I gave up" (U.S. Congress, 1965:107).

Proposition 8

Each participant in policy formulation and implementation has limited evaluation capacity. Even when the number of alternatives is large, the ability of any participant in policymaking to evaluate them comprehensively is limited. In reality, as Simon (1958) notes, decisionmaking often reduces to a choice between two alternatives: "doing X" or "not doing X." "Not doing X" may represent the whole set of possible alternatives that decisionmakers lack the resources, interest, information, or power to evaluate. These courses of action may be considered vaguely in terms of the opportunity costs of rejecting "doing X," or considered serially and incrementally only if alternative "doing X" is rejected, or if it is accepted and later proves to be ineffective (Braybrooke and Lindblom, 1963). But if "doing X" is considered satisfactory to the participating interest groups, alternatives may never be explicated.

The limited evaluation capacity of one congressional committee working on economic development legislation is not untypical. When a bill to amend the Appalachian Regional Development Act and Title V of EDA legislation was introduced in 1967, minority party members of the House Public Works Committee strongly opposed further expansion of these programs. They were at a loss, however, to offer positive alternatives to the amendments. They noted:

> When faced with the monumental task of searching and collecting information and data, visiting representative areas of the country to determine their problems and needs, conferring with state and local officials and business leaders in an effort to develop a really workable and effective program, we soon came to the conclusion that our limited, though capable, staff could not even make a dent in this workload in the time available to us. Reluctantly, we were forced to abandon, at this time, the development of a constructive alternative. (U.S. Congress, 1967a:90).

Proposition 9

Policy planning is done under conditions of uncertainty, risk, incomplete information, and partial ignorance of the situation in which problems evolve, the resources of interested groups, and the effectiveness of proposed solutions. Professional planners and public administrators have done little better than legislators in comprehensive policy analysis. Studies of the Federal Aid Highway Act of 1962—a law requiring that assisted highway projects be the result of a "cooperative, comprehensive and continuing planning process"—indicate that the Bureau of Public Roads lacks the political power to impose comprehensive analysis requirements (Morehouse, 1969). State, local, and metropolitan planning agencies lack the information, political resources, and analytical ability to comply with areawide planning provisions of later transportation programs (Levin and Abend, 1971). Greer (1965) suggests that local planners often found themselves in the same situation with the Federal Workable Program for 701 Assistance.

The Area Redevelopment Administration's attempts to implement congressional requirements for submission of overall economic development programs (OEDP's) by depressed areas as a condition for financial support were obstructed by uncertainty over congressional standards, lack of competent analysts at the local level, and by political pressures from congressmen themselves to speed up the process of aid distribution. ARA was not able to specify the requirements for comprehensive planning or even to evaluate the OEDP's that were submitted. Most local planning groups, therefore, simply filed superficial reports filled with masses of badly analyzed data to satisfy minimum standards. ARA could not disqualify localities for not performing a task that it could neither define nor evaluate. "The agency resolved this dilemma," reports Levitan (1964:200), "by accepting each OEDP submitted by communities as a token of good faith and an indication that the community desired to plan its economic future on a sound basis." Attempts to formulate Model Cities guidelines to allow maximum freedom for analysis and planning by localities failed miserably. "They did no good," one former Model Cities Administration deputy director complained. "Most of the cities didn't understand the process but were willing to play our silly little game for money. What was meant as a challenge, a prod, was interpreted as a regulation, a cage. Regulations you can relate to; freedom is something else" (Jorden, 1971: 46).

IMPLICATIONS FOR PLANNING

Policy analysis requires drastic modifications in the concept of and approaches to planning, and fundamental changes in planning education. Research, analytical techniques, and skills required for traditional plan-making are not adequate for policy planning. Planners trained as policy analysts must develop a view of the planning process that is substantially different from that of comprehensive planning. While existing planning curricula focus heavily on substantive urban problems, few provide the knowledge and skills required for effective intervention in the policymaking process. Conflict resolution and the management of social change are intrinsic to policy planning.

A Political Interaction View of Policy Planning

Comprehensive planning was prescriptive—seeking to design an ideal end-state for urban development—rather than interventional. The plan-making approach to education stressed objective, synoptic analysis, the search for endless numbers of alternatives and a combination of best choices into a long-range master plan for urban growth. Details of "routine" decisions were relegated to politicians and administrators. But grand schemes, long-range comprehensive plans, and systematic policy scenarios were ignored conveniently in a political system that renders rational, comprehensive evaluation of urban policies highly improbable and synoptic policy changes nearly impossible.

Analysis, to be of value to policymakers must isolate components of urban problems and reduce them to calculable proportions. Policy planners must indicate how resources can be mobilized and focused on remediable aspects of problems in such a way that urban areas can be moved marginally, through successive approximation, away from unsatisfactory social and economic conditions. Policy planners must delineate those alternatives upon which a variety of interest can act jointly and seek ways of binding together some of the disparate participants in policymaking to promote mutual cooperation along lines of specialization and common interest. An integral part of policy analysis is the search for ways of reconciling differences among specialized interests, where possible, and evaluating compromise positions, bases for mutual exchange, incentives, and instruments of manipulation and persuasion.

A political interaction view of policy planning defines one of the planner's roles as that of identifying "strategic factors." Strategic factors, Barnard (1938:203) notes, are those "whose control, in the right form, at the right place and time, will establish a new system or set of conditions which meets the purpose." Policy planning must search out limiting factors inhibiting desired social change and delineate the types of complementary factors needed to enact and implement appropriate programs or controls. Given the complexity of the pluralistic political system in which he must operate, the policy planner may focus on calculating the opportunity costs of pursuing alternative courses of action or of taking no deliberate action. By explicating the losses incurred by urban interests from the lag between socio-economic change and the public response to that change, strong incentives might be provided for the formation of effective coalitions to reduce their losses from inaction, delayed action, or inappropriate action. Policy planning is adjunctive—a process of facilitating adjustment among competing interests within a multi-nucleated governmental structure, to encourage policy outputs of marginally better quality measured against the status quo. (Rondinelli, 1971).

Research Needs and Planning Skills

The characteristics of public policymaking have been explored by the social sciences in recent years, but little thought has been given to manipulating processes of political interaction in order to plan urban policy more effectively. Nor have the skills and knowledge needed by policy planners been identified. Research is scarce on the relationships among the policymaking structures, the characteristics of the policymaking process, and techniques of interaction and knowledge needed to manage urban change and to design strategies of intervention. The attempt here is to raise research questions and to suggest some categories of skills and knowledge needed by policy planners to intervene effectively in urban policymaking (See Table 1).

Adaptive adjustments among groups seeking to influence policy through tacit interaction (Schelling, 1960; Lindblom, 1965) strongly characterized the evolution of urban development legislation during the 1960s (Rondinelli, 1969; Cleaveland, 1969). Indirect adjustments often take place without direct communication among policymaking participants, either because they cannot or do not want to communicate with each other. Each participant, instead, takes an action that he believes will avoid or resolve conflict based on expectations of what other participants will do or what they have done in the past. To some degree, it is based on intuitive rapport, "second guessing," or mutual recognition of a desirable goal. In other cases, it arises from uncoordinated reactions to the same basic conditions or perceptions of the same problem.

How do these techniques influence the content of policy proposals? How do they affect the structure and dynamics of conflict resolution? Are adaptive, noncentrally coordinated processes of interaction more successful in implementing policy proposals than techniques of direct coordination? In what types of issues are they least effective? Can groups be induced to tacit agreement by third parties? A planner attempting to use adaptive adjustment techniques to guide urban policies through formulation and implementation must understand processes of small group decisionmaking, organizational behavior, intragroup dynamics, and interorganizational interaction.

The pluralistic, multinucleated structure of policymaking involves vast networks of specialized groups linked together in intertwining "decision chains" (Wheaton, 1964). Through decision chains, coalitions create and participate in spheres of influence over specific types of issues and programs. To enact a policy or reform a program often requires that multiple consent

TABLE 1. Skills and Knowledge Needed in Urban Policymaking

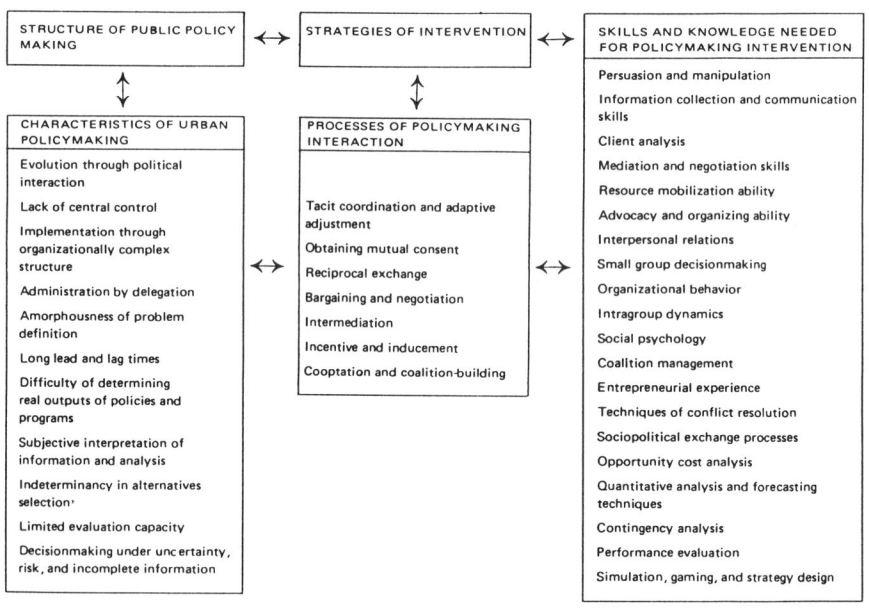

be obtained from the myriad of interests composing an organized sphere of influence. Indeed, failure to seek approval from the clientele of an established program, as proponents of a Federal Department of Urban Affairs discovered in the early 1960s (Parris, 1969), may activate a coalition of opposition to plans for policy change. What are the techniques of obtaining mutual consent? How do the techniques of obtaining formal, legal consent ("review and approval," "sign-off consent") differ from those of obtaining informal, political consent (logrolling, reciprocity, vote-swapping). What tradeoffs, exchanges, and spillovers arise in the act of obtaining mutual consent? Can some links in the decision chain be avoided or neglected in certain types of urban issues without jeopardizing the policy outcome? Can the process be standardized for particular issues to reduce lag and lead times in policy ratification and implementation? To deal effectively with decision chains in urban policymaking, planners must possess persuasion and manipulation skills, experience with client analysis, and information and communication skills. Knowledge of general principles of social psychology can assist in designing tactics of influence and manipulation (Mehrabian, 1970).

Policy conflicts are settled through processes of reciprocal exchange, negotiation, intermediation, and bargaining. The complex delegate agency arrangements characterizing urban policy implementation mandate the use of exchange-bargaining techniques among proponents and opponents of urban assistance policies. Failure to negotiate settlements among disparate groups—federal departments, state and local government agencies, clientele and target groups, and political factions—has led to serious complications in implementing Model Cities programs. What are the channels of exchange and bargaining among participants in urban policymaking? What groups and organizations serve as intermediaries in urban policy conflicts? What functions can the planning agency play in facilitating processes of exchange and negotiation? Which inputs into the bargaining processes influence policy decisions? Do quantitative analysis, evaluation of data, and trend projection play an important role in influencing the environment for negotiation and bargaining? What are the terms of and parameters on bargaining and exchange among opposing groups in urban policy formulation? Mediation and negotiation skills become important for planners involved in bargaining-exchange relationships in urban policymaking. Knowledge of organizational behavior, processes of conflict resolution, sociopolitical exchange processes, and strategy design are imperative. The ability to simulate and design games of strategy involving urban issues could provide a means of assisting political and administrative decisionmakers to test alternative proposals and political tactics.

Coalition-building is the essence of conflict management. Ultimately, urban policies evolve from compromises among groups with sufficient power and resources to persuade other participants of the desirability of a particular course of action. Incentives and inducements change both the parameters of decisionmaking and the costs and benefits of policy alternatives to interested groups. What are the techniques of coalition-building? How are interested groups brought together? How can initial policy proposals be designed so as to control the scope of conflict and attract allies into a coalition strong enough to insure enactment and effective implementation? How can conflict that is being repressed by groups attempting to prevent an issue from being discussed be socialized to ensure that the issues become the focus of public attention? Alternatively, how can issues that are being socialized to the point that effective coalition formation becomes impossible, be repressed? What are the costs of building urban policy coalitions? What are the dynamics of interaction among coalition participants? Which techniques are necessary to maintain a coalition of support for urban policies? The use of incentives requires entrepreneurial experience. Skills in organizational leadership, advocacy, resource mobilization, and coalition management are essential to this aspect of policy planning.

Intervention in policymaking is a continuous process of strategic analysis. Forecasting, quantitative measurement, contingency planning, and identification of opportunity costs are integral parts of strategy design. Monitoring and performance evaluation skills are as necessary for effective policy planning as substantive expertise in the urban problem issues. If planners are serious about redirecting the profession's energies toward policy planning, curricula must be redesigned to provide the skills, knowledge, and experience necessary for effective management of urban change.

REFERENCES

Altshuler, A. (1970) "Decision-making and the Trend Toward Pluralistic Planning" in E. Erber, ed., *Urban Planning in Transition*. New York: Grossman, pp. 183–186.

Bachrach, P., and M. S. Baratz (1970) *Power and Poverty*. New York: Oxford University Press.

Banfield, E. C. (1961) *Political Influence*. New York: The Free Press.

—— (1970) *The Unheavenly City*. Boston: Little, Brown.

Barnard, C. I. (1938) *The Functions of the Executive.* Cambridge, Mass.: Harvard University Press.

Bauer, R. I., de Sola Pool, and L. Dexter (1963) *American Business and Public Policy.* New York: Atherton.

Bauer, R. and K. Gergen (1968) *The Study of Policy Formation.* New York: The Free Press.

Bolan, R. S. (1967) "Emerging Views of Planning," *Journal of the American Institute of Planners* 33 (July): 233-245.

—— (1969) "Community Decision Behavior: The Culture of Planning," *Journal of the American Institute of Planners* 35 (Sept.): 301-310.

Braybrooke, D., and C. E. Lindblom (1963) *A Strategy of Decision: Policy Evaluation as a Social Process.* New York: The Free Press.

Cleaveland, F. (1969) *Congress and Urban Problems.* Washington, D.C.: The Brookings Institution.

Commonwealth of Pennsylvania, Governor's Office of Administration (1967) Executive Directive No. 18, "The Administration of the Appalachian Program in Pennsylvania," mimeographed, April 13.

Congressional Record (1961) 107, no. 4 (March 29): 521.

Diesing, P. (1955) "Noneconomic Decision-Making," *Ethics* 46 (Oct.): 18-35.

Donovan, J. C. (1967) *The Politics of Poverty.* New York: Western Publishing Company.

Dror, Y. (1968) *Public Policy Making Re-examined.* San Francisco: Chandler.

Friedmann, J. (1969) "Notes on Societal Action," *Journal of the American Institute of Planners* 35 (Sept.): 311-318.

Gans, H. J. (1970) "From Urbanism to Policy Planning," *Journal of the American Institute of Planners* 36 (July): 223-226.

Greer, S. (1965) *Urban Renewal and American Cities.* New York: Bobbs-Merrill.

Grodzins, M. (1966) *The American System.* Chicago: Rand McNally.

Hyman, A. A. (1971) "The Management of Planned Change," in S. E. Seashore and R. J. McNeill, eds., *Management of the Urban Crisis.* New York: The Free Press.

Jordan, Fred (1971) "The Confessions of a Former Grantsman," *City* (Summer): 45-47.

Lindblom, C. E. (1959) "The Handling of Policy Norms in Analysis," in M. Abromovitz et al., *Allocation of Economic Resources.* Stanford, Calif.: Stanford University Press.

—— (1965) *The Intelligence of Democracy.* New York: The Free Press.

Levin, M., and N. Abend (1971) *Bureaucrats in Collision: Case Studies in Area Transportation.* Cambridge, Mass.: The MIT Press.

Levitan, S. (1964) *Federal Aid to Depressed Areas.* Baltimore, Md.: Johns Hopkins Press.

Mehrabian, A. (1970) *Tactics of Social Influence.* Englewood Cliffs, N.J.: Prentice-Hall.

Morehouse, T. A. (1969) "The 1962 Highway Act: A Study in Artful Interpretation," *Journal of the American Institute of Planners* 35 (May): 160-168.

Parris, J. H. (1969) "Congress Rejects the President's Urban Department," in F. Cleaveland, ed., *Congress and Urban Problems.* Washington, D.C.: The Brookings Institution.

Perin, C. (1967) "The Noiseless Secession from the Comprehensive Plan," *Journal of the American Institute of Planners* 33 (Sept.): 336-346.

Rauner, R. M. (1967) "Regional and Area Planning: The EDA Experience." Washington, D.C.: U.S. Department of Commerce, Economic Development Administration, mimeographed.

Rondinelli, D. A. (1969) "Policy Analysis and Planning Administration: Toward Adjunctive Planning for Regional Development," unpublished PhD. dissertation, Cornell University.

—— (1971) "Adjunctive Planning and Urban Development Policy," *Urban Affairs Quarterly* 7 (Sept.): 13-39.

Schelling, T. C. (1960) *The Strategy of Conflict.* New York: Oxford University Press.

Simon, H. A. (1958) "The Role of Expectations in an Adaptive or Behavioristic Model," in M. J. Bowman, ed., *Expectations, Uncertainty and Business Behavior.* New York: Social Science Research Council.

U.S. Congress (1965) Senate Committee on Banking and Currency, "Public Works and Economic Development," Hearings on S. 1648, 89th Congress, 1st Session, (May).

U.S. Congress (1967a) House Committee on Public Works, "Appalachian Regional Development Act Amendments of 1967 and Amendments to the Public Works and Economic Development Act of 1965," Hearings, 90th Congress, 1st Session.

U.S. Congress (1967b) Senate Committee on Government Operations, "Creative Federalism," Hearings, 89th Congress, 2nd Session.

U.S. Congress (1969) Testimony of George Romney, Senate Committee on Banking and Currency, "Progress in the Model Cities Program," Hearings before the Subcommittee on Housing and Urban Affairs, 91st Congress, 1st Session.

Wheaton, W. L. C. (1964) "Public and Private Agents of Change in Urban Expansion," in M. Webber et al., *Explorations Into Urban Structure.* Philadelphia: University of Pennsylvania Press.

To Engineer the Metropolis: Sewers, Sanitation, and City Planning in Late-Nineteenth-Century America

STANLEY K. SCHULTZ
AND
CLAY MCSHANE

A Baltimore engineer who sought public construction and ownership of a city-wide sewer system drew a parallel in 1905 between the efficiency of sewers and the quality of a civilization. Referrring to Europe, he stated that "completely sewered, with a low death rate," Paris is "the center of all that is best in art, literature, science and architecture and is both clean and beautiful. In the evolution of this ideal attainment," he continued, "its sewers took at least a leading part, for we have only to look at conditions existing prior to their construction to see that such a realization would have been impossible before their existence." Although his sentiments were overblown, his statement conveyed some truth. A growing number of urbanites in early-twentieth-century America recognized an intimate relationship between technology and the social, economic, and governmental structure of cities. To harness new technologies to social needs was the aspiration of many so-called "progressives." As landscape architect John Nolen put it in 1909: "Intelligent city planning is one of the means toward a better utilization of our resources, toward an application of the methods of private business to public affairs, toward efficiency, toward a higher individual and higher collective life."[1]

The central watchwords of many political reformers during the late-nineteenth and early-twentieth centuries, as Nolen suggested, were conservation, corporate-like government, efficiency, and social engineering. Each goal required the application of technology to the solution of human problems. Each demanded innovative methods of

Stanley K. Schultz is associate professor of history in the University of Wisconsin. Clay McShane is assistant professor of history in Northeastern University.

[1] Baltimore *Sun*, April 24, 1905; John Nolen, "City Making," *The American City*, I (Sept. 1909), 19.

administration to serve best the public interest. The Baltimore engineer added his voice to a swelling chorus of city leaders and political pundits who urged stronger public control of such services as water and sewer systems, transportation facilities, electric lighting—indeed, all those services that improved the quality of the urban physical environment. To achieve these aims, numerous reformers called for municipal ownership of utilities and for new governmental institutions to administer the services.[2]

As the French philosopher Jacques Ellul observed, modern administrative organization in both the economic and political spheres matured with the application of formerly private techniques to questions of public concern. The moment that new techniques "proved themselves able to operate efficiently on the masses, they ceased to be purely private. The state could no longer remain disinterested." Twentieth-century economic and political administration emphasized several characteristics, including a centralized, permanent bureaucracy staffed by skilled experts, and a commitment to long-range, comprehensive planning. These served as goals for many political reformers during the late-nineteenth and early-twentieth centuries. Thus, if seeking the origins of modern municipal administration, especially if searching for the beginnings of so-called "comprehensive" city planning, scholars can do no better than to explore competing technological systems and ideas in cities over the last half of the nineteenth century. Sewers become important after all.[3]

Of the many crises confronting nineteenth-century urbanites, none loomed more obvious or important than environmental pollution. Unpaved or poorly paved streets, inefficient or non-existent collection of garbage, excrement from thousands of horses, the sooty dust from small manufacturing establishments—these and other problems threatened the physical comfort and safety of most urban Americans by mid-century. Successive cholera, typhoid, and diphtheria epidemics claimed the lives of thousands. With each epidemic city fathers established and then folded public boards of health, but made no permanent effort to enforce standards of hygiene until after 1866, when New York's newly-formed Metropolitan Board of Health served as a model. As late as 1850, only New York City, Boston, Chicago, and Philadelphia had even semi-

---

[2] The best summary of reformers' demands was by Frederic C. Howe, *The City The Hope of Democracy* (New York, 1906).

[3] Jacques Ellul, *The Technological Society* (New York, 1964), 234, 3–13, 171–83, 229–39. See also R. J. Forbes, *The Conquest of Nature: Technology and Its Consequences* (New York, 1968) and Herbert J. Muller, "The Social Environment: The City," *The Children of Frankenstein: A Primer on Modern Technology and Human Values* (Bloomington, Ind., 1970), 258–77.

adequate public water supplies. Integrated sewer systems were unknown; at best, cities depended upon a few private sewers or a few large storm sewers built only in part by tax monies. Add to those conditions the increasing density of urban populations and the pressures on the existent stock of housing, and who could have quibbled with the Massachusetts sanitary surveyors in 1850: "It has been ascertained that the inhabitants of densely populated places generally deteriorate in vitality.... This is a significant fact, which should be generally known. Cities are not necessarily unhealthy, but circumstances are permitted to exist, which make them so."[4]

To understand why citizens permitted such circumstances to exist, the structure of antebellum municipal government must be explored. During the late-eighteenth and early-nineteenth centuries the tasks of municipal administration began to shift from the exclusive promotion and regulation of trade to a more general concern for residents' well-being. By the eve of the Civil War, most city governments still more closely resembled their medieval predecessors than today's city administrations. State legislators saw cities principally as sources of patronage. Mayors were figureheads. Common councils exercised quasi-executive, quasi-judicial authority. Individual aldermen often retained control over most expenditures in their own wards. City employees such as policemen came into and left office in the revolving door of each election. Real estate speculators generally controlled land-use decisions and almost alone anticipated future growth; their major goal was to subdivide land to maximize short-run profits. Because of their traditional mistrust of centralized government, Americans usually turned to the local ward politicians or even to private groups or individuals for such vital urban services as water supply, street sanitation, and even fire protection. With the power to govern scattered in bits and pieces among

[4] *Report of a General Plan for the Promotion of Public and Personal Health, Devised, Prepared and Recommended by the Commissioners Appointed Under a Resolve of the Legislature of Massachusetts, Relating to a Sanitary Survey of the State* (Boston, 1850), 153–54. On pollution and attempts to deal with it, see Lawrence H. Larsen, "Nineteenth-Century Street Sanitation: A Study of Filth and Frustration," *Wisconsin Magazine of History*, 52 (Spring 1969), 239–47; Martin V. Melosi, " 'Out of Sight, Out of Mind': The Environment and Disposal of Municipal Refuse, 1860–1920," *The Historian*, XXXV (Aug. 1973), 621–40; Joel A. Tarr, "Urban Pollution—Many Long Years Ago," *American Heritage*, XXII (Oct. 1971), 65–69, 106; Nelson Manfred Blake, *Water for the Cities* (Syracuse, 1956). On public health boards see, among others, Barbara Gutman Rosenkrantz, *Public Health and the State: Changing Views in Massachusetts, 1842–1936* (Cambridge, 1972) and John Duffy, *A History of Public Health in New York City, 1625–1866* (New York, 1968).

a bewildering variety of offices, boards, and commissions, in effect no one governed.[5]

Changes in scientific knowledge and popular ideas about illness and death around the middle of the century fostered new perceptions of the urban environmental crisis. Many citizens, of course, still wanted to blame human frailty for the unhealthy conditions of the cities, and found convenient scapegoats in the growing numbers of native poor and foreign immigrants in their midst. But careful investigators of the cities' plight—such as physicians, sanitary surveyors, landscape architects, and civil engineers—began to identify other sources of urban ills. However much human attitudes and habits appeared at fault, the problems of environmental pollution were physical. Their solution would be physical and technological as well—or so an increasing number of urban Americans came to believe over the last half of the century.[6]

City officials had long appreciated the importance of adequate water supplies. Fear of epidemics and fires, coupled with the pollution of wells by seepage from graves and privies, forced city fathers to tap new sources and often to bring in water from outside municipal boundaries. Philadelphia built a public waterworks system in the 1790s. New York, Boston, and a few other large cities followed suit some forty years later. Various physicians and public health reformers advertised the sanitary reasons to provide not only water, but pure water. But who should construct and administer the new systems, the private sector or government? Until the 1850s most cities relied upon private firms, but in most cases the private efforts failed technically and economically, especially in the largest cities. Few private entrepreneurs or corporations had the capital, the condemnation power, the concern for public health, or the economic will to build and maintain water supply systems that would serve the entire public. Concerned about profits, few private companies proved to be willing to serve poorer people from whom they could expect meager revenues. Thus, municipal ownership and ad-

[5] Jon C. Teaford, *The Municipal Revolution in America: Origins of Modern Urban Government, 1650–1825* (Chicago, 1975), 47–110; Sam Bass Warner, Jr., *The Private City: Philadelphia in Three Periods of Its Growth* (Philadelphia, 1968), 49–157; Seymour J. Mandelbaum, *Boss Tweed's New York* (New York, 1965); Ernest S. Griffith, *A History of American City Government: The Conspicuous Failure, 1870–1900* (New York, 1974), 52–62.

[6] See, for example, Charles E. Rosenberg, *The Cholera Years: The United States in 1832, 1849 and 1866* (Chicago, 1962); George Rosen, *A History of Public Health* (New York, 1958), 237–46; Stanley K. Schultz, *The Culture Factory: Boston Public Schools, 1789–1860* (New York, 1973), 92–100, 209–51; and, for an apology about immigrants' part in fostering disease, absolving them and blaming instead the physical environment, see J. G. Pinkham, *The Sanitary Condition of Lynn, Including a Special Report on Diphtheria* (Boston, 1877), 58.

ministration gained slowly between the 1860s and the 1890s. By the turn of the century, however, only nine of the fifty largest cities still had privately owned water supplies. By 1910, more than 70 percent of cities over 30,000 population owned their waterworks. Over the last half of the century, city officials discerned sanitary, technological, and political reasons to provide this service at municipal expense and under municipal control.[7]

The addition of adequate water did not end environmental pollution. To some extent, it increased it, for now cities had to dispose of vast quantities of water brought in by the new aqueducts. Existent surface drainage was inadequate. The new water closets of the 1860s and 1870s overflowed the old privy waste disposal systems, soaked the urban water tables, and converted large portions of city land and streets into a stinking morass. Once again the solution was physical and technical. During the 1870s and 1880s, city leaders undertook expensive programs of sewer building. They also began massive paving programs to improve drainage and to cover the wastewater-saturated soil of urban streets. The engineers who shepherded these projects emphasized their sanitary functions nearly as much as their traffic-bearing functions.[8]

There was little doubt in the minds of many sanitarians, physicians, and engineers that a good sewer system meant investment in the present and future health of the citizenry. In Chicago during the mid-1850s, for example, Ellis S. Chesbrough, chief engineer of the first sewerage commission, was so persuasive that the city expended in excess of $10,000,000 to construct nearly fifty-four miles of sewers and to raise the grade of the street for drainage purposes by as much as twelve feet in

---

[7] Blake, *Water for the Cities*; M. N. Baker, ed., *The Manual of American Water Works* (New York, 1897); Samuel W. Abbott, *Past and Present Condition of Public Hygiene and State Medicine in the United States* (Boston, 1900); C.-E. A. Winslow, *The Evolution and Significance of the Modern Public Health Campaign* (New Haven, 1923), 38; J. J. Cosgrove, *History of Sanitation* (Pittsburgh, 1909), 87–88.

[8] Henry I. Bowditch, *Public Hygiene in America* (Boston, 1877), 103–04; "Early Sanitary History of Chicago, 1832–1874 and Sketch of the Early Drainage and Sewerage of Chicago 1847–1879," City of Chicago Municipal Reference Library, Frederick Rex, Librarian (n.p., n.d.); R. Isham Randolph, "A History of Sanitation in Chicago," *Journal of the Western Society of Engineers*, XLIV (Oct. 1939), 227–40; Samuel C. Busey, "History and Progress of Sanitation of the City of Washington and the Efforts of the Medical Profession in Relation Thereto," *The Sanitarian*, XLII (March, 1899), 205–16; Geo. W. Rafter and M. N. Baker, *Sewage Disposal in the United States* (New York, 1894), 169–86; Leonard Metcalf and Harrison P. Eddy, *American Sewerage Practice* (3 vols., New York, 1914), Vol. I: *Design of Sewers*; Richard Shelton Kirby and Philip Gustave Laurson, *The Early Years of Modern Civil Engineering* (New Haven, 1932), 185–239; Charles V. Chapin, *Municipal Sanitation in the United States* (Providence, 1901), 172–92; Henry B. Wood, "Street Work in Boston, As Applied to Brick Pavements, Filling Joints of Granite Pavements, Street Watering and Street Cleaning," *Association of Engineering Societies Journal*, XI (Aug. 1892), 427–38; and George W. Tillson, *Street Pavements and Paving Materials* (New York, 1901), 167. Joel Tarr and David Wojick of Carnegie-Mellon University made suggestions about the evolution and interdependence of water and wastewater systems.

the emerging central business district. John Bell, a Philadelphia physician reporting in 1859 for a committee on the internal hygiene of cities, argued that "paving ought to precede the erection of houses, and drainage follow habitation at a very early period. A neglect of these two preliminary conditions for public health has been productive, in all ages, of a fearful waste of life." By the late 1870s, George E. Waring, Jr., perhaps the most influential sanitary engineer of the late-nineteenth century, vividly stated the relationship between sewers and health. Speaking of the old sewers of New York and Boston, Waring charged that they were "highest at the lower end, lowest in the middle, biggest at the little end, receiving branch sewers from below, and discharging at their tops; elongated cesspools, half-filled with reeking filth, peopled [sic] with rats, and invaded by every tide...." He labeled such sewers "huge gasometers, manufacturing day and night a deadly aeriform poison, ever seeking to invade the houses along their course; reservoirs of liquid filth, ever oozing through the defective joints, and polluting the very earth upon which the city stands."[9]

Waring was a leading proponent of the sewer gas theory of disease, the notion that decaying organic matter, such as human and other animal wastes, exuded an odorless gas that caused innumerable infectious and non-infectious illnesses. Although widely debated, the idea was accepted by many involved in the public health movement. Engineering periodicals often supported the theory and offered technical schemes for preventing the escape of the gas. Not until the triumph of the germ theory of disease during the 1890s and early 1900s did the sewer gas theory completely evaporate.[10]

[9] E. S. Chesbrough, *Report and Plan of Sewerage for the City of Chicago, Illinois* (Chicago, 1855); "Up from the Mud: An Account of how Chicago's Streets and Buildings were Raised," Workers of the Writer's Program, WPA in Illinois for Board of Education (Chicago, 1941); Louis P. Cain, "Raising and Watering a City: Ellis Sylvester Chesbrough and Chicago's First Sanitation System," *Technology and Culture*, 13 (July 1972), 353–72; and James C. O'Connell, "Chicago's Quest for Pure Water" (Washington, 1976). John Bell, *Report on the Importance and Economy of Sanitary Measures to Cities* (New York, 1859), 35; and George E. Waring, Jr., *House-Drainage and Sewerage* (Philadelphia, 1878), 11.

[10] James H. Cassedy, "The Flamboyant Colonel Waring: An Anti-Contagionist Holds the American Stage in the Age of Pasteur and Koch," *Bulletin of the History of Medicine*, XXXVI (March-April 1962), 163–76. Among numerous contemporary comments about the sewer gas theory, see G. E. Waring, Jr., *Earth Closets and Earth Sewage* (New York, 1870); C. W. Chamberlain, "Erysipelas and Sewer Gas," *Public Health*, I (Aug. 9, 1879), 81–82; John Lambert, "Sanitary Reform and Preventive Medicine," *ibid.*, I (Aug. 16, 1879), 97–101; Victor C. Vaughan, "Healthy Homes and Foods for the Working Classes," *American Public Health Association* (Concord, N.H., 1886), 15–18; and the graphic depiction, "Sewer Gas Poisoning," *Scientific American*, LXIII (Nov. 29, 1890), 344. On the triumph of the germ theory see Charles V. Chapin, "The End of the Filth Theory of Disease," *Popular Science Monthly*, LX (Jan. 1902), 234–39; Rosen, *History of Public Health*, 285–335; and Richard Shryock, "The Medical History of the American People," Richard Shryock, *Medicine in America* (Baltimore, 1966), 22–30.

The discovery during the 1880s that many diseases, especially the killer typhoid, were waterborne accelerated campaigns for pure water, for sewer construction, and for the filtration of both water and sewage. In 1890 only twenty-six cities among those of 10,000 population or more had no sewers at all. By 1907, nearly every city in the nation had sewers. The filtration of water and sewage brought a dramatic drop in typhoid mortality rates, a drop that averaged sixty-five percent in selected major cities. The sewer gas theory, then, together with other theories and medical discoveries, lent weight to the arguments favoring technological solutions to public health problems.[11]

The lessons were clear. Water and sewer systems were a city's lifelines. As such, they were too vital to be left to either the good intentions or the caprices of private enterprise alone. On this point the opinion of the Massachusetts Drainage Commission of 1884–1885 was firm and typical of attitudes developing in a number of cities and states. The commission recommended that "the supervision of matters pertaining to water supply, sewerage, and the pollution of waters generally, be assigned to some board . . . to enable it to introduce system and method in these important departments of the common welfare." Municipal construction and control of water and wastewater systems grew so in public acceptance over the last three decades of the century that by 1910 the standard text on urban public health, *Municipal Sanitation in the United States* by Charles V. Chapin, could state succinctly: "Even the need for sewers has scarcely to be urged by health officers. The public so well appreciates their advantages that they are usually demanded when needed, even if they must be entirely paid for by the abutters." Chapin also pointed out that cities rarely called upon health officers to advise about sewer construction. "In recent times," he noted, "since sewers have been constructed by the municipality and with engineering advice, details have been wisely left to the engineers."[12]

By "wisely" leaving the matter to engineers, city administrators accomplished at least three results. First, they recognized and supported

[11] George C. Whipple, *Typhoid Fever, Its Causation, Transmission and Prevention* (New York, 1908); Frederic L. Hoffman, "American Mortality Progress," Mazÿck P. Ravenal, ed., *A Half Century of Public Health* (New York, 1921), 102; U.S. Bureau of the Census, *Financial Statistics of Cities Having a Population of Over 30,000: 1910* (Washington, 1913), 134–43; Cosgrove, *History of Sanitation*, 87–88; and Edward Meeker, "The Improving Health of the United States, 1850–1915," *Explorations in Economic History*, 9 (Summer 1972), 366–73 and Table 6; Edward Meeker, "The Social Rate of Return on Investment in Public Health, 1880–1910," *Journal of Economic History*, XXXIV (June 1974), 392–421.

[12] "Report of the Massachusetts Drainage Commission, 1884–85," portion reproduced in Rafter and Baker, *Sewage Disposal*, 115. Chapin, *Municipal Sanitation*, 296–97.

the growth of a new profession in the United States—municipal engineering. Second, they set in motion processes that ultimately would help restructure the organization of urban governments. Third, local administrations and the public at large implicitly came to accept the concept of comprehensive city planning, if not always the actual practice. From city-wide water and sewer systems to plans for every feature of the urban physical environment was but a short step of the imagination. A major engineering journal developed this logic in 1877:

> If the grading, drainage, paving, cleansing, and policing of towns are worthy of careful and systematic control, so are also the general shaping of the towns, the preservation or destruction of the natural features of their sites, and the distribution of their population and residence. Just what are the proper limits of public interference in such matters is a political question upon which we cannot venture; but public neglect has shown itself to be both costly and pernicious.

An examination of their part in reshaping the urban physical environment will underscore the importance of engineers to governmental reorganization and to city planning.[13]

Engineers did not raise solitary voices in calling for physical solutions to environmental problems. Sanitarians, landscape architects, and engineers formed a troika that tried to pull citizens and officials alike from the mire of governmental inaction to the higher ground of municipal planning and administration. Over the last half of the nineteenth century, urban public health officers assessed the spatial distribution of diseases, using the survey techniques of the engineers. Sanitarians supported municipal regulation of food, of air pollution, and of housing. They urged the rapid construction of water and sewer systems, rapid transit systems, and parks. But rarely, except in times of epidemics, did public health officers exert influence over most matters of municipal policy and administration. Landscape architects such as Frederick Law Olmsted, George Kessler, and Horace Shaler Cleveland—each of whom had some engineering training—propagandized planning concepts. Usually their physical solutions to health problems rested upon the construction of large urban parks as "lungs" for the city or upon the creation of upper-class suburbs as escape valves for the fortunate few. Occasionally their ideas roamed farther afield. Olmsted proposed parkways (even coining the term) as not only transportation

[13] Raymond H. Merritt, *Engineering in American Society, 1850–1875* (Lexington, Ky., 1969), 136–76; and, for the pre-Civil War experience, Daniel Calhoun, *The American Civil Engineer: Origins and Conflict* (Cambridge, 1960). The quotation appeared in *Engineering News*, IV (July 7, 1877), 173.

arteries, recreational areas, and pollution shields for urban watercourses, but also as hubs of comprehensively planned communities. He was an early advocate of restrictive covenants to regulate housing developments. Still, with few exceptions, the landscape architects contributed little to the reformulation of public policy or to changes in the administrative reach and authority of municipal governments. Although the troika often worked together, exchanged ideas, and supported similar goals, the municipal engineers were the most influential group.[14]

The functions of modern municipal administration were inherent in water and wastewater technology. Sewer and water supplies required permanent construction; hence they necessitated long-range planning. If engineers did not plan systems to accommodate future growth, the city would have to lay new aqueducts and trunk sewers each time the population increased even slightly. City officials learned that acquiring new sources of water or reconstructing sewer systems considerably increased costs over the long run. They also learned that if they ignored the use of experts in the construction and administration of sewer systems, disastrous health and financial consequences resulted. In the early 1870s, for example, Alexander Shepard, boss of the District of Columbia, wasted a $5,000,000 bond issue when contractors hired for political rather than engineering reasons built lateral sewers that ran uphill into the main sewers. Partly because of this fiasco, the District lost home rule to a federally-appointed commission which had to include at least one officer of the Army Corps of Engineers. St. Louis had to reconstruct its water supply and Cincinnati its sewer system within ten years after completion; both city administrations had rejected engineers' proposals in favor of politically popular decisions to cut costs. Hazen Pingree, Detroit's reform mayor during the 1890s, complained bitterly about politics having been more important than engineering in the construction of the sewer system when its concrete pipes began to crumble into dust during his regime. Of all major cities, Baltimore delayed longest in building a sewer system. The city paid for that folly with one of the two highest typhoid death rates in the nation. Not until

[14] For discussion of the sanitarians, in addition to those works on public health cited above, see James H. Cassedy, *Charles V. Chapin and the Public Health Movement* (Cambridge, 1962); Wilson G. Smillie, *Public Health, Its Promise for the Future: A Chronicle of the Development of Public Health in the United States, 1607-1914* (New York, 1955); Duncan R. Jamieson, "Towards a Cleaner New York: John H. Griscom and New York's Public Health, 1830-1870" (doctoral dissertation, Michigan State University, 1971); and Jon A. Peterson, "The Impact of Sanitary Reform upon American Urban Planning, 1840-1890" (paper delivered at the Organization of American Historians meeting, St. Louis, April 9, 1976).

1905–1906 did the city fathers begin to modernize and centralize the sewers under public control.[15]

Sewer and water systems required centralized administration. There were economies of scale in building only one reservoir and one main aqueduct. An integrated sewer system with a trunk sewer at the lowest grade level and an outfall at a site that minimized pollution problems also considerably reduced costs. Thus, the new technology necessitated a permanent bureaucracy to acquire land, oversee construction, administer on a day-by-day basis, and to plan for long-term needs. The public works could be built most efficiently by technological and managerial experts who could survey the topography, choose appropriate construction materials, and draw readily upon the experiences of their counterparts in other cities.

Engineers and their projects served to centralize metropolitan administration of problems common to areas larger than the central core city. Topography ignored municipal boundaries. An efficient sewer system that followed natural gradients to achieve a gravity flow usually violated a city's political limits. The dumping of one community's sewage might and often did pollute the system of a neighboring community. Newark, for instance, drew its water supply from the Passaic River at a point below the sewer outflows of Paterson and Passaic. Mill towns in the Merrimac Valley were notorious for fouling one another's water supplies. To combat pollution in such locales the engineering press began urging regional cooperation in water and sewer services during the early 1870s. Although there were earlier isolated examples of such metropolitan "authorities," usually public health boards and park planning commissions, permanent administrative bodies seem to have arisen in the late 1880s and early 1890s in response to pollution problems. City officials gained state legislative approval to create metropolitan water and sewer districts such as Boston's Metropolitan Sewage Commission (1889), and similar districts in Chicago, the Passaic Valley, and elsewhere. Municipal governments vested authority for such

[15] Busey, "History and Progress of Sanitation of the City of Washington," 210–12; Constance McLaughlin Green, *Washington, Village, and Capital, 1800–1878* (Princeton, 1962), 241–60; M. L. Holman, "Historical Aspects of the St. Louis Water Works," *Journal of the American Engineering Society*, XIV (Jan. 1895), 1–9; A. L. Anderson, "The Sanitary Conditions of the Cincinnati Sewer," *Engineering News*, V (Nov. 14, 21, 1878), 324, 372; Arthur S. Hobby, "The Sewerage of Cincinnati," *ibid.*, V (Nov. 28, 1878), 377–78; Melvin G. Holli, *Reform in Detroit: Hazen S. Pingree and Urban Politics* (New York, 1969), 26–27; William Travis Howard, Jr., *Public Health Administration and the Natural History of Disease in Baltimore, Maryland, 1797–1920* (Washington, 1924); and James B. Crooks, *Politics & Progress: The Rise of Urban Progressivism in Baltimore, 1895 to 1911* (Baton Rouge, 1968), 132–36.

extra-municipal projects in their city engineer's office. By the early 1890s, also, engineers in a few cities had obtained the power to approve plats in areas beyond city limits to ensure that subdividers used street plans that would facilitate travel and accommodate the installation of subsurface utilities. In some cities engineers could abate nuisances beyond city limits, thus gaining authority to protect watersheds and to engage in an early form of housing regulation as well.[16]

Engineers also contributed to the rationalization of fiscal techniques. Recurrently throughout the 1880s and 1890s articles in the engineering press outlined the organization and division of responsibility within engineering offices, provided model forms for paperwork, and suggested standardized systems for monitoring costs. Before organizations like the National Conference for Good City Government and the National Municipal League published data on tax and budgetary policies, the engineering press identified most of the major issues and shaped the framework for discussion.[17]

Labeling themselves neutral experts, engineers professed to work above the din of local politics. Usually they tried to isolate themselves from partisan wrangles, and often succeeded. In the creation of administrative bureaucracies, engineers apparently were the earliest municipal officials to achieve anything like job security. Chesbrough, chief engineer of the Chicago Board of Sewerage, 1855–1861, served as that community's first city engineer from 1861–1879, an extraordinary career at a time when most municipal jobs changed hands with every election. Others had equally long terms. E. P. North, director of the Croton Water Works for New York City; Robert Moore, municipal engineer of St. Louis; and, George Benzenberg, city engineer of Milwaukee, all had twenty years of continuous service before 1900.

[16] Rafter and Baker, *Sewage Disposal*, 579–85; Commonwealth of Massachusetts, *Acts of 1889* (Boston, 1890), Chap. 439, and *First Annual Report of the Board of Metropolitan Sewerage Commissioners* (Boston, 1890); "Troy, N.Y.," *Engineering News*, IV (Nov. 3, 1877), 359–69. "The Better Water Supply of Northeastern New Jersey," *Engineering News and American Railway Journal*, XIX (March 24, 1888), 230–31. See also "Municipal Co-operation a Possible Substitute for Consolidation," *Engineering News*, XLI (Feb. 16, 1899), 104–06; Paul Studenski, *The Government of Municipal Areas in the United States* (New York, 1930), 33–34, 49–59, 105–13. .On extra-municipal powers, see Nelson Tibbs, "The Sanitary Protection of the Watershed Supplying Water to Rochester, N.Y.," *Engineering News and American Railway Journal*, XIX (April 28, 1888), 531; Olmsted, Vaux & Co., *Report on the Parkway Proposed for the City of Brooklyn* (n.p., 1868); "How to Subdivide Land in Illinois," *The Engineer and Surveyor*, I (April 1874), 4; and Mel Scott, *American City Planning Since 1890* (Berkeley, 1969), 110–269.

[17] On the organization of offices in numerous cities, see, for example, *Journal of the Association of Engineering Societies* (March 1893) and the series that ran in *Engineering News* from Jan. 6, 1886 through Dec. 25, 1886.

Cost savings, of course, resulted from retention of an engineer familiar with the local system. In some jurisdictions, courts reinforced this tendency by declaring that engineers held title to whatever plans they made. A city that fired its engineer might lose the blueprint to its sewer system with his departure.[18] Still, longevity in office for engineers stemmed from more than simple cost considerations. Their political caution, growing stature as problem-solvers, and their professionalization all worked to the engineers' advantage.

Civil service reformers repeatedly praised engineers as models of efficient bureaucrats. Reform literature often cited the District of Columbia, largely administered by the Army Corps of Engineers, as an excellent example of good government. European cities with autonomous engineer-administrators, usually military officers like Baron Georges E. Haussman in Paris, also garnered plaudits from the reformers. Thus, engineers were among the earliest municipal employees to receive civil service protection, in most cases a *de jure* recognition of a *de facto* situation.[19]

Operating in a cosmopolitan, not a local context, engineers were as much responsive to their professional peers as to local pressures. They institutionalized the role of the consultant. Some, like Waring or Rudolph Hering, the two most prominent sanitary engineers of the period, worked only as consultants, moving from one city to another. Others, like Chesbrough, Benzenberg, Moses Lane of Milwaukee, Joseph P. Davis of Boston, and Colonel Julius W. Adams of Brooklyn were home based but traveled widely to consult on major projects in other cities. The consultant role was a measure of the status of engineers and of their independence from partisan politics. Nineteenth-century city leaders viewed their communities in keen competition with others for economic growth and population. A reputation for excellence in public works and health served local boosters well in the wars of urban imperialism. Yet, various city engineers were so important as in-house experts that local politicians could not deny them the opportunity of advising hated rival cities.

[18] American Society of Civil Engineers, *A Biographical Dictionary of American Civil Engineers* (New York, 1972), 23–24. Calhoun, *American Civil Engineer*, 68–78.

[19] Charles W. Eliot, "One Remedy for Municipal Misgovernment," *Forum*, XII (Oct. 1891), 153–68; "Engineers as Commissioners of Public Works," *Engineering News and American Railway Journal*, XXXI (Feb. 1, 1894), 82. References to Washington include: John Ficklen, "The Municipal Condition of New Orleans," *Proceedings of the Second National Conference on Good City Government* (Dec. 8–10, 1894), and "Municipal Reports," *Municipal Engineering*, XVII (Jan. 1900), 56–58. On civil service protection see A. Marston and G. W. Miller, "The Methods of Choosing City Engineers," *Engineering Record*, XLVII (Dec. 21, 1903), 198–99.

As an emerging "strategic elite," in sociologist Suzanne Keller's telling phrase, engineers secured job tenure through professionalization.[20] At a time when few if any clearinghouses for the exchange of ideas and practices benefited cities nationwide, the engineers built up a remarkable communications network among themselves. Their common training, whether in the relatively few engineering schools of the period or in shared apprenticeships, usually on the major railroads, bound them together. The practice of review by outside consultants reinforced these connections. Engineers belonged to the same national organizations. The majority held membership in the American Society of Civil Engineers that frequently published papers on municipal engineering with appended comments from experts throughout the nation. They also belonged to local professional clubs that corresponded with one another, publishing and exchanging reports about conditions in their individual cities. Numerous professional journals provided forums for discussion and debate. During the late-1870s and again in the late-1880s the most prestigious of these journals, the *Engineering News*, printed lengthy series comparing cities around the country. Reports described water supply, sewerage, streets, parks, housing design, transportation terminals, and other elements of municipal planning. They dealt also with administrative and legal questions, subjects on which some engineers had special competence. Of active civil engineers born before 1820, almost twenty-eight percent underwent legal training in addition to their technological training. The engineering press also published reports on European developments, paying particular attention to the important research trips abroad of Chesbrough and Hering. Finally, in 1894, the professionals involved principally with urban problems formed their own national organization, the American Society for Municipal Improvements.[21]

[20] Elites "refers first of all to a minority of individuals designated to serve a collectivity in a socially valued way. . . . Socially significant elites are ultimately responsible for the realization of major social goals and for the continuity of the social order." Furthermore, "only certain leadership groups have a general and sustained social impact. . . . We refer to these groups as *strategic elites* . . . [who] comprise not only political, economic, and military leaders, but also moral, cultural, and scientific ones. Whether or not an elite is counted as strategic does not depend on its specific activities but on the scope of its activities, that is, on how many members of society it directly impinges upon and in what respects." Suzanne Keller, *Beyond the Ruling Class: Strategic Elites in Modern Society* (New York, 1963), 4, 20.

[21] For example, see "European Systems of Sewerage," *Engineering News*, IX (Jan. 28, 1882), 33–35; "Municipal and Sanitary Engineering in the City of London," *Engineering News and American Contract Journal*, XVI (Aug. 21, 28, 1886), 122–23, 134–35. Information on the legal training of engineers may be found in American Society of Civil Engineers, *Biographical Dictionary of American Civil Engineers*. For the E. S. Chesbrough and Rudolph Hering reports see E. S. Chesbrough, *Report of the Results of Examinations Made in Relation to Sewerage in Several European Cities, in the Winter of 1856-7* (Chicago, 1858) and Rudolph Hering, "Reports of an Examination Made in 1880 of Several Sewerage Works in Europe," *Annual Report of the National Board of Health, 1881* (Washington, 1882), 200–12.

The engineers, then, were well aware of each other's activities, in contact with innovation in their profession, alert to employment opportunities throughout the nation, and not bound to the petty squabbles of local politics. Decades before early-twentieth-century political reformers depicted their ideal administrator, municipal engineers embodied all the administrator's attractive characteristics—efficiency, expertise, and an allegedly disinterested, incorruptible professionalism.

Over the last half of the nineteenth century, engineers often demonstrated the value of long-range planning to municipal administration. Not only did the profession offer solutions to physical problems such as water and sewer supply, it also contributed comprehensive planning schemes that repeatedly illustrated the interaction of technology with the social, economic, and political structure of cities. Planning ideas that evolved from the construction of water supply and sewer systems between the 1850s and the 1890s presaged the later city plans of men such as Nolen, Daniel Burnham, George B. Ford, and others. In many respects the engineers' proposals surveyed the physical city more thoroughly than did the plans of the early-twentieth century. Certainly the engineers, and their colleagues the landscape architects and the sanitarians, generally showed a deeper understanding of the health needs of the populace than did many planners after the turn of the century.

The engineering press propagated the ideas of the sanitarians. *Van Nostrand's Engineering Magazine*, for instance, reprinted in 1876 a utopian scheme of the British sanitarian B. W. Richardson. "Hygeia—A City of Health" outlined the elements of climate, site selection, water supply, sewerage, street layout, park system, and housing design that together could reduce mortality figures and transform the city into an ideal environment. The Chicago sanitarian J. M. Gregory told the Chicago Medical Society, in a speech promptly reprinted by *Engineering News*, that "a great city is a vast laboratory, in which the energies imported in the food supplies and stored in the atmosphere are transmitted into human life, or rather, into thousands of human lives, but which are momentarily and perpetually exposed to that further transmutation which crumbles organized being back to its chemical elements." Waring presented his utopian view of "New York, A.D., 1997—A Prophecy," predicting the city of the future built upon the solid foundations of well-designed transportation, adequate water and sewer systems, the use of electrical power, streets rid of the filth of horses and other domestic animals, universal public education, and efficient government freed of bossism and political corruption.

Engineers, accustomed to thinking about unified systems, joined with sanitarians in viewing the city as an ecosystem, a vast, integrated unit with the efficient functioning of one part dependent upon the efficient functioning of all the parts.[22]

Comprehensive planning meant nothing more nor less than focusing attention on all the interconnected parts of the urban system. A good example of this vision was the work prepared by the Engineer's Club of Philadelphia during the early-1880s. Lewis Haupt, an influential engineering professor at the University of Pennsylvania, presented a number of papers on street layout and the need for rapid transit. In form and recommendations, these proposals resembled but antedated the progressive-era transit and traffic surveys by engineer Bion Arnold and the consultant firm of Kelker, De Leuw. Haupt even tried to devise a method to forecast future population growth. Hering, then resident in Philadelphia, gave a paper on "The Future Sewerage Requirements of Philadelphia" that saw the city as a sprawling but integrated unit. Other papers dealt with housing regulation, water supply, bridge and harbor improvement. All the papers emphasized the necessity of comprehensive physical planning. Throughout the 1880s and the following decade, other local engineering clubs in St. Louis, Chicago, Cleveland, Kansas City, and elsewhere, prepared similar reports. Most reports stressed the engineers' role as planners and managers in sentiments like these expressed in 1894:

The city engineer is to the city very much what the family physician is to the family. He is constantly called upon to advise and direct in all matters pertaining to his profession. . . . He does know the character, constitution, particular needs and idiosyncrasies of the city, as the family physician knows the constitutions of the family. . . . The city engineer is becoming the most important director of the material development of cities, and his office is becoming more and more a permanent one. He is thus to a certain extent responsible for holding the successive political officials to a consistent, progressive policy in all the branches of work under his charge. To him, even more than to the successive mayors, falls the duty of serving as the intelligence and brains of the municipal government in all physical matters.[23]

[22] B. W. Richardson, "Modern Sanitary Science—A City of Health," *Van Nostrand's Eclectic Engineering Magazine*, XIV (Jan. 1876), 31–44. For a discussion of the issue, see James H. Cassedy, "Hygeia: A Mid-Victorian Dream of a City of Health," *Journal of the History of Medicine and Allied Sciences*, XVII (April 1962), 217–29. J. M. Gregory, "The Hygiene of Great Cities," *Engineering News*, VII (Jan. 10, 1880), 17; metaphors comparing the city to organisms or machines were frequent in the engineering press. George Waring's piece was published together with a biography in Albert Shaw, *Life of Col. Geo. E. Waring, Jr. The Great Apostle of Cleanliness* (New York, 1899).

[23] L. M. Haupt, "Rapid Transit," *Proceedings of the Engineering Club of Philadelphia*, IV (Aug. 1884), 135–38, which appeared to be modeled on an 1875 survey of rapid transit undertaken by the American Society of Civil Engineers for New York City, published as "Rapid

Engineers began promoting their "physician" role as early as the 1850s. During the immediate post-Civil War years a number of broad-ranging plans embodying the comprehensive viewpoint appeared. City fathers implemented some, others remained part of a paper brigade. Two examples—the development of Boston's Back Bay and a partially aborted plan for the Bronx—illustrated the scope of the planners' vision.

For two decades following the late 1850s Boston undertook a massive landfill operation and development project for its Back Bay area. Other historians have recounted the full story, but for present purposes several elements should be highlighted.[24] The city used restrictive covenants in deeds for lots on the newly filled land to establish common house setbacks, to impose height restrictions, and to limit nonresidential use of land—in other words, an early effort at zoning.[25] The entire area pivoted around a principal traffic artery, Commonwealth Avenue. On the model of European boulevards, the artery included a strip of park down the middle. Land-use restrictions and the boulevard served both to enhance the attractiveness of the area and to diminish the quantities of sewer gas and other miasmic materials in the air and thus, by contemporary standards, to ensure physical health. Boston also undertook a major reconstruction of its sewer system so that wastes drained into the South Bay rather than filling the more stagnant waters of the Back Bay. The city forced railroad lines to relocate from the Back Bay to a freight yard on newly filled land in the South Bay, thereby turning that district into an attractive site for industrial activities.

While the Back Bay project continued, an enterprising landscape architect, Robert Morris Copeland, seized the opportunity to advance a comprehensive plan for redoing all of Boston. "We have supposed that, for some unnamed reason," Copeland observed, "planning for a city's

Transit and Terminal Freight Facilities," *ASCE Transactions,* IV (1875), 1–80. Lewis Haupt, "The Growth of Cities as Exemplified in Philadelphia," *Proceedings of the Engineering Club of Philadelphia,* IV (Aug. 1884), 148–75. Rudolph Hering, "Future Sewerage Requirements," *ibid.,* II (1880), 36–50. Similar reports from other cities included "St. Louis Boulevards in the Business District," *Journal of the Association of Engineering Societies,* XII (March 1894), 190; "Civil Engineering," *Engineering Magazine,* III (June 1892), 418–20; Robert Gilliam, "Work for Our Engineers' Club," *Journal of the Association of Engineering Societies,* XII (June 1893), 305–13. The quotation appeared in John C. Olmsted, "Relation of the City Engineer to Public Parks," *Journal of the Association of Engineering Societies,* XIII (Oct. 1894), 594–95.

[24] Walter Muir Whitehill, *Boston, A Topographical History* (Cambridge, 1968), 141–73; Norman T. Newton, *Design on the Land: The Development of Landscape Architecture* (Cambridge, 1971), 290–306; Lawrence J. Friedman, *A History of American Law* (New York, 1973), 397.

[25] For an excellent discussion of this process in another city, see Andrew J. King, "Law and Land Use in Chicago: A Prehistory of Modern Zoning" (doctoral dissertation, University of Wisconsin, 1976).

growth and progress could only be done as it grows; . . . this is a fallacious belief." Directly confronting the tradition of unfettered individualism in American cities, he argued that the best way to protect private property rights was to plan carefully for the future. Boston's physical, economic, and social wants could be "digested for its future progress" by dividing the city into parts and by measuring the relationship of each of the parts to the whole. "The city whose area is carefully studied, which shows by plans where wharves may be built, where new avenues are to be laid out, and where factories may congregate; where parks, gardens, and palaces, if desired, may be made, will grow," Copeland predicted, "in a sure, orderly, and progressive way. . . ." He was certain that thoughtful engineering would satisfy all the city's needs: "merchandise can be easily transported, business done, water and gas supplied, amusements furnished, fires limited, and sewage provided for." Although the primary emphasis of his plan was to assure the rational conduct of business as vital to the strength of the community, Copeland demonstrated an understanding of the city as organism—a concept similar to that held by engineers. "A city or town," he affirmed, "is to be considered as a whole, and in relation to all of its wants, as well as its necessities. . . ." Boston did not adopt Copeland's plan. Still, he contributed significantly to the continuing public discussion over comprehensive planning for the urban future. Certainly his plan, in connection with the Back Bay project, taught Bostonians the importance of conceiving the city as a whole greater than the sum of its parts.[26]

Later, in the 1880s, when engineers and builders had finished most of the Back Bay development, the city sought to complete the project with yet another engineering scheme. To reduce further pollution of the bay and to provide additional recreational and health amenities, the city hired Olmsted to lay out a park system (the Back Bay Fens) along the Muddy River that drained into the bay. This carefully engineered project

[26] Robert Morris Copeland, *The Most Beautiful City in America. Essay and Plan for the Improvement of the City of Boston* (Boston, 1872), 10–12. In some specifics, tone, and in comprehensive sweep, Robert M. Copeland's plan resembled the much earlier work of Robert Fleming Gourlay, *Plans for Beautifying New York, and for Enlarging and Improving the City of Boston. Being, Studies to Illustrate the Science of City Building* (Boston, 1844). Today, Robert Gourlay is nearly forgotten as a pioneering city planner. Walter Muir Whitehill mentions him, but the only "modern" studies that exist are Janet Carnochan, "Robert Gourlay," *Publications of the Niagara Historical Society*, No. 18 (1909), 35–47 and Fletcher Steele, "Robert Fleming Gourlay, City Planner," *Landscape Architecture*, VI (Oct. 1915), 1–14.

was an example of intelligent planning that sparked enthusiasm for similar actions in other cities.[27]

Between 1865 and 1877, John J. R. Croes, a civil engineer, and Olmsted surveyed and prepared a thorough plan for a portion of territory in the Bronx recently annexed to New York City. Charged with the responsibility of planning a street system and a rapid-transit steam railroad to connect the annexed wards to the city, Croes and Olmsted instead proposed comprehensive development of the area as a suburb before any property could be sold to residents. Implicitly, their design argued for thorough planning of all the undeveloped areas that one day would comprise Greater New York City.

The Croes-Olmsted plans, presented in three reports, called for the development of a central business district bordered by a residential section on the high ground around the center of the area, with suburban homes on the northern and western edges. They offered street patterns that would provide drainage by gravity, thereby lessening the costs of subsurface water and sewer facilities. They urged construction of wide north-south avenues along valley bottoms and the tops of the ridges that dominated the topography of the Bronx. These avenues would cover water and sewer lines and also accommodate elevated railroads built up the middle, with consequent minimum disturbance to the surrounding environment. Parkways through proposed linear parks that would protect creeks and the Bronx River from pollution also would facilitate travel to the downtown. The most scenic lands in the area would be preserved for recreational and health purposes. Croes and Olmsted suggested granting of extra-municipal powers to city engineers to abate nuisances in the Westchester County headwaters of Bronx streams. Thus, the city could prevent industrial location along the small, slowly-flowing waterways and ensure the area's healthfulness.

Throughout their reports the two planners minimized private development decisions and elevated the role of the public agency, in this case the Board of Commissioners of Public Parks, in comprehensive planning. But the desires of the board and of real-estate speculators to populate the area quickly by the traditional means of private development won the day. Nuisance abatements, restrictive covenants as a land-use and housing control, and thorough planning before settlement were

[27] Laura Wood Roper, *FLO: A Biography of Frederick Law Olmsted* (Baltimore, 1973), 385–88; Newton, *Design on the Land*, 290–94.

too radical to please the special interest groups involved. Croes and Olmsted lost their battle.[28]

While nothing as comprehensive as the Back Bay development or the Bronx plan appeared again in the United States until after the turn of the new century, bits and pieces of these plans did recur elsewhere. By 1900, Chicago, Kansas City, and Buffalo, among others, had built or at least had begun multipurpose park systems that went far beyond the mere provision of recreational land usage. All of these plans protected streams and rivers from inordinate industrial pollution; all provided new transportation systems that improved travel conditions in and about the city; all promised solutions to the public health problems of the cities; and all projected the improvement of housing facilities for large numbers of the urban population.[29]

The last half of the nineteenth century thus saw remarkable innovations in technology, municipal administration, and city planning. Virtually the only problems successfully attacked by nineteenth-century urban leaders were those susceptible to engineering expertise. Cities dramatically lowered their disease and mortality rates with the construction of efficient water supply and sewage systems. The administrative techniques of engineers, and their reputations as problem-solvers, carried great prestige into the early years of the twentieth century. Within their specialized functions, engineers had developed centralized agencies capable of long-range, comprehensive planning and staffed by cosmopolitan experts. They also had advocated, with some success, the extension of their brand of organization to municipal administration as a whole. Albert F. Noyes, one of the leading city engineers of the period, echoed conventional wisdom among his

---

[28] The series of reports included *Preliminary Report of the Landscape Architect and the Civil and Topographical Engineer, upon the Laying Out of the Twenty-third and Twenty-fourth Wards, and Report of the Landscape Architect and the Civil Topographical Engineer, Accompanying a Plan for Laying out That Part of the Twenty-fourth Ward, Lying West of Riverdale Road* (New York, 1876); *Report of the Civil and Topographical Engineer and the Landscape Architect, Accompanying a Plan for Local Steam Transit Routes in the Twenty-third and Twenty-fourth Wards* (New York, 1877); and *Communication for the Landscape Architect and the Civil and Topographical Engineer, in Relation to the Proposed Plan for Laying out the Central District of the Twenty-third and Twenty-fourth Wards, Lying East of Jerome Avenue and West of Third Avenue and the Harlem Railroad* (New York, 1877). See also E. B. Van Winkle, "Drainage of the Twenty-third and Twenty-fourth Wards, This City," reprinted in *Engineering News*, VIII (Aug. 18, 20, 1881), 321–27, 337–49; S. S. Haight, "Surveying, Laying out and Monumenting the New Wards of New York," *Engineering News*, VIII (March 5, 1881), 96; Roper, *FLO*, 354–56; and Albert Fein, *Frederick Law Olmsted and the American Environmental Tradition* (New York, 1972), 50, 159, and fig. 78.

[29] Newton, *Design on the Land*, 307–36; and the voluminous collection of park planning reports in the Francis Loeb Library, Harvard School of Design (Cambridge).

colleagues in 1894 when he noted that "the office of the municipal engineer is of the greatest importance to the community.... In fact, the city government of today is in a large measure a matter of municipal engineering, and the character of the city engineer's department is a safe index to the intelligence shown in the development of a municipality."[30]

That city engineers trumpeted their own importance was not surprising. The core of professionalism is the assertion of knowledge and skills available only to in-group members. Although little contradictory evidence exists (and a great amount in support), the engineers' claims of political neutrality may be suspect. Surely their growing importance as managers of the physical city involved them intimately with elected officials and posed potential abuses of power similar to those associated with Robert Moses in twentieth-century New York City.[31] But, one fact is certain. Many political reformers of the early-twentieth century found themselves in agreement with the opinions of Noyes and other engineers. In both process and personnel, various changes in the structure of municipal government during the progressive era drew heavily on the technological and administrative skills exhibited by engineers over the last half of the nineteenth century. The cumulative impact of the engineers' contributions helped to create two new professions in early-twentieth-century America—city planners and city managers. Both substantially altered the administrative functions and reach of municipal government.[32]

The role of engineers in the emerging profession of city planning was considerable. Nelson P. Lewis, author of one of the earliest city-planning texts, dedicated his 1916 volume "To the Municipal Engineers of the United States, the first men on the ground in City Planning as in City

---

[30] Albert F. Noyes, "Organization and Management of a City Engineer's Office," *Journal of the Association of Engineering Societies*, XIII (Oct. 1894), 541, 544.

[31] Robert A. Caro, *The Power Broker: Robert Moses and the Fall of New York* (New York, 1974).

[32] On the planning profession see Scott, *American City Planning*; Roy Lubove, *The Progressives and the Slums: Tenement House Reform in New York City, 1890-1917* (Pittsburgh, 1962), 217-45; Roy Lubove, *The Urban Community: Housing and Planning in the Progressive Era* (Englewood Cliffs, 1967), 1-22; John L. Hancock, "Planners in the Changing American City, 1900-1940," *Journal of the American Institute of Planners*, XXXIII (Sept. 1967), 290-304; John W. Reps, *The Making of Urban America: A History of City Planning in the United States* (Princeton, 1965), 497-525; and Thomas S. Hines, *Burnham of Chicago: Architect and Planner* (New York, 1974). On the city manager profession, see John Porter East, *Council-Manager Government: The Political Thought of Its Founder, Richard S. Childs* (Chapel Hill, 1965); Clarence E. Ridley and Orin F. Nolting, *The City-Manager Profession* (Chicago, 1934); Richard J. Stillman II, *The Rise of the City Manager: A Public Professional in Local Government* (Albuquerque, 1974); and Harry Aubrey Toulmin, Jr., *The City Manager: A New Profession* (New York, 1915).

Building. . . ." Of the fifty-two charter members of the American Institute of Planning (AIP) in 1917 (then the American City Planning Institute), thirteen were engineers. Only the landscape architecture profession provided more members, and several of them had some engineering training. In that same year the American Institute of Architects published a nationwide survey, *City Planning Progress*, in which the editors noted that "the Committee has laid particular stress on the economic and engineering side of city planning, because it believes that that is fundamental to progress. . . ." The newly-formed AIP included the individuals, principally the engineers and the landscape architects, who had prepared most of the city plans advanced since 1905. Mel Scott, the plutarch of the planning profession, observed that during the 1920s most smaller cities still delegated responsibility for planning to their city engineer's office. With the solitary exception of Delos Wilcox, a political reformer, engineers dominated the most important of the new planning specialties, transportation planning.[33]

While engineers played a central part in the growth of the city-planning profession, their direct contributions to the restructuring of municipal governments during the early years of the twentieth century were even more impressive. However much reformers disagreed about specifics of structural change, they agreed that the proper direction lay in the professionalization and bureaucratization of government. No political change better reflected the emphasis on efficiency and the demands for accountability so characteristic of progressive structural reform than the managerial revolution in urban governments.

The new city manager form of government, as attested by the National Municipal League in 1913, promised administrative unity, clear lines of responsibility, expertise in the head of the administration, and discipline and harmony among the ranks of government servants. By 1919, the league incorporated the position of city manager into its model charter for urban governmental reform. The new professionals brought administrative expertise, a taste for bureaucracy, and the battle cry of "efficiency" to the management of scores of small and middle-sized cities over the first few decades of the twentieth century.[34]

A profile of members of the new profession revealed commonality of backgrounds. The first city managers of Staunton, Virginia, and Dayton,

[33] Nelson P. Lewis, *The Planning of the Modern City: A Review of the Principles Governing City Planning* (New York, 1916); Scott, *American City Planning*, 163–64, 228; George B. Ford and Ralph F. Warner, *City Planning Progress* (Washington, 1917), iii.
[34] Griffith, *A History of American City Government*, 167–68.

Ohio, the initial laboratories of the experiment, were both practicing civil engineers. H. M. Waite, who took up his Dayton post in 1914, came directly from a highly successful career as city engineer of Cincinnati. The 1919 *Yearbook* of the City Managers' Association showed that forty-eight percent of the total membership were engineers. In 1920, a survey of California city managers stated that of the twenty-one listing their backgrounds, thirteen were engineers. Surveys taken during the 1920s and 1930s demonstrated that less than three percent of all managers who graduated from college had majored in public administration or political science, the disciplines one might expect to have provided the best education for an administrator. Of those with B.A. degrees, seventy-five percent had trained as engineers. By the time the "typical" manager assumed his job, he had engaged in some engineering work and had held one or more posts in government, usually as a department head. As late as 1940, a major survey related that more than sixty-three percent of city managers over the previous twenty-five years had trained as engineers.[35]

Historians interested in tracing the strands of continuity in municipal government should find fascinating the engineering backgrounds of city managers. This new profession, which many contemporaries considered the high-water mark of progressive reforms in municipal administration, recruited primarily from another profession that long since had proved its central importance to the orderly functioning of cities. During the half-century preceding the progressive era, the job of municipal engineer developed into a profession that reshaped the physical landscape of urban America. But, of equal significance, it provided a corps of experienced experts and a model of administrative skill that later-day progressives would use as a basis for the structural reform of urban government.

Behind the political reforms of the progressive years lay decades of technological changes in the physical growth patterns of American cities. The increasingly complex metropolitan environment of the last half of the nineteenth century had deepened the awareness of urbanites about the role of technology in the comfort, health, and order of their daily lives. That awareness in turn helped foster new conceptions of the role of government in serving the expectations of the citizenry. Just as

[35] Lewis, *Planning of the Modern City*, 415; Toulmin, *The City Manager*, 78–81; "City Manager Plan Widely Endorsed," *Engineering News-Record*, LXXXV (Oct. 7, 1920), 703; Stillman, *Rise of the City Manager*, 38–39; Harold Stone, Don K. Price, and Kathryn H. Stone, *City Manager Government in the United States: A Review After Twenty-five Years* (Chicago, 1940), 57.

the physical problems of the expanding cities had called forth a new profession of experts to provide solutions, so did the political administrative problems require a new profession of skilled managers.

In both the technological and the political arenas, municipal engineers played an increasingly important part. They stamped their long-range visions of metropolitan planning on the public consciousness over the last half of the nineteenth century. Their successful demands for political autonomy in solving the physical problems of the cities contributed to the ultimate insistence for efficient government run by skilled professionals. At the heart of physical and political changes in the administration of American cities, indeed at the very core of city planning, stood the work of the municipal engineers.

Drainage, disease, comfort, and class: a history of Newark's sewers

STUART GALISHOFF

In the development and expansion of Newark's sewage disposal system can be seen, better perhaps than in the development of any other municipal service, the complete lack of city planning and the improvised manner in which municipal services evolved.[1]

IT would be difficult to find a more prosaic yet important subject than sewers. The introduction of sewage and indoor plumbing provided a measure of comfort to millions of persons who previously had suffered the indignities of outdoor toilets. Simultaneously, the elimination of privies and cesspools made cities more pleasant places in which to live and markedly reduced the incidence of cholera, typhoid fever, and other filth diseases. Recognizing the importance of good drainage and sanitary waste disposal, municipal leaders in the late nineteenth century undertook the building of sewer systems. Not everyone, however, shared in the blessings of sewerage. Since sewers were expensive, their use was limited to those who could afford the price of a sewer connection. Class membership thus determined who would gain access to a sewer and who would remain dependent upon outhouses.

Little has been written about the history of sewerage, and much of the literature on the subject deals only with its technical and scientific side. The social forces that shaped the development of sewerage, while equally important, are obscure. Similarly, there have been few studies of sewerage within the context of urban services. A detailed history of one community's sewerage therefore is needed to illuminate this long-neglected aspect of the American past.

The topography of much of the Newark area provides excellent natural drainage. The city is situated on the eastern side of the Orange Mountains on a gently sloping plain which extends to the Passaic River on the east and the meadows adjoining the river and Newark Bay on the south. Partly because of its advantageous location, Newark was without any sewers until 1854.[2]

In the two centuries following the establishment of Newark in 1636, the community expanded slowly along the axis formed by its principal thoroughfares, Broad and Market streets. Two blocks to the west of Broad Street there was a steep hillside, the first of a series of ridges which

121

extend to the Orange Mountains. From this elevated section several streams crossed the Newark plain before descending into the sea. Swelled by storms, they spilled over their banks turning the filthy, unpaved streets into liquid mud. Because of the city's failure to pave its thoroughfares and to provide sewerage, the natural drainage afforded by Newark's topography was lost. Newark's well-watered streets soon became a nuisance and a serious health hazard.[3]

Residents complained constantly about the wretchedness of the city streets but to little avail. During heavy rains, large sections of Newark became quagmires of liquid mud. The seeming intractability of the problem evoked a gallows humor. Following a January thaw which submerged Broad Street in liquid mud for several days, the *Newark Daily Advertiser* observed that enterprising citizens were seen navigating the street in a scow. On another occasion, the paper reported that strong ropes had to be used to extricate a mule caught in the mire. A few days later it solemnly recorded the death of the mule from injuries sustained in his rescue.[4]

Gutters, open drains that ran down the center of the street, were intended to remove the surface waters of the city. But they were poorly constructed and frequently were clogged with wood shavings, half-rotted straw, and other debris, preventing the water they carried from draining freely. Unsightly and malodorous, they were held responsible for the sickness which abounded in their environs. Some time prior to 1852 a resolution was passed to widen, deepen, and enclose one of the streams that crossed the city. Fearing a permanent nuisance in their midst, neighborhood people remonstrated and the plan was abandoned.[5]

Many inhabitants built drains from their homes to the gutters. The drains, which were used to remove basement water, household wastes and, occasionally excreta, were the cause of some of Newark's worst nuisances. In winter they froze and burst, causing the formation of large sheets of polluted ice. In the summer they emitted sickening stenches, drew flies, and provided breeding places for mosquitoes.[6]

The Newark board of health, which was responsible for the city's sanitary condition, lacked sufficient legal power to safeguard the public health. While the board was authorized to abate nuisances, it could not define their existence. To remove a nuisance not expressly covered in the statutes, the board had to secure a special legislative enactment or was constrained to prove in court that the public health was being endangered. In court "the defendants in the case would appeal and appeal until all the good that might have been done, and evil avoided by quick decisive action would be abrogated, and perhaps an epidemic or pestilence fostered by the want of action."[7] Despite the presence of slaughterhouses, breweries, tanneries, and fat- and bone-boiling establishments, whose failure to provide sanitary means of waste disposal constituted a standing danger to the community, the board was unable to secure summary powers to define and abate nuisances until 1885 when it was reorganized under state law.

Two unusually heavy August squalls, one occurring in 1843 and the other in 1853, revealed the city's precarious sanitary position. Besides destroying sidewalks and weakening foundations, the floods left in their wake large numbers of stagnant pools. It was feared that the "exhalations" from the pools would generate malaria. As the *Anopheles* mosquito was ubiquitous in Newark, there was indeed reason to be concerned. In addition there was the danger that fecal containers weakened by the storm would seep their contents into yards and cellars, thereby becoming a source of discomfort and disease. The flooding was particularly bad in the low-lying "Down Neck" section bordering the Newark meadows. This malaria-infested area was the center of the city's immigrant population. Because of its watery subsoil, lots reclaimed from the meadows had poor drainage. The land had been raised with garbage and subsequently had sunk. Throughout Newark lots and water-courses had been filled without regard to drainage. Even under the best of circumstances the residents of the Down Neck area were bedeviled with pools of fetid water and damp and flooded cellars. So great was the body of water left lying upon the ground by the 1853 storm that for many days cellars in the area could not be dried.[8]

Liquid wastes not absorbed by the soil drained into the city's waterways and into ditches and other open conduits. River and storm waters were relied upon to flush the sewage deposits that accumulated on the beds and the banks of the conduits. During times of drought or low tide the effluent decomposed in the sun and gave off a horrible stench. The odors emanating from the conduits were thought to poison the atmosphere and were held responsible for the so-called "intermittent fevers" that plagued nearby residents.[9]

Increased sickness in Newark affirmed the need for street improvements and better sanitation. After a seventeen-year absence, the dreaded scourge of cholera reappeared in 1849. Scattered cases occurred every year from 1850 to 1853, and in 1854 it struck more savagely than ever before. Since cholera was regarded as a "filth disease," there were urgent demands for sanitary reform.[10] In the winter of 1851-52, the city was beset by a pestilential fever. The fever was mistakenly thought to be malarial, though symptoms descriptive of typhoid fever, influenza, and typhus were also recorded. J. Henry Clark, a prominent local physician, traced the origin of the fever to odors arising from the Newark meadows.

While nothing could be done about the meadows, Clark warned that the existence of filth and stagnant ponds within the community was equally as dangerous and might at any time give rise to an epidemic.[11]

The deplorable condition of the streets was forcibly impressed upon the city fathers during a visit by the Hungarian patriot, Lajos Kossuth, on April 21, 1852. The event was marred by a spring torrent and by a demonstration of citizens angered by the city government's indifference to their appeals for municipal improvements. An ingenious plot was hatched. Just as the mayor started to welcome Kossuth and his procession at city hall, a boat dragged by horses appeared, and a trumpet proclaimed the arrival of "King Mud" and his royal retinue. The mayor's speech was drowned out, and the mud which rolled away from the boat's bow nearly reached the assembled dignitaries. A wagon crowded with curious onlookers collapsed, dumping twenty-five residents into the ooze. The city luminary who was leading the procession had his mount bolt and he also landed in the mud. A humorous account stated that "Kossuth was informed these events were not on the regular program."[12]

Kossuth's memorable visit was the last straw. By now, the harassed citizens had had a surfeit of mud and low comedy. At first it was proposed to alter all street grades to conform to a single grade.[13] When this remedy appeared to be unfeasible, a citizens' committee was formed to investigate the problem. The committee found great neglect everywhere in keeping the

> gutters properly cleaned out. In many streets the gutters are filled with dirt and filth to the top of the curbstones, so that the water has no passage; ... consequently, the streets are filled in wet weather with mud and water. This is the chief cause of the wretched condition of many of our streets.[14]

The committee proposed that the streets be paved or macadamized. It also suggested that the Morris Canal, which ran through the center of the city, be lowered so that it could be utilized for drainage, ignoring the likelihood that the canal would soon become an open sewer.[15]

Street improvements were one solution to achieving better sanitation and drainage. Another solution was suggested in a plan adopted by the common council about a week after the committee had made its report, in which it was proposed to build underground sewers to empty into the Passaic River. The plan had been devised after lengthy consultation with engineers employed in sewer construction in New York City. The council argued cogently that sewers "would provide permanent, useful and durable public works with little or no upkeep."[16]

In 1852 Newark began paving its streets and highways with round stones. By 1858 there was a little less than sixteen and one half miles of paved streets, about one-fifth the mileage of the city's thoroughfares. Work on the first sewer was begun in 1853 and completed in 1854. To accelerate construction, the city was authorized in 1857 to build sewers upon petition of a majority of the property owners fronting the proposed route.[17]

With the approach of the 1860 presidential election, Newarkers seemed to forget about their drainage problems as they became absorbed in the national drama over slavery. The threat of secession alarmed them because the South was their best customer. Southern plantations consumed nearly 65 percent of Newark's industrial output, no small consideration to a community that made its living from manufacturing. Democratic newspapers warned that Lincoln's election would bring ruin. Indeed, Lincoln ran poorly in Newark and did not secure the support of its citizens until the bombardment of Fort Sumter.[18]

The mass unemployment which had been predicted materialized during the first eighteen months of the civil war, but disappeared with the influx of war contracts. Newark's large population of skilled artisans made it an ideal center for the manufacture of war goods. Skillfully, city firms shifted their production from carriages and leather goods to outfitting the Union army. Lucrative contracts also resulted in a large accumulation of capital and began the process whereby local contractors and businessmen became industrial entrepreneurs whose market was the entire nation.[19]

Newark emerged from the civil war as an industrial giant. More than half of its wage earners in 1880 were employed in industry. Several new industries achieved prominence, revealing a shift from workshop to factory and from individually crafted wares to mass-produced goods. Newark was booming.[20]

Foreign-born immigrants provided the muscle and the hands for the factories. Nearness to New York City, the nation's largest port of entry, and the opportunities afforded unskilled labor in industry and municipal construction were powerful magnets attracting immigrants in large numbers to Newark. Thus, from 1860 to 1890 the city's population swelled from 72,000 to 190,000, an increase of more than 250 percent.[21]

Rapid development posed many problems for which there was virtually no planning. Though population increase put great pressure on municipal services, the city continued to provide them in a largely ad hoc manner. Moreover, while the perplexities of an urban-industrial society required additional government responsibilities, the triumph after the civil war of laissez-faire capitalism narrowly restricted the role of government to protecting property and maintaining order. Governmental concern did not extend to dilapidated housing or to hazardous employment, for these were areas in which individuals were expected to fend for themselves. It was thought that living conditions would gradually improve as the free enterprise system increased the wealth of society. Similarly, any imbalance in the community, as, for example, between population density and public transportation, or between suburban growth and inner-city decay, was left to be solved by the private money-making ventures that molded Newark's development.[22]

As population increased and the older areas of city became congested, real estate promoters began securing title to the western heights. In the years immediately following the civil war speculative mania swept the region and

> improvements ran mad.... Streets were laid out in pasture lands where they would not be needed for many years to come,.... Sewers were built in streets that were not graded, and while all this was going on, the center of the city was neglected.[23]

The curbing and grading of streets and the filling in of watercourses impeded drainage in the suburban uplands. Unable to find an outlet for their wastes, developers converted vacant lots into sewage repositories, endangering health and threatening property values. When citizens complained, the common council responded by undertaking an extensive program of sewer construction.[24]

The outlay of large sums of money for public improvements came to an abrupt end during the panic of 1873. Saddled with property they could not sell, promoters lost their zeal for speculation, and the construction of sewers was not fully revived for several years.[25]

With the return of prosperity in the early 1880's, property owners and civic and business leaders again began pleading for the building of additional sewers. "Our city," declared the president of the board of trade in 1884,

> has now reached a period where improvement in the system of our sewerage and the proper drainage of our meadows has become one of the vital questions to be met and determined. As to what is or is not done in this matter the growth of our city will be advanced or retarded.... Stagnant waters and imperfect sewerage means sickness and disease and an increased death rate and all this besides distress and sorrow means injury to our reputation as a healthful city and cause more ... loss to property interests [than] many times ... the cost of applying the remedy.[26]

The board of trade demonstrated how seriously it viewed the matter by employing a group of engineers to study Newark's sewer needs.[27]

For many years the sewerage question was entangled in the medical controversy over the origin of disease. Most physicians believed that disease was caused by "miasma," a loose term used to describe the noxious vapors emanating from decaying organic matter. That polluted air caused epidemics seemed apparent to physicians as far back as Hippocrates. When many persons suddenly became ill, there had to be a single cause — the air they all breathed. And, as the experience of the nineteenth century demonstrated, cities with their mounds of decomposing offal, garbage, and night soil were particularly subject to epidemics.[28]

The miasmatic theory of disease was challenged by Dr. John Snow, a distinguished London anaesthetist, in his study of cholera. He argued that cholera was caused by a specific poison which attacked the intestines and was excreted in the feces of the patient. Epidemics occurred, he asserted, when the patient's feces found its way into the water supply. In 1854 he had an opportunity to test his hypothesis, when cholera raged near Broad Street, London, killing 500 persons within a radius of 250 yards. Snow traced the origin of the epidemic to a polluted well. Simply by breaking the pump handle, he was able to end the outbreak. Shortly thereafter Snow demonstrated that almost all of London's cholera could be traced to one water company that obtained its supply from the sewage polluted lower section of the Thames River. The subscribers of London's other water company, whose intake pipes were located further upstream, remained free of the disease.[29]

What Snow did for cholera, William Budd and others accomplished for typhoid fever. Through the use of field studies, statistical evidence was obtained indicating that typhoid fever was caused by a minute organism which was transmitted through the fecal-oral route. Nevertheless, the miasmatic theory continued to exert a powerful influence. No one had ever looked under a microscope at the micro-organism responsible for typhoid fever much less identify it as the sole cause of the disease.[30]

The leading advocate of the miasmatic theory after the civil war was a German scientist, Professor Max von Pettenkofer. One of the most prominent figures in nineteenth-century medicine, he is best known for his pioneering studies in experimental hygiene. As health officer of Munich, Pettenkofer secured a new water supply and improved sanitation, effecting a marked reduction in the city's death rate. He was a convert of Snow but with this difference: he believed that the excreta of cholera victims was not dangerous unless allowed to ferment or germinate in the watery subsoil or in sewers. While accepting the notion of the specificity of disease, Pettenkofer maintained that epidemics could only occur where the necessary environmental conditions prevailed. He was convinced that sewers were dangerous for two reasons: (1) they hindered the drainage of the subsoil, increasing the likelihood of an epidemic; and (2) when not properly trapped, they emitted deadly sewer gas.[31]

Gradually the germ theory of disease began to gain ground against that of the miasmists. During the 1860's Louis Pasteur demonstrated the role of micro-organisms in fermentation and Joseph Lister established an antiseptic method of surgery which saved the lives of countless patients who otherwise would have died of post-operation infection. In the 1880's Robert Koch provided the long-awaited laboratory proof of the germ origin of disease. Soon bacteria were identified as the causes of several of man's most frightful diseases. The discovery in the early twentieth century of the part played by the carrier and the insect vector in transmitting infection provided the final missing links in the germ theory of disease and completed the rout of the miasmists.[32]

Meanwhile, the cause of sewer construction in Newark received an important boost in 1880, when Edgar Holden, president of the board of directors of the Mutual Benefit Life Insurance Company, revealed the city's poor health record in his treatise, *Mortality and sanitary records of Newark, New Jersey, 1859-1877.*[33] At the time there was widespread belief that sewer gas was responsible for cholera, diphtheria, scarlet fever, and other epidemic diseases. Thus, Newark mayor Henry J. Yates was convinced that much of the municipality's illness was caused by improperly constructed sewers and faulty drainage. In his annual message for 1878, Yates raised the question as to whether homeowners should be compelled to run pipes from drains to or above house roofs, where the gasses could be passed off safely. The mayor believed that roof pipes would protect the health of households while bringing about better ventilation of poorly trapped sewers.[34]

Holden also tended to think that sewers were detrimental to health. On two maps of Newark for the years 1872 and 1876, he plotted the location of every death from "preventable diseases" and the state of sewer development and was surprised to find an inverse correlation between sewers and fatalities. Similarly, a third map, "Showing the made land and the Different Depth of Filling and also the Old Water Courses," indicated that the death rate was lower in areas drained by sewers than in neighborhoods served by privies.[35] "In summing up the results of the investigation," Holden wrote, "I have been struck by the fact that theories, however plausible on the subject of a city's sanitary surroundings, are valueless against stubborn facts and figures."[36]

In deciding whether to live downtown or to move to the suburbs,

Newark residents had to weigh the advantages of more spacious houses and rural surroundings against a temporary loss of city services. Residents of Roseville, located on the western edge of Newark, chose trees and quiet over sewers, but they began to regret their decision when during the 1880's malaria and typhoid fever became endemic in the area. Community leaders blamed the increased sickness on the presence of disease-breeding filth. The Roseville Improvement Association in its annual report for 1883 pleaded with the Newark municipal fathers to extend sewerage to the Roseville border. Addressing itself also to Roseville property owners who opposed increased public expenditures, the Association declared that sewerage justified higher taxes since without health all the amenities of suburban life were a mirage. Sewers, it concluded, would provide a permanent relief from the malarial exhalations of Roseville's foul-smelling cesspools.[37]

In 1886 the *Sunday Call* reported that sewers were gaining support because of their supposed health benefits and attributed this development to the influence of Holden's treatise on mortality and sanitation.[38] At the same time there was a rapid increase in the demand for water closets and other bathroom fixtures. Indoor plumbing was becoming a standard feature in the construction of new houses and a necessity for the middle-class market. With the consequent increase in per capita consumption of water, it seems unlikely that the introduction of sewers could have been long delayed despite lingering fears that they might be dangerous.[39]

Newark was badly in need of sewerage. Only 49 miles of sewers existed in 1883, as contrasted with 131 miles of improved streets. About two-thirds of the city's residents, including many of those living in the central downtown area, were dependent upon privies and cesspools.[40] "Certain sections of our city are in such need of sewers," reported the board of health four years later, "as to constitute a constant source of danger and of high mortality to those in the immediate vicinity."[41]

Privies had been erected in Newark without regard for public comfort and safety. A house-to-house survey undertaken by the board of health in 1885 revealed that privies were often made of wood or had open bottoms and sides permitting their contents to contaminate the earth.[42] Fecal containers were not cleaned until the smell became intolerable or the night soil threatened to spill over the sides. Even worse, many homeowners had wells situated near cesspools and outhouses. The hazard posed by privies was somewhat exaggerated by the *Sunday Call*, which reported that the typhoid fever germs lurking in the excreta

> may be carried by the rains into streams from which drinking water is to be taken for the city. They may be conveyed into the human

stomach through the milk of cows which pasture upon the polluted ground and drink the tainted water. The germs, dried by the summer sun, may be driven over the city by the winds, or they may come to us in the ice cut from the shallow ponds which drain the land upon which night-soil has been deposited.[43]

A scavenger was employed by the city to remove night soil. To make his work easier, the city authorized the daytime cleaning of privies, provided the work was done under cover, away from the sun's destructive rays. Other than this restriction, the scavenger was a free agent.[44]

Unhappily, the scavenger did not reciprocate the favors bestowed upon him by the city. On the contrary, night soil was removed in a careless manner that offended the sensibilities of citizens. Excreta oozed from his wagons and its smell filled the air. A succinct analysis of the situation was made by the *Sunday Call*, when it asserted that the city could not

> hope for a remedy from a body of men [the common council] who are afraid of putting a few of their night soil scavenger constituents to an inconvenience....
>
> we need an ordinance to compel the use of some odorless system in cleansing out-houses. The present systems are merely travesties of the original plan, and an awning made of several old gunnybags gives the scavengers a license to perform their disgusting work by daylight.[45]

At Newark's request, a state law was enacted in 1882 making it easier for cities and property owners to secure sewers. The statute stipulated the construction of sewers upon the petition of any number of property owners along the route of the proposed sewer, provided not more than 50 percent of the affected parties objected. Municipalities were authorized to pay the cost of new sewers by the sale of three year Temporary Improvement Certificates, or bonds. The financing provision of the law was amended in 1886 to enable local governing councils to refinance the certificates by floating new bonds, thereby removing virtually all financial restraints on sewer building.[46]

The city's sewerage was augmented by private sewers. Newark authorities encouraged the installation of private sewers when the delays and expenses attendant upon the construction of public sewers threatened to preclude their undertaking.[47] Building a public sewer was a cumbersome affair. First, the common council's resolution of intention to construct one had to be published in at least two newspapers for ten consecutive days to provide time for property owners to object. Upon completion of the sewer, commissioners were appointed by the circuit court to assess the benefits conferred by the sewer. Property owners were then given three months in which to present objections to the commissioners, whose decision could be appealed to the circuit court for final adjudication.[48] The cost of advertisements, commission fees, and other miscellaneous expenses was between $350 and $400, which in some instances was more than the cost of the sewer. The city government in 1885 acknowledged the importance of private sewers by placing their construction under the supervision of the municipal surveyor. For the most part, private sewers were of two types: (1) very short sewers, from 50 to 200 feet in length; and (2) sewers built by land companies through large tracts of land being developed for sale.[49] By 1910, private sewers accounted for about 12 percent of the mileage of Newark sewers.[50]

Sewer construction, however, was not unopposed and for a time was successfully impeded. Sewers were resisted for several reasons: while a sewer connection increased the value of a house, property owners opposed them because the gain could not be realized until the house was sold, whereas the sewer had to be paid for annually in hard cash; given the poor construction of houses, home owners also objected because the indoor plumbing to which sewers were connected froze during cold weather. Moreover, sewers were expensive. The replacement value of Newark sewers in 1908 was several million dollars. Because of the opposition of Mayor Joseph E. Haynes and the editor of the influential *Sunday Call*, both of whom evinced an almost morbid fear of incurring debt, relatively few sewers were built between the years 1883 and 1893.[51]

In resisting appeals for more sewers, Mayor Haynes and the *Sunday Call* pointed out the inability of the city to pay for existing sewers. Often, after waiting several years for payment of sewer assessments, the city had to settle for one-quarter to one-half of the bill (which by then included interest on the assessment). Unable to pay off the bonds issued in 1882, Newark was constrained to issue new long-term bonds at the high interest rate of 6 percent.[52]

The manner in which sewer assessments were determined antagonized property owners, making the task of sewerage proponents that much more difficult. Property owners could only be assessed for the actual benefit derived from the sewer. In the case of laterals, or service sewers, the assessments were levied on the properties abutting the sewer. For collection sewers, intercepting sewers, and trunk sewers, assessments were levied on all property located within the drainage district served by the sewer.[53] But how does one measure the benefits gained from the installation of a sewer? The *Sunday Call* commented that most cities have adopted a sewerage plan for the whole community, with a consistent plan of paying the cost. They have fixed the price of sewer connection at so much a lot, or they have placed the cost of all sewers on the entire municipality, or they have assessed each lot according to frontage for the cost of the sewer, and charged the city at large with trunk sewer construction.[54]

In Newark no general plan existed, the method of sewer assessment having "grown upon the city." Since assessors had to treat each case individually, not infrequently the assessments were challenged and taken to court.[55]

Sewer construction in Newark proceeded without the benefit of a master plan and was nearly bereft of any planning whatsoever. Sewers were built "only as the needs of separate localities forced themselves upon public attention."[56] The municipal government did not even possess an accurate topographical map showing the region's watercourses, valleys, and elevations. Without such a map, engineers had no way of determining the best locations and outlets for sewers. When asked about the status of the city's sewerage program, the mayor's secretary admitted there was no general drainage plan covering the entire city, and that each locality was being serviced "according to its special requirements."[57]

Lack of planning delayed construction, complicated maintenance, and increased costs. In the absence of a master plan, sanitary engineers were hard put to determine the size, gradation, and depth of proposed sewers. Moreover, no records existed of private sewers built before 1885.[58] In some instances sewers were laid under unpaved streets where they were easily clogged by street dirt washing into them through the inlets. Moreover, because of faulty planning, sewers designed to carry storm water had to be used to carry sewage as well. The older sewers were made of earthenware and brick and were porous and expensive to maintain. Finally, decomposing deposits in poorly graded sewers emitted offensive odors making life unbearable for nearby residents. The only time sewers were adequately flushed was during a heavy rainfall.[59] Mayor J. A. Lebkuecher summarized the reasons for Newark's patchwork sewerage by declaring that "sewers have been constructed in piecemeal, at excessive expense, and in a way that has precluded the idea of permanent utility."[60]

Inadequate sewerage was an especially troublesome problem in the flat, low-lying southeastern quadrant of the city. The sewers in this section had little fall and emptied into sluggish tidal creeks which when swollen by high tide or heavy rains overflowed their banks and backed up on the meadows.⁶¹ "Under these circumstances," wrote one newspaper,

> it has been found almost impossible to get rid of the sewage. For the greater part of the twenty-four hours the sewage does not flow out at all, but remains dormant as in cesspools, from which, under the action of the sun, all kinds of foul odors arise and diseases are bred.⁶²

In June 1884, a newspaperman sent to investigate complaints in the area reported that "the stench arising from the black and sluggish water was so overpowering that only a strict sense of duty prevented a hasty retreat."⁶³ In one creek the reporter found the bloated carcasses of two large dogs, lying almost motionless upon the water, "upon which a cloud of flies were banquetting," while in an adjacent creek boys swam in the "dark green scum" unmindful or perhaps oblivious to the danger.⁶⁴

The matter became a *cause célèbre* and the object of the most ambitious public improvement undertaken in Newark to that date. It was first proposed to rid the area of sewage by harnessing the tide. This had been done successfully on the English coast in areas where the tide reached twenty feet. Despite warnings from experts that the plan was unworkable and absurd, the city forged ahead at a cost of $75,000. Two ditches were dug out to Newark Bay, one to hold the sewage, and the other to catch and impound the tide.

As had been predicted, the scheme was an utter fiasco. The common council now engaged the services of two prominent engineers who recommended the construction of a great intercepting sewer to service the sewers on the meadows. Work on the project was completed in 1887 at a cost of over $600,000. The sewage was brought to a pumping station on the edge of the meadows where it was lifted and pumped through culverts laid beneath the ground to an outlet some 200 feet into Newark Bay.⁶⁵ The success of the project led to proposals for linking up the great intercepting sewer to trunk sewers to be built in the city's other natural drainage districts. The pumps on the meadows had a capacity of about thirty million gallons per day, which was more than the combined sewage flow of the city. Through this scheme it was hoped to end Newark's chaotic sewerage and to reduce the pollution of the Passaic River, from which the city drew its drinking water. However, when in 1889, a new water supply was acquired, Newark lost its incentive for cleansing the Passaic River, and nothing more was heard of the plan.⁶⁶

Throughout the 1880's and early 1890's sewer construction failed to keep pace with the city's expansion. Though the city's sewerage more than doubled, there were more miles of paved streets without sewers at the end of Mayor Haynes' administration than there had been at its beginning.[67] In his inaugural message of 1894, Mayor Lebkuecher observed that Newark's sewers, "built in the main without regard to general utility or future requirements, fall far short of our needs, and the lack of them, in many sections, is a menace to the public health."[68]

But Lebkuecher was unaware of forces that would shortly bring about a dramatic increase in sewer construction. For one thing, the new science of bacteriology proved beyond a shadow of a doubt the perils of allowing excreta to accumulate in or near population centers. Then, too, homeowners were increasingly insisting on sewerage. Public health arguments and the growing demand for indoor sanitary facilities soon proved irresistible. In 1890 the board of health was authorized to require sewer connections in houses on streets with sewer lines.[69] Armed with this authority, the board began a vigorous drive to rid the city of outhouses, cesspools, manure pits, and other similar remnants of an unsanitary age. The years from 1894 to 1910 mark the greatest era of sewer construction in Newark. Approximately 200 miles of sewers were built, almost double the mileage which had heretofore existed.[70] To rectify the city's crazy-quilt sewer pattern, drainage districts were established and a series of large intercepting sewers were built.[71] Sewerage was extended to all areas of Newark except for the distant meadows. Devoid of human habitation, they were not in need of a sewage disposal system until World War I, when war plants were constructed in the area, and then septic tanks were used.[72] By 1919, 95 percent of the improved area of Newark was provided with sewers.[73]

Sewer building in Newark, 1854-1918[74]

Year ending	No. of miles of sewers
1854	—
1870	12.5
1883	49.0
1893	112.0
1910	310.6
1918	314.5

After considerable difficulties, sanitary reformers had succeeded in establishing facilities for ridding Newark of its liquid wastes. Yet the progress suggested by the extension of the city's sewerage was partly an illusion, since many citizens in areas served by sewers were still forced to rely on privies and cesspools. Though by 1919 nearly every section of Newark had sewers, the construction of sewer mains did not insure the use of flush toilets. The city's responsibility for providing sanitary services ended at the street line. A property owner could tap in at the curb, but it was at his own expense. This division of responsibility worked to the satisfaction of a majority of city dwellers, but left the poor without adequate sanitary facilities. Well-to-do home-owners were willing to pay the small costs involved in obtaining the latest improvements, but this was not true of slumlords, who generally provided the least amount of services the law allowed. The board of health was authorized to require property owners abutting on a sewer to tap in but was unwilling to risk antagonizing politically influential landlords. In a survey of Newark's impoverished "Ironbound" district, Willard D. Price, a social worker in the community, discovered that several old houses did not have water and sewer connections, which he attributed to the discretionary powers given the board of health in enforcing the sanitary code.

> The opportunities afforded by such powers for political and commercial favoritism are obvious, [wrote Price] and it is also obvious to anyone living in "The Ironbound District" that such opportunities are not always lost.[75]

Fear of disease and the comforts of indoor plumbing led Newark during the years 1854-1918 to construct a sewer system of over 300 miles valued at several million dollars. While sewer lines from the house to the street could have been provided at little extra cost and while tax monies had partly paid for the system, laissez-faire scriptures which removed private property from public policy and the unwillingness of affluent citizens to extend to the working class housing standards equal to that which they enjoyed prevented the city from making this humanitarian addition to its sewerage system. Thousands of city dwellers were thus denied the rudimentary essentials of a safe, sanitary environment because they were poor.[76]

[1] Samuel Harry Popper, "Newark, N.J., 1870-1910: chapters in the evolution of an American metropolis" (unpublished Ph.D. dissertation, New York University, 1952), p. 305.

[2] U.S., Bureau of the Census, *Tenth census of the United States, 1880: social statistics of cities* (Washington, 1886), Pt. I, 708-709.

[3] John T. Cunningham, *Newark* (Newark, 1966), p. 20; *Newark Daily Advertiser*, January 4, 6, 1847; April 17, 1852.

[4] *Newark Daily Advertiser*, January 4, 1847; April 9-10, 15, 1853.

[5] *Ibid.*, August 7, 1852, August 13, 1853.

[6] *Ibid.*

[7] *Newark Evening News*, September 6, 1883.

[8] *Newark Daily Advertiser*, August 7-16, 1853.

[9] *Report of the engineers to the special committee on sewerage, August 1, 1884* (Newark, 1884), pp. 8-9; Popper, "Newark, 1870-1910," p. 306.

[10] *Newark Daily Advertiser*, July 8, 12, 24, 28, August 24, 1854.

[11] *Ibid.*, May 13, 18, 1852.

[12] David L. Pierson, *Narratives of Newark, 1866-1919* (Newark, 1917), p. 276.

[13] *Newark Daily Advertiser*, May 14, 18, 1852.

[14] *Ibid.*, July 29, 1852.

[15] *Ibid.*

[16] *Ibid.*, August 7, 1852.

[17] Newark, *Charter of Newark and revised ordinances* (1858), pp. 58, 212-221.

[18] Cunningham, *Newark*, pp. 152-154.

[19] *Ibid.*, pp. 153-154; Popper, "Newark, 1870-1910," pp. 13-14.

[20] Popper, "Newark, 1870-1910," pp. 13-14.

[21] Cunningham, *Newark*, pp. 201-208; Popper, "Newark, 1870-1910," pp. 63, 126-135.

[22] Cunningham, *Newark*, pp. 222-223; Popper, "Newark, 1870-1910," p. 270.

[23] Anon., *Newark and its leading businessmen* (Newark, 1891), p. 12.

[24] Popper, "Newark, 1870-1910," p. 306. The project was made possible by the acquisition of a large new water supply in 1870.

[25] Cunningham, *Newark*, p. 222; Newark, *The mayor's message together with the reports of the city officers of the city of Newark, N.J., 1886, mayor's message*, pp. 44-45. Some reports of city officers were also published as separate volumes. When citing a report of a city department or officer that was published together with the mayor's message the citation will appear as follows: *Newark annual reports, year, name of reporting unit.*

[26] *Newark Evening News*, January 10, 1884.

[27] Popper, "Newark, 1870-1910," p. 308.

[28] Richard Harrison Shryock, *Medicine and society in America: 1660-1860* (New York, 1960), pp. 100, 134, 161.

[29] Charles-Edward Amory Winslow, *Man and epidemics* (Princeton, 1952), pp. 271-276; Charles E. Rosenberg, *The cholera years: the United States in 1832, 1849, and 1866* (Chicago, 1962), pp. 193-194.

[30] Wilson G. Smillie, *Public health, its promise for the future: a chronicle of the development of public health in the United States, 1607-1914* (New York, 1955), pp. 342-350.

[31] Charles-Edward Amory Winslow, *The conquest of epidemic diseases: a chapter in the history of ideas* (Princeton, 1943), pp. 311, 316; Rosenberg, *Cholera*, p. 194.

[32] George Rosen, *A history of public health* (New York, 1957), pp. 258-259, 287-288, 311-321.

[33] Edgar Holden, *Mortality and sanitary records of Newark, N.J., 1859-1879: a report presented to the president and director of the Mutual Benefit Life Insurance Company, January, 1880* (Newark, 1880), pp. 113-114.

[34] *Newark annual reports, 1878, board of health*, p. 28.

[35] Holden, *Mortality and sanitary records of Newark*, pp. 24ff.

[36] *Ibid.*, p. 24.

[37] Roseville Improvement Association, *Annual report of the secretary, 1883* (Newark, 1883), pp. 2-3.

[38] *Sunday Call* (Newark), August 8, 1886.
[39] *Ibid.*, December 28, 1884.
[40] *Newark Daily Journal*, August 7, 9, 1883; *Newark annual reports, 1883, board of health*, p. 426.
[41] *Newark annual reports, 1887, board of health*, pp. 475-476.
[42] *Newark Annual Reports, 1885, board of health*, p. 597.
[43] *Sunday Call*, March 1, 1885.
[44] Lott Southard, "Drainage and sewerage of the city of Newark, and their relation to the causation of diseases," *Transactions of the Medical Society of New Jersey, 1877* (hereafter *Trans. MSNJ*), pp. 198-199.
[45] *Sunday Call*, March 1, 1885. The board of health was also critical of the situation. See *Newark annual reports, 1886, board of health*, pp. 564-567. At this time the Odorless Excavating Machine was in operation in Boston. The apparatus consisted of a pumping mechanism, hose, and covered carts.
[46] New Jersey, *Legislative acts* (Trenton, 1882), pp. 60-65 (1886), pp. 119-120; *Newark annual reports, 1886, mayor's message*, pp. 44-45, *1892*, p. 7.
[47] *Newark annual reports, 1883, board of health*, p. 401.
[48] New Jersey, *Legislative acts* (Trenton, 1882), pp. 60-65; *Sunday Call*, December 28, 1884.
[49] *Newark annual reports, 1885, board of health*, p. 803; *1890, mayor's message*, p. 10; *1910, board of health*, p. 847; *Annual report of the Newark board of health, 1894*, p. 21.
[50] Popper, "Newark, 1870-1910," p. 309.
[51] *Sunday Call*, December 28, 1884, August 26, 1888, February 8, 1891; *Newark Evening News*, November 19, 1889.
[52] *Sunday Call*, December 28, 1884.
[53] *Ibid.*; Bureau of Municipal Research, New York, "A survey of the government, finances, and administration of the city of Newark, New Jersey" (November 1, 1919), pp. 318-319, Newark Public Library, New Jersey Reference Division (hereafter Bureau of Municipal Research, N.Y., "Survey").
[54] *Sunaay Call*, February 5, 1911.
[55] *Ibid.*
[56] *Annual report of the Newark board of health, 1894*, p. 19.
[57] *Report of the engineers*, p. 28.
[58] *Newark Evening News*, April 24, 1886, June 18, 1887, June 30, 1889; *Newark annual reports, 1885, board of health*, p. 803.
[59] Southard, "Drainage and sewerage of Newark," pp. 198-199; *Newark annual reports, 1883, board of health*, p. 426; *Newark Evening News*, June 18, 1887.
[60] *Annual report of the Newark board of health, 1894*, p. 21.
[61] New Jersey, Board of Health, *Annual report for 1880* (hereafter *ARNJBH*), p. 124; *Newark Daily Advertiser*, May 8, 1885; *Newark Annual Reports, 1883, board of health*, pp. 43-45.
[62] *Newark Daily Advertiser*, May 8, 1885.
[63] *Newark Evening News*, June 10, 1884.
[64] *Ibid.*
[65] *ARNJBH, 1884*, pp. 13-14, 189-190, *1887*, p. 187; *Newark Evening News*, June 18, 1884, June 18, 1887.
[66] *ARNJBH, 1884*, pp. 189-190; *Newark Daily Advertiser*, January 9, 1889; *Newark Evening News*, June 18, 1887. In 1891 it was revealed that shoddy construction had caused numerous breaks in the sewer. There were also suggestions of impropriety in the awarding of the contract.
[67] *Newark Daily Journal*, August 7, 9, 1883; *Annual report of the board of health, 1894*, p. 20.
[68] *Annual report of the board of health, 1894*, p. 5.
[69] Newark, *Supplement to the sanitary code . . . 1889*, sec. 5.
[70] *Annual report of the Newark board of health, 1894*, p. 20; *Newark annual reports, 1910, board of health*, p. 574.

[71] Frank John Urquhart, *A history of the city of Newark, New Jersey* (3 vols.; New York, 1913), II, 630; Bureau of Municipal Research, N.Y., "Survey," pp. 588-601.

[72] *Newark annual reports, 1915, board of health,* p. 985; see also report for 1916, pp. 1, 273.

[73] Bureau of municipal research, N.Y., "Survey," p. 588.

[74] Newark, Board of Education, *Newark study leaflets* (1914), No. 27, *Sewerage and its disposal,* p. 3; *Newark annual reports, 1870, mayor's message,* p. 11; *Newark Daily Journal,* August 7, 9, 1883; *Annual report of the board of health, 1894,* p. 20; *Newark annual reports, 1910, board of health,* p. 574; Bureau of Municipal Research, N.Y., "Survey," p. 588.

[75] Willard D. Price, *The Ironbound District: a study of a district in Newark, N.J.,* (Newark, 1912), pp. 24-25.

[76] Sam Bass Warner, Jr., *The urban wilderness: a history of the American city* (New York, 1972), pp. 202-205.

"Out of Sight, Out of Mind"
The Environment and Disposal of Municipal Refuse, 1860-1920

Martin V. Melosi*

THE unprecedented growth of American industry in the nineteenth century produced a marked increase in the size and number of urban centers in the United States. Where one of every four Americans had lived in a city or town in 1860, one of every two Americans was a city-dweller by 1910. The impact of "the rise of the city" was phenomenal. Urbanization epitomized the transformation of the United States from an agrarian, provincial society into an industrial, national culture and forged a new way of life for many Americans. Yet, urbanization did not end all vestiges of rural life, and even magnified many previously existing problems such as crime, housing, and public health. The disposal of solid waste was one of those problems which became a perpetual affliction of urban life.

Refuse is an age-old legacy of human society. With the emergence of congested cities, the mounds of public waste posed an increasingly serious menace that men were forced to acknowledge, if not immediately to reckon with. Not until the 1880s in the United States did the question of municipal refuse become so uncomfortably evident that a number of health experts and others publicly declared that "something had to be done."[1] This realization led to the first serious attempts in the United States to handle the collection and disposal of municipal solid waste on a major scale.

And a colossal problem it was! The character of municipal refuse was complex and the quantities were enormous. Generally speaking, there were seven types of solid waste: 1) garbage —

---

*This article won the Dr. George P. Hammond prize of $150 for the best paper submitted by a graduate student in the 1972 Student Essay Contest. Martin Melosi, a member of Beta Psi chapter at the University of Montana, is now at the Beta Alpha chapter, University of Texas at Austin.

[1] See William F. Morse, *The Collection and Disposal of Municipal Waste* (New York, 1908), v; George A. Soper, *Modern Methods of Street Cleaning* (New York, 1907), 163.

organic household or restaurant waste; 2) rubbish — inorganic waste such as paper, cans, and old shoes, 3) night soil or human excrement; 4) stable and street manure; 5) dead animals; 6) street sweepings; and 7) ashes.[2] Since each type was unique, individuals responsible for collection had to decide what methods, techniques, and equipment were necessary to deal with the "rejectamenta." The problem of collecting the refuse also posed a more fundamental question: Who was responsible? The householder? A private business? Public officials? This question plagued American cities for years without clear resolution.

Solving the problem of collection, however, would not solve the whole problem of municipal waste. Cities needed to decide upon a method(s) of final disposition of the refuse, taking into account geographical, climatic, economic, and technical considerations. A variety of methods were available — some primitive, some innovative — but few cities employed a systematic program of disposal prior to World War I.

The staggering quantities of municipal refuse graphically demonstrated the severity of the problem. For Manhattan alone, at the turn of the century, an average of 612 tons of garbage was collected daily — 1,100 tons on the heaviest days, 220 tons on the lightest.[3] Translated into national figures, one expert estimated at about the same time that each American contributed 300-1,200 pounds of ashes, 100-180 pounds of garbage, and 50-100 pounds of rubbish yearly.[4] Human waste was only part of the problem. The horse, the major source of transportation through the early twentieth century, contributed mountains of refuse. George A. Soper, a leading civil engineer, estimated that in every working day of eight hours, 1,000 horses deposited about 500 gallons of urine and ten tons of dung on the pavement.[5] Another report stated that the approximately 82,000 horses, mules, and cows maintained in the city of Chicago produced 600,000 tons of manure yearly.[6]

Americans eventually came to grips with the problem of

---

[2] Some of these types of refuse may be classified under other names according to regional and preferential differences.

[3] The city collected more garbage in the summer months because of the ease of transportation and the abundance of produce available to the consumers at that time of year. See John McGaw Woodbury, "The Wastes of a Great City," *Scribner's Magazine*, XXXIV (October 1903), 392.

[4] Rudolph Hering, "Disposal of Municipal Refuse," *Transactions of the American Society of Civil Engineers*, LIV, 263-308, cited in William Mayo Venable, *Garbage Crematories in America* (New York, 1906), 18-23.

[5] Soper, *Modern Methods of Street Cleaning*, 2.

[6] "Clean Streets and Motor Traffic," *The Literary Digest*, XLIX (September 5, 1914), 413.

Municipal Refuse

municipal solid waste in a forthright manner. Pleas for reform surfaced in the late 1880s initiating a flurry of rhetoric which made refuse disposal a public issue of considerable significance through the early twentieth century. Although recognition of the magnitude of the problem led to some positive action in many communities, the reforming spirit was the active concern of a relatively small group. Influenced by new methods of sanitation practiced in Europe and aware of the deplorable health conditions in most American cities, public health officials and other sanitarians were among the first to call for improved treatment of municipal waste.[7] Brandishing reams of statistics about the high death-rate and the myriad of diseases festering in the cities, the sanitarians sought to make municipal authorities and the public aware of the urgent need for hygienic living conditions. Their primary concern was organic refuse — a major source of urban disease and unsanitary conditions. At their annual meetings during the mid-1880s, the American Public Health Association labeled the disposal of garbage and night soil in populous communities the most significant practical sanitation problem of the time.[8] These pronouncements lent gravity to the general problem of municipal waste.

To some individuals concerned with urban sanitation, resolving the problem of refuse was the duty of "civilized" man. As one commentator put it: "Indeed, there is no more significant distinction between ancient and modern cities than their respective attitudes towards evils of this nature [the garbage problem]."[9] In an article about New York's garbage problem, H. S. Williams observed: "It is quite in order that New York should be grappling with the garbage problem at this time, for almost every other large city in the civilized world is in a similar predicament. . . ."[10] Williams also perceptively noted that no single method of collection suited every city because of the vast differences in the communities and their inhabitants. The level of intelligence of the citizenry was usually the most serious impediment to solving the problem. ("Intelligence" may have been a poor choice of words). Only the more intelligent person, he argued, would prepare garbage properly for collection.[11] As caustic as Williams, John S. Billings characterized the issue clearly:

[7] See "Disposal of Refuse in American Cities," *Scientific American*, LXV (August 29, 1891), 136.
[8] Cited in "Garbage-Cremation," *Science*, XII (December 7, 1888), 265.
[9] G. W. Hosmer, "The Garbage Problem," *Harper's Weekly*, XXXVIII (August 11, 1894), 750.
[10] Williams, "The Disposal of Garbage," *Harper's Weekly*, XXXVIII (September 1, 1894), 835.
[11] *Ibid.*

The Historian

> The great majority of the dwellers in our cities have not, heretofore, taken any active personal interest in the sanitary condition of their respective towns. They may grumble occasionally when some nuisance is forced on their notice, but, as a rule, they look on the city as a sort of hotel, with the details of the management of which they have no desire to become acquainted. They employ certain paid servants to look after municipal affairs: there is a Board of Health, or a Health Officer, whose business it is to prevent or mitigate nuisances, to stop epidemics, and to keep the death-rate low; there are engineers to manage the water works, sewage disposal, etc., and there are newspapers to criticise and instruct the authorities upon any and every possible subject connected with the cleanliness and healthfulness of the place. The individual citizen, if he thinks about the matter at all, usually concludes that this is all that need be done, and that if the results are not wholly satisfactory they must be accepted as the necessary outcome of politics or the weather, and do not involve him in any responsibility. Quite recently, however, there seems to be a growing interest in sanitary matters in our cities, and people are asking whether the death-rates are higher than they ought to be; whether the city is in good condition to resist the introduction or spread of cholera, and to what extent it is worth while to expend money to secure pure water, clean streets, odorless sewers, etc. . . . [12]

Despite the rhetoric of sanitarians, journalists, and others, the state of refuse collection and disposal in the 1880s and early 1890s was deplorable. Methods were erratic; technology in the United States was primitive; most individuals were unconcerned. In New York, street teams carelessly collected the garbage, loaded it on barges, and dumped it at sea. In Philadelphia, contractors, often inefficient and haphazard, were responsible for disposing of the city's wastes. In Chicago, St. Louis, Boston, and Baltimore, much of the refuse was simply carted to open dumps. And in Cleveland, there was no public provision for gathering household garbage at all.[13] "Out of sight, out of mind" was the typical reaction to the problem. And although the sanitarians tried to convince people that refuse was a major breeding ground for disease, almost everyone regarded municipal waste merely as a nuisance, a smell, to be removed from human senses.

The best example of this attitude and certainly the most

---

[12] Billings, "Municipal Sanitation: Defects in American Cities," *The Forum*, XV (May 1893), 304-05.

[13] From a report by Walter V. Hagt, General Sanitation Officer of the Chicago Board of Health, in *Sanitary News*, cited in "Disposal of Refuse in American Cities," *Scientific American*, LXV (August 29, 1891), 136. See also Billings, "Municipal Sanitation in Washington and Baltimore," *The Forum*, XV (August 1893), 727-37.

noisome method of disposal was dumping refuse into water. The practice for many years in New York was to load scows with refuse, tow them beyond the mouth of the harbor, and hope the tide would carry the "stuff" out. Besides the unrecognized danger to marine ecology, waste materials began to fill the harbor approaches, and polluted surrounding beaches. Citizens living on the New York and New Jersey shoreline eventually complained, but for some time the practice was not altered. This method of disposal was popular because it was simple. The ocean was a giant commode, and would swallow the discards of New Yorkers endlessly. As one journalist suggested: "For cities situated on the seaboard this question [refuse disposal] is not such a pressing one, as the refuse can be transported by water sufficiently far from shore, and deposited in the ocean. If it returns on the incoming tide, and is cast on the beach, this may in the future be avoided by carrying it still further...."[14] Dumping continued as a common means of disposal throughout the early twentieth century, though sanitarians unanimously condemned the practice.[15]

Yet some serious interest grew for cremating refuse as a viable alternative to less satisfactory methods of disposal. Although the use of chemical disinfectants to detoxify refuse prevailed in some sections of the United States, the successful use of cremation in England and the influence of American sanitarians inspired the widespread use of fire as a permanent disinfectant. Crematories of all types sprang up throughout the United States after the construction of the first American municipal incinerator in Allegheny, Pennsylvania in 1885. Numerous people extolled cremation as safe, efficient, and economical. The use of crematories in the late nineteenth century indicated, at least, that "out of sight, out of mind" had taken a sophisticated turn.[16]

The "rise of the crematory" also inspired a rash of technological innovations which considerably refined the method. The development of new techniques also had its lighter side. Two very distinctive types of crematories came into vogue in Chicago — the stationary furnace and the portable burner. The former handled much of the major refuse of the city, while the latter traveled the alleys and incinerated refuse. A dispute ensued between George S. Wells, creator of the portable burner, and A. M. Brainard, designer and operator of the stationary furnace, over the relative merits of

---

[14] "Garbage-Cremation," *Science*, XII, 265. See also "The Garbage Problem," *Harper's Weekly*, XXXVIII (July 28, 1894), 711.

[15] Williams, "The Disposal of Garbage," *Harper's Weekly*, XXXVIII, 835.

[16] See Hosmer, "The Garbage Problem," *Harper's Weekly*, XXXVIII, 750; "The Garbage Problem," *Harper's Weekly*, XXXVIII, 711; "Garbage-Cremation," *Science*, XII, 265-66; Morse, *The Collection and Disposal of Municipal Waste*, 99.

each crematory. Brainard, tinged with animosity and prone to cynicism, invited Wells to bring his portable burner to the stationary furnace with the expressed purpose of throwing it into the inferno. Wells responded by wagering $1,000 that he could fill the stationary furnace with ashes in ten days. Neither offer was accepted, but, "... out of this picturesque rivalry grew a startlingly clean condition of alleys in the city."[17]

With the appointment of Colonel George E. Waring, Jr. as Commissioner of the Department of Street-Cleaning in New York City in 1895, refuse disposal took on broader perspectives than sanitation alone. Waring was trained in agricultural chemistry, and devoted his early manhood to scientific agriculture and sewage disposal. The Civil War temporarily curtailed his various projects, but the ambitious and energetic young man worked his way up to the rank of colonel in the Missouri Cavalry of the United States Volunteers. Later he managed the Ogden Farm near Newport for ten years, and eventually turned full-time to the field of municipal engineering and sanitation. He developed a sewer system for Memphis, Tennessee and in 1879 served as special agent for the Tenth Census in charge of urban social statistics. After serving as Street-Cleaning Commissioner of New York from 1895 to 1898, he studied sanitary conditions in Cuba. Soon after returning to New York, he died from yellow fever contracted in Havana. His untimely death cut short an active public service and prolific writing career.[18]

Waring symbolized a shift from viewing refuse as purely a question of sanitation to realizing its other implications as an urban problem. He was infused with the progressive spirit which inspired so many reformers to reconcile long-standing American traditions with the new industrial age. Waring's comprehensive waste disposal program was not only meant to make New York City clean and free from disease, but to make urban life more orderly and aesthetically acceptable. He also sought to make collection and disposal of refuse a completely municipal responsibility. He was not the first to advocate such a change,[19] but was the first to implement it, and thus set standards for similar progress throughout the country.

Immediate reactions to Waring's reforms were not enthusiastic. The sanitarian and former military officer took his task seriously,

---

[17] Lane, "Chicago Garbage-Burning," *Harper's Weekly*, XXXVIII (January 27, 1894), 82. See also "The Traveling Garbage Burner in Chicago," *Scientific American*, LXIX (December 23, 1893), 408.

[18] Soper, "George Edwin Waring," *Dictionary of American Biography*, edited by Dumas Malone, XIX (New York, 1946), 456-57.

[19] Hosmer, "The Garbage Problem," *Harper's Weekly*, XXXVIII, 750.

Municipal Refuse

if not dramatically, and his organization of the Department of Street-Cleaning as a quasi-military outfit drew much ridicule from the press. Criticism soon turned to lavish praise when New Yorkers, for the first time in many years, could walk along uncluttered sidewalks and drive through streets free of garbage and manure. High praise of Waring's handiwork became widespread. As one writer stated: "Before the advent of his ever-memorable administration, the wastes of the city had been removed in a way which would have done credit to a medieval town, but which was shockingly discreditable to the most progressive community in the world." [20]

Until Waring's administration, the Department of Street-Cleaning was a fiasco. Politicians had controlled its finances and used the position of commissioner and other officials as patronage. [21] In an attempt to expose the New York politicians' mishandling of Street-Cleaning Department funds, F. W. Hewes prepared a comparative study of expenditures for street cleaning in ten American cities. [22] New York's outlay of funds was far higher than of any of the other cities surveyed. New York spent 71¢ per capita annually for street cleaning; the next highest cost, in Washington, D.C., was 31¢. In terms of yearly cost per mile of street cleaned, no city spent one fifth as much as New York. [23]

Much of Waring's success as Commissioner of Street-Cleaning came as a result of freeing himself from the politicians. He accepted the job with the positive assurance from Mayor William L. Strong that he would have "his own way." Waring immediately cleared "dead wood" from the department, filling the vacancies primarily with men of military or technical training and experience. He also was inclined to appoint young men; the superintendent of final disposition was twenty-five years old. In hiring men for menial tasks, especially sweepers, he put "a man instead of a voter" on the end of a broom. Waring relentlessly sought to develop an efficient and well-disciplined unit of men and instill an *esprit de corps* ". . . without which," he insisted, "no

---

[20] "The Disposal of New York's Refuse," *Scientific American*, LXXXIX (October 24, 1903), 292. See also Edward D. Very, "Modern Methods of Street Cleaning," *The American City*, VII (November, 1912), 434; Morse, *The Collection and Disposal of Municipal Waste*, 46.

[21] Before 1881, a bureau of the Police Department had been responsible for the cleaning of New York's streets, but the service was inadequate.

[22] The cities surveyed were New York, Buffalo, Chicago, Newark, Cleveland, Brooklyn, Philadelphia, St. Louis, and Washington, D.C. See Hewes, "Street Cleaning," *Harper's Weekly*, XXXIX (March 9, 1895), 233-34.

[23] Hewes qualified these figures by stating that the condition and type of streets found in New York were not substantially different than those in the other cities.

The Historian

organization of men can do its best, either in war or in peace."[24]

Waring's re-organization of the Department involved a full commitment to solving the problem of solid waste. As he stated:

> The "out-of-sight, out-of-mind" principle is an easy one to follow, but it is not an economical one, nor a decent one, nor a safe one. For other and more important reasons than the hope of getting money out of our wastes, should we pursue the study of the treatment of these wastes, and try to devise a less shiftless and uncivilized method than that which we now use.[25]

This statement epitomized Waring's reaction to the refuse issue, and was the basis for his reforms.

Waring urged a "radical change" in the collection of refuse, although he realized that many of the old practices and methods would have to remain until new means were found. His first step was to classify the various types of refuse, and initiate a system of "primary separation," i.e., each householder would be responsible for keeping organic waste, rubbish, and ashes in separate receptacles until the department collected them. In 1896, Mayor Strong assigned forty policemen to the Department of Street-Cleaning to be used to explain "primary separation" to each householder and to see that they complied with the standards.[26] Waring also ordered that householders discontinue the long-standing practice of placing refuse containers on the sidewalks.

In line with his new separation process, Waring advocated that the city not only profit from the collection of garbage and ashes, but rubbish as well. Scavengers ordinarily collected much resalable waste material from private homes. And on the garbage scows, "Scow-trimmers" as they were called, worked through the refuse and picked out items to be resold, such as old shoes, carpets, paper, and rags. Italian immigrants comprised most of the trimmers in New York. According to Waring, Italians were "... a race with a genius for rag-and-bone picking and for subsistency on rejected trifles of food."[27] Until 1878, the city had paid trimmers, allowing

---

[24] Waring, "The Cleaning of a Great City," *McClure's Magazine*, IX (September 1897), 914-17. See also Frank Hunter Potter, "Model Street-Cleaning," *The Outlook*, CXVI (August 1, 1917), 514-15.

[25] Waring, "The Disposal of a City's Waste," *North American Review*, CLXI (July 1895), 52. See also Waring, *Street-Cleaning and the Disposal of a City's Wastes: Methods and Results and the Effect upon Public Health, Public Morals, and Municipal Prosperity* (New York, 1898).

[26] Woodbury, "The Wastes of a Great City," *Scribner's Magazine*, XXXIV, 388-90; Waring, "The Utilization of a City's Garbage," *Cosmopolitan Magazine*, XXIV (February 1898), 411; Waring, "The Disposal of a City's Waste," *North American Review*, CLXI, 52-53.

[27] See Waring, "The Cleaning of a Great City," *McClure's Magazine*, IX, 917-19.

Municipal Refuse

them to keep what they salvaged; from 1878 to 1882, the city let them work through the refuse without cost to either party; beginning in 1882, the city charged a flat rate for the privilege of scavenging. Aware of the profit to be made in scavenging and trimming, Waring recommended that the city assume that phase of the operation. In time, New York took most of the resulting profits.[28]

Waring's most ambitious reforms applied to street cleaning, a monumental headache. Streets were often crudely constructed, easily erodable, especially if they were made of macadam, and improperly drained. Horses were a constant source of aggravation to the sweeper. Crowded conditions and littering compounded the already deplorable situation. Clamor perpetually had arisen from the "respectable areas of the city," but numerous attempts to keep the streets clean had failed miserably.[29] Waring immediately eliminated more than 60,000 unharnessed trucks and wagons abandoned on the public streets — a task most contemporaries believed was impossible. The removal of these vehicles was necessary, he argued, because they made street cleaning difficult, and were often dens of vice and corruption, "a veritable nocturnal hell."[30] Waring also relied heavily on his hierachy of superintendents and foremen to keep a careful eye on the daily street sweeping. Foremen were issued bicycles which increased the area of their surveillance threefold.[31]

To make street cleaning more efficient and thorough, Waring raised the competence, status and *esprit* of the menial workers. He placed more faith in a well-trained, well-disciplined force of men to keep the streets clean, than in any sophisticated machinery. The "White Wings," as the sweepers were called because of their white uniforms, were the department's trademark. The white outfits had no practical value, but symbolized cleanliness like a doctor's smock, and distinguished the sweepers. The feeling of belonging to a group gave the more than 2,000 sweepers and drivers an identity. Since most of the "White Wings" performed so admirably under Waring's leadership, this identity was almost flattering. Rarely were the sweepers of New York looked upon as dregs of society, as most men associated with refuse collection had been previously. The "White Wings" were a distinctive corps with a sublime purpose — to maintain a high level of cleanliness in the city. This

[28] See Waring, "The Disposal of a City's Waste," *North American Review*, CLXI, 49-52.

[29] General Emmons Clark, "Street-Cleaning in Large Cities," *Popular Science Monthly*, XXXVIII (April 1891), 748-55.

[30] Waring, "The Cleaning of a Great City," *McClure's Magazine*, IX, 911-14.

[31] *Ibid.*, 919-21.

The Historian

afforded them self-respect. Waring had also required his men to attend morning inspections, and he initiated yearly parades when the "White Wings" passed in review. The spectacle of the parade, which most New Yorkers enjoyed, continued throughout Waring's administration.[32]

The new Commissioner gave his men other cause to be content with their jobs. As one writer suggested:

> What of "White Wings" himself? He has little cause to complain. Street sweeping by contract went with the machines, and now by law not only has the city to employ him, but to pay him two dollars a day, which must not embrace more than eight hours of work, except in emergencies. The drivers of the rubbish carts get the same. This is more than unskilled labor commands in any other field....[33]

Besides the relatively good pay and working conditions, Waring instituted a viable system of committees to hear grievances and suggestions.[34]

The favorable results of Waring's reforms were soon evident. Collection was more efficient, and the daily cost per mile to clean the streets dropped to about half that of 1895.[35] Public health also improved. According to Waring and the Board of Health, the death-rate and sick-rate declined substantially. The average annual death-rate in New York was 26.78 per 1,000 in 1882-1894, but only 19.63 per 1,000 during the first half of 1897. Diarrheal diseases likewise decreased significantly.[36]

Because of a desire to make the public aware of the necessity of keeping the city clean, Waring initiated the Juvenile Street Cleaning League. The children received information about proper sanitation, and even sang songs with an obvious message:

> Do not drop the fruit you're eating,
> Neighbor mine,
> On the sidewalks, sewers, or grating,
> Neighbor mine!
> But lest you and I should quarrel,
> Listen to my little carol!
> Go and toss it in the barrel,
> Neighbor mine!

---

[32] See E. Burgoyne Baker, "The Refuse of a Great City," *Munsey's Magazine*, XXIII (April 1900), 83-84; "Street Cleaning," *The Outlook*, LXVI (October 1900), 427.

[33] Baker, "The Refuse of a Great City," *Munsey's Magazine*, XXIII, 83-84.

[34] Waring, "The Labor Question in the Department of Street Cleaning of New York," *Municipal Affairs*, I (September 1897), 515-24; Waring, "The Cleaning of a Great City," *McClure's Magazine*, IX, 921-23.

[35] Waring, "The Cleaning of a Great City," *McClure's Magazine*, IX, 921.

[36] The Board of Health of New York attributed much of the improved health conditions to Waring's reforms. *Ibid.*, 921-23.

630

Municipal Refuse

Initially, about 500 youngsters participated in the program, but the numbers increased substantially throughout the school system. Many children came from "the ignorant foreign populations in some East Side districts." It was hoped they would set an example for "less enlightened" parents. Thus, the Juvenile League was intended to promote civic pride and familiarize the children with the functions of city government as a positive good.[37]

In dealing with the final disposition of refuse, Waring again employed both old techniques and innovations. Although he considered dumping at sea a theoretically perfect disposal method, he realized its many serious pitfalls and relied on "primary separation" to allay a significant part of the problem. Most of the dry waste could still be dumped at sea — at least until experiments with scientific incineration had been completed and analyzed.[38] Until then, the Commissioner recommended the use of the Delehanty Dumping Scow, which was self-emptying and self-propelled. This new catamaran-type vessel replaced the less efficient and less sanitary deck scow and the Barney Self-Dumping Scow.[39]

With garbage, Waring relied more heavily on reduction and utilization. This reduction process extracted by-products from garbage, such as ammonia, glue, grease, and dry residuum for fertilizer. By salvaging these materials, the city could obtain substantial revenue. At the time of his administration, about 8.5% of the city's garbage was hauled to Barren Island where the Sanitary Utilization Company, under contract to the city, reduced it and sold the by-products. Waring encouraged experimentation to find more efficient and economical methods of reduction and utilization. He wanted to increase the amount of garbage reduced and place the whole process under municipal direction. Eventually, the city built a reduction plant on Barren Island, and began a land reclamation program on Rikers Island, using ashes and other incinerated materials as fill.[40]

Waring's projects inspired similar experiments throughout the country, but not every community accepted his methods and

---

[37] See Baker, "The Refuse of a Great City," *Munsey's Magazine*, XXIII, 90; Waring, "The Cleaning of a Great City," *McClure's Magazine*, IX, 921-23.

[38] At that time, about 6% of the rubbish in New York was incinerated. The experiments were to determine the economic feasibility and efficiency of burning more rubbish. See Baker, "The Refuse of a Great City," *Munsey's Magazine*, XXIII, 89.

[39] Waring, "The Cleaning of a Great City," *McClure's Magazine*, IX, 917-19; Baker, "The Refuse of a Great City," *Munsey's Magazine*, XXIII, 89; "The Delehanty Dumping-Scow," *Harper's Weekly*, XL (October 24, 1896), 1051.

[40] Waring, "The Utilization of a City's Garbage," *Cosmopolitan Magazine*, XXIV, 406-10; Baker, "The Refuse of a Great City," *Munsey's Magazine*, XXIII, 87.

techniques. Some cities experimented with other techniques or completely ignored any solution. The contrasts between New York's methods and San Francisco's were particularly marked. In San Francisco all refuse was mixed together and used predominantly for fill. When the noxious stench from the decomposing materials finally raised an inordinate number of complaints, the city fathers decided to burn all the refuse, unseparated. This incinerator system, the only one in the country that operated without fuel other than the waste itself, created a powdery residue used as a base for fertilizer, mortar, and ornamental brick.[41]

With relatively few exceptions, however, Waring contributed more than any one individual to reforming refuse collection and disposal in the United States. He organized a disciplined and efficient administrative system. He introduced the classification of refuse and "primary separation." He demonstrated that there was great monetary value in waste through proper methods of reduction and utilization, which meant revenue to the city. And he brought respectability to his occupation never known before.

Yet, Waring's greatest impact was to place the public good above private desires. A clean city was a healthy city; a clean city was also a pleasant place to live. He stressed that municipal government, free from bossism and patronage, should bear the full responsibility for collecting and disposing of refuse to insure the public good and provide the city with financial rewards. Waring also tried to inspire civic pride among New Yorkers, emphasizing the importance of personal responsibility. The high moral tone of Warings reforms placed the refuse question above "out of sight, out of mind." He fostered an urban progressive reform spirit in his field that led to a major shift in the manner in which civic reformers came to view the refuse problem. As one civil engineer stated:

> The reason why the problem of refuse disposal is receiving an ever-increasing amount of attention from engineers, municipal authorities, and from the American public does not lie in the newness of the problem, but rather in an intellectual awakening of the people. The same spirit that leads men to realize the corruption of politics and business, and to attempt to remedy those conditions by adopting new methods of administration and new laws, also leads to a realization of the primitiveness of the methods of waste

[41] "How San Francisco Disposes of Its Garbage," *Scientific American*, LXXIX (October 22, 1898), 260-61.

disposal still employed by many communities, and to a consequent desire for improvement.[42]

A professional aura rose amid the quest for cleaner cities. Increasing numbers of scientists and engineers joined the reform movement, sounding the call for a scientific response to municipal waste. In numerous textbooks and articles, civil engineers argued that unsatisfactory waste disposal in the United States was, in large part, a failure to recognize the problem as one requiring a high proficiency in engineering knowledge and skills.[43]

The advent of the sanitary engineer demonstrated that the engineering community, in a specific way, sought to direct its expertise toward refuse management. One contemporary defined sanitary engineering as "that branch of engineering which has for its object the improvement of the health of towns and cities, by bringing to them those things which promote health, and carrying from them those things which are injurious to it."[44] This new profession emerged only after the development of the biological sciences in the 1870s and 1880s, and was not distinct from other branches of engineering until the early twentieth century. Ventilation, sewage disposal, and water supply maintenance were the earliest concerns of sanitary engineers. By the 1880s and 1890s they turned more attention to waste disposal.[45] And by 1900 they were in the vanguard of refuse reform.

Women also contributed significantly to this movement. They had been involved in public health reform since its inception, and provided considerable information about home economics and the nature of household refuse. Individual women were important pioneers in some major cities. In Philadelphia, Mrs. Edith W. Pierce in 1916 became the first woman city inspector of street cleaning in the United States. She formed a Junior Sanitation League, on Waring's model, with about 10,000 members, and vigorously promoted other programs to improve Philadelphia's

[42] Venable, *Garbage Crematories in America*, 1. See also Woodbury, "The Wastes of a Great City," *Scribner's Magazine*, XXXIV, 387; Morse, *The Collection and Disposal of Municipal Waste*, v, 420; M. N. Baker, *Municipal Engineering and Sanitation* (New York, 1902), 5, 151; H. R. Crohurst, "Municipal Wastes; Their Character, Collection, Disposal," *Public Health Bulletin*, No. 107 (Washington, 1920), 7.

[43] See H. de B. Parsons, *The Disposal of Municipal Refuse* (New York, 1921), 8; Baker, *Municipal Engineering and Sanitation*, 164; Crohurst, *Public Health Bulletin*, No. 107, 84.

[44] See Carl S. Dow, "Sanitary Engineering," *The Chautauquan*, LXVI (March 1912), 80-98.

[45] R. Winthrop Pratt, "Sanitary Engineering," *Scientific American Supplement*, LXXVII (March 7, 1914), 150; "The Sanitary Engineer—A New Social Profession," *Charities and the Commons (The Survey)*, XVI (June 2, 1906), 286-87.

handling of its waste problem. Women, acting through civic groups throughout the country, lobbied for better methods of waste disposal. For example, a women's city club in Chicago led the way for scientific collection of garbage.[46]

Women were also an important force in a phenomenon of the Progressive Era — the city clean-up (or beautification) campaign. The clean-up campaign epitomized a growing civic awareness of the problem of refuse, especially in smaller communities. The women's league of Kirksville, Missouri promoted a clean-up campaign in the spring of 1912. The purpose of this drive was to beautify the city, and only indirectly led to increased concern about collection and disposal on a permanent basis.[47] Other communities attained more substantial results, however. In Sherman, Texas, the Civic League sponsored a campaign with the co-operation of the mayor and some of the city councilmen, who prepared an ordinance establishing four four-day clean-up periods yearly and a more diligent regulatory system to survey collection and disposal.[48] Similar programs appeared throughout the country.[49] There were also some serious attempts at public information programs. The Louisville Women's Civic Association, with help from other organizations, produced a film entitled "The Invisible Peril," which depicted the travels of a discarded hat and the disease it spread through open cans and open dumps.[50] But although these campaigns pervaded the country, they usually went little beyond the surface of the waste disposal problem. Still, they were graphic signs that some Americans were determined to improve the aesthetic quality of city life.

Despite the widespread appeal for a scientific solution to the refuse question and the apparently rising public awareness, American cities continued to be plagued with the growing mounds of "rejectamenta." As Commissioner, Waring had confronted his

[46] See "Chicago's Struggle for Scientific Garbage Collection and Disposal," *The Survey*, XXXI (March 21, 1914), 776-77; Mrs. C. J. Baxter, "A Woman's League that Keeps the Streets Clean," *The American City*, VI (June 1912), 898-99, 901; Samuel A. Greeley, "The Work of Women in City Cleaning," *The American City*, VI (June 1912), 873-75; Mildred Chadsey, "Municipal Housekeeping," *Journal of Home Economics*, VII (February 1915), 53-59; "A Street-Cleaning Nurse," *The Literary Digest*, LII (March 18, 1916), 709-10.

[47] Baxter, "A Women's League that Keeps the Streets Clean," *The American City*, VI, 898-99, 901.

[48] Ewing Galloway, "How Sherman Cleans Up," *The American City*, IX (July 1913), 40-41.

[49] "Clean Up American Cities," *The Survey*, XXV (October 1910), 83-84; "Children in City Clean-Up Work," *The American City*, XIV (February 1916), 156-61.

[50] About 20,000 people had viewed the film in its early distribution. Mrs. Lee Detheim, "A Campaign for Sanitary Collection and Disposal of Garbage," *The American City*, XV (August 1916), 134-36.

Municipal Refuse

task positively, certain that the refuse nuisance was ephemeral. This perhaps was naive, for the problem was far from resolved by 1898. Even in New York, the Tammany administration which followed Waring's death soon undid much of the Colonel's work. Finally, in 1903, an energetic new Street-Cleaning Commissioner, John McGaw Woodbury, reinstated and improved many of Waring's programs.[51] In New York as elsewhere, however, reformers could not be satisfied with the half-hearted responses to the waste problem.

The gasoline- or electric-powered motor truck gradually replaced the horse and cart as the primary collection vehicle in American cities, and helped to improve the efficiency of the collectors.[52] Yet, this and other technological advances did not fundamentally alter the manner in which most American cities collected refuse. In a study conducted by Massachusetts Institute of Technology in 1902, collection methods of 161 cities were examined.[53] Fifty-four cities had municipal collection systems; forty-eight had contract systems; forty-one used private or license systems; twelve had no system at all; and six did not report.[54] The survey demonstrated the wide variety of methods employed, many of which were ineffectual or obsolete. The contract system was particularly inefficient and costly.[55]

Cleaning streets remained a constant irritant.[56] Many of the experts followed Waring's lead and advocated hand-sweeping as the most thorough and inexpensive way to keep the streets clean. Others believed machines would replace the "White Wings." The street cleaning equipment was as varied as could possibly be imagined. Once again American technology had outdone itself. A popular device was the mechanical sweeper usually preceded by a sprinkling apparatus which was supposed to loosen the street grime. Sprinklers were also adapted for settling dust or flushing

---

[51] See "The Disposal of New York's Refuse," *Scientific American*, LXXXIX (October 24, 1903), 292-94; "Tammany and the Streets," *The Outlook*, LXVI (October 20, 1900), 427-28; Woodbury, "The Wastes of a Great City," *Scribner's Magazine*, XXXIV, 387-400.

[52] "Motor Trucks for Refuse Collection," *The American City*, XIV (March 1916), 239-43; "New York's Gasoline-Electric Trucks for Garbage-Collection and Snow Removal Service," *Scientific American*, CXIV (March 25, 1916), 327, 336.

[53] The cities were 28,000 or larger.

[54] Morse, *The Collection and Disposal of Municipal Waste*, 7-8. See also Charles V. Chapin, *Municipal Sanitation in the United States* (Providence, Rhode Island, 1901), 665-98.

[55] See Baker, *Municipal Engineering and Sanitation*, 165; George E. Hooker, "Cleaning Streets by Contract—A Sidelight from Chicago," *Review of Reviews*, XV (March 1897), 437-41.

[56] Soper, *Modern Methods of Street Cleaning*, 11-12.

the streets. Some cities used a squeegee system to scrape the streets clean; in still others a vacuum device was employed.[57] The usefulness of these contraptions could only be determined on a local level, since climatic conditions, the amount and kind of refuse, and the type of streets varied.

Yet, one important technological innovation, the automobile, had an immense, although indirect impact upon the problem of street cleaning. The automobile was a godsend to the street-sweeper, since manure was a major source, if not the major source of street debris. And although some could be sold as fertilizer, the smell, nuisance, and sanitary menace it created far outweighed economic benefits. Not only did the automobile help reduce the manure problem, but its rubber tires did less damage to the streets than horseshoes and iron wagon wheels.[58]

Despite the sophisticated machinery, most cities still employed a substantial number of sweepers. The respectability that the New York "White Wings" achieved was not widespread, however, and many people were convinced that the men behind the brooms and others associated with refuse collection were the dregs of society.[59] Even the high standards which Waring had set in New York got worse before they got better. By the turn of the century, labor problems increasingly plagued the Street-Cleaning Department. In November 1911, seven hundred drivers and sweepers went on strike, protesting night work instituted in April. This was one in a series of strikes the workers had staged since they joined the International Brotherhood of Teamsters in 1907. Repressive administrative policies — the antithesis of Waring's policies — brought on the 1911 strike and demonstrated the low ebb of the workers' morale.[60] By 1917, however, some important strides were made to improve employer/employee relations, and upgrade the department itself. Under Commissioner Fetherston, benefits for the men were raised, including medical and dental service, increased vacations, and a workable grievance system. A technical (or planning) division was added to the street cleaning army and

---

[57] William Parr Capes and Jeanne Daniels Carpenter, *Municipal Housecleaning;* . . . (New York, 1918), 17-18; "A Two Motor Street Flusher," *Scientific American,* CXVI (June 23, 1917), 623; "Motor-Driven Squeegees in Street Cleaning Service," *Scientific American,* CXV (July 15, 1916), 66; "Vacuum Street-Cleaning," *The Literary Digest,* XLVIII, 548.

[58] "Clean Streets and Motor Traffic," *Literary Digest,* XLIX, 413-14; Woodbury, "The Wastes of a Great City," *Scribner's Magazine,* XXXIV, 396-98; Hoffman, "The Municipal Collection of Manure in Columbus, Ohio," *The American City,* X (April 1914), 379.

[59] See Soper, *Modern Methods of Street Cleaning,* 13.

[60] "Strike of New York Street Cleaners," *The Survey,* XXVII (November 25, 1911), 1243ff.

Municipal Refuse

the clerical force. A model district was established where new techniques and methods were tested. Fetherston also initiated a school for "White Wings" to instruct the workers in new methods and demonstrate new equipment. Even officers met frequently at the school to keep abreast of technical advances in the field.[61]

At the turn of the century, methods of disposal improved as slowly as new collection practices. The MIT survey of 161 American cities graphically demonstrated this:

```
Dumping on land....................44
Burning in dumps................... 9
Dumping in water...................14
Plowing into ground................18
Feeding to stock...................41
Cremation .........................27
Reduction/utilization .............19
Irregular disposal ................11
```
[62]

Feeding garbage to hogs, a long-standing practice especially in rural communities, encountered controversy in the early twentieth century. Some experts argued that hogs fed on municipal waste were comparable on the market to hogs fed by other means.[63] Others believed that hogs fed on garbage were inferior, if not unhealthy.[64] The practice continued in many communities, but even where used, never was a complete answer to the problem of disposal. The heinous practice of dumping into water also continued well into the twentieth century in many parts of the country, although numerous reformers continued to condemn its use.[65]

And progress made in major cities rarely carried over into smaller communities. From the late 1880s until the turn of the century, only 6.3% of the towns with populations over 3,000 had made any real improvement on lines of the "enlightened and scientific disposition of the communal wastes."[66]

---

[61] "A School for White Wings," *The Outlook*, CXV (March 28, 1917), 542; Potter, "Model Street-Cleaning," *The Outlook*, 515.

[62] Morse, *The Collection and Disposal of Municipal Wastes*, 7-8. There is some evidence that reduction was beginning to replace cremation in a number of places. See Day Allen Willey, "Baltimore's System of Garbage Disposal," *Scientific American*, LXXXIX (October 31, 1903), 308.

[63] F. G. Ashbrook and A. Wilson, "Feeding Garbage to Hogs," *Farmer's Bulletin*, No. 1133 (Washington, 1921), 3.

[64] Some tests had shown that hogs fed on garbage alone were deficient in some nutritional elements.

[65] See Crohurst, "Municipal Wastes; . . ." *Public Health Bulletin*, No. 107, 42-43; Soper, *Modern Methods of Street Cleaning*, 35; Woodbury, "The Wastes of a Great City," *Scribner's Magazine*, XXXIV, 400.

[66] Morse, *The Collection and Disposal of Municipal Waste*, 9. See also Greeley, "Refuse Disposal in Small Cities and Towns," *The American City*, X (January 1914), 55-57.

The Historian

Innovations in disposal, however, came in more or less isolated situations. European experiments inspired the use of garbage to produce electricity. The "sanitary fill" became popular in some locations.[67] In Austin, Texas fuel bricks, called "oakoal," were produced from incinerated garbage.[68] The most noteworthy process developed at this time was recycling paper. In Philadelphia, a substantial quantity of discarded newspaper was converted into cardboard or pasteboard.[69] But the idea of recycling materials gained only a modicum of attention in the early twentieth century.

As the 1920s approached, a solution to the problem of municipal waste was not yet in sight. The 1880s to about 1917 was a period of sharp contrasts. A relatively small group of reformers had made refuse a public issue, and urged that urban centers implement new, more scientific methods of collection and disposal. Yet, most cities, inundated with growing amounts of garbage, ashes, rubbish and the like, took only half-way measures, if any. The populace was slow to accept reform, but many reformers, while clearly demonstrating that refuse was a major source of disease and discomfort, placed too much faith in a scientific solution. This overemphasized the reliance upon experts, and minimized concern for the underlying causes of the waste and the necessity of community involvement in solving the problem. Reformers made little attempt to "socialize" the dilemma of refuse.[70]

Consequently, refuse reformers to some degree perpetuated a more sophisticated application of the "out of sight, out of mind" principle. Sanitarians were primarily concerned with removing refuse from the urban centers as quickly as possible to prevent the spread of disease. Many civil engineers, impressed with Waring's highly organized Department of Street-Cleaning and imbued with

---

[67] In Seattle, treating raw waste with antiseptics and layering it with porous earth replaced incineration. See "Seattle Making a Profit from Disposal of Garbage," *World's Work*, XXVIII (August 1914), 472.

[68] According to a professor at the University of Texas, "oakoal" produced as many units of heat per pound as the best bituminous coal. See Robert H. Moulton, "Turning Garbage into Fuel," *Independent*, LXXXIX (February 5, 1917), 222.

[69] The most difficult technical problem was removing the printer's ink, but this was eventually overcome. See "Where Waste Newspapers Go," *Scientific American*, CXI (December 5, 1914), 471; Thomas J. Keenan, "How Wastepaper Is Treated to Make New Paper; An Account of Processes and the Difficulties To Be Overcome in Removing Printer's Ink," *Scientific American*, CXV (December 23, 1916), 574-75.

[70] Some contemporary sociologist had suggested that the sanitation movement needed to identify public health problems with the general problems of society. For some interesting reading, see William H. Allen, "Sanitation and Social Progress," *American Journal of Sociology*, VIII (March 1903), 631-43; Marion Talbot, "Sanitation and Sociology," *American Journal of Sociology*, II (July 1896), 74-81. See also Ellen H. Richards, *Conservation by Sanitation; Air and Water Supply, Disposal of Waste* (New York, 1911), v-vii, ix-x, 169-222.

Municipal Refuse

an abiding faith in science, viewed refuse as a strictly technical problem. The cry arose for efficiency. Confidence in technology was widespread. As a result, reformers who also preached the scientific solution were convinced they understood the problem. Unfortunately, their perspectives were narrow, for they advocated means without a clear sense of the causes.

While Waring shared many of the tenets of the reformers who preceded him and inspired those that followed, he and a few others attempted to develop a broad understanding of the refuse problem. He sensed that people confronted with new ideas for improving the collection and disposal of waste would first ask — "How much will it cost?" Waring increased the efficiency of his department and raised it above spoils politics; and he also played upon the sympathies and emotions of the city officials and citizenry. He tried to make officials aware of their responsibility to insure the public welfare, and convinced them that collecting and disposing of refuse had pecuniary rewards. Waring also sought to inspire a sense of civic pride in the community. Refuse was not merely a nuisance or a health hazard or an eyesore, but a blot upon a city's reputation. Everyone, he argued, had an obligation to remove that blot. In this sense, Waring idealized the city as the zenith of civilization. The whims and desires of the individual had to be sublimated to social progress. Thus, Waring placed the question of refuse on a high moral plane which many people could readily comprehend.

Yet, the Colonel did not understand the problem fully. To collect and dispose of refuse efficiently or to make the public aware of its responsibility not to litter did not eliminate the creation of waste. Only a few individuals linked the refuse problem directly to American attitudes toward wastefulness. Those who did were often associated with the rising concern for conservation that marked the Progressive Era. One such man stated:

> Nowhere in the world is there such a waste of material as in this country. In our eagerness to get the most results from our resources, and to get them quickly, we destroy perhaps as much as we use. Americans have not learned to save; and their wastefulness imperils their future. Our resources are fast giving out, and the next problem will be to make them last.
>
> In passing the alleys of an American city, a foreigner marvels at the quantity of produce in the garbage boxes. The thrifty Germans would have saved this; and there is no excuse for letting it spoil in these days of cold storage and quick transportation. . . .[71]

[71] Austin Bierbower, "American Wastefulness," *Overland Monthly*, XLIX (April 1907), 358-59.

The Historian

This problem of wastefulness arose, in large part, because of the high rate of consumption of goods that accompanied industrial growth in the nineteenth century. A contemporary expert noted that the garbage of New York, for instance, contained about 25% more water than English or Scottish refuse and about 50% more than German refuse. New York's waste contained more perishable goods, such as dairy products and citrus fruit, which were formerly considered luxury items.[72] The higher standard of living contributed to the mounting problem of urban refuse, as much as migration to the city and increasing population.

To expect the reformers of this period, and inevitably the citizenry, to perceive the refuse question in a broad environmental context was asking too much, since they had uncovered only the proverbial tip of the iceberg. Growing prosperity and the seeming abundance of natural resources helped conceal the immutable connection between wastefulness and the creation of refuse. Many people were convinced that by simply improving collection and disposal methods the solid waste problem would fade away. However, refuse production was intricately woven into the urban milieu, and solutions based upon considerations of health, convenience, efficiency, or aesthetics only flirted with underlying causes. It was easy to consider the "uncivilized" immigrant as a villain who cluttered the alleys and littered the streets; it was even simpler to believe that garbage dumps or massive incineration plants would digest the heaps of discards incessantly. These invalid and shortsighted assumptions accompanied the public interest in seeing that "rejectamenta" was hauled out of the city as quickly as possible and disposed of with the least effort and expense. By 1920, "out of sight, out of mind" had not been displaced — it had been honed, polished, and gilded.

---

[72] Woodbury, "The Wastes of a Great City," *Scribner's Magazine*, XXXIV, 390-91. For a more moderate view of these statistics, see Venable, *Garbage Crematories in America*, 18-23. See also Rudolph Hering and Samuel A. Greeley, *Collection and Disposal of Municipal Waste* (New York, 1921), 1; Waring, "The Utilization of City Garbage," *Cosmopolitan Magazine*, XXIV, 405; Capes and Carpenter, *Municipal Housecleaning;* . . ., Preface.

JOHN ELLIS AND
STUART GALISHOFF

ATLANTA'S WATER SUPPLY
1865-1918

We are convinced that this is the most important Department of the City, and probably more important than all the other Municipal Departments combined. Without water the Fire Department, Sanitation Department, and other Departments supplied with water, would be useless. Almost all of our manufacturing industries, hotels, railroads and other large consumers of water would have to close down. Our people would be seriously inconvenienced, our sewers would soon become clogged with filth, and life within our City almost unbearable. *

During Atlanta's early years most residents obtained their water from wells, the excavation of which often required the use of blasting powder in order to penetrate the rocky substrata. Private sources of water supply were supplemented by a few public wells and pumps located near the business district and maintained by a council Committee on Wells, Pumps and Cisterns. Ordinarily these facilities were used to fill large cisterns that were kept ready in the event of fire, but they were also available to the poor and the general public in times of drought.[1]

The inadequacy of Atlanta's water supply was dramatically underlined by Union bombardment during the summer of 1864 and by the fiery destruction wrought by General Sherman's departing troops. Early in 1866 Anthony Murphy, a lumber dealer and chairman of the Committee on Wells, Pumps and Cisterns, reported to the city council that building and industrial needs, as well as the city's sanitary and fire protection requirements, called for a larger and more dependable water supply. Atlanta had arisen from the ashes to become the state's leading transportation and commercial center with a population in 1870 of nearly twenty thousand persons. The council took no direct action on the report, but on March 7, 1866, a group of six incorporators obtained a charter for the Atlanta Canal and Waterworks Company with the stated purpose of providing the city a "constant and plentiful supply of water." The company was authorized to

---

JOHN ELLIS and STUART GALISHOFF are associate professors of history at Lehigh University and Georgia State University respectively.

*Atlanta Board of Water Commissioners, *Annual Report for 1914*, p. 18.

excavate a canal from any point on the Chattahoochee River and to lay mains and supply pipes in the city. The projected cost of the undertaking was $100,000, but no work was accomplished and the plan died.[2]

A second company with a similar name was incorporated on March 16, 1869. The Atlanta Canal and Water Company's charter authorized a capital stock issue of $100,000 (with the option of increasing it to $1,000,000) for the purpose of conveying water from Peachtree Creek "or any other stream" to the city. In October the city council appointed a special committee composed of councilmen and leading businessmen to consider the water question. Following the city election in December the committee sent Anthony Murphy, who had been re-elected to the council, to investigate and report on the water systems of northern cities. Dr. John G. Westmoreland, president of the Atlanta Canal and Water Company and founder of the Atlanta Medical College, submitted his company's proposal to build a waterworks southwest of the city on Utoy Creek. The proposal was rejected by the council on July 1, 1870. A short time later, on September 23, Governor Rufus B. Bullock approved an act that authorized the mayor and council of Atlanta to finance and construct a municipal waterworks and establish a city board of water commissioners. Anthony Murphy was the first president.[3]

Apparently the waterworks issue was deeply involved in both Reconstruction politics and the race question. The "restored" legislature of 1870, in which thirty-one Negroes were reseated along with twenty-four Republican replacements for expelled Democrats, enacted the public school law and passed the Atlanta waterworks bill. It also provided legislation enfranchising Negro residents of Atlanta in city elections and regularizing the procedure of ward voting for councilmen. In the city elections of 1870 a heavy black vote furnished the margin of victory for the Republican candidate, Judge D. F. Hammond, in the mayor's race, and two Negroes, William Finch and George Graham, were elected to the city council.[4] It was this council, acting with the board of water commissioners, that entered into a contract on May 29, 1871, with the Holly Manufacturing Company of Lockport, New York, for pumping machinery to be installed in a waterworks located on Peachtree Creek near the Air-Line Railroad. Opponents of the water commissioners, among them the Atlanta Canal and Water Company, responded with suits and injunctions prohibiting the city from issuing bonds and challenging the constitutionality of the legislative act. Finally, following two years of bitter litigation, the constitutional issues were resolved, and late in 1873 a decision was reached to locate the works at the Old Stephen Terry Mill (present site of Lakewood Park) on the South River. Construction contracts were let for a reservoir and a small building to house the machinery, and the facilities were built with convict labor. The waterworks, completed in September

ATLANTA'S WATER SUPPLY   7

1875 at a cost of $226,000, had a daily capacity of 2 million gallons. A single sixteen-inch main conveyed water from the works over a distance of approximately five miles into the city, and from there three additional miles of smaller mains fanned out to serve the business district.[5]

The waterworks, like the beginnings of the city's public school system, was one of the progressive contributions of Radical Reconstruction, but somehow things went wrong. Its major purpose was to provide an increased volume of water for business and industrial needs and fire protection; it seems to have been no part of the plan to furnish citizens with a potable supply for drinking and household uses. The South River reservoir was fed by rain washings from the city's natural drainage courses, which by the 1870s had become open sewers, and indeed perhaps the most important headwater of the city waterworks pond was the notorious Lloyd Street sewer. The initial proposals for waterworks in the 1860s had emphasized the value of water for sanitary purposes, but the limited capacity of the waterworks was wholly inadequate for flushing the crude rock sewers built after 1873. Even for the main purposes it proposed to serve, the waterworks was inadequate the day it went into operation. The chances for obtaining sufficient pressure to combat fire were best at night when industrial use was minimal, but the pumping machinery was often under repair in the evenings from the daily overload that was placed on it. Consequently, there were numerous causes for dissatisfaction with the Atlanta waterworks, and perhaps not least among them was the discrepancy between a cost of $226,000 and a municipal bond issue exceeding $400,000.[6]

In the absence of a dependable municipal water supply, some well-to-do residents purchased drinking water delivered from Ponce de Leon and outlying springs, but the great majority of citizens continued to drink from public and private wells. In 1878 the Committee on Wells, Pumps and Cisterns maintained twenty-three public pumps and seven drinking fountains for purposes of fire protection and watering livestock, yet hundreds of persons living in the central portion of the city relied chiefly on the public wells for drinking water. A larger number of citizens in the same area drew water from their own wells or purchased it from a neighbor. The results of a study published in the *Atlanta Medical Register* in 1883 indicated that many wells were badly contaminated, and shortly thereafter the *Constitution* contended in an editorial that "a large class of people actually suffer for [want of] good water."[7] The main sufferers were Negroes, whose relation to the city's topography corresponded with their social status; their lots and wells received the drainage from the premises above, since the extension of sewer outfalls invariably stopped in black neighborhoods. Lack of pure, wholesome water combined with poor drainage in the hollows of the city led to increased sickness among the poor. The lower sections of the city were literally drained on from above by the downtown business area and the homes of the wealthy that occupied the higher elevations. Commenting on the fact that the death rate among Atlanta's Negroes in 1885 was 2½ times greater than that for whites, Mayor George Hillyer said: "I believe that if good clear water were supplied to all the lower levels of the city, where so many of the colored people live, and their contaminated wells were all filled up and obliterated, a very marked change for the better would immediately appear."[8]

By 1884 a growing realization on the part of the general public that most shallow wells were contaminated by sewage and that their use was connected with a great deal of sickness brought forth demands that something be done. Numerous newspaper articles and editorials pointed to the efficacy of artesian wells elsewhere, and in March 1884 the *Constitution* took the position that it was the duty of the municipal authorities to conduct a similar experiment for Atlanta. On August 21 an independent contractor began drilling a deep well in the center of the city (near the present site of Five Points) which ultimately reached a depth of more than two thousand feet. In 1886, amidst considerable rejoicing, the completed artesian well was incorporated into the municipal waterworks system. Within eighteen months reports of Waterworks Superintendent William G. Richards showed that 6¼ miles of distributing pipes and seventy-three hydrants had been installed in the central part of town. However, the flow of municipal self-congratulation at having obtained a limited but potable supply of water for human consumption was of short duration. The city chemist found that the artesian well was contaminated by surface drainage, and in its report for 1888 the board of health declared the well unsafe.[9]

The remaining source of Atlanta's water supply was the city waterworks authorized by the legislature in 1870 and finally completed in 1875. Its principle function under the direction of a board of water commissioners, which shared administrative authority with the council's Committee on Waterworks, was to provide water in sufficient volume for adequate fire protection and to meet the requirements of railroad and industrial concerns. Yet Atlanta's growth during the seventies was so rapid that the small reservoir and pumping station on South River were obsolete before they were finished. A severe drought in 1881 and business losses of nearly $1 million from fires the next winter spurred the water commissioners to increase the plants' capacity from 2 million to 6 million gallons per day. New pumping machinery and a partial twenty-inch main were installed at the waterworks in July 1882. These attempts to increase both volume and pressure, however, met with only limited success, and in August 1883 the 400-room Kimball House, Atlanta's finest hotel, burned to the ground.[10]

Fire insurance rates on business houses and dwellings rose sharply, as much as 100 percent in some sections of town. One irate citizen complained in 1884 that while South River water was excellent for drowning puppies, killing crabgrass, and dyeing white goods buff-brown, it was unsuitable for bathing, cooking, and drinking purposes. One pump at the waterworks was down for nearly a whole year, and shortly following its repair in April 1885, the badly overloaded sixteen-inch supply main burst, leaving the city without water, bringing industry to a standstill, and generally creating alarm.

At this juncture, the Hillyer administration proposed selling the works to a private company, but 500 of Atlanta's businessmen, meeting in May 1885 at the Chamber of Commerce building, expressed their strong opposition to such a move. Instead, a special committee of forty business leaders, including former Governor Joseph E. Brown, Samuel Inman, and Joel Hurt, recommended the use of meters and filtration of the South River water. Accordingly, the board of water commissioners began to require subscribers to purchase meters that year, and a city contract for a Hyatt filter system was signed in 1886.[11] The increased cost of the water kept down the number of subscribers and thereby increased volume and pressure, enabling industrialists and businessmen to benefit from their access to the clear water. The meter rate of seventeen cents per 1,000 gallons, with a minimum charge of ten dollars per year in advance, was allegedly designed to curtail waste. It did reduce consumption greatly, particularly for sanitary purposes, a result which the *Constitution* related to the increasingly foul condition of city sewers. "Water that cleanses and drenches and purifies," noted an editorial in the spring of 1887, "is not water wasted."[12]

Initially, the cost of waterworks service was charged at a flat rate for each faucet opening. There were 1,009 entries in the waterworks superintendent's tap book in 1879, an increase of but 200 over the previous year. During the ensuing eight years the number of taps increased to 2,077, but of these only 1,372 were in service by 1886. At that time less than one-third of the area within the city limits was accessible to waterworks mains, and out of approximately 9,000 houses and buildings, little more than 10 per cent were regularly supplied with water. However, a substantial minority of Atlanta's citizens used the waterworks product for drinking and other domestic purposes, and perhaps they were in as great a danger as the poor who drank mainly from wells. The two spring branches that fed the South River reservoir—Hardin's branch and Todd's branch—rose within the corporate limits of Atlanta, and during rains they became channels for the washings from hundreds of lots plus stables, tanneries, slaughter pens, railroad shops, the county convict camps, and the outfalls of sewers. Beginning in 1879 the board of health regularly saw to the removal of dead animals from the branches and began prohibiting tanneries and livestock pens from locating in the watershed. Yet as the city grew, given the absence of a planned drainage system, the contents of the reservoir became increasingly foul. The board of health's campaign against contaminated water beginning in 1886 finally resulted in the construction of a by-pass canal in 1888; the flow of the particularly notorious Todd's branch could then be diverted from the reservoir during rains.[13] Still, the volume of water available was inadequate, and business and industrial needs as well as planning for a new drainage system in 1888 demanded that a more abundant supply be obtained.

In 1889 a committee of businessmen and public officials asked the noted sanitary engineer, Rudolph Hering, to study Atlanta's water needs. Hering's report recommended that Atlanta abandon the South River for a copious supply of pure mountain water to be drawn from the Chattahoochee River. In 1891 the city purchased a 100-acre site for a pumping station on the Chattahoochee River above the mouth of Peachtree Creek and another site for a 176-million-gallon reservoir and relay station at an elevated point 3½ miles from the city. Construction of the Chattahoochee and Hemphill pumping stations began in 1892, and on September 29, 1893, the new system, furnishing a capacity of 20 million gallons per day, went into operation.[14]

The opening of the Chattahoochee plant, however, did not end the city's water crisis. When the water came into the city reservoir it was badly discolored by red clay particles. While the Chattahoochee River was relatively free of fecal contamination and other harmful wastes, it was filled with sand, necessitating that its waters be treated before being piped to Atlanta residents. Some of the sand settled to the bottom of the reservoir, a process known as sedimentation. Other impurities in the water were removed by filters that had been installed at the time of the water plant's construction. The filters, which were of the "Hyatt sectional wash type," were among the best available. But Atlanta's population was skyrocketing, and within a few years the filters were overloaded and ineffective.[15]

Even worse than dirty water was no water at all. Interruptions in water service due to machinery problems at the pumping stations occurred sporadically, and in the summer of 1900 the city experienced a water famine as a result of a series of mechanical malfunctions extending over a period of a month and a half. Water was cut off for ten hours on July 3 and 4 when both pumps at the Hemphill station went down. On July 5 the board of water works advised residents to store water in vessels and tubs as a precautionary measure. It was prudent advice, for during subsequent weeks the water that ran from faucets was muddy. The filter plant was simply inadequate in warm weather when water consumption increased. The filters could handle 7 million gallons of water per day, which was 40 to 80 percent less than the demand during periods of peak consumption. Another interruption in water service occurred on July 23, when the thirty-inch main between the Hemphill pumping station and the reservoir broke. The poor suffered especially from the water crisis. On one street in an impoverished neighborhood a well-owner was charging five cents for a small can of what was probably polluted well-water and ten cents for a larger container. Noting that for years the board of water works had warned of the peril facing the city, the *Constitution* took the General Council to task for inaction, adding that the want of water threatened property and endangered life.[16]

Judge George Hillyer of the board of waterworks believed that the water crisis had been brought on by human failure rather than the strains produced by increased water consumption. Hillyer charged that the pumps had broken down because the engineers employed by the board were not skilled machinists. A citizens' committee composed of ten businessmen and mechanical experts was formed to investigate Hillyer's charges and to put pressure on the General Council for a permanent solution to the city's water problems. Desirous of getting expert technical advice, the committee raised $1,000 through public subscription to hire Peter Milne, a prominent New York civil engineer, to make a complete study of the pumping stations, filter plant, reservoir, and water mains. Milne's study concluded that the breakdowns had occurred because the city had outgrown its water supply. The heavy demands placed on the pumps during warm weather far exceeded their ordinary or normal guaranteed capacity, leading to mechanical failures. Moreover, the congested condition of the distribution system stirred up the sediment in the pipes and muddied the water. Milne recommended that large mains be laid in the heart of the city, a 15-million-gallon pump be added to the Hemphill station, and the capacity of the filters be expanded by 4 million gallons. He also suggested the city give thought to building a second reservoir.[17]

On the basis of Milne's recommendations a $200,000 water bond issue was authorized in 1901. Water bond issues, however, had been defeated in both 1898 and 1899, and a difficult struggle lay ahead. To insure passage of the bond issue citizens' committees were organized in each ward district to get out the vote. Residents were reminded by mail of the importance of voting and were helped in getting to the polls on election day. The committees also enlisted the support of fire officials, board of health physicians, and other friends of the waterworks. Fire wagons were decked out with painted banners calling attention to the bond issue, and on election day the firemen's drum corps paraded downtown to Five Points. Fire chief Joyner warned that Atlanta was not a "cross-roads village" anymore and that the water mains downtown were too small to cope with a conflagration. Significant aid was also given by the club women of the city, led by Mrs. W.P. Patillo and Mrs. Nellie Peters Black. The opposition countered

357

with cards and circulars and was helped by a persistent morning rain that kept many persons from voting. On March 20, 1901, the bond issue was approved by a margin of thirty-eight votes.[18]

With the money from the 1901 bond issue, large water mains, including a thirty-inch pipe, were laid downtown and were credited with successfully combating several large fires in 1902 in the business district. The addition of a 15-million-gallon pump at the Hemphill station, the other major improvement brought about by the bond issue, did not show such dramatic benefits, but did help reduce the pressure on the pumps and diminish the chance of another interruption in water service. Mayor Livingston Mims, in his January 1903 valedictory address, commented on the benefits that had accrued from the expansion of the waterworks and reminded his constituents that every dollar expended on the waterworks was a large dividend-paying investment. Mims also noted that two-thirds of the city was still without water.[19]

The improvements brought about by the 1901 bond issue barely enabled the waterworks to keep abreast of population growth. One of the most frequent complaints about the city water supply was its high content of sand and mud. The smell, taste, and appearance of the water became alarmingly worse after the building of Bull Sluice Dam about twelve miles above the reservoir intake. The dam forced water from the bed of the river onto previously dry land. The lake formed behind the dam was therefore polluted with decayed leaves and other filth, which greatly increased the amount of silt that flowed into the reservoirs.[20]

In 1904 the *Constitution* asked W. C. King of New York, the representative of an eastern firm that furnished parts to the Atlanta waterworks, to comment on the adequacy of the city's water supply. King, while in Atlanta visiting his in-laws, remarked that the waterworks was only half the size it should be. If an accident interrupted service at the waterworks, said King, residents would be forced to resort to well water, and a typhoid and malaria epidemic would ensue. King also cited the report on Atlanta's water supply by the state chemist, J. M. McCandless. Finding evidence of fecal pollution, McCandless recommended that residents boil their water before drinking it. Alarmed city officials called in Dr. Ephraim Smith, a well-known bacteriologist, to examine Atlanta's drinking water. Smith did not find any dangerous micro-organisms, but he cautioned Atlantans that daily drinking of muddy water was bound to irritate the stomach, intestines, and kidneys.[21]

An important step in purifying Atlanta's water was taken in 1905 with the completion of the waterwork's first coagulating basin. The basin was designed to precipitate 80 to 90 per cent of the silt from the water. First the water was taken by suction from the intake well to the reservoir where sedimentation took place. The water, drawn from the surface where it was exposed to the purifying effects of sunshine and air, then flowed by gravity into the coagulating basins. Before entering the basin, a small amount of alum (aluminum sulphate) in solution was put into the water. The alum united with the alkali (soluble lime) found in the waters of the Chattahoochee River to form flakes of aluminum hydrate, a sticky, insoluble, gelatinous substance much like the white of an egg. While the water passed through the basin the jellylike flakes caught the clay and other foreign matter contained in the water and settled to the bottom. The improved water then flowed by gravity to the filters, which were cylindrical shells twenty feet long and eight feet in diameter, filled with sand and gravel. As the water percolated through the filters the remaining aluminum hydrate fell on the sand, forming a thick gelatinous blanket known as the schmurzdecke. The water that passed through the gravel at the bottom of the filters was virtually free of all suspended matter, bacteria, and foreign substances.[22]

The waterworks thus had the technical means for cleansing the city's water supply, but the capacity of the existing purifying equipment was still limited. With both per capita and total water consumption rising, Atlantans continued to live with sand and mud in their faucets for some time. The remedy, of course, was to spend more money on expanding the filtering plant. Thus the coagulating basin had no sooner been completed than the board of water commissioners asked that another one be built. The board explained that until this was done the water would run muddy for several days every time the coagulating basin was cleaned.[23]

Another problem that plagued the operation of the waterworks was the lack of adequate storage capacity. Beginning in the late 1890s the board of waterworks asked for a second reservoir. The city reservoir, when constructed in 1893, held a thirty- to forty-day supply. At the time, the waterworks was pumping about 2½ million gallons per day. By 1901 the waterworks was supplying an average of 7 million gallons a day. If the reservoir and the connections to the filter house broke, every city industry would stop within twelve hours, and in three days there would be no drinking water. In his report of 1904 Dr. Smith recommended the construction of a second reservoir to aid purification. With two reservoirs in use, new water from the river could undergo sedimentation, while water that had already settled would be sent to the coagulating basin for further treatment. As it was, the water passed in and out of the reservoir so quickly that the suspended matter in the water did not have sufficient time to settle to the bottom. A second reservoir would also enable the waterworks to suspend pumping when the water in the river was particularly turbulent. A site for a second reservoir was acquired in 1903, but the city dragged its heels in releasing money for completion of the project. Despite the urgent entreaties of the board of waterworks, the reservoir was not finished for several more years.[24]

Atlanta also experienced sewerage problems, which led the Georgia legislature in 1902 to authorize two bond issues of $400,000 each for sewer extentions and water improvements. But this was a greater debt than the fiscally conservative General Council wished to incur. The following year the bonds were cut back to $250,000 for sewers and $150,000 for water. In his final address to the city, Mayor Mims urged support for the bond issues and commented that well water was responsible for much of Atlanta's sickness. Mayor-elect Howell P. Evans warned residents who already had piped-in water that disease and illness caused by lack of water and poor sanitation in one part of town could quickly spread to other areas. The voters obviously agreed with the mayors, for the bond issue was passed. The $150,000 made available to the board of waterworks was used to build a new coagulating basin and to lay a thirty-six-inch water main from the Chattahoochee pumping station to the city reservoir.[25]

In 1905 the need for rapid expansion of the waterworks was emphasized in the recommendations made by the Committee of Twenty from the National Board of Fire Underwriters in its investigation of the city's buildings and fire hazards. The committee recommended that the pumping capacity of the Hemphill station be increased by at least 20 million gallons per day and that the distribution system be strengthened by the addition of one sixteen-inch and eight twelve-inch arteries in the congested downtown district. It further suggested that the city install only mains of eight-inch diameter for residential districts and not less than twelve-inch diameter for mercantile districts.[26]

The Committee of Twenty's report sparked a heated argument between the waterworks board and the city's elected officials. The mayor and

Table 1. Atlanta's Water Supply, 1909-1913

Years	Average Daily Consumption in Gallons	Estimated Population Supplied	Gals. per Capita	Number of taps	Number of meters
1909	11,450,000	138,700	83	19,061	19,261
1910	13,613,000	146,100	93	20,817	20,941
1911	14,914,000	153,500	97	23,349	23,358
1912	15,992,000	160,900	99	25,434	25,620
1913	16,313,000	168,300	97	27,132	27,120

Source: National Board of Fire Underwriters, *Report on the City of Atlanta, Georgia*, p. 4.

the General Council intimated that the management of the water department was not acquainted with the department's needs. Park Woodward, the department's general manager, replied that whatever deficiencies existed were caused by the failure of politicians to heed the department's appeals for waterworks improvements.[27] The president of the board of water commissioners impressed upon the General Council the department's need for funds "to meet the demands made upon it by the people, who are clamoring before our Board at each and every meeting for extension of mains."[28] He estimated that it would take $500,000 to implement the recommendations made by the National Board of Fire Underwriters, but to delay would "leave us in a very precarious condition in the very near future."[29] At one point in the controversy Woodward engaged in a personal attack against the mayor, dismissing his criticism of the water department as "the vaporings of a diseased mind or worse."[30]

Woodward was particularly incensed about proposals to end municipal ownership of the waterworks and the mayor's support for such proposals. "There is no surer way to bring about a state of feeling in the public mind adverse to the Water Works, and in favor of its sale," commented Woodward, "than to create the impression that it is not properly managed."[31] Attempts to sell or lease the waterworks to private interests were defeated in the General Council in 1906 and 1911 and were rejected by the citizens of Atlanta in the charter revision vote of 1913.[32]

Despite a $350,000 bond issue approved in April 1907 that permitted significant enlargements in the distribution and purification systems, the water situation continued to grow more perilous. In July 1907 Atlanta suffered another water famine. On Independence Day Atlantans turned on their faucets and got "yellow, ugly water." Lack of water prevented flushing the sewers and caused the development of stagnant pools along the sewer trunks, where mosquitoes bred. The bacteria count of the water jumped from its normal average of 15 to 20 per cubic centimeter to 1,500 to 2,000.[33]

The immediate cause of the crisis was the lack of sufficient water in the reservoir to activate the filters. To remedy the situation, the waterworks board proposed the immediate construction of a thirty-six-inch main from the river to the reservoir to supplement the existing thirty-inch main. The pipe for the main had already been ordered, when it was discovered that the purchase was illegal. An ordinance introduced early in the year by Alderman James L. Key forbade the city from spending money on the waterworks until all of the 1907 bond issue was sold and the money put in the city treasury. The waterworks board, anxious to head off a water famine, had ordered the pipes before the bond sales had been completed.[34]

Mayor Joyner called the General Council into special session to see what could be done to relieve the water crisis. The council first heard testimony from Woodward, who reminded the council that for several years he had "warned, begged, and prophesized" about the dangers of a water shortage. Woodward blamed the city's present emergency on Key's ordinance, while Key accused the management of the waterworks of "gross, miserable, inexcusable and damnable incompetence." Shortly thereafter, a city council committee appointed to investigate the conduct and management of the Atlanta waterworks exonerated the water department of any malfeasance. The committee reported that the water crisis could have been avoided had the General Council listened to the warnings of the water department. Atlanta's government, the committee stated, had been "parsimonious" in making needed improvements in the water supply system, despite the fact that the waterworks annually paid in about $200,000 to the city treasury, none of which could be used for maintenance or expansion without a council appropriation.[35]

Despite several bond issues, the building of water mains and sewer lines failed to keep pace with the city's surging growth. In 1908, one-third of the city's area and 40 per cent of the population did not have water mains or sewers, a condition which the chamber of commerce described as being "worthy of the plague-stricken cities of the middle ages." Moreover, it was the richer, less populous areas that enjoyed modern sanitary facilities. Streets without water had an average of 132 houses to the mile, whereas those with water showed 104 to the mile. In the absence of sewerage and running water, large numbers of Atlantans were forced to rely upon surface privies and wells, most of which were polluted. In addition, Atlanta had no sewage treatment facilities. Trunk sewers took the bodily wastes of 80,000 persons to or near the city limits, where the sewage was dumped into streams. The streams were the favorite resort of flies and mosquitoes, who carried back to the city the germs found in the sewers. Because of these unsanitary conditions, the city continued to suffer grievously from water-borne diseases. From 1906 to 1910, Atlanta had an annual typhoid-fever death rate of 62.1 per 100,000 population, second highest in the nation of any city with over 100,000 population.[36]

Atlanta's reputation as an unhealthy city led the chamber of commerce to lobby for major improvements in the city's water supply and sewers. In 1908 the chamber published *Urgent Needs of Atlanta*. It presented statistics gathered from the 1905 U.S. census report on mortality in American cities to support its call for a new bond issue for public health reforms. The report showed that Atlanta's death rate exceeded the national average by 47 per cent and was higher than all but 12 of the 388 cities surveyed. The city's health record was particularly bad with regard to typhoid fever, tuberculosis, and pneumonia. While Atlanta fared better when compared to other southern cities or to cities with large Negro populations, the chamber warned against complacency and argued that Atlanta's position as the region's leading city required it to become the examplar of southern cities in sanitation and public health.[37]

The chamber of commerce gave four reasons for the city's high death rate: the dependence of large numbers of persons on unsafe surface privies and polluted wells; the occasional impurity of the water supply because of improper filtration; the dirty, dusty condition of the streets; and the existence of overcrowded and poorly ventilated schoolrooms. To improve the city's sanitary condition, the chamber asked that city water be supplied to the 11,000 homes in Atlanta without it, the water purification plant be enlarged, and sewerage be extended throughout the city.[38] Commenting on the importance of public health to a city's economic welfare, the chamber noted that

it is only within the recent past that the interest of the community, in a financial or commercial sense, in the health of the individuals composing it has been aroused. Formerly the health question was viewed from the selfish standpoint of the individual or the family. . . . But now municipal governments have come to realize that to them the general health is quite as important and profitable as to the individual. With communities, as with individuals, it has developed that it is impossible to prosper without health, as it is to build a house without a foundation.[39]

In 1910, a $3,000,000 bond issue was proposed, of which $900,000 was earmarked for the waterworks and $1,350,000 for sewage disposal plants. The chamber of commerce pointed out that laying water mains and sewers in the areas presently without those amenities would save the city $20,000 each year on night soil removal. That money would pay the interest on the sewer bonds. The interest on the water bonds could easily be paid for by raising the city's low water fees. Saving money on water and sewers was criminal when it threatened health and life. The chamber noted that if Atlanta only succeeded in reducing the death rate to the national average of American cities it would save 1,200 lives each year.[40]

In the months preceding the referendum the chamber of commerce, with the blessings of Mayor Robert Maddox, waged an all-out fight for the bond issue. To spearhead the campaign, the chamber appointed a special bond committee with a war chest of $3,500. The chief efforts of the committee were directed toward two goals: registering voters and getting out the vote on election day. The chamber of commerce was responsible for registering voters in the commercial classes. The Atlanta Federation of Trades was assigned the workingmen, and the Federation of Women's Clubs did the door-to-door canvassing. Every person in Atlanta was listed according to occupation and assigned to an organization for purposes of registration. The chamber of commerce alone had thirty-two committees at work canvassing business houses.[41] The chamber boasted that "no campaign in Atlanta's history was ever more systematically made. Each ward is divided into districts and every street is polled by committees."[42]

As in any election, there were special interest groups to be courted. Over eight-thousand families in Atlanta lived on streets without water mains. Those voters would almost certainly favor the bond issue if they could be assured it would bring them running water. After considerable effort, Walter G. Cooper, secretary of the chamber of commerce, secured the names and addresses of the heads of those families and personally promised them that water mains would be laid in front of their homes if the bond issue were carried.[43]

In order to secure passage of the bond issue, two-thirds of those registered had to cast affirmative ballots. Polls early in January showed about 88 per cent in favor of the bonds. Still not satisfied, the chamber intensified its efforts and by late January had reduced the opposition to about 5 per cent. All of the chamber's efforts, however, would be wasted if the persons they had painstakingly registered failed to vote. To insure that they did turn out, employers were asked to give their workers time off to vote on election day. A new feature of the bond drive was the use of a telephone corps organized by Secretary Cooper. On election day, forty-five women telephoned the voters all day reminding them to vote. The chamber's efforts paid off handsomely. On February 15, by the lopsided vote of 8,409 to 66, the bond issue was approved.[44]

Between 1910 and 1914 extensive improvements were made in the Atlanta waterworks. With the money provided by the 1910 bond issue, two new coagulating basins were added, bringing their number to four. A contract was signed with the New York Continental Jewell Filtration Company for filters with a 10-million-gallon daily capacity, bringing the system's total filtration capacity to 21 million. In 1911 the second reservoir was finally completed. It reduced the likelihood of future water famines and improved the water's quality. These additions gave Atlanta one of the best water supplies in the South.[45] In its annual report for 1911 the board of waterworks stated that "the character of water now furnished to the city is entirely satisfactory, the bacterial and chemical tests showing. . .a most excellent water; free from discoloration, pure and wholesome."[46]

Extensive additions were also made in the waterworks distributing system. In 1910 alone nearly forty-one miles of water mains were laid, providing thousands of Atlantans with running water for the first time. By 1917 nearly every house in Atlanta had piped-in water. The water mains in the central business district were augmented, thereby affording greater fire protection and lower insurance rates for downtown businessmen. By 1914, two thirty-inch mains and one thirty-six-inch main extended from the Hemphill pumping station well into the distributing system. These mains supplied a number of secondary feeders, well located and connected in the congested district, which in turn supplied numerous ten- and twelve-inch lines. Outlying residential areas were served mainly by six-inch pipe, though the National Board of Fire Underwriters had recommended the adoption of eight-inch pipe as the minimum size.[47]

By 1914 the waterworks was supplying over 16 million gallons of water daily, and still the water supply was inadequate. In its annual report for 1910 the board of waterworks had asked for an additional 20-million-gallon pump for both the Chattahoochee and Hemphill stations to insure a sufficient reserve capacity in case of accident. Within a few years, however, the additional pumps were needed, not as security against accidents but to satisfy the city's continually growing demand for water. Only twice in fourteen years had the board of waterworks expressed optimism about the future, first in 1907, after the bond issue had been passed, and again in 1910. Both times surging population growth and increased per capita consumption of water had dashed the board's hopes and forced it again to begin sounding the alarm. Between 1900 and 1910 Atlanta's population increased from 90,000 to 150,000, and by 1922 it reached 240,000. In its annual report for 1914, the board of water commissioners warned that during the summer months the water department had been sorely pressed to meet the demands of its regular customers. If called upon, it could not have furnished the fire department with adequate water pressure. The danger was underscored by a disastrous fire on May 21, 1917, in which over 1,900 buildings were damaged causing as estimated $5 million in property losses.[48]

The new waterworks and sewerage facilities built with the money from the 1910 bond issue did result in a marked improvement in the city's public health. As city water and sewerage became available, wells and surface closets were abandoned, although there were still 4,000 surface closets in use in 1917. In the years 1911 to 1916, the typhoid fever death rate fell from 56 to 17 per 100,000 population, a 70 per cent reduction.[49]

Between 1865 and 1918, Atlanta businessmen and water officials fought an up-hill battle to keep the city's water supply abreast of rapid population growth. Throughout the period, fear of illness and the threat of fire were used to convince taxpayers and politicians alike of the need for expensive improvements in the water supply system. By 1918 a wholesome if not quite copious water supply was being piped-in to nearly all residents of Atlanta, and the city was well on the way to solving its water supply problems.

NOTES

[1] F. D. Thurman, "Healthfulness of Atlanta," *Atlanta Medical and Surgical Journal* 3 (July 1858): 650; Richard J. Hopkins, "Public Health in Atlanta: The Formative Years, 1865-1879," *Georgia Historical Quarterly* 53 (September 1969): 297.

[2] John R. Hornaday, *Atlanta Yesterday, Today and Tomorrow* (n.p., 1922), pp. 105-06.

[3] Franklin M. Garrett, *Atlanta and Environs: A Chronicle of Its People and Events*, 3 vols. (New York, 1954), 1: 914-16.

[4] Edgar G. Epps, "The Participation of the Negro in the Municipal Politics of the City of Atlanta, 1867-1908" (M.A. thesis, Atlanta University, 1955), pp. 10-15.

[5] Garrett, *Atlanta and Environs*, 1: 916-18; Atlanta *Constitution*, Feb. 4, 1885.

[6] Garrett, *Atlanta and Environs*, 2: 260; U.S., Department of Commerce, Bureau of the Census, *Tenth Census of the United States, 1880*, vol. 14, 160; Atlanta *Constitution*, June 6, 21, 1879, and July 9, 1881.

[7] Atlanta *Constitution*, Jan. 30, 1885; see also Ibid., Sept. 5, 1883; "Annual Report of the Committee on Wells, Pumps, and Cisterns for the Year 1878," in Minutes of the City Council of Atlanta, City Hall, Atlanta, Georgia, vol. 9, n.d. (hereafter cited as Minutes of the City Council).

[8] *Annual Report of the Officer of the City of Atlanta for the Year Ending December 31, 1885, Showing the Condition of Municipal Affairs* (Atlanta, 1886), p. 22 (hereafter cited as *AAR*, year, name of reporting unit); see also *AAR, 1887, Board of Health*, pp. 18-19. The board of health urged the city council (unsuccessfully) to grant it authority to have condemned wells filled up.

[9] *AAR, 1886, Superintendent of Waterworks*, p. 44; *AAR, 1887, Water Works Committee*, p. 19; *AAR, 1888, Water Works Committee*, p. 23; *AAR, 1888, Superintendent of Water Works*, p. 27; *AAR, 1888, Board of Health*, p. 29; Atlanta *Constitution*, Mar. 11, Aug. 22, 1884, Feb. 15, Dec. 6, 1885, and Aug. 29, 1886; Atlanta *Journal*, July 13, 1886. Since the water from the well was "perfectly clear," it was initially assumed to be "absolutely pure."

[10] *AAR, 1881, Board of Health*, p. 4; *AAR, 1883, Board of Health*, pp. 9-10; *AAR, 1883, Superintendent of Water Works*, pp. 64-66; *AAR, 1883, Water Commissioners*, 61-62; Atlanta *Constitution*, July 9, 1881, Mar. 1, 29, 1882, Aug. 18, Oct. 27, 1883.

[11] *AAR, 1886, Superintendent of Water Works*, pp. 44-45; Atlanta *Journal*, Nov. 5, 1884; Atlanta *Constitution*, June 24, July 13, 1884, Jan. 31, Apr. 15, May 17, 24, 30, June 16, 1885, and Nov. 19, 1886.

[12] Atlanta *Constitution*, Apr. 21, 1887.

[13] "Valedictory Address of Hon. N. L. Angier—retiring," Minutes of the City Council, vol. 9, Jan. 1, 1879; "Waterworks Superintendent's Report for 1879," Ibid., Jan. 5, 1880; *AAR, 1885, The Mayor's Address*, p. 12; *AAR, 1885, Superintendent of Water Works*, pp. 42-44; *AAR, 1888, Board of Water Commissioners*, p. 24; *AAR, 1888, Superintendent of Water Works*, pp. 25-26; Atlanta *Constitution*, June 2, 1885, Apr. 12, May 7, 1886, Aug. 19, 1887, and Dec. 16, 1888.

[14] *AAR, 1889, Mayor John T. Glenn's Address*, pp. 14-15; Rudolph Hering, "Report on Water Supply for Atlanta, Ga.," *AAR, 1890, Mayor John T. Glenn's Address*, pp. 254-72; Atlanta *Constitution*, Dec. 16, 1888, Sept. 3, 1889, Dec. 3, 1891, and Sept. 30, 1893.

[15] *Points of Information of the Atlanta Water Works* (Atlanta, 1913), pp. 6-7; Moses Nelson Baker, *The Quest for Pure Water: The History of Water Purification from the Earliest Records to the Twentieth Century* (New York, 1948), p. 184.

[16] Atlanta *Constitution*, July 5, 10, 12, 24, 25, 1900.

17*AAR, 1900, Board of Water Commissioners,* pp. 533-34, 37-38, 58-59, 77-78; Atlanta *Constitution,* July 12, 24-26, and Aug. 11, 12, 14, 1900.

18Atlanta *Constitution,* Mar. 17, 18, 21, 1901; Thomas M. Deaton, "Atlanta During the Progressive Era" (Ph.D. diss., University of Georgia, 1969), pp. 198-99.

19*AAR, 1901, Board of Water Commissioners,* p. 472; *AAR, 1902, Board of Water Commissioners,* pp. 114-15; *AAR, 1903, Mayor's Message,* pp. 22-23.

20Atlanta *Constitution,* Aug. 14, 1904.

21Alton Timothy Dial, "Public Health in Atlanta During the Progressive Era" (M.A. thesis, Georgia State University, 1970), pp. 45-46; Atlanta *Constitution,* Aug. 14, 16, 28, and Sept. 6, 1904.

22*AAR, 1905, Board of Water Commissioners,* p. 32; Henry Reid Hunter, *Outline: Government of the City of Atlanta,* 2 vols. (Atlanta, 1919), 1: 24-26.

23*AAR, 1905, Board of Water Commissioners,* p. 32.

24*AAR, 1901, Board of Water Commissioners,* pp. 467-68; see also the reports for 1902 (p. 318), 1903 (p. 483), and 1904 (p. 486); Atlanta *Constitution,* Aug. 28, and Sept. 6, 1904.

25Deaton, "Atlanta During the Progressive Era," p. 195; *AAR, 1902, Mayor's Message,* 35-37, 55-56.

26*AAR, 1905, Board of Water Commissioners,* pp. 17-19.

27Ibid., pp. 13-14.

28*AAR, 1906, Board of Water Commissioners,* p. 9.

29Ibid., p. 11.

30*AAR, 1905, Board of Water Commissioners,* p. 14.

31Ibid., p. 15.

32Deaton, "Atlanta During the Progressive Era," pp. 199-200.

33Atlanta *Constitution,* July 9, 1907; *Atlanta Journal-Record of Medicine* 10 (April 1908): 53.

34Atlanta *Constitution,* July 8-9, 1907.

35Ibid., July 9, 21, 1907; *AAR, 1907, Board of Water Commissioners,* p. 12.

36Atlanta Chamber of Commerce, *Urgent Needs of Atlanta* (Atlanta, 1908), pp. 7-8; Department of Commerce, Bureau of the Census, *Mortality Statistics, 1910,* p. 24; Atlanta Chamber of Commerce, *Annual Report, 1909,* p. 5; *Progress,* May 1909, p. 5.

37*Urgent Needs of Atlanta,* pp. 6-7; *Mortality Statistics, 1910,* pp. 15-18; *Progress,* Oct. 1909, p. 3.

38*Urgent Needs of Atlanta,* pp. 6-7; Atlanta Chamber of Commerce, *Annual Report, 1909,* p. 5; *Progress,* May 1909, p. 87.

39*Progress,* Jan. 1910, p. 10.

40*Urgent Needs of Atlanta,* pp. 7-8; Atlanta Chamber of Commerce, *Annual Report, 1909,* p. 5; *Progress,* May 1909, p. 5.

41Garrett, *Atlanta,* 2: 559; *Progress,* Feb. 1910, p. 13-14.

42*Progress,* Feb. 1910, p. 14.

43Garrett, *Atlanta,* 2: 559.

44*Progress,* Feb. 1910, pp. 13-14, and Jan. 1912, p. 4.

45*AAR, 1910, Board of Water Commissioners,* p. 13.

46*AAR, 1911, Board of Water Commissioners,* p. 8.

⁴⁷Atlanta *Constitution,* Jan. 3, 1911; National Board of Fire Underwriters Committee on Fire Prevention Report No. 100, *Report on the City of Atlanta, Georgia, May 1914,* pp. 4-5.

⁴⁸National Board of Fire Underwriters, *Report on the City of Atlanta,* p. 4; *AAR, 1910, Board of Water Commissioners,* p. 47; *AAR, 1914, Board of Water Commissioners,* p. 7.

⁴⁹Hugh M. Willet, *Public Health in Atlanta* (Atlanta, 1917), p. 7.

JOURNAL of the WEST®

Los Angeles Aqueduct: A Search for Water

By William K. Jones
Museum Curator, Dwight D. Eisenhower Library

Water has always been a problem to Los Angeles. This major city, founded in 1781 as Pueblo de Nuestra Senora la Reina de Los Angeles, received most of its water until 1913 from the Los Angeles River by means of a primitive municipal system.[1] In 1868, a private company, the Los Angeles City Water Company, obtained a franchise to operate the public water works for thirty years. After four years of litigation, beginning in 1898, the city recovered control of the system. In the period 1868 to 1900, Los Angeles' population increased from less than 5,000 to more than 100,000 people.[2]

Most of Los Angeles' growth took place in the two

Los Angeles Department of Water and Power

The builders (left to right) — J.B. Lippincott, Fred Eaton and William Mulholland.

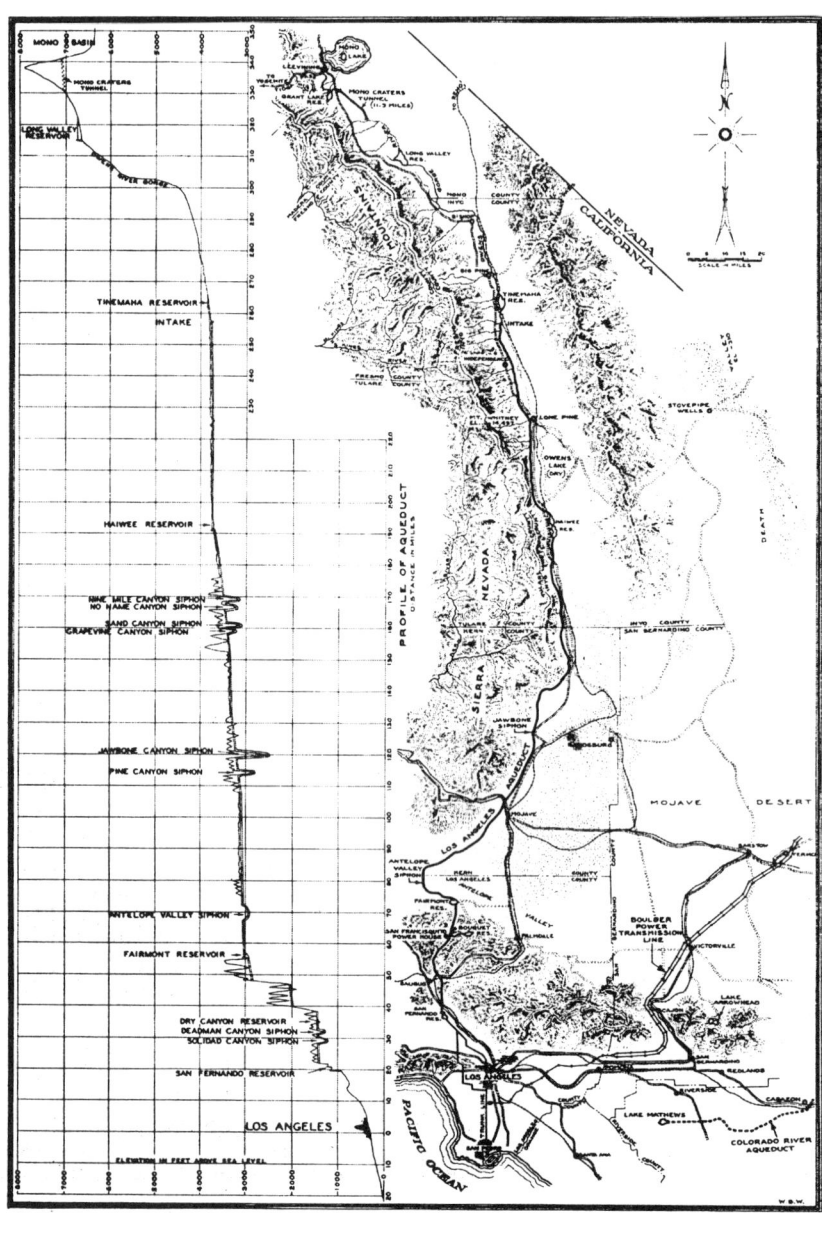

decades preceding 1900, doubling in the ten years from 1880 to 1890, and again from 1890 to 1900. City planners, assuming that the astonishing growth would continue, estimated that with conservative use existing water resources would be adequate until about 1920. But four years after the turn of the century, the city's population again doubled, and the safety margin of fifteen years was cut to four years. At this time two surveys of the Los Angeles area were made to determine the quantity of water that could be obtained near the city.[3]

William Mulholland, Chief Engineer and General Manager of the City Bureau of Water Works and Supply, examined the water resources of the southern part of the state. His report stated that a ten to twenty year supply could be obtained at a reasonable cost by building reservoirs in the San Gabriel Valley or on the coastal plain. He pointed out, however, this would lead to rapid exhaustion of water resources required by communities commercially and politically tributary to Los Angeles.[4]

Joseph B. Lippincott, survising engineer of the United States Reclamation Service for the Southwest, prepared the second report for the city. His survey pointed out that water sources tapped in the Los Angeles area would be expensive and temporary.[5]

The Mulholland-Lippincott reports suggested that the municipality should go to a remote region where a minimum of injury would be caused by the acquisition and removal of water. After considerable searching Los Angeles city leaders selected the Owens River, situated between the eastern base of the Sierra Nevada Mountains and the Inyo Mountain Range, as the new water source. The valley is about 120 miles long, from two to ten miles wide, and lies at an elevation of between 3,500 and 6,000 feet. It is situated approximately in the center of California, north to south and is isolated from the San Joaquin Valley by the "High Sierras" and from Los Angeles by the Mojave Desert.[6]

The Owens River has its source in the Sierra Nevada Mountains. The snowfall on western slopes is extremely heavy and nearly every canyon carries a fine stream of water throughout the year. These gentle brooks become veritable rivers in the spring and summer months. Thirty-five such tributaries flow into Owens River from a drainage area of 2,800 square miles. The 150 mile long river is supplied entirely by this run-off. There is enough water in the river to irrigate the Owens Valley, and according to one report the water wasted, which runs into the Owens Lake, a salt *playa* of about seventy-five square miles at the end of the Owens River, could amply supply a city of two million people.[7]

Fred Eaton, engineer, rancher and ex-mayor of Los Angeles, first suggested to Los Angeles water officials that they turn to the Owens River. Eaton had been Chief Engineer and Superintendent of the Los Angeles City Water Company, and his experience working for both the city and the old franchised water company had given him insight into water needs. Thirteen years before the valley was chosen, Eaton had seen its potential and had begun to buy water options and land in the area. In the fall of 1904 he began extensive purchasing of contracts and options on water-bearing property, so that by the time he presented his idea to the representatives of the city, he had obtained over 30,000 dollars worth of property. Eaton first proposed a combined private and municipal project in which the city would receive 10,000 miner's[8] inches of water for domestic uses with the surplus water to be available to Eaton and his associates for disposal outside the city.[9]

Mulholland accompanied Eaton to Owens Valley in September of 1904. As the two engineers traveled by wagon over the 250 miles of desert to the valley, Eaton pointed out that in some past geologic period a river had apparently flowed from the eastern foot of the Sierras to within a few miles of the Southern California Plain. The flow of this river had been cut off by volcanic action which had formed a barrier across the southern end of Owens Valley. The two men say, however, that the barrier was low and that after it was passed the only obstacle in the way of an aqueduct would be the mountain range north of Los Angeles. They decided that if the city could take advantage of this old river course, a water line could be built at a minimum cost and without the use of a single pump.[10]

Because of the growing interest in water and electrical power in the West, Los Angeles met competition in Owens Valley. Two other groups had seen the possibilities of the Owens River. One, a local electrical power company, made plans to build an aqueduct and a power transmission line to Los Angeles, but this endeavor was being checked by the city's second rival, the United States Reclamation Service. The Reclamation Service presented the greatest obstacle to Los Angeles' bid to obtain water from the Sierras.

As early as June, 1903, J. C. Clausen, an engineer for the Service, had surveyed Owens Valley as a possible location for a federal irrigation project. Although this examination was merely preliminary and the local residents were warned that the survey might result in the condemning of the area, they doubted that the federal project would materialize. When Los Angeles eventually won Owens Valley, the local farmers and ranchers believed that the Reclamation Service had sold out their interests. In 1904, one month before his trip to the valley with Mulholland, Eaton had accompanied a Reclamation Service crew on a survey into this area. Eaton realized that he and city officials must act quickly to obtain it as a source of water for Los Angeles.[11]

To resolve the conflict of interest with the Reclamation Service, the city had to show a definite need for the area and to receive a commitment from Los Angeles taxpayers indicating their support of such a project. On his return from the valley, Mulholland began a detailed study of the proposed line. He plotted an approximate route and made an estimate of the cost and time that would be involved. He believed that 25,000,000 dollars would cover the purchase of land and water rights and the cost of construction and that it could be built in five years. Mulholland completed the plans by early 1905 and presented them to the Los Angeles Water Board. After approving them the Board announced that Lippincott had sent word that the government might step aside if the city's project were publicly owned from one end to the other. The ruling made in May of 1905 stated:

> Against a private enterprise, the Reclamation Service could exercise the right of condemnation. As against a municipality seeking water for a large urban population, the government would not persist in its project, its policy being to promote the good of the greatest number.[12]

Eaton, after being notified of this ruling, decided to sell.

This presented still another problem for the Los Angeles Water Board. Because the options were about to expire, there was no time for a bond issue to raise the money to purchase Eaton's holdings. If the city allowed the options to expire, the cost of re-purchase would be exorbitant. The city's plans for Owens Valley were not publicly known, but there had been enough activity and interest in the area to arouse curiosity and to raise the price of water options. With these problems in mind the city water board authorized William H. Workman, City Treasurer, to take 150,000 dollars from the board's funds to purchase Eaton's property. Had the bond issue which was held later in the fall failed, city leaders having used public funds to buy land over 200 miles from Los Angeles would have been in an embarrassing position. On May 22, 1905, the city bought out Fred Eaton.[13]

As soon as the water board notified the Reclamation Service that it had taken steps to make the planned water project entirely a public venture, the Service called a meeting of a board of engineers to decide the fate of the federal plan for Owens Valley. This three man board met in San Francisco in late July and held hearings on the Owens Valley Reclamation Project. Testifying at these meetings were Clausen, who had supervised the survey of the area, and Lippincott. Clausen's testimony favored continuation of the federal government plans, but Lippincott urged that regardless of the plan's feasibility the government should not continue surveys and the whole idea should be abandoned in favor of Los Angeles. The board issued its decision on July 28, 1905. The engineers stated that they favored the federal project and believed it should be completed, but that since Los Angeles had made it impractical by purchasing land and water options in the area, the government should stop work in the valley.[14]

On the last day of July, 1905, the Los Angeles *Times* released the news of the proposed aqueduct. Previously the water board had informed the newspapers of their actions but had requested that the project be kept out of the news. The official explanation of the board's secrecy was that:

> Any advance knowledge of the intentions of the City of Los Angeles to purchase great tracts of land and water rights in Owens Valley would certainly have led to local excitement and loss to the City. The City officials, therefore, conducted preliminary negotiations in this quiet and businesslike manner before making public announcements.[15]

Not only were the people of Los Angeles and Owens Valley not publicly informed of what was happening, but neither was the City Council which had no advance notice of the plans.[16]

In trying to keep their plans for Owens Valley secret and to prevent exploitation of the city by valley land owners and speculators, the water board unknowingly allowed a syndicate of newspapermen, realtors, and one of their own board colleagues to make a fortune by giving them privileged information. This wealth was made not in Owens Valley but almost 200 miles away in the San Fernando Valley. As early as 1903 investors had seen the possibilities of the San Fernando Valley as an agricultural area to supply Los Angeles, but the lack of water presented a problem. Despite this drawback a group of investors, including Harrison Gray Otis, owner of the Los Angeles *Times,* Edwin T. Earl, owner of the Los Angeles *Express,* L. C. Brand, president of the Title Guarantee and Trust Company, and Henry Edwards Huntington, owner of the electric inter-urban railroad that served Los Angeles, began purchasing land in the San Fernando Valley. They planned to extend an electric railroad line into the valley and to subdivide the land for sale to settlers.[17]

On November 28, 1904, General Moses Hazeltine Sherman, a member of the Los Angeles Water Board, joined the San Fernando developers in a syndicate to buy land in the valley. Their company, the San Fernando Mission Land Company, purchased over 16,000 acres of land at thirty-five dollars per acre. When the proposed Los Angeles Aqueduct was announced the following July, the price of the same land went to over three hundred dollars per acre. This jump was caused because existing water laws stated that Los Angeles had to find a current use for its future water supplies. If the city failed to use the water, it would relinquish its claims to it and would have to re-negotiate for more when the demand increased. Because of this law Mulholland suggested that the surpluses be used to irrigate sections of the San Fernando Valley.[18] He also recommended locating the terminal reservoir of the aqueduct in the valley.[19]

Soon after the water board plans for an aqueduct from Owens Valley were made public, Mr. J. O. Koepfli, President of the Chamber of Commerce of Los Angeles, was asked for his support and for the backing of the Chamber of Commerce. In August of 1905 this city body and other commercial interests sent a special committee to investigate the Owens River Valley. This group took samples of the water for analysis, made an estimate of construction costs, and examined the general feasibility of the project. On their return these men made public their finding in a report presented to the Chamber of Commerce. They outlined six reasons why Los Angeles had to turn to Owens Valley and stated they "heartily" approved the entire plan and urged public support for the bonds needed to finance the water line.[19]

In September the water board asked the city to issue bonds for 1,500,000 dollars for the purchase of land and water and to inaugurate work on the aqueduct. Support for these bonds came from the city government, the Chamber of Commerce and all city newspapers except one, the *Daily News*.[20] On September 7, 1905, by a vote of 10,787 to 755 or over fourteen to one, the citizens of Los Angeles approved the bonds and endorsed the Owens River Project.[21]

While consulting engineers examined the valley, the water board sent a delegation to Washington, D. C. to obtain a right-of-way across government lands for the aqueduct and to gain permission for Los Angeles to control surplus water in Owens Valley. Since Congress would have to pass on Los Angeles' request, the leader chosen for this delegation was Senator Frank P. Flint. This veteran lawmaker from Los Angeles enjoyed a prominence in the national Republican Party that made him valuable to the city's cause. The people of Owens Valley presented the city with its major obstacle in Washington. Unhappy with the Reclamation Service and demanding Lippincott's removal from the Service, valley farmers felt they had been robbed of their future by a great thirsty giant. Most of them believed that both the valley and the city could use water from the Owens River and that plans to obtain control of the surplus was merely a "water grab" to make San Fernando Valley speculators rich. To act for them in Washington they enlisted the aid of Representative Sylvester C. Smith from the Inyo District which includes part of Owens Valley.[22]

Smith was unable to stop Flint who, with the aid of Secretary of the Interior Ethan A. Hitchcock, Chief of the Forest Service Gifford Pinchot, and President Theodore Roosevelt, received both the right-of-way for the line across federal lands and the right of use of the Owens River surplus flow. Pinchot went so far as to declare 298,880 acres of treeless land in Owens Valley a national forest, thus closing it to homesteading. Taft later reversed Pinchot's move, but by that time Los Angeles had completed its aqueduct.[23]

On June 20, 1906, Congress passed an act known as "Public Law Number 395" which granted to Los Angeles all necessary rights-of-way for canals and reservoirs for carrying and storing water and the rights-of-way for electric plants and transmission lines. This act also provided for the sale of public land and reservoir sites to the city at a rate of $1.25 per acre. Besides this federal grant the Southern Pacific Railroad Company sold about 1,000 acres it held in the San Fernando Valley to Los Angeles for five dollars per acre.[24]

After approval by consulting engineers and the federal government were received, the next step for William Mulholland and the water board was to obtain approval for a final bond issue for 23,000,000 dollars by Los Angeles voters. The city charter stated that this was the maximum amount for which the city could bond itself. Such a bond would place a tax of eighty-eight dollars on every man, woman, and child within the corporate limits.[25] Opposition to the aqueduct project came from a small group of Los Angeles citizens led by newspaperman Samuel I. Clover who felt the plan was a water grab to help the Otis-Huntington syndicate. Clover published articles stating that water from Owens River held too much alkali to be used for municipal purposes and that city water shortages had been created by the water department to scare the people into backing the Owens Valley Plan.

Mulholland had the backing of the Los Angeles Chamber of Commerce, the Merchants and Manufacturers Association, newspapers and most civic organizations. The opposition unintentionally promoted passage of the bond issue by rallying supporters. Pamphlets were distributed, slide shows were presented in theaters, school children debated the subject, Mulholland made speeches and Owens Valley water was used at tea parties to disprove Clover's alkali story. On June 12, 1907, the electorate passed the aqueduct bond issue by a vote of ten to one.[26]

The project was then taken out of the hands of the water board and placed under a newly formed Board of Public Works. This new body worked closely with the Water Commissioners. Because of public trust in them, Mulholland and Lippincott were appointed to an advisory committee to handle the details and supervise building the Los Angeles Aqueduct.

Preparations for construction of the aqueduct began soon after the June 12, 1907 bond issue election. The preliminary work rivaled in magnitude the actual excavation and pipe-laying. Mulholland divided the route of the aqueduct into eleven sections which varied in length from six to twenty-three miles depending upon the nature of the terrain.[27] For each of these divisions roads, telephone and power lines, and quarters and offices had to be constructed and, most important, water had to be supplied.

Only one road, a dusty wagon trail, connected Los Angeles and Owens Valley. It led through the little desert town of Mojave, which for half a century prospectors had made their last stop before entering Death Valley, and ore wagons laden with gold and silver from the Sierra Nevada Mountains made it their first stop. Mulholland decided on Mojave as his central distribution point.

Tons of freight and machinery had to be moved by mule train and railroads to the construction sites. Each day the railroad carried detachments of engineers, laborers and equipment. Workmen who lacked train fare walked along the railroad right-of-way. All the men and equipment went first to Mojave and then were distributed to division headquarters along the line.[28]

When the crews began to arrive for work assignments, they built construction camps at various points along the line of stakes that marked the route of the aqueduct. The engineers had planned camp buildings well adapted to the climatic conditions of the region with many windows and doors. Some were portable to allow them to be moved from point to point as construction progressed. The city spent an average of twenty-five dollars to house each man. One hundred eighty-five major buildings were constructed on the line, all lighted by electricity from the city's hydro-electric plants in Owens Valley.[29]

Each camp consisted of an office building, which also included quarters for the engineers and their assistants, a row of bunk houses and a camp store constructed half of wood and half of canvas to supply the necessities of desert living from clothing to tobacco. Each bunkhouse, built to withstand the extremes of desert temperatures, was divided into rooms with two men sharing each room. Every camp also had a mess hall with enough room to feed the hundreds of men who composed each working shift; corrugated iron warehouses and machine shops to store and repair heavy steam shovels, caterpillars, traction engines and drills, and barns and corrals for the livestock. In addition, each major camp had a hospital staffed with a surgeon and steward.[30]

While some crews built the camps, others were hard at work searching out water and laying lines to supply men, animals and equipment. This precious liquid was found in streams and springs in the mountains along the course of the aqueduct. Four systems with three and four inch mains were laid across the desert giving the appearance that men had walked along dragging them as though they were hoses. These four original systems served the whole project for the five-year construction period.[31]

While not discounting the importance of thorough planning and preparation, the engineers believed that completion of the water carrier within five years depended on the speed with which the tunnels could be driven. In September, 1907, at the same time other preparations were beginning, a crew of forty men set up

Section of open canal work showing "stakers" and steam shovel.

Los Angeles Department of Water and Power

camp in San Francisquito Canyon and broke ground at the south portal of the five mile Elizabeth Tunnel. Early in October a second crew started on its north face. While digging this tunnel, the crews set several American records for hardrock tunnel driving, the last being 604 feet in one month. Mulholland and his engineers had estimated it would take five years to complete the tunnel; it took only forty months.[32]

When construction began, the engineers projected that a reasonable progress for each end of the tunnel would be eight feet per day with three crews of eight hours each making one day's work. Soon after work started, the Board of Public Works set up a system of bonuses in which each man in the tunnel received forty cents above his regular wage for every foot exceeding the eight foot quota. The effect of the bonuses was to increase the daily wage of the laborers about thirty percent and to decrease the cost of digging from ten to fifteen percent. Besides the savings made in tunnel construction, the equipment that had been used in the tunnel was released for some other phase of the aqueduct much earlier than had been anticipated.[33]

By October 1, 1908, the date construction officially began, the preliminary work was finished. At this time 215 miles of road, 230 miles of pipeline, 218 miles of power transmission line and 377 miles of telegraph and telephone line were in service. Also, the problem of transporting material from Mojave to Owens Valley had been overcome by building a branch of the Southern Pacific Railroad, known as the Nevada and California Railroad. Finally, a cement plant had been built with a daily capacity of 1,000 barrels of Portland cement.[34]

The army of men who started work on the line came from every level of society. Among them were highly experienced engineers like Mulholland and Lippincott, young engineers just out of college, clerks and draftsmen, mechanics and miners, heavy equipment operators and mule skinners, but most of them were rank and file laborers. These men known as "stakers" worked in the ditch. To maintain a high level of competence, everyone on the payroll except day laborers had to be certified by the City Civil Service Commission of Los Angeles. City officials believed this would minimize political jobs and help remove unproductive laborers.[35]

Los Angeles Department of Water and Power

General work scene on the canal section of the Aqueduct, showing "staker" laborers.

The stakers, over 4,000 of them, came mainly from the gold fields of California and Colorado. They were experienced in digging and tunneling. The work force was domestic. Not a single foreign laborer was imported to work on the project.[36] The workers were soon tagged with the name "hobo" labor because of their habit of working at one division only long enough to be eligible for a bonus. The bonus system, started at the Elizabeth Tunnel, was soon extended to the whole project. It was based on a ten working day period, at the end of which time all bonuses were paid. On payday many took their blanket rolls and bottles and water and set out for the nearest ragtown. After walking at least four miles they would reach these half-wood, half-tent towns made up almost entirely of saloons and bawdy houses. The long walk was required because Los Angeles had persuaded the state legislature to pass a law that saloons and brothels had to be at least four miles from the construction project. After several days of pleasure, the staker would set out for the next division to start the pattern all over again. The tunnel crews usually stayed at their divisions longer than the ditch laborers, but one tunnel foreman recalled in a newspaper interview that he regularly had "one crew drunk, one crew sobering up, and one crew working."[37]

Wherever the stakemen worked along the line, they found one condition that had not existed in the mines, overall use of the most modern construction equipment and techniques. Mulholland believed that if the line were to be completed in five years — and for under 24,000,000 dollars — he must remain aware of the newest construction methods and be ready to use anything that would improve the efficiency of his workers. Mulholland's foresight and that of his assistants paid off for the city. His decision to use the Leyner air hammer drill in the tunnels saved some twenty months of hard rock driving. These light weight drills, designed and built by J. George Leyner of Denver, Colorado, used a light, high-speed oscillating piston or "hammer," striking the end of the drill rod, to drive the drill into the rock rather than the slow action of the piston drill, then standard, in which the entire drill rod was driven in and out.[38]

In addition to the air drill, a new kind of blasting cap was introduced, first in the Elizabeth Tunnel and then, over the entire project. This German-made fuse proved

Los Angeles Department of Water and Power
The Soledad inverted siphon, one of the longest sections of the Los Angeles Aqueduct.

more reliable and much safer than the American-made blasting cap. Over 6,000,000 pounds of blasting powder were used in building the aqueduct, yet only five men were killed by accidents due to explosives in underground work.[39]

Also pioneered on the aqueduct was the electricity-driven shovel. Due to the scarcity of water in the desert, steam power was not always practical. The two hydroelectric plants that had been built in Owens Valley to supply power to the camps were used to run much of the heavy equipment, making this the first major engineering project in America to utilize electricity in this way. These electric shovels reduced expenses by cutting down the need for coal and fuel oil.[40]

Not all of the new equipment proved successful. One example was the Caterpillar tractor. Before its introduction all material for the project had been carried over the precipitous mountain roads and across the desert on wagons pulled by jerk-line mule teams. Moving materials and heavy equipment this way was slow and difficult. The shovels had to be dismantled and packed in several wagons before they could be transported from one location to another. To overcome this Mulholland decided to try the newly invented traction engine, called by its manufacturer the "Caterpillar" because of its resemblance to a caterpillar as it moved across the ground. With this new tractor a shovel could be moved easily by simply hooking on two "Cats" in tandem and pulling it. Here again the savings were substantial since one tractor could do the work of hundreds of animals at less than half the cost. But after several months of work in the desert the Caterpillars began to cost more and more to maintain as fine blowing sand destroyed vital parts. After repeated breakdowns and repairs, Mulholland abandoned them. The slower but more reliable mule once more became the method of transportation in the desert.[41]

Construction was not the only phase of the Los Angeles Aqueduct in which new techniques were used. In designing the water carrier, engineers employed the inverted siphon, a new method for transporting water across ravines and canyons. The inverted siphon is a steel or concrete pipe designed to handle extremely high heads of water pressures that build up as water descends into and rises out of canyons. Before their development water had to be gradually lowered into a

Jerk-line mule teams pulling section of steel pipe used on the Soledad siphon.

Los Angeles Department of Water and Power

canyon by a long sloping decline. With the inverted siphon the water could be dropped over the edge of a canyon wall. It had limited use on the Catskill Mountain Aqueduct and at Niagara Falls. Construction design called for a total of over nine miles of siphon, with three sections over a mile in length and twenty shorter ones. One of the longest sections, called the Soledad siphon, was 8,060 feet long and eleven feet in diameter and was, except for a steel main imbedded in concrete near Madrid, Spain, the largest steel pipe in use by 1912.[42]

Eastern companies that supplied steel for the siphons built thirty-foot sections of large diameter pipe with one-half inch thick steel walls and shipped them to the project on railroad flat cars. Each of these sections made up a full carload. Some of the steel for the smaller siphons was cut and shaped at the factory and shipped unriveted. This reduced shipping expense by making it possible to place more than one section on a railroad car.[43]

Trouble developed with the siphons after their installation. At Sand Canyon where the design called for a steel siphon, the engineers decided to experiment by drilling a pressure tunnel in rock on both inclines. The rock formation of the canyon walls seemed to be massive granite. But when the first pressure hit the siphon, fissures and leaks began to appear. When full pressure was turned into the conduit, the south incline blew out spectacularly, and the whole side of the mountain crashed to the canyon floor.[44]

Another problem occurred soon after completion of the aqueduct when unusually heavy rains washed out concrete piers which supported the siphon across Antelope Valley. When the siphon sagged from loss of these supports, a circular seam broke. Water burst out at a head pressure of 200 pounds per square inch. As the water left the lower portion of the siphon a vacuum was created in the upper portion subjecting the pipe to atmospheric pressure and "the steel pipe collapsed like an emptied fire hose for nearly two miles of its length."[45] In places the top and bottom of the pipe were forced to within a few inches of each other. On examining the damage, many engineers pronounced it a total loss, saying that the thick pipe would have to be taken up, the 1/4 to 5/16 inch thick steel plate rerolled and the siphon rebuilt.

The section was repaired, however, by turning water slowly into the pipe after the break had been mended. The hydraulic pressure created as the water started down the siphon restored its circular form. By gradually increasing the head of water the engineers allowed the pipe to take its original form without breaking joints or shearing rivets. Common sense and ingenuity saved the city over 245,000 dollars in repair expense, and the line was working in less than a month.[46]

With excellent supervision, new building techniques and bonus incentives, the aqueduct was far ahead of the construction timetable. Work had been going so well

Los Angeles Department of Water and Power
Collapsed inverted siphon at Antelope Valley

that the New York investment companies were buying bonds ahead of schedule. In mid-May, 1910, a currency shortage caused the financing firms to stop purchasing bonds in advance and to inform the city that they would supply no more money until the construction schedule caught up with the bonds already purchased.

This financial stricture hit at a time when there was only enough money on hand for one month's work at the regular pace. In order to conserve funds, Mulholland reduced the size of his crews, retaining only enough men to prevent completed work from falling into disrepair. Only in the tunnels did he maintain full work gangs. In a few days the work force dropped from over 4,000 men to less than 1,000. Whole divisions were shut down, and Mojave, ordinarily booming with the trade of 3,000 workers, became a dead camp. Since he was ahead of schedule, Mulholland believed he could ride out the money strain, but his well-organized crews were broken down and scattered.

During the slow-down, trouble erupted among the remaining workers. On July 19 the mess contractor asked to raise the price of food in order to compensate for the smaller number of boarders. Aqueduct officials, in answer to these demands, raised the price of meals five cents on condition that the food would be improved. This rate increase went into effect in November, 1910, and was branded by the Western Federation of Miners, who were trying to organize the aqueduct workers, as unfair. The union, at this time, linked with the Industrial Workers of the World, had already made considerable headway in organizing the tunnel crews of the Little Lake, Grapevine and Elizabeth Divisions. The union gained enough strength to call a strike two weeks after the meal price increase. More that seven hundred men walked off the line leaving only skeleton crews at most construction sites and closing Elizabeth tunnel completely.[47]

By the end of 1910 the financial crisis was over, and Mulholland was able to weaken the hold of the union by lowering meal prices and raising bonuses. The temporary slowdown cost Los Angeles more than 250,000 dollars but did not necessitate an extension in construction time.

After a slight delay in May, 1913, when a section of the pipeline burst, Owens River water arrived at the San Fernando reservoir on November 5, 1913. After being treated at the reservoir, the water was pumped into city mains. Over 30,000 people watched as the water poured out of the last tunnel and down an artificial waterfall. As the water rushed in, Mulholland is quoted as saying, "There it is. Take it."[48]

Los Angeles did take the water, and virtually overnight the city turned from water famine to water flood. The San Fernando Valley, where the aqueduct dumped its precious load into the Upper Van Norman Lake, changed from a grain growing center dependent on intermittent rainfall to one of the richest truck garden and orchard communities in the United States. By 1915 most of the valley was annexed by Los Angeles. With the lure of what was thought to be an inexhaustible water supply, one community after another joined Los Angeles. The belief that they had solved their water problems was short lived for Angelenos. While it lasted, they made the most of it.

For William Mulholland the period following completion of the line was a time of reward. Most of the population is Los Angeles and the nation believed that his boundless energy and confidence had made the aqueduct a reality. All the animosity for his role in the acquisition of water rights in Owens Valley seemed to

Typical construction camp located in the Grapevine Division, in the Mojave Desert.

Los Angeles Department of Water and Power

South portal of the Elizabeth Lake Tunnel during construction.

dissolve. National magazines acclaimed the aqueduct to be a "splendid monument to Chief Engineer Mulholland and his assistants" and an engineering feat second only to the Panama Canal.⁴⁹ The University of California gave Mulholland an honorary doctorate in engineering, and wherever he went he was introduced as the "Goliath of the West" and as "California's greatest man."⁵⁰

Leaders in Los Angeles now felt that they were totally independent of the limitations nature placed on their region. As early as 1905 they realized that because of the uncertain condition of their water supply, it was unlikely factories, mills and other long term investment enterprises would be located in the Los Angeles area. Also, because a large percentage of the city's income was from tourism which would be one of the first activities to be curtailed during a depression, Los Angeles would be directly affected by every shift in the national economy. Many people now believed that even if no new industry moved to the area a large population could support itself on the irrigated land in the suburbs. One engineer estimated that he could sustain himself and his family on only one acre of irrigated land in the Hollywood area. With over a hundred thousand acres of such land to be irrigated this would mean that Los Angeles could now maintain over a half a million people living in a radius of twenty-five miles of City Hall.⁵¹

Unfortunately, despite the engineering genius that had gone into the aqueduct, one vital feature of the Owens Valley project had been omitted — a major reservoir. With the pressing need for water, Los Angeles simply built the aqueduct and tapped into the lower end of Owens River. The only reservoirs built were small ones that served the month-to-month operation of the aqueduct. During normal climatic conditions there was enough water in Owens River for both Owens Valley farmers to irrigate their fields and the water board to supply the city. But without a major reservoir water could not be stored during wet years to provide for dry ones.⁵²

In a normal year most of the water that flowed into Owens Valley from the Sierra Nevada Mountains went unused.⁵³ Most of the precipitation in this area occurs in the form of snow. As a result streams feeding Owens River are at their minimum discharge between September and April although about eighty percent of the moisture falls in this period. During early April snow begins to melt and between June 15 and July 15 the river reaches its maximum flow. The discharge then begins to decline until by mid-September it once again reaches its minimum which remains regular because of percolating ground water.⁵⁴

Between 1913 and 1920 exceptionally heavy snowfall in the mountains provided enough water to allow the ground water level to remain high, thus insuring a supply during the long months when stream discharge into the river was low. But beginning in 1922 a succession of abnormally dry years started to affect the flow of Owens River making it inadequate to supply both the needs of the valley and the demand of the rapidly growing city. Had Los Angeles followed early recommendations to built a major reservoir at Long Valley in the upper reaches of Owens Valley above Bishop (see map) problems of later years could have been avoided.⁵⁵

This decrease in water came at a time of unprecedented and unforeseen population growth in both Owens Valley and Los Angeles after World War I. William Mulholland's intolerant attitude toward valley residents, and a feud between Mulholland and several Los Angelenos, including Fred Eaton, who had large ranches in Long Valley, gave rise to a violent period in Southern California history. The events of the next few years have been described as "California's Little Civil War"⁵⁶ or simply as the "Water War."⁵⁷

Trouble broke out in the summer of 1922 when water reaching the aqueduct intake proved to be insufficient to meet the city's needs. More water was required. The first step taken by the city was to buy irrigated lands and the ditches that served them and allow the water allotted for that property to go on down river toward the intake.⁵⁸ This action by the city caused deep alarm among the valley people. They feared that their oasis would soon return to desert. The remaining farmers countered the city first by diverting more water into their fields⁵⁹ and second by attempting to form the Owens Valley Irrigation District to hold all remaining water rights. Late in 1922 the plan for the formation of this irrigation district was approved by a vote of the farmers. Before the water titles could be turned over to the new district, two agents from Los Angeles moved along the McNalley Ditch, one of the oldest and largest irrigation canals, offering high prices for water rights.⁶⁰

During 1922 and 1923 Los Angeles spent over 12,000,000 dollars purchasing water-bearing lands, but this did not help the ever decreasing water supply in Los Angeles and the San Fernando Valley. Early in 1923 farmers in the San Fernando Valley were told that supplying domestic needs of the city had priority over irrigating the valley, therefore, they would have to curtail the watering of their fields. Mulholland protested this move, holding that water once put on the land should never be removed.⁶¹

In the summer of 1923 Los Angeles began drilling water wells near the aqueduct intake. An effort was made by the overlying farmers to block this action, but for each case that was tried and an injunction issued, the city would buy out the landowner.⁶² At this same time the Los Angeles Department of Public Service tried to purchase the water rights along the Big Pine Canal, the last big ditch out from the mouth of the aqueduct. All water that was not taken by canals upstream was being siphoned off by Big Pine. When their move to buy the land failed, the city resorted to more "primitive measures." The Big Pine intake was on a U-bend in the meandering river. A construction crew was sent into the area with instructions to cut a canal across the bend, diverting the river and leaving the Big Pine Canal high and dry.

When the Big Piners discovered the city workmen, they formed a posse of about twenty armed men and moved on the construction site. They charged across the river and with what one of them called a "shotgun injunction" told the laborers that if the work stopped no one would be shot. The farmers took all the city equipment and dumped it into the river. Faced with armed force the city reopened negotiations for purchase of water rights and soon met the farmers' demand of 1,100,000 dollars, thus making many of the farmers wealthy.[63]

By October, 1923, the water problem was so critical in Los Angeles that Mulholland recommended to the Department of Public Service that another area would have to be opened up to serve the city's increasing needs. He proposed that a survey be made of the Colorado Rover to determine the feasibility of importing water from it. This recommendation was approved, and on October 29, 1923, William Mulholland led the first reconnaissance party of the Colorado River aqueduct survey into the field.

Colorado River water was many millions of dollars and a decade away. What Los Angeles needed was immediate help. By 1924, water flowing into the aqueduct had dropped from 355 to 262.5 cubic feet per second. The local rainfall in Owens Valley had declined from an average of over sixteen inches per year to 6.67 inches.[64]

By March, 1924, farmers in the San Fernando Valley faced the possibility of financial ruin if Los Angeles did not receive enough water to allow them to irrigate their fields. They sent a delegation up to Owens Valley to buy water. The delegates were escorted along brim-full irrigation canals and were told that not a drop of it was for sale but that they could buy out the entire upper valley in forty-eight hours for 8,000,000 dollars. At this point the controversy changed from farmers fighting to keep their homes and lands productive to farmers trying to get as much money from the city as they could possible force them to pay. The Owens Valley farmers told the San Fernandoans that if they needed the water so badly they should be willing to pay what was asked for it.

The delegation returned home and within two months the city gave its answer. A suit was filed against the upper valley in an effort to recover the McNally and Big Pine water that Los Angeles had purchased. Fearing they could never defeat the city in court, the Owens Valley people prepared for violence.[65]

The suit was filed in early May, 1924. On May 20, three boxes of dynamite were taken from a Bishop powder house owned by Wilfred and Mark Watterson, leaders of the settlers fighting Los Angeles. Wilfred Watterson owned five banks in eastern California and dominated the economic life of Owens Valley. The destination of the dynamite was a section of the aqueduct a few miles north of the town of Lone Pine.

Here shortly after one a.m. on May 21, 1924, a charge was set off that shook the lower valley like an earthquake. Almost before the dynamiters could leave the scene, the aqueduct employees were swarming over the area. They found that a forty-foot section of the line had been blown away.[66]

The water crisis had reached another turning point. It now became a shooting war. Soon after the dynamiting an attorney representing Los Angeles in Owens Valley was kidnapped and ordered to leave the valley.[67] Mulholland, enraged by the attack on his aqueduct, hurled a diatribe at the Owens Valley ranchers calling them "yellow" and "barking dogs." The ranchers countered this name calling with a warning that if he set one foot in Bishop he would be lynched.[68]

In the valley demands that the city buy all of the ranches grew to include demands that the town properties be included in Los Angeles' purchasing and that reparation be made to the business communities for intangible damage done by the loss of customers due to their moving after selling out to the city. In July, 1924, Los Angeles mayor George E. Cryer went to Owens Valley to investigate the problem and to try to bring it to a reasonable solution. Upon his return to Los Angeles he recommended that the city purchase all of the remaining land in Owens Valley. To this Mulholland, who questioned the integrity of the valley leaders, answered that most of the water-bearing land in the area had been purchased and that the settlers were trying to force the city to buy land it did not need.[69]

Two months later Mulholland, in open defiance of the Bishop settlers' threats, led a party of reporters, committeemen, engineers and the entire Los Angeles Water Board to Owens Valley. They were met by Watterson and were told that the only fair solution was to buy the whole district. On their return to Los Angeles the commissioners drew up a plan of compensation for losses accrued by business by previous land purchases and promised to aid the valley economy. This plan submitted by the Los Angeles Board of Public Service Commissioners to the Owens Valley residents in October proposed:

> ...a reservation of thirty thousand acres in the upper part of the valley for agricultural purposes, the development of surface and underground water supplies, the construction of paved highways, and a systematic plan for the upbuilding of the valley towns.[70]

This proposal was aimed at increasing tourist travel in the area besides improving the farmers' situation. But this effort was met by criticism and was denounced in the valley as a "vague declaration...that in effect, said nothing, meant nothing and guaranteed nothing."[71]

The valley leaders saw that this fairly generous proposal and early snowstorms which promised more water for the next spring were diminishing their prospects for forcing the lucrative sale of their properties. They felt that more vigorous steps were needed to coerce the city to buy their land. Early on the morning of November 16, 1924, Mark Watterson led a force of between sixty and a hundred men in autos down the length of Owens valley. When this parade neared the town of Lone Pine (see map) it turned eastward toward the aqueduct which lay in the tortuous Alabama Hills. Here these men, many of them prominent Valley citizens, seized a set of waste gates and turned the water out of the aqueduct through an overflow spillway to flow into the Owens River. This water, amounting to 200,000,000 gallons per day, flowed downriver, eventually to be evaporated as it lay in the dry basin of Owens Lake.

The first representative of the city to reach the scene was Edward F. Leaney, who was Los Angeles' chief delegate in Owens Valley. Although warned not to leave his car, he climbed into the main wheelhouse. Here, while swinging a noose in front of him, the settlers explained their reasons for forcibly taking the Alabama Gates. In essence the demonstration was aimed at publicizing their demands throughout California. Also they hoped that direct action might help force Los Angeles to make a decision to buy out the valley. Their hopes for publicity were soon fulfilled by the arrival of a large number of reporters from throughout the nation.[72]

After Leaney's unsuccessful attempt to reason with the settlers, Los Angeles turned to legal action. Seventy-five copies of a restraining order were issued and given to the sheriff of Inyo County, Charles Collins. Armed with these orders he arrived at the gates the day after they had been taken. He found that the settlers had strung barbed wire around the gates and wheelhouse and were waiting for a contingent of detectives and investigators that were rumored on their way to the site from Los Angeles. Collins' efforts were at best half-hearted. The documents he issued were thrown into the river, and he was picked up and carried to his car.[73]

By the second day the siege at the waste gates had become a valley-wide picnic. Wives of the insurgents brought baskets of food; children played in and around the wheelhouse; and in store windows were signs that read, "If I am not on the job, you will find me at the Aqueduct." A similar sign was flown from the flagpole in Bishop. One preacher who was asked why he was condoning this act of lawlessness by being present at the site answered that his whole congregation was there. This holiday was costing Los Angeles an estimated 15,000 dollars per day.[74]

In desperation Los Angeles sent out a request to sheriffs throughout southern California for their aid. Once these law officers agreed to give their support to the sheriff of Inyo, word was sent to Sheriff Collins. His office reported that he had left the county to go to the state capitol to plead with Governor F.W. Richardson to call out the National Guard. The Governor steadfastly refused to take any such action.[75]

The Owens Valley farmers' hopes that Los Angeles businessmen would not stand behind the water department when the reputation of the city for fair dealing was questioned were thwarted. The water supply was not immediately cut off because of reservoirs near the city, and most Angelenos believed that the valley action was an attempt to terrorize them. The attitude of the city went against the farmers' cause, and instead of aiding them, it was the businessmen who finally broke the beleaguerment.[76]

The farmers were finally driven from the Alabama Gates by economic pressure. When the demonstration broke out, Wilfred Watterson was meeting with fellow bankers of the Clearinghouse Association in Los Angeles. At this meeting Watterson called for the adoption of a resolution supporting the "embattled farmers" and calling for the outright purchase of all the land in question. But instead of supporting Watterson the bankers told him that unless he got the gates closed, they would cut off his bank's credit.[77] He immediately returned to Owens Valley, and on the evening of the nineteenth he met with a twelve-man delegation from the spillway at his soda works at Keeler on Owens Lake. He explained that the business community in Los Angeles had agreed to aid the farmers, and he advised them to return to their homes. Before sunup the next morning, the settlers broke camp and turned the Alabama Gates to city employees, who promptly diverted the water back into the aqueduct.[78]

No legal action was taken against the men who had seized the spillway, but their return of it to city control did not end hostilities. Though tempers seemed to cool during the rest of 1924 and 1925, the following year a new series of dynamitings began on the line. These continued in the valley. These crimes too went unpunished.[79] Between May and August of 1927, dynamitings were almost a weekly if not a nightly affair. City agents armed with Winchesters, tommyguns and sawed off shotguns raced up and down the line only to have the saboteurs slip in behind them and blow gaping holes in the aqueduct.[80]

What Los Angeles could not do by offering to buy all the land in Owens Valley at appraised prices and by sending great armies of armed World War I veterans into the valley was accomplished by a simple newspaper notice that appeared in a Bishop newspaper on August 4, 1927. The announcement stated that N.N. and M.G. Watterson were closing their banks in Owens Valley. An audit by State Superintendent of Banks Will C. Woods showed a shortage in excess of two million dollars.

The collapse of the banks in Inyo County coupled with the arrest of their leaders stunned the valley farmers and delighted Los Angeles citizens. The failure of the Wattersons' banks explained why the brothers had been so eager to get Los Angeles money and why they had not allowed the farmers to carry their fight to the courtroom. Both the Wattersons were convicted of thirty-six counts of embezzlement on November 11,

1927, and sentenced to long prison terms in San Quentin. Los Angeles quickly moved to clean up Owens Valley by starting a program of land and business purchasing.[81] Under this program, augmented by a twelve million dollar bond issue, Los Angeles, by the mid-1930's, had bought more than ninety percent of the privately-owned land, both business and rural in Owens Valley.[82]

The conviction of the Watterson brothers marked the end of organized resistance to Los Angeles in Owens Valley. Most of the families that had remained in the valley were ruined financially by the failure of the banks. Los Angeles offered jobs to many men as a measure to relieve the wide-spread distress in the area. In some cases they were set to work repairing the damage they had done on the aqueduct. Also, though the nation was suffering a severe depression in the 1930's, Los Angeles continued to offer and to pay land prices that it had originally set in the early 1920's. As another method of stabilizing the supporting area's economy, the city, working with the people of Inyo County, began leasing its properties for continued operation. In many cases these properties, both rural and business, remained in the hands of the former owners.[83]

The disaster that broke Owens Valley's will to fight was soon equalled by a disaster that broke the spirit not only of William Mulholland but of the entire Los Angeles Water and Power Department. In August of 1924, Los Angeles had begun construction of a reservoir in San Francisquito Canyon. This reservoir was to catch and store water that had been used to create electricity. Formerly the water that was released from the San Fernando Reservoir power generator had been lost. Mulholland suggested that the city build a dam on the Santa Clara River to save this water. Also, concern over the fact that the Elizabeth Tunnel pierced the San Andreas Fault and that emergency storage was needed below the fault was a prime factor in the need for a dam.[84]

By May, 1926, work was completed, and the structure was christened the St. Francis Dam. Almost as soon as it was finished, problems arose. The dam site lay along the San Andreas Fault, and the rock formation on which the base of the dam sat was permeated by fractures and cracks. The fact that these hazards were overlooked or ignored can probably be explained by the constant pressure that was on the Department of Water and Power to find new sources of water to supply Los Angeles. Soon after construction was completed, leaks began to develop, and by the end of 1927 it was evident that the valley walls, made up of mica schist and conglomerate, were soaking up water and swelling, causing two major dam cracks. Appearing in January of 1928 they started at the top center of the structure and sloped out to each side, indicating that the sides of the dam were being forced upward.[85]

Early in March the water below the dam turned muddy, indicating to many that the abutment ground was giving way. On March 12, 1928, Mulholland and Harvey A. Van Norman, Mulholland's assistant, inspected the dam. They explained that the muddy water was due to a nearby road construction project, and although the dam leaked, all concrete dams leak slightly. A few hours later at 11:57½ a.m. the entire structure gave way, sending a hundred and eighty-five foot wall of water down the San Francisquito Canyon. Five hours later, the crest, now twenty-five feet high, rushed out of the mouth of the Santa Clara River into the Pacific Ocean, some sixty miles from the dam, leaving a wake of terror and destruction that destroyed the towns of Piru, Castaic Junction, Fillmore, Santa Paula and Ventura plus several construction camps and numerous isolated farms and ranches. The official death toll was fixed at between 385 and 420, but there was no way of knowing the exact number. Over 1,250 homes and 7,900 acres of farmland lay desolated, making it one of America's worst flood disasters.[86]

William Mulholland bore the brunt of the wrath of the people in the Santa Clara Valley. At the coroner's inquest that followed the tragedy, Mulholland accepted full responsibility for the dam. "Don't blame anybody else," his statement began. "You just fasten it on me. If there was an error of human judgment, I was the human."[87] It is interesting to note the use of the word "if" in Mulholland's testimony. He believed that the dam had been dynamited by Owens Valley hotheads. This belief was shared by only a few experts, one being Frank Rieber, consulting engineer for San Francisco. No definite proof was ever presented for this theory.[88]

The St. Francis Dam experience left the Los Angeles Department of Water and Power without the leadership of Mulholland. He retired immediately after the coroner's inquest, much mellower toward the Owens Valley problem. From March 1928 the rift between the valley farmers and the city seemed to lessen. There were occasional flareups and dynamitings, but nothing to compare with the previous hostilities.

REFERENCES

1. Robert Glass Cleland, *From Wilderness to Empire: A History of California* (New York: Alfred A. Knopf, 1959), 336.
2. U.S. Census Office, 9th Census, 1870, *Ninth Census of the United States, Statistics of Population* (Washington: Government Printing Office, 1872), 90; and U.S. Census Office, 12th Census, 1900, *Twelfth Census of the United States, Population, I* (Washington: Government Printing Office, 1901), 126.
3. Charles Anaden Moody, "Los Angeles and the Owens River," *Out West*, XXIII, No. 4 (October, 1905), 428.
4. City of Los Angeles, *Complete Report on Construction of the Los Angeles Aqueduct* (Los Angeles: Department of Public Service, 1916), 9.
5. Joseph B. Lippincott, "William Mulholland—Engineer, Pioneer, Raconteur —Part II," *Civil Engineering*, 11 (March, 1941), 162.
6. City of Los Angeles, 51.
7. Henry Z. Osborne, "The Completion of the Los Angeles Aqueduct," *Scientific American*, CIX, No. 19 (November 8, 1913), 364.

8. A miner's inch of water is equal to one and one-half cubic feet per minute or 13,000 gallons per day.
9. U.S. Congress, House, *Fourth Annual Report of the Reclamation Service, 1904-1905*, 59th Cong., 1st sess., 1906, House Doc. 86, 97.
10. City of Los Angeles, 13.
11. Remi Nadeau, *The Water Seekers* (New York: Doubleday and Co., 1950) 12.
12. City of Los Angeles, 10.
13. Margaret Romer, "The Story of Los Angeles," *Journal of the West*, III (January, 1964), 17.
14. U.S. Congress, House, 97.
15. City of Los Angeles, 48.
16. William R. Stewart, "A Desert City's Far Reach for Water," *The World's Work* XV, No. 1 (November, 1907), 9538-39.
17. Nadeau, 33.
18. Remi Nadeau, "Water War," *American Heritage*, XIII, No. 1 (December, 1961), 32.
19. City of Los Angeles, 14.
20. Romer, 17.
21. City of Los Angeles, 14.
22. Nadeau, *Water Seekers*, 35.
23. Oscar Osburn Winther, "Los Angeles: It's Aqueduct Life Lines," *The Journal of Geography*, XLIX (February, 1950), 48.
24. City of Los Angeles, 71-72.
25. Burt A. Heinly, "Carrying Water Through A Desert: The Story of the Los Angeles Aqueduct," *The National Geographic Magazine*, XXI (July, 1910), 585.
26. Vincent Ostrum, *Water and Politics: A Study of Water Policies and Adminstration in the Development of Los Angeles* (Los Angeles: The Haynes Foundation, 1953), 55.
27. Burt A. Heinly, "Carrying Water Through a Desert: The Story of the Los Angeles Aqueduct," *The National Geographic Magazine*, XXI (July, 1910), 585.
28. Roscoe E. Schrader, "A Ditch in the Desert," *Scribner's Magazine*, LI, No. 5 (May, 1912), 541.
29. Burt A. Heinly, "The Longest Aqueduct in the World," *The Outlook*, XCIII (September 25, 1909), 218.
30. Schrader, 544.
31. *Ibid.*, 542.
32. Remi Nadeau, *The Water Seekers*, 47.
33. City of Los Angeles, *Complete Report on Construction of the Los Angeles Aqueduct* (Los Angeles: Department of Public Service, 1916), 21.
34. City of Los Angeles, 22.
35. Heinly, "Carrying Water Through...," 588.
36. Morrow Mayo, *Los Angeles* (New York: Alfred A. Knopf, 1933), 238.
37. Heinly, "The Longest Aqueduct...," 219; and Nadeau, 47.
38. City of Los Angeles, 21.
39. *Ibid.*, 25.
40. Schrader, 544.
41. Nadeau, 49.
42. Heinly, "The Longest Aqueduct...," 476.
43. "Nine Miles of Siphons," *The Literary Digest*, XLVI, No. 9, Whole No. 1193 (March 1, 1913), 452.
44. City of Los Angeles, 26.
45. *Ibid.*, 29.
46. *Ibid.*, 29.
47. Nadeau, 52-53; and City of Los Angeles, 26.
48. Remi Nadeau, "Water War," *American Heritage*, XIII (December, 1961), 35.
49. Henry Z. Osborne, "The Completion of the Los Angeles Aqueduct," *Scientific American*, CIX, No. 19 (November 8, 1913), 372.
50. Remi Nadeau, "Water War," *American Heritage*, XIII, 35.
51. William E. Smythe, "The Social Significance of the Owens River Project," *Out West*, XXIII, No. 4 (Octtober, 1905), 443-45.
52. Nadeau, 35.
53. Morrow Mayo, *Los Angeles* (New York: Alfred A. Knopf, 1933), 230.
54. Vincent Ostrum, *Water and Politics: A Study of Water Policies and Administration in the Development of Los Angeles* (Los Angeles: The Haynes Foundation, 1953), 55.
55. In 1941 a reservoir was finally built at Long Valley.
56. "California's Little Civil War," *Scribner's Magazine*, LI, No. 8 (May, 1912), 15.
57. Nadeau, 30.
58. A Special Correspondent, "The Owens Valley Controversy," *The Outlook*, CXLVI, No. 11 (July 13, 1927), 342.
59. Robert Glass Cleland, *California in Our Time, 1900-1940* (New York: Alfred A. Knopf, 1947), 185.
60. Nadeau, 103.
61. Joseph B. Lippincott, "William Mulholland—Engineer, Pioneer, Raconteur—Part II," *Civil Engineering*, 11 (March, 1941), 163.
62. Ostrum, 132.
63. Nadeau, 103.
64. Ostrum, 15-16.
65. Nadeau, 104.
66. "California's Little Civil War," 15.
67. *Ibid.*
68. Nadeau, 104.
69. Ostrum, 62.
70. Cleland, 188.
71. *Ibid.*
72. A Special Correspondent, 343.
73. Nadeau, 87.
74. *Ibid.*, 88-89.
75. Nadeau, "Water War", 104.
76. A Special Correspondent, 343.
77. Nadeau, "Water War", 105.
78. "California's Little Civil War," 15.
79. Cleland, 189.
80. Nadeau, "Water Seekers", 104-107.
81. Nadeau, "Water War," 106.
82. Inyo County Board of Supervisors, *Inyo 1866-1966* (Bishop, California: Chalfant Press, 1966), 70.
83. *Ibid.*
84. Charles Outland, *Man-Made Disaster: The Story of the St. Francis Dam* (Glendale, California: The Arthur H. Clark Co., 1965), 30.
85. *Ibid.*, 49-58.
86. *Ibid.*, 79, Appendix v, vi.
87. *Ibid.*, 211.
88. *Ibid.*, 193.

A Neglected Aspect of the Owens River Aqueduct Story: The Inception of the Los Angeles Municipal Electric System

BY NELSON VAN VALEN

The Owens River aqueduct has long been a favorite topic for investigation among scholars and journalists concerned with California south of the Tehachapi.[1] Recently the aqueduct story even provided the basis for the Oscar-winning screenplay of the highly successful commercial film "Chinatown." Yet for all of the attention it has received, one significant aspect of the aqueduct story — the electric power aspect — has been consistently neglected. This essay seeks to remedy that neglect.

On Saturday morning, July 29, 1905, residents of the City of Los Angeles on picking up their copies of the Los Angeles *Times* read of a decidedly ambitious undertaking — a project to bring water to the city from the Owens River, 250 miles to the north.[2] The project had its origins in a growing population's pressure on scarce water resources. A quarter of a century earlier, at the beginning of the boom of the eighties, Los Angeles had a population of 11,000. At the end of the decade, the city's population stood at 50,000, and at the turn of the century, at 100,000. At the date of the *Times* story, the population of Los Angeles was approaching 200,000. Especially during the last dozen years of this quarter-century of extraordinarily rapid population growth, the problem of supplying the city's increasingly numerous inhabitants with water became critical. In the eighties, there seemed no cause for concern, for the peak of the boom coincided with the beginning of a wet period during which the Los Angeles River, the city's principal source of water, rose to a record mean annual flow of 100 cubic feet per second. "We have water enough here in the river to supply the city for the next fifty years," declared

[85]

the future Chief Engineer and General Manager of the city's water system, William Mulholland. But the mid-nineties witnessed the beginning of a dry period that continued for a decade. By 1900, the mean annual flow of the Los Angeles River had fallen to 57 second feet. In 1901 the river's flow was 53.5 feet, and in 1902, 45 feet. The Board of Water Commissioners insisted, "There is ample water" — but installed meters and raised rates in order to "stop waste." In 1903, the river's flow dropped another foot. In 1904 the river's flow reached a record low of 42.8 second feet. For ten days in the summer of that year, water was drawn out of Los Angeles reservoirs faster than it flowed into them — and newcomers continued to arrive. Mulholland summed up the situation, "Our population climbed to the top and the bottom appeared to drop out of the river."[3] Out of this combination of circumstances emerged the Owens River project.

Although the preponderant majority of Los Angeles residents first learned of the project when they picked up their copies of the *Times* that summer morning in 1905, the idea was an old one; it had been put forward in the public press a quarter-century earlier.[4] The idea first began to take the form of a specific project in the mid-nineties in the mind of Fred Eaton. In turn superintendent of the Los Angeles City Water Company, Los Angeles City Engineer, and in 1899-1900 Mayor of Los Angeles, Eaton was thoroughly familiar with the city's water problem. He early came to believe that Los Angeles must someday supplement the flow of the Los Angeles River with water from an additional source, and in the mid-nineties concluded that that source would be the Owens River.

> Mr. Eaton did not publicly discuss his ideas . . . [Mulholland explained in his first annual report as Chief Engineer of the Los Angeles Aqueduct]. In the fall of 1904 and the early spring of 1905, Mr. Eaton on his own responsibility and at his own expense, began obtaining contracts and options on water-bearing property in Owens Valley. With these contracts and options in hand, he first presented the matter to representatives of the City of Los Angeles in the fall of 1904 and early in the year 1905.

Convinced, after months of investigation, both of the sufficiency of the Owens River water supply and of the feasibility of the aqueduct necessary to carry the water from the valley to the city, the Water Board came to an agreement with Eaton. Two days after the Owens River project became public knowledge, the Board requested the City Council to call a special election to authorize a preliminary $1,500,000 bond issue to purchase the necessary lands, water rights, and right of way in Owens Valley, and to make the necessary preliminary engineering investigation prior to the beginning of actual construction of the aqueduct.[6]

Fifty miles from Los Angeles the proposed aqueduct dropped precipitously at two points a total distance of almost fifteen hundred feet. Thus the Owens River project was not only a water project; it was also a hydroelectric power project. Initially, however, there was little general awareness of the power implications of the project. That

> Little drops of water
> On little grains of sand
> Make a hell of a difference
> In the price of land

was immediately apparent to virtually everyone, and virtually everyone also recognized quickly that an ample supply of water was essential to the prosperity not only of Los Angeles real estate operators but of the city generally. But that a plentiful supply of cheap electricity might also have some bearing on the city's prosperity and that the proposed aqueduct might provide that supply — these facts were neither so immediately nor so generally apparent. City officials, perhaps fearful of arousing the opposition of the private electric utility companies, said almost nothing about the power potential of the aqueduct.[7] Nor did the press have much to say about that potential. The *Times*, for example, in breaking the story of the Owens River project made but one brief reference to electric power.[8]

Within a week after the announcement of the Owens River project, however, the press began to recognize the project's potential for electric power development. "With electric power at nominal cost," declared a *Times* editorial, "the entire city — or at least all the principal streets — might be illuminated with brilliantly lighted lamps on ornamental candelabra." But the *Times* was clearly more interested in power than in light. "Look at the

[87]

question of power for manufacturing," the editorial continued.

> Power to run factories could be supplied at about cost . . . and that cost would be so trifling as to be scarcely worth mentioning. Just think what such an inducement would mean in the way of transforming Los Angeles into one of the most important manufacturing cities in the country.[9]

Yet despite the trifling cost at which aqueduct electricity would be sold, another *Times* editorial asserted, receipts from power and light sales would net the city $2,000,000 annually, a sum more than sufficient to discharge all expenses of aqueduct construction within a twenty-five year period. Other Los Angeles newspapers presented much the same argument.[10]

In mid-August the City Council called the special election requested by the Water Board to authorize the $1,500,000 preliminary bond issue. Los Angeles voters approved the issue by a margin greater than that given any previous municipal issue.[11] They did so, no doubt, primarily because they believed additional water was essential for the city's continued growth. "If we don't get the water," Mulholland once observed, "we won't need it." It seems highly probable, however, that the overwhelming nature of the vote was in part traceable to the assurances that electricity to be developed along the aqueduct would pay the cost of constructing the aqueduct and also assure the industrialization of Los Angeles. The city could, indeed, eat its cake and have it, too.

From the voting of these bonds, interest in the power side of the Owens River project increased markedly. Only two days after approval of the issue, Eaton called attention to what the *Times* called a "NEW SIDE TO OWENS PROJECT" — the power side. Eaton asserted that 65,000 horse power could be developed within twenty miles of Los Angeles and an additional 25,000 horse power one hundred miles from the city. Eaton's estimate of the city's annual revenue from the sale of aqueduct power was $1,000,000, a figure but half that put forward by the *Times* during the bond campaign but equivalent to four percent interest on $25,000,000, the estimated cost of building the aqueduct.[12]

In part because they saw in cheap power a way of paying for expensive water, city officials were only slightly less enthusiastic than Eaton and the press. The Board of Water Commissioners,

[88]

in its annual report for 1905, while clearly stating that the Owens River project was chiefly a water project, also called attention to the opportunities for power development. The Commissioners estimated the amount of electricity that might be generated along the aqueduct at 80,000 horse power — an amount so large that even after meeting street lighting and other municipal needs, the city would have a large surplus available for sale. The Board concluded only slightly less optimistically than Eaton and the press, "The amount of revenue that might be derived from this source, together with the net income of the water department, would be sufficient to meet, if not the whole, at least a substantial part, of the indebtedness to be incurred by the city in completing this project."[13]

In the summer of 1906, the Water Board — with the advice of other city officials and of the presidents of the Merchants and Manufacturers Association, the Municipal League, and the Voters' League — appointed a board of consulting engineers to review the city's aqueduct plans. Of eleven subjects for investigation assigned the engineers, only one pertained to power — the engineers were to estimate the amount of power that might be developed along the aqueduct — but of a half dozen major modifications of the city's plan recommended by the engineers, three dealt with power. The consultants estimated that 49,000 horse power "would be available twenty-four hours per day, and seven days a week," but by raising the elevation of the aqueduct, adding storage reservoirs, and enlarging conduits the city could have available during hours of peak demand a total of 93,000 horse power. The engineers concluded their report with the statement,

> The conditions for the economic development and maintenance of the power are very favorable, and its safety against interruption or diminution by drought and the permanent character of the aqueduct, tend to make the power development feature particularly attractive and valuable.[14]

"The Board felt," according to one of the consultants, "as a power proposition alone, the aqueduct would be worth constructing . . . ." He estimated the annual revenue to be derived from the sale of aqueduct power at $1,400,000, a sum sufficient to "pay all interest on the cost of the entire project."[15]

[89]

As the engineering feasibility and financial attractiveness of aqueduct power development became thoroughly established, it became increasingly likely that aqueduct power would, indeed, be developed. But developed by what agency? By the private electric utility companies already in the field? Or by the city of Los Angeles itself? Although in a few years the issue of public versus private power would become one of the most important and most durable in Los Angeles politics, initially it aroused little interest. The *Times*, in a few years to become a principal champion of private power, declared that aqueduct power might be exploited by either private or public agencies.[16] And the Board of Water Commissioners, soon to be charged with the development of what was to become the largest public power enterprise in the United States, in its annual report for 1905 ignored the issue completely.[17]

What makes this lack of public discussion of the issue of public or private development especially striking is that the issue was present from the very inception of the aqueduct project, for private development was an important part of Eaton's plan. John Steven McGroarty, picturesque annalist of Los Angeles history, while likening Eaton to Moses and seeing him "permeated to the very soul" with "a great dream" "for the relief of a city that was well beloved by him," also notes Eaton's awareness of the opportunity for personal profit in the exploitation of aqueduct power.[18] A less romantic chronicler of the city's growth, Boyle Workman, similarly credits Eaton with "a blinding vision," but adds, "As an engineer, he knew it was feasible. He knew, also, that there lay an opportunity to build a personal fortune."[19] Nor did Eaton himself make any effort to hide either his conception of the Owens River project as "a splendid opportunity to make money," an opportunity he had "had in view for a dozen years," or his reluctance to forgo that opportunity.[20] According to Mulholland, when he first conceived of the aqueduct project, Eaton thought of it as a project for private capital, but by the time he presented the project to the city, he was prepared to carry it out as a private project only if the city failed to act. The plan that Eaton finally presented to the city called for a marriage of private and public enterprise. Eaton was to secure and deliver to the city without

[90]

cost all necessary land and water rights. In return he was to receive "the right to develop and own all the water power incident to construction."[21]

But Eaton and the city were not the only parties interested in the Owens River. So, too, was the federal government. And Eaton's inability to promote the aqueduct as a combined public and private enterprise was in part the result of the opposition of federal officials. In the spring of 1902, President Theodore Roosevelt had signed the Newlands Act. The Reclamation Service created by that act soon began to investigate seven possible reclamation projects in California, among them one in Owens Valley. It was clear to city officials that if the Reclamation Service began actual construction work on the Owens Valley project, Los Angeles would be denied Owens River water and the city's future growth would be very seriously curtailed. Hence the "aid" of the Reclamation Service was absolutely essential. Los Angeles officials sounded out Reclamation Service officials on Eaton's proposal of a combined public and private project. These officials, in Mulholland's words, "took the stand that they could not aid the City . . . unless the project was exclusively a municipal one." As the *Complete Report* explained a decade later, "Against a municipality seeking water for a large urban population, the government would not persist in its project, its policy being to promote the good of the greatest number." City officials promptly rejected Eaton's plan, insisting on "exclusive municipal ownership and control," and the Reclamation Service stopped all work in Owens Valley.[22]

A few months after rejecting Eaton's plan for a combined public and private aqueduct project, the city received from another source a plan that called for a much larger ingredient of private enterprise. A local engineer, allegedly representing Eastern financiers, tentatively offered to build the aqueduct in exchange for power rights. Private capital could build and operate the aqueduct at far less cost than the city, the engineer urged, because private capital would be "out of the pale of political influences . . . which always arise when any municipality undertakes some project on a gigantic scale."[23] Although nothing came of this proposal, it is significant both as an indicator of the grow-

[91]

ing awareness of the importance of the power side of the aqueduct project and as a foretaste of the impending conflict over the issue of public versus private exploitation.

Still another sign of increasing awareness of the issue of municipal or private development was the increasing frequency with which Los Angeles newspapers accused electric utility companies operating in Los Angeles of seeking to gain control of aqueduct power or, failing that, to block the entire Owens River project. No sooner did the *Times* discover the power potential of the aqueduct project than it also discovered that that potential perhaps fatally endangered the project's chances of adoption. The paper had heard what it termed "well-grounded rumors of a quiet combination of certain large interests against the Owens River scheme for business reasons." Although the *Times* named no names, it declared that if opposition to the aqueduct project did, indeed, develop, the opposition would "come in strongest force from the power and light interests." "A stream running 33,000 inches of water is enough to make any power producer jealous," the *Times* concluded. Mulholland was more specific, "The only opposition we are meeting is the Edison people. They fear Los Angeles will have too much power if we run this water down here from those mountains." Such allegations became so prevalent that the president of the Edison Electric Corporation, John B. Miller, felt called upon to write to the Board of Water Commissioners to deny them. Miller wrote, "I desire to say to you as emphatically and as unequivically as English can express it, that this company has not in any way opposed the city's plans for bringing water from Owens River."[24]

Six months later the *Times* again charged that there was "underhand knocking" of the Owens River project by electric company officers. It was clear to the *Times* that whoever controlled the 100,000 horse power of aqueduct electricity could "fix the price of power and light in Los Angeles," and this fact explained why the power companies were "knocking" the aqueduct. The *Times* charged specifically that the general manager of the Pacific Light and Power Company, Allan C. Balch, and an engineer retained by the Edison Company, F. C. Finkle, were "going about telling their friends and business acquaintances that the Owens River project is 'a scheme of graft,' an engineering absurdity,

[92]

a financial chimera and an utterly impracticable proposition." Both men were said to have stressed engineering obstacles. Finkle, in addition, was said to have stated that he had made a survey of the flow of the Owens River for the Edison Company, the results of which were considerably less optimistic than those of the Reclamation Service survey on which the city was basing its plans. The *Times* feared that because Finkle was an engineer, his words would carry weight with business men innocent of engineering knowledge. The paper particularly feared Finkle's influence on bankers, "whose opinion might influence public action on a proposition to issue bonds."[25]

Finkle categorically denied that the Edison Company had sought to have him "knock" the aqueduct project. He declared plausibly,

> The power companies now operating here would benefit vastly by the attainment of such a result, even should the city secure 100,000 horse power in San Fernando Valley, because the 20,000 inches of additional water would so increase the population and industrial activity in Southern California as to consume all the output both of the power companies and the city at prices very profitable to the owners of power.

The data resulting from his investigation were the property of the Edison Company; Finkle had "never used them either for or against the city's Owens River project." Finkle also denied that he had made any allegations of graft — past, present, or prospective.[26]

A few weeks later, the *Times* called attention to still another "knocker" of the aqueduct project — Samuel T. Clover, maverick Republican editor of the recently founded Los Angeles *Evening News*. The *News*, the *Times* charged, was the "subsidized organ" of the power corporations opposing the Owens River project, "the nominal editor . . . their employee." "Subsidized Sammy's" *Evening News* was doing openly what Balch and Finkle were doing under cover. According to the *Times*, the power companies were "knocking" the aqueduct project in order to impair the city's credit when it became time to sell aqueduct bonds. Alarmed at the prospect of municipal development of aqueduct power, the companies were determined to block the aqueduct

[93]

395

project entirely or, at the very least, reduce its flow, and hence its power production, to a trickle.[27]

The alleged power company opposition to the aqueduct project was not confined to the local scene. In June, 1906, Mulholland and City Attorney W. B. Mathews, accompanied by a Chamber of Commerce delegation, went to Washington to work for passage of an act giving the city a right of way through certain public lands between Owens Valley and the San Fernando Valley. They found that a representative of the Edison Company had been on the ground for two weeks and that Balch had "used the wires" to block the bill. By the time the spokesmen for the city arrived, this opposition, together with that of the congressman representing the settlers of Owens Valley, apparently had begun to have some influence on Interior Secretary Frank H. Hitchcock. Mulholland found the Secretary "a very positive, domineering man," according to the *Times*. "But," the *Times* continued, "Mulholland was loaded with facts, and his emphatic way of stating facts had its effect." Furthermore, the city had on its side Frank P. Flint, Republican Senator from California and member of the Senate Committee on Public Lands, who had introduced the right of way measure, presumably at the behest of Los Angeles city officials. And the city also had on its side "two strong friends close to the President" — Chief Forester Gifford Pinchot and Geological Survey Director Charles D. Walcott. The whole matter was thrashed out in a conference with President Theodore Roosevelt. Roosevelt opened the conference by saying to the city's representatives, "You'll get your bill." He then proceeded to dictate a characteristic letter to Secretary Hitchcock, seated at his elbow, in which he said,

> I am also impressed by the fact that the chief opposition to this bill, aside from the opposition of the few settlers in Owens Valley (whose interest is genuine, but whose interest unfortunately must be disregarded in view of the infinitely greater interest to be served by putting the water in Los Angeles), comes from certain private power companies whose object evidently is for their own pecuniary interest to prevent the municipality from furnishing its own water. The people at the head of these companies are doubtless respectable citizens, and if there is no law they have a right to seek their own pecuniary advantage in securing control of this

necessity of life for the City. Nevertheless, their opposition seems to me to afford one of the strongest arguments for passing the law, inasmuch as it ought not to be within the power of private individuals to control such a necessity of life as against the municipality.

The *Times* commented, "When the letter was completed and read, the Secretary found that he agreed with the President." The aqueduct right of way bill became law five days later.[28]

But even after the passage of the aqueduct right of way act, the *Times* continued to fear power company opposition to the aqueduct. The "pin-head managers" of the power companies had said in public that they were friendly toward the aqueduct project, but in private they continued to fight it. Unable to defeat the aqueduct at the polls, power company agents were boasting that they would tie the project up in litigation, which even if unsuccessful, would so impair the city's credit that aqueduct bonds could be sold. The *Times* made it quite clear, however, that the ultimate goal of the power companies was no longer permanently to block the aqueduct project. Persistent efforts of the companies to kill the project had failed. Consequently "the power company schemers" had now "put about on another tack." The direction of this new course had been given in an "unauthorized and wholly baseless statement of the city's plans in "their organ," the *Evening News*: "It is not the purpose of the city to supply electricity, and a lease will be made to a corporation, the revenues to go to an expense fund. If a lease is not desirable, the right to use the power will be sold." As the *Times* pointed out, no one had been authorized to define the city's power plans, and no city official had presumed to do so. "The corporation organ" alone was responsible for the statement. The *Times* thought the statement highly significant. To the *Times*, it meant that the power companies, recognizing that they could not block the Owens River project, were trying "to hold up the project . . . until the city shall be forced to make an arrangement with them by which they can control the power."[29]

As the issue of public versus private exploitation of aqueduct power slowly emerged, planning for the financing of the aqueduct continued. City officials wrestled with the problem of whether to install the proposed power plants concurrently with the construction of the aqueduct, or to delay power plant installation until the aqueduct was completed. The *Times* recalled "conservative" estimates that the power to be developed at the mouth of the aqueduct would yield an annual revenue sufficient to "provide for interest and sinking fund on the bond issues of $25,000,000 and leave about half a million a year to be used otherwise." Common sense, therefore, seemed to dictate that the power plants should be installed concurrently with the construction of the aqueduct, in order that they could go into operation and start yielding revenue when the first Owens River water rushed down San Francisquito Canyon. The *Times* estimated the cost of installing the power plants, transmission lines, and substations at $3,000,000.[30] But Mulholland had earlier declared, "It will be time enough to take up the power end of it when we get the water down here,"[31] and he concluded his first annual report as Chief Engineer of the Los Angeles Aqueduct with this typical paragraph:

> The proposed plan is to build the Aqueduct for the purpose of supplying water for municipal purposes, and after its completion, if the citizens of Los Angeles consider it desirable to install these power plants, they may subsequently be built as independent works. The installation of power has not been included in the Aqueduct estimates because the power situation is considered as wholly independent of the proposition of supplying water, and should stand on its own merits.[32]

Surprisingly, in light of the expectation that aqueduct power would pay for aqueduct water, city officials adopted Mulholland's position. The City Council voted to submit a bond issue in the amount of $23,000,000 solely for the construction of the aqueduct; a power bond issue would be submitted independently at a later date.[33]

At the beginning of the aqueduct bond campaign, the press appeared quite fearful of power company opposition to the bonds. In an editorial titled "The City's Enemies," the *Times* quoted at length from the Roosevelt letter, and charged that the chief opposition to the bonds was coming from the same power companies that the President had charged with opposing the right of way bill. The companies had offered to cease their op-

[96]

position if the city would give them control of aqueduct power. The city had rejected their offer, however, and consequently the companies were seeking to defeat the bonds. The *Times* urged its readers not to forget that all of the opposition to the bonds was being inspired by power companies whose sole aim was, in the words of the President of the United States, "their own pecuniary interest."[34] The liberal press, too, saw the hand of the private power companies raised against the aqueduct bond issue.[35]

A fortnight before election day, however, the opposition of the power companies waned. "Their attempt to bluff and bully the city into giving them control of the power developed by the aqueduct had failed," the *Times* declared, "and they cannot make good their threat to defeat the Owens River bond issue." The companies had abandoned their fight against the Owens River project and their presidents had "publicly and unqualifiedly" endorsed it.[36] The opposition that remained was insignificant; only the *Evening News* continued to oppose the bonds.

Support for the bonds was overwhelming. All of the city's major business and civic groups — coordinated by the Chamber of Commerce, the Merchants and Manufacturers Association, and the Municipal League — joined together to form an Owens River Campaign Committee. The city's major newspapers were also unanimously in support of the aqueduct bond issue. Supporters of the bonds, while primarily concerned with assuring the city an abundant supply of water, gave considerable attention to the power and light side of the project. Mayor A. C. Harper, for example, called attention to the power that would be developed along the aqueduct, and declared that in anticipation of the development of this power the city had already planned to establish its own municipal lighting system. City Attorney Leslie R. Hewitt pointed out that the aqueduct would provide Los Angeles with abundant power not just for lighting but for manufacturing as well.[37] Equally important, receipts from the sale of aqueduct power would also assure the financial success of the entire aqueduct project.[38] The *Times*, for example, again reassured its readers that the revenue to be derived from the sale of aqueduct power would be "more than enough to provide

[97]

for interest and sinking fund on the entire cost of the aqueduct and power plants."³⁹

Lured by a vision of a great city, a city with ample water and abundant electricity, an increasingly industrialized city, and convinced that this vision would become a reality at no cost to them, on election day Los Angeles voters went to the polls in greater numbers than at any previous special election and voted ten to one in favor of the aqueduct bonds, the bonds carrying in every precinct.⁴⁰

With completion of the aqueduct scheduled for the spring of 1912, city officials were obliged to turn to power development. A Bureau of Los Angeles Aqueduct Power was established; Ezra F. Scattergood, previously a consulting engineer for the Henry Huntington interests and for the aqueduct, was named Chief Electrical Engineer; and a second board of consulting engineers was appointed.⁴¹

This second board of engineers was even more enthusiastic than the earlier board about the opportunities for power development along the aqueduct. A maximum delivery of 120,000 horse power and 64,000 horse power for a twenty-four hour period, an amount thirty percent larger than that estimated by the first board, could be developed at "an unusually low first cost." The completed system, furthermore, would be characterized by "the very highest degree of reliability in operation," and by unusually low costs of operation. In concluding their report, the consultants pointed out that in the preceding thirteen years, the demand for electricity in Los Angeles and vicinity had increased tenfold, from 5,000 kilowatts in 1897 to 50,000 kilowatts at the time of their report. The city had "an assured and early market" for its aqueduct power."⁴² The *Times* commented, "If a private corporation received such a report as this from its examining engineers its stock would immediately jump twenty-five points . . . ."⁴³

At the same time that they gave attention to the engineering side of the aqueduct power project, city officials also wrestled with the financial side. The Board of Public Works recommended to the City Council that it call a special election to authorize a power bond issue of $4,500,000. Although an issue in that amount would not be sufficient to complete an aqueduct power system — to do that an additional million dollars would be required — it would be sufficient to carry aqueduct power development to the point where it would be "commercially serviceable." Mayor George Alexander sent a special message to the Council urging prompt submission. The Council fixed April 19, 1910, as the date of the special election.

Although for a quarter-century afterwards almost all Los Angeles power bond elections were bitterly contested, the city's first such election was "a formality." Support for the power bonds was almost as overwhelming as it had been for the aqueduct bonds. City officials were particularly active in urging adoption. Mayor Alexander issued a proclamation calling on the voters to approve the issue; Scattergood appeared before the City Club to urge that influential civic group to support the bonds; City Attorney Hewitt addressed the Federated Improvement Associations; and Mulholland and Mathews, the latter now Special Counsel for the Aqueduct Bureau, issued strong pro bond statements. Perhaps even more influential was the virtually unanimous backing given the bonds by the city's business and civic organizations. The Chamber of Commerce, the Merchants and Manufacturers Association, the Federated Improvement Associations, and the Municipal League — all of these potent organizations, among others, urged the adoption of the power bonds. The city's newspapers unanimously endorsed the issue. The bonds carried by a margin of seven to one.[45]

City officials in proposing municipal development of aqueduct power, business and civic groups and newspapers in endorsing the proposal, and voters in approving it were guided by several considerations. For one, almost from the first public announcement of the Owens River project five years earlier, and especially during the 1907 aqueduct bond election, voters had been assured that revenues to be received from the sale of aqueduct power would be sufficient both to meet the interest charges on the aqueduct bonds and to provide a sinking fund that would retire them in twenty years. In an expansive moment, Mayor Alexander had gone so far as to assert that power revenues together with those from the newly improved harbor would "wipe out the entire city indebtedness." Good judgment seemed to indicate, therefore, that installation of aqueduct power plants should begin promptly in order that the city could begin to realize large revenues from the sale of aqueduct power just as soon as Owens Rivers waters began to flow through the aqueduct.[46] Another compelling argument in favor of voting the 1907 aqueduct bonds had been the role of cheap power in the industrialization of Los Angeles; this argument, too, was now widely used in favor of the power bonds.[47] And common sense reasons of economy also called for the earliest possible exploitation of the power potential of the aqueduct. If construction of power facilities were delayed until after the aqueduct was in actual operation, "hundreds of thousands" of dollars would have to be spent to detour water past construction work at the power sites; concurrent construction of the aqueduct and aqueduct power plants would obviate this waste.[48] In sum, city officials and voters saw aqueduct power development as "a corollary of the aqueduct." "The voting of the power bonds was guaranteed when the aqueduct was undertaken," one newspaper observed. "It was an essential part of the project."[49]

What needs to be explained, however, is not only why the power resources of the Los Angeles aqueduct were developed, but also why they were developed by the city of Los Angeles itself, rather than by the private electric utility companies already operating in the area. Benjamin Franklin is reputed to have asserted that the wisest measures of statesmanship are not the product of previous wisdom, but rather are forced by the occasion. In the decision of the city of Los Angeles to go into the business of generating electricity, however, both forces were at work. Clearly the construction of the aqueduct furnished the occasion for that decision. It is equally clear, however, that the decision was also the product of previous wisdom.

During the first decade and a half of the present century, Los Angeles was the scene of a movement for municipal reform.[50] A major impetus to reform was acute dissatisfaction with private utility companies. For a generation, city officials in their eagerness to obtain water, gas, electricity, telephone service, and street railways had granted extremely liberal franchises to entrepreneurs who would undertake to provide them. Poor service,

[100]

A Neglected Aspect of the Owens

high rates, and interference in the city's governance had ensued. Hence a primary aim of the reformers was to bring utilities under municipal control.[51] Electric utilities were a prime target.

During the early years of the electric light and power industry, years of extraordinarily rapid growth, there was a general belief that it was inherently the least monopolistic of the public utilities. City councils looked to competition to prevent abuses in rates and services. Indeed so thoroughly was competition thought to be the natural and effective way to prevent abuses that virtually every city in the country granted several general franchises, some simultaneously, and some granted franchises to all applicants. It quickly became evident, however, that the electric utility industry was a natural monopoly, for competition produced a wasteful duplication of investment.[52] Some other means must be found to control rates and services.

One proposed way to control the rates and services of electric utilities was government regulation. The earliest attempts were made on the municipal level. Some municipalities attempted regulation through ordinances or franchises; others established utility commissions. But regulation through ordinances proved to be "rigid, spasmodic and inept, if not corrupt," and regulation through franchises was similarly "inflexible, difficult to enforce and sometimes corrupt," while even large cities seldom could command the administrative and technical skills necessary to establish utility commissions worthy of the name. At best the jurisdiction of a municipality was too confined for effective regulation of a large utility system embracing several communities. Municipal regulation became widespread, but only rarely was it effective.[53]

The evident general failure of municipal regulation gave rise to a widespread demand first for state and later for federal regulation.[54] From the first, however, there were those who were skeptical of the ability of regulation by any level of government to control the electric utility industry.[54]

During the years of the reform movement, three companies — the Los Angeles Gas and Electric Corporation, the Pacific Light and Power Company, and the Edison Electric Corporation — distributed electricity in Los Angeles. Yet the three companies

[101]

did not directly compete, for they served different geographic areas of the city. The gas company — a product of earlier consolidations and a subsidiary of a San Francisco holding company, the Pacific Lighting Corporation, which also controlled the Pacific Gas and Electric Corporation and the Southern California and Southern Counties Gas companies, and the only one of the three companies that distributed most, 87 percent, of its current for lighting purposes — operated principally in the lucrative central business district, where it also had a contract to furnish current for lighting the city streets. The Pacific Light and Power Company supplied most, 90 percent, of its current for power purposes, principally to Henry E. Huntington's electric railways, the Los Angeles Railway and the Pacific Electric, but it also furnished electricity for lighting in the southern and northeastern portions of the city. The Edison Company also supplied most, 75 percent, of its current for power purposes, but its lines reached 75 percent of the city's area and served almost half of the city's domestic consumers.[56]

Although a provision of the city charter of 1889 authorized the City Council to regulate utility rates, not until 1904 did the Council pass the necessary ordinance implementing the charter provision, and not until 1907 did the Council actually exercise its authority. At that time the Council simply approved most of the existing rates. Mayor Arthur C. Harper, however, vetoed the domestic rate of eleven cents per kilowatt-hour. After a conference with the Mayor and the Councilmen, representatives of the electric companies agreed to accept a nine cent domestic rate, but the Councilmen were obliged to enter into a secret "gentlemen's agreement" not to fix a lower rate for three years.[57]

Despite the "gentlemen's agreement" of 1907, the following year the Council entered upon its rate-fixing task much more earnestly. The electric companies, however, filed reports that City Auditor W. C. Mushet called incomplete and misleading, and refused the City Auditor access to their books. Mushet none the less thought the nine cent domestic rate too high and urged a two cent reduction. He was convinced that the companies were exploiting the small light consumers for the benefit of the large power consumers. Mushet asserted, for example, that the Pacific Light and Power Corporation was selling power below cost to

[102]

the street railway companies. Interested citizens presented similar charges. The Council, however, was unconvinced and perhaps also influenced by the "gentlemen's agreement" continued the nine cent rate.[58]

By 1909 both the reformers and the companies were convinced of the failure of rate regulation by councilmanic ordinance. In its place both would substitute regulation by a permanent, non-political public utility commission. A utility commission bill largely reflecting the desires of the companies was approved by the Council but vetoed by Mayor George Alexander. The Council sustained the veto. The Council then passed a second bill and overrode the Mayor's veto of it. This ordinance was superceded, however, when at the December general election the voters approved an initiative creating the type of public utility commission desired by the reformers. The Commission employed a group of nationally known utility experts that surveyed Los Angeles utilities and recommended upward adjustments of telephone and electric rates. The Commission forwarded these recommendations to the Council, but that body refused to adopt them. In July, 1911, the members of the Commission resigned. Municipal regulation of utilities suffered further blows when in a number of disputes between the city and the companies the courts decided in favor of the companies. Thereafter the task of regulating public utilities was gradually assumed by the state. This failure of municipal regulation, either by councilmanic ordinance or by utility commission, to control the rates of the electric utility companies provided the reformers with considerable reason to adopt the alternative of municipal ownership.

But there was a second important, and closely related, influence making for municipal ownership of electric utilities in Los Angeles during the Progressive era. The city had received as part of its Spanish-Mexican heritage a tradition of municipal ownership and distribution of the water of the Los Angeles River. During the Spanish-Mexican period, the city held full title to the water of the river. The water was diverted from the river in publicly controlled ditches, called *zanjas*, from which all inhabitants might draw for irrigation or domestic purposes. Private enterprise was represented only by Indian women carrying on their heads jugs of water that they peddled from door to door for

[103]

domestic use or by a water bartel mounted on a horse-drawn cart. After California was annexed to the United States, Los Angeles city officials felt obliged to provide an improved system for supplying water for domestic purposes. In 1868, apparently against the wishes of the majority of the city's voters, the city sold to a group of private capitalists a thirty-year contract to provide the city with water, from the Los Angeles River, for domestic purposes. The Los Angeles City Water Company — the name the capitalists gave to their organization — was to install an adequate distributing system, which the city was to have the right to purchase at the expiration of the contract. From the first the "thirty year lease" was attacked on the ground that the company was making profits from the water owned by the people of Los Angeles. In the municipal election of 1896, the Republican platform charged that water could be supplied at one-tenth the rate charged by the company. In addition, the company's 200 miles of two-inch mains provided inadequate volume and pressure for fire protection or even for domestic service. Hence in 1898 the city authorities decided not to renew the contract. After a great deal of litigation, in 1902 the company reluctantly relinquished its properties, and the city returned to municipal distribution of its water resources. A charter amendment approved the following year precluded any future alienation of water resources from municipal control. The amendment required approval of two-thirds of the voters of any proposal to sell or lease any of the city's water or water rights. Municipal distribution brought improved service at substantially lower rates.[60] The unhappy experience with private operation of the city's water system and the later success of municipal operation considerably strengthened the emerging sentiment for municipal ownership of utilities generally and of electric utilities in particular. This sentiment became especially evident when, with the inception of the Los Angeles Aqueduct project, water and power became so closely linked as to be almost interchangeable.

    That the power resources of the Los Angeles Aqueduct would be exploited was a foregone conclusion. It was the considered opinion of two boards of consulting engineers that the opportunities for the economical generation of electricity along the line of the aqueduct were truly exceptional. Cheap electricity would find eager purchasers among manufacturers and householders alike — and attract additional manufacturers and home-seekers to Los Angeles — and power receipts would go a long way toward paying the high costs of constructing the aqueduct.

What is surprising is that the city of Los Angeles, instead of delegating the task to private capital, itself undertook to exploit aqueduct power. This action was the product of several forces. The Spanish-Mexican heritage of municipal ownership and operation of the Los Angeles water system combined during the American period with an unsuccessful experiment with private distribution of domestic water and a subsequent successful return to municipal distribution to produce an overwhelming general sentiment in favor of municipal operation of the city's water system. This sentiment embraced the water system's hydroelectric by-product. Municipal electricity was a corollary of municipal water.

Los Angeles was not, as were most American municipalities that resorted to municipal electric systems at the beginning of the present century, a small community neglected by private electric companies. Los Angeles was a sizable and rapidly growing city served by three electric companies. Reformers were convinced, however, that the companies did not compete but rather cooperated to maintain high rates. Regulation, by city council and by public utility commission, had also failed to secure low rates. The aqueduct offered a third means of control. Perhaps municipal competition in the generation of electricity might secure lower rates.

Public reaction to the repeated charges that the already unpopular private power companies were seeking to block the aqueduct project or, failing in that, to get control of aqueduct power sites, and the determination of the conservation-minded Roosevelt administration to prevent private expropriation of water power resources were additional forces leading to the inception of the Los Angeles municipal power enterprise.

[105]

Historical Society of Southern California

NOTES

[1] For a brief, incisive analysis of aqueduct literature, see Abraham Hoffman, "Joseph Barlow Lippincott and the Owens Valley Controversy: Time for Revision," *Southern California Quarterly* LIV (Fall 1972), 239-40.

[2] Even the most casual of *Times* readers could scarcely have avoided reading of the project, for news of it covered the entire front page of the local news section. Only *Times* readers could have read of the project because only the *Times* violated a gentlemen's agreement not to break the story until the project was further advanced.

[3] Minutes of the Board of Water Commissioners of the City of Los Angeles, September 22, 1902, Los Angeles City, Department of Public Service, *Complete Report on Construction of the Los Angeles Aqueduct; with Introductory Historical Sketch* (Los Angeles, 1916), p. 9; Vincent Ostrom, *Water & Politics; A Study of Water Politics and Administration in the Development of Los Angeles* (Los Angeles: The Haynes Foundation, 1953), pp. 8-10, 13. For the gradual realization that Los Angeles was outgrowing its water supply, the futile search for additional local sources of water, and the final turning to distant sources see the *Annual Reports* of the Board of Water Commissioners for the years 1902-1905 (Los Angeles, 1903-1906).

[4] Los Angeles *Express*, 29 July, 31 July 1880.

[5] Los Angeles City, Department of Public Works, Los Angeles Aqueduct, *First Annual Report of the Chief Engineer of the Los Angeles Aqueduct to the Board of Public Works*, March 15, 1907 (Los Angeles: 1907), p. 17. The Board of Water Commissioners also credited Eaton with conceiving the project. Board of Water Commissioners, *Fourth Annual Report*, p. 47. Eaton had served the Board as consulting engineer in 1902. Minutes of the Board of Water Commissioners, February 24, March 3, 17, 1902.

[6] Minutes of the Board of Water Commissioners, May 22, 29, June 6, July 31, 1905; Department of Public Works, Los Angeles Aqueduct, *First Annual Report*, pp. 18-19; Department of Public Service, *Complete Report*, p. 47; Board of Water Commissioners, *Fourth Annual Report*, p. 5.

[7] Boyle Workman, *The City That Grew* (Los Angeles: The Southland Publishing Company, 1935), p. 301; Ostrom, *Water & Politics*, p. 49.

[8] Los Angeles *Times*, 29 July 1905.

[9] *Ibid.*, 6 August 1905. Not until three months later did the *Times* belatedly point out another advantage to be derived from aqueduct power — cheaper lighting for domestic consumers. *Ibid.*, 16 November 1905.

[10] *Ibid.*, 24 August 1905; Los Angeles *Record*, 30 August, 6 September 1905; Los Angeles *Express*, 29, 31 July 1905.

[11] Minutes of the City Council of the City of Los Angeles, August 9, 1905; Los Angeles *Times*, 5 September 1905. The vote was 10,787 to 755. In only a single precinct did the bonds fail to receive a two-thirds majority. Los Angeles *Times*, 8 September 1905.

[12] Los Angeles *Times*, 10 September 1905.

[13] Board of Water Commissioners, *Fourth Annual Report*, p. 6.

[14] Department of Public Works, Los Angeles Aqueduct, *First Annual Report*, pp. 69-84.

[15] James D. Schuyler, quoted in Los Angeles *Express*, 26 December 1906.

[16] Los Angeles *Times*, 6 August 1905.

[17] Board of Water Commissioners, *Fourth Annual Report*, p. 6.

[18] John Steven McGroarty, *Los Angeles, from the Mountains to the Sea* (Chicago: The American Historical Society, 1921), pp. 229-230.

[19] Workman, *The City That Grew*, p. 303.

[106]

²⁰ Fred Eaton, quoted in Los Angeles *Express*, 4 August 1905.
²¹ Department of Public Service, *Complete Report*, pp. 13, 47; Department of Public Works, Los Angeles Aqueduct, *First Annual Report*, pp. 17-18.
²² Department of Public Works, Los Angeles Aqueduct, *First Annual Report*, pp. 17-18, 21-22; Department of Public Service, *Complete Report*, pp. 13, 47. It is bitterly ironic that almost simultaneously with the Reclamation Service's abandonment of reclamation work in Owens Valley, William E. Smythe published a revised edition of his *Conquest of Arid America* in which he not only declared that because its water resources had already been fully utilized the "charming district" of southern California was "not within the field of largest future development," but added that the "finest field for development in California, and one of the finest in the United States," was what he called "Undiscovered California" — the regions of the eastern slope of the Sierra Nevada, especially Inyo County, the site of Owens Valley. "There can be no question," Smythe wrote, "that during this century they will become the homes of hundreds of thousands of people and the seat of manifold industrial life." William E. Smythe, *The Conquest of Arid America* (New York: The Macmillan Company, 1905), pp. 139-140, 150-151, 157.
²³ Los Angeles *Times*, 28 October, 26 November 1905. The Pacific Light and Power Company also tentatively offered to lease aqeduct power rights. *Times*, 25 December 1905.
²⁴ *Ibid.*, 7 August 1905; William Mulholland quoted in Los Angeles *Examiner*, 15 August 1905; John B. Miller to John B. Fay, 18 August 1905, quoted in Los Angeles *Times*, 19 August 1905.
²⁵ Los Angeles *Times*, 11 March 1906. A few days later, the *Times* printed a cartoon captioned "Shoo Fly" that showed "Miss Los Angeles" shooing various anti-Owens River project flies, conspicuous among them one labeled "Power Company Hireling." *Times*, 14 March 1906.
²⁶ F. C. Finkle, quoted in *Ibid.*, 12 March 1906.
²⁷ Los Angeles *Times*, 8, 18 April 1906.
²⁸ *Ibid.*, 4 July 1906; United States, *Congressional Record*, 59 Cong., 1st Sess., 1906, XL, Part 9, p. 8307; Theodore Roosevelt, quoted in Department of Public Works, Los Angeles Aqueduct, *First Annual Report*, pp. 26-27; Department of Public Service, *Complete Report*. pp. 68-71.
²⁹ Los Angeles *Times*, 2, 25 December 1906.
³⁰ *Ibid.*, 28 December 1906.
³¹ Mulholland, quoted in Los Angeles *Examiner*, 15 August 1905.
³² Department of Public Service, Los Angeles Aqueduct, *First Annual Report*, pp. 56-58.
³³ City Council Minutes, April 1, 1907.
³⁴ Los Angeles *Times*, 7, 17 May 1907.
³⁵ Los Angeles *Express*, 3 May 1907; *Pacific Outlook* II (May 25, 1907), 3-5.
³⁶ Los Angeles *Times*, 29 May 1907.
³⁷ *Ibid.*, 1, 4 June 1907.
³⁸ Los Angeles *Express*, 1, 31 May 1907.
³⁹ Los Angeles *Times*, 6 June 1907.
⁴⁰ *Ibid.*, 13 June 1907.
⁴¹ Los Angeles City, Department of Public Works, Bureau of Los Angeles Aqueduct Power, *First Annual Report of the Bureau of Los Angeles Aqueduct Power to the Board of Public Works* (Los Angeles, 1910), pp. 8-9; City Council Minutes, September 14, 21, 1909; Los Angeles *Times*, 27, 28 August, 3 October, 27 November 1909.
⁴² Los Angeles City, Department of Public Works, Bureau of Los Angeles Aqueduct Power, Board of Consulting Engineers, *Preliminary Report of Consulting Board of Engineers Bureau of Los Angeles Aqueduct Power* (Los Angeles, 1910), pp. 4-9. In June, Scattergood submitted the first annual report

of the Bureau of Los Angeles Aqueduct Power. He estimated the average peak load in the Los Angeles-Long Beach-San Bernardino triangle at 90,000 horse power — 30,000 horse power less than the potential peak generating capacity of the proposed aqueduct power plants. Scattergood added, however, that the average annual consumption of electricity in the triangle had increased from 80 million kilowatts in 1905 to 280 million kilowatts in 1909. Not only had consumption of electricity increased, it had increased at an increasing rate. Assuming even a constant rate of increase, about twenty percent per year — and assuming that no other new sources of power would be developed — an assumption Scattergood thought "very probable" — the entire generating capacity of the proposed aqueduct power plants would be absorbed within six or seven years after the plants went into operation, presumably in 1912. Bureau of Los Angeles Aqueduct Power, *First Annual Report*, p. 13.

[43] Los Angeles *Times*, 5 March 1910.

[44] City Council Minutes, November 2, 1909; Los Angeles *Times*, 9 September, 15 October, 2 December 1909, 13, 30 January, 2 March 1910.

[45] Los Angeles *Times*, 30 January, 13, 17, 18, 19, 24 April 1910; Los Angeles *Herald*, 15 April 1910; Los Angeles *Express*, 20 May 1910. The *Evening News*, which had opposed the aqueduct bonds, had ceased publication in April, 1908.

[46] Bureau of Los Angeles Aqueduct Power, *First Annual Report*, p. 8; Chairman of Board of Water Commissioners, quoted in Los Angeles *Times*, 9 September 1909; Mayor Alexander, quoted in Los Angeles *Times*, 15 October 1909; Los Angeles *Times*, 9 September, 15 October 1909, 13, 15, 20 April 1910; Los Angeles *Express*, 1, 4, 6, 12, 13 April 1910.

[47] Joint statement of Hewitt and Mathews, quoted in Los Angeles *Times*, 15 October 1909; Los Angeles *Times*, 11, 13 April 1910; Los Angeles *Record*, 16 April 1910; Los Angeles *Express*, 4, 6, 7, 12 April 1910. Scattergood was apparently unique in advancing an additional telling argument for developing aqueduct power — "guaranteeing to the inhabitants of the city reasonable rates for light and power." Los Angeles *Times*, 17 April 1910.

[48] Bureau of Los Angeles Aqueduct Power, *First Annual Report*, p. 8; Chairman of Board of Water Commissioners, quoted in Los Angeles *Times*, 9 September 1909; Scattergood, quoted in Los Angeles *Times*, 17 April 1910; Los Angeles *Times*, 9 September, 15 October 1909.

[49] Los Angeles *Times*, 11, 19 April 1910.

[50] Albert Howard Clodius, "The Quest for Good Government in Los Angeles, 1890-1910" (Ph.D. dissertation, Claremont Graduate School, 1953), p. 793; Jancie Jacques, "The Political Reform Movement in Los Angeles, 1900-1910" (M.A. thesis, Claremont Graduate School, 1948), p. 115.

[51] Clodius, "Quest for Good Government," pp. 102-103, 116; George E. Mowry, *The California Progressives* (Berkeley: University of California Press, 1951), p. 55.

[52] Delos F. Wilcox, *Municipal Franchises*, 2 Vols. (Rochester, New York: The Gervaise Press, 1910), I, 212-213; II, 803; Harry W. Laidler, *Concentration of Control in American Industry* (New York: Thomas Y. Crowell Company, 1931), pp. 150-151; National Civic Federation, Commission on Publi cOwnership, *Municipal and Private Operation of Public Utilities*, 3 vols. (New York: National Civic Federation, 1907), I, 23; Raymond C. Miller, *Kilowatts at Work: A History of the Detroit Edison Company* (Detroit: Wayne State University Press, 1957), pp. 37, 60.

[53] National Civic Federation, *Municipal and Private Operation*, I, pp. 23, 26; Twentieth Century Fund, pp. 3, 42; 106-116; Wilcox, *Municipal Franchises*, II, 803.

[54] Twentieth Century Fund, pp. 3, 42-43, 116-162.

[55] H. S. Raushenbush and Harry W. Laidler, *Power Control* (New York: New Republic, Inc., 1928), pp. 158-159.

[56] Clodius, "Quest for Good Government," pp. 107-112; Los Angeles City, Board of Public Utilities, *First Annual Report of the Board of Public Utilities* (Los Angeles: Press of Will A. Kistler Co., 1910), pp. 63, 93; Charles M. Coleman, *P.G. and E. of California; The Centennial Story of Pacific Gas and Electric Company, 1852-1952* (New York: McGraw-Hill Book Company, Inc., 1952), pp. 188-189; Los Angeles *Times*, 16 November 1916, 23 May 1917.

[57] Clodius, "Quest for Good Government," pp. 292-293.

[58] *Ibid.*, pp. 294, 297-308.

[59] *Ibid.*, pp. 314-336, 520-522; Board of Public Utilities, p. 5.

[60] Clodius, "Quest for Good Government," pp. 78-83; Ostrom, *Water & Politics*, pp. 27-48.

Acknowledgments

Bender, Thomas. "The 'Rural' Cemetery Movement: Urban Travail and the Appeal of Nature." *New England Quarterly* 47, No.2 (1974): 196–211. Reprinted with the permission of the New England Quarterly, Inc.

Stewart, Ian R. "Politics and the Park: The Fight for Central Park." *New York Historical Society Quarterly* 61, No.3–4 (1977): 124–55. Reprinted with the permission of the New York Historical Society.

Holt, Glen E. "Private Plans for Public Spaces: The Origins of Chicago's Park System, 1850–1875." *Chicago History* 8, No.3 (1979): 173–84. Reprinted with the permission of the Chicago Historical Society.

Blodgett, Geoffrey. "Frederick Law Olmsted: Landscape Architecture as Conservative Reform." *Journal of American History* 62, No.4 (1976): 869–89. Reprinted with the permission of the *Journal of American History*.

Miller, Ross L. "The Landscaper's Utopia Versus the City: A Mismatch." *New England Quarterly* 49, No.2 (1976): 179–93. Reprinted with the permission of the New England Quarterly, Inc.

Johnston, Norman J. "The Frederick Law Olmsted Plan for Tacoma." *Pacific Northwest Quarterly* 66, No.3 (1975): 97–104. Reprinted with the permission of the University of Washington.

Peterson, Jon A. "The City Beautiful Movement: Forgotten Origins and Lost Meanings." *Journal of Urban History* 2, No.4 (1976): 415–34. Copyright 1976 Sage Publications, Inc. Reprinted with the permission of Sage Publications, Inc.

Kantor, Harvey A. "The City Beautiful in New York." *New York Historical Society Quarterly* 57, No.2 (1973): 148–71. Reprinted with the permission of the New York Historical Society.

Bach, Ira J. "A Reconsideration of the 1909 'Plan of Chicago.'" *Chicago History* 2, No.3 (1973): 132–41. Reprinted with the permission of the Chicago Historical Society.

Brownell, Blaine A. "The Commercial-Civic Elite and City Planning in Atlanta, Memphis, and New Orleans in the 1920s." *Journal of Southern History* 41, No.3 (1975): 339–68. Copyright (1975) by the Southern Historical Association. Reprinted by permission of the Managing Editor.

Lapping, Mark B. "Radburn: Planning the American Community." *New Jersey History* 95, No.2 (1977): 85–100. Reprinted with the permission of the New Jersey Historical Society.

Myhra, David. "Rexford Guy Tugwell: Initiator of America's Greenbelt New Towns, 1935 to 1936." *Journal of the American Institute of Planners* 40, No.3 (1974): 176–88. Reprinted with the permission of the *Journal of the American Institute of Planners*.

Grabow, Stephen. "Frank Lloyd Wright and the American City: The Broadacres Debate." *Journal of the American Institute of Planners* 43, No.2 (1977): 115–24. Reprinted with the permission of the *Journal of the American Institute of Planners*.

Foster, Mark. "City Planners and Urban Transportation: The American Response, 1900–1940." *Journal of Urban History* 5, No.3 (1979): 365–96. Copyright 1979 Sage Publications, Inc. Reprinted with the permission of Sage Publications, Inc.

Goldfield, David R. "Historic Planning and Redevelopment in Minneapolis." *Journal of the American Institute of Planners* 42, No.1 (1976): 76–86. Reprinted with the permission of the *Journal of the American Institute of Planners*.

Rondinelli, Dennis A. "Urban Planning as Policy Analysis: Management of Urban Change." *Journal of the American Institute of Planners* 39, No.1 (1973): 13–22. Reprinted with the permission of the *Journal of the American Institute of Planners*.

Schultz, Stanley K. and Clay McShane. "To Engineer the Metropolis: Sewers, Sanitation, and City Planning in Late-Nineteenth-Century America." *Journal of American History* 65, No.2 (1978): 389–411. Reprinted with the permission of the *Journal of American History*.

Galishoff, Stuart. "Drainage, Disease, Comfort, and Class: A History of Newark's Sewers." *Societas* 6, No.2 (1976): 121–38.

Melosi, Martin V. "'Out of Sight, Out of Mind': The Environment and Disposal of Municipal Refuse, 1860–1920." *Historian* 35, No.4 (1973): 621–40. Reprinted with the permission of the International Honor Society in History.

Ellis, John and Stuart Galishoff. "Atlanta's Water Supply, 1865–1918." *Maryland Historian* 8, No.1 (1977): 5–22. Reprinted with the permission of the University of Maryland, Department of History.

Jones, William K. "Los Angeles Aqueduct: A Search for Water." *Journal of the West* 16, No.3 (1977): 5–21. Reprinted with the permission of the *Journal of the West*.

Van Valen, Nelson. "A Neglected Aspect of the Owens River Aqueduct Story: The Inception of the Los Angeles Municipal Electric System." *Southern California Quarterly* 59, No.1 (1977): 85–109. Reprinted with the permission of the Historical Society of Southern California.